MW01626235

About Pearson

Pearson is the world's learning company, with presence across 70 countries worldwide. Our unique insights and world-class expertise comes from a long history of working closely with renowned teachers, authors and thought leaders, as a result of which, we have emerged as the preferred choice for millions of teachers and learners across the world.

We believe learning opens up opportunities, creates fulfilling careers and hence better lives. We hence collaborate with the best of minds to deliver you class-leading products, spread across the Higher Education and K12 spectrum.

Superior learning experience and improved outcomes are at the heart of everything we do. This product is the result of one such effort.

Your feedback plays a critical role in the evolution of our products and you can contact us – reachus@pearson.com. We look forward to it.

The Dark Side of Valuation

Second Edition

Valuing Young, Distressed, and Complex Businesses

Aswath Damodaran

Original edition, entitled *The Dark Side of Valuation: Valuing Young, Distressed, and Complex Businesses*, 2nd Edition, by Damodaran, Aswath Published by Pearson Education, Limited.
Copyright © 2010 by Pearson Education, Inc.

Indian Edition

Copyright © 2017 Pearson India Education Services Pvt. Ltd

All rights reserved. This book is sold subject to the condition that it shall not, by way of trade or otherwise, be lent, resold, hired out, or otherwise circulated without the publisher's prior written consent in any form of binding or cover other than that in which it is published and without a similar condition including this condition being imposed on the subsequent purchaser and without limiting the rights under copyright reserved above, no part of this publication may be reproduced, stored in or introduced into a retrieval system, or transmitted in any form or by any means (electronic, mechanical, photocopying, recording or otherwise), without the prior written permission of both the copyright owner and the above-mentioned publisher of this book.

Although the author and publisher have made every effort to ensure that the information in this book was correct at the time of editing and printing, the author and publisher do not assume and hereby disclaim any liability to any party for any loss or damage arising out of the use of this book caused by errors or omissions, whether such errors or omissions result from negligence, accident or any other cause. Further, names, pictures, images, characters, businesses, places, events and incidents are either the products of the author's imagination or used in a fictitious manner. Any resemblance to actual persons, living or dead or actual events is purely coincidental and do not intend to hurt sentiments of any individual, community, sect or religion.

In case of binding mistake, misprints or missing pages etc., the publisher's entire liability and your exclusive remedy is replacement of this book within reasonable time of purchase by similar edition/reprint of the book.

ISBN 978-93-868-7325-5

First Impression, 2018

This edition is manufactured in India and is authorized for sale only in India, Bangladesh, Bhutan, Pakistan, Nepal, Sri Lanka and the Maldives. Circulation of this edition outside of these territories is UNAUTHORIZED.

Published by Pearson India Education Services Pvt. Ltd, CIN: U72200TN2005PTC057128.

Head Office: 15th Floor, Tower-B, World Trade Tower, Plot No. 1, Block-C, Sector 16, Noida 201 301, Uttar Pradesh, India.

Registered Office: 7th Floor, SDB2, ODC 7, 8 & 9, Survey No.01 ELCOT IT/ ITES SEZ, Sholinganallur, Chennai – 600119, Tamil Nadu, India.

Website: in.pearson.com, Email: companysecretary.india@pearson.com

Digitally printed in India by Saurabh Printers Pvt. Ltd. in the year of 2022.

To my family, who remind me daily of the things that truly matter in life

(and valuation is not in the top-ten list)

CONTENTS

PREFACE

The Dark Side of Valuation, Second Edition

The first edition of this book is showing its age and origins. The idea for the first edition of *The Dark Side of Valuation* was born at the end of 1999, toward the end of the dot-com boom. It was triggered by two phenomena:

- The seeming inability of traditional valuation models to explain stratospheric stock prices for technology (especially new technology) companies
- The willingness of analysts to abandon traditional valuation metrics and go over to the "dark side" of valuation, where prices were justified using a mix of new metrics and storytelling

The publication of the first edition coincided with the bursting of that bubble.

As markets have evolved and changed, the focus has shifted. The bubble and the concurrent rationalization using new paradigms and models have shifted to new groups of stocks (Chinese and Indian equities) and new classes of assets (subprime mortgages). I have come to the realization that the dark side of valuation beckons any time analysts have trouble fitting companies into traditional models and metrics. This second edition reflects that broader perspective. Rather than focusing on just young, high-tech (Internet) companies, as I did in the first edition, I want to look at companies that are difficult to value across the spectrum.

Chapters 2 through 5 review the basic tools available in valuation. In particular, they summarize conventional discounted cash flow models, probabilistic models (simulations, decision trees), relative valuation models, and real options. Much of what is included in this part has already been said in my other books on valuation.

Chapters 6 through 8 examine some of the estimation questions and issues surrounding macro variables that affect all valuation. Chapter 6 looks at the risk-free rate, the building block for all other inputs, and challenges the notion that government bond rates are always good estimates of risk-free rates. Chapter 7 expands the discussion to look at equity risk premiums. This is another number that is often taken as a given in valuation, primarily because risk premiums in mature markets have been stable for long periods. In shifting and volatile markets, risk premiums can change significantly over short periods. Failing to recognize this reality will create skewed valuations. Chapter 8 examines other macroeconomic assumptions that are often implicit in valuations about growth in the real economy. It also looks at exchange rates and inflation and how inconsistencies in these valuations affect the conclusions we draw.

Chapters 9 through 12 look at valuation challenges across a firm's life cycle. Figure P.1 shows the challenges.

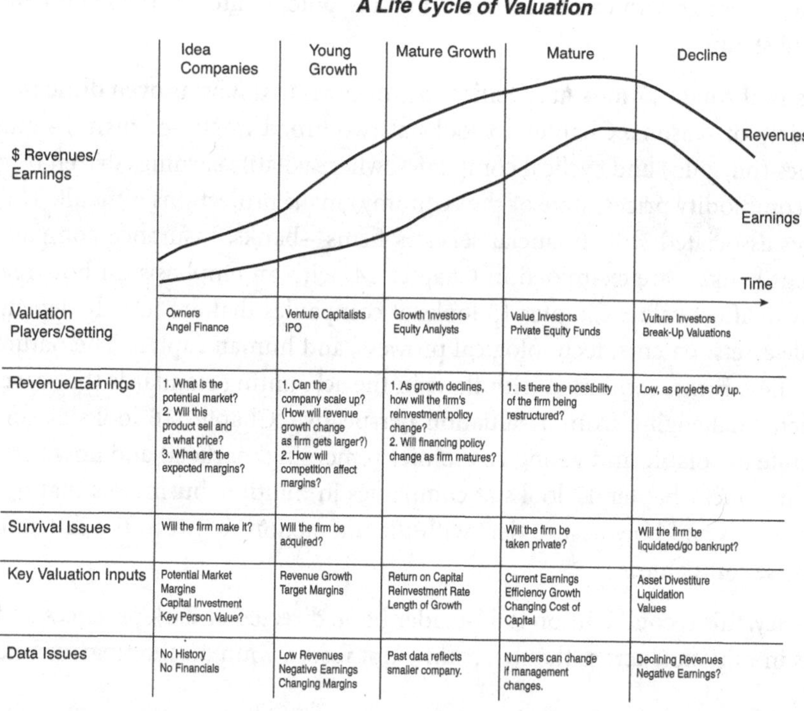

Figure P.1: A Life Cycle View of Valuation

Chapter 9 reviews the challenges faced in valuing young and "idea" businesses, which have an interesting idea for a product or service but no tangible commercial product yet. It also considers the baby steps involved as the idea evolves into a commercial product, albeit with very limited revenues and evidence of market success. Thus, it looks at the challenges faced in the first stages of entrepreneurial valuation. These are the challenges that venture capitalists have faced for decades when providing "angel financing" to small companies. Chapter 10 climbs the life cycle ladder to look at young growth companies, whose products and services have found a market and where revenues are growing fast. This chapter also examines the valuation implications of going public as opposed to staying private and the sustainability of growth. In addition, this chapter looks at growth companies that have survived the venture capital cycle and have gone public. These companies have a well-established track record of growth, but their size is working against them. Chapter 11 looks at "mature companies," where growth is in the past, and the efforts made by these firms to increase value, including acquisitions, operating restructuring, and financial restructuring. In the process, we also consider how a private equity investor may view value in a "mature" company in the context of a leveraged buyout and the value of control in this company. Chapter 12 considers firms in decline, where growth can be negative, and the potential for distress and bankruptcy may be substantial.

Chapters 13 through 17 look at specific types of firms that have proven difficult to value for a variety of reasons. Chapter 13 looks at two broad classes of firms—commodity companies (oil, gold) and cyclical companies, where volatile earnings driven by external factors (commodity prices, state of the economy) make projections difficult. The special challenges associated with financial services firms—banks, insurance companies, and investment banks—are examined in Chapter 14, with an emphasis on how regulatory changes can affect value. Chapter 15 looks at companies that are heavily dependent on intangible assets: patents, technological prowess, and human capital. The nature of the assets in these firms, combined with flaws in the accounting standards that cover them, make them challenging from a valuation perspective. Chapter 16 looks at companies that operate in volatile and young economies (emerging markets) and how best to estimate their value. Chapter 17 looks at companies in multiple businesses that operate in many countries and how best to deal with the interactions between the different pieces within these companies.

In summary, this second edition is a broader book directed at dark practices and flawed methods in valuation across the spectrum—not just in young technology companies.

ABOUT THE AUTHOR

Aswath Damodaran is Professor of Finance at the Stern School of Business at New York University. He teaches the corporate finance and equity valuation courses in the MBA program. He received his MBA and Ph.D from the University of California at Los Angeles. He has written several books on corporate finance, valuation, and portfolio management. He has been at NYU since 1986 and has received the Stern School of Business Excellence in Teaching Award (awarded by the graduating class) eight times. He was profiled in *BusinessWeek* as one of the top twelve business school professors in the United States in 1994.

1

The Dark Side of Valuation

I have always believed that valuation is simple and that practitioners choose to make it complex. The intrinsic value of a cash flow-generation asset is a function of how long you expect it to generate cash flows, as well as how large and predictable these cash flows are. This is the principle that we use in valuing businesses, private as well as public, and in valuing securities issued by these businesses.

Although the fundamentals of valuation are straightforward, the challenges we face in valuing companies shift as firms move through the life cycle. We go from idea businesses, often privately owned, to young growth companies, either public or on the verge of going public, to mature companies, with diverse product lines and serving different markets, to companies in decline, marking time until they are liquidated. At each stage, we are called on to estimate the same inputs—cash flows, growth rates, and discount rates—but with varying amounts of information and different degrees of precision. All too often, when confronted with significant uncertainty or limited information, we are tempted by the dark side of valuation, in which first principles are abandoned, new paradigms are created, and common sense is the casualty.

This chapter begins by describing the determinants of value for any company. Then it considers the estimation issues we face at each stage in the life cycle and for different types of companies. We close the chapter by looking at manifestations of the dark side of valuation.

Foundations of Value

We will explore the details of valuation approaches in the next four chapters. But we can establish the determinants of value for any business without delving into the models themselves. In this section, we will first consider a very simple version of an intrinsic value model. Then we will use this version to list the classes of inputs that determine value in any model.

Intrinsic Valuation

Every asset has an intrinsic value. In spite of our best efforts to observe that value, all we can do, in most cases, is arrive at an estimate of value. In discounted cash flow (DCF) valuation, the intrinsic value of an asset can be written as the present value of expected cash flows over its life, discounted to reflect both the time value of money and the riskiness of the cash flows.

$$\text{Value of Asset} = \sum_{t=1}^{t=N} \frac{E(CF_t)}{(1+r)^t}$$

In this equation, $E(CF_t)$ is the expected cash flow in period t, r is the risk-adjusted discount rate for the cash flow, and N is the life of the asset.

Now consider the challenges of valuing an ongoing business or company, which, in addition to owning multiple assets, also has the potential to invest in new assets in the future. Consequently, not only do we have to value a portfolio of existing assets, but we also have to consider the value that may be added by new investments in the future. We can encapsulate the challenges by framing a financial balance sheet for an ongoing firm, as shown in Figure 1.1.

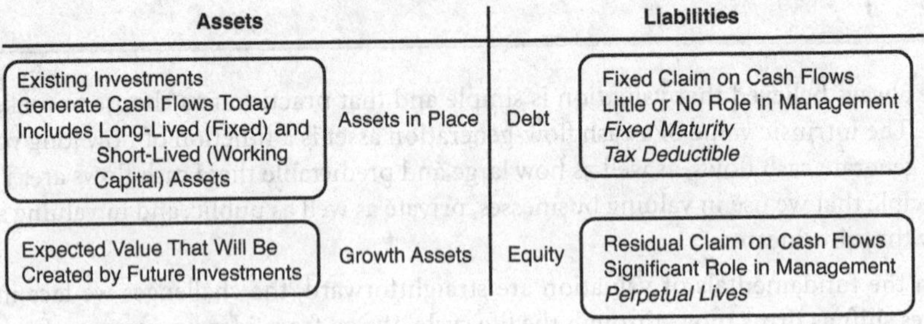

Figure 1.1: A Financial Balance Sheet

Thus, to value the company, we have to value both the investments already made (assets in place) and growth assets (investments that are expected in the future) while factoring in the mix of debt and equity used to fund the investments. A final complication must be considered. At least in theory, a business, especially if it is publicly traded, can keep generating cash flows forever, thus requiring us to expand our consideration of cash flows to cover this perpetual life:

$$\text{Value of Business} = \sum_{t=1}^{t=\infty} \frac{E(CF_t)}{(1+r)^t}$$

Because estimating cash flows forever is not feasible, we simplify the process by estimating cash flows for a finite period (N) and then a "terminal value" that captures the value of all cash flows beyond that period. In effect, the equation for firm value becomes the following:

$$\text{Value of Business} = \sum_{t=1}^{t=N} \frac{E(CF_t)}{(1+r)^t} + \frac{\text{Terminal Value}_N}{(1+r)^N}$$

Although different approaches can be used to estimate terminal value, the one most consistent with intrinsic value for a going concern is to assume that cash flows beyond year N grow at a constant rate forever, yielding the following variation on valuation:

$$\text{Value of Business} = \sum_{t=1}^{t=N} \frac{E(CF_t)}{(1+r)^t} + \frac{E(CF_{N+1})}{(r-g_n)(1+r)^N}$$

Because no firm can grow at a rate faster than the overall economy forever, this approach to estimating terminal value can be used only when the firm becomes a mature business. We will examine the details of estimating the inputs—cash flows, discount rates, and growth rates—in Chapter 2, "Intrinsic Valuation."

Determinants of Value

Without delving into the details of estimation, we can use the equation for the intrinsic value of the business to list the four broad questions that we need to answer in order to value any business:

- What are the cash flows that will be generated by the existing investments of the company?
- How much value, if any, will be added by future growth?
- How risky are the expected cash flows from both existing and growth investments, and what is the cost of funding them?
- When will the firm become a stable growth firm, allowing us to estimate a terminal value?

What Are the Cash Flows Generated by Existing Assets?

If a firm has already made significant investments, the first inputs into valuation are the cash flows from these existing assets. In practical terms, this requires estimating the following:

- How much the firm generated in earnings and cash flows from these assets in the most recent period
- How much growth (if any) is expected in these earnings/cash flows over time
- How long the assets will continue to generate cash flows

Although data that allows us to answer all these questions may be available in current financial statements, it might be inconclusive. In particular, cash flows can be difficult to obtain if the existing assets are still not fully operational (infrastructure investments that have been made but are not in full production mode) or if they are not being efficiently utilized. There can also be estimation issues when the firm in question is in a volatile business, where earnings on existing assets can rise and fall as a result of macroeconomic forces.

How Much Value Will Be Added by Future Investments (Growth)?

For some companies, the bulk of value is derived from investments you expect them to make in the future. To estimate the value added by these investments, you have to make judgments on two variables. The first is the magnitude of these new investments relative to the size of the firm. In other words, the value added can be very different if you assume that a firm reinvests 80% of its earnings into new investments than if you assume that it reinvests 20%. The second variable is the quality of the new investments measured in terms of excess returns. These are the returns the firm makes on the investments over and above the cost of funding those investments. Investing in new assets that generate returns of 15%, when the cost of capital is 10%, will add value, but investing in new assets that generate returns of 10%, with the same cost of capital, will not. In other words, it is growth with excess returns that creates value, not growth per se.

Because growth assets rest entirely on expectations and perception, we can make two statements about them. One is that valuing growth assets generally poses more challenges than valuing existing assets; historical or financial statement information is less likely to provide conclusive results. The other is that there will be far more volatility in the value of growth assets than in the value of existing assets, both over time and across different people valuing the same firm. Not only will analysts be likely to differ more on the inputs into growth asset value—the magnitude and quality of new investments—but they will also change their own estimates more over time as new information about the firm comes out. A poor earnings announcement by a growth company may alter the value of its existing assets just a little, but it can dramatically shift expectations about the value of growth assets.

How Risky Are the Cash Flows, and What Are the Consequences for Discount Rates?

Neither the cash flows from existing assets nor the cash flows from growth investments are guaranteed. When valuing these cash flows, we have to consider risk somewhere, and the discount rate is usually the vehicle that we use to convey the concerns that we may have about uncertainty in the future. In practical terms, we use higher discount rates to discount riskier cash flows and thus give them a lower value than more predictable cash flows. While this is a commonsense notion, we run into issues when putting this into practice when valuing firms:

- **Dependence on the past:** The risk that we are concerned about is entirely in the future, but our estimates of risk are usually based on data from the past—historical prices, earnings, and cash flows. While this dependence on historical data is understandable, it can give rise to problems when that data is unavailable, unreliable, or shifting.
- **Diverse risk investments:** When valuing firms, we generally estimate one discount rate for its aggregate cash flows, partly because of how we estimate risk parameters and partly for convenience. Firms generate cash flows from multiple assets, in different locations, with varying amounts of risk, so the discount rates we use should be different for each set of cash flows.
- **Changes in risk over time:** In most valuations, we estimate one discount rate and leave it unchanged over time, again partly for ease and partly because we feel uncomfortable changing discount rates over time. When valuing a firm, though, it is entirely possible, and indeed likely, that its risk will change over time as its asset mix changes and it matures. In fact, if we accept the earlier proposition that the cash flows from growth assets are more difficult to predict than cash flows from existing assets, we should expect the discount rate used on the cumulative expected cash flows of a growth firm to decrease as its growth rate declines over time.

When Will the Firm Become Mature?

The question of when a firm will become mature is relevant because it determines the length of the high-growth period and the value we attach to the firm at the end of the period (the terminal value). This question may be easy to answer for a few firms. This includes larger and more stable firms that are either already mature businesses or close to maturity, or firms that derive their growth from a single competitive advantage with an expiration date (for instance, a patent). For most firms, however, the conclusion will be murky for two reasons:

- Making a judgment about when a firm will become mature requires us to look at the sector in which the firm operates, the state of its competitors, and what they will do in the future. For firms in sectors that are evolving, with new entrants and existing competitors exiting, this is difficult to do.
- We are sanguine about mapping pathways to the terminal value in discounted cash flow models. We generally assume that every firm makes it to stable growth and goes on. However, the real world delivers surprises along the way that may impede these paths. After all, most firms do not make it to the steady state that we aspire to and instead get acquired, are restructured, or go bankrupt well before the terminal year.

In summary, not only is estimating when a firm will become mature difficult to do, but considering whether a firm will make it as a going concern for a valuation is just as important.

Pulling together all four questions, we get a framework for valuing any business, as shown in Figure 1.2.

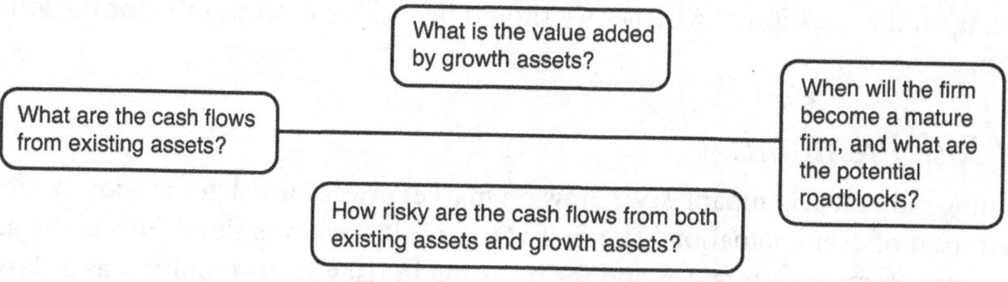

Figure 1.2: The Fundamental Questions in Valuation

Although these questions may not change as we value individual firms, the ease with which we can answer them can change. This happens not only as we look across firms at a point in time, but also across time, even for the same firm. Getting from the value of the business to the value of the equity in the business may seem like a simple exercise: subtracting the outstanding debt. But the process can be complicated if the debt is not clearly defined or is contingent on an external event (a claim in a lawsuit). Once we have the value of equity, getting the value of a unit claim in equity (per share value) can be difficult if different equity claims have different voting rights, cash flow claims, or liquidity.

Valuation Across Time

Valuing all companies becomes more complicated in an unsettled macroeconomic environment. In fact, three basic inputs into every valuation—the risk-free rate, risk premiums, and overall economic growth (real and nominal)—can be volatile in some cases, making it difficult to value any company. In this section, we will look at the reasons for volatility in these fundamental inputs and how they can affect valuations.

Interest Rates

To value a risky asset, we have to answer a fundamental question: What can you expect to earn as a rate of return on a riskless investment? The answer to this question is the risk-free rate. Although we take it as a given in most valuations, it can sometimes be difficult to identify. When the risk-free rate is unknown, everything else in the valuation is open to question as well.

To understand why estimating the risk-free rate can be problematic, let us define a risk-free rate. It is the rate of return you can expect to make on an investment with a guaranteed return. For an investment to deliver such a return, it must have no default risk, which is why we use government bond rates as risk-free rates. In addition, the notion of a risk-free rate must be tied to your time horizon as an investor. The guaranteed return for a six-month investment can be very different from the guaranteed return over the next five years.

So, what are the potential issues? The first is that, with some currencies, the governments involved either do not issue bonds in those currencies, or the bonds are not traded. This makes it impossible to get a long-term bond rate in the first place. The second issue is that not all governments are default-free, and the potential for default can inflate the rates on bonds issues by these entities, thus making the observed interest rates not risk-free. The third issue is that the riskless rate today may be (or may seem to be) abnormally high or low, relative to fundamentals or history. This leaves open the question of whether we should be locking in these rates for the long term in a valuation.

Market Risk Premiums

When valuing individual companies, we draw on market prices for risk for at least two inputs and make them part of every valuation. The first is the equity risk premium. This is the additional return that we assume investors demand for investing in risky assets (equities) as a class, relative to the risk-free rate. In practice, this number is usually obtained by looking at long periods of historical data, with the implicit assumption that future premiums will converge to this number sooner rather than later. The second input is the default spread for risky debt, an input into the cost of debt in valuation. This number is usually obtained by either looking at the spreads on corporate bonds in different ratings classes or looking at the interest rates a company is paying on the debt it has on its books right now.

In most valuations, the equity risk premium and default spread are assumed to be either known or a given. Therefore, analysts focus on company-specific inputs—cash flows, growth, and risk—to arrive at an estimate of value. Furthermore, we usually assume that the market prices for risk in both equity and debt markets remain stable over time. In emerging markets, these assumptions are difficult to sustain. Even in mature markets, we face two dangers. The first is that economic shocks can change equity risk premiums and default spreads significantly. If the risk premiums that we use to value companies do not reflect these changes, we risk undervaluing or overvaluing all companies (depending on whether risk premiums have increased or decreased). The second danger is that there are conditions, especially in volatile markets, where the equity risk premium that we estimate for the near term (the next year or two) will be different from the equity risk premium that we believe will hold in the long term (after year 5, for instance). To get realistic valuations of companies, we have to incorporate these expected changes into the estimates we use for future years.

The Macro Environment

It is impossible to value a company without making assumptions about the overall economy in which it operates. Since instability in the economy feeds into volatility in company earnings and cash flows, it is easier to value companies in mature economies, where inflation and real growth are stable. Most of the changes in company value over time, then, come from changes in company-specific inputs. We face a very different challenge when we value companies in economies that are in flux, because changes in the macroeconomic environment can dramatically change values for all companies.

In practice, three general macro economic inputs influence value. The first is the growth in the real economy. Changes in that growth rate will affect the growth rates (and values) of all companies, but the effect will be largest for cyclical companies. The second is expected inflation; as inflation becomes volatile, company values can be affected in both positive and negative ways. Companies that can pass through the higher inflation to their customers will be less affected than companies without pricing power. All companies can be affected by how accounting and tax laws deal with inflation. The third and related variable is exchange rates. When converting cash flows from one currency into another, we have to make assumptions about expected exchange rates in the future.

We face several dangers when valuing companies in volatile economies. The first is that we fail to consider expected changes in macroeconomic variables when making forecasts. Using today's exchange rate to convert cash flows in the future, from one currency to another, is an example. The second danger is that we make assumptions about changes in macroeconomic variables that are internally inconsistent. Assuming that inflation in the local currency will increase while also assuming that the currency will become stronger over time is an example. The third danger is that the assumptions we make about macroeconomic changes are inconsistent with other inputs we use in the valuation. For instance, assuming that inflation will increase over time, pushing up expected cash flows, while the risk-free rate remains unchanged, will result in an overvaluation of the company.

Valuation Across the Life Cycle

Although the inputs into valuation are the same for all businesses, the challenges we face in making the estimates can vary significantly across firms. In this section, we first break firms into four groups based on where they are in the life cycle. Then we explore the estimation issues we run into with firms in each stage.

The Business Life Cycle

Firms pass through a life cycle, starting as young idea companies, and working their way to high growth, maturity, and eventual decline. Because the difficulties associated with estimating valuation inputs vary as firms go through the life cycle, it is useful to start with the five phases that we divide the life cycle into and consider the challenges in each phase, as shown in Figure 1.3.

Note that the time spent in each phase can vary widely across firms. Some, like Google and Amazon, speed through the early phases and quickly become growth companies. Others make the adjustment much more gradually. Many growth companies have only a few years of growth before they become mature businesses. Others, such as Coca-Cola, IBM, and Wal-Mart, can stretch their growth periods to last decades. At each phase in the cycle, some companies never make it through, either because they run out of cash and access to capital or because they have trouble making debt payments.

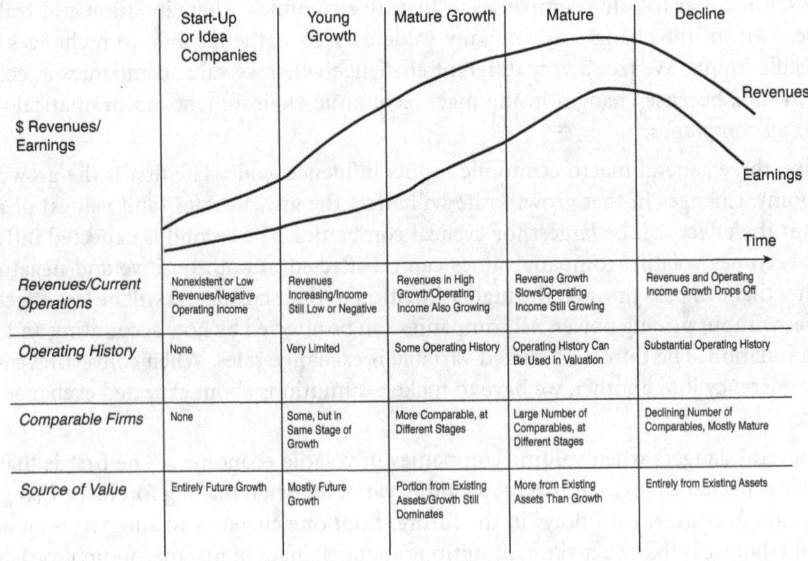

Figure 1.3: Valuation Issues Across the Life Cycle

Early in the Life Cycle: Young Companies

Every business starts with an idea. The idea germinates in a market need that an entrepreneur sees (or thinks he sees) and a way of filling that need. Most ideas go nowhere, but some individuals take the next step of investing in the idea. The capital to finance the investment usually comes from personal funds (from savings, friends, and family), and in the best-case scenario, it yields a commercial product or service. Assuming that the product or service finds a ready market, the business usually needs to access more capital. Usually it is supplied by venture capitalists, who provide funds in return for a share of the equity in the business. Building on the most optimistic assumptions again, success for the investors in the business ultimately is manifested as a public offering to the market or sale to a larger entity.

At each stage in the process, we need estimates of value. At the idea stage, the value may never be put down on paper, but it is the potential for this value that induces the entrepreneur to invest both time and money in developing the idea. At subsequent stages of the capital-raising process, the valuations become more explicit, because they determine what the entrepreneur must give up as a share of ownership in return for external funding. At the time of the public offering, the valuation is key to determining the offering price.

Using the template for valuation that we developed in the preceding section, it is easy to see why young companies also create the most daunting challenges for valuation. There are few or no existing assets; almost all the value comes from expectations of future growth. The firm's current financial statements provide no clues about the potential margins and returns that will be generated in the future, and little historical data can be used to develop risk measures. To cap the estimation problem, many young firms will not make it to stable growth, and estimating when that will happen for firms that survive is difficult to do. In addition, these firms are often dependent on one or a few key people for their success, so losing them can have significant effects on value. A final valuation challenge we face with valuing equity in young companies is that different equity investors have different claims on the cash flows. The investors with the first claims on the cash flows should have the more valuable claims. Figure 1.4 summarizes these valuation challenges.

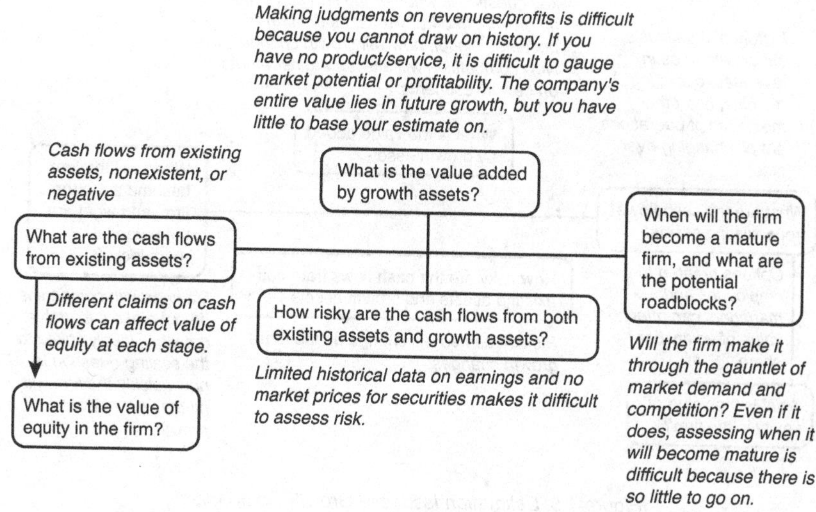

Figure 1.4: Valuation Challenges

Given these problems, it is not surprising that analysts often fall back on simplistic measures of value, "guesstimates," or rules of thumb to value young companies.

The Growth Phase: Growth Companies

Some idea companies make it through the test of competition to become young growth companies. Their products or services have found a market niche, and many of these companies make the transition to the public market, although a few remain private. Revenue growth is usually high, but the costs associated with building market share can result in losses and negative cash flows, at least early in the growth cycle. As revenue growth persists, earnings turn positive and often grow exponentially in the first few years.

Valuing young growth companies is a little easier than valuing start-up or idea companies. The markets for products and services are more clearly established, and the current financial statements provide some clues to future profitability. Five key estimation issues can still create valuation uncertainty. The first is how well the revenue growth that the company is reporting will scale up. In other words, how quickly will revenue growth decline as the firm gets bigger? The answer will differ across companies and will be a function of both the company's competitive advantages and the market it serves. The second issue is determining how profit margins will evolve over time as revenues grow. The third issue is making reasonable assumptions about reinvestment to sustain revenue growth, with concurrent judgments about the returns on investment in the business. The fourth issue is that as revenue growth and profit margins change over time, the firm's risk will also shift, with the requirement that we estimate how risk will evolve in the future. The final issue we face when valuing equity in growth companies is valuing options that the firm may grant to employees over time and the effect that these grants have on value per share. Figure 1.5 captures the estimation issues we face in valuing growth companies.

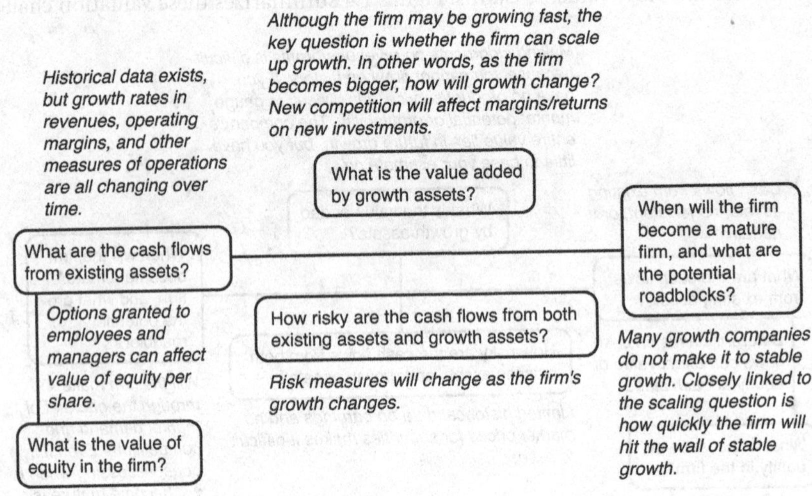

Figure 1.5: Estimation Issues in Growth Companies

As firms move through the growth cycle, from young growth to more established growth, some of these questions become easier to answer. The proportion of firm value that comes from growth assets declines as existing assets become more profitable and also accounts for a larger chunk of overall value.

Maturity—a Mixed Blessing: Mature Firms

Even the best of growth companies reach a point where size works against them. Their growth rates in revenues and earnings converge on the growth rate of the economy. In this phase, the bulk of a firm's value comes from existing investments, and financial statements become more informative. Revenue growth is steady, and profit margins have settled into a pattern, making it easier to forecast earnings and cash flows.

Although estimation does become simpler with these companies, analysts must consider potential problems. The first is that the results from operations (including revenues and earnings) reflect how well the firm is utilizing its existing assets. Changes in operating efficiency can have a large impact on earnings and cash flows, even in the near term. The second problem is that mature firms sometimes turn to acquisitions to re-create growth potential. Predicting the magnitude and consequences of acquisitions is much more difficult to do than estimating growth from organic or internal investments. The third problem is that mature firms are more likely to look to financial restructuring to increase their value. The mix of debt and equity used to fund the business may change overnight, and assets (such as accounts receivable) may be securitized. The final issue is that mature companies sometimes have equity claims with differences in voting right and control claims, and hence different values. Figure 1.6 frames the estimation challenges at mature companies.

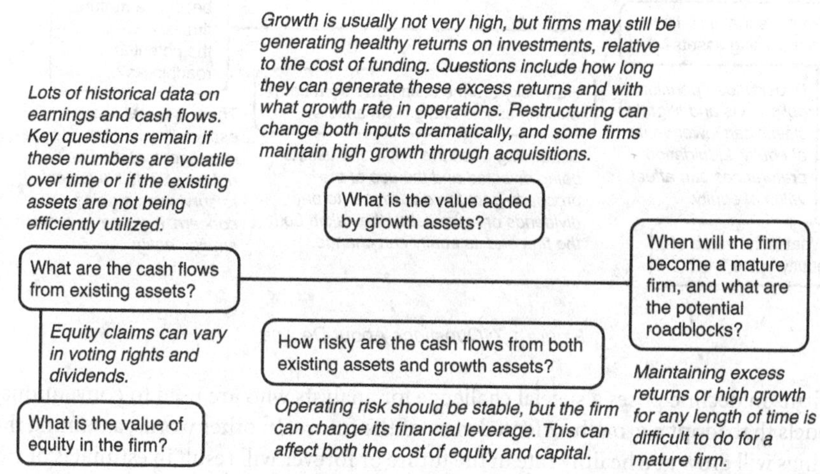

Figure 1.6: Estimation Challenges in Mature Companies

Not surprisingly, mature firms usually are targeted in hostile acquisitions and leveraged buyouts, where the buyer believes that changing how the firm is run can result in significant increases in value.

Winding Down: Dealing with Decline

Most firms reach a point in their life cycle where their existing markets are shrinking and becoming less profitable, and the forecast for the future is more of the same. Under these circumstances, these firms react by selling assets and returning cash to investors. Put another way, these firms derive their value entirely from existing assets, and that value is expected to shrink over time.

Valuing declining companies requires making judgments about the assets that will be divested over time and the profitability of the assets that will be left in the firm. Judgments about how much cash will be received in these divestitures and how that cash will be utilized (pay dividends, buy back shares, retire debt) can influence the value attached to the firm. Another concern overhangs this valuation. Some firms in decline that have significant debt obligations can become distressed. This problem is not specific to declining firms but is more common with them. Finally, the equity values in declining firms can be affected significantly by the presence of underfunded pension obligations and the overhead of litigation costs—more so than with other firms. Figure 1.7 shows these questions.

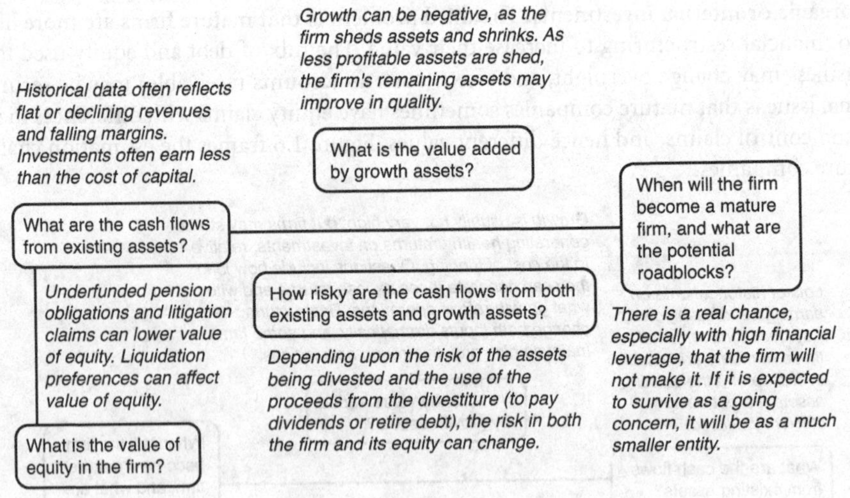

Figure 1.7: Questions About Decline

Valuing firms in decline poses a special challenge for analysts who are used to conventional valuation models that adopt a growth-oriented view of the future. In other words, assuming that current earnings will grow at a healthy rate in the future or forever will result in estimates of value for these firms that are way too high.

Valuation Across the Business Spectrum

The preceding section considered the different issues we face in estimating cash flows, growth rates, risk, and maturity across the business life cycle. In this section, we consider how firms in some businesses are more difficult to value than others. We consider five groups of companies:

- Financial services firms, such as banks, investment banks, and insurance companies
- Cyclical and commodity businesses
- Businesses with intangible assets (human capital, patents, technology)
- Emerging-market companies that face significant political risk
- Multibusiness global companies

With each group, we examine what it is about the firms within that group that generates valuation problems.

Financial Services Firms

While financial services firms have historically been viewed as stable investments that are relatively simple to value, financial crises bring out the dangers of this assumption. In 2008, for instance, the equity values at most banks swung wildly, and the equity at many others, including Lehman Brothers, Bear Stearns, and Fortis, lost all value. It was a wake-up call to analysts who had used fairly simplistic models to value these banks and had missed the brewing problems.

So what are the potential problems with valuing financial services firms? We can frame them in terms of the four basic inputs into the valuation process:

- The existing assets of banks are primarily financial, with a good portion being traded in markets. While accounting rules require that these assets be marked to market, these rules are not always consistently applied across different classes of assets. Since the risk in these assets can vary widely across firms, and information about this risk is not always forthcoming, accounting errors feed into valuation errors.
- The risk is magnified by the high financial leverage at banks and investment banks. It is not uncommon to see banks have debt-to-equity ratios of 30 to 1 or higher, allowing them to leverage up the profitability of their operations.
- Financial services firms are, for the most part, regulated, and regulatory rules can affect growth potential. The regulatory restrictions on book equity capital as a ratio of loans at a bank influence how quickly the bank can expand over time and how profitable that expansion will be. Changes in regulatory rules therefore have big effects on growth and value, with more lenient (or stricter) rules resulting in more (or less) value from growth assets. Finally, since the damage created by a troubled bank or investment bank can be extensive, it is also likely that problems at these entities will evoke much swifter reactions from authorities than at other firms. A troubled bank will be quickly taken over to protect depositors, lenders, and customers, but the equity in the banks will be wiped out in the process.
- As a final point, getting to the value of equity per share for a financial services firm can be complicated by the presence of preferred stock, which shares characteristics with both debt and equity. Figure 1.8 summarizes the valuation issues at financial services firms.

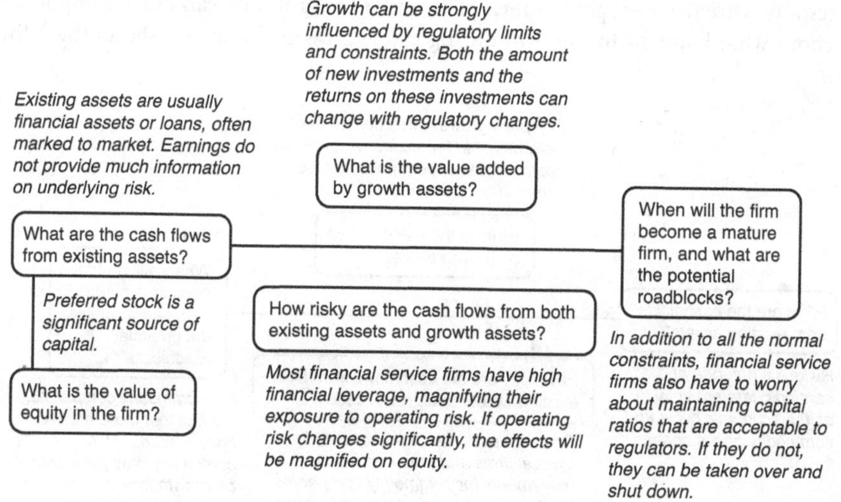

Figure 1.8: Valuation Issues at Financial Services Firms

Analysts who value banks go through cycles. In good times, they tend to underestimate the risk of financial crises and extrapolate from current profitability to arrive at higher values for financial services firms. In crises, they lose perspective and mark down the values of both healthy and unhealthy banks, without much discrimination.

Cyclical and Commodity Companies

If we define a mature company as one that delivers predictable earnings and revenues, period after period, cyclical and commodity companies will never be mature. Even the largest, most established of them have volatile earnings. The earnings volatility has little to do with the company. It is more reflective of variability in the underlying economy (for cyclical firms) or the base commodity (for a commodity company).

The biggest issue with valuing cyclical and commodity companies lies in the base year numbers that are used in valuation. If we do what we do with most other companies and use the current year as the base year, we risk building into our valuations the vagaries of the economy or commodity prices in that year. As an illustration, valuing oil companies using earnings from 2007 as a base year will inevitably result in too high a value. The spike in oil prices that year contributed to the profitability of almost all oil companies, small and large, efficient and inefficient. Similarly, valuing housing companies using earnings and other numbers from 2008, when the economy was drastically slowing down, will result in values that are too low. The uncertainty we feel about base year earnings also percolates into other parts of the valuation. Estimates of growth at cyclical and commodity companies depend more on our views of overall economic growth and the future of commodity prices than they do on the investments made at individual companies. Similarly, risk that lies dormant when the economy is doing well and commodity prices are rising can manifest itself suddenly when the cycle turns. Finally, for highly levered cyclical and commodity companies, especially when the debt was accumulated during earnings upswings, a reversal of fortune can very quickly put the firm at risk. In addition, for companies like oil companies, the fact that natural resources are finite—only so much oil is under the ground—can put a crimp in what we assume about what happens to the firm during stable growth. Figure 1.9 shows the estimation questions.

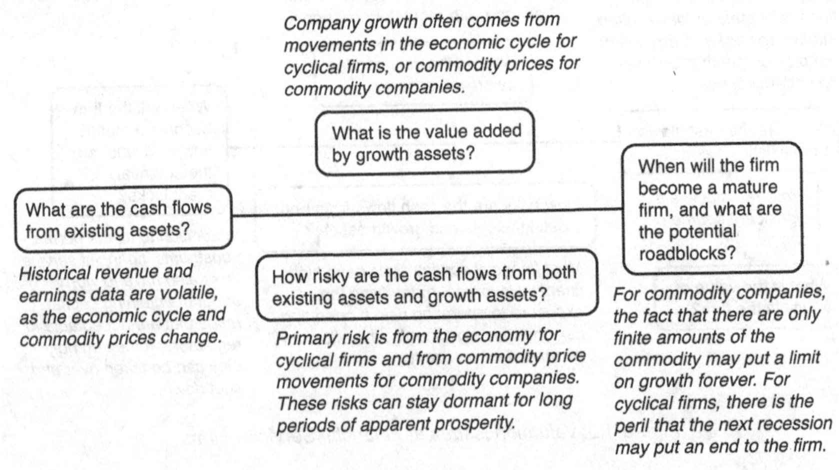

Figure 1.9: Estimation Questions for Cyclical and Commodity Companies

When valuing cyclical and commodity companies, analysts often make implicit assumptions about the economy and commodity prices by extrapolating past earnings and growth rates. Many of these implicit assumptions turn out to be unrealistic, and the valuations that lead from them are equally flawed.

Businesses with Intangible Assets

In the last two decades, we have seen mature economies, such as the U.S. and Western Europe, shift from manufacturing to services and technology businesses. In the process, we have come to recognize how little of the value at many of our largest companies today comes from physical assets (like land, machinery, and factories) and how much of the value comes from intangible assets. Intangible assets range from brand name at Coca-Cola to technological know-how at Google and human capital at firms like McKinsey. As accountants grapple with how best to deal with these intangible assets, we face similar challenges when valuing them.

Let us state at the outset that there should be no reason why the tools that we have developed over time for physical assets cannot be applied to intangible assets. The value of a brand name or patent should be the present value of the cash flows from that asset, discounted at an appropriate risk-adjusted rate. The problem that we face is that the accounting standards for firms with intangible assets are not entirely consistent with the standards for firms with physical assets. An automobile company that invests in a new plant or factory is allowed to treat that expenditure as a capital expenditure, record the item as an asset, and depreciate it over its life. A technology firm that invests in research and development, with the hope of generating new patents, is required to expense the entire expenditure and record no assets, and it cannot amortize or depreciate the item. The same can be said of a consumer products company that spends millions on advertising with the intent of building a brand name. The consequences for estimating the basic inputs for valuation are profound. For existing assets, the accounting treatment of intangible assets makes both current earnings and book value unreliable. The former is net of R&D, and the latter does not include investments in the firm's biggest assets. Since reinvestment and accounting return numbers are flawed for the same reasons, assessing expected growth becomes more difficult. Since lenders tend to be wary about lending to firms with intangible assets, they tend to be funded predominantly with equity, and the risk of equity can change quickly over a firm's life cycle. Finally, estimating when a firm with intangible assets gets to steady state can be complex. On the one hand, easy entry into and exit from the business and rapid changes in technology can cause growth rates to drop quickly at some firms. On the other hand, the long life of some competitive advantages like brand name and the ease with which firms can scale up (they do not need heavy infrastructure or physical investments) can allow other firms to maintain high growth, with excess returns, for decades. The problems that we face in valuing companies with intangible assets are shown in Figure 1.10.

When faced with valuing firms with intangible assets, analysts tend to use the accounting earnings and book values at these firms, without correcting for the miscategorization of capital expenditures. Any analyst who compares the price earnings (PE) ratio for Microsoft to the PE ratio for GE is guilty of this error. In addition, there is also the temptation, when doing valuations, to add arbitrary premiums to estimated value to reflect the value of intangibles. Thus, adding a 30% premium to the value estimate of Coca-Cola is not a sensible way of capturing the value of a brand name.

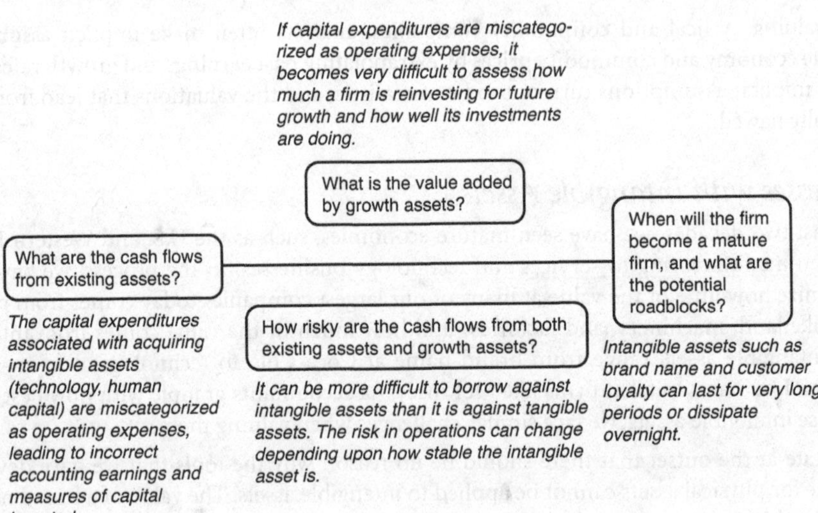

Figure 1.10: Questions About Valuing Companies with Intangible Assets

Emerging-Market Companies

In the last decade, the economies that have grown the fastest have been in Asia and Latin America. With that growth, we have also seen an explosion of listings in financial markets in these emerging economies and increased interest in valuing companies in these markets.

In valuing emerging-market companies, the overriding concern that analysts have is that the risk of the countries that these companies operate in often overwhelms the risk in the companies themselves. Investing in a stable company in Argentina will still expose you to considerable risk, because country risk swings back and forth. While the inputs to valuing emerging-market companies are familiar—cash flows from existing and growth assets, risk and getting to stable growth—country risk creates estimation issues with each input. Variations in accounting standards and corporate governance rules across emerging markets often result in a lack of transparency when it comes to current earnings and investments, making it difficult to assess the value of existing assets. Expectations of future growth rest almost as much on how the emerging market that the company is located in will evolve as they do on the company's own prospects. Put another way, it is difficult for even the best-run emerging-market company to grow if the market it operates in is in crisis. In a similar vein, the overlay of country risk on company risk indicates that we have to confront and measure both if we want to value emerging-market companies. Finally, in addition to economic crises that visit emerging markets at regular intervals, putting all companies at risk, there is the added risk that companies can be nationalized or appropriated by the government. The challenges associated with valuing emerging-market companies are shown in Figure 1.11.

Analysts who value emerging-market companies develop their own coping mechanisms for dealing with the overhang of country risk, with some mechanisms being healthier than others. In its most unhealthy form, analysts avoid even dealing with the risk. They switch to more stable currencies for their valuations and adopt very simple measures of country risk, such as adding a fixed premium to the cost of capital to every company in a market. In other cases, their preoccupation with country risk leads them to double-count and triple-count the risk and pay insufficient attention to the company being valued.

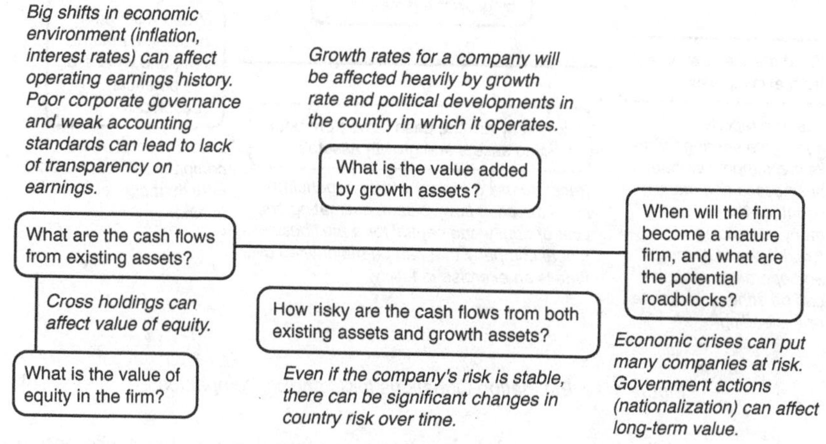

Figure 1.11: Challenges Associated with Valuing Emerging-Market Companies

Multibusiness and Global Companies

As investors globalize their portfolios, companies are also becoming increasingly globalized, with many of the largest ones operating in multiple businesses. Give that these businesses have very different risk and operating characteristics, valuing the multibusiness global company can be a challenge to even the best-prepared analyst.

The conventional approach to valuing a company has generally been to work with the consolidated earnings and cash flows of the business and to discount those cash flows using an aggregated risk measure for the company that reflects its mix of businesses. Although this approach works well for firms in one or a few lines of business, it becomes increasingly difficult as companies spread their operations across multiple businesses in multiple markets. Consider a firm like General Electric, a conglomerate that operates in dozens of businesses and in almost every country around the globe. The company's financial statements reflect its aggregated operations, across its different businesses and geographic locations. Attaching a value to existing assets becomes difficult, since these assets vary widely in terms of risk and return-generating capacity. While GE may break down earnings for its different business lines, those numbers are contaminated by the accounting allocation of centralized costs and intrabusiness transactions. The expected growth rates can be very different for different parts of the business, in terms of not only magnitude but also quality. Furthermore, as the firm grows at different rates in different businesses, its overall risk changes to reflect the new business weights, adding another problem to valuation. Finally, different pieces of the company may approach stable growth at different points in time, making it difficult to stop and assess the terminal value. Figure 1.12 summarizes the estimation questions that we have to answer for complex companies.

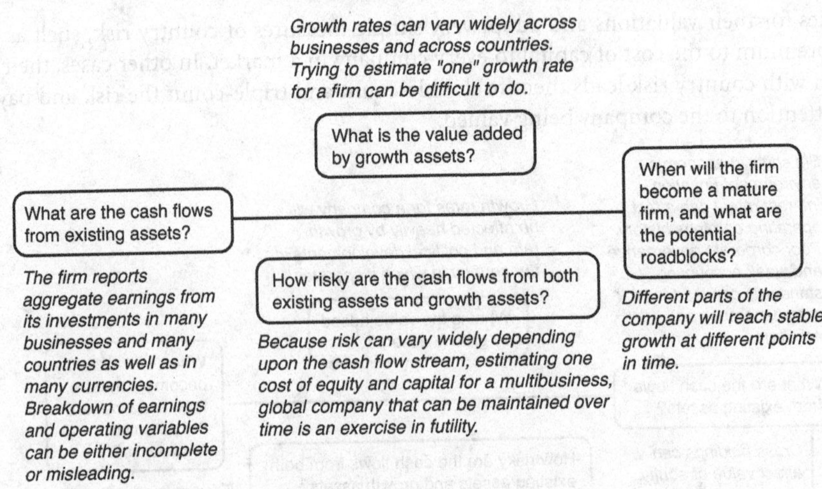

Figure 1.12: Estimation Questions for Complex Companies

Analysts who value multibusiness and global companies often draw on the averaging argument to justify not knowing as much as they should about individual businesses. Higher growth (or risk) in some businesses will be offset by lower growth (or risk) in other businesses, they argue, thus justifying their overall estimates of growth and risk. They underestimate the dangers of the unknown. All too often, with companies like these, what you do not know is more likely to contain bad news than good news.

Seeing the Dark Side of Valuation

When confronted with estimation challenges, analysts have one of two choices. The healthy response is to confront the challenge and adapt existing models to reflect the differences in the company being valued. The more common response is to bend the rules of valuation and use shortcuts to justify whatever price they are predisposed to pay for the company. The latter approach is "the dark side of valuation." This section looks at its many manifestations.

Input Phase

In the input phase, we look for the standard starting points for valuing individual companies—earnings and operating details from the most recent financial statements; forecasts for the future, provided by analysts and management; and data for macroeconomic inputs such as risk-free rates, risk premiums, and exchange rates. We see some standard patterns in valuations:

- **Base year fixation:** Analysts often treat the current year as the base year in valuation and build these numbers in making forecasts. While this is understandable, it can also lead to serious errors in valuation when either of the following occurs:
  - Current numbers do not reflect the firm's long-term earnings capability. As we noted earlier, this is especially true of commodity and cyclical companies, but it is also the case for young and start-up companies.

- Inconsistencies in the accounting treatment of operating and capital expenditures are skewing current values for earnings and book value. With technology and human capital companies, this will be an issue.

- **Outsourcing key inputs:** When it comes to macroeconomic inputs, analysts usually go to outside sources. This is especially true with equity risk premiums and betas, where services offer estimates of the numbers, backed up by volumes of data. While this may give analysts someone else to blame if things go wrong, it also means that little independent thought goes into whether the numbers being used actually make sense.
- **Trusting management forecasts:** The most difficult task in valuing a company is forecasting future revenues, earnings, and reinvestment. This is especially true with younger companies that have significant growth prospects. When managers offer to provide forecasts of these numbers, analysts, not surprisingly, jump at the opportunity and rationalize their use of these forecasts by arguing that managers know more about the company than they do. What they fail to consider is that these forecasts are likely to be biased.

Valuation Phase

The inputs feed into valuation models and metrics to provide the final judgments on value. At this stage in the process, it is natural for analysts to feel uncertain about the reliability of these numbers—more so for some companies than others. In the process of dealing with this uncertainty, some common errors show up in valuations:

- **Ignoring the scaling effect:** As firms get larger, it becomes more and more difficult to maintain high growth rates. In making forecasts, analysts often fail to consider this reality and continue to use growth rates derived from history long into their forecast periods.
- **Inconsistencies in valuation:** Good valuations should be internally consistent, but it is easy for inconsistencies to enter valuations. As you will see in the coming chapters, assumptions about growth, reinvestment, and risk not only have to make sense individually but also have to tie together. Estimating high growth rates with little or no reinvestment into the business to generate this growth may be possible, but it is unlikely. The assumptions that we make about inflation in our cash flow estimates have to be consistent with the assumptions (often implicit) about expected inflation in interest rates and exchange rates.
- **Valuing for the exception:** Analysts often draw on anecdotal evidence to justify their assumptions. The fact that Wal-Mart was able to continue growing, even as it became larger, is used to justify maintaining high revenue growth rates for firms for long periods. Analysts point to companies like Coca-Cola and Microsoft to justify assumptions about maintaining high margins and returns on investment for small-growth companies. It is worth nothing that Wal-Mart, Coca-Cola, and Microsoft are the exceptions, rather than the rule.
- **Paradigm shifts:** When analysts abandon age-old principles of economics and valuation, talking about how the rules have changed, it is time to be skeptical. It is true that economies and markets change, and we have to change with them. But we cannot repeal

the laws of demand and supply or the notion that businesses eventually have to make money to be valuable.

- **Black-box models**: As data becomes more easily accessible and building bigger models becomes more feasible, one response to uncertainty is to build bigger and more complex models. Two problems come out of more detailed models. One is the fact that they require far more inputs to arrive at a number. Uncertainty often multiplies as we add more detail, and it is "garbage in, garbage out." The other problem is that the model becomes a black box, with analysts having little sense of what happens inside the box.
- **Rules of thumb**: If one response to complexity is to build bigger and better models, the other response is to look for a simple solution. In many valuations, this takes the form of using a rule of thumb to arrive at the value of an asset. An analyst faced with a particularly troublesome set of inputs may decide to value a company at three times revenues because that is what investors have traditionally paid for companies in this sector. While using these shortcuts may provide the illusion of precision, it is far better to confront uncertainty than to ignore it.

Post-Valuation Phase

In many cases, the real damage to valuation principles occurs after the valuation has been done—at least in terms of mechanics. At least two common practices wreak havoc on valuations:

- **Valuation garnishing**: This is the all-too-common practice of adding premiums and discounts to estimated value to reflect what the analyst believes are missed components. It is not uncommon in acquisition valuations, for instance, to add a 20% premium for control, just as it is standard practice in private company valuation to reduce value by 20 to 25% to reflect illiquidity. Similar premiums/discounts are added/subtracted to reflect the effects of brand names and other intangibles and emerging-market risk. The net result of these adjustments is that the value reflects whatever preconceptions the analyst might have had about the company.
- **Market feedback**: With publicly traded companies, the first number that we look at after we have done a valuation is the market price. When analysts are uncertain about the numbers that go into their valuations, big differences between the value and the market price lead to their revisiting the valuation. As inputs change, the value drifts inexorably toward the market price, rendering the entire process pointless. If we believe that markets are right, why bother doing valuation in the first place?

In summary, the dark side of valuation can take many different forms, but the end result is always the same. The valuations we arrive at for individual businesses reflect the errors and biases we have built into the process. All too often, we find what we want to find rather than the truth.

Conclusion

Some companies are easier to value than others. When we have to leave the comfort zone of companies with solid earnings and predictable futures, we invariably stray into the dark side of valuation. Here we invent new principles, violate established ones, and come up with unsustainable values for businesses.

This chapter described the four inputs that we have to estimate to value any company:

- The expected cash from investments that the business has already made (existing assets)
- The value that will be added by new investments (growth assets)
- The risk in these cash flows
- The point in time where we expect the firm to become a mature firm

The estimation challenges we face will vary widely across companies, so we must consider how estimation issues vary across a firm's life cycle. For young and start-up firms, the absence of historical data and the dependence on growth assets make estimating future cash flows and risk particularly difficult. With growth firms, the question shifts to whether growth rates can be maintained and, if so, for how long, as firms scale up. With mature firms, the big issue in valuation shifts to whether existing assets are being efficiently utilized and whether the financial mix used by the firm makes sense. Restructuring the firm to make it run better may dramatically alter value. For declining firms, estimating revenues and margins as assets get divested is messy, and considering the possibility of default can be tricky. The estimation challenges we face can also be different for different subsets of companies. Cyclical and commodity companies have volatile operating results. Companies with intangible assets have earnings that are skewed by how accountants treat investments in these assets. The risk in emerging-market and global companies can be difficult to assess. Finally, valuing any company can become more difficult in economies where the fundamentals—risk-free rates, risk premiums, and economic growth—are volatile.

In the last part of the chapter, we turned our attention to how analysts respond to uncertainty, with an emphasis on some of the more unhealthy responses. The dark side of valuation manifests itself at each phase of a valuation; our task for the rest of the book is clear. Accepting the fact that uncertainty will always be with us and that we have to sometimes value "difficult" businesses, we will look at healthy ways of responding to uncertainty.

2

Intrinsic Valuation

Every asset that generates cash flows has an intrinsic value that reflects both its cash flow potential and its risk. Many analysts claim that when significant uncertainty about the future exists, estimating intrinsic value becomes not just difficult but pointless. But we disagree. Notwithstanding this uncertainty, we believe that it is important to look past market perceptions and gauge, as best we can, the intrinsic value of a business or asset. This chapter considers how discounted cash flow valuation models attempt to estimate intrinsic value and describes estimation details and possible limitations.

Discounted Cash Flow Valuation

In discounted cash flow (DCF) valuation, an asset's value is the present value of the expected cash flows on the asset, discounted back at a rate that reflects the riskiness of these cash flows. This section looks at the foundations of the approach and some of the preliminary details of how we estimate its inputs.

The Essence of DCF Valuation

We buy most assets because we expect them to generate cash flows for us in the future. In discounted cash flow valuation, we begin with a simple proposition. The value of an asset is not what someone perceives it to be worth; it is a function of the expected cash flows on that asset. Put simply, assets with high and predictable cash flows should have higher values than assets with low and volatile cash flows.

The notion that the value of an asset is the present value of the cash flows that you expect to generate by holding it is neither new nor revolutionary. The earliest interest rate tables date back to 1340, and the intellectual basis for discounted cash flow valuation was laid by Alfred Marshall and Bohm-Bawerk in the early part of the twentieth century.[1] The principles of modern valuation were developed by Irving Fisher in two books—*The Rate of Interest* in 1907 and *The Theory of Interest* in 1930.[2] In these books, he presented the notion of the internal rate of return. In the last 50 years, we have seen discounted cash flow models extend their reach into security and business valuation, and the growth has been aided and abetted by developments in portfolio theory.

1 Marshall, A., 1907, *Principles of Economics*, Macmillan, London; Bohm-Bawerk, A. V., 1903, *Recent Literature on Interest*, Macmillan.

2 Fisher, I., 1907, *The Rate of Interest*, Macmillan, New York; Fisher, I., 1930, *The Theory of Interest*, Macmillan, New York.

Using discounted cash flow models is in some sense an act of faith. We believe that every asset has an intrinsic value, and we try to estimate that intrinsic value by looking at an asset's fundamentals. What is intrinsic value? Consider it the value that would be attached to an asset by an all-knowing analyst with access to all information available right now and a perfect valuation model. No such analyst exists, of course, but we all aspire to be as close as we can to this perfect analyst. The problem lies in the fact that none of us ever gets to see the true intrinsic value of an asset. Therefore, we have no way of knowing whether our discounted cash flow valuations are close to the mark.

Equity Versus Firm Valuation

Of the approaches for adjusting for risk in discounted cash flow valuation, the most common one is the risk-adjusted discount rate approach. Here we use higher discount rates to discount expected cash flows when valuing riskier assets and lower discount rates when valuing safer assets. We can approach discounted cash flow valuation in two ways, and they can be framed in terms of the financial balance sheet introduced in Chapter 1, "The Dark Side of Valuation." The first is to value the entire business, with both existing assets (assets-in-place) and growth assets; this is often called firm or enterprise valuation. Figure 2.1 shows an example.

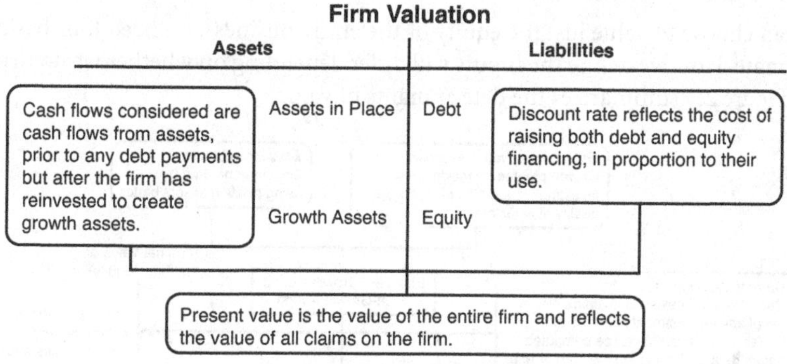

Figure 2.1: Valuing a Firm (Business)

The cash flows before debt payments and after reinvestment needs are called *free cash flows to the firm*, and the discount rate that reflects the composite cost of financing from all sources of capital is the *cost of capital*.

The second way is to value just the equity stake in the business; this is called equity valuation. Figure 2.2 shows an example.

The cash flows after debt payments and reinvestment needs are called free cash flows to equity, and the discount rate that reflects just the cost of equity financing is the cost of equity. With publicly traded firms, it can be argued that the only cash flow equity investors get from the firm is dividends, and that discounting expected dividends back at the cost of equity should yield the value of equity in the firm.

Note also that we can always get from the former (firm value) to the latter (equity value) by netting out the value of all nonequity claims from firm value. Done right, the value of equity should be the same whether it is valued directly (by discounting cash flows to equity at the cost of equity) or indirectly (by valuing the firm and subtracting the value of all nonequity claims).

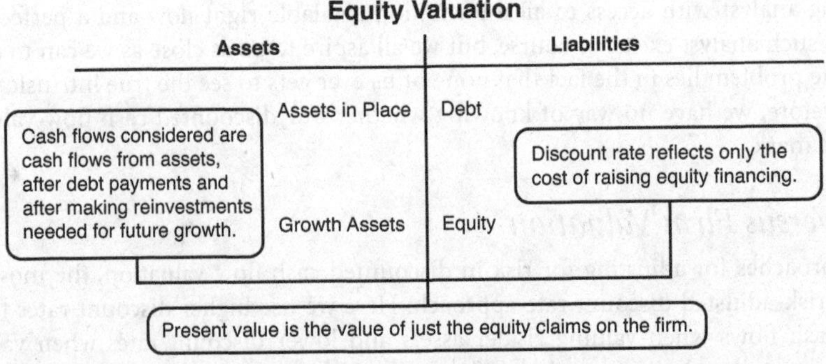

Figure 2.2: Valuing Equity

Inputs to a DCF Valuation

While we can choose to value just the equity or the entire business, we need four basic inputs for a value estimate. How we define the inputs will differ depending on whether we do firm or equity valuation. Figure 2.3 summarizes the determinants of value.

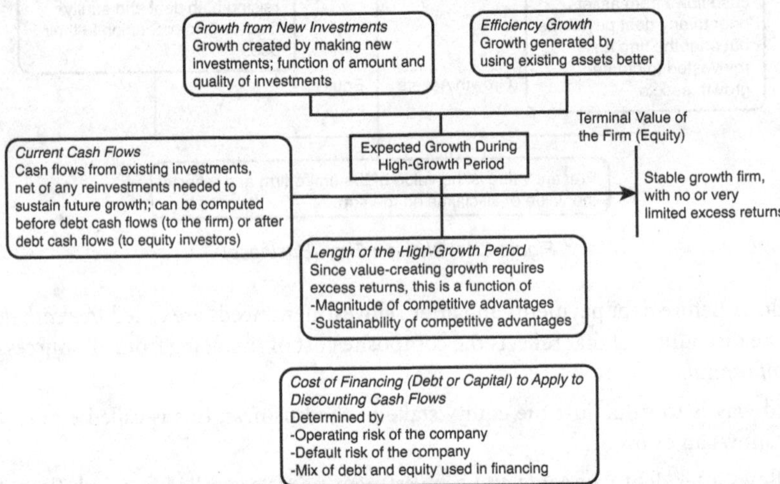

Figure 2.3: Determinants of Value

The first input is the cash flow from existing assets. This is defined as either pre-debt (and to the firm) or post-debt (and to equity) earnings, net of reinvestment to generate future growth. With equity cash flows, we can use an even stricter definition of cash flow and consider only dividends paid. The second input is growth. Growth in operating income is the key input when valuing the entire business. Growth in equity income (net income or earnings per share) is the focus when valuing equity. The third input is the discount rate. This is defined as the cost of the firm's overall capital when valuing the business and as cost of equity when valuing equity. The final input, allowing for closure, is the terminal value, defined as the firm's (equity's) estimated value at the end of the forecast period in firm (equity) valuation.

The rest of this section will focus on estimating the inputs into discounted cash flow models. We will start with cash flows and then move on to risk (and discount rates). We will close with a discussion of how best to estimate the growth rate for the high-growth period and the value at the end of that period.

Cash Flows

Leading up to this section, we noted that cash flows can be estimated either to just equity investors (cash flows to equity) or to all suppliers of capital (cash flows to the firm). This section begins with the strictest measure of cash flow to equity—the dividends received by investors. Then it will move to more expansive measures of cash flows, which generally require more information.

Dividends

When an investor buys stock in a publicly traded company, he generally expects to get two types of cash flows—dividends during the holding period, and an expected price at the end of the holding period. Since this expected price is itself determined by future dividends, the value of a stock is the present value of just expected dividends. If we accept this premise, the only cash flow to equity that we should be considering in valuation is the dividend paid. Estimating that dividend for the last period should be a simple exercise. Since many firms do not pay dividends, this number can be zero, at least for the near term, but it should never be negative.

Augmented Dividends

One of the limitations of focusing on dividends is that many companies, especially in the U.S. but increasingly around the world, have shifted from dividends to stock buybacks as their mechanism for returning cash to stockholders. While only stockholders who sell back their stock receive cash, it still represents cash returned to equity investors. In 2007, for instance, firms in the U.S. returned twice as much cash in the form of stock buybacks as they did in dividends. Focusing only on dividends will result in the undervaluation of equity. One simple way of adjusting for this is to *augment the dividend* with stock buybacks and look at the cumulative cash returned to stockholders:

Augmented Dividends = Dividends + Stock Buybacks

One problem, though, is that unlike dividends that are smoothed out over time, stock buybacks can spike in some years and be followed by years of inaction. Therefore, we must normalize buybacks by using average buybacks over a period of time (say, five years) to arrive at more reasonable annualized numbers.

Potential Dividends (Free Cash Flow to Equity)

With both dividends and augmented dividends, we trust managers at publicly traded firms to return to pay out to stockholders any excess cash left over after meeting operating and reinvestment needs. However, we do know that managers do not always follow this practice, as evidenced by the large cash balances that you see at most publicly traded firms. To estimate what managers could have returned to equity investors, we develop a measure of potential dividends that we call the *free cash flow to equity*. Intuitively, this measures the cash left over after taxes, reinvestment needs, and that debt cash flows have been met. It is measured as follows:

FCFE = Net Income – Reinvestment Needs – Debt Cash Flows
= Net Income – (Capital Expenditures – Depreciation + Change in Noncash Working Capital) – (Principal Repayments – New Debt Issues)

Consider the equation in pieces. We begin with net income, since that is the earnings generated for equity investors; it is after interest expenses and taxes. We compute what the firm has to reinvest in two parts:

- *Reinvestment in long-lived assets* is measured as the difference between capital expenditures (the amount invested in long-lived assets during the period) and depreciation (the accounting expense generated by capital expenditures in prior periods). We net the latter because it is not a cash expense and hence can be added back to net income.
- *Reinvestment in short-lived assets* is measured by the change in noncash working capital (Δ working capital). In effect, increases in inventory and accounts receivable represent cash tied up in assets that do not generate returns—wasting assets. The reason we don't consider cash in the computation is because we assume that companies with large cash balances generally invest them in low-risk, marketable securities like commercial paper and Treasury bills. These investments earn a low but fair rate of return and therefore are not wasting assets.[3] To the extent that they are offset by the use of supplier credit and accounts payable, the effect on cash flows can be muted. The overall change in noncash working capital therefore is investment in short-term assets.

Reinvestment reduces cash flow to equity investors, but it provides a payoff in terms of future growth. We will reconsider whether the net effect is positive or negative after we consider how best to estimate growth. The final input into the process are the negative cash flows associated with the repayment of old debt and the positive cash flows to equity investors from raising new debt. If old debt is replaced with new debt of exactly the same magnitude, this term will be zero, but it will generate positive (or negative) cash flows when debt issues exceed (or are less than) debt repayments.

Focusing on just debt cash flows allows us to zero in on a way to simplify this computation. In the special case where the capital expenditures and working capital are expected to be financed at a fixed debt ratio δ, and principal repayments are made from new debt issues, the FCFE is measured as follows:

FCFE = Net Income + (1 – δ) (Capital Expenditures – Depreciation) + (1 – δ) Δ Working Capital

3 Note that we do not make the distinction between operating and nonoperating cash that some analysts do (they proceed to include operating cash in working capital). Our distinction is between wasting cash (which would include currency or cash earning below-market rate returns) and nonwasting cash. We are assuming that the former will be a small or negligible number at a publicly traded company.

In effect, we are assuming that a firm with a 30% debt ratio that is growing through reinvestment will choose to fund 30% of its reinvestment needs with new debt and replace old debt that comes due with new debt.

There is one more way in which we can present the free cash flow to equity. If we define the portion of the net income that equity investors reinvest into the firm as the equity reinvestment rate, we can state the FCFE as a function of this rate:

$$\text{Equity Reinvestment Rate} = \frac{(\text{Capital Expenditures} - \text{Depreciation} + \Delta\ \text{Working Capital})\ (1 - \delta)}{\text{Net Income}}$$

$$\text{FCFE} = \text{Net Income}\ (1 - \text{Equity Reinvestment Rate})$$

A final note is needed on the contrast between the first two measures of cash flows to equity (dividends and augmented dividends) and this measure. Unlike those measures, which can never be less than zero, the free cash flow to equity can be negative for a number of reasons. The first is that the net income could be negative, a not-uncommon phenomenon even for mature firms. The second reason is that reinvestment needs can overwhelm net income, which is often the case for growth companies, especially early in the life cycle. The third reason is that large debt repayments coming due that have to be funded with equity cash flows can cause negative FCFE. Highly levered firms that are trying to bring down their debt ratios can go through years of negative FCFE. The fourth reason is that the quirks of the reinvestment process, where firms invest large amounts in long-lived and short-lived assets in some years and nothing in others, can cause the FCFE to be negative in the big reinvestment years and positive in others. As with buybacks, we have to consider normalizing reinvestment numbers across time when estimating cash flows to equity. If the FCFE is negative, the firm needs to raise fresh equity.

Cash Flow to the Firm

The cash flow to the firm should be both after taxes and after all reinvestment needs have been met. Since a firm raises capital from debt and equity investors, the cash flow to the firm should be before debt cash flows—interest expenses, debt repayments, and new debt issues. The cash flow to the firm can be measured in two ways. One is to add up the cash flows to all the different claim holders in the firm. Thus, the cash flows to equity investors (estimated using one of the three measures described in this section) are added to the cash flows to debt holders (interest and net debt payments) to arrive at the cash flow. The other approach is to start with operating earnings and to estimate the cash flows to the firm prior to debt payments but after reinvestment needs have been met:

$$\text{Free Cash Flow to Firm (FCFF)} = \text{After-Tax Operating Income} - \text{Reinvestment}$$

$$= \text{After-Tax Operating Income} - (\text{Capital Expenditures} - \text{Depreciation} + \Delta\ \text{Working Capital})$$

It is easiest to understand FCFF by contrasting it with FCFE. First, we begin with after-tax operating income instead of net income. The former is before interest expenses, whereas the latter is after interest expenses. Second, we adjust the operating income for taxes, computed as if we were taxed on the entire income, whereas net income is already an after-tax number.[4] Third, while we subtract reinvestment, just as we did to arrive at free cash flows to equity, we do not net out the effect of debt cash flows, since we are now looking at cash flows to all capital, not just to equity.

Another way of presenting the same equation is to cumulate the net capital expenditures and working capital change into one number and state it as a percentage of the after-tax operating income. This ratio of reinvestment to after-tax operating income is called the reinvestment rate, and the free cash flow to the firm can be written as follows:

$$\text{Reinvestment Rate} = \frac{(\text{Capital Expenditures} - \text{Depreciation} + \Delta\,\text{Working Capital})}{\text{After-Tax Operating Income}}$$

$$\text{Free Cash Flow to the Firm} = \text{EBIT}\,(1-t)\,(1-\text{Reinvestment Rate})$$

Note that the reinvestment rate can exceed 100%[5] if the firm has substantial reinvestment needs. The reinvestment rate can also be less than zero for firms that are divesting assets and shrinking capital.

A few final thoughts about free cash flow to the firm are worth noting before we move on to discount rates. First, the free cash flow to the firm can be negative, just as the FCFE can, but debt cash flows can no longer be the culprit. Even highly levered firms that are paying down debt will report positive FCFF while also registering negative FCFE. If the FCFF is negative, the firm will raise fresh capital, with the mix of debt and equity being determined by the mix used to compute the cost of capital. Second, the cash flow to the firm is the basis for all cash distributions made by the firm to its investors. Dividends, stock buybacks, interest payments, and debt repayments all have to be made out of these cash flows.

Estimating Cash Flows for a Firm: 3M in 2007

Minnesota Mining and Manufacturing (3M) is a large market capitalization company with operations in transportation, health care, office supplies, and electronics.

- In 2007, the firm reported operating income, before taxes, of $5,344 million and net income of $4,096 million. Interest expenses for the year amounted to $210 million, and interest income on cash and marketable securities was $132 million. The firm also paid dividends of $1,380 million during the year and bought back $3,239 million of stock. The effective tax rate during the year was 32.1%, but the marginal tax rate is 35%.

4 In effect, when computing taxes on operating income, we act like we have no interest expenses or tax benefits from those expenses while computing the cash flow. This is because we will be counting the tax benefits from debt in the cost of capital (through the use of an after-tax cost of debt). If we use actual taxes paid or reflect the tax benefits from interest expenses in the cash flows, we are double-counting its effect.

5 In practical terms, this firm will have to raise external financing, either from debt or equity or both, to cover the excess reinvestment.

- During 2007, 3M reported $1,422 million in capital expenditures and cash acquisitions of $539 million. The depreciation and amortization charges for the year amounted to $1,072 million. The noncash working capital increased by $243 million during 2007.
- Finally, 3M repaid $2,802 million of debt during the year but raised $4,024 million in new debt.

With this data, we can first estimate the free cash flows to equity, as shown in Figure 2.4.

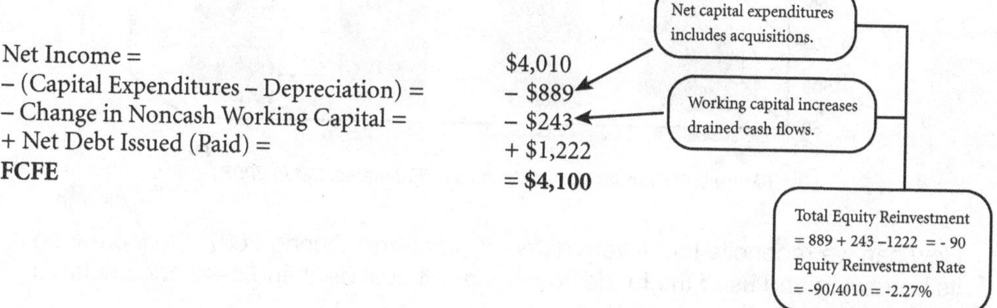

Figure 2.4: Free Cash Flows to Equity

Note that the net debt issued reflects the new debt issues, netted out against debt repaid. The free cash flow to the firm for 2007 can also be computed, as shown in Figure 2.5.

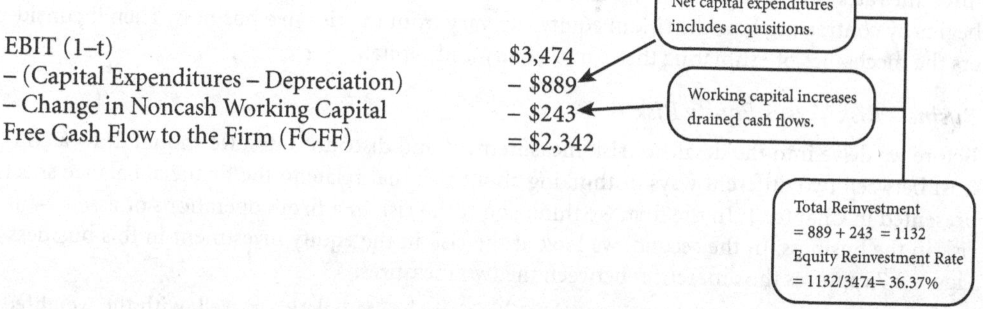

Figure 2.5: Free Cash Flow to 3M

Figure 2.6 summarizes all four estimates of cash flows for 3M for 2007—dividends, augmented dividends, free cash flows to equity, and free cash flows to the firm.

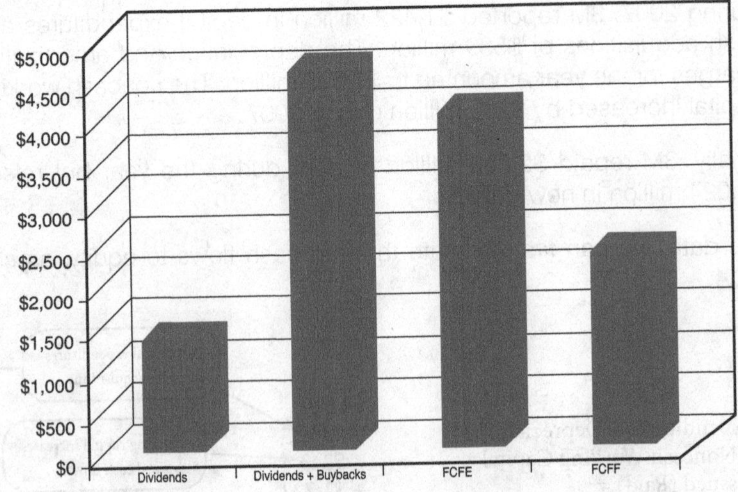

Figure 2.6: Comparison of Cash Flow Estimates: 3M in 2007

How can we reconcile these very different numbers? During 2007, 3M increased its borrowing and used the funds from the additional debt and cash accumulated in prior years to buy back stock.

Risk

Cash flows that are riskier should be assessed a lower value than more stable cash flows, but how do we measure risk and reflect it in value? In conventional discounted cash flow valuation models, the discount rate becomes the vehicle for conveying our concerns about risk. We use higher discount rates on riskier cash flows and lower discount rates on safer cash flows. This section begins by contrasting how the risk in equity can vary from the risk in a business. Then it considers the mechanics of estimating the cost of equity and capital.

Business Risk Versus Equity Risk

Before we delve into the details of risk measurement and discount rates, we should draw a contrast between two different ways of thinking about risk that relate to the financial balance sheet presented in Chapter 1. In the first, we think about the risk in a firm's operations or assets—the risk in the business. In the second, we look at the risk in the equity investment in this business. Figure 2.7 captures the differences between the two measures.

As with any other aspect of the balance sheet, this one has to balance as well, with the weighted risk in the assets being equal to the weighted risk in the ingredients to capital—debt and equity. Note that the risk in the equity investment in a business is determined partly by the risk of the business the firm is in and partly by its choice of how much debt to use to fund that business. The equity in a safe business can be rendered risky if the firm uses substantial debt to fund that business.

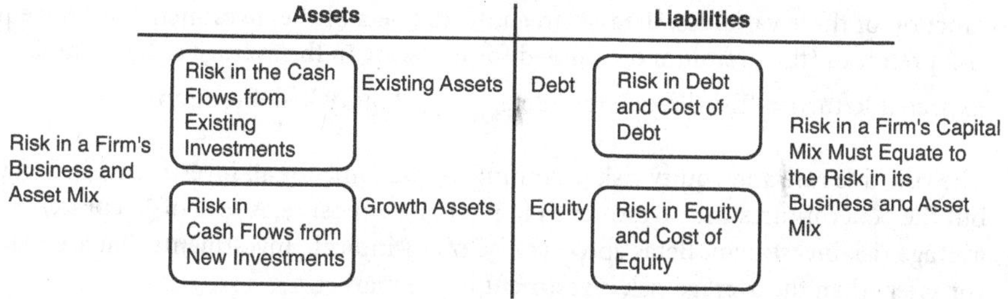

Figure 2.7: Risk in Business Versus Risk in Equity

In discount rate terms, the risk in the equity in a business is measured with the cost of equity, whereas the risk in the business is captured in the cost of capital. The latter is a weighted average of the cost of equity and the cost of debt, with the weights reflecting the proportional use of each source of funding.

Measuring Equity Risk and the Cost of Equity

Measuring the risk in equity investments and converting that risk measure into a cost of equity is rendered difficult by two factors. The first is that equity has an implicit cost, which is unobservable, unlike debt, which comes with an explicit cost in the form of an interest rate. The second factor is that risk in the eyes of the beholder and different equity investors in the same business can be very different. Therefore, they might demand different expected returns as a consequence.

The Diversified Marginal Investor

If a company had only one equity investor, estimating equity risk and the cost of equity would be far simpler. We would measure the risk to the investor of investing in equity in that company. Then we would assess a reasonable rate of return, given that risk. In a publicly traded company, we run into the practical problem that the equity investors number in the hundreds, if not the thousands. They vary not only in size, from small to large investors, but also in risk aversion. So, whose perspective should we take when measuring risk and cost of equity? In corporate finance and valuation, we develop the notion of the *marginal investor*—the investor most likely to influence the market price of publicly traded equity. The marginal investor in a publicly traded stock has to own enough stock in the company to make a difference and must be willing to trade on that stock. The common theme shared by risk-and-return models in finance is that the marginal investor is diversified, and we measure the risk in an investment as the risk added to a diversified portfolio. Put another way, only that portion of the risk in an investment that can be attributed to the broader market or economy, and hence is not diversifiable, should be built into expected returns.

Models for Expected Return (Cost of Equity)

It is on the issue of how best to measure this nondiversifiable risk that the different risk-and-return models in finance part ways. Let us consider the alternatives:

- In the *capital asset pricing model (CAPM)*, this risk is captured in the *beta* that we assign an asset/business. That number has the burden of measuring exposure to all the components of market risk. The expected return on an investment can then be specified as a function of three variables: the risk-free rate, the beta of the investment, and the equity risk premium (the premium demanded for investing in the average risk investment):

$$\text{Expected Return} = \text{Risk-Free Rate} + \text{Beta}_{\text{investment}} \text{ (Equity Risk Premium)}$$

The risk-free rate and equity risk premium are the same for all investments in a market, but the beta captures the investment's market risk exposure. A beta of 1 represents an average risk investment. Betas above (or below) 1 indicate investments that are riskier (or safer) than the average risk investment in the market.

- The arbitrage pricing and multifactor models allow for multiple sources of nondiversifiable (or market) risk and estimate betas against each one. The expected return on an investment can be written as a function of the multiple betas (relative to each market risk factor) and the risk premium for that factor. If the model has k factors, with β_{ji} and risk premium$_j$ representing the beta and risk premium of factor j, the expected return on the investment can be written as follows:

$$\text{Expected Return} = \text{Risk-Free Rate} + \sum_{j=1}^{j=k} \beta_j \text{ (Risk Premium}_j)$$

Note that the capital asset pricing model can be written as a special case of these multifactor models, with a single factor (the market) replacing the multiple factors.

- The final class of models can be categorized as proxy models. With these models, we essentially give up on measuring risk directly. Instead, we look at historical data for clues on what types of investments (stocks) have earned high returns in the past. Then we use the common characteristic(s) they share as a measure of risk. For instance, researchers have found that market capitalization and price-to-book ratios are correlated with returns. Stocks with small market capitalization and low price-to-book ratios have historically earned higher returns than large market stocks with higher price-to-book ratios. Using the historical data, we can then estimate the expected return for a company based on its market capitalization and price-to-book ratio:

$$\text{Expected Return} = a + b(\text{Market Capitalization}) + c(\text{Price-to-Book Ratio})$$

Since we are no longer working within the confines of an economic model, it is not surprising that researchers keep finding new variables (trading volume, price momentum) that improve the predictive power of these models. The open question, though, is whether these variables are truly proxies for risk or indicators of market inefficiency. In effect, we may be explaining away the market's misvaluation of classes of stock by using proxy models for risk.

Estimation Issues

With the CAPM and multifactor models, the inputs that we need for the expected return are straightforward. We need to come up with a risk-free rate and an equity risk premium (or premiums in the multifactor models) to use across all investments. Once we have these market-wide estimates, we measure the risk (beta or betas) in individual investments. This section lays out the broad principles that govern these estimates. Future chapters will return to the details of how best to make these estimates for different types of businesses.

- The risk-free rate is the expected return on an investment with guaranteed returns; in effect, your expected return is also your actual return. Since the return is guaranteed, an investment must meet two conditions to be risk-free. The first is that the entity making the guarantee can have no default risk; this is why we use government securities to derive risk-free rates, a necessary though not always sufficient condition. As you will see in Chapter 6, default risk in many government securities is priced into the expected return. The second condition is that the time horizon matters. A six-month Treasury bill is not risk-free if you are looking at a five-year time horizon, since we are exposed to reinvestment risk. In fact, even a five-year Treasury bond may not be riskless, since the coupons received every six months have to be reinvested. Clearly, getting a risk-free rate is not as simple as it looks at the outset.
- The equity risk premium is the premium that investors demand for investing in risky assets (or equities) as a class, relative to the risk-free rate. It is a function not only of how much risk investors perceive in equities as a class, but also the risk aversion that they bring to the market. It also follows that the equity risk premium can change over time, as market risk and risk aversion both change. The conventional practice for estimating equity risk premiums is to use the historical risk premium—the premium investors have earned over long periods (say, 75 years) investing in equities instead of risk-free (or close to risk-free) investments. Chapter 7, "Risky Ventures: Assessing the Price of Risk," questions the efficacy of this process and offers alternatives.
- To estimate the beta in the CAPM and betas in multifactor models, we draw on statistical techniques and historical data. The standard approach for estimating the CAPM beta is to run a regression of returns on a stock against returns on a broad equity market index. The slope captures how much the stock moves for any given market move. To estimate betas in the arbitrage pricing model, we use historical return data on stocks and factor analysis to extract both the number of factors in the models and factor betas for individual companies. As a consequence, the beta estimates that we obtain always look backward (since they are derived from past data) and are noisy (they are statistical estimates, with standard errors). In addition, these approaches clearly will not work for investments that do not have a trading history (young companies, divisions of publicly traded companies). One solution is to replace the regression beta with a *bottom-up beta*—one that is based on industry averages for the businesses that the firm is in, adjusted for differences in financial leverage.[6] Since industry averages are more precise than individual regression betas, and the weights on the businesses can reflect a firm's current mix, bottom-up betas generally offer better estimates for the future.

6 The simplest and most widely used equation relating betas to debt-to-equity ratios is based on the assumption that debt provides a tax advantage and that the beta of debt is 0:

Beta for Equity = Beta of Business * (1 + (1 – Tax Rate) (Debt / Equity))

The beta for equity is a levered beta, whereas the beta of the business is called an unlevered beta. Regression betas are equity betas and thus are levered. The debt-to-equity ratio over the regression period is embedded in the beta.

Estimating the Cost of Equity for 3M

Because 3M is a publicly traded stock with a long history, we can use its price history to run a regression against the market index to derive a regression beta. Figure 2.8 provides a regression beta for 3M against the S&P 500 using two years of weekly returns against the S&P 500. The regression (raw) beta is 0.79; the adjusted beta, which is the raw beta moved toward the market average beta of 1, is 0.86.

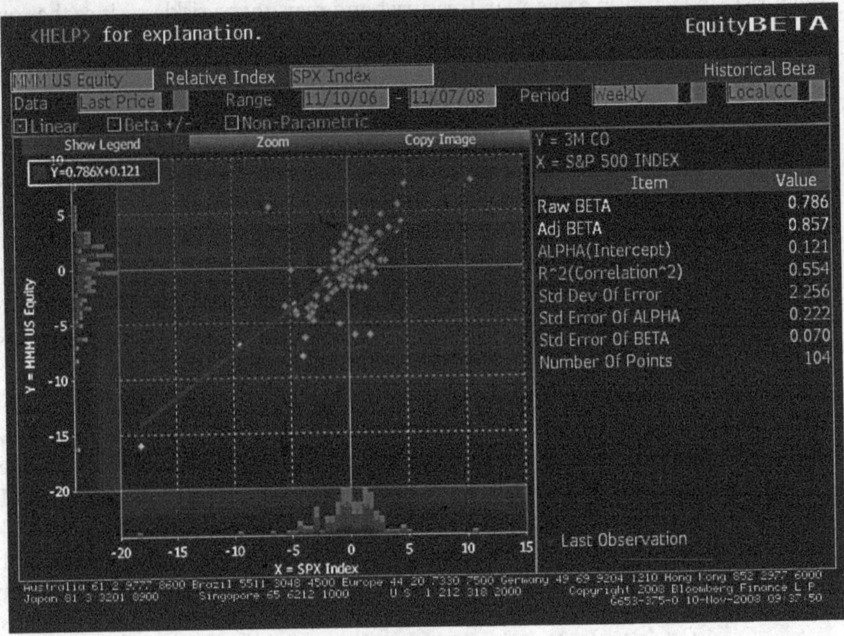

Figure 2.8: Regression Beta for 3M

Although we do have a regression beta, all the normal caveats we listed in the preceding section apply. It is backward-looking (for the last two years) and has a standard error (albeit a small one of 0.07). The regression results would have been very different if we had run the regression using a different time period (say, five years) and different return intervals (daily or monthly) and if we had used a different market index.

To yield a contrasting value, we estimated a beta for 3M by breaking it into individual businesses and taking a weighted average of the business betas (see Table 2.1).

Table 2.1 Bottom-Up Beta Estimate for 3M

Business	Revenues	EV/Sales	Estimated Value	Weight in Firm	Unlevered Beta
Industrial and transportation	$7,724	1.07	$8,265	27.42%	0.82
Health care	$3,968	1.83	$7,261	24.09%	1.40
Display and graphics	$3,892	1.63	$6,344	21.04%	1.97
Consumer and office	$3,403	0.78	$2,654	8.80%	0.99
Safety, security, and protection	$3,070	1.09	$3,346	11.10%	1.16
Electronics and communications	$2,775	0.82	$2,276	7.55%	1.32
3M as a firm			**$30,146**	**100.00%**	**1.29**

The unlevered betas of the businesses are obtained by averaging the regression betas of publicly traded firms in each business and adjusting the average regression beta for the average financial leverage (D/E ratio) in each business. The EV/sales ratio measures the typical multiple of revenues that firms in each business trade for. Applying 3M's debt-to-equity ratio of 8.80% in 2007 (based on market values for debt and equity) to the unlevered beta of 1.29 yields an equity beta of 1.36 for 3M:

Levered (Equity) Beta = 1.29 (1 + (1 – .35) (8.80%)) = 1.36

Using the ten-year Treasury bond rate of 3.72% in September 2007 as the risk-free rate and a 4% equity risk premium yields a cost of equity of 9.16%:

Cost of Equity = Risk-Free Rate + Beta * Equity Risk Premium
= 3.72% + 1.36 * 4% = 9.16%

Obviously, using a higher equity risk premium would have led to a higher cost of equity.

The Cost of Debt

While equity investors receive residual cash flows and bear the bulk of the operating risk in most firms, lenders to the firm also face the risk that they will not receive their promised payments—interest expenses and principal repayments. To cover this default risk, lenders add a "default spread" to the riskless rate when they lend money to firms; the greater the perceived risk of default, the greater the default spread and the cost of debt. The other dimension on which debt and equity can vary is in their treatment for tax purposes, with cash flows to equity investors (dividends and stock buybacks) coming from after-tax cash flows, whereas interest payments are tax-deductible. In effect, the tax law provides a benefit to debt and lowers the cost of borrowing to businesses.

To estimate the cost of debt for a firm, we need three components. The first is the risk-free rate, an input to the cost of equity as well. As a general rule, the risk-free rate used to estimate the cost of equity should be used to compute the cost of debt as well. If the cost of equity is based on a long-term risk-free rate, as it often is, the cost of debt should be based on the same rate. The second component is the default spread. Three approaches are used, depending on the firm being analyzed:

- If the firm has traded bonds outstanding, the current market interest rate on the bond (yield to maturity) can be used as the cost of debt. This is appropriate only if the bond is liquid and is representative of the firm's overall debt; even risky firms can issue safe bonds, backed up by the firms' most secure assets.
- If the firm has a bond rating from an established ratings agency such as S&P or Moody's, we can estimate a default spread based on the rating. In September 2008, for instance, the default spread for BBB-rated bonds was 2% and would have been used as the spread for any BBB-rated company.
- If the firm is unrated and has debt outstanding (bank loans), we can estimate a "synthetic" rating for the firm based on its financial ratios. A simple, albeit effective, approach for estimating the synthetic rating is to base it entirely on a firm's interest coverage ratio (EBIT/interest expense); higher interest coverage ratios yield higher ratings and lower interest coverage ratios.

The final input needed to estimate the cost of debt is the tax rate. Since interest expenses save you taxes at the margin, the tax rate that is relevant for this calculation is not the effective tax rate but the marginal tax rate. In the U.S., where the federal corporate tax rate is 35% and state and local taxes add to this, the marginal tax rate for corporations in 2008 was close to 40%, much higher than the average effective tax rate, across companies, of 28%. The after-tax cost of debt for a firm therefore is as follows:

After-Tax Cost of Debt = (Risk-Free Rate + Default Spread) (1 – Marginal Tax Rate)

The after-tax cost of debt for most firms will be significantly lower than the cost of equity for two reasons. First, debt in a firm generally is less risky than its equity, leading to lower expected returns. Second, a tax saving is associated with debt that does not exist with equity.

Estimating the Cost of Debt for 3M

To estimate the synthetic rating for 3M, we begin with an estimate of the interest coverage ratio in 2007:

$$\text{Interest Coverage Ratio} = \frac{\text{After-Tax Operating Income}}{\text{Interest Expenses}} = \frac{\$5{,}361}{\$227} = 23.63$$

Given its large market capitalization (more than $50 billion), we use Table 2.2 to extract the synthetic rating and the default spread on 3M debt.

Table 2.2 **Interest Coverage Ratios, Ratings, and Default Spreads—October 2008**

Interest Coverage Ratio	Rating	Typical Default Spread
> 12.5	AAA	0.75%
9.50 to 12.50	AA	1.25%
7.50 to 9.50	A+	1.40%
6.00 to 7.50	A	1.50%
4.50 to 6.00	A–	1.70%
4.00 to 4.50	BBB	2.50%
3.50 to 4.00	BB+	3.20%
3.00 to 3.50	BB	3.65%
2.50 to 3.00	B+	4.50%
2.00 to 2.50	B	5.65%
1.50 to 2.00	B–	6.50%
1.25 to 1.50	CCC	7.50%
0.80 to 1.25	CC	10.00%
0.50 to 0.80	C	12.00%
< 0.50	D	20.00%

The rating that we assign to 3M is AAA, with a default spread of 0.75%. Adding this spread to the ten-year Treasury bond rate of 3.72% results in a pre-tax cost of debt of 4.49%. Just as a contrast, we compute the book interest rate by dividing the interest expenses in 2007 by the book value of debt:

$$\text{Book Interest Rate} = \frac{\text{Interest Expenses}}{\text{Book Value of Debt}} = \frac{\$210}{\$4920} = 4.27\%$$

Given how sensitive the book interest rate is to different definitions of book value of debt, we remain skeptical about its usefulness. Using the marginal tax rate of 35% on the pre-tax cost of debt of 4.49%, we derive an after-tax cost of debt of 2.91% for the company:

$$\begin{aligned}\text{After-Tax Cost of Debt} &= (\text{Risk-Free Rate} + \text{Default Spread for Debt})\,(1 - \text{Marginal Tax Rate})\\ &= (3.72\% + 0.75\%)\,(1 - .35) = 2.91\%\end{aligned}$$

Debt Ratios and the Cost of Capital

After we have estimated the costs of debt and equity, we still have to assign weights to the two ingredients. To come up with this value, we could start with the mix of debt and equity that the firm uses right now. In making this estimate, the values that we should use are market values, rather than book values. For publicly traded firms, estimating the market value of equity is usually a trivial exercise, where we multiply the share price by the number of shares outstanding. Estimating the market value of debt usually is a more difficult exercise, since most firms have some debt that is not traded. Though many practitioners fall back on book value of debt as a proxy of market value, estimating the market value of debt is still a better practice.

Once we have the current market value weights for debt and equity for use in the cost of capital, we have a follow-up judgment to make in terms of whether these weights will change or remain stable. If we assume that they will change, we have to specify both what the right or target mix for the firm will be and how soon the change will occur. In an acquisition, for instance, we can assume that the acquirer can replace the existing mix with the target mix instantaneously. As passive investors in publicly traded firms, we have to be more cautious, since we do not control how a firm funds its operations. In this case, we may adjust the debt ratio from the current mix to the target over time, with concurrent changes in the costs of debt, equity, and capital. In fact, the last point about debt ratios and costs of capital changing over time is worth reemphasizing. As companies change over time, we should expect the cost of capital to change as well.

Estimating the Cost of Capital for 3M

In the second sidebar, we estimated a cost of equity of 9.16% for 3M, based on a bottom-up beta estimate of 1.36. In the third sidebar, we concluded that the after-tax cost of debt for 3M is 2.91%, based on the synthetic AAA rating we assigned the firm. We estimated the market values of equity and debt for the firm in September 2008 (with the resulting weights and overall costs of capital) and derived the cost of capital for the firm. Table 2.3 shows the results.

Table 2.3 3M's Cost of Capital

	Market Value	Proportion of Capital	Cost
Equity	$57,041	91.50%	9.16%
Debt	$5,297	8.50%	2.91%
Capital	$62,338	100.00%	8.63%

At its current debt ratio of 8.50%, the cost of capital for 3M is 8.63%.

Growth Rates

No other ingredient in discounted cash flow valuation evokes as much angst as estimating future growth. Unlike cash flows and discount rates, where we often have the security of historical data, growth rates require us to grapple with the future. This section looks at why growth rates can be different for equity and operating earnings. It examines two of the standard approaches for estimating growth (looking at the past, and using analyst estimates). This section closes with a discussion of the fundamentals that determine growth.

Equity Versus Operating Earnings

As with cash flows and discount rates, a contrast has to be drawn between growth in equity earnings and growth in operating earnings. To make the distinction, consider the simplified version of an income statement shown in Table 2.4.

Table 2.4 **An Income Statement: Revenues to Earnings per Share**

Item	Factors That Explain Differences in Growth
Revenues	
– Operating expenses	Changes in operating efficiency/performance Operating leverage
EBITDA	
– Depreciation and amortization	Changes in depreciation schedules/rules Amortization of intangibles
EBIT	
– Interest expenses	Changes in financial leverage (debt)
+ Income from cash holdings	Changes in cash holdings/interest rates
– Taxes	Changes in tax rates/rules
Net Income	
/ Number of shares	Stock buybacks and issues Exercise of past option grants
Earnings per Share	

We are assuming that the firm has no minority holdings in other companies, which would result in an additional line item, just above the net income line, for income from these holdings.

The growth rates in different measures of earnings (operating income, net income, and earnings per share) generally will be different for most firms. This is especially true of growth firms and firms in transition.

- **Share issues and buybacks:** If the number of shares remains fixed, the growth rate in earnings per share should be the same as the growth rate in net income. Firms that generate excess cash flows and use these cash flows to buy back stock register higher growth rates in earnings per share than in net income. Conversely, firms that make a practice of raising new equity (issuing new shares) to fund investments or acquisitions can have higher growth rates in net income than in earnings per share.
- **Financial leverage:** The growth rates in operating and net income can diverge if the net interest expense (interest expense minus interest income) grows at a rate different from operating income. Firms that use increasing amounts of debt to fund their operations generally report higher growth rates in operating income than net income. However, if that debt is used to buy back shares, the earnings per share growth reflect the fewer shares outstanding.

- **Operating leverage:** The growth in operating income can also be very different from the growth in revenues, primarily because some operating expenses are fixed and others are variable. The higher the proportion of the costs that are fixed (higher operating leverage), the greater the growth rate in operating income relative to the growth in revenues.

In effect, when asked to estimate growth rates, the first question an analyst has to ask is, "In what item?" If our task is to estimate growth in operating income, we cannot use growth rates in earnings per share as substitutes.

Historical and Forecasted Growth Rates

When confronted with the task of estimating growth, it is not surprising that analysts turn to the past. In effect, they use growth in revenues or earnings in the recent past as a predictor of growth in the future. Before we put this practice under the microscope, we should add that the historical growth rates for the same company can yield different estimates for the following reasons:

- **Earnings measure:** As we noted, the growth rates in earnings per share, net income, operating income, and revenues can be very different for the same firm over a specified time period.
- **Period of analysis:** For firms that have been in existence for a long time, the growth rates can be very different if we look at ten years of history as opposed to five years.
- **Averaging approach:** Even if we agree on an earnings measure and time period for the analysis, the growth rates we derive can be different, depending on how we compute the values. We could, for instance, compute the growth rate in each period and average the growth rates over time, yielding an arithmetic average. Alternatively, we could use just the starting and ending values for the measure and compute a geometric average. For firms with volatile earnings, the latter can generate a very different (and lower) value for growth than the former.

A debate on how best to estimate historical growth makes sense only if it is a good predictor of future growth. Unfortunately, studies that have looked at the relationship have generally concluded that

- The relationship between past and future growth is a very weak one.
- Scaling matters, with growth dropping off significantly as companies grow.
- Firms and sectors grow through growth cycles, with high growth in one period followed by low growth in the next.

If historical growth is not a useful predictor of future growth, we can use another source for future growth. We can draw on those who know the firm better than we do—equity research analysts who have tracked the firm for years, or the managers in the firm—and use their estimates of growth. On the plus side, these forecasts should be based on better information than we have available. After all, managers should have a clearer sense of how much they will reinvest in their own businesses and what the potential returns on investments are when they do. And equity research analysts have sector experience and informed sources they can draw on for better information. On the minus side, neither managers nor equity research analysts are objective about the future; managers are likely to overestimate their capacity to generate growth, and analysts have their own biases. In addition, both analysts and managers can get caught up in the mood of the moment, overestimating growth in buoyant times and underestimating growth in down times. As with historical growth, studies indicate that neither analyst estimates nor management forecasts are good predictors of future growth.

Fundamental Growth Rates

If we cannot draw on history or trust managers and analysts, how, then, do we estimate growth? The answer lies in the fundamentals within a firm that ultimately determine its growth rate. This section considers the two sources of growth—new investments that expand the business, and improved efficiency on existing investments.

Decomposing Growth

The best way to consider earnings growth is to break it down algebraically into its constituent parts. Define E_t to be the earnings in period t, I_t to be the investment at the start of period t, and ROI_t as the return on that investment. Thus, we can rewrite E_t as follows:

$$E_t = ROI_t * I_t$$

The change in earnings from period t–1 to t, ΔE, can then be written as follows:

$$\Delta E = E_t - E_{t-1} = ROI_t * I_t - ROI_{t-1} * I_{t-1}$$

The growth rate is written in terms of ΔE and E_{t-1}:

$$g = \Delta E / E_{t-1} = (ROI_t * I_t - ROI_{t-1} * I_{t-1}) / E_{t-1}$$

Consider the simplest scenario, in which the ROI is stable and does not change from period to period ($ROI = ROI_t = ROI_{t-1}$). The expected growth rate in earnings for this firm is as follows:

$$g = \Delta E / E_{t-1} = ROI\,(I_t - I_{t-1}) / E_{t-1}$$

$$= ROI * (\Delta I/E_{t-1})$$

In other words, the firm's growth rate is a function of only two variables—the return it makes on new investments (ROI), and the proportion of its earnings that are put into new investments ($\Delta I/E_{t-1}$).

The more general scenario is one in which the return on investment does change from period to period. In this case, the expected growth rate can be written as:

$$g = \Delta E / E_{t-1} = ROI_t * (\Delta I/E_{t-1}) + (ROI_t - ROI_{t-1}) / ROI_{t-1}$$

This equation is based on the assumption that the return on new investments in period t is identical to the return earned on existing investments in that period. In fact, this can be generalized even further. If we allow the return on new investments, $ROI_{New,t}$, to be different from the return on existing assets, $ROI_{Existing,t}$, the expected growth rate can be written as:

$$g = \Delta E / E_{t-1} = ROI_{New,t} * (\Delta I/E_{t-1}) + (ROI_{Existing,t} - ROI_{Existing,t-1}) / ROI_{Existing,t-1}$$

The first term in this equation captures the growth from new investments, determined by the marginal return on those investments and the proportion invested in these investments. The second term captures the effect of changes in the return on investment on existing assets, a component that we will call *efficiency growth.* Increasing the return on investment (improving efficiency) will create additional earnings growth, whereas declining efficiency (with drops in the return on investment) will reduce earnings growth.

Growth from New Investments

While investment and return on investment are generic terms, how we define them depends on whether we are looking at equity earnings or operating income. When looking at equity earnings, our focus is on the investment in equity, and the return is the return on equity. When looking at operating earnings, the focus is on the investment in capital, and the return is the return on capital. In the cash flow definitions introduced at the start of this chapter, the change in investment is computed as the reinvestment, and the measurement of the reinvestment again varies, depending on the cash flow being discounted. In dividend discount models, reinvestment is defined as retained earnings (any income not paid out as dividends). In free cash flow to equity (firm) models, reinvestment is defined in terms of the equity reinvestment rate (reinvestment rate).

Central to any estimate of fundamental growth is the estimate of return on capital or equity. Table 2.5 summarizes the inputs for each measure, depending on the measure of cash flow that we are focused on.

Table 2.5 Measuring Investment and Return on Investment

	Change in Investment	Return on Investment
Operating income	Reinvestment Rate = $\frac{(\text{Cap Ex} - \text{Deprec'n} + \Delta\text{WC})}{\text{EBIT}(1-t)}$	Return on invested capital (ROC or ROIC)
Net income (noncash)	Equity Reinvestment Rate = $\frac{(\text{Cap Ex} - \text{Deprec'n} + \Delta\text{WC} - \Delta\text{Debt})}{\text{Net Income}}$	Noncash return on equity (NCROE)
Earnings per share	Retention Ratio = $1 - \frac{\text{Dividends}}{\text{Net Income}}$	Return on equity (ROE)

It is conventional practice to use accounting measures of investment and return on investment. Thus, the book values of equity and invested capital and accounting earnings are used to compute returns on equity and capital:

$$\text{Return on Capital (ROIC)} = \frac{\text{Operating Income}_t\ (1 - \text{Tax Rate})}{\text{Book Value of Invested Capital}_{t-1}}$$

$$\text{Noncash Return on Equity (NCROE)} = \frac{\text{Net Income}_t - \text{Interest Income from Cash}_t\ (1 - \text{Tax Rate})}{\text{Book Value of Equity}_{t-1} - \text{Cash}_{t-1}}$$

$$\text{Return on Equity (ROE)} = \frac{\text{Net Income}_t}{\text{Book Value of Equity}_{t-1}}$$

The problem with accounting measures on both dimensions is well documented. Accounting choices on restructuring charges, amortization, and capitalization all make a difference in the final number.[7]

The final issue that we have to consider is the difference between marginal and average returns. Note that the return on investment that we use to compute the growth from new investments should be the return earned on those investments alone—a marginal return. The return on existing assets is an average return on a portfolio of investments already made. While we often use the same value for both numbers in valuation, they can be different in practice.

Efficiency Growth

For many mature firms with limited investment opportunities, the potential for growth from new investments is limited. These firms cannot maintain a high reinvestment rate and deliver a high return on capital with that reinvestment. However, they can still grow at healthy rates if they can improve the returns that they earn on existing assets. Conversely, declines in returns on existing assets can translate into drops in earnings growth rates. Stated again in terms of different measures of earnings, efficiency growth can be written as shown in Table 2.6.

Table 2.6 Determinants of Efficiency Growth in Earnings

	Measure of Return on Existing Assets	Efficiency Growth
Operating income	Return on capital	$\frac{(ROC_t - ROC_{t-1})}{ROC_{t-1}}$
Net income (noncash)	Noncash return on equity	$\frac{(NCROE_t - NCROE_{t-1})}{NCROE_{t-1}}$
Earnings per share	Return on equity	$\frac{(ROE_t - ROE_{t-1})}{ROE_{t-1}}$

When valuing companies, efficiency growth is pure gravy in terms of value created, since the growth comes with no concurrent cost. Unlike growth from new investments, where the positive effects of growth have to be offset against the negative effect of more investment, improving the return on capital on existing assets increases the growth rate without adversely affecting the cash flows. It should as come as no surprise, then, that analysts who want to increase a company's value draw on the efficiency argument to justify much higher growth rates than those estimated using fundamentals.

While the potential for efficiency growth is always there, we should put some commonsense constraints on how much we can draw on this growth:

- Mature firms have more potential for efficiency growth, with poor returns on capital (equity), than firms that are performing well. This is true for two reasons. First, improving the return on capital is a much more feasible option for a firm that generates a

7 To get a sense of the problems with using accounting numbers, and how best to correct for them, see Damodaran, A., 2007, "Return on Capital, Return on Invested Capital and Return on Equity: Measurement and Implications," working paper, SSRN.

return on capital that is well below the sector average than at a firm that already outperforms the sector. Second, the effect of an improvement in returns on growth is much greater when the return on capital is low than when it is high. A firm that improves its return on capital from 5% to 6% will report a 20% growth rate from efficiency in that period. On the other hand, a firm that improves its return on capital from 25% to 26% will generate a 4% growth rate from efficiency in that period.

- You can draw on increased efficiency to justify growth only for finite periods. After all, a firm cannot be infinitely inefficient. Once the inefficiencies, no matter how significant, are fixed, the firm must revert to its sustainable growth rate, based on new investments. In discounted cash flow valuation, this has a practical consequence: You can draw on both efficiency and new investments to justify growth during the high-growth period, but only on new investments to justify growth forever (in the terminal value computation).

In closing, growth in a specific firm can come from new investments or improved efficiency, but it has to be earned either way. None of us has the power to endow companies with higher growth rates just because we like the managers or want to make the firms' value increase.

Estimating Growth for 3M

It makes sense to start with an estimate of historical growth in earnings at 3M. Figure 2.9 presents different estimates of past earnings growth for 3M, given different definitions of earnings and different time periods.

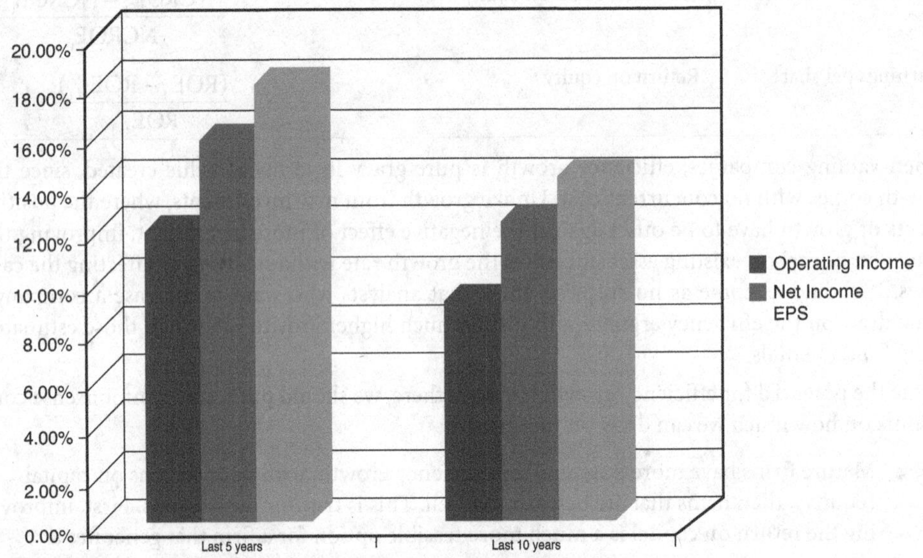

Figure 2.9: Historical Growth Rates in Earnings for 3M

Note the wildly divergent numbers that we get for past growth. In September 2008, analysts were estimating growth in earnings per share at 3M of between 8 and 9% a year for the next five years.

Looking at the fundamentals, it seems unlikely that 3M, given its high existing return on capital and equity, can generate much in terms of efficiency growth. It is, however, reinvesting in new assets. This reinvestment, in conjunction with high returns on capital on new investments, will generate growth. Table 2.7 summarizes growth in dividends, noncash net income, and after-tax operating income using the reinvestment and return characteristics we have estimated for 3M.

Table 2.7 Dividends, Net Income, and After-Tax Operating Income: Fundamentals

	In the Last Financial Year, 2007			Expected for the Next Five Years		
	Reinvestment	Return	Expected Growth	Reinvestment	Return	Expected Growth
Dividends	66.31%	33.93%	22.50%	Not forecast		
Noncash net income	–2.27%	47.65%	–1.08%	25.00%	30.00%	7.50%
After-tax operating income	36.37%	25.31%	9.21%	30.00%	25.00%	7.50%

Note that we have stayed fairly close to last year's estimates of the reinvestment rate and return on capital for 3M. However, we changed the equity reinvestment rate substantially for the next few years to reflect the historical average for this number from 2003 to 2007.

Terminal Value

Publicly traded firms do not have finite lives. We cannot estimate cash flows forever. Therefore, we generally impose closure in valuation models by stopping our estimation of cash flows sometime in the future and then computing a terminal value that reflects all cash flows beyond that point. Three approaches generally are used to estimate the terminal value. The most common approach, which is to apply a multiple to earnings in the terminal year to arrive at the terminal value, is inconsistent with intrinsic valuation. Since these multiples are usually obtained by looking at what comparable firms are trading at in the market today, this is a relative valuation, rather than a discounted cash flow valuation. Two more legitimate ways of estimating terminal value exist. The first is to estimate a liquidation value for the firm's assets, assuming that the assets are sold in the terminal year. The other is to estimate a going concern or a terminal value.

Liquidation Value

If we assume that the business will be ended in the terminal year and that its assets will be liquidated at that time, we can estimate the proceeds from the liquidation. This liquidation value still has to be estimated, using a combination of market-based numbers (for assets that have ready markets) and cash flow-based estimates. For firms that have finite lives and marketable assets (like real estate), this represents a fairly conservative way of estimating terminal value. For other firms, estimating liquidation value becomes more difficult, either because the assets are not separable (brand-name value in a consumer product company) or because there is no market for the individual assets. One approach is to use the estimated book value of the assets as a starting point and to estimate the liquidation value based on the book value.

Going Concern or Terminal Value

If we treat the firm as a going concern at the end of the estimation period, we can estimate the value of that concern by assuming that cash flows will grow at a constant rate forever afterwards. This perpetual growth model draws on a simple present-value equation to arrive at terminal value:

$$\text{Terminal Value}_n = \frac{\text{Cash Flow in Year n+1}}{(\text{Discount Rate} - \text{Perpetual Growth Rate})}$$

Our definitions of cash flow and growth rate have to be consistent with whether we are valuing dividends, cash flows to equity, or cash flows to the firm. The discount rate is the cost of equity for the first two and the cost of capital for the last. The perpetual growth model is a powerful one, but it can be easily misused. In fact, analysts often use it as a piggy bank that they go to whenever they feel that the value they have derived for an asset is too low or high. Small changes in the inputs can alter the terminal value dramatically. Consequently, three key constraints should be imposed on its estimation:

- **Cap the growth rate**: Small changes in the stable-growth rate can change the terminal value significantly, and the effect gets larger as the growth rate approaches the discount rate used in the estimation. The fact that a stable-growth rate is constant forever, however, puts strong constraints on how high it can be. Since no firm can grow forever at a rate higher than the growth rate of the economy in which it operates, the constant growth rate cannot be greater than the overall growth rate of the economy. So, what is the maximum stable-growth rate that you can use in a valuation? The answer depends on whether the valuation is being done in real or nominal terms. If it's the latter, the currency used to estimate cash flows will determine what the contraint on the growth rate will be. With the former, you would use the real-growth rate in the economy as your constraint. With the latter, you would add expected inflation in the currency to the real growth. Setting the stable-growth rate to be less than or equal to the economy's growth rate is not only the consistent thing to do, but it also ensures that the growth rate will be less than the discount rate. This is because of the relationship between the riskless rate that goes into the discount rate and the economy's growth rate. Note that the riskless rate can be written as follows:

  Nominal Riskless Rate = Real Riskless Rate + Expected Inflation Rate

  In the long term, the real riskless rate converges on the economy's real-growth rate, and the nominal riskless rate approaches the economy's nominal growth rate. In fact, a simple rule of thumb about the stable-growth rate is that it should not exceed the riskless rate used in the valuation.

- **Use mature company risk characteristics:** As firms move from high growth to stable growth, we need to give them the characteristics of stable-growth firms. A firm in stable growth is different from that same firm in high growth on a number of dimensions. In general, you would expect stable-growth firms to be less risky and use more debt. In practice, we should move betas toward one for even high-risk firms toward stable growth and give them debt ratios more consistent with larger, more stable cash flows.
- **Reinvestment and excess-return assumptions:** Stable-growth firms tend to reinvest less than high-growth firms. It is critical that we both capture the effects of lower growth on reinvestment and ensure that the firm reinvests enough to sustain its stable-growth rate in the terminal phase. Given the relationship between growth, reinvestment rate, and returns that we established in the section "Decomposing Growth," we can estimate the reinvestment rate that is consistent with expected growth in Table 2.8.

Table 2.8 Reinvestment in Stable Growth

Model	Reinvestment Rate in Stable Growth
Dividend	$\frac{\text{Stable Growth Rate}}{\text{Return on Equity in Stable Growth}}$
FCFE	$\frac{\text{Stable Growth Rate}}{\text{Noncash Return on Equity in Stable Growth}}$
FCFF	$\frac{\text{Stable Growth Rate}}{\text{Return on Capital in Stable Phase}}$

Linking the reinvestment rate and retention ratio to the stable-growth rate also makes the valuation less sensitive to assumptions about stable growth. Although increasing the stable-growth rate while holding all else constant can dramatically increase value, changing the reinvestment rate as the growth rate changes creates an offsetting effect:

$$\text{Terminal Value} = \frac{\text{EBIT}_{n+1}(1-t)(1-\text{Reinvestment Rate})}{\text{Cost of Capital}_n - \text{Stable Growth Rate}}$$

The gains from increasing the growth rate are partially or completely offset by the loss in cash flows because of the higher reinvestment rate. Whether value increases or decreases as the stable growth increases depends entirely on what you assume about excess returns. If the return on capital is higher than the cost of capital in the stable-growth period, increasing the stable-growth rate increases value. *If the return on capital is equal to the cost of capital in stable growth, increasing the stable-growth rate has no effect on value.* Substituting the stable-growth rate as a function of the reinvestment rate from before, you get this:

$$\text{Terminal Value} = \frac{\text{EBIT}_{n+1}(1-t)(1-\text{Reinvestment Rate})}{\text{Cost of Capital}_n - (\text{Reinvestment Rate} * \text{Return on Capital})}$$

Setting the return on capital equal to the cost of capital, you arrive at the following:

$$\text{Terminal Value}_{\text{ROC=Cost of Capital}} = \frac{\text{EBIT}_{n+1}(1-t)}{\text{Cost of Capital}_n}$$

You could establish the same propositions with equity income and cash flows and show that the terminal value of equity is a function of the difference between the return on equity and cost of equity:

$$\text{Terminal Value of Equity} = \frac{\text{Net Income}_{n+1}\left(1 - \frac{g_n}{\text{ROE}_n}\right)}{(\text{Cost of Equity}_n - g_n)}$$

$$\text{Terminal Value}_{\text{ROE =Cost of Equity}} = \frac{\text{Net Income}_{n+1}}{\text{Cost of Equity}_n}$$

In closing, the key assumption in the terminal value computation is not what growth rate you use in the valuation, but what excess returns accompany that growth rate. If you assume no excess returns, the growth rate becomes irrelevant. Some valuation experts believe that this is the only sustainable assumption, since no firm can maintain competitive advantages forever. In practice, though, there may be some wiggle room, insofar as the firm may become a stable-growth firm before its excess returns go to zero. If that is the case and the firm's competitive advantages are strong and sustainable (even if they do not last forever), we may be able to give the firm some excess returns in perpetuity. As a simple rule of thumb, these excess returns forever should be modest (<4 to 5%) and will affect the terminal value.

High Growth Versus Terminal Value Assumptions at 3M

Table 2.9 lists our assumptions about 3M in both the high-growth phase and steady state.

Table 2.9 Valuing 3M: High-Growth Versus Stable-Growth Phases

	High Growth	**Stable Growth**
Length of High-Growth Period	**Next Five Years**	**After Year 5**
Growth rate	7.50%	3.00%
Debt ratio used in cost-of-capital calculation	8.48%	20.00%
Beta used for stock	1.36	1.00

Length of High-Growth Period	High Growth Next Five Years	Stable Growth After Year 5
Risk-free rate	3.72%	3.72%
Risk premium	4.00%	4.00%
Cost of debt	4.47%	4.47%
Tax rate	35.00%	35.00%
Cost of capital	8.63%	6.76%
Return on capital	25.00%	6.76%
Reinvestment rate	30.00%	44.40%

Note that as the growth declines after year 5, the beta is adjusted toward 1, and the debt ratio is raised to the industry average of 20% to reflect the company's overall stability. Since the cost of debt is relatively low, we leave it unchanged, resulting in a drop in the cost of capital to 6.76%. We do change the reinvestment rate in stable growth to reflect the assumption that there will be no excess returns in stable growth (return on capital = cost of capital). Using the predicted stable-growth rate of 3% and the return on capital of 6.76% (equal to cost of capital), we derive a reinvestment rate of 44.4%:

$$\text{Reinvestment Rate in Stable Growth} = \frac{\text{Expected Growth}}{\text{Stable ROC}} = \frac{3.00\%}{6.76\%} = 44.40\%$$

Tying up Loose Ends

We have covered the four inputs that go into discounted cash flow valuation models—cash flows, discount rates, growth rates, and the terminal value. The present value we arrive at when we discount the cash flows at the risk-adjusted rates should yield an estimate of value. But getting from that number to what we would be willing to pay per share for equity does require us to consider a few other factors:

- **Cash and marketable securities:** Most companies have cash balances that are not insignificant in magnitude. Is this cash balance already incorporated into the present value? The answer depends on how we estimated cash flows. If the cash flows are based on operating income (free cash flow to the firm) or noncash net income, we have not valued cash yet, and it should be added to the present value. On the other hand, if we estimate cash flows from the cumulative net income or use the dividend discount model, cash already has been implicitly valued. The income from cash is part of the final cash flow, and the discount rate presumably has been adjusted to reflect the presence of cash.
- **Cross-holdings in other companies:** Companies sometimes invest in other firms, and these cross-holdings can generally be categorized as either minority or majority holdings. With the former, the holdings are usually less than 50%, and the income from the holdings is reported in the income statement below the operating income line. If we

use free cash flow to the firm to value the operating assets, we have not valued these minority holdings yet, and they have to be valued explicitly and added to the present value. With majority holdings, which generally exceed 50%, firms usually consolidate the entire subsidiary in their financials and report 100% of the operating income and the subsidiary's assets. To reflect the portion of the subsidiary that does not belong to them, they report the book value of that portion as minority interest in a balance sheet. If we compute cash flows from consolidated financial statements, we have to subtract the estimated market value of the minority interest.

- **Potential liabilities (not treated as debt)**: Since we are interested in the value of equity in the firm, we have to consider any potential liabilities we may face that reduce that value. Thus, items like underfunded pension obligations and health care obligations may not meet the threshold to be categorized as debt for cost-of-capital purposes but should be considered when valuing equity. In other words, we would subtract the values of these and other claims (such as potential costs from lawsuits against the firm) on equity from firm value to arrive at equity value.
- **Employee options**: Having arrived at the value of equity in the firm, we must make a final estimate, especially if the firm has made it a practice to grant options to managers. Since many of these options will still be outstanding, we have to consider them as another (and different) claim on equity. While analysts often use shortcuts (such as adjusting the number of shares for dilution) to deal with these options, the right approach is to value the options (using an option pricing model), reduce the value of equity by the option value, and then divide by the actual number of shares outstanding.

Table 2.10 summarizes the loose ends and how to deal with them in the different models.

Table 2.10 Dealing with Loose Ends in Valuation

Loose End	Dividend Discount Model	FCFE Model	FCFF Model
Cash and marketable securities	Ignore, since net income includes interest income from cash.	Ignore if FCFE is computed using total net income. Add if FCFE is computed using noncash net income.	Add value of cash and marketable securities. Operating income does not include income from cash.
Cross-holdings	Ignore, since net income includes income from cross-holdings.	Ignore, since net income includes income from cross-holdings.	Add market value of minority holdings and subtract market value of minority interests.

Loose End	Dividend Discount Model	FCFE Model	FCFF Model
Other liabilities	Ignore. The assumption is that the firm considers costs when setting dividends.	Subtract expected litigation costs.	Subtract underfunded pension obligations, health care obligations, and expected litigation costs.
Employee options	Ignore.	Subtract value of equity options outstanding.	Subtract value of equity options outstanding.

A Valuation of 3M

In the earlier sidebars, we estimated the inputs for 3M, ranging from existing cash flows (in the first sidebar) to cost of capital (in the fourth sidebar) to the terminal value computation (in the preceding sidebar). We first use the expected growth rate of 7.5% and the reinvestment rate of 30% that we estimated for the first five years to obtain the expected FCFF each year, as shown in Table 2.11.

Table 2.11 Expected FCFF to 3M: The Next Five Years

	Currently	Year 1	Year 2	Year 3	Year 4	Year 5
After-tax operating income (growing at 7.5% a year)	$3,586	$3,854	$4,144	$4,454	$4,788	$5,147
– Reinvestment (30% of income)		$1,156	$1,243	$1,336	$1,437	$1,544
= FCFF		$2,698	$2,900	$3,118	$3,352	$3,603

At the end of the fifth year, we assume that 3M becomes a stable-growth firm with a growth rate of 3% a year forever. Staying consistent with the parameters (44.4% reinvestment rate and 6.76% cost of capital), we estimated for 3M in stable growth in the preceding sidebar, we derive the FCFF in year 6 and the firm's terminal value:

Expected After-Tax Operating Income in Year 6 = $5,147 * 1.03 = $5,302 million

Reinvestment Rate in Year 6 (44.4% of Income) = $2,355 million

FCFF in Year 6 = $5,302 – $2,355 = $2,947 million

Terminal Value at End of Year 5 = $2,947 / (.0676 – .03) = $78,464 million

Using the cost of capital of 8.63% for the first five years, we discount back the cash flows for the next five years and the terminal value to arrive at an estimate of value for the operating assets of $64,036 million.

Value of Operating Asset= PV of FCFF in Years 1-5 + PV of Terminal Value

$$= \frac{2698}{1.0863} + \frac{2900}{1.0863^2} + \frac{3118}{1.0863^3} + \frac{3352}{1.0863^4} + \frac{(3603 + 78464)}{1.0863^5} = \$64{,}036 \text{ million}$$

Adding on the existing cash balance of $2,475 million and the value of existing minority cross-holdings in other firms of $778 million results in an overall value for 3M of $67,289 million:

Value of Operating Asset:	$64,036 million
+ Cash and Marketable Securities:	$2,475 million
+ Cross-Holdings in Other Companies:	$778 million
= Value of 3M as a Firm:	$67,289 million

Subtracting the debt outstanding in the firm yields the value of the equity in 3M:

Value of Equity = Value of Firm – Value of Outstanding Debt
= $67,289 million – $5,297 million = $61,992 million

Finally, we estimate a value of $1,216 million for the equity options that have been granted over time to the managers at 3M and that are still outstanding:[8]

Value of Equity in Common Stock = Value of Equity – Value of Option Overhang
= $61,992 million – $1,216 million = $60,776 million

Dividing by the actual number of shares outstanding results in a value per share of $86.95, slightly higher than the stock price prevailing in early September 2008 of $80 a share.

Variations on DCF Valuation

The discounted cash flow model described so far in this chapter is still the standard approach for estimating intrinsic value. However, variations on that approach also have the same objective. This section begins with a model in which we adjust the cash flows for risk, rather than the discount rate. Then we move on to the adjusted present-value model (where the effect of debt on value is separated from the operating assets) and excess-return models (where value is derived from earning excess returns on new investments).

Certainty-Adjusted Cash Flow Models

While most analysts adjust the discount rate for risk in DCF valuation, some prefer to adjust the expected cash flows for risk. In the process, they replace the uncertain expected cash flows with

8 58.82 million options were outstanding at the end of 2007, with a weighted average strike price of $66.83 and 5.5 years left to expiration. We valued these options using a Black-Scholes option pricing model.

the certainty equivalent cash flows, using a risk-adjustment process akin to the one used to adjust discount rates.

Misunderstanding Risk Adjustment

At the outset of this section, it should be emphasized that many analysts misunderstand what risk-adjusting the cash flows requires them to do. Some consider the cash flows of an asset under a variety of scenarios, ranging from best-case to catastrophic, assign probabilities to each one, take an expected value of the cash flows, and consider it risk-adjusted. While it is true that bad outcomes have been weighted to arrive at this cash flow, it is still an expected cash flow and is not risk-adjusted. To see why, assume that you are given a choice between two alternatives. In the first one, you are offered \$95 with certainty. In the second, you will receive \$100 with probability 90% and only \$50 the rest of the time. The expected values of both alternatives are \$95, but risk-averse investors would pick the first investment with guaranteed cash flows over the second one.

Ways of Computing Certainty Equivalent Cash Flows

The practical question that we will address in this section is how best to convert uncertain expected cash flows into guaranteed certainty equivalents. While we do not disagree with the notion that it should be a function of risk aversion, the estimation challenges remain daunting.

Risk Adjustments Based on Utility Models

The first (and oldest) approach to computing certainty equivalents is rooted in the utility functions for individuals. If we can specify the utility function of wealth for an individual, we are well set to convert risky cash flows to certainty equivalents for that individual. For instance, an individual with a log utility function would have demanded a certainty equivalent of \$93.90 for the risky gamble presented in the last section (90% chance of \$100 and 10% chance of \$50):

$$\text{Utility from Gamble} = .90 \ln(100) + .10 \ln(50) = 4.5359$$
$$\text{Certainty Equivalent} = \exp^{4.5359} = \$93.30$$

The certainty equivalent of \$93.30 delivers the same utility as the uncertain gamble with an expected value of \$95. This process can be repeated for more complicated assets, and each expected cash flow can be converted into a certainty equivalent.

One quirk of using utility models to estimate certainty equivalents is that the certainty equivalent of a positive expected cash flow can be negative. Consider, for instance, an investment where you can make \$2,000 with probability 50% and lose \$1,500 with probability 50%. The expected value of this investment is \$250, but the certainty equivalent may very well be negative, with the effect depending on the utility function assumed.[9]

Using this approach in practice has two problems. The first is that specifying a utility function for an individual or analyst is very difficult, if not impossible, to do with any degree of precision. In fact, most utility functions that are well behaved (mathematically) do not seem to explain actual

9 The certainty equivalent will be negative in this example for some utility functions for wealth. Intuitively, this would indicate that an investor with this utility function would actually pay to avoid being exposed to this gamble (even though it has a positive expected value).

behavior very well. The second problem is that, even if we could specify a utility function, this approach requires us to lay out all the scenarios that can unfold for an asset (with corresponding probabilities) for every time period. Not surprisingly, certainty equivalents from utility functions have been largely restricted to analyzing simple gambles in classrooms.

Risk-and-Return Models

A more practical approach to converting uncertain cash flows into certainty equivalents is offered by risk-and-return models. In fact, we would use the same approach to estimating risk premiums that we employ while computing risk-adjusted discount rates, but we would use the premiums to estimate certainty equivalents instead:

Certainty Equivalent Cash Flow = Expected Cash Flow / (1 + Risk Premium in Risk-Adjusted Discount Rate)

In the 3M valuation, for instance, note that the cost of capital of 8.63% is a risk-adjusted discount rate, based on its market risk exposure and current market conditions; the risk-free rate used was 3.72%. Instead of discounting the expected cash flow of $2,698 million in year 1 at 8.63%, we would decompose the discount rate into a risk-free rate of 3.72% and a compounded risk premium of 4.73%.[10]

$$\text{Risk Premium} = \frac{(1 + \text{Risk-Adjusted Discount Rate})}{(1 + \text{Risk Free Rate})} - 1 = \frac{(1.0863)}{(1.0372)} - 1 = .0473$$

Using this risk premium, we can compute the certainty equivalent cash flow for 3M in year 1:

Certainty Equivalent Cash Flow in Year 1 = $2,698 million / 1.0473 = $2,576 million

The present value of this certainty equivalent cash flow can then be computed at the risk-free rate:

Present Value of Certainty Equivalent Cash Flow = $2,576 million / 1.0372 = $2,484 million

This process would be repeated for all the expected cash flows:

$$CE\,(CF_t) = \alpha_t\, E(CF_t) = \frac{(1+r_f)^t}{(1+r)^t} E(CF_t)$$

This adjustment has two effects. The first is that expected cash flows with higher uncertainty associated with them have lower certainty equivalents than more predictable cash flows at the same point in time. The second effect is that the effect of uncertainty compounds over time. This makes the certainty equivalents of uncertain cash flows further into the future lower than uncertain cash flows that will occur sooner.

Cash Flow Haircuts

A far more common approach to adjusting cash flows for uncertainty is to "haircut" the uncertain cash flows subjectively. With this approach, an analyst faced with uncertainty replaces

10 A more common approximation used by many analysts is the difference between the risk-adjusted discount rate and the risk-free rate. In this case, that would have yielded a risk premium of 4.91% (8.63% – 3.72% = 4.91%).

uncertain cash flows with conservative or lowball estimates. This weapon is commonly employed by analysts who are forced to use the same discount rate for projects of different risk levels and who want to level the playing field. They haircut the cash flows of riskier projects to make them lower, thus hoping to compensate for the failure to adjust the discount rate for the additional risk.

In a variation on this approach, some investors consider only cash flows on an asset that are predictable; they ignore risky or speculative cash flows when valuing the asset. Warren Buffet expresses his disdain for the CAPM and other risk-and-return models and claims to use the risk-free rate as the discount rate. We suspect that he can get away with doing so because of a combination of the types of companies he chooses to invest in and his inherent conservatism when it comes to estimating the cash flows.

While cash flow haircuts retain their intuitive appeal, we should be wary of their usage. After all, gut feelings about risk can vary widely across analysts looking at the same asset; more risk-averse analysts will tend to haircut the cash flows on the same asset more than less risk-averse analysts. Furthermore, the distinction we drew between diversifiable and market risk when developing risk-and-return models can be lost when analysts make intuitive adjustments for risk. In other words, the cash flows may be adjusted downward for risk that will be eliminated in a portfolio. The absence of transparency about the risk adjustment can also lead to the double counting of risk, especially when the analysis passes through multiple layers of analysis. For example, after the first analyst looking at a risky investment decides to use conservative estimates of the cash flows, the analysis may pass to a second stage, where his superior may decide to make an additional risk adjustment to the already risk-adjusted cash flows.

Risk-Adjusted Discount Rate or Certainty Equivalent Cash Flow

Adjusting the discount rate for risk or replacing uncertain expected cash flows with certainty equivalents are alternative approaches to adjusting for risk, but do they yield different values? If so, which one is more precise? The answer lies in how we compute certainty equivalents. If we use the risk premiums from risk-and-return models to compute certainty equivalents, the values obtained from the two approaches will be the same. After all, adjusting the cash flow using the certainty equivalent and then discounting the cash flow at the risk-free rate is equivalent to discounting the cash flow at a risk-adjusted discount rate. To see this, consider an asset with a single cash flow in one year. Assume that r is the risk-adjusted cash flow, r_f is the risk-free rate, and RP is the compounded risk premium, computed as described earlier in this section:

$$\text{Certainty Equivalent Value} = \frac{CE}{(1+r_f)} = \frac{E(CF)}{(1+RP)(1+r_f)} = \frac{E(CF)}{\frac{(1+r)}{(1+r_f)}(1+r_f)} = \frac{E(CF)}{(1+r)}$$

This analysis can be extended to multiple time periods and will still hold.[11] Note, though, that if the approximation for the risk premium, computed as the difference between the risk-adjusted return and the risk-free rate, had been used, this equivalence will no longer hold. In that case, the certainty equivalent approach will give lower values for any risky asset, and the difference will increase with the size of the risk premium.

11 The proposition that risk-adjusted discount rates and certainty equivalents yield identical net present values is shown in Stapleton, R. C., 1971.

There are other scenarios in which the two approaches yield different values for the same risky asset. The first is when the risk-free rates and risk premiums change from time period to time period; the risk-adjusted discount rate also changes from period to period. Some argue that the certainty equivalent approach yields more precise estimates of value in this case. The other scenario is when the certainty equivalents are computed from utility functions or subjectively, whereas the risk-adjusted discount rate comes from a risk-and-return model. The two approaches can yield different estimates of value for a risky asset. Finally, the two approaches deal with negative cash flows differently. The risk-adjusted discount rate discounts negative cash flows at a higher rate, and the present value becomes less negative as the risk increases. If certainty equivalents are computed from utility functions, they can yield certainty equivalents that are negative and that become more negative as you increase risk—a finding that is more consistent with intuition.

The biggest dangers arise when analysts use an amalgam of approaches, in which the cash flows are adjusted partially for risk, usually subjectively, and the discount rate is also adjusted for risk. It is easy to double-count risk in these cases, and the risk adjustment to value often becomes difficult to decipher.

Adjusted Present-Value Models

In the *adjusted present value (APV) approach*, we separate the effects on value of debt financing from the value of a business's assets. In contrast to the conventional approach, where the effects of debt financing are captured in the discount rate, the APV approach attempts to estimate the expected dollar value of debt benefits and costs separately from the value of the operating assets.

Basis of the APV Approach

In the APV approach, we begin with the firm's value without debt. As we add debt to the firm, we consider the net effect on value by considering both the benefits and costs of borrowing. In general, using debt to fund a firm's operations creates tax benefits (because interest expenses are tax-deductible) on the plus side and increases bankruptcy risk (and expected bankruptcy costs) on the minus side. A firm's value can be written as follows:

Value of Business = Value of Business with 100% Equity Financing + Present Value of Expected Tax Benefits of Debt – Expected Bankruptcy Costs

The first attempt to isolate the effect of tax benefits from borrowing was in Miller and Modigliani (1963). They valued the present value of the tax savings in debt as a perpetuity using the cost of debt as the discount rate. The adjusted present-value approach in its current form was first presented in Myers (1974) in the context of examining the interrelationship between investment and financing decisions.[12]

Implicitly, the adjusted present-value approach is built on the presumption that it is easier and more precise to compute the valuation impact of debt in absolute terms rather than in proportional terms. Firms, it is argued, do not state target debt as a ratio of market value (as implied by the cost-of-capital approach) but in dollar value terms.

12 Modigliani, F. and M. Miller, 1958, "The Cost of Capital, Corporation Finance and the Theory of Investment," *American Economic Review*, v48, 261-297; Myers, S., 1974, "Interactions in Corporate Financing and Investment Decisions—Implications for Capital Budgeting," *Journal of Finance*, v29, March, 1-25.

Measuring APV

In the adjusted present value approach, we estimate the firm's value in three steps. We begin by estimating the firm's value with no leverage. We then consider the present value of the interest tax savings generated by borrowing a given amount of money. Finally, we evaluate the effect of borrowing the amount on the probability that the firm will go bankrupt, and the expected cost of bankruptcy.

The first step in this approach is estimating the value of the unlevered firm. This can be accomplished by valuing the firm as if it has no debt—by discounting the expected free cash flow to the firm at the unlevered cost of equity. In the special case where cash flows grow at a constant rate in perpetuity, the firm's value is easily computed:

$$\text{Value of Unlevered Firm} = \frac{FCFF_0(1+g)}{\rho_u - g}$$

where $FCFF_0$ is the current after-tax operating cash flow to the firm, ρ_u is the unlevered cost of equity, and g is the expected growth rate. In the more general case, we can value the firm using any set of growth assumptions we believe are reasonable for the firm. The inputs needed for this valuation are the expected cash flows, growth rates, and unlevered cost of equity.

The second step in this approach is calculating the expected tax benefit from a given level of debt. This tax benefit is a function of the firm's tax rate and is discounted to reflect the riskiness of this cash flow:

$$\text{Value of Tax Benefits} = \sum_{t=1}^{t=\infty} \frac{\text{Tax Rate}_t \text{ X Interest Rate}_t X \text{Debt}_t}{(1+r)^t}$$

We must address three estimation questions. The first is what tax rate to use in computing the tax benefit and whether that rate can change over time. The second is the dollar debt to use in computing the tax savings and whether that amount can vary across time. The final issue relates to what discount rate to use to compute the present value of the tax benefits. In the early iterations of APV, the tax rate and dollar debt were viewed as constants (resulting in tax savings as a perpetuity), and the pre-tax cost of debt was used as the discount rate leading to a simplification of the tax benefit value:

$$= \frac{(\text{Tax Rate})(\text{Cost of Debt})(\text{Debt})}{\text{Cost of Debt}}$$

$$\text{Value of Tax Benefits} = (\text{Tax Rate})(\text{Debt})$$

$$= t_c D$$

Subsequent adaptations of the approach allowed for variations in both the tax rate and the dollar debt level and raised questions about whether it was appropriate to use the cost of debt as the discount rate. In other versions of the models, the present value of the tax benefits has been computed using the cost of capital and the unlevered cost of equity as discount rates. The argument about which one of these rates is right is really one about how predictable the tax benefits from debt are.

The third step is to evaluate the effect of the given level of debt on the firm's default risk and on expected bankruptcy costs. In theory, at least, this requires estimating the probability of default with the additional debt and the direct and indirect cost of bankruptcy. If π_a is the probability of default after the additional debt, and BC is the present value of the bankruptcy cost, the present value of expected bankruptcy cost can be estimated:

$$\text{PV of Expected Bankruptcy Cost} = (\text{Probability of Bankruptcy})(\text{PV of Bankruptcy Cost}) = \pi_a BC$$

This step of the adjusted present-value approach poses the most significant estimation problem, since neither the probability of bankruptcy nor the bankruptcy cost can be estimated directly. The probability of bankruptcy can be estimated indirectly in two basic ways. One is to estimate a bond rating, as we did in the cost-of-capital approach, at each level of debt and use the empirical estimates of default probabilities for each rating. The other is to use a statistical approach to estimate the probability of default, based on the firm's observable characteristics, at each level of debt. The bankruptcy cost can be estimated, albeit with considerable error, from studies that have looked at the magnitude of this cost in actual bankruptcies. Research that has looked at the direct cost of bankruptcy concludes that it is small[13] relative to firm value. In fact, the costs of distress stretch far beyond the conventional costs of bankruptcy and liquidation. The perception of distress can do serious damage to a firm's operations as employees, customers, suppliers, and lenders react. Firms that are viewed as distressed lose customers (and sales), have higher employee turnover, and have to accept much tighter restrictions from suppliers than healthy firms. These indirect bankruptcy costs can be catastrophic for many firms and essentially make the perception of distress into a reality. The magnitude of these costs has been examined in studies and can range from 10 to 25% of firm value.[14]

Cost of Capital Versus APV Valuation

In an APV valuation, the value of a levered firm is obtained by adding the net effect of debt to the unlevered firm value:

$$\text{Value of Levered Firm} = \frac{FCFF_o(1+g)}{\rho_u - g} + t_c D - \pi_a BC$$

The tax savings from debt are discounted back at the cost of debt. In the cost-of-capital approach, the effects of leverage show up in the cost of capital. The tax benefit is incorporated into the after-tax cost of debt and the bankruptcy costs in both the levered beta and the pre-tax cost of debt.

13 Warner, J.N., 1977, "Bankruptcy Costs: Some Evidence," *Journal of Finance*, v32, 337-347; he studied railroad bankruptcies and concluded that the direct cost of bankruptcy was only 5% on the day before bankruptcy. And it is even lower when assessed five years before the bankruptcy.

14 For an examination of the theory behind indirect bankruptcy costs, see Opler, T. and S. Titman, 1994, "Financial Distress and Corporate Performance," *Journal of Finance*, v49, 1015-1040. For an estimate of how large these indirect bankruptcy costs are in the real world, see Andrade, G. and S. Kaplan, 1998, "How Costly Is Financial (not Economic) Distress? Evidence from Highly Leveraged Transactions That Become Distressed," *Journal of Finance*, v53, 1443-1493. They looked at highly levered transactions that subsequently became distressed and concluded that the magnitude of these costs ranges from 10 to 23% of firm value.

Will these approaches yield the same value? Not necessarily. The first reason for the differences is that the models consider bankruptcy costs very differently. The adjusted present-value approach provides more flexibility in allowing you to consider indirect bankruptcy costs. To the extent that these costs do not show up or show up inadequately in the pre-tax cost of debt, the APV approach yields a more conservative estimate of value. The second reason is that the conventional APV approach considers the tax benefit from a fixed-dollar debt value, usually based on existing debt. The cost-of-capital approach estimates the tax benefit from a debt ratio that may require the firm to borrow increasing amounts in the future. For instance, assuming a market debt-to-capital ratio of 30% in perpetuity for a growing firm will require it to borrow more in the future, and the tax benefit from expected future borrowings is incorporated into value today. Finally, the discount rate used to compute the present value of tax benefits is the pre-tax cost of debt in the conventional APV approach. It is the unlevered cost of equity in the cost-of-capital approach. The conventional APV approach yields a higher value than the cost of capital approach because it views the tax savings from debt as less risky and assigns a higher value to these savings.

Which approach yields more reasonable estimates of value? The dollar debt assumption in the APV approach is a more conservative one, but the fundamental flaw with the APV model lies in the difficulties associated with estimating expected bankruptcy costs. As long as that cost cannot be estimated, the APV approach will continue to be used in half-baked form. The present value of tax benefits will be added to the unlevered firm value to arrive at total firm value.

Excess-Return Models

The model that we have presented in this section, where expected cash flows are discounted back at a risk-adjusted discount rate, is the most commonly used discounted cash flow approach, but variations exist. In the excess-return valuation approach, we separate the cash flows into excess-return cash flows and normal return cash flows. Earning the risk-adjusted required return (cost of capital or equity) is considered a normal return cash flow, but any cash flows above or below this number are categorized as excess returns. Therefore, excess returns can be either positive or negative. With the *excess-return valuation* framework, the value of a business can be written as the sum of two components:

Value of Business = Capital Invested in Firm Today + Present Value of Excess-Return Cash Flows from Both Existing and Future Projects

Suppose we assume that the accounting measure of capital invested (book value of capital) is a good measure of capital invested in assets today. This approach implies that firms that earn positive excess-return cash flows will trade at market values higher than their book values. It also implies that the reverse will be true for firms that earn negative excess-return cash flows.

Basis of the Models

Excess-return models have their roots in capital budgeting and the net present-value rule. In effect, an investment adds value to a business only if it has positive net present value, no matter how profitable it may seem on the surface. This also implies that earnings and cash flow growth have value only when they are accompanied by excess returns—returns on equity (capital) that exceed the cost of equity (capital). Excess-return models take this conclusion to the logical next step and compute a firm's value as a function of expected excess returns.

Although numerous versions of excess-return models exist, this section considers one widely used variant—economic value added (EVA). EVA measures the surplus value created by an investment or a portfolio of investments. It is computed as the product of the "excess return" made on an investment or investments and the capital invested in that investment or investments:

$$\begin{aligned}\text{Economic Value Added} &= (\text{Return on Capital Invested} - \text{Cost of Capital})\ (\text{Capital Invested})\\ &= \text{After-Tax Operating Income} - (\text{Cost of Capital})\ (\text{Capital Invested})\end{aligned}$$

EVA is a simple extension of the net present-value rule. The project's net present value (NPV) is the present value of the economic value added by that project over its life:[15]

$$\text{NPV} = \sum_{t=1}^{t=n} \frac{\text{EVA}_t}{(1+k_c)^t}$$

where EVA_t is the economic value added by the project in year t, the project has a life of n years, and k_c is the cost of capital.

This connection between EVA and NPV allows us to link a firm's value to the economic value added by that firm. To see this, let us begin with a simple formulation of firm value in terms of the value of assets in place and expected future growth:

$$\text{Firm Value} = \text{Value of Assets in Place} + \text{Value of Expected Future Growth}$$

Note that in a discounted cash flow model, the values of both assets in place and expected future growth can be written in terms of the net present value created by each component:

$$\text{Firm Value} = \text{Capital Invested}_{\text{Assets in Place}} + \text{NPV}_{\text{Assets in Place}} + \sum_{t=1}^{t=\infty} \text{NPV}_{\text{Future Projects, t}}$$

Substituting the economic value added version of net present value into this equation, we get the following:

$$\text{Firm Value} = \text{Capital Invested}_{\text{Assets in Place}} + \sum_{t=1}^{t=\infty} \frac{\text{EVA}_{\text{t, Assets in Place}}}{(1+k_c)^t} + \sum_{t=1}^{t=\infty} \frac{\text{EVA}_{\text{t, Future Projects}}}{(1+k_c)^t}$$

Thus, a firm's value can be written as the sum of three components:

- The capital invested in assets in place
- The present value of the economic value added by these assets
- The expected present value of the economic value that will be added by future investments

Note that the reasoning used for firm value can be applied just as easily to equity value, leading to the following equation, stated in terms of equity excess returns:

15 This is true, though, only if the expected present value of the cash flows from depreciation is assumed to be equal to the present value of the return of the capital invested in the project.

$$\text{Equity Value} = \text{Equity Invested}_{\text{Assets in Place}} + \sum_{t=1}^{t=\infty} \frac{\text{Equity EVA}_{\text{t, Assets in Place}}}{(1+k_e)^t} + \sum_{t=1}^{t=\infty} \frac{\text{Equity EVA}_{\text{t, Future Projects}}}{(1+k_e)^t}$$

$$\text{Equity EVA} = (\text{Return on Equity} - \text{Cost of Equity}) * \text{Equity Invested}_{\text{Assets in Place}}$$

Note that k_e is the cost of equity.

Measuring EVA

The definition of EVA outlines three basic inputs we need for its computation—the return on capital earned on investments, the cost of capital for those investments, and the capital invested in them. We talked about the first inputs in the context of conventional DCF models. Everything we said in that context applies to measuring EVA as well.

The last input—capital invested in existing assets—is a key input to excess-return models, since it represents the base on which the excess returns are computed. One obvious measure is the firm's market value, but market value includes capital invested not just in assets in place but in expected future growth.[16] Since we want to evaluate the quality of assets in place, we need a measure of the capital invested in these assets. Given the difficulty of estimating the value of assets in place, it is not surprising that we turn to the book value of capital as a proxy for the capital invested in assets in place. The book value, however, is a number that reflects not just the accounting choices made in the current period, but also accounting decisions made over time on how to depreciate assets, value inventory, and deal with acquisitions. The older the firm, the more extensive the adjustments that have to be made to book value of capital to get to a reasonable estimate of the market value of capital invested in assets in place. Since this requires that we know and take into account every accounting decision over time, sometimes the book value of capital is too flawed to be fixable. Here, it is best to estimate the capital invested from the ground up, starting with the assets owned by the firm, estimating the market value of these assets, and cumulating this market value.

Equivalence of Excess Return and DCF Valuation Models

It is relatively simple to show that a firm's discounted cash flow value should match the value you obtain from an excess-return model if you are consistent in your assumptions about growth and reinvestment. In particular, excess-return models are built around a link between reinvestment and growth. In other words, a firm can generate higher earnings in the future only by reinvesting in new assets or using existing assets more efficiently. Discounted cash flow models often do not make this linkage explicit, even though you can argue that they should. Thus, analysts often estimate growth rates and reinvestment as separate inputs and don't make explicit links between the two.

The model values can diverge because of differences in assumptions and ease of estimation. Penman and Sourgiannis (1998) compared the dividend discount model to excess-return models. They concluded that the valuation errors in a discounted cash flow model with a ten-year horizon significantly exceeded the errors in an excess-return model. They attributed the difference

16 As an illustration, computing the return on capital at Google using the firm's market value in 2009, instead of book value, results in a return on capital of about 5%. It would be a mistake to view this as a sign of poor investments on the part of the firm's managers.

to generally accepted accounting principles (GAAP) accrual earnings being more informative than either cash flows or dividends. Francis, Olson, and Oswald (1999) concurred with Penman and also found that excess-return models outperform dividend discount models. Courteau, Kao, and Richardson (2001) argued that the superiority of excess-return models in these studies can be attributed entirely to differences in the terminal value calculation. They also said that using a terminal price estimated by Value Line (instead of estimating one) results in dividend discount models outperforming excess-return models.[17]

What Do Intrinsic Valuation Models Tell Us?

All the approaches described in this chapter try to estimate the intrinsic value of an asset or business. However, it is important that we understand exactly what we are doing in the process. We are estimating what an asset or business is worth, given its cash flows and the risk in those cash flows. To the extent that the value is dependent on the assumptions we make about cash flows, growth, and risk, it represents what we think the intrinsic value is at any point in time.

So, what if the intrinsic value we derive is very different from the market price? Several explanations are possible. One is that we have made erroneous or unrealistic assumptions about a company's future growth potential or riskiness. A second and related explanation is that we have made incorrect assessments of risk premiums for the entire market. A third is that the market is, in fact, making a mistake in its assessment of value.

Even in the last scenario, where our assessment of value is right and the market price is wrong, we have no guarantee that we can make money on our valuations. For that to occur, markets have to correct their mistakes, and that may not happen in the near future. In fact, we can buy stocks that we believe are undervalued and find that they become more undervalued over time. That is why a long time horizon is almost a prerequisite for using intrinsic valuation models. Giving the market more time (say, three to five years) to fix its mistakes provides better odds than hoping it will happen in the next quarter or the next six months.

Conclusion

A company's intrinsic value reflects its fundamentals. The primary tool for estimating intrinsic value is the discounted cash flow model. We started by looking at the contrast between valuing the equity in a business and valuing the entire business, and then we moved on to the four inputs we need for the model. The cash flows to equity investors can be defined strictly as dividends, more expansively as dividends augmented with stock buybacks, and most generally as free cash flows to equity (potential dividends). The cash flow to the firm is the cumulative cash flow to both equity investors and lenders and thus is a predebt cash flow. The discount rates we apply have to be consistent with the cash flow definition, with the cost of equity used to discount cash

17 Penman, S. and T. Sougiannis, 1998, "A Comparison of Dividend, Cash Flow, and Earnings Approaches to Equity Valuation," *Contemporary Accounting Research*, v15, 343-383; Francis, J., P. Olsson, and D. Oswald, 2000, "Comparing the Accuracy and Explainability of Dividend, Free Cash Flow and Abnormal Earnings Equity Value Estimates," *Journal of Accounting Research*, v38, 45-70; Courteau, L., J. Kao, and G.D. Richardson, 2001, "The Equivalence of Dividend, Cash Flow and Residual Earnings Approaches to Equity Valuation Employing Ideal Terminal Value Calculations," *Contemporary Accounting Research*, v18, 625–661.

flows to equity and the cost of capital to discount cash flows to the firm. When estimating growth, we noted the limitations of historical growth numbers and outside estimates and the importance of linking growth to fundamentals. Finally, we applied closure to the models by assuming that cash flows will settle into stable growth sometime in the future, but we imposed constraints on what this growth rate can be and the characteristics of stable-growth companies.

We closed the chapter by looking at three variations on the discounted cash flow model. In the certainty equivalent approach, we adjusted the cash flows for risk and discounted back at the risk-free rate. In the adjusted present-value approach, we separated debt from the firm's operating assets and valued its effects independently of the firm. In the excess-return model, we zeroed in on the fact that it is not growth per se that creates value but growth with excess returns. However, we noted that the models agree at the core, although there are minor differences in assumptions.

3

Probabilistic Valuation: Scenario Analysis, Decision Trees, and Simulations

The preceding chapter examined ways in which we can adjust the value of a business for its risk. Notwithstanding their popularity, all the approaches we described share a common theme. The riskiness of an asset or business is encapsulated in one number—a higher discount rate, or lower cash flows. This computation almost always requires us to make assumptions (often unrealistic) about the nature of risk.

This chapter considers a different and potentially more informative way of assessing and presenting the risk in an investment. Rather than compute an expected value for an asset or firm that tries to capture the expected value across different possible outcomes, we could provide information on what the value of the asset will be under each outcome or at least a subset of outcomes. We will begin this section by looking at the simplest version, which is an analysis of an asset's value under three scenarios—a best case, most likely case, and worst case. Then we will extend the discussion to look at scenario analysis more generally. We will move on to examine the use of decision trees, a more complete approach to dealing with discrete risk. We will close the chapter by evaluating Monte Carlo simulations, the most complete approach to assessing risk across the spectrum.

Scenario Analysis

The expected cash flows that we use to value risky assets can be estimated in one of two ways. They can represent a probability-weighted average of cash flows under all possible scenarios, or they can be the cash flows under the most likely scenario. The former is the more precise measure, but it is seldom used simply because it requires far more information to compile. In both cases, there are scenarios in which the cash flows will be different from expectations—higher than expected in some and lower than expected in others. In scenario analysis, we estimate expected cash flows and asset value under various scenarios, with the intent of getting a better sense of the effect of risk on value. In this section, we first consider an extreme version of scenario analysis where we consider the value in the best and the worst case scenarios and then a more generalized version of scenario analysis.

Best Case/Worst Case

With risky assets, the actual cash flows can be very different from expectations. At the minimum, we can estimate the cash flows if everything works to perfection (a best-case scenario) and if nothing does (a worst-case scenario). In practice, this analysis can be structured in two ways. In the first, each input into asset value is set to its best (or worst) possible outcome, and the cash flows are estimated with those values. Thus, when valuing a firm, you may set the revenue growth rate and operating margin at the highest possible level while setting the discount rate at its lowest level. Then you compute the value as the best-case scenario. The problem with this approach is that it may not be feasible. After all, to get the high revenue growth, the firm may have to lower prices and accept lower margins. With the second method, the best possible scenario is defined in terms of what is feasible while allowing for the relationship between the inputs. Thus, instead of assuming that revenue growth and margins will both be maximized, we will choose a combination of growth and margin that is feasible and yields the maximum value. Although this approach is more realistic, it requires more work to put into practice.

How useful is best-case/worst-case analysis? The results from this analysis can be useful to decision makers in two ways. First, the difference between the best-case and worst-case values can be used as a measure of risk on an asset; the range in value (scaled to size) should be higher for riskier investments. Second, firms that are concerned about the potential spillover effects on their operations of an investment going bad may be able to gauge the effects by looking at the worst-case outcome. Thus, a firm that has significant debt obligations may use the worst-case outcome to decide whether an investment has the potential to push it into default.

In general, though, best-case/worst-case analyses are not very informative. After all, there should be no surprise in knowing that an asset will be worth a lot in the best case and not very much in the worst case. Thus, an equity research analyst who uses this approach to value a stock priced at $50 may arrive at values of $80 for the best case and $10 for the worst case. With a range that large, it is difficult to decide whether the stock is a good investment.

Multiple Scenario Analysis

Scenario analysis does not have to be restricted to the best and worst cases. In its most general form, the value of a risky asset can be computed under a number of different scenarios, varying the assumptions about both macroeconomic and asset-specific variables. The concept of sensitivity analysis is simple; it has four critical components:

- **Deciding which factors the scenarios will be built around**: These factors can range from the state of the economy, for an automobile manufacturer; to the response of competitors, for a consumer products firm; to the behavior of regulatory authorities, for a phone company. In general, analysts should focus on the two or three most critical factors that will determine the asset's value and then build scenarios around these factors.
- **Determining how many scenarios to analyze for each factor**: While more scenarios may be more realistic than fewer, it becomes more difficult to collect information and differentiate between the scenarios in terms of asset cash flows. Thus, estimating cash flows under each scenario is easier if we lay out five scenarios, for instance, instead of 15. The question of how many scenarios to consider depends on how different the scenarios are and how well the analyst can forecast cash flows under each scenario.
- **Estimating asset cash flows under each scenario**: It is to ease the estimation at this step that we focus on only two or three critical factors and build relatively few scenarios for each factor.

- **Assigning probabilities to each scenario**: For some scenarios, involving macroeconomic factors such as exchange rates, interest rates, and overall economic growth, we can draw on the expertise of services that forecast these variables. For other scenarios, involving either the sector or competitors, we have to draw on our knowledge of the industry. Note, though, that this makes sense only if the scenarios cover the full spectrum of possibilities. If the scenarios represent only a subset of the possible outcomes on an investment, the probabilities will not add up to 1.

The output from a scenario analysis can be presented as values under each scenario and as an expected value across scenarios (if the probabilities can be estimated in the fourth step).

Multiple scenario analysis provides more information than a best-case/worst-case analysis by providing asset values under each of the specified scenarios. However, it has its own set of problems:

- **Garbage in, garbage out**: It goes without saying that the key to doing scenario analysis well is setting up the scenarios and the estimation of cash flows under each one. Not only must the outlined scenarios be realistic, but they also have to try to cover the spectrum of possibilities. Once the scenarios have been laid out, the cash flows have to be estimated under each one. You must consider this trade-off when determining how many scenarios will be run.
- **Continuous risk**: Scenario analysis is better suited for dealing with risk that takes the form of discrete outcomes than it is for continuous risk. An example of the former is a shift in regulatory rules. Changes in margins or market share are an example of the latter.
- **Double counting of risk**: As with the best-case/worst-case analysis, a danger exists that decision-makers will double-count risk when they do scenario analysis. Thus, an investor looking at the output from a scenario analysis may decide not to invest in an undervalued stock, because its value under some scenarios is lower than the market price. Since the expected value is already risk-adjusted, this would represent a double counting of potentially the same risk or risk that should not be a factor in the decision in the first place (because it is diversifiable).

Valuing a Company with Scenario Analysis

To illustrate scenario analysis, consider a simple example. Assume that you are valuing TechSmart, a manufacturing company that gets 20% of its revenues and half its operating profits from Wal-Mart. The contract with Wal-Mart is up for renewal at the start of next year. Assume that there are three scenarios. The first and most likely one is that the contract will be renewed with the existing terms. The second is that the contract will be renewed, but with more restrictive (and less profitable) terms for TechSmart. The third is that the contract will not be renewed. Your valuation of the company depends greatly on whether the contract is renewed. Therefore, you estimate three sets of numbers for expected revenues and after-tax operating income next year, depending on what happens with the contract. Table 3.1 summarizes the estimates for each scenario. (Dollar amounts are in millions.)

Table 3.1 Expected Revenues and Operating Earnings Next Year: Contract Scenarios

Scenario	Revenues	After-Tax Operating Income
Contract renewed	$1,500	$240
Contract renewed with restrictions	$1,500	$180
Contract not renewed	$1,200	$120

Under every scenario, the firm is expected to see stable growth, with a growth rate of 3% and a cost of capital of 8%. However, the returns on capital vary under each scenario, leading to differences in reinvestment needed to sustain the expected growth rate (see Table 3.2).

Table 3.2 Return on Capital (ROC) and Reinvestment Rate: Contract Scenarios

Scenario	Growth Rate	ROC	Reinvestment Rate (g/ROC)
Contract renewed	3%	12%	25.00%
Contract renewed with restrictions	3%	9%	33.33%
Contract not renewed	3%	6%	50.00%

Using the estimates of expected after-tax operating income from Table 3.1 and the reinvestment rate from Table 3.2, we estimate the firm's value under each scenario as follows:

$$\text{Value of Firm} = \frac{\text{Expected After-Tax Operating Income } (1 - \text{Reinvestment Rate})}{(\text{Cost of Capital} - \text{Expected Growth Rate})}$$

The results are shown in Table 3.3.

Table 3.3 Value of the Firm: Contract Scenarios

Scenario	Operating Income	Reinvestment Rate	Value of Firm
Contract renewed	$240	25.00%	$3,600
Contract renewed with restrictions	$180	33.33%	$2,400
Contract not renewed	$120	50.00%	$1,200

Finally, let us assume that the probabilities for the three scenarios are as follows: contract renewal without restrictions is 50%, contract renewal with restrictions is 30%, and contract cancellation is 20%. The expected value of the firm across the scenarios is as follows:

Value of Firm = (.50) (3,600) + (.30) (2,400) + .20 (1,200) = $2,760 million

Note that we could have arrived at precisely the same value using expected values for the operating income and return on capital in a single discounted cash flow valuation.

Decision Trees

In some valuations, risk is not only discrete, but sequential. In other words, for the asset to have value, it must pass through a series of tests. Failure at any point potentially can translate into a complete loss of value. This is the case, for instance, with a pharmaceutical drug that is just being tested on human beings. The three-stage FDA approval process lays out the hurdles that must be passed for this drug to be sold. Failure at any of the three stages dooms the drug's chances. Decision trees allow us not only to consider the risk in stages but also to devise the right response to outcomes at each stage.

Steps in Decision Tree Analysis

The first step in understanding decision trees is to distinguish between root nodes, decision nodes, event nodes, and end nodes:

- The *root node* represents the start of the decision tree, where a decision-maker can be faced with a decision choice or an uncertain outcome. The objective of the exercise is to evaluate what a risky investment is worth at this stage.
- *Event nodes* represent the possible outcomes on a risky gamble; whether a drug passes the first stage of the FDA approval process is a good example. We have to figure out the possible outcomes and the probabilities of the outcomes occurring based on the information we have available today.
- *Decision nodes* represent choices that the decision-maker can make—to expand from a test market to a national market after a test market's outcome is known.
- *End nodes* usually represent the final outcomes of earlier risky outcomes and decisions made in response.

Consider a very simple example. You are offered a choice of accepting $20 or partaking in a gamble in which you have a 50% chance of winning $50 and a 50% chance of winning $10. Figure 3.1 shows the decision tree for this offered gamble.

Note the key elements in the decision tree. First, only the event nodes represent uncertain outcomes and have probabilities attached to them. Second, the decision node represents a choice. On a pure expected value basis, the gamble is better (with an expected value of $30) than the guaranteed amount of $20; the double slash on the latter branch indicates that it would not be selected. While this example may be simplistic, it contains the elements of building a decision tree:

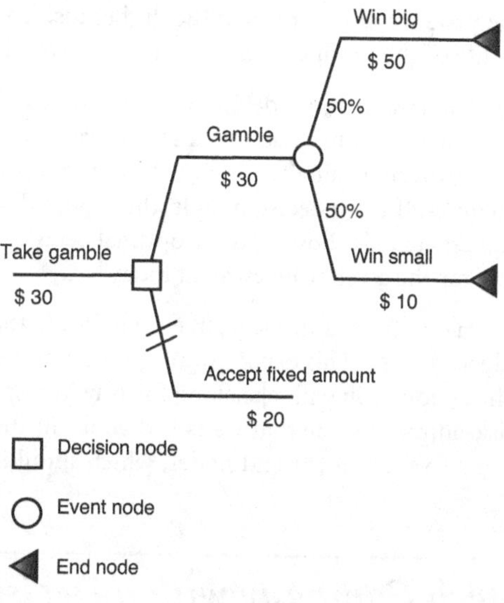

Figure 3.1: Simple Decision Tree

1. **Divide analysis into risk phases.** The key to developing a decision tree is outlining the phases of risk that you will be exposed to in the future. In some cases, such as the FDA approval process, this is easy, since there are only two outcomes. Either the drug gets approved to move on to the next phase, or it does not. In other cases, this is more difficult. For instance, a test market of a new consumer product can yield hundreds of potential outcomes; here, you will have to create discrete categories for the success of the test market.

2. **In each phase, estimate the probabilities of the outcomes.** After the phases of risk and the outcomes at each phase are defined, the probabilities of the outcomes must be computed. In addition to the obvious requirement that the probabilities across outcomes must add up to 1, the analyst must consider whether the probabilities of outcomes in one phase can be affected by outcomes in earlier phases. For example, how does the probability of a successful national product introduction change when the test market outcome is only average?

3. **Define decision points.** Embedded in the decision tree are decision points. These are where you get to determine, based on observing the outcomes at earlier stages, and expectations of what will occur in the future, your best course of action. With the test market example, for instance, you get to determine, at the end of the test market, whether you want to conduct a second test market, abandon the product, or move directly to a national product introduction.

4. **Compute cash flows/value at end nodes.** The next step in the decision tree process is estimating what the final cash flow and value outcomes will be at each end node. In some cases, such as abandonment of a test market product, this is easy to do and represents the money spent on the test marketing of the product. In other cases, such as a national

launch of the same product, this is more difficult, because you must estimate expected cash flows over the life of the product and discount these cash flows to arrive at value.

5. **Fold back the tree.** The last step in a decision tree analysis is "folding back" the tree, in which the expected values are computed working backwards through the tree. If the node is a chance node, the expected value is computed as the probability weighted average of all the possible outcomes. If it is a decision node, the expected value is computed for each branch, and the highest value is chosen (as the optimal decision). The process culminates in an expected value for the asset or investment today.[1]

Two key pieces of output emerge from a decision tree. The first is the expected value today of going through the entire decision tree. This expected value incorporates the potential upside and downside from risk and the actions you will take along the way in response to this risk. In effect, this is analogous to the risk-adjusted value that we talked about in the last chapter. The second piece of output is the range of values at the end nodes, which should encapsulate the potential risk in the investment.

Valuing a Biotech Company with a Decision Tree

To illustrate the steps involved in developing a decision tree, we will value a small biotechnology company that has only one product: a drug for treating type 1 diabetes that has gone through preclinical testing and is about to enter phase 1 of the FDA approval process.[2] Assume that you are provided with additional information on each of the three phases:

- Phase 1 is expected to cost $50 million and will involve 100 volunteers to determine safety and dosage; it is expected to last one year. There is a 70% chance that the drug will successfully complete the first phase.

- In phase 2, the drug will be tested on 250 volunteers for effectiveness in treating diabetes over a two-year period. This phase will cost $100 million, and the drug will have to show a statistically significant impact on the disease to move on to the next phase. There is only a 30% chance that the drug will prove successful in treating type 1 diabetes. There is a 10% chance that it will be successful in treating both type 1 and type 2 diabetes. There also is a 10% chance that it will succeed in treating only type 2 diabetes.

- In phase 3, the testing will expand to 4,000 volunteers to determine the long-term consequences of taking the drug. If the drug is tested

1 A significant body of literature examines the assumptions that have to hold for this folding-back process to yield consistent values. In particular, if a decision tree is used to portray concurrent risks, the risks should be independent of each other. See Sarin, R. and P. Wakker, 1994, "Folding Back in Decision Tree Analysis," *Management Science*, v40, pp. 625–628.

2 In type 1 diabetes, the pancreas does not produce insulin. The patients are often children, and the disease is unrelated to diet and activity; they must receive insulin to survive. In type 2 diabetes, the pancreas produces insufficient insulin. The disease manifests itself in older people and can sometimes be controlled by changing lifestyle and diet.

on only type 1 or type 2 diabetes patients, this phase will last four years and will cost $250 million; there is an 80% chance of success. If it is tested on both types, the phase will last four years and cost $300 million; there is a 75% chance of success.

If the drug passes through all three phases, the costs of developing the drug and the annual cash flows are as shown in Table 3.4.

Table 3.4 Development Costs and Annual Cash Flows

Disease Treatment	Cost of Development	Annual Cash Flow
Type 1 diabetes only	$500 million	$300 million for 15 years
Type 2 diabetes only	$500 million	$125 million for 15 years
Type 1 and 2 diabetes	$600 million	$400 million for 15 years

Assume that the firm's cost of capital is 10%.

We now have the information to draw the decision tree for this drug. We will first draw the tree shown in Figure 3.2, specifying the phases, the cash flows at each phase, and the probabilities.

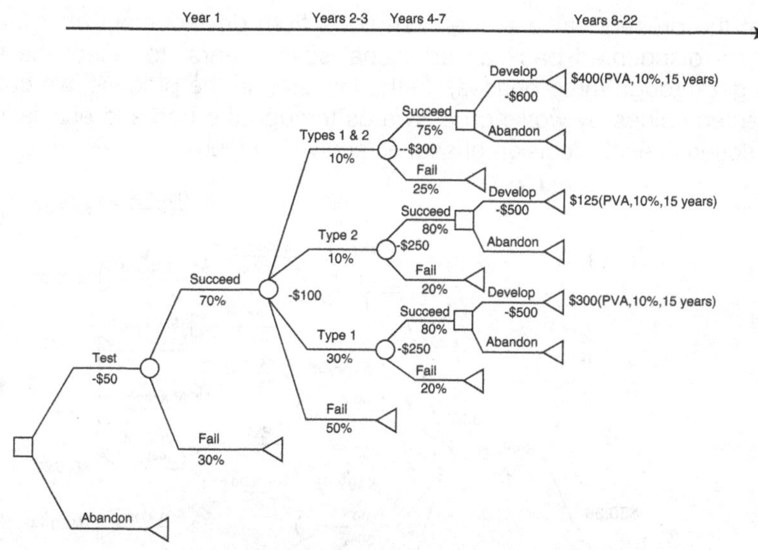

Figure 3.2: Decision Tree for Drug Development

The decision tree shows the probabilities of success at each phase and the additional cash flow or marginal cash flow associated with each step. Since it takes time to go through the phases, a time-value effect must be built into the expected cash flows for each path. We introduce the time-value effect and compute the cumulative present value (today) of cash flows from each path, using the 10% cost of capital as the discount rate, as shown in Figure 3.3.

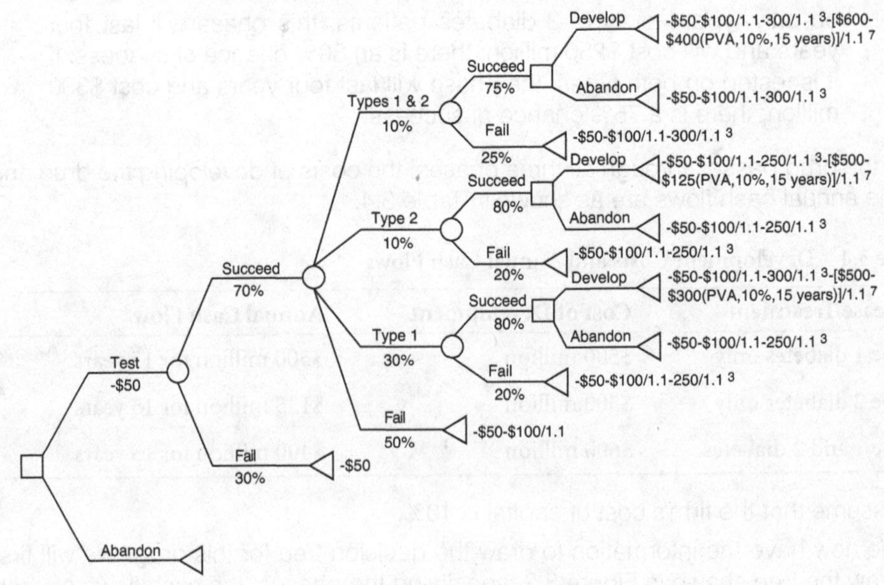

Figure 3.3: Present Value of Cash Flows at End Nodes: Drug Development Tree

Note that the present value of the cash flows from development after the third phase gets discounted back an additional seven years (to reflect the time it takes to get through three phases). In the last step in the process, we compute the expected values by working backwards through the tree and estimating the optimal action in each decision phase, as shown in Figure 3.4.

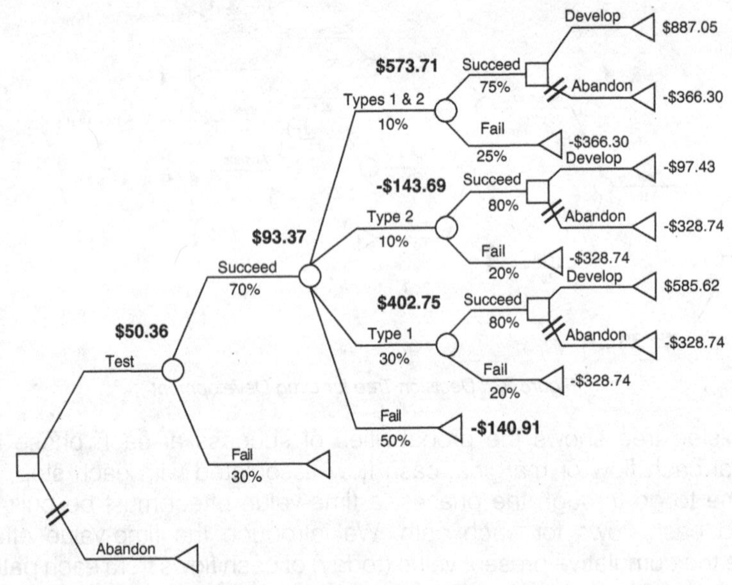

Figure 3.4: Drug Decision Tree Folded Back

The expected value of the drug today, given the uncertainty over its success, is $50.36 million. This value reflects all the possibilities that can unfold over time and shows the choices at each decision branch that are suboptimal and thus should be rejected.

For example, once the drug passes phase 3, developing the drug beats abandoning it in all three cases—as a treatment for type 1, type 2, or both. The decision tree also provides a range of outcomes. The worst-case outcome is failure in phase 3 of the drug as a treatment for both type 1 and 2 diabetes (–$366.30 million in today's dollars). The best-case outcome is approval and development of the drug as treatment for both types of diabetes ($887.05 million in today's dollars).

One element in the last set of branches might seem puzzling. The present value of developing the drug as a treatment for just type 2 diabetes is negative (–$97.43 million). Why would the company still develop the drug? Because the alternative of abandoning the drug at the late stage in the process has an even more negative net present value (–$328.74 million). Another way to see this is to look at the marginal effect of developing the drug just for type 2 diabetes. Once the firm has expended the resources to go through all three phases of testing, the testing cost becomes a sunk cost and is not a factor in the decision.[3] The marginal cash flows from developing the drug after phase 3 yield a positive net present value of $451 million (in year 7 cash flows):

Present Value of Developing Drug to Treat Type 2 Diabetes in Year 7 = -500 + 125(PV of Annuity, 10%, 15 Years) = $451 million

At each stage in the decision tree, you make your judgments based on the incremental cash flows at that juncture. Rolling back the decision tree allows you to see what the value of the drug is at each phase in the process.

In summary, this decision tree would lead us to assess a value of $50.36 million for the diabetes drug and, by extension, the firm that owns the rights to the drug. The decision tree provides information on the value that we should attach to the firm as it moves through the phases. If the initial test succeeds, for instance, the firm's value will jump to $93.37 million. In the follow-up test, if the drug has promise for treating both type 1 and 2 diabetes, the firm's value will jump to $573.71 million.

Estimation Issues

Decision trees can handle some types of risk but not others. In particular, decision trees are best suited for risk that is sequential; the FDA process where approval occurs in phases is a good example. Risks that affect an asset concurrently cannot be easily modeled in a decision tree.[4] As

3 It would be more accurate to consider only the costs of the first two phases as sunk, because by the end of phase 2, the firm knows that the drug is effective only against type 2 diabetes. Even if we consider only the costs of the first 2 phases as sunk, it still makes sense on an expected-value basis to continue to phase 3.

4 If we choose to model such risks in a decision tree, they have to be independent of each other. In other words, the sequencing should not matter.

with scenario analysis, decision trees generally look at risk in terms of discrete outcomes. Again, this is not a problem with the FDA approval process, which has only two possible outcomes—success or failure. Most other risks have a much wider range of outcomes, so we have to create discrete categories for the outcomes to stay within the decision tree framework.

Assuming that risk is sequential and can be categorized into discrete boxes, we are faced with estimation questions to which there may be no easy answers. In particular, we have to estimate the cash flow under each outcome and the associated probability. With the drug development example, we had to estimate the cost and the probability of success of each phase. The advantage that we have when it comes to these estimates is that we can draw on empirical data on how frequently drugs that enter each phase make it to the next one and historical costs associated with drug testing. To the extent that there may be wide differences across different phase 1 drugs in terms of success—some may be longer shots than others—errors can still creep into decision trees.

The expected value of a decision tree is heavily dependent on the assumption that we will stay disciplined at the tree's decision points. In other words, if the optimal decision is to abandon if a test market fails, and the expected value is computed based on this assumption, the integrity of the process and the expected value will quickly fall apart if managers decide to overlook the market testing failure and go with a full launch of the product anyway.

Finally, decision trees are most useful when valuing companies that are entirely dependent on a single product or asset for their value. In the biotechnology company valuation described in the preceding sidebar, we assumed that the entire value was derived from the single diabetes drug working its way through the pipeline. The valuations that we obtain, though, may not be realistic if we assume that the firm has the research potential to develop other drugs in the future. In that case, additional value might be generated from these new drugs.

Risk-Adjusted Value and Decision Trees

Are decision trees an alternative or an addendum to discounted cash flow valuation? The question is an interesting one. Some analysts believe that decision trees, by factoring in the possibility of good and bad outcomes, are already risk-adjusted. In fact, they go on to make the claim that the right discount rate to use in estimating present value in decision trees is the risk-free rate. Using a risk-adjusted discount rate, they argue, would be double-counting the risk. Barring a few exceptional circumstances, they are incorrect in their reasoning:

- **Expected values are not risk-adjusted**: Consider decision trees, where we estimate expected cash flows by looking at the possible outcomes and their probabilities of occurrence. The probability-weighted expected value that we obtain is not risk-adjusted. The only rationale that can be offered for using a risk-free rate is that the risk embedded in the uncertain outcomes is asset-specific and will be diversified away. In that case, the risk-adjusted discount rate would be the risk-free rate. In the FDA drug development example, for instance, this may be offered as the rationale for why we would use the risk-free rate to discount cash flows for the first seven years when the only risk we face is drug approval risk. After year 7, though, the risk is likely to contain a market element, and the risk-adjusted rate will be higher than the risk-free rate.

- **Double counting of risk:** We do have to be careful about making sure that we don't double-count for risk in decision trees by using risk-adjusted discount rates that are set high to reflect the possibility of failure at the earlier phases. One common example of this phenomenon is in venture capital valuation. A conventional approach that venture capitalists have used to value young start-up companies is to estimate an exit value, based on projected earnings and a multiple of those earnings in the future, and then to discount the exit value at a target rate. Using this approach, for instance, the value today for a firm that is losing money currently but is expected to make $10 million in five years (when the earnings multiple at which it will be taken public is estimated to be 40) can be computed as follows (if the target rate is 35%):

  Value of the Firm in 5 Years = Earnings in Year 5 * PE = 10 * 40 = $400 million

  Value of Firm Today = $ $400/1.35^5$ = $89.20 million

  Note, however, that the target rate is set at a high level (35%) because of the probability that this young firm will not make it to a public offering. In fact, we could frame this as a simple decision tree, as shown in Figure 3.5.

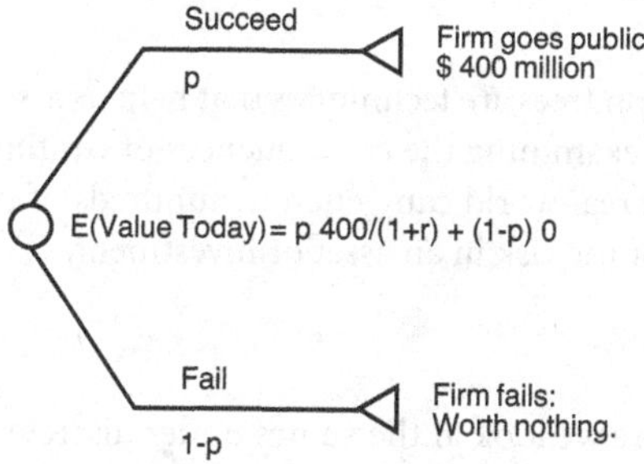

Figure 3.5: Decision Tree for a Start-Up Firm

  Assume that r is the correct discount rate, based on the risk that the venture capitalist faces on this venture. Going back to the numeric example, assume that this discount rate would have been 15% for this venture. We can solve for the implied probability of failure, embedded in the venture capitalist's estimate of value of $89.20 million:

  $$\text{Estimated Value} = \$89.20 = \frac{\$400}{1.15^5}(p)$$

  Solving for p, we estimate the probability of success at 44.85%. With this estimate of probability in the decision tree, we would have arrived at the same value as the venture capitalist, assuming that we use the right discount rate. Using the target rate of 35% as the discount rate in a decision tree would lead to a drastically lower value, because risk would have been counted twice. Using the same reasoning, we can see why using a high discount rate in assessing the value of a biotechnology drug in a decision tree will undervalue the drug. This is especially true if the discount rate already reflects the probability that the drug will not make it to commercial production. If the risk of the approval process is drug-specific and thus diversifiable, this suggests that discount rates should be moderate in decision tree analysis, even for drugs with a very high likelihood of not making it through the approval process.

- **The right discount rate**: If the right discount rate to use in a decision tree should reflect the nondiversifiable risk looking forward, it is not only possible but likely that discount rates will be different at different points in the tree. For instance, extraordinary success at the test market stage may yield more predictable cash flows than an average test market outcome. This would lead us to use a lower discount rate to value the former and a higher discount rate to value the latter. In the drug development example, it is possible that the expected cash flows, if the drug works for both types of diabetes, will be more stable than if it is a treatment for only one type. It would follow that a discount rate of 8% may be best for the first set of cash flows, whereas a 12% discount rate may be more appropriate for the second.

Reviewing the discussion, decision trees are not alternatives to risk-adjusted valuation. Instead, they can be viewed as a different way of adjusting for discrete risk that may be difficult to bring into expected cash flows or risk-adjusted discount rates.

Simulations

If scenario analysis and decision trees are techniques that help us assess the effects of discrete risk, simulations provide a way of examining the consequences of continuous risk. To the extent that most risks that we face in the real world can generate hundreds of possible outcomes, a simulation gives us a fuller picture of the risk in an asset or investment.

Steps in Simulation

Unlike scenario analysis, where we look at the values under discrete scenarios, simulations allow for more flexibility in how we deal with uncertainty. In their classic form, distributions of values are estimated for each parameter in the valuation (growth, market share, operating margin, beta). In each simulation, we draw one outcome from each distribution to generate a unique set of cash flows and value. Across a large number of simulations, we can derive a distribution for the value of investment or an asset that will reflect the underlying uncertainty we face in estimating the inputs to the valuation. The steps associated with running a simulation are as follows:

1. **Determine "probabilistic" variables.** Any analysis has potentially dozens of inputs, some of which are predictable and some of which are not. Unlike scenario analysis and decision trees, where the number of variables that are changed and the potential outcomes have to be few in number, there is no constraint on how many variables can be allowed to vary in a simulation. At least in theory, we can define probability distributions for every input in a valuation. The reality, though, is that this would be time-consuming and may not provide much of a payoff, especially for inputs that have only marginal impact on value. Consequently, it makes sense to focus on a few variables that have a significant impact on value.
2. **Define probability distributions for these variables.** This is a key and the most difficult step in the analysis. Generically, we can go about defining probability distributions in three ways:

a. **Historical data**: For variables that have a long history and reliable data over that history, it is possible to use the historical data to develop distributions. Assume, for instance, that you are trying to develop a distribution of expected changes in the long-term Treasury bond rate (to use as an input in investment analysis). You could use the histogram shown in Figure 3.6, based on the annual changes in Treasury bond rates every year from 1928 to 2005, as the distribution for future changes.

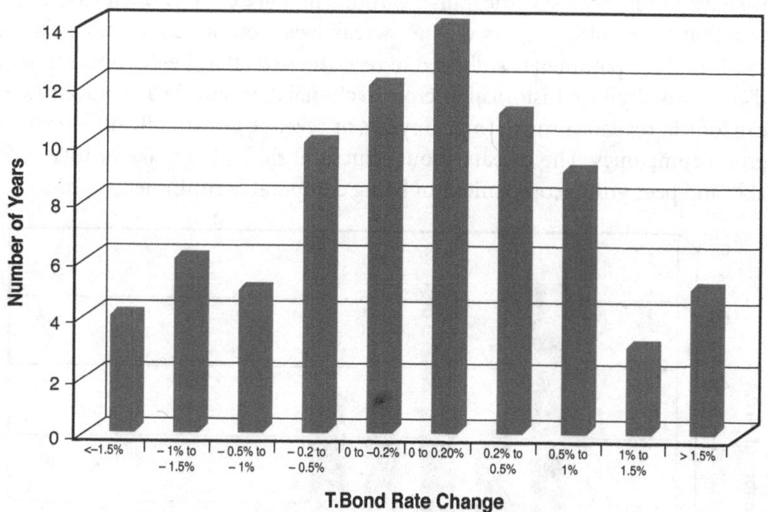

Figure 3.6: Change in the Treasury Bond Rate, 1928 to 2005

Implicit in this approach is the assumption that there have been no structural shifts in the market that will render the historical data unreliable.

b. **Cross-sectional data**: In some cases, you may be able to substitute data on differences in a specific variable across existing investments that are similar to the investment being analyzed. Consider two examples. Assume that you are valuing a software firm and are concerned about the volatility in operating margins. Figure 3.7 shows the distribution of pretax operating margins across software companies in 2006.

   If we use this distribution, we are in effect assuming that the underlying distribution of margins is the same across software firms. In a second example, assume that you work for Target, the retailer, and that you are trying to estimate the sales per square foot for a new store investment. Target could use the distribution on this variable across existing stores as the basis for its simulation of sales at the new store.

c. **Statistical distribution and parameters**: For most variables that you are trying to forecast, the historical and cross-sectional data will be insufficient or unreliable. In these cases, we have to pick a statistical distribution that best captures the variability in the input and estimate the parameters for that distribution. Thus, we may conclude that operating margins will be distributed uniformly, with a minimum of 4% and a maximum of 8%. We may also conclude that revenue growth is normally distributed with an expected value of 8% and a standard deviation of 6%. Many simulation packages available for personal computers now provide a rich array of distributions, but picking the right distribution and the parameters for the distribution remains difficult for two reasons. The first is that few inputs we see in practice meet the stringent requirements that statistical distributions demand. Revenue growth, for instance, cannot really be normally distributed, because the lowest value it can take on is –100%. Consequently, we have to settle for statistical distributions that are close enough to the real distribution that the resulting errors will not wreak havoc on our conclusion. The second reason is that the parameters still need to be estimated after the distribution is chosen. For this, we can draw on historical or cross-sectional data. For the revenue growth input, we can look at revenue growth in prior years or revenue growth rate differences across peer group companies. The caveats about structural shifts that make historical data unreliable and peer group companies not being comparable continue to apply.

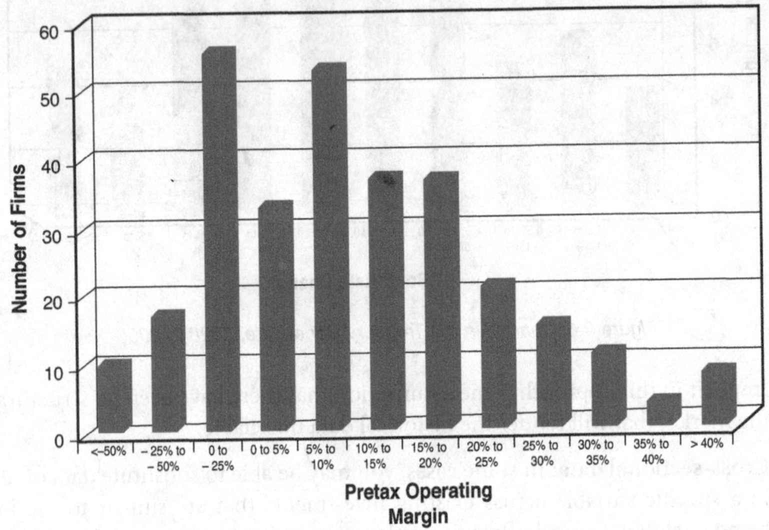

Figure 3.7: Pretax Operating Margin Across U.S. Software Companies, January 2006

The probability distributions for discrete for some inputs and continuous for other inputs and should be based on historical data for some and statistical distributions for others.

3. **Check for correlation across variables.** While it is tempting to begin running simulations right after the distributions have been specified, it is important that we check for correlations across variables. Assume, for instance, that you are developing probability distributions for both interest rates and inflation. Although both inputs may be critical in determining value, they are likely to be correlated with each other; high inflation is usually accompanied by high interest rates. When strong correlation (positive or negative) exists across inputs, you have two choices. One is to pick only one of the two inputs to vary; it makes sense to focus on the input that has the bigger impact on value. The other is to build the correlation explicitly into the simulation. This requires more sophisticated simulation packages and adds more detail to the estimation process.

4. **Run the simulation.** For the first simulation, you draw one outcome from each distribution and compute the value based on those outcomes. This process can be repeated as many times as you want, although the marginal contribution of each simulation drops off as the number of simulations increases. The number of simulations you run should be determined by the following:

    a. **Number of probabilistic inputs**: The larger the number of inputs that have probability distributions attached to them, the greater the required number of simulations.

    b. **Characteristics of probability distributions**: The greater the diversity of distributions in an analysis, the larger the number of required simulations. Thus, the number of required simulations will be smaller in a simulation where all the inputs have normal distributions than in one where some have normal distributions, some are based on historical data distributions, and some are discrete.

    c. **Range of outcomes**: The greater the potential range of outcomes on each input, the greater the number of simulations.

    Most simulation packages allow users to run thousands of simulations, with little or no cost attached to increasing that number. Given that reality, it is better to err on the side of too many simulations rather than too few.

There have generally been two impediments to good simulations. The first is informational: estimating distributions of values for each input into a valuation is difficult. In other words, it is far easier to estimate an expected growth rate of 8% in revenues for the next five years than it is to specify the distribution of expected growth rates—the type of distribution, parameters for that distribution—for revenues. The second is computational. Until the advent of personal computers, simulations tended to be too time- and resource-intensive for the typical analyst. Both these constraints have eased in recent years, and simulations have become more feasible.

Valuing 3M: Monte Carlo Simulation

In Chapter 2, "Intrinsic Valuation," we valued 3M using a conventional discounted cash flow model. We discounted expected cash flows at a risk-adjusted rate to arrive at an estimated value of $86.95 per share. In the process, though, we did make a number of assumptions about not only how the company would evolve over time, but also about risk-free rates and risk premiums in the future. To run a simulation on 3M's value, we will make the following assumptions:

- **Equity risk premium**: In the base case valuation, we used an equity risk premium of 4%, reflecting the historical average of implied premiums in the S&P 500 from 1960 to 2007. This estimate has some error associated with it. Therefore, we will assume that the equity risk premium is normally distributed with an expected value of 4% and a standard deviation of 0.80%, as shown in Figure 3.8.

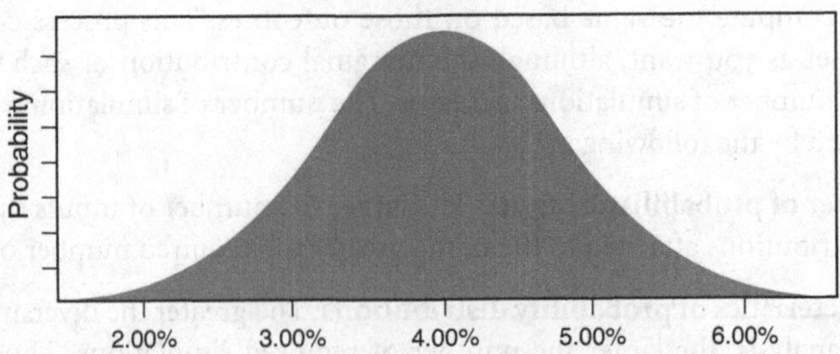

Figure 3.8: Equity Risk Premium: Distribution

- **Length of the growth period**: We assumed that 3M would be able to continue to grow at rates higher than the economy for the next five years. To reflect the uncertainty in this estimate, we allowed the length of the growth period to vary from two to eight years, with equal probabilities attached to each time period (see Figure 3.9).

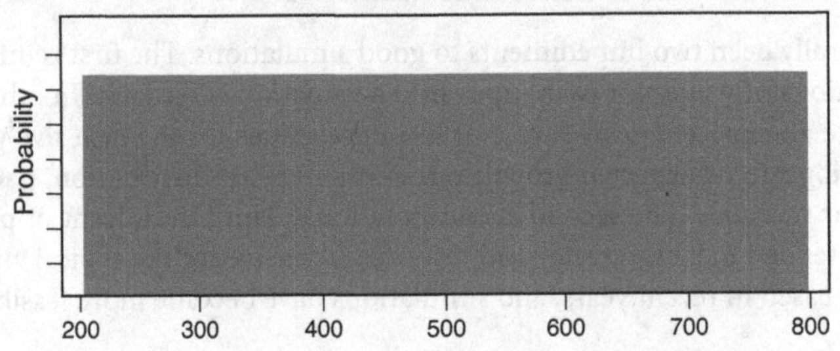

Figure 3.9: Length of the Growth Period: Distribution

- **Return on capital**: When valuing 3M, a key component determining value was the assumption that the firm would be able to maintain its existing return on capital (approximately 25%) for the next five years. Since returns on capital can shift over time, as competition increases, we assumed the distribution shown in Figure 3.10.

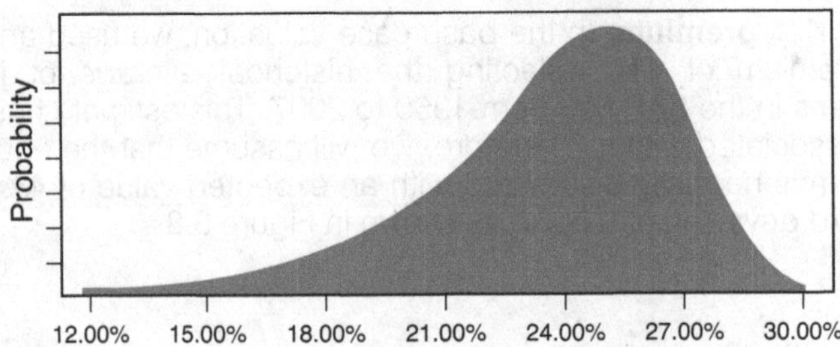

Figure 3.10: Return on Invested Capital: Distribution

Note that we are assuming that although the expected return on capital is 25%, it is unlikely that the return will exceed 30%, and there is a possibility of much lower returns in future years. We obtained this distribution by looking at the distribution of returns on capital across companies in this sector.

- **Reinvestment rate**: In the base case valuation, we assumed that 3M would maintain a reinvestment rate of 30% for the next five years, based on past history. However, the firm might ramp up or lower this reinvestment rate. Using the standard deviation in past reinvestment rates at 3M as guidance, we assumed that the reinvestment rate would be normally distributed, with an expected value of 30% and a standard deviation of 5%, as shown in Figure 3.11.

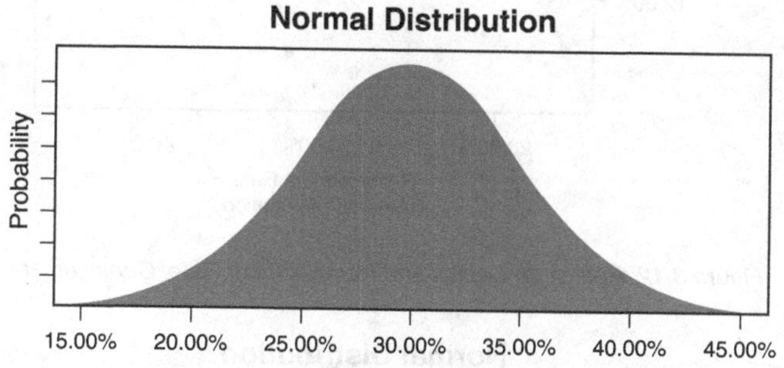

Figure 3.11: Reinvestment Rate: Distribution

However, it is very likely that the reinvestment rate will be a function of the return on capital, with high reinvestment rates occurring if the returns on capital are high. We capture this comovement between return on capital and the reinvestment rate by assuming a correlation of 0.40 between the two. This results in the scatter plot shown in Figure 3.12.

Thus, if the return on capital is close to 30%, the reinvestment rate will be approximately 40%. If the return on capital drops to 12%, the reinvestment rate will decline to 20%.

- **Beta**: In the base case valuation, we estimated a beta of 1.36, based on the businesses that 3M operated in. We used this beta for the high-growth period. It is possible that this beta estimate could be incorrect. To reflect this imprecision, we assume that the beta is normally distributed with a mean of 1.36 and a standard error of 0.07, as shown in Figure 3.13.

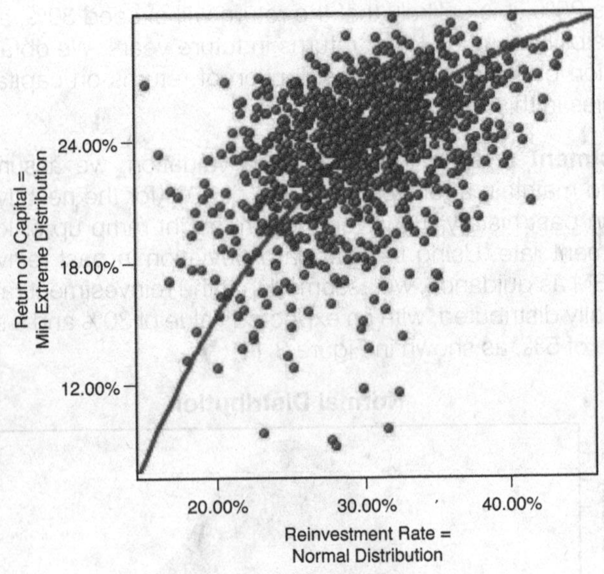

Figure 3.12: Return on Capital and Reinvestment Rate: Comovement

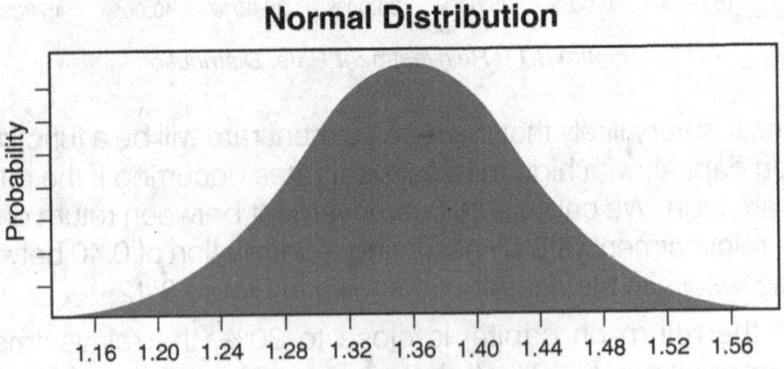

Figure 3.13: Beta Distribution

With these inputs in place, we can estimate the value per share for 3M, allowing the parameters just specified to vary across simulations. Figure 3.14 shows the results of the simulation in the distribution we obtain (across 10,000 simulations). Here are the key statistics on the values obtained across the 10,000 runs:

- The average value across the simulations was $87.35 a share, a trifle higher than the risk-adjusted value of $86.95 a share. The median value was $87.10 a share.

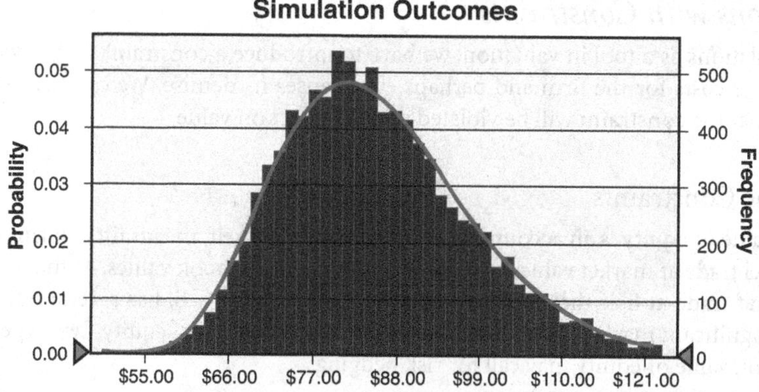

Figure 3.14: Value of Equity Per Share at 3M: Simulation Results

- There was substantial variation in values. The lowest value across all runs was $55.22 a share, and the highest value was $121 a share. The standard deviation in values per share was $16.15.

Use in Decision Making

A well-done simulation provides us with more than just an expected value for an asset or business:

- **Better input estimation:** In an ideal simulation, analysts examine both the historical and cross-sectional data on each input variable before deciding what distribution to use and the parameters of the distribution. In the process, they may be able to avoid the sloppiness that is associated with the use of point estimates. Many discounted cash flow valuations are based on expected growth rates that are obtained from services such Zack's or IBES, which report analysts' consensus estimates.
- **It yields a distribution for expected value rather than a point estimate:** Consider the valuation example that we completed in the preceding section. In addition to reporting an expected value of $87.35 a share, we estimated a standard deviation of $16.15 million in that value and a breakdown of the values by percentile. The distribution reinforces the obvious but important point that valuation models yield estimates of value for risky assets that are imprecise. It also explains why different analysts valuing the same asset may arrive at different estimates of value.

Note that we are unwilling to make two claims about simulations. The first is that simulations yield better estimates of expected value than conventional risk-adjusted value models. In fact, the expected values from simulations should be fairly close to the expected value that we would obtain using the expected values for each of the inputs (rather than the entire distribution). The second claim is that simulations, by providing estimates of the expected value and the distribution in that value, lead to better investment decisions. This may not always be the case. The benefits that decision-makers receive by getting a fuller picture of the uncertainty in value in a risky asset may be more than offset by misuse of that risk measure. As we will argue later in this chapter, it is all too common for risk to be double-counted in simulations and for decisions to be based on the wrong type of risk.

Simulations with Constraints

To use simulations as a tool in valuation, we have to introduce a constraint that, if violated, creates very large costs for the firm and perhaps even causes its demise. We can then evaluate the likelihood that the constraint will be violated and the effect on value.

Book Value Constraints

The book value of equity is an accounting construct and, by itself, means little. Firms like Microsoft and Intel trade at market values that are several times their book values. At the other extreme are firms that trade at half their book value or less. In fact, the U.S. has several hundred firms, some with significant market values that have negative book values of equity. Two types of restrictions on book value of equity may call for risk hedging:

- **Regulatory capital restrictions**: Financial services firms such as banks and insurance companies are required to maintain book equity as a fraction of loans or other assets at or above a floor ratio specified by the authorities. Firms that violate these capital constraints can be taken over by the regulatory authorities; the equity investors lose everything if that occurs. Not surprisingly, financial services firms not only keep a close eye on their book value equity (and the related ratios), but they also are conscious of the possibility that the risk in their investments or positions can manifest itself as a drop in book equity. In fact, value at risk (VAR) represents the efforts by financial services firms to understand the potential risks in their investments and to be ready for the possibility of a catastrophic outcome, even though the probability of its occurring might be very small. By simulating the values of their investments under a variety of scenarios, these firms can not only identify the possibility of falling below the regulatory ratios but also look for ways of hedging against this occurring. When valuing a bank using a discounted cash flow model, a simulation might indicate the risk that an investor is exposed to that the bank may run afoul of its regulatory capital ratios.
- **Negative book value of equity**: As noted, hundreds of firms in the U.S. with negative book values of equity survive its occurrence and have high market values of equity. In some countries, a negative book value of equity can create substantial costs for the firm and its investors. For instance, companies with negative book values of equity in parts of Europe are required to raise fresh equity capital to bring their book values above 0. In some countries in Asia, companies that have negative book values of equity are barred from paying dividends. Even in the U.S., lenders to firms can have loan covenants that allow them to gain at least partial control of a firm if its book value of equity turns negative. As with regulatory capital restrictions, we can use simulations to assess the probability of a negative book value of equity and to adjust the value for that possibility.

Earnings and Cash Flow Constraints

Earnings and cash flow constraints can be either internally or externally imposed, and both can affect the value of firms. In some firms, managers may decide that the consequences of reporting a loss or not meeting analysis estimates of earnings are so dire (including, perhaps, the loss of their jobs) that they are willing to expend the resources on risk-hedging products to prevent this from happening. The cost of hedging risk can reduce earnings, cash flows, and value. In other firms, the constraints on earnings and cash flows can be externally imposed. For instance, loan covenants can be related to earnings outcomes. Not only can the loan's interest rate be tied to whether a company makes money, but control over the firm can itself shift to lenders in some cases if the firm loses money. In either case, we can use simulations both to assess the likelihood that these constraints will be violated and to examine the effect of this likelihood on value.

Market Value Constraints

In discounted cash flow valuation, the firm's value is computed as a going concern by discounting expected cash flows at a risk-adjusted discount rate. Deducting debt from this estimate yields equity value. The possibility and potential costs of not being able to meet debt payments is considered only peripherally in the discount rate. In reality, the costs of not meeting contractual obligations can be substantial. In fact, these costs generally are categorized as indirect bankruptcy costs. They could include the loss of customers, tighter supplier credit, and higher employee turnover. The perception that a firm is in trouble can lead to further trouble. By allowing us to compare the value of a business to its outstanding claims in all possible scenarios (rather than just the most likely one), simulations allow us to not only quantify the likelihood of distress but also build the cost of indirect bankruptcy costs into valuation. In effect, we can explicitly model the effect of distress on expected cash flows and discount rates.

Issues with Using Simulations

The use of simulations in investment analysis was first suggested in an article by David Hertz in the *Harvard Business Review*.[5] He argued that using probability distributions for input variables, rather than single-best estimates, would yield more informative output. He used simulations to compare the distributions of returns of two investments. The investment with the higher expected return also had a greater chance of losing money (which was viewed as an indicator of its riskiness). In the aftermath, several analysts jumped on the simulation bandwagon, with mixed results. Recent years have seen a resurgence in interest in simulations as a tool for risk assessment, especially in the context of derivatives. However, we have to deal with several key issues in the context of using simulations in risk assessment:

- **Garbage in, garbage out**: For simulations to have value, the distributions chosen for the inputs should be based on analysis and data, rather than guesswork. It is worth noting that simulations yield great-looking output, even when the inputs are random. Unsuspecting decision-makers therefore may receive meaningless pictures of the risk in an investment. It is also worth noting that simulations require more than a passing knowledge of statistical distributions and their characteristics. Analysts who cannot assess the difference between normal and lognormal distributions should not be doing simulations.
- **Real data may not fit distributions:** The problem with the real world is that the data seldom fits the stringent requirements of statistical distributions. Using probability distributions that bear little resemblance to the true distribution underlying an input variable will yield misleading results.

5 Hertz, D., 1964, "Risk Analysis in Capital Investment," *Harvard Business Review.*

- **Nonstationary distributions**: Even when the data fits a statistical distribution or where historical data distributions are available, shifts in the market structure can lead to shifts in the distribution as well. In some cases, this can change the form of the distribution; in others, it can change the parameters of the distribution. Thus, the mean and variance estimated from historical data for an input that is normally distributed may change for the next period. What we would really like to use in simulations, but seldom can assess, are forward-looking probability distributions.
- **Changing correlation across inputs**: Earlier in this chapter, we noted that correlation across input variables can be modeled into simulations. However, this works only if the correlations remain stable and predictable. To the extent that correlations between input variables change over time, it becomes far more difficult to model them.

Risk-Adjusted Value and Simulations

In our discussion of decision trees, we mentioned the common misconception that decision trees are risk-adjusted because they consider the likelihood of adverse events. The same misconception is prevalent in simulations. The argument is that the cash flows from simulations are somehow risk-adjusted because of the use of probability distributions and that the risk-free rate should be used in discounting these cash flows. With one exception, this argument does not make sense. Looking across simulations, the cash flows we obtain are expected cash flows and are not risk-adjusted. Consequently, we should discount these cash flows at a risk-adjusted rate.The exception occurs when you use the standard deviation in values from a simulation as a measure of investment or asset risk and make decisions based on that. In this case, using a risk-adjusted discount rate will result in a double counting of risk. Consider a simple example. Assume that you are trying to choose between two investments, both of which you have valued using simulations and risk-adjusted discount rates. Table 3.5 summarizes your findings.

Table 3.5 Simulation Results for Two Investments

Asset	Risk-Adjusted Discount Rate	Simulation Expected Value	Simulation Standard Deviation
A	12%	$100	15%
B	15%	$100	21%

Note that you consider asset B riskier and have used a higher discount rate to compute value. If you now reject asset B because the standard deviation is higher across the simulated values, you would be penalizing it twice. You can redo the simulations using the risk-free rate as the discount rate for both assets, but a note of caution needs to be mentioned. If you then base your choice between these assets on the standard deviation in simulated values, you are assuming that all risk matters in investment choice, rather than only the risk that cannot be diversified away. Put another way, you may end up rejecting an asset because it has a high standard deviation in simulated values, even though adding that asset to a portfolio may result in little additional risk (because much of its risk can be diversified away).

This is not to suggest that simulations are not useful to us in understanding risk. Looking at the variance of the simulated values around the expected value provides a visual reminder that we are estimating value in an uncertain environment. It is also conceivable that we can use it as a decision tool in portfolio management in choosing between two stocks that are equally undervalued but have different value distributions. The stock with the less volatile value distribution may be considered a better investment than another stock with a more volatile value distribution.

An Overall View of Probabilistic Risk Assessment Approaches

Now that we have looked at scenario analysis, decision trees, and simulations, we can consider not only when each one is appropriate but also how these approaches complement or replace risk-adjusted value approaches.

Comparing the Approaches

Assuming that you decide to use a probabilistic approach to assess risk and can choose between scenario analysis, decision trees, and simulations, which one should you pick? The answer depends on how you plan to use the output and what types of risk you are facing:

- **Selective versus full-risk analysis**: In the best-case/worst-case scenario analysis, we look at only three scenarios (the best case, most likely case, and worst case) and ignore all other scenarios. Even when we consider multiple scenarios, we do not have a complete assessment of all possible outcomes from risky investments or assets. With decision trees and simulations, we attempt to consider all possible outcomes. In decision trees, we try to accomplish this by converting continuous risk into a manageable set of possible outcomes. With simulations, we can use distributions to capture all possible outcomes. Put in terms of probability, the sum of the probabilities of the scenarios we examine in scenario analysis can be less than 1. On the other hand, the sum of the probabilities of outcomes in decision trees and simulations must equal 1. As a consequence, we can compute expected values across outcomes in the latter using the probabilities as weights. These expected values are comparable to the single-estimate risk-adjusted values we talked about in Chapter 2.
- **Discrete versus continuous risk**: As noted, scenario analysis and decision trees generally are built around discrete outcomes in risky events, whereas simulations are better suited for continuous risks. Focusing on just scenario analysis and decision trees, the latter are better suited for sequential risks, since risk is considered in phases. The former is easier to use when risks occur concurrently.
- **Correlation across risks**: If the various risks that an investment is exposed to are correlated, simulations allow for explicitly modeling these correlations (assuming that you can estimate and forecast them). In scenario analysis, we can deal with correlations subjectively by creating scenarios that allow for them. The high (or low) interest rate scenario will also include slower (or higher) economic growth. Correlated risks are difficult to model in decision trees.

Table 3.6 summarizes the relationship between risk type and the probabilistic approach used.

Table 3.6 Risk Type and Probabilistic Approaches

Discrete/ Continuous	Correlated/ Independent	Sequential/ Concurrent	Risk Approach
Discrete	Independent	Sequential	Decision tree
Discrete	Correlated	Concurrent	Scenario analysis
Continuous	Either	Either	Simulations

Finally, the quality of the information will be a factor in your choice of approach. Because simulations depend largely on being able to assess probability distributions and parameters, they work best when substantial historical and cross-sectional data can be used to make these assessments. With decision trees, you need estimates of the probabilities of the outcomes at each chance node. This makes them best suited for risks that can be assessed either using past data or population characteristics. Thus, it should come as no surprise that when confronted with new and unpredictable risks, analysts continue to fall back on scenario analysis, notwithstanding its slapdash and subjective ways of dealing with risk.

A Complement to or Replacement for Risk-Adjusted Value

As we noted in our discussion of both decision trees and simulations, these approaches can be used as either complements to or substitutes for risk-adjusted value. Scenario analysis, on the other hand, always complements risk-adjusted value, since they do not look at the full spectrum of possible outcomes.

When any of these approaches are used as complements to risk-adjusted value, the caveats that we offered earlier in the chapter continue to apply and bear repeating. All these approaches use expected rather than risk-adjusted cash flows, and *the discount rate that is used should be a risk-adjusted discount rate*. The risk-free rate cannot be used to discount expected cash flows. In all three approaches, though, we still preserve the flexibility to change the risk-adjusted discount rate for different outcomes. Since all these approaches also provide a range for estimated value and a measure of variability (in terms of value at the end nodes in a decision tree or as a standard deviation in value in a simulation), it is important that we do not double-count for risk. In other words, it is patently unfair to risky investments to discount their cash flows at a risk-adjusted rate (in simulations and decision trees) and then reject them because the variability in value is high.

Both simulations and decision trees can be used as alternatives to risk-adjusted valuation, but the process has constraints. The first is that the cash flows will be discounted at a risk-free rate to arrive at value. The second is that we now use the measure of variability in values that we obtain in both these approaches as a measure of risk in the investment. Comparing two assets with the same expected value (obtained with riskless rates as discount rates) from a simulation, we pick the one with the lower variability in simulated values as the better investment. If we do this, we are assuming that all the risks we have built into the simulation are relevant for the investment decision. In effect, we are ignoring the line drawn between risks that could have been diversified away in a portfolio and asset-specific risk on which much of modern finance is built. For an investor considering investing all his or her wealth in one asset, this should be reasonable. For a portfolio manager comparing two risky stocks that he or she is considering adding to a diversified portfolio, it can yield misleading results. The rejected stock with the higher variance in simulated values may be uncorrelated with the other investments in the portfolio and thus have little marginal risk.

Conclusion

Estimating the risk-adjusted value for a risky asset or investment may seem like an exercise in futility. After all, the value is a function of the assumptions we make about how the risk will unfold in the future. With probabilistic approaches to risk assessment, we not only estimate an expected value but also get a sense of the range of possible outcomes for value, across good and bad scenarios:

- In the most extreme form of scenario analysis, you look at the value in the best-case and worst-case scenarios and contrast them with the expected value. In its more general form, you estimate the value under a small number of likely scenarios, ranging from optimistic to pessimistic.
- Decision trees are designed for sequential and discrete risks. Here the risk in an investment is considered in phases, and the risk in each phase is captured in the possible outcomes and the probabilities that they will occur. A decision tree provides a complete assessment of risk. It can be used to determine the optimal course of action at each phase and an expected value for an asset today.
- Simulations provide the most complete assessments of risk because they are based on probability distributions for each input (rather than just discrete outcomes). The output from a simulation takes the form of an expected value across simulations and a distribution for the simulated values.

With all three approaches, the keys are to avoid double-counting risk (by using a risk-adjusted discount rate and considering the variability in estimated value as a risk measure) and to avoid making decisions based on the wrong types of risk.

4

Relative Valuation

In discounted cash flow valuation, the objective is to find the value of an asset given its cash flow, growth, and risk characteristics. In relative valuation, the objective is to value an asset based on how similar assets are currently priced by the market. Consequently, relative valuation has two components. The first is that to value assets on a relative basis, prices have to be standardized, usually by converting prices into multiples of some common variable. While this common variable varies across assets, it usually takes the form of earnings, book value, or revenues for publicly traded stocks. The second component is to find similar assets. This is difficult to do, because no two assets are identical. With real assets, as with antiques and baseball cards, the differences may be small and easily controlled for when pricing the assets. In the context of valuing equity in firms, the problems are compounded, because firms in the same business can still differ in risk, growth potential, and cash flows. The question of how to control for these differences, when comparing a multiple across several firms, becomes a key one.

While relative valuation is easy to use and intuitive, it is also easy to misuse. This chapter develops a four-step process for doing relative valuation. In the process, we will also develop a series of tests that can ensure that multiples are used correctly.

What Is Relative Valuation?

Relative valuation values an asset based on how similar assets are priced in the market. A prospective house buyer decides how much to pay for a house by looking at the prices paid for similar houses in the neighborhood. A baseball card collector makes a judgment on how much to pay for a Mickey Mantle rookie card by checking transaction prices on other Mickey Mantle rookie cards. In the same vein, a potential investor in a stock tries to estimate its value by looking at the market pricing of "similar" stocks.

Embedded in this description are the three essential steps in relative valuation. The first step is *finding comparable assets that are priced by the market*, a task that is easier to accomplish with real assets like baseball cards and houses than it is with stocks. All too often, analysts view other companies in the same sector as comparable, comparing a software firm to other software firms or a utility to other utilities. However, we will question whether this practice really yields similar companies later in this chapter. The second step is *scaling the market prices to a common variable* to generate standardized prices that are comparable. While this may not be necessary when comparing identical assets (Mickey Mantle rookie cards), it is necessary when comparing assets that vary in size or units. Other things remaining equal, a smaller house or apartment should trade at a lower price than a larger residence. In the context of stocks, this equalization usually requires converting the market value of equity or the firm into multiples of earnings, book value, or revenues. The third and last step in the process is *adjusting for differences across assets* when comparing their standardized values. Again, using the example of a house, a newer house with more updated amenities should be priced higher than a similar-sized older house that needs renovation. Differences in pricing across stocks can be attributed to all the fundamentals we talked about with discounted cash flow valuation. Higher-growth companies, for instance, should trade at higher multiples than lower-growth companies in the same sector. Many analysts adjust for these differences qualitatively, making every relative valuation a storytelling experience; analysts with better and more believable stories are given credit for better valuations.

There is a significant philosophical difference between discounted cash flow and relative valuation. In discounted cash flow valuation, we attempt to estimate the intrinsic value of an asset based on its capacity to generate cash flows in the future. In relative valuation, we make a judgment about how much an asset is worth by looking at what the market is paying for similar assets. If the market is correct, on average, in how it prices assets, discounted cash flow and relative valuations may converge. However, if the market is systematically overpricing or underpricing a group of assets or an entire sector, discounted cash flow valuations can deviate from relative valuations.

The Ubiquity of Relative Valuation

Notwithstanding the focus on discounted cash flow valuation in classrooms and in theory, evidence exists that most assets are valued on a relative basis. In fact, consider the following:

- Most equity research reports are based on multiples. Price/earnings (PE) ratios, enterprise value to earnings before interest, taxes, depreciation, and amortization (EBITDA), price, and price-to-sales ratios are but a few examples. In a study of 550 equity research reports in early 2001, relative valuations outnumbered discounted valuations almost ten to one.[1] While many equity research reports included the obligatory cash flow tables, values were estimated and recommendations were made by looking at comparable firms and using multiples. Thus, when analysts contend that a stock is under- or overvalued, they are usually making that judgment based on a relative valuation.
- Discounted cash flow techniques are more common in acquisitions and corporate finance. While casual empiricism suggests that almost every acquisition is backed up by a discounted cash flow valuation, the value paid in the acquisition is often determined using a multiple. In acquisition valuation, many discounted cash flow valuations are themselves relative valuations in disguise, because the terminal values are computed using multiples.
- Most investment rules of thumb are based on multiples. For instance, many investors consider companies that trade at less than book value as cheap, as well as stocks that trade at PE ratios that are less than the expected growth rates.

Given that relative valuation is so dominant in practice, it would be a mistake to dismiss it as a tool of the unsophisticated. As we will argue in this chapter and the next two, relative valuation has a role to play that is separate and different from discounted cash flow valuation.

1 The study by the author included sell-side equity research reports from different investment banks in the U.S., London, and Asia. About 75% were from the U.S., about 15% from Europe, and 10% for Asia.

Reasons for Popularity and Potential Pitfalls

Why is the use of relative valuation so widespread? Why do managers and analysts relate so much better to a value based on a multiple and comparables than to discounted cash flow valuation? This section considers some of the reasons for the popularity of multiples.

- **It is less time- and resource-intensive than discounted cash flow valuation**: Discounted cash flow valuations require substantially more information than relative valuation. For analysts who are faced with time constraints and limited access to information, relative valuation offers a less time-intensive alternative.
- **It is easier to sell**: In many cases, analysts in particular and salespeople in general use valuations to sell stocks to investors and portfolio managers. It is far easier to sell a relative valuation than a discounted cash flow valuation. After all, discounted cash flow valuations can be difficult to explain to clients, especially when working under a time constraint. Many sales pitches are made over the phone to investors who have only a few minutes to spare. Relative valuations, on the other hand, fit neatly into short sales pitches. In political terminology, it is far easier to spin a relative valuation than it is to spin a discounted cash flow valuation.
- **It is easy to defend**: Analysts are often called on to defend their valuation assumptions in front of superiors, colleagues, and clients. Discounted cash flow valuations, with their long lists of explicit assumptions, are much more difficult to defend than relative valuations, where the value used for a multiple often comes from what the market is paying for similar firms. It can be argued that the brunt of the responsibility in a relative valuation is borne by financial markets. In a sense, we are challenging investors who have a problem with a relative valuation to take it up with the market if they have a problem with the value.
- **Market imperatives**: Relative valuation is much more likely to reflect the current mood of the market, since it attempts to measure relative and not intrinsic value. Thus, in a market where all technology stocks see their prices bid up, relative valuation is likely to yield higher values for these stocks than discounted cash flow valuations. In fact, by definition, relative valuations generally yield values that are closer to market prices than discounted cash flow valuations, across all stocks. This is particularly important for investors whose job it is to make judgments on relative value and who are themselves judged on a relative basis. Consider, for instance, managers of technology mutual funds. These managers are judged based on how their funds do relative to other technology funds. Consequently, they are rewarded if they pick technology stocks that are undervalued relative to other technology stocks, even if the entire sector is overvalued.

The strengths of relative valuation are also its weaknesses. First, the ease with which a relative valuation can be put together, pulling together a multiple and a group of comparable firms, can also result in inconsistent estimates of value, where key variables such as risk, growth, or cash flow potential are ignored. Second, the fact that multiples reflect the market mood also implies that using relative valuation to estimate an asset's value can result in values that are too high, when the market is overvaluing comparable firms, or too low, when it is undervaluing these firms. Third, while there is scope for bias in any type of valuation, the lack of transparency regarding the underlying assumptions in relative valuations makes them particularly vulnerable to manipulation. A biased analyst who is allowed to choose the multiple on which the valuation is based and to choose the comparable firms can essentially ensure that almost any value can be justified.

Standardized Values and Multiples

When comparing identical assets, we can compare the prices of these assets. Thus, the price of a Tiffany lamp can be compared to the price at which an identical item was bought or sold in the market. However, comparing assets that are not exactly similar can be a challenge. If we have to compare the prices of two buildings of different sizes in the same location, the smaller building will look cheaper unless we control for the size difference by computing the price per square foot. Things get even messier when comparing publicly traded stocks across companies. After all, the price per share of a stock is a function of both the value of the equity in a company and the number of shares outstanding in the firm. Thus, a stock split that doubles the number of units will approximately halve the stock price. To compare the values of "similar" firms in the market, we need to standardize the values in some way by scaling them to a common variable. In general, values can be standardized relative to the earnings firms generate, to the book value or replacement value of the firms themselves, to the revenues that firms generate, or to measures that are specific to firms in a sector.

Earnings Multiples

One of the more intuitive ways to think of the value of any asset is as a multiple of the earnings that asset generates. When buying a stock, it is common to look at the price paid as a multiple of the earnings per share generated by the company. This PE ratio can be estimated using current earnings per share, yielding a current PE; earnings over the last four quarters, resulting in a trailing PE; or an expected earnings per share in the next year, providing a forward PE.

When buying a business, as opposed to just the equity in the business, it is common to examine the value of the firm as a multiple of the operating income or the EBITDA. For a buyer of the equity or the firm, a lower multiple is better than a higher one, but these multiples are affected by the growth potential and risk of the business being acquired.

Book Value or Replacement Value Multiples

While financial markets provide one estimate of the value of a business, accountants often provide a very different estimate of value for the same business. The accounting estimate of book value is determined by accounting rules and is heavily influenced by the original price paid for assets and any accounting adjustments (such as depreciation) made since. Investors often look at the relationship between the price they pay for a stock and the book value of equity (or net worth) as a measure of how over- or undervalued a stock is. The price/book value ratio that emerges can vary widely across industries, depending again on the growth potential and the quality of the investments in each. When valuing businesses, we estimate this ratio using the value of the firm and the book value of all assets or capital (rather than just the equity). For those who believe that book value is not a good measure of the true value of the assets, an alternative is to use the replacement cost of the assets; the ratio of the value of the firm to replacement cost is called Tobin's Q.

Revenue Multiples

Both earnings and book value are accounting measures and are determined by accounting rules and principles. An alternative approach, which is far less affected by accounting choices, is to use the ratio of the value of a business to the revenues it generates. For equity investors, this ratio is the price/sales (PS) ratio, where the market value of equity is divided by the revenues generated by the firm. For firm value, this ratio can be modified as the enterprise value/sales (VS) ratio, where the numerator becomes the market value of the firm's operating assets. Again, this ratio varies widely across sectors, largely as a function of the profit margins in each. The advantage of using revenue multiples, however, is that it becomes far easier to compare firms in different markets, with different accounting systems at work, than to compare earnings or book value multiples.

Sector-Specific Multiples

While earnings, book value, and revenue multiples are multiples that can be computed for firms in any sector and across the entire market, some multiples are specific to a sector. For instance, when Internet firms first appeared on the market in the late 1990s, they had negative earnings and negligible revenues and book value. Analysts looking for a multiple to value these firms divided the market value of each firm by the number of hits generated by that firm's website. Firms with lower market value per customer hit were viewed as undervalued. More recently, cable companies have been judged by the market value per cable subscriber, regardless of the longevity and profitably of having these subscribers.

Although sector-specific multiples can be justified under some conditions, they are dangerous for two reasons. First, since they cannot be computed for other sectors or for the entire market, sector-specific multiples can result in persistent over- or undervaluations of sectors relative to the rest of the market. Thus, investors who would never consider paying 80 times revenues for a firm might not have the same qualms about paying $2,000 for every page hit (on the website). This is largely because they have no sense of what high, low, or average is on this measure. Second, it is far more difficult to relate sector-specific multiples to fundamentals, which is an essential ingredient of using multiples well. For instance, does a visitor to a company's website translate into higher revenues and profits? Not only will the answer vary from company to company, but it also will be difficult to estimate looking forward.

The Four Basic Steps of Using Multiples

Multiples are easy to use and easy to misuse. There are four basic steps to using multiples wisely and for detecting misuse in the hands of others. The first step is to ensure that the multiple is defined consistently and that it is measured uniformly across the firms being compared. The second step is to be aware of the multiple's cross-sectional distribution, not only across firms in the sector being analyzed, but also across the entire market. The third step is to analyze the multiple and understand not only what fundamentals determine the multiple but also how changes in these fundamentals translate into changes in the multiple. The final step is finding the right firms to use for comparison and controlling for differences that may persist across these firms.

Definitional Tests

Even the simplest multiples are defined differently by different analysts. Consider, for instance, the PE ratio, the most widely used multiple in valuation. Analysts define it as the market price divided by the earnings per share, but that is where the consensus ends. The PE ratio has a number of variants. While the current price is conventionally used in the numerator, some analysts use the average price over the last six months or year. The earnings per share in the denominator can be the earnings per share from the most recent financial year (yielding the current PE), the last four quarters of earnings (yielding the trailing PE), or expected earnings per share in the next financial year (resulting in a forward PE). In addition, earnings per share can be computed based on primary shares outstanding or fully diluted shares and can include or exclude extraordinary items. Figure 4.1 shows some of the PE ratios for Google in November 2008 using different estimates of earnings per share.

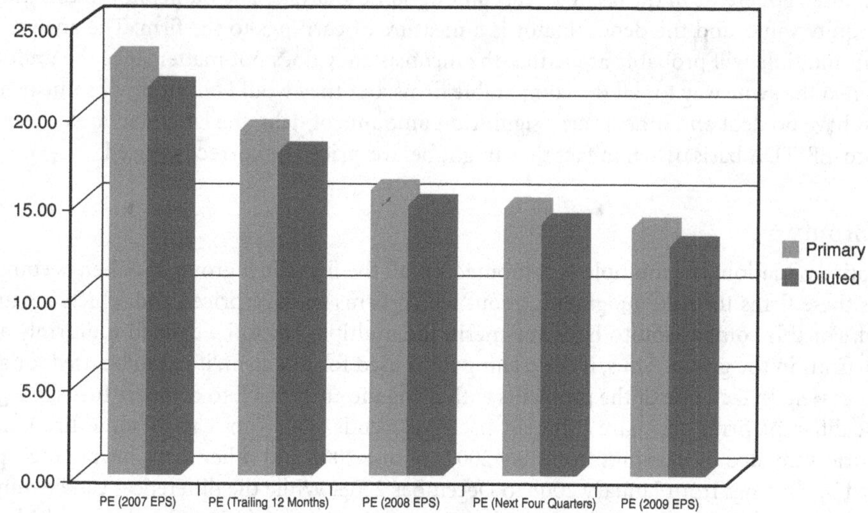

Figure 4.1: Google: PE Ratios in November 2008

Not only can these variants on earnings yield vastly different values for the PE ratio, but the one that gets used by analysts depends on their biases. For instance, in periods of rising earnings, the forward PE yields consistently lower values than the trailing PE, which, in turn, is lower than the current PE. A bullish analyst tends to use the forward PE to make the case that the stock is trading at a low multiple of earnings. A bearish analyst focuses on the current PE to make the case that the multiple is too high. The first step when discussing a valuation based on a multiple is to ensure that everyone in the discussion is using the same definition for that multiple.

Consistency

Every multiple has a numerator and a denominator. The numerator can be either an equity value (such as market price or value of equity) or a firm value (such as enterprise value, which is the sum of the values of debt and equity, net of cash). The denominator can be an equity measure (such as earnings per share, net income, or book value of equity) or a firm measure (such as operating income, EBITDA, or book value of capital).

One of the key tests to run on a multiple is to examine whether the numerator and denominator are defined consistently. If the numerator for a multiple is an equity value, the denominator should be an equity value as well. If the numerator is a firm value, the denominator should be a firm value as well. To illustrate, the PE ratio is a consistently defined multiple, since the numerator is the price per share (which is an equity value) and the denominator is earnings per share (which is also an equity value). The enterprise value to EBITDA also is a multiple, since the numerator and denominator are both firm-value measures. The enterprise value measures the market value of a company's operating assets, and the EBITDA is the cash flow generated by the operating assets prior to taxes and reinvestment needs.

Are any multiples in use inconsistently defined? Consider the price-to-EBITDA multiple, which has acquired adherents in the last few years among some analysts. The numerator in this multiple is an equity value, and the denominator is a measure of earnings to the firm. The analysts who use this multiple will probably argue that the inconsistency does not matter since the multiple is computed the same way for all the comparable firms, but they would be wrong. If some firms on the list have no debt and others carry significant amounts of debt, the latter will look cheap on a price-to-EBITDA basis, when in fact they might be overpriced or correctly priced.

Uniformity

In relative valuation, the multiple is computed for all the firms in a group and then is compared across these firms to make judgments about which firms are overpriced and which are underpriced. For this comparison to have any merit, the multiple has to be defined uniformly across all the firms in the group. Thus, if the trailing PE is used for one firm, it has to be used for all the others as well. In fact, one of the problems with using the current PE to compare firms in a group is that different firms can have different fiscal-year ends. This can lead to some firms having their prices divided by earnings from July 2007 to June 2008 and other firms having their prices divided by earnings from January 2008 to December 2008. While the differences can be minor in mature sectors, where earnings do not make quantum leaps over six months, they can be large in high-growth sectors.

Both earnings and book value measures have another component to be concerned about—the accounting standards used to estimate earnings and book values. Differences in accounting standards can result in very different earnings and book value numbers for similar firms. This makes comparisons of multiples across firms in different markets, with different accounting standards, very difficult. Even with the same accounting standards governing companies, differences in firms can arise because of discretionary accounting choices. An additional problem is posed by the fact that some firms use different accounting rules (on depreciation and expensing) for reporting purposes and tax purposes, and others do not.[2] In summary, companies that use aggressive assumptions to measure earnings will look cheaper on earnings multiples than firms that adopt conservative accounting practices.

2 Firms that adopt different rules for reporting and tax purposes generally report higher earnings to their stockholders than they do to tax authorities. When they are compared on a price/earnings basis to firms that do not maintain different reporting and tax books, they look cheaper (a lower PE).

Descriptive Tests

When using a multiple, it is always useful to have a sense of what a high value, a low value, or a typical value for that multiple is in the market. In other words, knowing the distributional characteristics of a multiple is a key part of using that multiple to identify under- or overvalued firms. In addition, we need to understand the effects of outliers on averages and unearth any biases in these estimates introduced in the process of estimating multiples. The final part of this section looks at how the distributions of multiples shift over time.

Distributional Characteristics

Many analysts who use multiples have a sector focus and have a good sense of how different firms in their sector rank on specific multiples. What is often lacking, however, is a sense of how the multiple is distributed across the entire market. Why should a software analyst care about PE ratios of utility stocks? Because both software and utility stocks are competing for the same investment dollar, they have to, in a sense, play by the same rules. Furthermore, an awareness of how multiples vary across sectors can be very useful in detecting when the sector we are analyzing is over- or undervalued.

Which distributional characteristics matter? The standard statistics—the *average* and *standard deviation*—are where we should start. Markets like the U.S., characterized by diverse companies in very different businesses, have significant variation across companies on any multiple at any point in time. Table 4.1 summarizes the average and standard deviation for three widely used multiples—PE ratios, price-to-book value ratios, and enterprise value (EV) to EBITDA multiple—in January 2008 in the U.S. In addition, the maximum and minimum values for each multiple are reported.

Table 4.1 Summary Statistics on Multiples—January 2008

	Current PE	**Price-to-Book Equity**	**EV/EBITDA**
Average	45.02	5.15	37.40
Median	18.16	2.07	7.36
Standard Deviation	299.11	23.17	331.98
Standard Error	4.64	0.31	4.76
Minimum	0.50	0.00	0.69
Maximum	15,126.20	998.63	11,120.00

Note that the lowest value that any company can register on any of these multiples is 0, whereas the highest values are unbounded. As a result, the distributions of these multiples are skewed toward the positive values. Figure 4.2 compares the distribution of values for a typical multiple to a normal distribution.

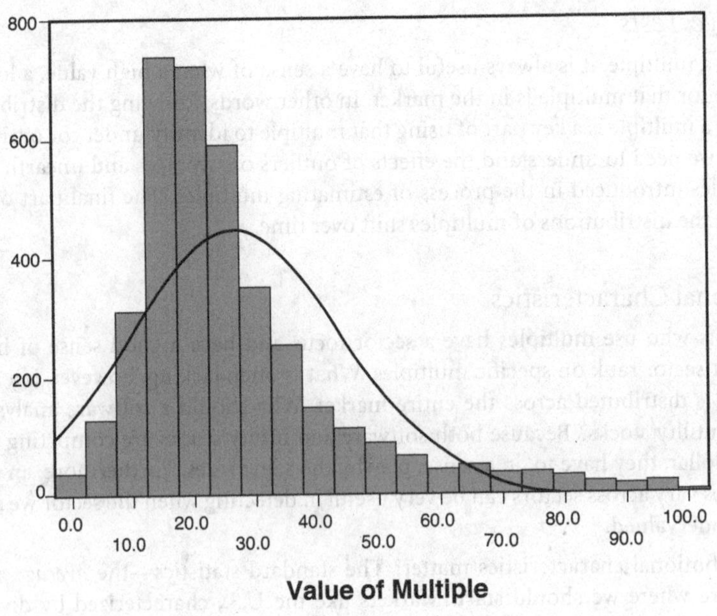

Figure 4.2: Distribution of a Multiple Versus Normal Distribution

The consequences of asymmetric distributions for investors and analysts are significant:

- **Average versus median values**: As a result of the positively skewed distributions, the average values for multiples are higher than *median* values.[3] For instance, the median PE ratio in January 2008 was 18, well below the average PE reported in Table 4.1, and this is true for all multiples. The median value is much more representative of the typical firm in the group, and any comparisons should be made to medians. The standard sales pitch of a stock being cheap because it trades at a multiple less than the average for the sector should be retired in favor of one that compares the stock's pricing to the median for the sector.
- **Probabilistic statements**: As a result of the focus on normal distributions in most statistics classes, we begin attributing their properties to all distributions. For instance, it is true that the probability of values in a normal distribution falling more than two standard deviations away from the mean is very small. In the case of the PE ratio, this rule would suggest that few companies should have PE ratios that fall below 35.74 (which is the average of 45.02 minus two standard errors) or above 54.30 (the average plus two standard errors). The reality is that thousands of firms fall outside this range. While the maximum and minimum values are usually of limited use, the percentile values (10th percentile, 25th percentile, 75th percentile, 90th percentile, and so on) can be useful in judging what a high or low value for the multiple in the group is.

3 With the median, half of all firms in the group fall below this value, and half lie above.

Outliers and Averages

As noted earlier, multiples are unconstrained on the upper end, and firms can trade at multiples of 500 or 2,000 or even 10,000. This can occur not only because of high stock prices but also because earnings at firms can sometimes drop to a few cents or even a fraction of a cent. These outliers result in averages that are not representative of the sample. In many cases, data-reporting services (such as Value Line and Standard & Poor's) that compute and report average values for multiples either throw out these outliers when computing the averages or constrain the multiples to be less than or equal to a fixed number. For instance, any firm that has a PE ratio greater than 500 will be assumed to have a PE ratio of 500. The consequence is that the averages reported by two services for the same sector or market will almost never match up, because they deal with outliers differently. In November 2008, for instance, the average PE reported for the S&P 500 varied widely across services, from a low value of 11.5 on Yahoo! Finance to 14.2 on Morningstar. It is incumbent on investors using these numbers to be clear about how they are computed and consistent in their comparisons.

Biases in Estimating Multiples

Every multiple has firms for which the multiple cannot be computed. Consider again the PE ratio. When the earnings per share are negative, the PE ratio for a firm is not meaningful and usually is not reported. When looking at the average PE ratio across a group of firms, the firms with negative earnings all drop out of the sample, because the PE ratio cannot be computed. Why should this matter when the sample is large? The fact that the firms that are taken out of the sample are the firms losing money creates a bias in the selection process. In fact, the average PE ratio for the group is biased upward because of the elimination of these firms.

This problem has three solutions. The first is to be aware of the bias and build it into the analysis. In practical terms, this means adjusting the average PE down to reflect the elimination of the money-losing firms. The second solution is to aggregate the market value of equity and net income (or loss) for all the firms in the group, including the money-losing ones, and compute the PE ratio using the aggregated values. Figure 4.3 summarizes the average PE ratio, the median PE ratio, and the PE ratio based on aggregated earnings for three sectors—semiconductors, telecom services, and trucking—in January 2008.

Note that the median PE ratio is significantly lower than the average PE in the telecom services and semiconductor business, indicating the presence of large outliers (PE) for some firms in both businesses. In both these businesses, the PE ratio based on the aggregate market cap and net income is closer to the median than the average. In the trucking sector, all three values are close, indicating that this business has few outliers and that the PE ratios for firms tend to be bunched together. The third solution is to use a multiple that can be computed for all the firms in the group. The inverse of the PE ratio, which is called the earnings yield, can be computed for all firms, including those losing money. It is not exposed to the same biases as the PE ratio.

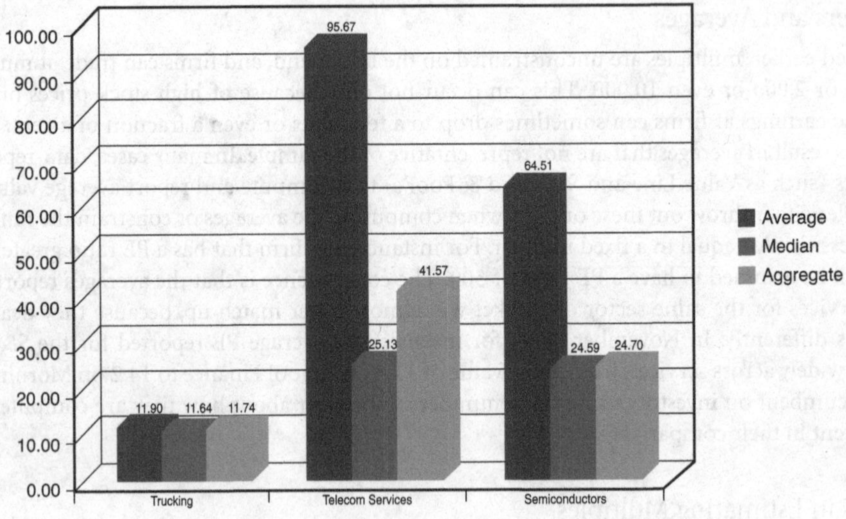

Figure 4.3: Sector PE: Average, Median, and Aggregate Values

Time Variation in Multiples

As any investor who has tracked the market for any length of time knows, multiples change over time for the entire market and for individual sectors. To provide a measure of how much multiples can change over time, Table 4.2 shows the average and median PE ratios each year from 2000 to 2009 for the U.S.

Table 4.2 PE Ratios Across Time: U.S. Stocks

Date	Average	Median	Percentage of Firms with PE Ratios
January 2000	52.16	24.55	65.33%
January 2001	44.99	14.74	63.00%
January 2002	43.44	15.5	57.06%
January 2003	33.36	16.68	49.99%
January 2004	41.4	20.76	58.18%
January 2005	48.12	23.21	56.43%
January 2006	44.33	22.40	56.89%
January 2007	40.77	21.21	57.50%
January 2008	45.02	18.16	56.42%
January 2009	18.91	9.80	58.36%

The last column notes the percentage of firms in the overall sample for which we can compute PE ratios. Note that the beginning of 2000 was the peak of the market bubble; the high values for the PE ratios attest to this. Note also the dramatic drop off in the values between January 2008 and January 2009, attesting to the severity of the market correction that occurred in the last few months of 2008.

Why do multiples change over time? Some of the change can be attributed to fundamentals. As interest rates and economic growth shift over time, the pricing of stocks changes to reflect these shifts. Lower interest rates, for instance, played a key role in the rise of earnings multiples through the 1990s. Some of the change, though, comes from changes in market perception of risk. As investors become more risk-averse, which tends to happen during recessions, multiples paid for stocks decrease. This is captured in Figure 4.4, which shows the earnings yield (earnings/price) ratio for the S&P 500 and the Treasury bond rate over time.

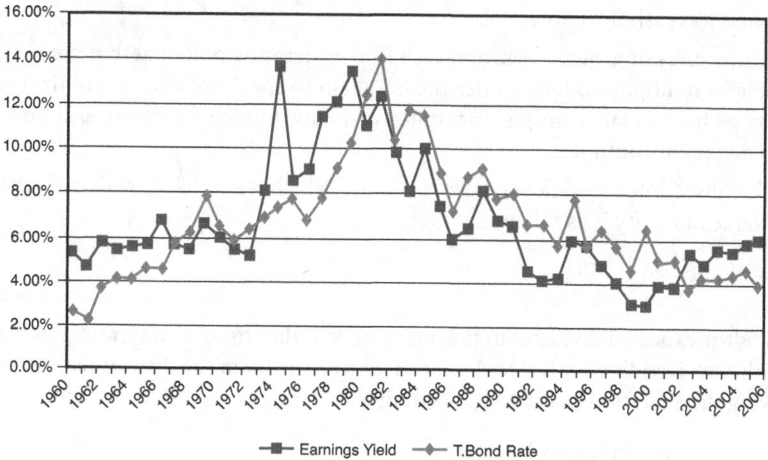

Figure 4.4: U.S. Market: E/P and Interest Rates, 1960 to 2008

Note that the earnings yield rose with the Treasury bond rate in the 1970s and declined as rates went down in the 1980s and 1990s. From a practical standpoint, what are the consequences? The first is that comparisons of multiples across time are fraught with danger. For instance, the common practice of branding a market to be under- or overvalued based on comparing the PE ratio today to historical PE ratios will lead to misleading judgments when interest rates are higher or lower than historical norms. The second consequence is that relative valuations have short shelf lives. A stock may look cheap relative to comparable companies today, but that assessment can shift dramatically over the next few months. Intrinsic valuations are inherently more stable than relative valuations.

Analytical Tests

In discussing why analysts were so fond of using multiples, we argued that relative valuations require fewer assumptions than discounted cash flow valuations. While this is technically true, it is only so on the surface. In reality, we make just as many assumptions when we do a relative valuation as we do in a discounted cash flow valuation. The difference is that the assumptions in a relative valuation are implicit and unstated, whereas those in discounted cash flow valuation are explicit and stated. The two primary questions that we need to answer before using a multiple are What fundamentals determine at what multiple a firm should trade? and How do changes in the fundamentals affect the multiple?

Determinants

In the introduction to discounted cash flow valuation, we observed that a firm's value is a function of three variables—its capacity to generate cash flows, its expected growth in these cash flows, and the uncertainty associated with these cash flows. Every multiple, whether it is of earnings, revenues, or book value, is a function of the same three variables—risk, growth, and cash flow-generating potential. Intuitively, then, firms with higher growth rates, less risk, and greater cash flow-generating potential should trade at higher multiples than firms with lower growth, higher risk, and less cash flow potential.

The specific measures of growth, risk, and cash flow-generating potential that are used will vary from multiple to multiple. To look under the hood (so to speak) of equity and firm value multiples, we can go back to fairly simple discounted cash flow models for equity and firm value and use them to derive the multiples.

In the simplest discounted cash flow model for equity, which is a stable growth dividend discount model, the value of equity is as follows:

$$\text{Value of Equity} = P_0 = \frac{DPS_1}{k_e - g_n}$$

where DPS_1 is the expected dividend in the next year, k_e is the cost of equity, and g_n is the expected stable growth rate. Dividing both sides by the earnings, we obtain the discounted cash flow equation specifying the PE ratio for a stable growth firm:

$$\frac{P_0}{EPS_0} = PE = \frac{\text{Payout Ratio} * (1 + g_n)}{k_e - g_n}$$

The key determinants of the PE ratio are the expected growth rate in earnings per share (EPS), the cost of equity, and the payout ratio. Other things remaining equal, we would expect higher growth, lower risk, and higher payout ratio firms to trade at higher multiples of earnings than firms without these characteristics.

Dividing both sides by the book value of equity, we can estimate the price/book value (PBV) ratio for a stable growth firm:

$$\frac{P_0}{BV_0} = PBV = \frac{ROE * \text{Payout Ratio} * (1 + g_n)}{k_e - g_n}$$

where ROE is the return on equity. ROE is the only variable in addition to the three that determine PE ratios (growth rate, cost of equity, and payout) that affects price-to-book equity.

Dividing by the sales per share, the price/sales ratio for a stable growth firm can be estimated as a function of its profit margin, payout ratio, risk, and expected growth:

$$\frac{P_0}{Sales_0} = PS = \frac{\text{Net Margin} * \text{Payout Ratio} * (1+g_n)}{k_e - g_n}$$

The net margin is the new variable that is added to the process. While all these computations are based on a stable growth dividend discount model, we will show that the conclusions hold even when we look at companies with high growth potential and with other equity valuation models. We can do a similar analysis to derive the firm value multiples. The value of a firm in stable growth can be written as follows:

$$\text{Value of Firm} = V_0 = \frac{FCFF_1}{k_c - g_n}$$

Dividing both sides by the expected free cash flow to the firm yields the value/FCFF multiple for a stable growth firm:

$$\frac{V_0}{FCFF_1} = \frac{1}{k_c - g_n}$$

The multiple of FCFF that a firm commands depends on two variables—its cost of capital and its expected stable growth rate. Since the firm's free cash flow is its after-tax operating income netted against the net capital expenditures and working capital needs, the multiples of revenues, earnings before interest and taxes (EBIT), and after-tax EBIT can also be estimated similarly:

$$\frac{V_0}{EBIT_1(1-t)} = \frac{(1 - \text{Reinvestment Rate})}{k_c - g_n}$$

$$\frac{V_0}{EBIT_1} = \frac{(1 - \text{Reinvestment Rate})(1-t)}{k_c - g_n}$$

$$\frac{V_0}{Sales} = \frac{\text{After-tax Operating Margin } (1 - \text{Reinvestment Rate})}{k_c - g_n}$$

Table 4.3 summarizes the multiples and key variables that determine each multiple, with the sign of the relationship in parentheses next to each variable. ↑ indicates that an increase in this variable increases the multiple, whereas ↓ indicates that an increase in this variable decreases the multiple, with everything else being constant.

Table 4.3 **Fundamentals Determining Multiples**

Multiple	Fundamental Determinants
Price/earnings ratio	Expected growth (↑), payout (↑), risk (↓)
Price-to-book equity ratio	Expected growth (↑), payout (↑), risk (↓), ROE (↑)
Price-to-sales ratio	Expected growth (↑), payout (↑), risk (↓), net margin (↑)
EV to FCFF	Cost of capital (↓), growth rate (↑)
EV to EBITDA	Expected growth (↑), reinvestment rate (↓), risk (↓), ROC (↑), tax rate (↓)
EV to capital ratio	Expected growth (↑), reinvestment rate (↓), risk (↓), ROC (↑)
EV to sales	Expected growth (↑), reinvestment rate (↓), risk (↓), operating margin (↑)

The point of this analysis is not to suggest that we go back to using discounted cash flow valuation, but to understand the variables that may cause these multiples to vary across firms in the same sector. If we ignore these variables, we might conclude that a stock with a PE of 8 is cheaper than one with a PE of 12. But the true reason may be that the latter has higher expected growth. Or we might decide that a stock with a PBV ratio of 0.7 is cheaper than one with a PBV ratio of 1.5. But the true reason may be that the latter has a much higher return on equity.

Companion Variable

The variables that determine a multiple can be extracted from a discounted cash flow model, and the relationship between each variable and the multiple can be developed by holding all else constant and asking what-if questions. However, a single variable dominates when it comes to explaining each multiple (and it is not the same for every multiple). The *companion variable* is critical to using multiples wisely in making valuation judgments. You can identify it by looking for the variable that best explain differences across firms using a particular multiple.

So, what are the companion variables for the most widely used multiples? To arrive at this judgment, we looked at which of the variables listed in Table 4.3 were most useful in explaining differences across firms with each multiple. We came up with the list shown in Table 4.4.

Table 4.4 **Companion Variables**

Multiple	Companion Variable	Valuation Mismatch
PE ratio	Expected growth	Low PE stock with high expected growth rate in earnings per share
PBV ratio	ROE	Low PBV stock with high ROE
PS ratio	Net margin	Low PS stock with high net profit margin

Multiple	Companion Variable	Valuation Mismatch
EV/EBITDA	Reinvestment rate	Low EV/EBITDA stock with low reinvestment needs
EV/capital	Return on capital	Low EV/capital stock with high return on capital
EV/sales	After-tax operating margin	Low EV/sales ratio with a high after-tax operating margin

Relationship

Knowing the fundamentals that determine a multiple is a useful first step, but understanding how the multiple changes as the fundamentals change is just as critical to using the multiple. To illustrate, knowing that higher-growth firms have higher PE ratios is not a sufficient insight if we are called on to analyze whether a firm with a growth rate that is twice as high as the average growth rate for the sector should have a PE ratio that is 1.5 times or 1.8 times or 2 times the average PE ratio for the sector. To make this judgment, we need to know how the PE ratio changes as the growth rate changes.

A surprisingly large number of valuation analyses are based on the assumption that a linear relationship exists between multiples and fundamentals. For instance, consider the PEG ratio, which is the ratio of the PE to a firm's expected growth rate. It is widely used to analyze high-growth firms. It implicitly assumes that PE ratios and expected growth rates are linearly related.

One of the advantages of deriving the multiples from a discounted cash flow model, as was done in the preceding section, is that we can analyze the relationship between each fundamental variable and the multiple by keeping everything else constant and changing the value of that variable. When we do this, we will find that valuation has very few linear relationships.

Application Tests

When multiples are used, they tend to be used in conjunction with comparable firms to determine a firm's value or equity. But what is a comparable firm? The conventional practice is to look at firms within the same industry or business, but this is not necessarily always the correct or the best way of identifying these firms. In addition, no matter how carefully we choose comparable firms, differences will remain between the firm we are valuing and the comparable firms. Figuring out how to control for these differences is a significant part of relative valuation.

What Is a Comparable Firm?

A comparable firm is one with cash flows, growth potential, and risk similar to the firm being valued. It would be ideal if we could value a firm by looking at how a firm that is identical—in terms of risk, growth, and cash flows—is priced. Nowhere in this definition is there a component that relates to the industry or sector to which a firm belongs. Thus, a telecommunications firm can be compared to a software firm if the two are identical in terms of cash flows, growth, and risk. In most analyses, however, analysts define comparable firms to be other firms in the firm's business or businesses. If there are enough firms in the industry to allow for it, this list is pruned further using other criteria. For instance, only firms of similar size may be considered. The implicit assumption being made here is that firms in the same sector have similar risk, growth, and cash flow profiles and therefore can be compared with much more legitimacy.

This approach becomes more difficult to apply when a sector has relatively few firms. In most markets outside the U.S., the number of publicly traded firms in a particular sector, especially if it is defined narrowly, is small. It is also difficult to define firms in the same sector as comparable firms if differences in risk, growth, and cash flow profiles across firms within a sector are large. Hundreds of computer software companies are listed in the U.S., but the differences across these firms are large. The trade-off, therefore, is a simple one. Defining an industry more broadly increases the number of comparable firms, but it also results in a more diverse group of companies.

Alternatives exist to the conventional practice of defining comparable firms. One is to look for firms that are similar in terms of valuation fundamentals. For instance, to estimate the value of a firm with a beta of 1.2, an expected growth rate in earnings per share of 20%, and a return on equity of 40%,[4] we would find other firms across the entire market with similar characteristics.[5] The other alternative is to consider all firms in the market as comparable firms and to control for differences on the fundamentals across these firms using statistical techniques.

Controlling for Differences Across Firms

No matter how carefully we construct our list of comparable firms, we will end up with firms that are different from the firm we are valuing. The differences may be small on some variables and large on others; we will have to control for these differences in a relative valuation. There are three ways of doing so, as discussed in the following sections.

Subjective Adjustments

Relative valuation begins with two choices: the multiple used in the analysis, and the group of comparable firms. In many relative valuations, the multiple is calculated for each of the comparable firms, and the average is computed. To evaluate an individual firm, the analyst then compares the multiple it trades at to the average computed. If it is significantly different, the analyst can make a subjective judgment about whether the firm's individual characteristics (growth, risk, or cash flows) may explain the difference. Thus, a firm may have a PE ratio of 22 in a sector where the average PE is only 15, but the analyst may conclude that this difference can be justified because the firm has higher growth potential than the average firm in the industry. If, in the judgment of the analyst, the difference on the multiple cannot be explained by the fundamentals, the firm is viewed as overvalued (if its multiple is higher than the average) or undervalued (if its multiple is lower than the average).

The weakness in this approach is not that analysts are called on to make subjective judgments, but that the judgments are often based on little more than guesswork. All too often, these judgments confirm their biases about companies.

4 The return on equity of 40% becomes a proxy for cash flow potential. With a 20% growth rate and a 40% return on equity, this firm can return half its earnings to its stockholders in the form of dividends or stock buybacks.

5 Finding these firms manually may be tedious when your universe includes 10,000 stocks. You could draw on statistical techniques such as cluster analysis to find similar firms.

Modified Multiples

In this approach, we modify the multiple to take into account the most important variable that determines it—the companion variable. For example, analysts who compare PE ratios across companies with very different growth rates often divide the PE ratio by the expected growth rate in EPS to determine a growth-adjusted PE ratio (the PEG ratio). This ratio is then compared across companies with different growth rates to find under- and overvalued companies.

We make two implicit assumptions when using these modified multiples. The first is that these firms are comparable on all the other measures of value, other than the one being controlled for. In other words, when comparing PEG ratios across companies, we assume that they all have equivalent risk. The other assumption generally made is that the relationship between the multiples and fundamentals is linear. Again using PEG ratios to illustrate the point, we are assuming that as growth doubles, the PE ratio will double. If this assumption does not hold up and PE ratios do not increase proportional to growth, companies with high growth rates will look cheap on a PEG ratio basis.

Comparing PE Ratios and Growth Rates Across Firms: Beverage Companies—January 2004

Table 4.5 shows the PE ratios and expected growth rates in EPS over the next five years, based on consensus estimates from analysts, for firms that are categorized as beverage firms.

Table 4.5 Beverage Companies

Company Name	Trailing PE	Expected Growth	Standard Deviation	PEG
Andres Wine Ltd. A	8.96	3.50%	24.70%	2.56
Anheuser-Busch	24.31	11.00%	22.92%	2.21
Boston Beer A	10.59	17.13%	39.58%	0.62
Brown-Forman B	10.07	11.50%	29.43%	0.88
Chalone Wine Group Ltd.	21.76	14.00%	24.08%	1.55
Coca-Cola	44.33	19.00%	35.51%	2.33
Coca-Cola Bottling	29.18	9.50%	20.58%	3.07
Coca-Cola Enterprises	37.14	27.00%	51.34%	1.38
Coors (Adolph) B	23.02	10.00%	29.52%	2.30
Corby Distilleries Ltd.	16.24	7.50%	23.66%	2.16
Hansen Natural Corp	9.70	17.00%	62.45%	0.57
Molson Inc. Ltd. A	43.65	15.50%	21.88%	2.82
Mondavi (Robert) A	16.47	14.00%	45.84%	1.18

Table 4.5 Beverage Companies *continued*

Company Name	Trailing PE	Expected Growth	Standard Deviation	PEG
PepsiCo, Inc.	33.00	10.50%	31.35%	3.14
Todhunter International	8.94	3.00%	25.74%	2.98
Whitman Corp.	25.19	11.50%	44.26%	2.19
Average	**22.66**	**12.60%**	**33.30%**	**2.00**

Source: Value Line

Is Andres Wine undervalued on a relative basis? A simple view of multiples would lead us to conclude this, because its PE ratio of 8.96 is significantly lower than the average for the industry.

In making this comparison, we assume that Andres Wine has growth and risk characteristics similar to the average for the sector. One way of bringing growth into the comparison is to compute the PEG ratio, which is reported in the last column. Based on the average PEG ratio of 2.00 for the sector and the estimated growth rate for Andres Wine, we obtain the following value for the PE ratio for Andres:

PE Ratio = 2.00 * 3.50% = 7.00

Based on this adjusted PE, Andres Wine looks overvalued even though it has a low PE ratio. While this may seem like an easy adjustment to resolve the problem of differences across firms, the conclusion holds only if these firms are of equivalent risk. Implicitly, this approach assumes a linear relationship between growth rates and PE.

Statistical Techniques

Subjective adjustments and modified multiples are difficult to use when the relationship between multiples and the fundamental variables that determine them becomes complex. Some statistical techniques offer promise when this happens. This section considers the advantages of these approaches and potential concerns.

Sector Regressions

In a regression, we attempt to explain a dependent variable by using independent variables that we believe influence the dependent variable. This mirrors what we are attempting to do in relative valuation, where we try to explain differences across firms on a multiple (PE ratio, EV/EBITDA) using fundamental variables (such as risk, growth, and cash flows). Regressions offer three advantages over the subjective approach:

- The output from the regression gives us a measure of how strong the relationship is between the multiple and the variable being used. Thus, if we are contending that higher-growth companies have higher PE ratios, the regression should yield clues about both how growth and PE ratios are related (through the coefficient on growth as an independent variable) and how strong the relationship is (through the t statistics and R squared).

- If the relationship between a multiple and the fundamental we are using to explain it is nonlinear, the regression can be modified to allow for the relationship.
- Unlike the modified multiple approach, where we could control for differences on only one variable, a regression can be extended to allow for more than one variable and even for cross-effects across these variables.

In general, regressions seem particularly suited to our task in relative valuation, which is to make sense of voluminous and sometimes contradictory data. We face two key questions when running sector regressions:

- The first relates to how we define the sector. If we define sectors too narrowly, we run the risk of having small sample sizes, which undercut the usefulness of the regression. Defining sectors broadly entails fewer risks. While there may be large differences across firms when we do this, we can control for those differences in the regression.
- The second question involves the independent variables that we use in the regression. While the focus in statistics classes is increasing the explanatory power of the regression (through the R-squared) and including any variables that accomplish this, the focus of regressions in relative valuations is narrower. Since our objective is not to explain away all differences in pricing across firms but only differences that are explained by fundamentals, we will use only variables that are related to those fundamentals. The preceding section, where we analyzed multiples using DCF models, should yield valuable clues. As an example, consider the PE ratio. Since it is determined by the payout ratio, expected growth, and risk, we will include only those variables in the regression. We will not add other variables to this regression, even if doing so increases the explanatory power, if there is no fundamental reason why these variables should be related to PE ratios.

Revisiting the Beverage Sector: Sector Regression

The PE ratio is a function of the expected growth rate, risk, and payout ratio. None of the firms in the beverage sector pays significant dividends, but they differ in terms of risk and growth. Table 4.6 summarizes the PE ratios, betas, and expected growth rates for the firms on the list.

Table 4.6 Beverage Firms: PE, Growth, and Risk

Company Name	Trailing PE	Expected Growth	Standard Deviation
Andres Wine Ltd. A	8.96	3.50%	24.70%
Anheuser-Busch	24.31	11.00%	22.92%
Boston Beer A	10.59	17.13%	39.58%
Brown-Forman B	10.07	11.50%	29.43%
Chalone Wine Group Ltd.	21.76	14.00%	24.08%

Table 4.6 **Beverage Firms: PE, Growth, and Risk** *continued*

Company Name	Trailing PE	Expected Growth	Standard Deviation
Coca-Cola	44.33	19.00%	35.51%
Coca-Cola Bottling	29.18	9.50%	20.58%
Coca-Cola Enterprises	37.14	27.00%	51.34%
Coors (Adolph) B	23.02	10.00%	29.52%
Corby Distilleries Ltd.	16.24	7.50%	23.66%
Hansen Natural Corp	9.70	17.00%	62.45%
Molson Inc. Ltd. A	43.65	15.50%	21.88%
Mondavi (Robert) A	16.47	14.00%	45.84%
PepsiCo, Inc.	33.00	10.50%	31.35%
Todhunter International	8.94	3.00%	25.74%
Whitman Corp.	25.19	11.50%	44.26%

Source: Value Line Database

Since these firms differ on both risk and expected growth, a regression of PE ratios on both variables is presented:

$$PE = \underset{(3.01)}{20.87} - \underset{(2.63)}{63.98}\ \text{Standard Deviation} + \underset{(3.66)}{183.24}\ \text{Expected Growth} \quad R^2 = 51\%$$

The numbers in parentheses are t-statistics and suggest that the relationships between PE ratios and both variables in the regression are statistically significant. The R-squared indicates the percentage of the differences in PE ratios that is explained by the independent variables. Finally, the regression[6] itself can be used to get predicted PE ratios for the companies in the list. Thus, the predicted PE ratio for Coca-Cola, based on its standard deviation of 35.51% and the expected growth rate of 19%, would be as follows:

$$\text{Predicted } PE_{\text{Coca-Cola}} = 20.87 - 63.98\,(0.3551) + 183.24\,(0.19) = 32.97$$

Since the actual PE ratio for Coca-Cola was 44.33, this suggests that the stock is overvalued, given how the rest of the sector is priced.

If the assumption is that the relationship between PE and growth is not linear, we could either run nonlinear regressions or modify the variables in the regression to make the relationship more linear. For instance, using the ln(growth rate) instead of the growth rate in the preceding regression yields a more linear relationship.

6 Both approaches described here assume that the relationship between a multiple and the variables driving value are linear. Since this is not always true, you might have to run nonlinear versions of these regressions.

Market Regression

Searching for comparable firms within the sector in which a firm operates is fairly restrictive, especially when the sector has relatively few firms or when a firm operates in more than one sector. The definition of a comparable firm is not one that is in the same business but one that has the same growth, risk, and cash flow characteristics as the firm being analyzed. Therefore, we need not restrict our choice of comparable firms to those in the same industry. The regression introduced in the preceding section controls for differences on the variables we believe cause multiples to vary across firms. Based on the variables that determine each multiple, we should be able to regress each multiple against the variables that should affect them. Using Table 4.3, which lists the determinants of each multiple, as a guide, we ran market-wide regressions on each of the multiples in January 2009. The results are summarized in Table 4.7. The t-statistics are in parentheses below the coefficients.

Table 4.7 Market-Wide Regressions of Multiples: U.S. Companies in January 2009

Regression	R^2
PE = 7.62 + 77.98 g + 7.67 payout – 5.37 beta (8.77) (26.71) (13.09) (7.21)	28.6%
PBV = 1.28 + 6.72 g + 0.33 payout – 1.65 beta + 8.67 ROE (10.09) (15.85) (4.95) (11.70) (38.48)	68.3%
PS = 0.29 + 4.32 g + 0.31 payout – 0.86 beta + 11.42 net margin (2.48) (9.52) (4.58) (8.60) (35.72)	62.3%
EV/capital = 1.10 + 3.99 g + 5.06 ROIC – 2.59 (debt/capital) (10.23) (6.60) (20.59) (6.60)	50.1%
EV/sales = 1.72 + 1.94 g + 5.58 operating margin – 4.87 tax rate (16.46) (3.32) (29.00) (18.80)	50.3%
EV/EBITDA = 6.68 + 25.34 g – 7.99 tax rate – 1.59 (debt/capital) – 0.50 RIR (18.58) (12.35) (9.78) (3.84) (1.94)	19.3%

g = expected growth rate in EPS for next five years (analyst estimates)

payout = dividends/earnings

ROIC = return on invested capital = EBIT (1 – tax rate)/book value of capital invested

ROE = net income/book value of equity

debt/capital = debt/(market value of equity + debt)

RIR = reinvestment rate = (capital expenditures – depreciation + change in WC)/EBIT (1 – t)

The proportion of the variation explained by the independent variables varies across multiples, with book value and revenue multiples generally having a higher R-squared than earnings multiples. However, it is possible that the proxies that we use for risk (beta, debt/capital), growth (expected growth rate in earnings per share), and cash flow (payout, reinvestment rate) may be imperfect and that the relationship may not be linear. To deal with these limitations, we can add more variables to the regression. For example, the size of the firm may operate as a good proxy for risk.

This market-wide approach has some advantages over the subjective, sector-focused comparison that is often used in relative valuation. It quantifies, based on actual market data, the degree to which higher growth or risk should affect the multiples. It is true that these estimates can contain errors, but those errors reflect the reality that many analysts choose not to face when they make subjective judgments. Second, by looking at all firms in the market, this approach allows us to make more meaningful comparisons of firms that operate in industries with relatively few firms. Third, it allows us to examine whether all firms in an industry are under- or overvalued by estimating their values relative to other firms in the market.

Limitations of Statistical Techniques

Statistical techniques are not a panacea for research or qualitative analysis. They are tools that every analyst should have access to, but they should remain tools. In particular, when applying regression techniques to multiples, we need to be aware of both the distributional properties of multiples, which we talked about earlier in the chapter, and the relationships among the independent variables used in the regression.

- The fact that multiples are not normally distributed can pose problems when using standard regression techniques. These problems are accentuated with small samples, where the asymmetry in the distribution can be magnified by the existences of a few large outliers.
- In a multiple regression, the independent variables are themselves supposed to be independent of each other. Consider, however, the independent variables that we have used to explain valuation multiples—cash flow potential or payout ratio, expected growth, and risk. Across a sector and over the market, it is quite clear that high-growth companies tend to be risky and have low payout. This correlation across independent variables creates "multicolinearity," which can undercut the explanatory power of the regression.
- Earlier in the chapter, we noted how much the distributions for multiples changed over time, making comparisons of PE ratios or EV/EBITDA multiples across time problematic. By the same token, a multiple regression, in which we explain differences in a multiple across companies at a point in time, will itself lose predictive power as it ages. A regression of PE ratios against growth rates in early 2008 therefore may not be very useful in valuing stocks in early 2009.
- As a final caution, the R-squared on relative valuation regressions will almost never be higher than 70%. It is common to see it drop to 30 or 35%. Rather than ask how high an R-squared has to be to be meaningful, we would focus on the predictive power of the regression. When the R-squared decreases, the ranges on the forecasts from the regression will increase. For example, the beverage sector regression (in the last sidebar) yields a forecasted PE of 32.97, but the R-squared of 51% generates a range of 27.11 to 38.83 for the forecast with 95% accuracy. If the R-squared had been higher, the range would have been tighter.

Reconciling Relative and Intrinsic Valuations

The two approaches to valuation—discounted cash flow valuation and relative valuation—generally yield different estimates of value for the same firm at the same point in time. It is even possible for one approach to generate the result that the stock is undervalued while the other concludes that it is overvalued. Furthermore, even within relative valuation, we can arrive at different estimates of value depending on which multiple we use and what firms we based the relative valuation on.

The differences in value between discounted cash flow valuation and relative valuation come from different views of market efficiency or, put more precisely, market inefficiency. In discounted cash flow valuation, we assume that markets make mistakes, that they correct these mistakes over time, and that these mistakes can often occur across entire sectors or even the entire market. In relative valuation, we assume that while markets make mistakes on individual stocks, they are correct on average. In other words, when we value a new software company relative to other small software companies, we are assuming that the market has priced these companies correctly, on average, even though it might have made mistakes in pricing each of them individually. Thus, a stock may be overvalued on a discounted cash flow basis but undervalued on a relative basis if the firms used for comparison in the relative valuation are all overpriced by the market. The reverse would occur if an entire sector or market were underpriced.

Conclusion

In relative valuation, we estimate the value of an asset by looking at how similar assets are priced. To make this comparison, we begin by converting prices into multiples—standardizing prices. Then we compare these multiples across firms that we define as comparable. Prices can be standardized based on earnings, book value, revenue, or sector-specific variables.

The allure of multiples remains their simplicity. There are four steps in using them soundly. First, we have to define the multiple consistently and measure it uniformly across the firms being compared. Second, we need a sense of how the multiple varies across firms in the market. In other words, we need to know what a high value, low value, and typical value are for the multiple in question. Third, we need to identify the fundamental variables that determine each multiple and how changes in these fundamentals affect the value of the multiple. Finally, we need to find truly comparable firms and adjust for differences between the firms on fundamental characteristics.

5

Real Options Valuation

The approaches we have described in the last three chapters for assessing the value of an asset are mainly focused on the negative effects of risk. Put another way, they are all focused on the downside of risk; they miss the opportunity component that provides the upside. The real options approach is the only one that gives prominence to the upside potential for risk. Uncertainty can sometimes be a source of additional value, especially to those who are poised to take advantage of it.

We begin this chapter by describing in very general terms the argument behind the real options approach, noting its foundations in two elements:

- The capacity of individuals or entities to learn from what is happening around them
- Their willingness and ability to modify their behavior based on that learning

We then describe the various forms that real options can take in practice and how they can affect how we assess the value of investments and our behavior. The last section considers some of the potential pitfalls of using the real options argument and how it can be best incorporated into a portfolio of risk-assessment tools. Because the chapter assumes some familiarity with option payoffs and option pricing, we provide a short overview of both in the appendix at the end of this chapter.

The Essence of Real Options

To understand the basis of the real options argument and the reasons for its allure, it is easiest to go back to the risk-assessment tool unveiled in Chapter 3—decision trees. Figure 5.1 shows a simple example of a decision tree.

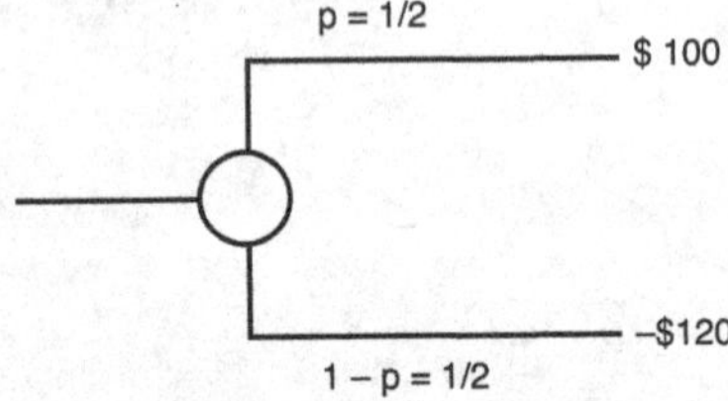

Figure 5.1: Simple Decision Tree

Given the equal probabilities of up and down movements, and the larger potential loss, the expected value for this investment is negative:

Expected Value = 0.50 (100) + 0.5 (–120) = –$10

Now contrast this with the slightly more complicated two-phase decision tree shown in Figure 5.2.

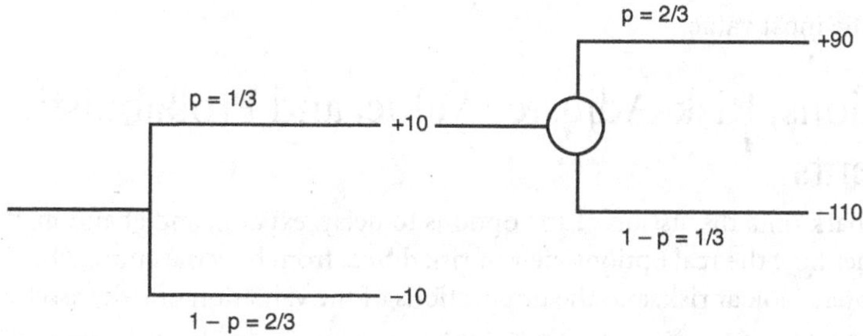

Figure 5.2: Two-Phase Decision Tree

Note that the total potential profits and losses over the two phases in the tree are identical to the profit and loss of the simple tree shown in Figure 5.1; your total gain is \$100, and your total loss is \$120. Note also that the cumulative probabilities of success and failure remain at the 50% we used in the simple tree. When we compute the expected value of this tree, though, the outcome changes:

$$\text{Expected Value} = (2/3)(-10) + 1/3\,[10 + (2/3)(90) + (1/3)(-110)] = \$4.44$$

What is it about the second decision tree that makes a potentially bad investment (in the first tree) into a good investment (in the second)? We can attribute the change to two factors. First, by allowing for an initial phase where you get to observe the cash flows on a first and relatively small try at the investment, we allow for *learning*. Thus, getting a bad outcome in the first phase (–10 instead of +10) is an indicator that the overall investment is more likely to be money-losing than money-making. Second, you act on the learning by abandoning the investment if the outcome from the first phase is negative; we will call this *adaptive behavior*.

In essence, the value of real options stems from the fact that when investing in risky assets, we can learn from observing what happens in the real world. We can adapt our behavior to increase our potential upside from the investment and decrease the possible downside. In the real options framework, we use updated knowledge or information to expand opportunities while reducing danger. In the context of a risky investment, you can take three potential actions based on this updated knowledge. The first is that you build on good fortune to increase your possible profits; this is the *option to expand*. For instance, a market test that suggests that consumers are far more receptive to a new product than you expected them to be could be used as a basis for expanding the project's scale and speeding its delivery to market. The second potential action is to scale down or even abandon an investment when the information you receive contains bad news; this is the *option to abandon*, and it can allow you to cut your losses. The third action is to hold off on making further investments if the information you receive suggests ambivalence about future prospects; this is the *option to delay or wait*. You are, in a sense, buying time for the investment, hoping that product and market developments will make it attractive in the future.

We would add one final piece to the mix that is often forgotten but is just as important as the learning and adaptive behavior components in terms of contributing to the real options arguments. The value of learning is greatest when you and only you have access to that learning and can act on it. After all, the expected value of knowledge that is public, where anyone can act on it, is close to zero. We will term this third condition *exclusivity* and use it to scrutinize when real options have the most value.

Real Options, Risk-Adjusted Value, and Probabilistic Assessments

Before we embark on a discussion of the options to delay, expand, and abandon, it is important that we consider how the real options view of risk differs from how the approaches laid out in the last three chapters look at risk, and the implications of the valuation of risky assets.

When computing the risk-adjusted value for risky assets, we generally discount back the expected cash flows using a discount rate adjusted to reflect risk. We use higher discount rates for riskier assets and thus assign a lower value for any given set of cash flows. In the process, we are faced with the task of converting all possible outcomes in the future into one expected number. The real options critique of discounted cash flow valuation can be boiled down simply. The expected cash flows for a risky asset, where the holder of the asset can learn from observing what happens in early periods and adapting, is understated. It does not capture the diminution of the downside risk from the option to abandon and the expansion of upside potential from the options to expand and delay. To provide a concrete example, assume that you are valuing an oil company. You estimate the cash flows by multiplying the number of barrels of oil that you expect the company to produce each year by the expected oil price per barrel. While you may have reasonable and unbiased estimates of both these numbers (the expected number of barrels produced and the expected oil price), what you are missing in your expected cash flows is the interplay between these numbers. Oil companies can observe the price of oil and adjust production accordingly; they produce more oil when oil prices are high and less when oil prices are low. In addition, their exploration activity ebbs and flows as the oil price moves. As a consequence, their cash flows computed across all oil price scenarios will be greater than the expected cash flows used in the risk-adjusted value calculation, and the difference will widen as the uncertainty about oil prices increases. So, what would real options proponents suggest? They would argue that the risk-adjusted value, obtained from conventional valuation approaches, is too low and that a premium should be added to it to reflect the option to adjust production inherent in these firms.

The approach that is closest to real options in terms of incorporating adaptive behavior is the decision tree approach, where the optimal decisions at each stage are conditioned on outcomes at prior stages. The two approaches, though, usually yield different values for the same risky asset for two reasons. The first is that the decision tree approach is built on probabilities and allows for multiple outcomes at each branch. On the other hand, the real options approach is more constrained in its treatment of uncertainty. In its binomial version, there can be only two outcomes at each stage, and the probabilities are not specified. The second reason is that the discount rates used to estimate present values in decision trees, at least in conventional usage, tend to be risk-adjusted. They are not conditioned on which branch of the decision tree you are looking at. When computing the value of a diabetes drug in a decision tree in Chapter 3, we used a 10% cost of capital as the discount rate for all cash flows from the drug in both good and bad outcomes. In the real options approach, the discount rate varies, depending on the branch of the tree being analyzed. In other words, the cost of capital for an oil company if oil prices increase may very well be different from the cost of capital when oil prices decrease. Copeland and Antikarov provide persuasive proof that the value of a risky asset is the same under real options and decision trees if we allow for path-dependent discount rates.[1]

Simulations and real options are not so much competing approaches for risk assessment as they are complementary. Two key inputs into the real options valuation—the value of the underlying asset and the variance in that value—are often obtained from simulations. To value a patent, for instance, we need to assess the present value of cash flows from developing the patent today and the variance in that value given the uncertainty about the inputs. Since the underlying product is not traded, it is difficult to get either of these inputs from the market. A Monte Carlo simulation can provide both values.

Real Options Examples

As we noted in the introductory section, three types of options are embedded in investments—the option to expand, delay, and abandon an investment. In this section, we will consider each of these options and how they add value to an investment, as well as potential implications for valuation.

The Option to Delay an Investment

Investments typically are analyzed based on their expected cash flows and discount rates at the time of the analysis. The net present value computed on that basis is a measure of its value and acceptability at that time. The rule that emerges is a simple one: negative net present value investments destroy value and should not be accepted. Expected cash flows and discount rates change over time, however, and so does the net present value. Thus, a project that has a negative net present value now may have a positive net present value in the future. In a competitive environment, in which individual firms have no special advantages over their competitors in taking projects, this may not seem significant. In an environment in which a project can be taken by only one firm (because of legal restrictions or other barriers to entry to competitors), however, the changes in the project's value over time give it the characteristics of a call option.

Basic Setup

In the abstract, assume that a project requires an initial up-front investment of X, and that the present value of expected cash inflows computed right now is V. The net present value (NPV) of this project is the difference between the two:

$$NPV = V - X$$

Now assume that the firm has exclusive rights to this project for the next n years. Also assume that the present value of the cash inflows may change over that time, because of changes in either the cash flows or the discount rate. Thus, the project may have a negative net present value right now,

1 Copeland, T. E. and V. Antikarov, 2003, *Real Options: A Practitioner's Guide*, Texere. For an alternate path to the same conclusion, see Brandao, L. E., J. S. Dyer, and W. J. Huhn, 2005, "Using Binomial Decision Trees to Solve Real-Option Valuation Problems," *Decision Analysis*, v2, 69–88. They use the risk-neutral probabilities from the option pricing model in the decision tree to solve for the option's value.

but it may still be a good project if the firm waits. Defining V again as the present value of the cash flows, the firm's decision rule on this project can be summarized as follows:

If V > X, take the project: The project has positive net present value.

If V < X, do not take the project: The project has negative net present value.

If the firm does not invest in the project, it incurs no additional cash flows, though it will lose what it originally invested in the project. This relationship can be presented in a payoff diagram of cash flows on this project, as shown in Figure 5.3. This assumes that the firm holds out until the end of the period for which it has exclusive rights to the project.[2]

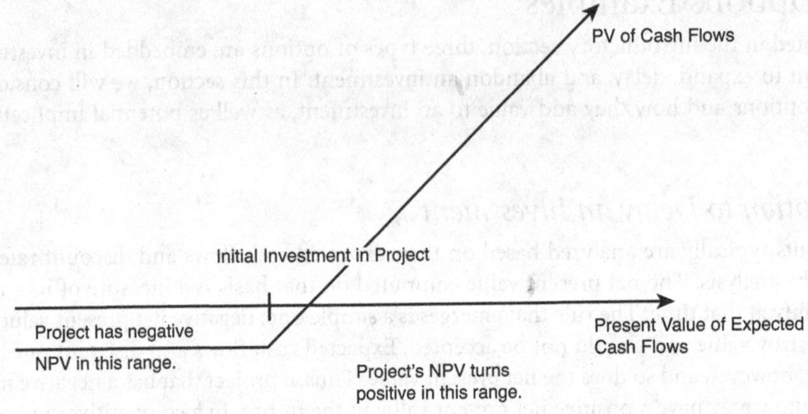

Figure 5.3: Payoff Diagram on Option to Delay

Note that this payoff diagram is that of a call option. The underlying asset is the investment. The option's strike price is the initial outlay needed to initiate the investment. The option's life is how long the firm has rights to the investment. The present value of the cash flows on this project and the expected variance in this present value represent the value and variance of the underlying asset.

Valuing an Option to Delay

On the surface, the inputs needed to apply option pricing theory to valuing the option to delay are the same as those needed for any option. We need the value of the underlying asset, the variance in that value, the time to expiration on the option, the strike price, the riskless rate, and the equivalent of the dividend yield (cost of delay). Actually estimating these inputs for product patent valuation can be difficult, however:

- **Value of the underlying asset**: In this case, the underlying asset is the investment itself. The current value of this asset is the present value of expected cash flows from initiating the project now, not including the up-front investment, which can be obtained by doing a standard capital budgeting analysis. There is likely to be a substantial amount of error

2 McDonald, R. and D. Siegel, 2002, "The Value of Waiting to Invest," *Quarterly Journal of Economics*, v101, 707–728.

in the cash flow estimates and the present value, however. Rather than being viewed as a problem, this uncertainty should be viewed as the reason why the project delay option has value. If the expected cash flows on the project were known with certainty and were not expected to change, there would be no need to adopt an option pricing framework, because the option would have no value.

- **Variance in the value of the asset**: The present value of the expected cash flows that measures the value of the asset will change over time. This is partly because the product's potential market size may be unknown and partly because technological shifts can change the product's cost structure and profitability. The variance in the present value of cash flows from the project can be estimated in one of three ways:
  - If similar projects have been introduced in the past, the variance in the cash flows from those projects can be used as an estimate. This may be how a consumer products company like Gillette might estimate the variance associated with introducing a new blade for its razors.
  - Probabilities can be assigned to various market scenarios, cash flows estimated under each scenario, and the variance estimated across present values. Alternatively, the probability distributions can be estimated for each of the inputs into the project analysis—the size of the market, the market share, and the profit margin, for instance—and simulations used to estimate the variance in the present values that emerge.
  - The variance in the market value of publicly traded firms involved in the same business (as the project being considered) can be used as an estimate of the variance. Thus, the average variance in firm value of firms involved in the software business can be used as the variance in present value of a software project.

  The value of the option is largely derived from the variance in cash flows—the higher the variance, the higher the value of the project delay option. Thus, the value of an option to delay a project in a stable business will be less than the value of a similar option in an environment where technology, competition, and markets are all changing rapidly.
- **Exercise price on option**: A project delay option is exercised when the firm owning the rights to the project decides to invest in it. The cost of making this investment is the option's exercise price. The underlying assumption is that this cost remains constant (in present-value dollars) and that any uncertainty associated with the product is reflected in the present value of cash flows on the product.
- **Expiration of the option and the riskless rate**: The project delay option expires when the rights to the project lapse. Investments made after the project rights expire are assumed to deliver a net present value of 0 as competition drives returns down to the required rate. The riskless rate to use in pricing the option should be the rate that corresponds to the option's expiration. While this input can be estimated easily when firms have explicit rights to a project (through a license or patent, for instance), it becomes far more difficult to obtain when firms have only a competitive advantage to take a project.
- **Cost of delay (dividend yield)**: There is a cost to delaying taking a project once the net present value turns positive. Since the project rights expire after a fixed period, and

excess profits (which are the source of positive present value) are assumed to disappear after that time as new competitors emerge, each year of delay translates into one less year of value-creating cash flows.[3] If the cash flows are evenly distributed over time, and the patent's life is n years, the cost of delay can be written as follows:

Thus, if the project rights are for 20 years, the annual cost of delay works out to 5% a year. Note, though, that this cost of delay rises each year, to 1/19 in year 2, 1/18 in year 3, and so on, making the cost-of-delay exercise larger over time.

$$\text{Annual Cost of Delay} = \frac{1}{n}$$

Practical Considerations

While it is quite clear that the option to delay is embedded in many investments, several problems are associated with the use of option pricing models to value these options. First, the *underlying asset in this option, which is the project, is not traded,* making it difficult to estimate its value and variance. We would argue that the value can be estimated from the expected cash flows and the discount rate for the project, albeit with error. The variance is more difficult to estimate, however, since we are attempting to estimate a variance in project value over time.

Second, the *behavior of prices over time may not conform to the price path assumed by the option pricing models.* In particular, the assumption that prices move in small increments continuously (an assumption of the Black-Scholes model), and that the variance in value remains unchanged over time, may be difficult to justify in the context of a real investment. For instance, a sudden technological change may dramatically change a project's value, either positively or negatively.

Third, *there may be no specific period for which the firm has rights to the project.* For instance, a firm may have significant advantages over its competitors. This may, in turn, provide it with virtually exclusive rights to a project for a period of time. The rights are not legal restrictions, however, and they could erode faster than expected. In such cases, the expected life of the project itself is uncertain and is only an estimate. Ironically, uncertainty about the option's expected life can increase the variance in present value, and through it, the expected value of the rights to the project.

Applications of the Option to Delay

The option to delay provides interesting perspectives on three common investment problems. The first is in the valuation of patents, especially those that are not viable today but could be viable in the future. By extension, this also allows us to look at whether R&D expenses deliver value. The second is in the analysis of natural resource assets such as vacant land and undeveloped oil reserves.

Patents

A product patent gives a firm the right to develop and market a product. But the firm will do so only if the present value of the expected cash flows from the product sales exceed the cost of

3 A value-creating cash flow is one that adds to the net present value because it is in excess of the required return for investments of equivalent risk.

development, as shown in Figure 5.4. If this does not occur, the firm can shelve the patent and not incur any further costs. If I is the present value of the costs of developing the product, and V is the present value of the expected cash flows from development, the payoffs from owning a product patent can be written as follows:

$$\text{Payoff from Owning a Product Patent} = V - I \quad \text{if } V > I$$
$$= 0 \quad \text{if } V \leq I$$

Thus, a product patent can be viewed as a call option, where the product itself is the underlying asset.[4]

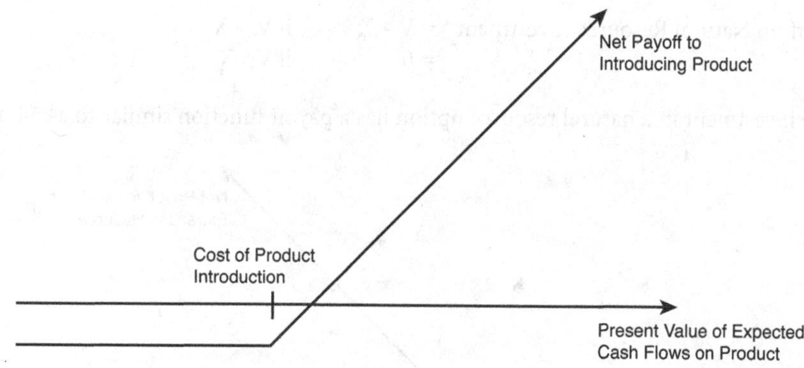

Figure 5.4: Payoff to Introducing Product

The implications of viewing patents as options can be significant. First, it implies that nonviable patents will continue to have value, especially in businesses that have substantial volatility. Second, it indicates that firms may hold off on developing viable patents if they feel that they gain more from waiting than they lose in terms of cash flows. This behavior is more common if no significant competition is on the horizon. Third, the value of patents will be higher in risky businesses than in safe businesses, since option value increases with volatility. If we consider R&D to be the expense associated with acquiring these patents, this would imply that research should have its biggest payoff when directed to areas where less is known and more uncertainty exists. Consequently, we should expect pharmaceutical firms to spend more of their R&D budgets on gene therapy than on flu vaccines.[5] We return to examine this issue in more depth in Chapter 15, "Invisible Investments: Firms with Intangible Assets."

4 Schwartz, E., 2002, "Patents and R&D as Real Options," working paper, Anderson School at UCLA.

5 Pakes, A., 1986, "Patents as Options: Some Estimates of the Value of Holding European Patent Stocks," *Econometrica*, v54, 755–784. While this paper does not explicitly value patents as options, it examines the returns investors would have earned investing in companies that derive their value from patents. The return distribution resembles that of a portfolio of options, with most investments losing money but the winners providing disproportionate gains.

Natural Resource Options

In a natural resource investment, the underlying asset is the natural resource, and the asset's value is based on two variables: the estimated quantity and the price of the resource. Thus, in a gold mine, for example, the value of the underlying asset is the value of the estimated gold reserves in the mine, based on the current price of gold. In most such investments, an initial cost is associated with developing the resource. The difference between the value of the asset extracted and the cost of the development is the profit to the owner of the resource (see Figure 5.5). Defining the cost of development as X, and the estimated value of the developed resource as V, the potential payoffs on a natural resource option can be written as follows:

$$\text{Payoff on Natural Resource Investment} = V - X \quad \text{if } V > X$$
$$= 0 \quad \text{if } V \leq X$$

Thus, the investment in a natural resource option has a payoff function similar to a call option.[6]

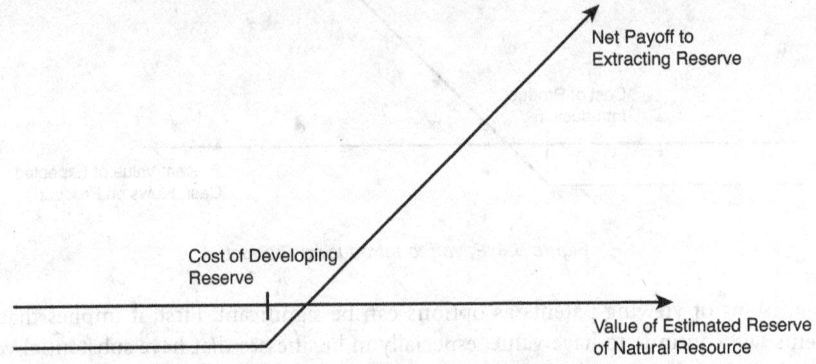

Figure 5.5: Payoff from Developing Natural Resource Reserves

What are the implications of viewing natural resource reserves as options? The first is that the value of a natural resource company can be written as a sum of two values: the conventional risk-adjusted value of expected cash flows from developed reserves, and the option value of undeveloped reserves. While both will increase in value as the price of the natural resource increases, the latter will respond positively to increases in price volatility. Thus, the values of oil companies should increase if oil price volatility increases, even if oil prices themselves do not go up. The second implication is that conventional discounted cash flow valuation will understate the value of natural resource companies, even if the expected cash flows are unbiased and reasonable, because it will miss the option premium inherent in their undeveloped reserves. The third implication is that development of natural resource reserves will slow down as the volatility in prices increases. The time premium on the options will increase, making exercise of the options (development of the reserves) less likely. The same type of analysis can be extended to any other commodity company (gold and copper reserves, for instance) and even to vacant land or real estate properties.

6 Brennan, M. and E. Schwartz, 1985, "Evaluating Natural Resource Investments," *The Journal of Business*, v58, 135–157.

The owner of vacant land in Manhattan can choose whether and when to develop the land and will make that decision based on real estate values.[7]

Mining and commodity companies have been at the forefront of using real options in decision making. Their usage of the technology predates the current boom in real options. One reason is that natural resource options come closest to meeting the prerequisites for the use of option pricing models. Firms can learn a great deal by observing commodity prices and can adjust their behavior (in terms of development and exploration) quickly. In addition, if we consider exclusivity to be a prerequisite for real options to have value, that exclusivity for natural resource options derives from their natural scarcity. After all, only a finite amount of oil and gold is under the ground, and there's only so much vacant land in Manhattan. Finally, natural resource reserves come closest to meeting the arbitrage/replication requirements that option pricing models are built on; both the underlying asset (the natural resource) and the option can often be bought and sold. We will examine the use of real options models in commodity company valuations in more depth in Chapter 13, "Ups and Downs: Cyclical and Commodity Companies."

The Option to Expand an Investment

In some cases, a firm takes an investment because doing so allows it either to make other investments or to enter other markets in the future. In such cases, it can be argued that the initial investment provides the firm with an option to expand, and the firm should therefore be willing to pay a price for such an option. Consequently, a firm may be willing to lose money on the first investment because it perceives the option to expand as having a large-enough value to compensate for the initial loss.

To examine this option, assume that the present value of the expected cash flows from entering the new market or taking the new project is V, and the total investment needed to enter this market or take this project is X. Furthermore, assume that the firm has a fixed time horizon, at the end of which it must decide whether to take advantage of this opportunity. Finally, assume that the firm cannot move forward on this opportunity if it does not take the initial investment. This scenario implies the option payoffs shown in Figure 5.6.

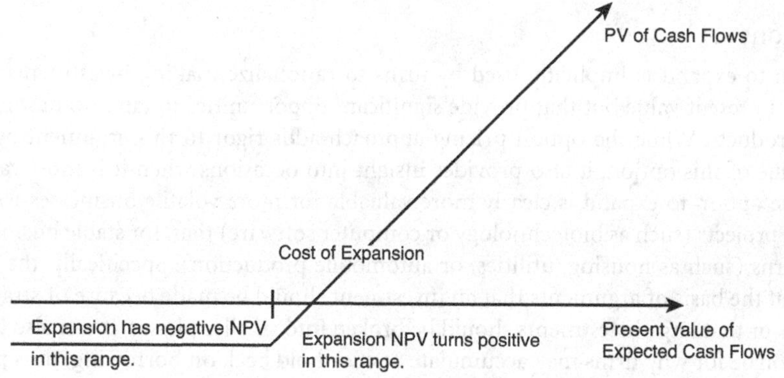

Figure 5.6: Cash Flows on Expansion

7 Quigg, L., 1993, "Empirical Testing of Real Option-Pricing Models," *Journal of Finance*, vol. 48, 621–640. The author examined transaction data on 2,700 undeveloped and 3,200 developed real estate properties between 1976 and 1979 and found evidence of a premium arising from the option to wait in the former.

As you can see, at the expiration of the fixed time horizon, the firm enters the new market or takes the new investment if the present value of the expected cash flows at that point in time exceeds the cost of entering the market.

Consider a simple example of an option to expand. Disney is considering starting a Spanish version of the Disney Channel in Mexico. It estimates the investment will lose money and have a negative net present value. The negative net present value normally would suggest that rejecting the investment is the best course. However, assume that if the Mexican venture does better than expected, Disney plans to expand the network into the rest of Latin America at a significant cost. Based on its current assessment of this market, Disney believes that the present value of the expected cash flows on this investment will be less than the cost, yielding a negative net present value for that investment as well. The saving grace is that the latter present value is an estimate and Disney does not have a firm grasp of the market, and there is significant uncertainty about that value. Finally, assume that Disney will have to make this expansion decision within a fixed period (say, five years) of the Mexican investment.

We can value the Latin American expansion as an option, with the uncertainty about its value generating the value for the option. If the value of the expansion option is greater the value lost on the initial investment in Mexico, Disney could justify the investment.

The practical considerations associated with estimating the value of the option to expand are similar to those associated with valuing the option to delay. In most cases, firms with options to expand have no specific time horizon by which they have to make an expansion decision, making these open-ended options or, at best, options with arbitrary lives. Even in cases where a life can be estimated for the option, neither the size nor the product's potential market may be known, and estimating either can be problematic. To illustrate, consider again the Disney example. While we adopted a period of five years, at the end of which Disney must decide on its future expansion into Latin America, it is entirely possible that this time frame is not specified when the Mexican channel goes on the air. Furthermore, we have assumed that both the cost and present value of expansion are known initially. In reality, the firm may not have good estimates for either before making the first investment, since it does not have much information on the underlying market.

Implications

The option to expand is implicitly used by firms to rationalize making investments that have negative net present value but that provide significant opportunities to tap into new markets or sell new products. While the option pricing approach adds rigor to this argument by estimating the value of this option, it also provides insight into occasions when it is most valuable. In general, the option to expand is clearly more valuable for more volatile businesses with higher returns on projects (such as biotechnology or computer software) than for stable businesses with lower returns (such as housing, utilities, or automobile production). Specifically, the option to expand is at the basis of arguments that an investment should be made because of strategic considerations or that large investments should be broken into smaller phases. It can also be considered a rationale for why firms may accumulate cash or hold back on borrowing, thus preserving financial flexibility.

Strategic Considerations

In many acquisitions or investments, the acquiring firm believes that the transaction will give it competitive advantages in the future. These competitive advantages run the gamut:

- **Entry into a growing or large market:** An investment or acquisition may allow the firm to enter a large or potentially large market much sooner than it otherwise would have been able to. A good example of this is the acquisition of a Mexican retail firm by a U.S. firm, with the intent of expanding into the Mexican market.
- **Technological expertise:** In some cases, the acquisition is motivated by the desire to acquire a proprietary technology that will allow the acquirer to either expand its existing market or expand into a new market.
- **Brand name:** Firms sometimes pay large premiums over market price to acquire firms with valuable brand names, because they believe that these brand names can be used to expand into new markets in the future.

While all these potential advantages may be used to justify initial investments that do not meet financial benchmarks, not all of them create valuable options. The value of the option is derived from the degree to which these competitive advantages, assuming that they do exist, translate into sustainable excess returns. As a consequence, these advantages can be used to justify premiums only in cases where the acquiring firm believes that it has some degree of exclusivity in the targeted market or technology. Two examples can help illustrate this point. A telecommunications firm should be willing to pay a premium for a Chinese telecomm firm if the latter has exclusive rights to service a large segment of the Chinese market. The option to expand into the Chinese market could be worth a significant amount.[8] On the other hand, a developed market retailer should be wary about paying a real options premium for an Indian retail firm, even though it may believe that the Indian market could grow to be a lucrative one. The option to expand into this lucrative market is open to all entrants, not just existing retailers, so it might not translate into sustainable excess returns.

Multistage Projects and Investments

When entering new businesses or making new investments, firms sometimes can enter the business in stages. While doing so may reduce potential upside, it also protects the firm from downside risk by allowing it, at each stage, to gauge demand and decide whether to go on to the next stage. In other words, a standard project can be recast as a series of options to expand, with each option being dependent on the previous one. Two propositions follow:

- Some projects that do not look good on a full investment basis may be value-creating if the firm can invest in stages.
- Some projects that look attractive on a full investment basis may become even more attractive if taken in stages.

The gain in value from the options created by multistage investments must be weighed against the cost. Taking investments in stages may allow competitors who decide to enter the market on a

8 A note of caution needs to be added here. If the exclusive rights to a market come with no pricing power—in other words, the government sets the price you charge your customers—it may very well translate into zero excess returns (and no option value).

full scale to capture the market. It may also lead to higher costs at each stage, since the firm is not taking full advantage of economies of scale.

Several implications emerge from viewing this choice between multistage and one-time investments in an option framework. Here are some cases where the gains will be largest from making the investment in multiple stages:

- **Projects that have significant barriers to entry** from competitors entering the market and that take advantage of delays in full-scale production. Thus, a firm with a patent on a product or other legal protection against competition pays a much smaller price for starting small and expanding as it learns more about the product.
- **Projects that have significant uncertainty about the size of the market and the project's eventual success:** Here, starting small and expanding allows the firm to reduce its losses if the product does not sell as well as anticipated and to learn more about the market at each stage. This information can then be useful in subsequent stages in both product design and marketing. Hsu argues that venture capitalists invest in young companies in stages. This is partly to capture the value option of waiting/learning at each stage and partly to reduce the likelihood that the entrepreneur will be too conservative in pursuing risky (but good) opportunities.[9]
- **Projects that need a substantial investment in infrastructure (large fixed costs) and high operating leverage**: Since the savings from doing a project in multiple stages can be traced to investments needed at each stage, they are likely to be greater in firms where those costs are large. Capital-intensive projects as well as projects that require large initial marketing expenses (a new brand-name product for a consumer product company) will gain more from the options created by taking the project in multiple stages.

Growth Companies

In the stock market boom of the 1990s, we witnessed the phenomenon of young start-up Internet companies with large market capitalizations but little to show in terms of earnings, cash flows, or even revenues. Conventional valuation models suggested that it would be difficult, if not impossible, to justify these market valuations with expected cash flows. In an interesting twist on the option-to-expand argument, some people argued that investors in these companies were buying options to expand to be part of a potentially huge e-commerce market, rather than conventional stock.[10]

While the argument is alluring and serves to pacify investors in growth companies who may feel that they are paying too much, clear dangers exist in making this stretch. The biggest one is that the "exclusivity" component that is necessary for real options to have value is being given short shrift. Suppose that you invested in an Internet stock in 1999, and assume that you are paying a premium to be part of a potentially large online market today. Assume further that this market comes to fruition. Could you partake in this market without paying that upfront premium for a

9 Hsu, Y., 2002, "Staging of Venture Capital Investment: A Real Options Analysis," working paper, University of Cambridge.

10 Schwartz, E. S. and M. Moon, 2001, "Rational Pricing of Internet Companies Revisited," *The Financial Review*, 36, pp. 7–26. A simpler version of the same argument was made in Mauboussin, M., 1998, "Get Real: Using Real Options in Security Analysis," CSFB Publication, June 23, 1999.

dot-com company? We don't see why not. After all, GE and Nokia were just as capable of being part of this online market, as were any number of new entrants into the market.

Financial Flexibility

When making decisions about how much to borrow and how much cash to return to stockholders (in dividends and stock buybacks), managers should consider the effects that such decisions will have on their capacity to make new investments or meet unanticipated contingencies in the future. Practically, this translates into firms maintaining excess debt capacity or larger cash balances than are warranted by current needs, to meet unexpected future requirements. While maintaining this financing flexibility has value for firms, it also has costs. The large cash balances might earn below-market returns, and excess debt capacity implies that the firm is giving up some value by maintaining a higher cost of capital.

Using an option framework, it can be argued that a firm that maintains a large cash balance and preserves excess debt capacity does so to have the option to invest in *unexpected* projects with *high returns* that may arise in the future. To value financial flexibility as an option, consider the following framework: A firm has expectations about *how much it will need to reinvest* in future periods, based on its own history and current conditions in the industry. On the other side of the ledger, a firm also has expectations about *how much it can raise* from internal funds and its normal access to capital markets in the future. Assume that actual reinvestment needs can be very different from the expected reinvestment needs. For simplicity, we will assume that the firm knows its capacity to generate funds. The advantage (and value) of having excess debt capacity or large cash balances is that the firm can meet any reinvestment needs in excess of funds available using its excess debt capacity and surplus cash. The payoff from these projects, however, comes from the excess returns that the firm expects to make on them.

Looking at financial flexibility as an option yields valuable insights into when financial flexibility is most valuable. Using the framework we just developed, for instance, we would argue the following:

- Other things remaining equal, firms operating in businesses where projects earn substantially higher returns than their hurdle rates should value flexibility more than those that operate in stable businesses where excess returns are small. This would imply that firms that earn large excess returns on their projects can use the need for financial flexibility as the justification for holding large cash balances and excess debt capacity.
- Since a firm's ability to fund these reinvestment needs is determined by its capacity to generate internal funds, other things remaining equal, financial flexibility should be worth less to firms with large and stable earnings as a percent of firm value. Young and growing firms that have small or negative earnings, and therefore much lower capacity to generate internal funds, will value flexibility more. As supporting evidence, note that technology firms usually borrow very little and accumulate large cash balances.
- Firms with limited internal funds can still get away with little or no financial flexibility if they can tap external markets for capital—bank debt, bonds, and new equity issues. Other things remaining equal, the greater a firm's capacity (and willingness) to raise funds from external capital markets, the less should be the value of flexibility. This may explain why private or small firms, which have far less access to capital, value financial flexibility more than larger firms. The existence of corporate bond markets can also

make a difference in how much flexibility is valued. In markets where firms cannot issue bonds and have to depend entirely on banks for financing, there is less access to capital and a greater need to maintain financial flexibility.

- The need for and value of flexibility is a function of how uncertain a firm is about future reinvestment needs. Firms with predictable reinvestment needs should value flexibility less than firms in sectors where reinvestment needs are volatile on a period-to-period basis.

In conventional corporate finance, the optimal debt ratio is the one that minimizes the cost of capital. There is little incentive for firms to accumulate cash balances. This view of the world, though, flows directly from the implicit assumption we make that capital markets are open and can be accessed with little or no cost. Introducing external capital constraints, internal or external, into the model leads to a more nuanced analysis where rational firms may borrow less than optimal and hold back on returning cash to stockholders.

The Option to Abandon an Investment

The final option to consider is the option to abandon a project when its cash flows do not measure up to expectations. One way to reflect this value is through decision trees, as discussed in Chapter 3. The decision tree has limited applicability in most real-world investment analyses; it typically works only for multistage projects, and it requires inputs on probabilities at each stage of the project. The option pricing approach provides a more general way of estimating and building the value of abandonment into investment analysis. To illustrate, assume that V is the remaining value on a project if it continues to the end of its life, and L is the liquidation or abandonment value for the same project at the same point in time. If the project has a life of n years, the value of continuing the project can be compared to the liquidation (abandonment) value. If the value from continuing is higher, the project should be continued; if the value of abandonment is higher, the holder of the abandonment option could consider abandoning the project:

Payoff from Owning an Abandonment Option	$= 0$	if $V > L$
	$= L - V$	if $V \leq L$

These payoffs are graphed in Figure 5.7 as a function of the expected value from continuing the investment.

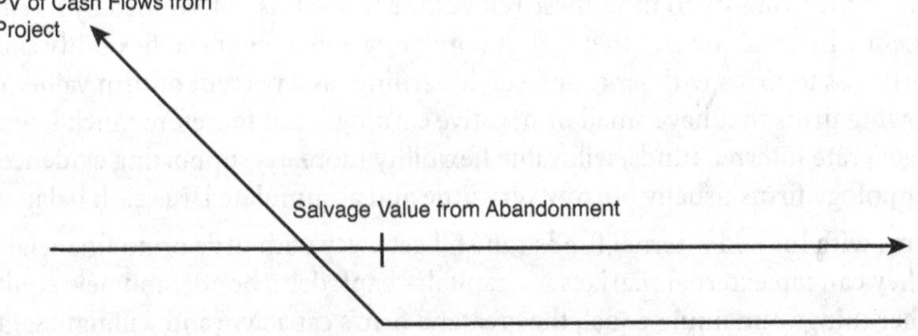

Figure 5.7: Payoff Diagram on the Abandonment Option

Unlike the prior two cases, the option to abandon takes on the characteristics of a put option.

Consider a simple example. Assume that a firm is considering taking a ten-year project that requires an initial investment of $100 million in a real estate partnership, where the present value of expected cash flows is $90 million. While the net present value of –$10 million is negative, assume that the firm has the option to abandon this project anytime in the next ten years by selling its share of the ownership to the other partners in the venture for $50 million.

If the value of this abandonment option is greater than $10 million (which is the negative net present value of the investment), the investment makes sense. Note, though, that abandonment becomes a more and more attractive option as the remaining project life decreases, since the present value of the remaining cash flows decreases.

In the preceding analysis, we assumed, rather unrealistically, that the abandonment value was clearly specified up front and that it did not change during the life of the project. This may be true in some very specific cases, in which an abandonment option is built into the contract. More often, however, the firm has the option to abandon, and the salvage value from doing so has to be estimated (with error) up front. Further, the abandonment value may change over the life of the project, making it difficult to apply traditional option pricing techniques. Finally, it is entirely possible that abandoning a project may not bring in a liquidation value, but may create costs instead. A manufacturing firm may have to pay severance to its workers, for instance. In such cases, it would not make sense to abandon, unless the present value of the expected cash flows from continuing with the investment are even more negative.

Implications

The fact that the option to abandon has value provides a rationale for firms to build in operating flexibility to scale back or terminate projects if they do not measure up to expectations. It also indicates that firms that focus on generating more revenues by offering their customers the option to walk away from commitments may be giving up more than they gain.

Escape Clauses

When a firm enters into a long-term risky investment that requires a large up-front investment, it should do so with the clear understanding that it may regret making this investment fairly early in its life. Being able to get out of such long-term commitments that threaten to drain more resources in the future is at the heart of the option to abandon. It is true that some of this flexibility is determined by the business you are in; getting out of bad investments is easier to do in service businesses than in heavy infrastructure businesses. However, it is also true that firms can take actions at the time of making these investments that give them more choices if things do not go according to plan.

The first and most direct way is to build operating flexibility contractually with the parties that are involved in the investment. First, contracts with suppliers may be written on an annual basis rather than long-term, and employees may be hired on a temporary basis rather than permanently. The physical plant used for a project may be leased on a short-term basis rather than bought, and the financial investment may be made in stages rather than as an initial lump sum. While there is a cost to building in this flexibility, the gains may be much larger, especially in volatile businesses. Second, the initial capital investment can be shared with another investor, presumably with deeper pockets and a greater willingness to stay with the investment, even if it turns sour. This provides a rationale for joint venture investing, especially for small firms that have limited resources; finding a cash-rich, larger company to share the risk may well be worth the cost.

None of these actions is costless. Entering into short-term agreements with suppliers and leasing the physical plant may be more expensive than committing for the life of the investment, but that additional cost has to be weighed against the benefit of maintaining the abandonment option.

Customer Incentives

Firms that are intent on increasing revenues sometimes offer customers abandonment options to induce them to buy their products and services. Consider a firm that sells its products on multiyear contracts and that offers customers the option to cancel their contracts at any time, with no cost. While this may sweeten the deal and increase sales, a substantial cost is likely. In the event of a recession, customers who are unable to meet their obligations are likely to cancel their contracts. In effect, the firm has made its good times better and its bad times worse. The cost of this increased volatility in earnings and revenues has to be measured against the potential gain in revenue growth to see if the net effect is positive.

This discussion should also be a cautionary note for firms that are run with marketing objectives such as maximizing market share or posting high-revenue growth. Those objectives can often be accomplished by giving customers valuable options. Salespeople will want to meet their sales targets and are not particularly concerned about the long-term costs they may create with their commitments to customers—and the firm may be worse off as a consequence.

Switching Options

While the abandonment option considers the value of shutting down an investment, an intermediate alternative is worth examining. Firms can sometimes alter production levels in response to demand. Being able to do so can make an investment more valuable. Consider, for instance, a power company that is considering a new plant to generate electricity. Assume that the company can run the plant at full capacity and produce 1 million kilowatt-hours of power or run it at half capacity (and substantially less cost) and produce 500,000 kilowatt-hours of power. In this case, the company can observe both the demand for power and the revenues per kilowatt-hour and decide if it makes sense to run at full or half capacity. The value of this switching option can then be compared to the cost of building in this flexibility in the first place.

The airline business provides an interesting case study in how different companies manage their cost structure and the payoffs to their strategies. One reason that Southwest Airlines has been able to maintain its profitability in a deeply troubled airline sector is that the company has made cost flexibility a central component of its decision process. From its choice of using only one type of aircraft for its entire fleet[11] to its refusal, for the most part, to fly into large urban airports (with high gate costs), the company's operations have created the most flexible cost structure in the business. Thus, when revenues dip (as they inevitably do when the economy weakens), Southwest can trim its costs and stay profitable while other airlines teeter on the brink of bankruptcy.

11 From its inception until recently, Southwest used the Boeing 737 as its workhorse, thus reducing the need to keep different maintenance crews at each airport it flies into.

Caveats for Real Options

The discussion of the potential applications of real options should provide a window into why they are so alluring to practitioners and businesses. In essence, we are ignoring the time-honored rules of capital budgeting, which include rejecting investments that have negative net present value, when real options are present. Not only does the real options approach encourage you to make investments that do not meet conventional financial criteria, it also makes it more likely that you will do so the less you know about the investment. Ignorance, rather than being a weakness, becomes a virtue, because it increases the uncertainty in the estimated value and the resulting option value. To prevent the real options process from being hijacked by managers who want to rationalize bad (and risky) decisions, we have to impose some reasonable constraints on when it can be used. And when it *is* used, we have to specify how to estimate its value.

First, not all investments have options embedded in them, and not all options, even if they do exist, have value. To assess whether an investment creates valuable options that need to be analyzed and valued, three key questions need to be answered affirmatively:

- **Is the first investment a prerequisite for the later investment/expansion?** If not, how necessary is the first investment for the later investment/expansion? Consider our earlier analysis of the value of a patent or the value of an undeveloped oil reserve as options. A firm cannot generate patents without investing in research or paying another firm for the patents, and it cannot get rights to an undeveloped oil reserve without bidding on it at a government auction or buying it from another oil company. Clearly, the initial investment here (spending on R&D, bidding at the auction) is required for the firm to have the second option. Now consider the Disney expansion into Mexico. The initial investment in a Spanish channel provides Disney with information about market potential, without which presumably it is unwilling to expand into the larger Latin American market. Unlike the examples of patents and undeveloped reserves, the initial investment is not a prerequisite for the second, although management might view it as such. The connection gets even weaker when we look at one firm acquiring another to have the option to be able to enter a large market. Acquiring an Internet service provider to have a foothold in the Internet retailing market or buying a Brazilian brewery to preserve the option to enter the Brazilian beer market are examples of such transactions.
- **Does the firm have an exclusive right to the later investment/expansion?** If not, does the initial investment provide the firm with significant competitive advantages on subsequent investments? The value of the option ultimately derives not from the cash flows generated by the second and subsequent investments, but from the excess returns generated by these cash flows. The greater the potential for excess returns on the second investment, the greater the value of the option in the first investment. The potential for excess returns is closely tied to how much of a competitive advantage the first investment provides the firm when it takes subsequent investments. At one extreme, again, consider investing in research and development to acquire a patent. The patent gives the firm that owns it the exclusive rights to produce that product and, if the market potential is large, the right to the excess returns from the project. At the other extreme, the firm might get no competitive advantages on subsequent investments. In that case, it is questionable whether these investments can generate any excess returns. In reality, most investments

fall in between these two extremes, with greater competitive advantages being associated with higher excess returns and larger option values.

- **How sustainable are the competitive advantages?** In a competitive marketplace, excess returns attract competitors, and competition drives out excess returns. The more sustainable the competitive advantages possessed by a firm, the greater the value of the options embedded in the initial investment. The sustainability of competitive advantages is a function of two forces. The first is the nature of the competition; other things remaining equal, competitive advantages fade much more quickly in sectors that have aggressive competitors. The second is the nature of the competitive advantage. If the resource controlled by the firm is finite and scarce (as is the case with natural resource reserves and vacant land), the competitive advantage is likely to be sustainable for longer periods. Alternatively, if the competitive advantage comes from being the first mover in a market or technological expertise, it will come under assault far sooner. The most direct way of reflecting this in the value of the option is in its life. The option's life can be set to the period of competitive advantage. Only the excess returns earned over this period count toward the value of the option.

Second, when real options are used to justify a decision, the justification has to be in more than qualitative terms. In other words, managers who argue for taking a project with poor returns or for paying a premium on an acquisition on the basis of real options should be required to value these real options. They also should be required to show that the economic benefits exceed the costs. Two arguments can be made against this requirement. The first is that real options cannot be easily valued, since the inputs are difficult to obtain and often noisy. The second is that the inputs to option pricing models can be easily manipulated to back up whatever the conclusion might be. While both arguments have some basis, an estimate with error is better than no estimate at all. The process of quantitatively trying to estimate the value of a real option is, in fact, the first step to understanding what drives its value.

We should mention a final note of caution about the use of option pricing models to assess the value of real options. Option pricing models, whether they are of the binomial or Black-Scholes variety, are based on two fundamental precepts—replication and arbitrage. For either to be feasible, you have to be able to trade on the underlying asset and on the option. This is easy to accomplish with a listed option on a traded stock; you can trade on both the stock and the listed option. It is much more difficult to pull off when valuing a patent or an investment expansion opportunity. Neither the underlying asset (the product that emerges from the patent) nor the option itself is traded. This does not mean that you cannot estimate the value of a patent as an option, but it does indicate that monetizing this value will be much more difficult. In the Avonex example from earlier in the chapter, the option value for the patent was \$907 million, whereas the conventional risk-adjusted value was only \$547 million. Much as you may believe in the former as the right estimate of value, it is unlikely that any potential buyer of the patent will come close to paying that amount.

Conclusion

In contrast to the approaches that focus on downside risk—risk-adjusted value, simulations, and decision trees—the real options approach brings an optimistic view to uncertainty. While conceding that uncertainty can create losses, it argues that uncertainty can also be exploited for potential gains and that updated information can be used to augment the upside and reduce the downside risks inherent in investments. In essence, you are arguing that the conventional risk-adjustment approaches fail to capture this flexibility and that you should add an option premium to the risk-adjusted value.

This chapter considered three potential real options and applications of each. The first is the option to delay. This is where a firm with exclusive rights to an investment has the option of deciding when to take that investment and to delay taking it, if necessary. The second is the option to expand. This is where a firm may be willing to lose money on an initial investment in the hopes of expanding into other investments or markets further down the road. The third is the option to abandon an investment if it looks like a money loser, early in the process.

While it is clearly appropriate to attach value to real options in some cases—patents, reserves of natural resources, or exclusive licenses—the argument for an option premium gets progressively weaker as we move away from the exclusivity inherent in each of these cases. In particular, a firm that invests in an emerging market in a money-losing enterprise, using the argument that the market is a large and potentially profitable one, could be making a serious mistake. After all, the firm could be right in its assessment of the market, but absent barriers to entry, it may not be able to earn excess returns in that market or keep out the competition. Not all opportunities are options, and not all options have significant economic value.

Appendix 5.1: Basics of Options and Option Pricing

An option provides the holder with the right to buy or sell a specified quantity of an *underlying asset* at a fixed price (called a *strike price* or an *exercise price*) at or before the expiration date of the option. Because it is a right and not an obligation, the holder can choose not to exercise the right and allow the option to expire. There are two types of options—*call options* and *put options*.

Option Payoffs

A call option gives the option buyer the right to buy the underlying asset at a fixed price, called the strike or the exercise price, at any time prior to the expiration date of the option: The buyer pays a price for this right. If at expiration the value of the asset is less than the strike price, the option is not exercised and expires worthless. If, on the other hand, the value of the asset is greater than the strike price, the option is exercised—the option buyer buys the stock at the exercise price and the difference between the asset value and the exercise price comprises the gross profit on the investment. The net profit on the investment is the difference between the gross profit and the price paid for the call initially. A payoff diagram illustrates the cash payoff on an option at expiration. For a call, the net payoff is negative (and equal to the price paid for the call) if the value of the underlying asset is less than the strike price. If the price of the underlying asset exceeds the strike price, the gross payoff is the difference between the value of the underlying asset and the strike price, and the net payoff is the difference between the gross payoff and the price of the call. This is illustrated in the Figure 5A.1.

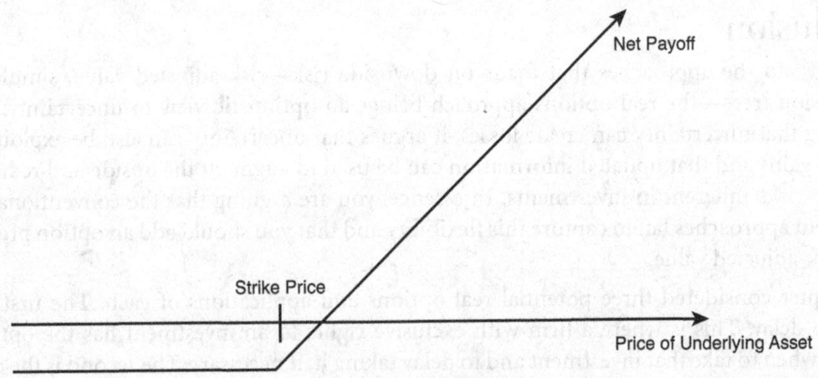

Figure 5A.1: Payoff on Call Option

A put option gives the option buyer the right to sell the underlying asset at a fixed price, again called the strike or exercise price, any time prior to the expiration date of the option. The buyer pays a price for this right. If the price of the underlying asset is greater than the strike price, the option will not be exercised and will expire worthless. If, on the other hand, the price of the underlying asset is less than the strike price, the owner of the put option will exercise the option and sell the stock at the strike price, claiming the difference between the strike price and the market value of the asset as the gross profit. Again, netting out the initial cost paid for the put yields the net profit from the transaction. A put has a negative net payoff if the value of the underlying asset exceeds the strike price and has a gross payoff equal to the difference between the strike price and the value of the underlying asset if the asset value is less than the strike price. This is summarized in Figure 5A.2.

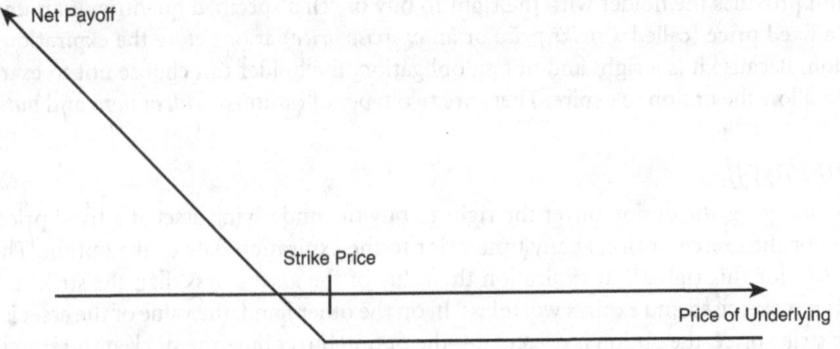

Figure 5A.2: Payoff on Put Option

There is one final distinction that needs to be made. Options are usually categorized as American or European options. A primary distinction between the two is that American options can be exercised at any time prior to their expiration, whereas European options can be exercised only at expiration. The possibility of early exercise makes American options more valuable than otherwise similar European options; it also makes them more difficult to value. There is one compensating factor that enables the former to be valued using models designed for the latter. In most cases, the time premium associated with the remaining life of an option and transactions costs makes early exercise suboptimal. In other words, the holders of in-the-money options will generally get much more by selling the option to someone else than by exercising the options.[1]

Determinants of Option Value

The value of an option is determined by a number of variables relating to the underlying asset and financial markets.

1. **Current value of the underlying asset**: Options are assets that derive value from an underlying asset. Consequently, changes in the value of the underlying asset affect the value of the options on that asset. Because calls provide the right to buy the underlying asset at a fixed price, an increase in the value of the asset will increase the value of the calls. Puts, on the other hand, become less valuable as the value of the asset increases.

2. **Variance in value of the underlying asset**: The buyer of an option acquires the right to buy or sell the underlying asset at a fixed price. The higher the variance in the value of the underlying asset, the greater the value of the option. This is true for both calls and puts. Although it might seem counterintuitive that an increase in a risk measure (variance) should increase value, options are different from other securities because buyers of options can never lose more than the price they pay for them; in fact, they have the potential to earn significant returns from large price movements.

3. **Dividends paid on the underlying asset**: We can expect the value of the underlying asset to decrease if dividend payments are made on the asset during the life of the option. Consequently, the value of a call on the asset is a *decreasing* function of the size of expected dividend payments, and the value of a put is an *increasing* function of expected dividend payments. A more intuitive way of thinking about dividend payments, for call options, is as a cost of delaying exercise on in-the-money options. To see why, consider an option on a traded stock. Once a call option is in the money, that is, the holder of the option will make a gross payoff by exercising the option; exercising the call option will provide the holder with the stock and entitle him or her to the dividends on the stock in subsequent periods. Failing to exercise the option means that these dividends are foregone.

4. **Strike price of option**: A key characteristic used to describe an option is the strike price. In the case of calls, where the holder acquires the right to buy at a fixed price, the value of the call declines as the strike price increases. In the case of puts, where the holder has the right to sell at a fixed price, the value increases as the strike price increases.

5. **Time to expiration on option**: Both calls and puts become more valuable as the time to expiration increases. This is because the longer time to expiration provides more time for

1 Although early exercise is not optimal generally, there are at least two exceptions to this rule. One is a case in which the underlying asset pays large dividends, thus reducing the value of the asset and any call options on that asset. In this case, call options may be exercised just before an ex-dividend date, if the time premium on the options is less than the expected decline in asset value as a consequence of the dividend payment. The other exception arises when an investor holds both the underlying asset and deep in-the-money puts on that asset at a time when interest rates are high. In this case, the time premium on the put may be less than the potential gain from exercising the put early and earning interest on the exercise price.

the value of the underlying asset to move, increasing the value of both types of options. Additionally, in the case of a call, where the buyer has to pay a fixed price at expiration, the present value of this fixed price decreases as the life of the option increases, increasing the value of the call.

6. **Riskless interest rate corresponding to life of option:** Because the buyer of an option pays the price of the option up front, an opportunity cost is involved. This cost depends on the level of interest rates and the time to expiration on the option. The riskless interest rate also enters into the valuation of options when the present value of the exercise price is calculated because the exercise price does not have to be paid (received) until expiration on calls (puts). Increases in the interest rate increase the value of calls and reduce the value of puts.

Table 5A.1 summarizes the variables and their predicted effects on call and put prices.

Table 5A.1 Summary of Variables Affecting Call and Put Prices

	Effect on	
Factor	**Call Value**	**Put Value**
Increase in underlying asset's value	Increases	Decreases
Increase in strike price	Decreases	Increases
Increase in variance of underlying asset	Increases	Increases
Increase in time to expiration	Increases	Increases
Increase in interest rates	Increases	Decreases
Increase in dividends paid	Decreases	Increases

Option Pricing Models

Option pricing theory has made vast strides since 1972, when Black and Scholes published their path-breaking paper providing a model for valuing dividend-protected European options. Black and Scholes used a "replicating portfolio"—a portfolio composed of the underlying asset and the risk-free asset that had the same cash flows as the option being valued—to derive their final formulation. Although their derivation is mathematically complicated, there is a simpler binomial model for valuing options that draws on the same logic.

The Binomial Model

The *binomial option pricing model* is based on a simple formulation for the asset price process, in which the asset can move to one of two possible prices in any time period. The general formulation of a stock price process that follows the binomial is shown in Figure 5A.3.

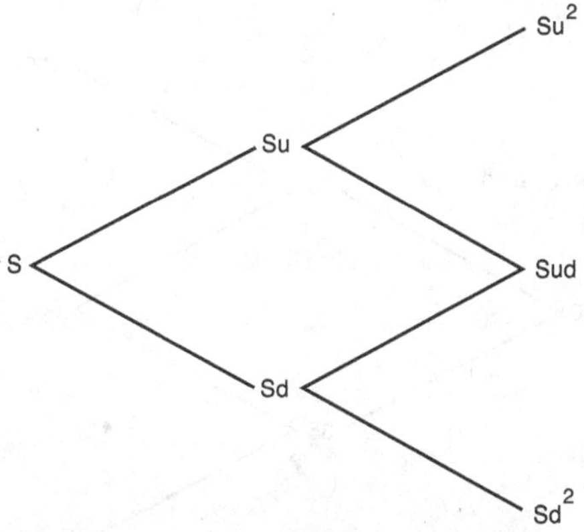

Figure 5A.3: General Formulation for Binomial Price Path

In this figure, S is the current stock price; the price moves up to Su with probability p and down to Sd with probability 1–p in any time period.

The objective in creating a replicating portfolio is to use a combination of risk-free borrowing/lending and the underlying asset to create the same cash flows as the option being valued. The principles of arbitrage apply here, and the value of the option must be equal to the value of the replicating portfolio. In the case of the preceding general formulation, where stock prices can either move up to Su or down to Sd in any time period, the replicating portfolio for a call with strike price K involves borrowing $B and acquiring Δ of the underlying asset, where:

$$\Delta = \text{Number of Units of the Underlying Asset Bought} = (C_u - C_d)/(Su - Sd)$$

where

C_u = Value of the Call If the Stock Price Is Su

C_d = Value of the Call If the Stock Price Is Sd

In a multiperiod binomial process, the valuation has to proceed iteratively; that is, starting with the last time period and moving backward in time until the current point in time. The portfolios replicating the option are created at each step and valued, providing the values for the option in that time period. The final output from the binomial option pricing model is a statement of the value of the option in terms of the replicating portfolio, composed of Δ shares (option delta) of the underlying asset and risk-free borrowing/lending:

Value of the Call = Current Value of Underlying Asset * Option Delta – Borrowing Needed to Replicate the Option

Consider a simple example. Assume that the objective is to value a call with a strike price of 50, which is expected to expire in two time periods, on an underlying asset whose price currently is 50 and is expected to follow a binomial process:

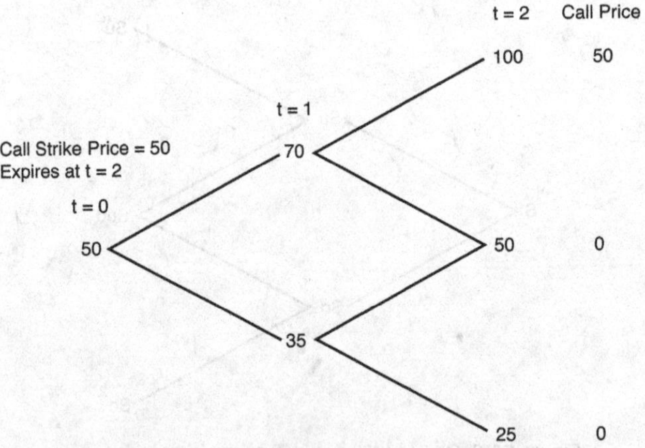

Now assume that the interest rate is 11%. In addition, define the following:

Δ = Number of Shares in the Replicating Portfolio

B = Dollars of Borrowing in the Replicating Portfolio

The objective is to combine Δ shares of stock and B dollars of borrowing to replicate the cash flows from the call with a strike price of $50. This can be done iteratively, starting with the last period and working back through the binomial tree.

Step 1: Start with the end nodes and work backwards:

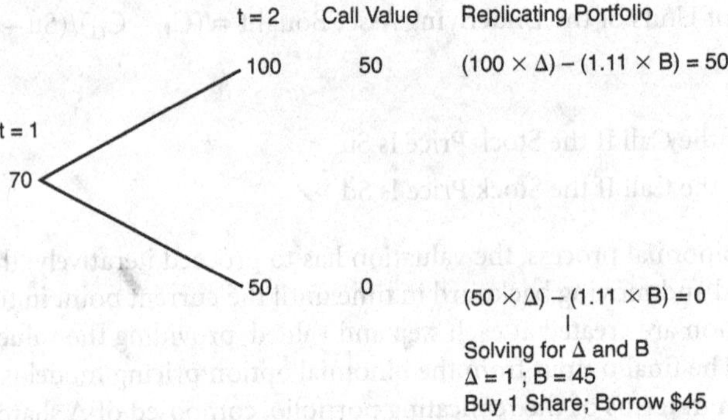

Thus, if the stock price is $70 at t = 1, borrowing $45 and buying 1 share of the stock will give the same cash flows as buying the call. The value of the call at t = 1, if the stock price is $70, is therefore:

Value of Call = Value of Replicating Position = 70 Δ – B = 70 – 45 = 25

Considering the other leg of the binomial tree at t = 1,

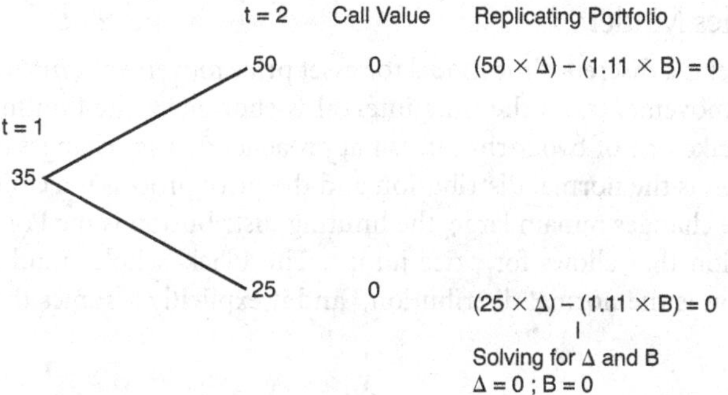

If the stock price is 35 at t = 1, then the call is worth nothing.

Step 2: Move backwards to the earlier time period and create a replicating portfolio that will provide the cash flows the option will provide.

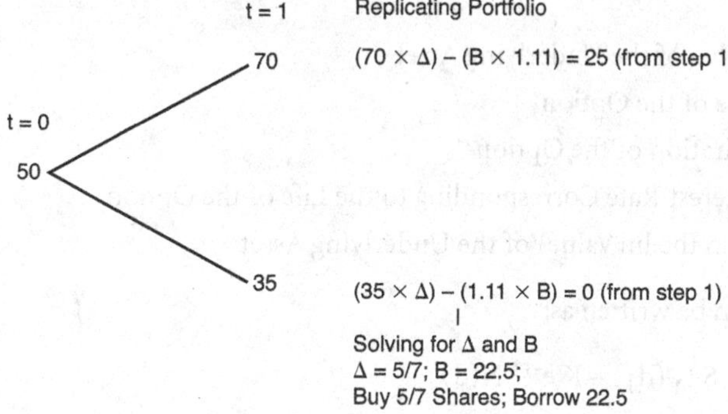

In other words, borrowing $22.50 and buying 5/7 of a share will provide the same cash flows as a call with a strike price of $50. The value of the call therefore has to be the same as the value of this position:

Value of Call = Value of Replicating Position = 5/7 * Current Stock Price – $22.50 = $13.20

The binomial model provides insight into the determinants of option value. The value of an option is not determined by the *expected* price of the asset but by its *current* price, which, of course, reflects expectations about the future. This is a direct consequence of arbitrage. If the option value deviates from the value of the replicating portfolio, investors can create an arbitrage position—that is, one that requires no investment, involves no risk, and delivers positive returns. To illustrate, if the portfolio that replicates the call costs more than the call does in the market, an investor could buy the call, sell the replicating portfolio, and be guaranteed the difference as a profit. The cash flows on the two positions offset each other, leading to no cash flows in subsequent periods. The option value also increases as the time to expiration is extended, as the price movements (u and d) increase, and with increases in the interest rate.

The Black-Scholes Model

The binomial model is a discrete-time model for asset price movements, including a time interval (t) between price movements. As the time interval is shortened, the limiting distribution, as t approaches 0, can take one of two forms. If, as t approaches 0, price changes become smaller, the limiting distribution is the normal distribution and the price process is a continuous one. If, as t approaches 0, price changes remain large, the limiting distribution is the Poisson distribution—that is, a distribution that allows for price jumps. The Black-Scholes model applies when the limiting distribution is the normal distribution,[2] and it explicitly assumes that the price process is continuous.

The Model

The original Black-Scholes model was designed to value European options, which were dividend-protected. Thus, neither the possibility of early exercise nor the payment of dividends affects the value of options in this model. The value of a call option in the Black-Scholes model can be written as a function of the following variables:

S = Current Value of the Underlying Asset

K = Strike Price of the Option

t = Life to Expiration of the Option

r = Riskless Interest Rate Corresponding to the Life of the Option

σ^2 = Variance in the ln(Value) of the Underlying Asset

The model itself can be written as:

$$\text{Value of Call} = S\,N(d_1) - K\,e^{-rt}\,N(d_2)$$

where

$$d_1 = \frac{\ln\left(\frac{S}{K}\right) + \left(r + \frac{\sigma^2}{2}\right)t}{\sigma\sqrt{t}}$$

$$d_2 = d_1 - \sigma\sqrt{t}$$

The process of valuation of options using the Black-Scholes model involves the following steps:

Step 1: The inputs to the Black-Scholes model are used to estimate d_1 and d_2.

Step 2: The cumulative normal distribution functions, $N(d_1)$ and $N(d_2)$, corresponding to these standardized normal variables are estimated.

Step 3: The present value of the exercise price is estimated, using the continuous time version of the present value formulation:

2 Stock prices cannot drop below zero because of the limited liability of stockholders in publicly listed firms. Hence, stock prices by themselves cannot be normally distributed because a normal distribution requires some probability of infinitely negative values. The distribution of the natural logs of stock prices is assumed to be log-normal in the Black-Scholes model. This is why the variance used in this model is the variance in the log of stock prices.

Present Value of Exercise Price = $K e^{-rt}$

Step 4: The value of the call is estimated from the Black-Scholes model.

The determinants of value in the Black-Scholes model are the same as those in the binomial—the current value of the stock price, the variability in stock prices, the time to expiration on the option, the strike price, and the riskless interest rate. The principle of replicating portfolios that is used in binomial valuation also underlies the Black-Scholes model. In fact, embedded in the Black-Scholes model is the replicating portfolio:

$$\text{Value of Call} = \underbrace{S\,N(d_1)}_{\text{Buy } N(d_1) \text{ Shares}} - \underbrace{K e^{-rt} N(d_2)}_{\text{Borrow This Amount}}$$

N(d1), which is the number of shares that are needed to create the replicating portfolio, is called the *option delta*. This replicating portfolio is self-financing and has the same value as the call at every stage of the option's life.

Model Limitations and Fixes

The version of the Black-Scholes model presented previously does not take into account the possibility of early exercise or the payment of dividends, both of which impact the value of options. Adjustments exist, which although not perfect, provide partial corrections to value.

Dividends

The payment of dividends reduces the stock price. Consequently, call options become less valuable and put options more valuable as dividend payments increase. One approach to dealing with dividends is to estimate the present value of expected dividends paid by the underlying asset during the option life and subtract it from the current value of the asset to use as S in the model. Because this becomes impractical as the option life becomes longer, we would suggest an alternate approach. If the dividend yield (y = Dividends/Current Value of the Asset) of the underlying asset is expected to remain unchanged during the life of the option, the Black-Scholes model can be modified to take dividends into account:

$$C = S e^{-yt} N(d_1) - K e^{-rt} N(d_2)$$

where

$$d_1 = \frac{\ln\left(\frac{S}{K}\right) + (r - y + \frac{\sigma^2}{2})t}{\sigma\sqrt{t}}$$

$$d_2 = d_1 - \sigma\sqrt{t}$$

From an intuitive standpoint, the adjustments have two effects. First, the value of the asset is discounted back to the present at the dividend yield to take into account the expected drop in value from dividend payments. Second, the interest rate is offset by the dividend yield to reflect the lower carrying cost from holding the stock (in the replicating portfolio). The net effect is a reduction in the value of calls, with the adjustment, and an increase in the value of puts.

Early Exercise

The Black-Scholes model is designed to value European options, whereas most options that we consider are American options, which can be exercised anytime before expiration. Without working through the mechanics of valuation models, an American option should always be worth at least as much and generally more than a European option because of the early exercise option. There are three basic approaches for dealing with the possibility of early exercise. The first is to continue to use the unadjusted Black-Scholes model and regard the resulting value as a floor or conservative estimate of the true value. The second approach is to value the option to each potential exercise date. With options on stocks, this basically requires that we value options to each ex-dividend day and choose the maximum of the estimated call values. The third approach is to use a modified version of the binomial model to consider the possibility of early exercise.

Although it is difficult to estimate the prices for each node of a binomial, variances estimated from historical data can be used to compute the expected up and down movements in the binomial. To illustrate, if σ^2 is the variance in ln(stock prices), the up and down movements in the binomial can be estimated as follows:

$$u = \text{Exp}\ [(r - s2/2)(T/m) + \sqrt{(s2T/m)}]$$

$$d = \text{Exp}\ [(r - \sigma^2/2)(T/m) - \sqrt{(\sigma^2 T/m)}]$$

where u and d are the up and down movements per unit time for the binomial, T is the life of the option, and m is the number of periods within that lifetime. Multiplying the stock price at each stage by u and d yields the up and the down prices. These can then be used to value the asset.

The Impact of Exercise on the Value of the Underlying Asset

The derivation of the Black-Scholes model is based on the assumption that exercising an option does not affect the value of the underlying asset. This may be true for listed options on stocks, but it is not true for some types of options. For instance, the exercise of warrants increases the number of shares outstanding and brings fresh cash into the firm, both of which affect the stock price.[3] The expected negative impact (dilution) of exercise decreases the value of warrants compared to otherwise similar call options. The adjustment for dilution in the Black-Scholes to the stock price is fairly simple. The stock price is adjusted for the expected dilution from the exercise of the options. In the case of warrants, for instance:

$$\text{Dilution-Adjusted } S = (S\ n_S + W\ n_W)/(n_S + n_w)$$

where

S = Current Value of the Stock n_W = Number of Warrants Outstanding

W = Market Value of Warrants Outstanding n_S = Number of Shares Outstanding

When the warrants are exercised, the number of shares outstanding increases, reducing the stock price. The numerator reflects the market value of equity, including both stocks and warrants outstanding. The reduction in S reduces the value of the call option.

3 Warrants are call options issued by firms, either as part of management compensation contracts or to raise equity.

There is an element of circularity in this analysis because the value of the warrant is needed to estimate the dilution-adjusted S, and the dilution-adjusted S is needed to estimate the value of the warrant. This problem can be resolved by starting off the process with an estimated value of the warrant (say, the exercise value) and then iterating with the new estimated value for the warrant until there is convergence.

Valuing Puts

The value of a put can be derived from the value of a call with the same strike price and the same expiration date through an arbitrage relationship that specifies that:

$$C - P = S - K e^{-rt}$$

where C is the value of the call and P is the value of the put (with the same life and exercise price). This arbitrage relationship can be derived fairly easily and is called *put-call parity*. To see why put-call parity holds, consider creating the following portfolio:

(a) Sell a call and buy a put with exercise price K and the same expiration date "t"

(b) Buy the stock at current stock price S

The payoff from this position is riskless and always yields K at expiration (t). To see this, assume that the stock price at expiration is S*:

Position	**Payoffs at t if S*>K**	**Payoffs at t if S*<K**
Sell call	-(S* – K)	0
Buy put	0	K – S*
Buy stock	S*	S*
Total	*K*	*K*

Because this position yields K with certainty, its value must be equal to the present value of K at the riskless rate ($K e^{-rt}$):

$$S + P - C = K e^{-rt}$$

$$C - P = S - K e^{-rt}$$

This relationship can be used to value puts. Substituting the Black-Scholes formulation for the value of an equivalent call,

$$\text{Value of Put} = S e^{-yt} (N(d_1) - 1) - K e^{-rt} (N(d_2) - 1)$$

where

$$d_1 = \frac{\ln\left(\frac{S}{K}\right) + (r - y + \frac{\sigma^2}{2})t}{\sigma\sqrt{t}}$$

$$d_2 = d_1 - \sigma\sqrt{t}$$

6

A Shaky Base: A "Risky" Risk-Free Rate

Most risk-and-return models in finance start with an asset that is defined as risk-free and use the expected return on that asset as the risk-free rate. The expected returns on risky investments are then measured relative to the risk-free rate, with the risk creating an expected risk premium that is added to the risk-free rate.

But what makes an asset risk-free? And how do we estimate a risk-free rate? We will consider these questions in this chapter. In the process, we have to grapple with why risk-free rates may be different in different currencies and how to adapt discounted cash flow valuations to reflect these differences. We will also look at cases where estimating a risk-free rate becomes difficult, and mechanisms that we can use to meet the challenges. Furthermore, we will look at the dark side of valuation when it comes to risk-free rates, and the consequences for valuations.

What Is a Risk-Free Asset?

To understand what makes an asset risk-free, let us go back to how risk is measured in investments. Investors who buy assets have returns *that they expect to make* over the time horizon that they will hold the asset. The *actual returns* that they make over this holding period may by very different from the expected returns, and this is where the risk comes in. Risk in finance is viewed in terms of the variance in actual returns around the expected return. For an investment to be risk-free in this environment, then, the actual returns should always be equal to the expected return.

To illustrate, consider an investor with a one-year time horizon buying a one-year Treasury bill (or any other default-free one-year bond) with a 5% expected return. At the end of the one-year holding period, the actual return that this investor would have on this investment will always be 5%, which is equal to the expected return. Figure 6.1 shows the return distribution for this investment.

This investment is risk-free because there is no variance around the expected return.

We can think of a risk-free investment in a second way—in the context of how the investment behaves, relative to other investments. A risk-free investment should have returns that are uncorrelated with risky investments in a market. Note that if we accept the first definition of a risk-free asset as an investment with a guaranteed return, this property always follows. An investment that delivers the same return, no matter what the scenario, should be uncorrelated with risky investments with returns that vary across scenarios.

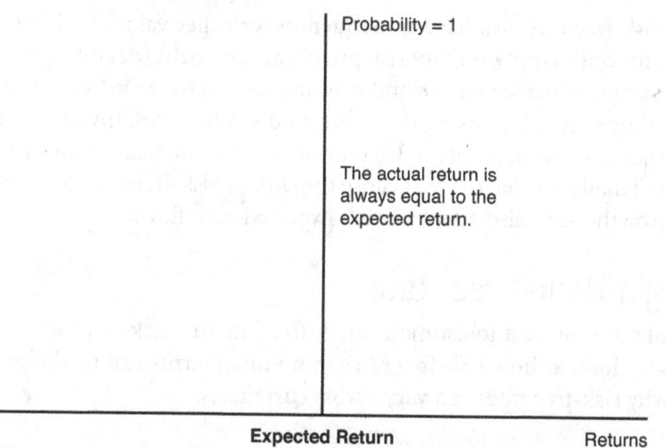

Figure 6.1: Probability Distribution for a Risk-Free Investment

Why Do Risk-Free Rates Matter?

The risk-free rate is the building block for estimating both the cost of equity and capital. The cost of equity is computed by adding a risk premium to the risk-free rate, with the magnitude of the premium being determined by the risk in an investment and the overall equity risk premium (for investing in the average risk investment). The cost of debt is estimated by adding a default spread to the risk-free rate, with the magnitude of the spread depending on the credit risk in the company. Thus, using a higher risk-free rate, holding all else constant, increases discount rates and reduces present value in a discounted cash flow valuation.

The level of the risk-free rate matters for other reasons as well. As the risk-free rate rises, and the discount rates rise with it, the breakdown of a firm's value into growth assets and assets in place also shifts (see Figure 6.2). Since growth assets deliver cash flows further into the future, the value of growth assets decreases more than the value of assets in place as risk-free rates rise.

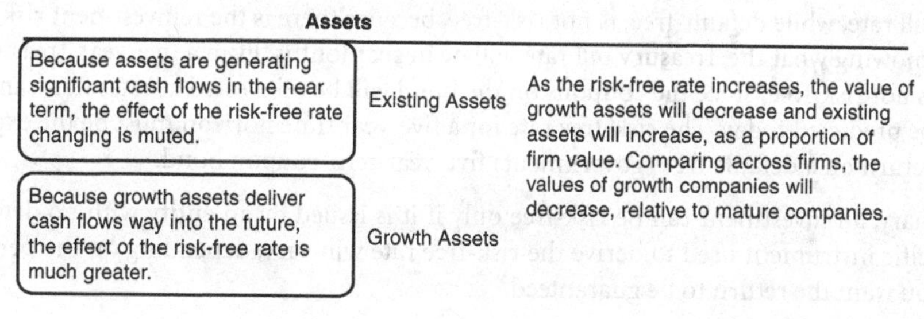

Figure 6.2: Effects on Value-Asset Type

If we categorize companies, based on assets in place and growth assets, growth companies should be affected much more adversely than mature companies when the risk-free rate increases, holding all else constant.

Changes in the risk-free rate also have consequences for other valuation inputs. The risk premiums that we use for both equity (equity risk premium) and debt (default spreads) may change as risk-free rates change. In particular, a significant increase in the risk-free rate generally results in higher risk premiums, thus increasing the effect on discount rates. Investors who settle for a 4% risk premium when the risk-free rate is 3% may demand a much larger risk premium if risk-free rates rise to 10%. Finally, the factors that cause the shift in risk-free rates—expected inflation and real economic growth—can also affect a firm's expected cash flows.

Estimating a Risk-Free Rate

This section looks at how best to estimate a risk-free rate in markets where a default-free entity exists. We will also look at how risk-free rates in nominal terms can be different from real risk-free rates, and why risk-free rates can vary across currencies.

Requirements for an Investment to Be Risk-Free

If we define a risk-free investment as one where we know the expected return with certainty, under what conditions will the actual return on an investment always be equal to the expected return? In general, two basic conditions must be met:

- The first is that *there can be no default risk*. Essentially, this rules out any security issued by a private entity, since even the largest and safest firms have some measure of default risk. The only securities that have a chance of being risk-free are government securities—not because governments are better run than corporations, but because they control the printing of currency. At least in nominal terms, they should be able to fulfill their promises. Even this assumption, straightforward though it may seem, does not always hold up, especially when governments refuse to honor claims made by previous regimes and when they borrow in currencies other than their own.
- Riskless securities need to fulfill a second condition that is often forgotten. For an investment to have an actual return equal to its expected return, *there can be no reinvestment risk*. To illustrate this point, assume that you are trying to estimate the expected return over a five-year period, and that you want a risk-free rate. A six-month Treasury bill rate, while default-free, is not risk-free, because there is the reinvestment risk of not knowing what the Treasury bill rate will be in six months. Even a five-year Treasury bond is not risk-free, since the coupons on the bond will be reinvested at rates that cannot be predicted today. The risk-free rate for a five-year time horizon must be the expected return on a default-free (government) five-year zero-coupon bond.

In summary, an investment can be risk-free only if it is issued by an entity with no default risk. The specific instrument used to derive the risk-free rate will vary, depending on the period over which you want the return to be guaranteed.

The Purist Solution

If we accept both requirements—no default risk and no reinvestment risk—as prerequisites for an investment to be risk-free, the risk-free rates will vary with the time horizon. Thus, we would use a one-year default-free bond to derive the risk-free rate for a one-year cash flow and a five-year default-free bond to derive the risk-free rate for a five-year cash flow.

As noted earlier, a conventional five-year bond will not yield a risk-free return over five years, even if it is issued by a default-free entity, because the coupons every six months will have to be reinvested at uncertain rates. The solution is to strip the coupons from the bond and make it a zero-coupon bond. Thus, the risk-free rates for each period will be measured by using the rate on a zero-coupon default-free bond maturing in that period. In the U.S., where zero-coupon treasuries have been traded for several years now, this is a simple task. Even if zero-coupon bonds are not traded, we can estimate zero-coupon rates for each period by using the rates on coupon-bearing bonds. To do this, we start with the single-period bond and set the rate on it as the zero-coupon rate for that period. We then can move up the maturity ladder progressively, solving for the zero-coupon rates for each subsequent period. For example, assume that coupons are annual and that you are provided with the following information on one-year and two-year coupon bonds:

Price of a 2% One-Year Coupon Bond = 1,000

Price of a 2.5% Two-Year Coupon Bond = 990

Setting up the one-year coupon bond, we can solve for the one-year rate:

$$\text{Price of Bond} = 1000 = \frac{(\text{Principal} + \text{Coupon})}{(1 + 1\text{ - Year Zero Rate})} = \frac{(1000 + 20)}{(1 + r_1)}$$

Since the bond trades at par, the one-year zero rate = coupon rate on the bond = 2%.

Moving to the two-year coupon bond, we can solve for the two-year rate:

$$\text{Price of Bond} = 990 = \frac{\text{Coupon}_1}{(1+r_1)} + \frac{(\text{Coupon}_2 + \text{Principal})}{(1+r_2)^2} = \frac{25}{(1.02)} + \frac{1025}{(1+r_2)^2}$$

Solving for the two-year rate, we get r_2 = 3.03%. We can then use the one-year and two-year rates in conjunction with the three-year bond to get the three-year rate, and so on. In September 2008, we used the information available on U.S. treasuries (prices and coupons) to extract the zero-coupon rates shown in Table 6.1.

Table 6.1 Zero-Coupon Rates: U.S. Treasuries in September 2008

Maturity	Coupon Rate	Price	Yield	Zero Rate
1	1.50%	100.00	1.50%	1.5000%
2	1.75%	99.00	1.77%	2.2739%
3	2.00%	98.00	2.04%	2.7172%
4	2.25%	97.50	2.31%	2.9411%
5	2.50%	98.00	2.55%	2.9543%
6	2.75%	99.00	2.78%	2.9510%
7	3.00%	98.00	3.06%	3.3789%
8	3.25%	97.00	3.35%	3.7884%

Table 6.1 Zero-Coupon Rates: U.S. Treasuries in September 2008

Maturity	Coupon Rate	Price	Yield	Zero Rate
9	3.50%	99.00	3.54%	3.7174%
10	3.75%	98.00	3.83%	4.1522%

If we accept the proposition that the risk-free rate should be matched to the time period of the cash flow, we would use the rates in this table as the risk-free rates by period—1.5% for year 1, 2.27% for year 2, and so on.

From a pragmatic standpoint, refining risk-free rates to make them year-specific may not be worth the effort in mature markets for two reasons. The first is that with any reasonably well-behaved yield curve,[1] the effect on present value of using year-specific risk-free rates is likely to be small, since the rates do not deviate significantly across time. The second reason is that the rest of the parameters we use in analysis now have to be defined relative to these risk-free rates. The equity risk premium we use for the cost of equity in year 1 has to be defined relative to a one-year risk-free rate rather than the more conventional computation, which uses ten-year rates. This usually results in higher equity risk premiums for the short-term risk-free rates, which may nullify the eventual impact on the cost of equity. For instance, assume that the one-year rate is 2% and that the ten-year rate is 4%. Further assume that the equity risk premium relative to the ten-year rate is 4.5% but is 6% against a one-year rate. The cost of equity for an average risk investment then is 8% for the one-year cash flow (2% + 6%) and 8.5% for the ten-year cash flow (4% + 4.5%).

When would it make sense to use year-specific risk-free rates? If the yield curve is downward-sloping (short-term rates are much higher than long-term rates) or excessively upward-sloping, with long-term rates exceeding short-term rates by more than 4%, there is a payoff to being year-specific. In market crises, for instance, it is not uncommon to see big differences (in either direction) between short-term and long-term rates. If we decide to use year-specific rates, we should also estimate year-specific equity risk premiums and default spreads to be consistent.

A Practical Compromise

If we decide not to estimate year-specific risk-free rates, we have to come up with one risk-free rate to use on all the cash flows. But what rate should we use? One answer is duration matching. Its roots are in an interest-rate risk management strategy that is widely used by banks. Put simply, banks that face interest rate risk in their assets (generally loans made to corporate and individual borrowers) have two choices. The first is to try to match the cash flows on each asset with a liability that has equivalent cash flows. This would neutralize interest rate risk but would be difficult to put into practice. The other is to match the average duration of the assets to the average duration of the liabilities, resulting in less complete risk hedging, but with far less cost.

1 We use historical norms to define "well behaved." In the U.S., for instance, yield curves over the last century have been upward-sloping, with long-term (ten-year) Treasury bill rates about 2% higher than short-term (three-month) Treasury bill rates.

In valuation, we could use a variation on this duration-matching strategy. We would use one risk-free rate on all the cash flows. Then we would set the duration of the default-free security used as the risk-free asset to the duration[2] of the cash flows in the analysis. In most firm valuations, we can safely assume that the duration of the cash flows will be high, especially if we assume that cash flows continue into perpetuity. In 2004, S&P used the dividend discount model to estimate the duration of equity in the S&P 500 to be about 16 years.[3] Since dividends are lower than cash flows to equity, we would expect the true duration to be lower and closer to eight or nine years for the S&P 500. Since the duration of a 10-year coupon bond (with a coupon rate of about 4%) priced at par is close to eight years,[4] we would use the 10-year Treasury bond rate as the risk-free rate on all cash flows for most mature firms. The duration of equity will rise for higher-growth firms and could be as high as 20 to 25 years for young firms with negative cash flows in the initial years. In valuing these firms, an argument can be made that we should be using a 30-year Treasury bond rate as the risk-free rate.[5]

The difference between the 10-year and 30-year bond rates is small.[6] It is much easier to estimate equity risk premiums and default spreads against the former rather than the latter. Therefore, we believe that using the 10-year bond rate as the risk-free rate on all cash flows is a good practice in valuation, at least in mature markets. In exceptional circumstances, where year-specific rates vary widely across time, we should consider using risk-free rates that vary across time.

The Currency Effect

Even if we accept the proposition that the 10-year default-free bond rate is the risk-free rate, the number we obtain at any point in time can vary, depending on which currency you use for your analysis. On October 20, 2008, for instance, the market interest rate on a 10-year U.S. Treasury bond rate was 3.9%. If we assume that the U.S. Treasury is default-free, this would be the risk-free rate in U.S. dollars. On the same date, the market interest rate on a ten-year Japanese government bond, denominated in yen, was 1.53%. If we assume that the Japanese government will fulfill its contractual obligations with certainty, this would be the risk-free rate in Japanese yen. Using the same logic, Figure 6.3 shows the two-year and ten-year government bond rates in various currencies, at least for governments that are rated AAA by S&P and thus are unlikely to default.

One currency that is missing from this list is the euro. At least 11 different governments that are part of the European Union issue ten-year bonds, all denominated in euros, but with differences in interest rates. Figure 6.4 summarizes the two-year and ten-year rates on October 20, 2008.

2 In investment analysis, where we look at projects, these durations usually are between three and ten years. In valuation, the durations tend to be much longer, because firms are assumed to have infinite lives. The duration in these cases is often more than ten years and increases with the firm's expected growth potential.

3 The duration of equity in the dividend discount model can be written as
Duration of Equity = $1 / (\text{Cost of Equity} - g)\ (1 - \delta g/\sigma r)$ where r is the risk-free rate.

4 The duration of a 10-year 4% coupon bond trading at par is 8.44 years.

5 The duration of a 30-year 4% coupon bond trading at par is close to 18 years.

6 In the U.S. market, which is the only one with a long history of both bonds, the difference between the two rates has been less than 0.5% for the last 40 years.

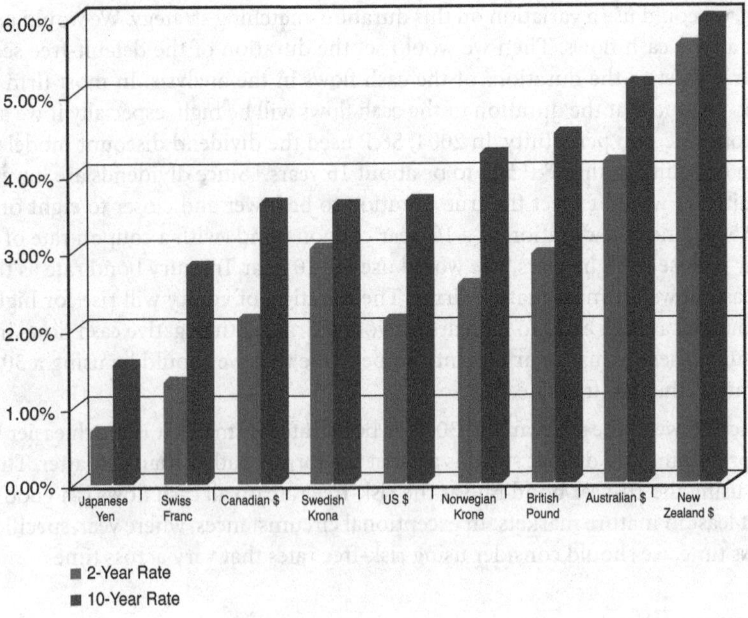

Figure 6.3: Risk-Free Rates by Currency

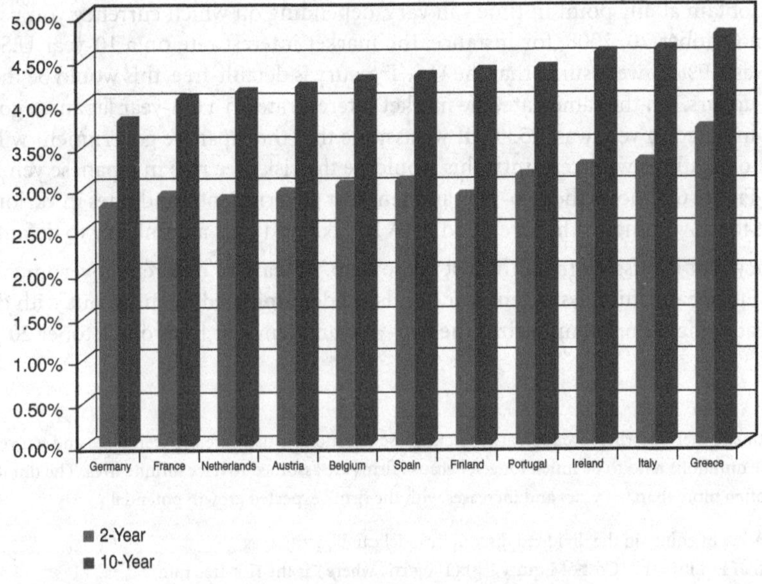

Figure 6.4: Government Bond Rates in Euros

Since none of these governments technically control the printing of the euro, all of them have some default risk. However, the market clearly sees more default risk in the Greek and Portuguese government bonds than it does in the German and French issues. To get a risk-free rate in euros, we use the lowest of the ten-year government euro bond rates as the risk-free rate; in October 2008, the German ten-year euro bond rate of 3.81% would then have been the risk-free rate.[7]

So the risk-free rate on October 20, 2008 would have ranged from a low of 1.53% in Japanese yen to 5.95% in British pounds. This gives rise to two follow-up questions:

- **Why does the risk-free rate vary across currencies?** Since the rates that we have specified as risk-free are all over the same maturity (ten years) and are default-free, the only significant factor that can cause differences is expected inflation. High inflation currencies have higher risk-free rates than low inflation currencies. With our numbers, for instance, the market is expecting greater inflation in British pounds than it is in U.S. dollars, and greater inflation in U.S. dollars than in Japanese yen.
- **Which risk-free rate should we use in valuation?** If higher risk-free rates lead to higher discount rates and, holding all else constant, reduce present value, using a yen risk-free rate seemingly should give a company a higher value than using a U.S. dollar risk-free rate. The fact that expected inflation is the key cause for differences in risk-free rates, though, should give us pause. If we decide to value a company in Japanese yen because of the allure of the lower risk-free rate and lower discount rates, the cash flows also have to be in Japanese yen. If expected inflation in the yen is lower, the expected growth rate and cash flows estimated in yen reflect that fact. Consequently, whatever we gain by using a lower yen-based discount rate will be exactly offset by the loss of having to use yen-based cash flows.

Summarizing, the risk-free rate used to come up with expected returns should be measured consistently with the cash flows that are measured. Thus, if cash flows are estimated in nominal U.S. dollar terms, the risk-free rate is the U.S. Treasury bond rate. This is the case whether the company being analyzed is Brazilian, Indian, or Russian. While this may seem illogical, given the higher risk in these countries, the risk-free rate is not the vehicle for conveying concerns about this risk. This also implies that it is not where a project or firm is domiciled that determines the choice of a risk-free rate, but the currency in which the cash flows on the project or firm are estimated. Thus, Nestlé can be valued using cash flows estimated in Swiss francs, discounted back at an expected return estimated using a Swiss long-term government bond rate as the risk-free rate. Or Nestlé can be valued in British pounds, with both the cash flows and the risk-free rate being British pound rates.

If the difference in interest rates across two currencies does not adequately reflect the difference in expected inflation in these currencies, the values obtained using the different currencies can be different. In particular, projects and assets are valued more highly when the currency used is the one with low interest rates relative to inflation. The risk, however, is that the interest rates will have to rise at some point to correct for this divergence, at which point the values also converge.

Real Versus Nominal Risk-Free Rates

Under conditions of high and unstable inflation, valuation is often done in real terms. Effectively, this means that cash flows are estimated using real growth rates and without allowing for the

7 If you believe that default risk is inherent even in this rate, you could subtract a small default spread from the German rate to get to a euro risk-free rate.

growth that comes from price inflation. To be consistent, the discount rates used in these cases have to be real discount rates. To get a real expected rate of return, we need to start with a real risk-free rate. While government bonds may offer returns that are risk-free in nominal terms, they are not risk-free in real terms, since expected inflation can be volatile. The standard approach of subtracting an expected inflation rate from the nominal interest rate to arrive at a real risk-free rate provides at best an estimate of the real risk-free rate.

Until recently, few traded default-free securities could be used to estimate real risk-free rates, but the introduction of inflation-indexed treasuries has filled this void. A Treasury inflation-protected security (TIPS) does not offer a guaranteed nominal return to buyers but instead provides a guaranteed real return. Thus, an inflation-indexed Treasury bond that offers a 3% real return yields approximately 7% in nominal terms if inflation is 4% and only 5% in nominal terms if inflation is only 2%. Figure 6.5 shows the rate on ten-year inflation-indexed treasuries in the U.S., relative to the nominal ten-year Treasury bond rate, from January 2003 to September 2008.

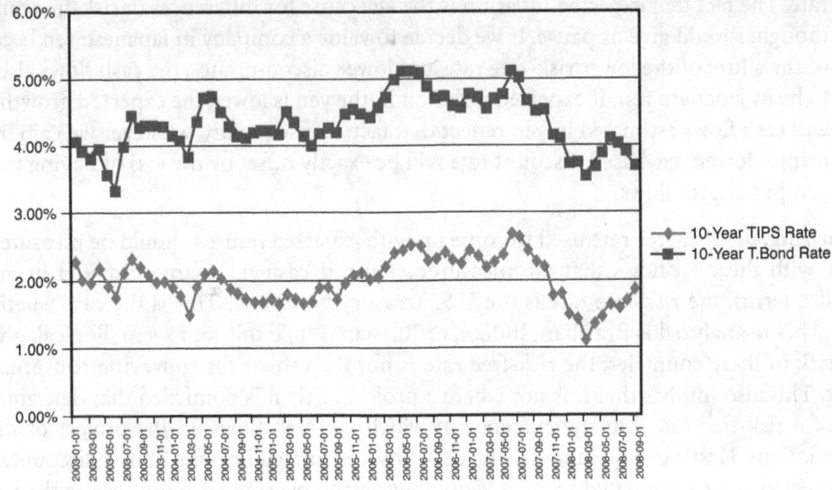

Figure 6.5: TIPS Versus Ten-Year Treasury

Note that the difference between the nominal and the real Treasury rate can be viewed as a market expectation of inflation.[8] During this period, the average expected inflation based on these rates was 2.29%.

We could use the inflation-indexed Treasury rate as a real risk-free rate in the U.S. The only problem is that real valuations are seldom called for or done in markets like the U.S., which has stable and low expected inflation. The markets where we would most need to do real valuations, unfortunately, are markets without inflation-indexed default-free securities. The real risk-free rates in these markets can be estimated by drawing on one of two arguments:

8 The difference between the Treasury and the TIPS rate is an approximate measure of expected inflation. The more precise number is obtained as follows:
Expected Inflation Rate = (1 + Nominal Treasury Rate)/(1+TIPs Rate) – 1

- The first argument is that as long as capital can flow freely to those economies with the highest real returns, there can be no differences in real risk-free rates across markets. Using this argument, the real risk-free rate for the U.S., estimated from the inflation-indexed Treasury, can be used as the real risk-free rate in any market.
- The second argument applies if frictions and constraints exist in capital flowing across markets. In that case, the expected real return on an economy, in the long term, should be equal to the expected real growth rate, again in the long term, of that economy, for equilibrium. Thus, the real risk-free rate for a mature economy like Germany should be much lower than the real risk-free rate for an economy with greater growth potential, such as Hungary.

Done consistently, a company's value should be the same whether we discount real cash flows at a real discount rate or nominal cash flows, in any currency, at a nominal discount rate in the same currency.

Issues in Estimating Risk-Free Rates

In the preceding section, we assumed that government bonds were for the most part default-free and that the government bond rate therefore was risk-free. Even with the euro, which was the only currency that had no government that could print more currency, we assumed that the German government was close to default-free and made our estimates accordingly. In this section, we will consider the tougher cases, where governments either have no long-term bonds outstanding in the local currency or, even if they do, are exposed to default risk. We will also look at the special case where we distrust the existing risk-free rate and believe it to be either too low or too high, given history and fundamentals.

There Are No Long-Term Traded Government Bonds

In the last section, we used the current market interest rate on government bonds issued by the U.S., Japan, and the UK as the risk-free rates in the respective currencies. But what if there are no long-term government bonds in a specific currency or, even if there are, they are not traded? This section examines the consequences.

The Scenario

In many countries (and their associated currencies), the biggest roadblock to finding a risk-free rate is that the government does not issue long-term bonds in the local currency. So how do they borrow? Many choose to use bank loans, the World Bank, or the International Monetary Fund (IMF) for their borrowing, thus bypassing the rigors of the market. This is true for most of the countries that comprise sub-Saharan Africa, for instance. Quite a few other governments issue bonds, but in the currencies of more mature markets, rather than their own currencies. From 1992 to 2006, the Brazilian government issued long-term bonds denominated in U.S. dollars rather than Brazilian reais. In 2008, only three of the 12 South American countries had long-term bonds denominated in local currencies. Finally, some governments issue long-term bonds but then proceed to either offer special incentives to domestic investors (such as tax breaks) or use coercion to place these bonds, resulting in unrealistic rates on these bonds.

The Dark Side

When no long-term government bonds in the local currency are widely traded, analysts valuing companies in that market often take the path of least resistance when estimating both cash flows and discount rates. This results in *currency mismatches in their valuations.* With discount rates, analysts decide that it is easier to estimate risk-free rates and risk premiums in a mature market currency. With Latin American companies, for instance, the currency of choice is the U.S. dollar, and the discount rates are estimated in U.S. dollars. With cash flows, analysts either stick with local currency cash flows or convert those cash flows at the current exchange rate into a mature market currency. Again, with Latin American companies, the cash flows in the local currency are converted into U.S. dollars using current exchange rates. If the value of the company is computed using these cash flows and discount rates, the resulting value will be fatally flawed, because the expected inflation built into the cash flows will be different from the expected inflation built into discount rates. Consider, for instance, a Mexican company where the cash flows are estimated in pesos and the discount rate is estimated in U.S. dollars. Since, in early 2009, the expected inflation rate in pesos is about 5% and the inflation rate built into the U.S. dollar discount rate is only 2%, we will overvalue the company. Note that converting the peso cash flows into dollar cash flows using current exchange rates does nothing to alleviate this problem.

Currency Mismatch Effects on Valuation

Assume that you are valuing a Brazilian company and have been provided with the following estimates of cash flows in nominal Brazilian reais (BR) for the next three years and beyond:

Year	Expected Cash Flow in BR
1	100 million BR
2	110 million BR
3	121 million BR
Beyond	Grow at 6% a year forever

Assume that the current exchange rate is two BR per U.S. dollar and that the current cost of capital computed in U.S. dollars, based on the current Treasury bond rate of 4%, is 9%. Finally, assume that the inflation rate in U.S. dollars is 2% and that the inflation rate in BR is 6%. If we use the current exchange rate to convert the cash flows and leave the growth rate after year 3 intact, the value of the business we arrive at will be $1,789.55 million (3,579.10 million BR), as shown in Table 6.2.

Table 6.2 Cash Flows and Exchange Rates

Year	Cash Flow in BR	Exchange Rate	Cash Flow in U.S. $	Present Value
1	100	0.50	$50.00	$45.87
2	110	0.50	$55.00	$46.29
3	121	0.50	$60.50	$46.72

Year	Cash Flow in BR	Exchange Rate	Cash Flow in U.S. $	Present Value
Terminal value			$2,137.67	$1,650.67
Value of firm				$1,789.55

Note that the terminal value is computed at the end of year 3:

Terminal Value = 60.50 (1.06) / (.09 – .06) = $2,137.67

By using the current exchange rate to convert future BR cash flows into U.S. dollars, we have in effect built in the 6% inflation rate in BR into the expected cash flows while using a discount rate that reflects the 2% inflation rate in U.S. dollars. In addition, the terminal value has been computed using a growth rate in nominal BR and a discount rate in U.S. dollars. Not surprisingly, the mismatch in inflation rates leads us to overvalue the company.

Solutions

If the government does not issue long-term local currency bonds (or at least ones that you can trust to deliver a market interest rate), two solutions preserve consistency. One is to estimate discount rates in a mature market currency (rather than the local currency) and then convert the cash flows into the mature market currency as well. The other is to try to estimate a local currency discount rate, troubles with the risk-free rate notwithstanding.

Mature Market Currency Valuation

Since the value of a company, done right, should not be a function of what currency we choose to do the valuation in, one solution is to value the company in an alternate (mature market) currency. If getting a risk-free rate in Brazilian reais is too difficult, a Brazilian company can be valued entirely in U.S. dollars or euros. To do this right, we have to first estimate the discount rate in U.S. dollars. As we noted in the preceding section, the right risk-free rate to use is the U.S. Treasury bond rate (and not the ten-year dollar-denominated Brazilian bond rate, which has an embedded default spread in it). To be consistent, the cash flows, which generally will be in reais, will have to be converted into U.S. dollar cash flows. This conversion has to be done using the expected U.S. dollar/reais exchange rate and not the current exchange rate. While forward or future markets may provide estimates for the near term, the best way to estimate future exchange rates is by using purchasing power parity, based on expected inflation in the two currencies:

$$\text{Expected Reais/\$ in Period t} = \text{Current Rate}^* \frac{(1 + \text{Expected Inflation Rate}_{\text{Brazilian Reai}})^t}{(1 + \text{Expected Inflation Rate}_{\text{US \$}})^t}$$

Using this expected exchange rate ensures that the inflation built into the expected cash flows is consistent with the inflation embedded in the discount rate.

Valuing in Mature Market Currency

Let us revisit the valuation from the preceding sidebar. Instead of using the current exchange rate, we will use the expected BR/$ exchange rate, estimated using the inflation rates of 6% in BR and 2% in U.S. dollars, to convert the cash flows into dollars. Table 6.3 shows the results.

Table 6.3 Cash Flows and Exchange Rates Revisited

Year	Cash Flow in BR	Exchange Rate (BR/$)	Exchange Rate ($/BR)	Cash Flow in U.S. $	Present Value
1	100	2.0784	0.481132075	$48.11	$44.14
2	110	2.1599	0.462976148	$50.93	$42.86
3	121	2.2446	0.44550535	$53.91	$41.63
Terminal value				$785.49	$606.54
					$735.17

The higher inflation rate in BR leads to a depreciation in the currency's value over time. In addition, the terminal value is computed using the U.S. dollar cash flow of $53.91 million in year 3 and an expected growth rate of 2% (reflecting the inflation rate in U.S. dollars and not in BR):

Terminal Value = $53.91 (1.02) / (.09 – .02) = $785.49 million

The value that we derive for the firm today is $735.17 million (1,470.35 million BR). It reflects more consistent assumptions about inflation in the cash flows and discount rates. It is much lower than the value of $1,789.55 million that we derived in the first sidebar.

Local Currency Valuation

The valuation can be done in the local currency, with the discount rate converted into a local currency discount rate. The expected cash flows in this case remain in the local currency. We can overcome the absence of a local currency in three ways:

- **The build-up option:** Since the risk-free rate in any currency can be written as the sum of expected inflation in that currency and the expected real rate, we can try to estimate the two components separately. To estimate expected inflation, we can start with the current inflation rate and extrapolate from that to expected inflation in the future. For the real rate, we can use the rate on the inflation-indexed U.S. Treasury bond rate, with the rationale that real rates should be the same globally. In 2009, for instance, adding the expected inflation rate of 6% in India to the interest rate of 2.55% on the inflation-indexed U.S. Treasury would have yielded a risk-free rate of 8.55% in Indian rupees.

- **The forward exchange rate**: Forward and futures contracts on exchange rates provide information about interest rates in the currencies involved, because interest rate parity governs the relationship between spot and forward rates. For instance, the forward rate between the Thai baht and U.S. dollar can be written as follows:

$$\text{Forward Rate}^{t}_{\text{Baht, \$}} = \text{Spot Rate}_{\text{Baht,\$}} \frac{(1+\text{Interest Rate}_{\text{Thai Baht}})^{t}}{(1+\text{Interest Rate}_{\text{US dollar}})^{t}}$$

If the current spot rate is 38.10 Thai baht per U.S. dollar, the ten-year forward rate is 61.36 baht per dollar, and the current ten-year U.S. Treasury bond rate is 5%, the ten-year Thai risk-free rate (in nominal baht) can be estimated as follows:

$$61.36 = 38.10\ \frac{(1+\text{Interest Rate}_{\text{Thai Baht}})^{10}}{(1.05)^{10}}$$

Solving for the Thai interest rate yields a ten-year risk-free rate of 10.12%. The biggest limitation of this approach, however, is that forward rates are difficult to come by for periods beyond a year[9] for many of the emerging markets, where we would be most interested in using them.

- **The discount rate conversion**: Since it far easier to estimate the other inputs to the discount rate computation, such as the equity risk premium and default spreads, in a mature market currency, the third option is to compute the entire discount rate in the mature market currency and to convert that discount rate (r) into the local currency as the last step:

$$r_{\text{Local Currency}} = (1 + r_{\text{Foreign Currency}})^{*}\frac{(1+\text{Expected Inflation}_{\text{Local Currency}})}{(1+\text{Expected Inflation}_{\text{Foreign Currency}})} - 1$$

For example, assume that the cost of capital computed for an Indonesian company in U.S. dollars is 14% and that the expected inflation rate in Indonesian rupiah is 11% (compared to the 2% inflation rate in U.S. dollars). The Indonesian rupiah cost of capital can be written as follows:

$$\text{Cost of Capital}_{\text{Rupiah}} = (1.14)^{*}\frac{(1.11)}{(1.02)} - 1 = 0.24058 \text{ or } 24.06\%$$

Note that we are building on our earlier theme that the only difference between currencies should be expected inflation. To make this conversion, we still have to estimate the expected inflation in the local currency and the mature market currency.

With all three approaches, we end up with local currency cash flows and local currency discount rates and a consistent value at the end.

9 In cases where only a one-year forward rate exists, an approximation of the long-term rate can be obtained by backing out the one-year local currency borrowing rate, taking the spread over the one-year Treasury bill rate, and adding this spread to the long-term Treasury bond rate. For instance, with a one-year forward rate of 39.95 on the Thai bond, we obtain a one-year Thai baht riskless rate of 9.04% (given a one-year Treasury bill rate of 4%). Adding the spread of 5.04% to the ten-year Treasury bond rate of 5% provides a ten-year Thai baht rate of 10.04%.

Valuing in the Local Currency

In the preceding sidebar, we corrected the inflation mismatch from the first sidebar by doing the entire valuation in U.S. dollars. In this sidebar, we will stay with nominal BR cash flows and convert the dollar cost of capital of 9% into a BR cost of capital, using the expected inflation rates of 2% in U.S. dollars and 6% in BR:

$$\text{Cost of Capital in BR} = \text{Cost of Capital in US \$} * \frac{(1+\text{Expected Inflation}_{BR})}{(1+\text{Expected Inflation}_{US\$})} - 1$$

$$= (1.09) * \frac{(1.06)}{(1.02)} - 1 = .1327 \text{ or } 13.27\%$$

The cash flows in nominal BR are discounted back at 13.27% to estimate the value today, as shown in Table 6.4.

Table 6.4 Cash Flows

Year	Cash Flow in BR	Present Value
1	100	88.28111477
2	110	85.72910747
3	121	83.25087292
Terminal value	1763.142857	1213.084148
Value of firm		1470.345243

The terminal value is estimated using the nominal growth of 6% in BR and the BR cost of capital:

Terminal Value = 121 (1.06) / (.1327 – .06) = 1,763.1428 million BR

Note that the value of the firm is 1,470.35 million BR. That's the same as the valuation we obtained when we valued the company in U.S. dollars in the second sidebar.

The Government Is Not Default-Free

We have so far assumed that governments are default-free, at least when it comes to borrowing in the local currency. That assumption, reasonable though it may seem, can be challenged in some countries where investors built in the likelihood that governments will default even on local currency borrowings.

The Scenario

Our discussion so far has been predicated on the assumption that governments do not default, at least on local currency borrowing. In many emerging-market economies, this assumption might be viewed as unreasonable. Governments in these markets are perceived as capable of defaulting, even on local borrowing. The ratings agencies capture this potential by providing two sovereign ratings for most countries—one for foreign currency borrowing, and the other for local currency borrowing. While the latter is usually higher than the former, several countries have local currency ratings that are not Aaa (the standard from Moody's for a default-free country). Table 6.5 lists local and foreign currency ratings for selected emerging markets. (See Appendix 6.1, at the end of this chapter, for the complete listing.)

Table 6.5 Local and Foreign Currency Ratings for Selected Markets: October 2008

Country	Local Currency Rating	Foreign Currency Rating
Brazil	Ba1	Ba1
China	A1	A1
India	Baa3	Baa2
Russia	Baa2	Baa2

To the extent that we accept Moody's assessment of country risk, the long-term bonds issued by each of these governments will have default risk embedded in them. The risk is greater in the Brazilian government bond than it is in the Chinese government bond.

The Dark Side

When there are local currency long-term bonds, analysts often choose to use the market interest rate on these bonds, notwithstanding the default risk embedded in them, as risk-free rates. For example, the interest rate on long-term rupee-denominated bonds issued by the Indian government in October 2008, which was 10.7%, would be used as the risk-free rate in computing the rupee cost of equity and capital for an Indian company. As shown in Table 6.5, India's local currency rating of Baa3 suggests that the Indian rupee bond has default risk and that some of the observed interest rate can be attributed to this risk. While it may seem reasonable that rupee discount rates should be higher to reflect the Indian government risk, the danger of building it into the risk-free rate is that the risk may end up being double-counted. Analysts who use 10.7% as the risk-free rate for rupee discount rates often also use higher equity risk premiums for India. In fact, one approach to adjusting equity risk premiums in emerging markets is to add the default spread for the country to mature market equity risk premiums.

The Solution

Since the problem in this case is that the local currency bond rate includes a default spread, the solution is fairly simple. If we can estimate how much of the current market interest rate on the bond can be attributed to default risk, we can strip this default spread from the rate to arrive at an estimate of the risk-free rate in that currency. Again using the Indian rupee bond as the illustration, we use the local currency rating for India as the measure of default risk to arrive at a default spread of 2.6%. Subtracting this from the market interest rate yields a risk-free rupee rate of 8.10%:

Risk-Free Rate in Indian Rupees = Market Interest Rate on Rupee Bond – Default Spread$_{India}$

= 10.70% – 2.60% = 8.10%

How did we go from a rating to a default spread? Table 6.6 estimates the typical default spreads for bonds in different sovereign ratings classes in September 2008, computed by comparing sovereign bonds issued in Euros or dollars, where a risk-free rate can be obtained. One problem that we had in estimating the numbers for this table is that relatively few emerging markets have dollar- or euro-denominated bonds outstanding. Consequently, some ratings classes had only one country with data, and several ratings classes had none. To mitigate this problem, we used spreads from the Credit Default Swap (CDS) market. We were able to get default spreads for almost 40 countries, categorized by rating class, and we averaged the spreads across multiple countries in the same ratings class.[10] An alternative approach to estimating default spread is to assume that sovereign ratings are comparable to corporate ratings. In other words, a Ba1-rated country bond and a Ba1-rated corporate bond have equal default risk. In this case, we can use the default spreads on corporate bonds for different ratings classes. Table 6.6 summarizes the typical default spreads for corporate bonds in different ratings classes in September 2008.

Table 6.6 Default Spreads by Sovereign Ratings Class: September 2008

Rating	Sovereign Bonds/CDS	Corporate Bonds
Aaa	0.15%	0.50%
Aa1	0.30%	0.80%
Aa2	0.60%	1.10%
Aa3	0.80%	1.20%
A1	1.00%	1.35%
A2	1.30%	1.45%
A3	1.40%	1.50%
Baa1	1.70%	1.70%
Baa2	2.00%	2.00%
Baa3	2.25%	2.60%
Ba1	2.50%	3.20%
Ba2	3.00%	3.50%
Ba3	3.25%	4.00%
B1	3.50%	4.50%
B2	4.25%	5.50%
B3	5.00%	6.50%

10 For instance, Turkey, Indonesia, and Vietnam all share a Ba3 rating, and the CDS spreads as of September 2008 were 2.95%, 3.15%, and 3.65%, respectively. The average spread across the three countries is 3.25%.

Rating	Sovereign Bonds/CDS	Corporate Bonds
Caa1	6.00%	7.00%
Caa2	6.75%	9.00%
Caa3	7.50%	11.00%

Note that the corporate bond spreads, at least in September 2008, were larger than the sovereign spreads. Using this approach to estimate the default spread for Brazil, with its rating of Ba1, would result in a spread of 2.50% (or 3.20%) if we use sovereign spreads (or corporate spreads).

The Risk-Free Rate May Change Over Time

The default-free long-term interest rate in a currency is the risk-free rate that we use to estimate the costs of equity and capital. However, that rate will change over time, and as it does, so will the valuation. While this is always true, there may be times when the current risk-free rate may seem abnormally high or low, relative to history or fundamentals, and the change over time seems more likely to be in one direction than in the other.

The Scenario

Looking at the history of interest rates in the U.S., we can draw two conclusions. The first is that they are volatile and change over time, more so in some periods than others. The other is that evidence suggests that interest rates in most periods stay within a "normal" range and that deviations above or below this range are corrected over time. Figure 6.6 illustrates both findings by looking at the Treasury bond rate from 1928 to 2008.

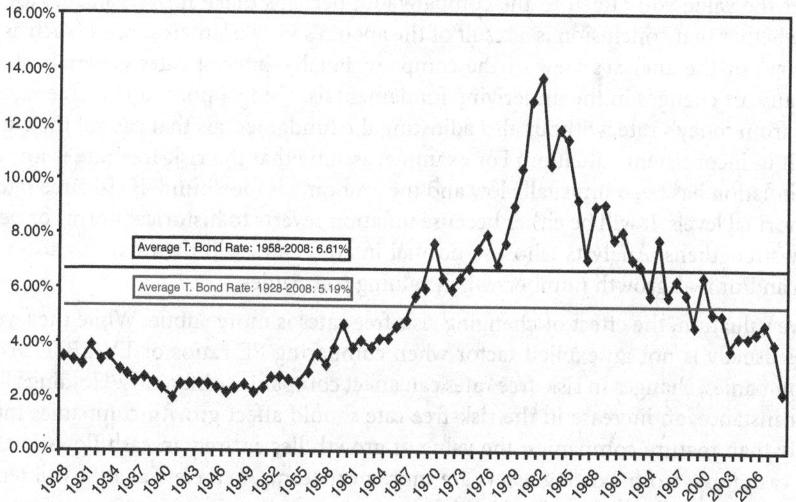

Figure 6.6: U.S. Dollar Risk-Free Rates: 1928 to 2008

Although long periods of interest rate stability occurred, they were interspersed with periods of interest rate volatility. Thus, a long period of stable interest rates in the 1960s was followed by a decade of interest rate volatility in the 1970s. In addition, note that interest rates seem to revert toward a range of 5 to 7% over time; this corresponds to a normal range of rates for the U.S. Note, though, that a degree of subjective judgment goes into estimating this range, because it depends on the time period we look at. For instance, the normal interest rate is much higher if we look at only the last 30 years (average rate = 7.40%) rather than the last 50 years (average rate = 6.61%) or the last 80 years (average rate = 5.19%).

Less historical data exists on long-term interest rates outside the U.S., but we can safely argue that the volatility in interest rates has been far higher in emerging markets, especially in Latin America. The volatility has been driven primarily by changes in inflation expectations over time. In addition, it is far more difficult to set a normal range for rates in these markets, where interest rates have been in triple digits in some periods and single digits in others.

The Dark Side

When confronted with rates that deviate from what they regard as "normal," analysts often substitute what they feel is a more normal rate when valuing companies. If the Treasury bond rate is 3.5%, an analyst may decide to use 5% as the normal risk-free rate in a valuation. Although this may seem logical, three potential problems exist. The first is that "normal" is in the eyes of the beholder. Different analysts make different judgments on what comprises that number. To provide a simple contrast, analysts who started working in the late 1980s in the U.S. use higher normal rates than analysts who joined in 2002 or 2003, reflecting their experiences. The second potential problem is that using a normal risk-free rate, rather than the current interest rate, will have valuation consequences. For instance, using a 5% risk-free rate when valuing a company will lower the value you attach to the company and perhaps make it overvalued. However, it is unclear whether that conclusion is a result of the analyst's view of interest rates (such as that they are too low) or the analyst's view of the company. Finally, interest rates generally change over time because of changes in the underlying fundamentals. Using a normal risk-free rate, which is different from today's rate, without also adjusting the fundamentals that caused the current rate, will result in inconsistent valuation. For example, assume that the risk-free rate is low currently, because inflation has been unusually low and the economy is moribund. If risk-free rates bounce back to normal levels, it will be either because inflation reverts to historical norms or because the economy strengthens. Analysts who use normal interest rates will then have to also use higher inflation and/or real-growth numbers when valuing companies.

In relative valuation, the effect of changing risk-free rates is more subtle. While the level of risk-free rates usually is not an explicit factor when comparing PE ratios or EV/EBITDA multiples across companies, changes in risk-free rates can affect companies differently. Holding all else constant, for instance, an increase in the risk-free rate should affect growth companies much more negatively than mature companies; the value of growth lies entirely in cash flows in the future, whereas cash flows from existing assets are more near-term. A careless analyst will tend to find growth companies to be undervalued in high-interest-rate scenarios and mature companies to be bargains in low-interest-rate scenarios.

Interest Rate Views and Valuation

You are valuing Dow Chemical as a stable growth firm in September 2008, and you make the following assumptions:

- You expect the operating income next year, after taxes, to be $3 billion. This income is expected to grow 3% a year in perpetuity.
- Dow Chemical generated a return on capital of 15% in 2007, and you expect it to maintain this return on capital forever.
- The Treasury bond rate is 4%, and the cost of capital based on this risk-free rate is 8%.

You believe that the Treasury bond rate is too low and that it will revert to its normalized level, which you estimate to be 5%. The cost of capital based on this normalized risk-free rate is 9%.

If you value Dow Chemical using the cost of capital of 9%, your estimate of value for the firm is as follows:

After-Tax Operating Income Next Year = $3 billion

Reinvestment Rate = Expected Growth Rate / Return on Capital = 3 / 15 = 20%

Expected FCFF Next Year = EBIT (1 – t) (1 – Reinvestment Rate)

= 3,000 (1 – .2) = $2,400 million

Value of Firm = Expected FCFF Next Year / (Cost of Capital – g)

= 2,400 / (.09 – .03) = $40,000 million

Because the market value of the firm was $44 billion at the time of the analysis, you would have concluded that the firm was overvalued. However, one reason for your lower value was your use of the normalized risk-free rate of 5%, instead of the actual rate of 4%. Suppose the firm had been valued using the actual cost of capital of 8%:

Value of Firm = Expected FCFF Next Year / (Cost of Capital – g)

= 2,400 / (.08 – .03) = $48,000 million

At its current market value, the firm would have been undervalued. In effect, your initial conclusion about Dow Chemical being overvalued reflected both your assumptions about the company and your views on interest rates. The latter was the main reason for your final conclusion. In effect, your belief that interest rates are too low reduced the value of the firm by $8 billion (from $48 billion to $40 billion).

Solutions

As a general rule, it is not a good idea to bring our idiosyncratic views on interest rates, no matter how well thought-out and reasoned they may be, into individual company valuations. Does this mean we are stuck using the current risk-free rate when valuing companies today? Not necessarily. We can still draw on market expectations of interest rates in valuing companies. For instance, assume that the current ten-year Treasury bond rate is 3.5%. That will be the risk-free rate for the next ten years. However, we can use futures or forward markets on Treasury bonds to get a sense of what the market sees as the expected interest rate ten years from now. Then we can use that as the risk-free rate in the future (perhaps in computing terminal value). Our views on market interest rates can be offered separately, because they do have consequences for the overall value of equities and asset allocation decisions. In effect, we let the users of our research decide what aspect of the research they trust more. If they trust our macro views but not the micro views, they will attach more weight to the interest rate and asset allocation views we present. On the other hand, if they feel more confident in our company analyses than in our interest rate views, they will focus on the corporate valuation and recommendation.

Closing Thoughts on Risk-Free Rates

Looking at the bigger picture, we can break the estimation of a risk-free rate into steps, starting with a choice of currency and working down to include views on future rate levels. The steps are captured in Figure 6.7.

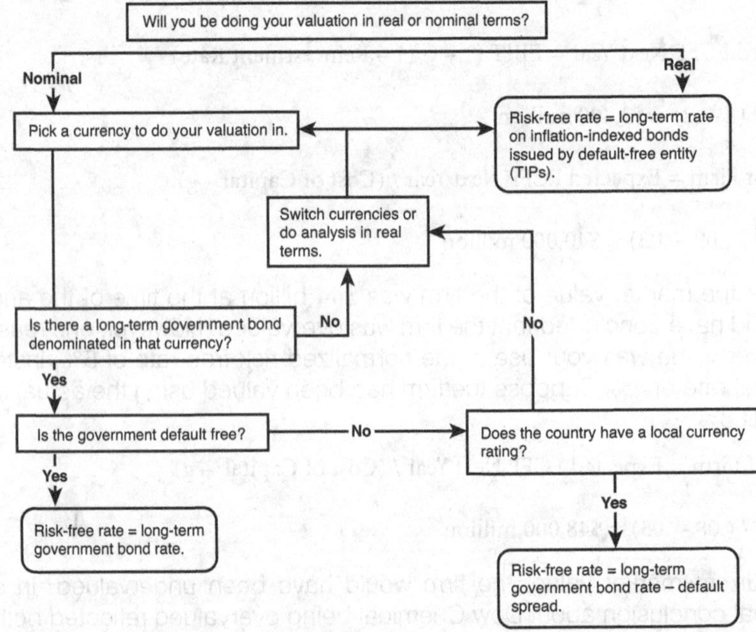

Figure 6.7: A Framework for Estimating Risk-Free Rates

Summarizing the key points made in this chapter, we would list the following as the key rules to follow when it comes to risk-free rates:

- **A risk-free rate should be truly free of risk.** A rate that has risk spreads embedded in it for default or other factors is not a risk-free rate. This is why we argued that local currency government bond rates in many emerging markets cannot be used as the risk-free rate.
- **Choose a risk-free rate that is consistent with how cash flows are defined.** Thus, if the cash flows are real, the risk-free rate should also be real. If the cash flows are in a specific currency, the risk-free rate has to be defined in that currency. In other words, once you choose a currency, the risk-free rate should be for that currency and should not be a function of where a company is incorporated or the investor for whom the valuation is done. When valuing a Russian company in euros, the risk-free rate should be the euro risk-free rate (the German ten-year bond rate).
- **If you have strong views on interest rates, try to keep them out of the valuation of individual companies.** In other words, even if you believe that risk-free rates will rise or fall over time, it is dangerous to reflect those views in your valuation. If you do so, your final valuation will be a joint result of your views on interest rates and your views on the company, with no easy way of deciphering the results of each effect.

Conclusion

The risk-free rate is the starting point for all expected return models. For an investment to be risk-free, it has to meet two conditions. The first is that no risk of default can be associated with its cash flows. The second is that the investment can have no reinvestment risk. Using these criteria, the appropriate risk-free rate to use to obtain expected returns should be a default-free (government) zero coupon rate that is matched up to when the cash flow or flows that are being discounted occur. In practice, however, it is usually appropriate to match up the duration of the risk-free asset to the duration of the cash flows being analyzed. In corporate finance and valuation, this will lead us toward long-term government bond rates as risk-free rates.

This chapter considered three problem scenarios. The first is when there are no long-term, traded government bonds in a specific currency. We suggested either doing the valuation in a different currency or estimating the risk-free rate from forward markets or fundamentals. The second scenario is when the long-term government bond rate has potential default risk embedded in it. In this case, we argued that the risk-free rate in that currency has to be net of the default spread. The third scenario is when the current long-term risk-free rate seems too low or too high, relative to historic norms. Without passing judgments on the efficacy of this view, we noted that it is better to separate our views on interest rates from our assessment of companies.

Appendix 6.1

Table 6A.1 Sovereign Ratings by Country (Moody's)

Country	Foreign	Local	Country	Foreign	Local	Country	Foreign	Local
Albania	B1	B2	Guatemala	Ba2	Ba1	Peru	Ba2	Baa3
Alderney	Aaa	Aaa	Guernsey	Aaa	Aaa	Philippines	B1	B1
Andorra	Aaa	Aaa	Honduras	B2	B2	Poland	A2	A2
Argentina	B3	B3	Hong Kong	Aa2	Aa2	Portugal	Aa2	Aa2
Armenia	Ba2	Ba2	Hungary	A2	A2	Qatar	Aa2	Aa2
Australia	Aaa	Aaa	Iceland	Aaa	Aaa	Romania	Baa3	Baa3
Austria	Aaa	Aaa	India	Baa3	Ba2	Russia	Baa2	Baa2
Azerbaijan	Ba1	Ba1	Indonesia	Ba3	Ba3	San Marino	Aaa	Aaa
Bahamas	A3	A1	Ireland	Aaa	Aaa	Sark	Aaa	Aaa
Bahrain	A2	A2	Isle of Man	Aaa	Aaa	Saudi Arabia	A1	A1
Barbados	Baa2	A3	Israel	A1	A1	Singapore	Aaa	Aaa
Belarus	B1	B1	Italy	Aa2	Aa2	Slovakia	A1	A1
Belgium	Aa1	Aa1	Jamaica	B1	Ba2	Slovenia	Aa2	Aa2
Belize	Caa1	Caa1	Japan	Aaa	A1	South Africa	Baa1	A2
Bermuda	Aa1	Aaa	Jersey	Aaa	Aaa	Spain	Aaa	Aaa
Bolivia	B3	B3	Jordan	Ba2	Baa3	St. Vincent & Grenadines	B1	B1
Bosnia & Herzegovina	B2	B2	Kazakhstan	Baa2	Baa1	Suriname	B1	Ba3
Botswana	A2	A1	Korea	A2	A2	Sweden	Aaa	Aaa
Brazil	Ba1	Ba1	Kuwait	Aa2	Aa2	Switzerland	Aaa	Aaa
Bulgaria	Baa3	Baa3	Latvia	A2	A2	Taiwan	Aa3	Aa3
Cambodia	B2	B2	Lebanon	B3	B3	Thailand	Baa1	Baa1
Canada	Aaa	Aaa	Liechtenstein	Aaa	Aaa	Trinidad & Tobago	Baa1	Baa1
Cayman Islands	Aa3	Aa3	Lithuania	A2	A2	Tunisia	Baa2	Baa2
Chile	A2	A1	Luxembourg	Aaa	Aaa	Turkey	Ba3	Ba3

Country	Foreign	Local	Country	Foreign	Local	Country	Foreign	Local
China	A1	A1	Macao	Aa3	Aa3	Turkmenistan	B2	B2
Colombia	Ba2	Baa3	Malaysia	A3	A3	Ukraine	B1	B1
Costa Rica	Ba1	Ba1	Malta	A1	A1	United Arab Emirates	Aa2	Aa2
Croatia	Baa3	Baa1	Mauritius	Baa2	Baa2	United Kingdom	Aaa	Aaa
Cuba	Caa1	NR	Mexico	Baa1	Baa1	United States	Aaa	Aaa
Cyprus	Aa3	Aa3	Moldova	Caa1	Caa1	Uruguay	B1	B1
Czech Republic	A1	A1	Monaco	Aaa	Aaa	Venezuela	B2	B1
Denmark	Aaa	Aaa	Mongolia	B1	B1	Vietnam	Ba3	Ba3
Dominican Republic	B2	B2	Montenegro	Ba2	—			
Ecuador	B3	—	Morocco	Ba1	Ba1			
Egypt	Ba1	Baa3	Netherlands	Aaa	Aaa			
El Salvador	Baa3	Baa2	New Zealand	Aaa	Aaa			
Estonia	A1	A1	Nicaragua	Caa1	B3			
Eurozone	Aaa	Aaa	Norway	Aaa	Aaa			
Fiji Islands	Ba2	Ba2	Orman	A2	A2			
Finland	Aaa	Aaa	Pakistan	B1	B1			
France	Aaa	Aaa	Panama	Ba1	—			
Germany	Aaa	Aaa	Papua New Guinea	B1	B1			
Greece	A1	A1	Paraguay	B3	B3			

7

Risky Ventures: Assessing the Price of Risk

Most investments and assets that we are called on to value have some or a great deal of risk embedded in them. While part of the challenge in valuing a business is assessing the risk in that business, it is just as important that we estimate the price the market is demanding for taking this risk. The former is specific to individual assets, and the latter is a more general assessment that affects how we value all assets.

This chapter considers two inputs that affect every valuation. The first is the equity risk premium—the premium that investors demand for investing in the average-risk equity investment. The second is default spreads, which lenders charge as premiums over the risk-free rate for lending money to a business. We begin by looking at why the price of risk matters across valuations, and we move on to consider the determinants of risk premiums and why these premiums may change over time. We then look at conventional practices used to estimate these numbers and the potential problems in these practices. Finally, we look at scenarios where assessing a price for risk becomes difficult, how the dark side beckons, and some ways to avoid going over to the dark side.

Why Do Risk Premiums Matter?

The price of risk is key to assessing the cost of funding to a firm. We can use the financial balance sheet introduced in Chapter 1 to illustrate this concept, as shown in Figure 7.1.

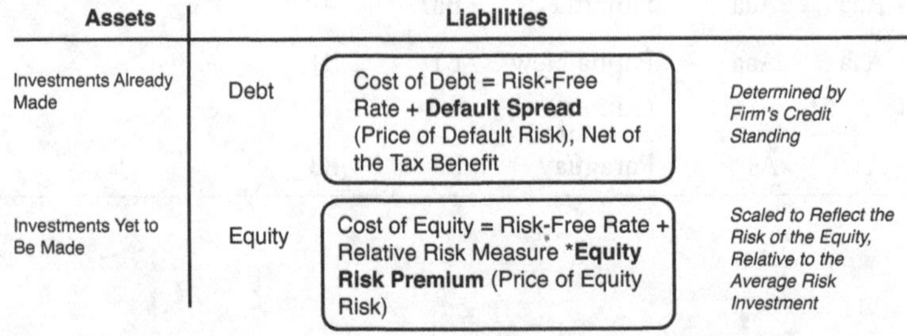

Figure 7.1: The Price of Risk: Effects on Funding Costs

Note that both the cost of equity and the cost of debt are a function not only of the risk characteristics of the business being analyzed—its credit standing and relative risk measure—but also of the market prices that we attach to default risk (default spread) and the equity risk (equity risk premium). The latter applies across all investments, whereas the former is investment-specific.

Consider the cost of equity first. Chapter 2, "Intrinsic Valuation," noted that all the risk-and-return models we use to estimate the cost of equity share a common focus on measuring only the risk that cannot be diversified away. The differences are in how we measure the nondiversifiable risk. In the capital asset pricing model (CAPM), the market risk is measured with a beta. When multiplied by the equity risk premium, this beta yields the total risk premium for a risky asset. In the competing models, such as the arbitrage pricing and multifactor models, betas are estimated against individual market risk factors, and each factor has it own price (risk premium). Table 7.1 summarizes four models and the role that equity risk premiums play in each one.

Table 7.1 Equity Risk Premiums in Risk-and-Return Models

	Model	Equity Risk Premium
CAPM	Expected Return = Risk-Free Rate + $\text{Beta}_{\text{Asset}}$ (Equity Risk Premium)	Risk premium for investing in the market portfolio, which includes all risky assets, relative to the riskless rate
Arbitrage pricing model (APM)	$\text{Expected Return} = \text{Risk-Free Rate} + \sum_{j=1}^{j=k} \beta_j (\text{Risk Premium}_j)$	Risk premiums for individual (unspecified) market risk factors
Multifactor model	$\text{Expected Return} = \text{Risk-Free Rate} + \sum_{j=1}^{j=k} \beta_j (\text{Risk Premium}_j)$	Risk premiums for individual (specified) market risk factors
Proxy models	Expected Return = a + b (Proxy 1) + c (Proxy 2) (Where the Proxies Are Firm Characteristics Such as Market Capitalization, Price-to-Book Ratios, or Return Momentum)	No explicit risk premium computation, but coefficients on proxies reflect risk preferences

All the models other than proxy models require three inputs. The first is the risk-free rate. This is easy to estimate in currencies where a default-free entity exists, but it's more complicated in markets that have no default-free entities. The second input is the beta (in the CAPM) or betas (in the APM or multifactor models) of the investment being analyzed. We considered the challenges associated with estimating the risk-free rate in the preceding chapter. We will return to the question of how best to estimate betas for individual firms in the coming chapters. The third input is the appropriate risk premium for the portfolio of all risky assets (in the CAPM) and the factor risk premiums for the market risk factors in the APM and multifactor models. Note that the equity risk premium in all these models is a market-wide number, in the sense that it is not company-specific or asset-specific but affects expected returns on all risky investments. Using a larger equity risk premium increases the expected returns for all risky investments and, by extension, reduces their value. Consequently, the choice of an equity risk premium may have much larger consequences for value than firm-specific inputs such as cash flows, growth, and even firm-specific risk measures (such as betas).

The cost of debt is a function of the firm's default risk and the price that the market attaches in the form of a default spread (over and above the risk-free rate) to reflect that risk:

Cost of Debt = Risk-Free Rate + Default Spread, Given Default Risk

Again, while the first input is company-specific, the second is market-wide. When default spreads increase, the cost of debt rises for all firms, although the magnitude of the increase will vary across firms.

The price of risk encompasses both the equity risk premium and the default spread. While these two variables may not always move together, we would expect them to be affected by the same factors. If investors become more worried about risk and demand a larger premium when investing in equities, we would also expect default spreads to go up. We will look at the determinants of both measures in the next section.

What Are the Determinants of Risk Premiums?

If equity risk premiums and default spreads were constant, estimating them would be much easier. However, both measures change over time. This section considers the determinants of equity risk premiums and then extends the discussion to cover default spreads.

Equity Risk Premiums

The equity risk premium reflects the "extra" return that investors demand for investing in equities (or risky assets) as a class, relative to the risk-free investment. Not surprisingly, it is affected by almost everything that occurs in the overall economy. In particular, we would expect it to be a function of the following:

- **Risk aversion**: The first and most critical factor, obviously, is the risk aversion of investors in the markets. As investors become more risk-averse, equity risk premiums climb, and as risk aversion declines, equity risk premiums fall. While risk aversion varies across investors, it is the collective risk aversion of investors that determines equity risk premium. Changes in that collective risk aversion manifest themselves as changes in the equity risk premium. Relating risk aversion to expected equity risk premiums is not as easy as it looks. The direction of the relationship is fairly simple to establish—higher risk aversion should translate into higher equity risk premiums. But getting beyond that requires us to be more precise in our judgments about investor utility functions, specifying how investor utility relates to wealth (and variance in that wealth). As we will see later in this chapter, it is widely believed that most conventional utility models do not do a good job of explaining observed equity risk premiums.
- **Economic risk**: The risk in equities as a class comes from more general concerns about the health and predictability of the overall economy. Put in more intuitive terms, the equity risk premium should be lower in an economy with predictable inflation, interest rates, and economic growth than in one where these variables are volatile.

  A related strand of research examines the relationship between equity risk premium and inflation, with mixed results. Studies that look at the relationship between the level of inflation and equity risk premiums find little or no correlation. In contrast, Brandt and Wang (2003) argue that news about inflation dominates news about real economic growth and consumption in determining risk aversion and risk premiums.[1] They present evidence that equity risk premiums tend to increase if inflation is higher than anticipated and decrease when it is lower than expected. Reconciling the findings, it seems reasonable to conclude that it is not so much the level of inflation that determines equity risk premiums but uncertainty about that level.

- **Information**: When you invest in equities, the risk in the underlying economy is manifested in volatility in the earnings and cash flows reported by individual firms in that economy. Information about these changes is transmitted to markets in multiple ways. It is clear that significant changes have occurred in both the quantity and quality of information available to investors over the last two decades. During the market boom of the late 1990s, some people argued that the lower equity risk premiums we observed in that period reflected the fact that investors had access to more information about their investments, leading to higher confidence and lower risk premiums in 2000. After the accounting scandals that followed the market collapse, others attributed the increase in the equity risk premium to deteriorating quality of information as well as information overload. In effect, they argued that easy access to large amounts of information of varying reliability was making investors less certain about the future. Information differences may therefore be one reason why investors demand larger risk premiums in some emerging markets than in others. After all, markets vary widely in terms of transparency and information disclosure requirements. Markets like Russia, where firms provide little (and often flawed) information about operations and corporate governance, should have higher risk premiums than markets like India, where information on firms is not only more reliable but also much more easily accessible to investors.
- **Liquidity**: In addition to the risk from the underlying real economy and imprecise information from firms, equity investors also have to consider the additional risk created by illiquidity. If investors have to accept large discounts on estimated value or pay high transaction costs to liquidate equity positions, they will pay less for equities today (and thus demand a larger risk premium). The notion that the market for publicly traded stocks is wide and deep has led to the argument that the net effect of illiquidity on aggregate equity risk premiums should be small. However, there are two reasons to be skeptical about this argument. The first is that not all stocks are widely traded, and illiquidity can vary widely across stocks; the cost of trading a widely held, large market cap stock is very small, but the cost of trading an over-the-counter stock is much higher. The second reason is that the cost of illiquidity in the aggregate can vary over time, and even small variations can have significant effects on equity risk premiums. In particular, the cost of illiquidity seems to increase when economies slow down and during periods of crisis, thus exaggerating the effects of both phenomena on the equity risk premium.
- **Catastrophic risk**: When investing in equities, the potential for catastrophic risk always exists. These are events that occur infrequently but can cause dramatic drops in wealth. Examples in equity markets include the Great Depression from 1929 to 1930 in the U.S. and the collapse of Japanese equities in the late 1980s. In cases like these, many investors exposed to the market declines saw the values of their investments drop so much that it

1 Brandt, M. W. and K. Q. Wang (2003). "Time-varying risk aversion and unexpected inflation," *Journal of Monetary Economics*, v50, pp. 1457–1498.

was unlikely that they would be made whole again in their lifetimes.[2] While the possibility of catastrophic events may be low, they cannot be ruled out, and the equity risk premium has to reflect that risk.

Default Spreads

Equity risk premiums measure what investors demand for investing in equities. Default spreads are the risk premium for investing in risky corporate bonds. Therefore, at least some of the determinants of both should overlap. The twist is that lenders are (or should be) far more concerned about downside risk—especially about whether they will receive their promised payments (interest and principal).

Two of the key determinants of equity risk premiums also play a role in determining default spreads. The first is risk aversion. As investors in bond markets become more (or less) risk-averse, we would expect default spreads to increase (or decrease). Since the same investors often invest in both stock and bond markets, movements in risk aversion tend to affect both equity risk premiums and default spreads in the same direction at the same time. The second determinant is economic risk. As economies become more volatile, the earnings at companies reflect that volatility. While equity investors react to this increased volatility by demanding a higher equity risk premium, bond investors also are affected, since more volatile earnings increase the likelihood that firms will be unable to make their interest payments in the future. As you will see in the next section, default spreads have generally widened during periods of economic slowdown and uncertainty and have shrunk when economies are healthy and stable.

Standard Approaches for Estimating Risk Premiums

How do analysts estimate the equity risk premium(s) and default spreads to use when doing valuation? The answer may vary across analysts, but we will focus on the most common approaches used to estimate the two measures.

Equity Risk Premiums

The most widely used approach to estimating equity risk premiums is the historical premium approach. The actual returns earned on stocks over a long time period are estimated and are compared to the actual returns earned on a default-free (usually government) security. The difference, on an annual basis, between the two returns is computed; it represents the historical risk premium. This section takes a closer look at this approach. While users of risk-and-return models may have developed a consensus that historical premium is the best estimate of the risk premium looking forward, there are surprisingly large differences in the actual premiums we observe being used in practice. The numbers range from 3% at the lower end to 12% at the upper end. Given that we are almost all looking at the same historical data, these differences may seem surprising. However, three reasons explain the divergence in risk premiums: different time periods for estimation, differences in risk-free rates and market indices, and differences in how returns are averaged over time.

2 An investor in the U.S. equity markets who invested just prior to the crash of 1929 would not have seen index levels return to precrash levels until the 1940s. An investor in the Nikkei in 1987, when the index was at 40000, would still be facing a deficit of 50% (even after counting dividends) in 2008.

- **Time period used**: Even if we agree that historical risk premiums are the best estimates of future equity risk premiums, we can still disagree about how far back in time we should go to estimate this premium. Ibbotson Associates, which is the most widely used estimation service, has stock return data and risk-free rates going back to 1926.[3] Other less widely used databases go back to 1871 or even 1802.[4] Although many analysts use all the data going back to the inception date, almost as many analysts use data over shorter time periods, such as 50, 20, or even 10 years, to come up with historical risk premiums.
- **Risk-free rate and market index**: We can compare the expected return on stocks to either short-term government securities (Treasury bills) or long-term government securities (Treasury bonds). The risk premium for stocks can be estimated relative to either. Given that the yield curve in the U.S. has been upward-sloping for most of the last eight decades, the risk premium is larger when estimated relative to short-term government securities (such as Treasury bills) than when estimated against Treasury bonds. The historical risk premium may also be affected by how stock returns are estimated. Using an index with a long history, such as the Dow 30, seems like an obvious solution, but returns on the Dow may not be a good reflection of overall returns on stocks. Consequently, many services fall back on broader indices such as the S&P 500 to estimate stock returns on an annual basis.
- **Averaging approach**: The final sticking point when it comes to estimating historical premiums relates to how the average returns on stocks, Treasury bonds, and bills are computed. The arithmetic average return measures the simple mean of the series of annual returns, whereas the geometric average looks at the compounded return.[5]

$$\text{Geometric Average} = \left(\frac{\text{Value}_N}{\text{Value}_0}\right)^{1/N} - 1$$

The questions of how far back in time to go, what risk-free rate to use, and how to average returns (arithmetic or geometric) may seem trivial—until you see the effect that the choices you make have on your equity risk premium. Rather than rely on the summary values that are provided by data services, we will use raw return data on stocks, Treasury bills, and Treasury bonds from 1928 to 2008 to make this assessment.[6] How much will the premium change if we make different choices on historical time periods, risk-free rates, and averaging approaches? To answer this question, Table 7.2 estimates the arithmetic and geometric risk premiums for stocks over both Treasury bills and bonds over different time periods.

3 Ibbotson Associates, Stocks, Bonds, Bills and Inflation, 2007 Edition.

4 Siegel, in his book *Stocks for the Long Run*, estimates the equity risk premium from 1802 to 1870 to be 2.2% and from 1871 to 1925 to be 2.9%. (Siegel, Jeremy J., *Stocks for the Long Run*, Second Edition, McGraw Hill, 1998.)

5 The compounded return is computed by taking the value of the investment at the start of the period (Value_0) and the value at the end (Value_N) and then computing the following:

6 The raw data for Treasury rates is obtained from the Federal Reserve data archive at the Fed site in St. Louis. The six-month Treasury bill rate is used for Treasury bill returns. The ten-year Treasury bond rate is used to compute the returns on a constant-maturity ten-year Treasury bond. The stock returns represent the returns on the S&P 500.

Table 7.2 **Historical Equity Risk Premiums (ERP): Estimation Period, Risk-Free Rate, and Averaging Approach**

	ERP: Stocks Minus Treasury Bills		ERP: Stocks Minus Treasury Bonds	
	Arithmetic	**Geometric**	**Arithmetic**	**Geometric**
1928–2008	7.30%	5.32%	5.65%	3.88%
1967–2008	5.14%	3.77%	3.33%	2.29%
1997–2008	-2.53%	-4.53%	-6.26%	-7.96%

Note that, even considering only three slices of history, the premiums can range from -7.96% to 7.30%, depending on the choices made. It is not surprising, therefore, that the equity risk premiums used by analysts reflect this uncertainty, with wide differences across analysts on the number used.

Default Spreads

Unlike the equity risk premium, which is an implicit number that is built into stock prices and difficult to decipher, the default spread should be observable at the time a company borrows. In effect, the interest rate on the debt should provide the default spread at least at the time the debt is raised. Two basic approaches are used to estimate the default spread. The first approach is more prevalent among firms that have traded bonds outstanding. The second is used more when a firm has only nontraded (usually bank) debt.

- **Ratings/bond spread approach**: Firms that have bonds outstanding are generally rated for default risk by ratings agencies such as S&P, Moody's, and Fitch. These letter grade ratings reflect how much default risk the agencies see in each firm at the time of the assessment. Moody's, for instance, assigns ratings for bonds that range from Aaa for the safest firms to D for firms that are in default. Going from a rating to a default spread is a simple exercise. Because each ratings class has publicly traded bonds, we can look at the market interest rates that these bonds trade at and back out a default spread for each rating. Table 7.3 summarizes default spreads as of June 2008.

Table 7.3 **Bond Ratings and Default Spreads**

Rating	Typical Default Spread
AAA	0.75%
AA	1.25%
A+	1.40%
A	1.50%
A–	1.70%
BBB	2.50%
BB+	3.20%

Rating	Typical Default Spread
BB	3.65%
B+	4.50%
B	5.65%
B–	6.50%
CCC	7.50%
CC	10.00%
C	12.00%
D	20.00%

Based on this table, a firm with a BBB rating would be assigned a default spread of 2.50% in June 2008. Adding this spread to the risk-free rate will yield a pre-tax cost of debt for the company.

- **Book interest rate approach**: Even in markets like the U.S., where corporate bond issues are common, most companies raise their debt primarily from bank loans. Most of these companies are not rated, thus eliminating the option of using a default spread based on the rating. With these companies, analysts fall back on the debt that is on the books and the interest expense that the firm incurs to estimate a "book interest rate."

$$\text{Book Interest Rate} = \frac{\text{Annual Interest Expense}}{\text{Book Value of Debt}}$$

Thus, if a company reports interest expenses of $10 million on book value of debt of $200 million,s the book interest rate used would be 5%.

Problem Scenarios

The values that we use for the equity risk premium and default spreads clearly have an impact on valuations. This section considers three scenarios in which assessing these numbers may be difficult. The first is in markets that have relatively little historical data, as is the case in many emerging markets. In addition, most companies have only bank loans outstanding and no bond ratings. The second scenario is in markets with historical data, but the data gives mixed signals about the risk premiums to use in the future. The third scenario is when risk premiums are changing as a result of shifting fundamentals, leading to uncertainty about what to use in the future.

No Historical Data and Bond Ratings

We do not realize how dependent we are on historical data for our future estimates of the equity risk premium and default spreads until we are asked to assess these numbers for markets with little or no historical data. This section looks at this scenario, some unhealthy responses to the absence of data, and potential solutions.

The Scenario

Although obtaining historical data for the U.S. market for long periods is easy, that task is much more difficult, if not impossible, in many other markets. This is clearly the case for emerging markets, where equity markets have often been in existence for only a short time (Eastern Europe, China) or have seen substantial changes over the last few years (Latin America, India). This is also true for many West European equity markets. While the economies of Germany, Italy, and France can be categorized as mature, their equity markets did not share the same characteristics until recently. They tended to be dominated by a few large companies, many businesses remained private, and trading was thin except on a few stocks. To add to the estimation problems, most companies in markets like these tend to not issue bonds or have a rating that can be used to assess a cost of debt.

The Dark Side

- **Use a historical risk premium anyway:** Notwithstanding these issues, services have tried to estimate historical risk premiums for non-U.S. markets with the data they have available. To capture some of the danger in this practice, Table 7.4 summarizes historical arithmetic average equity risk premiums for major non-U.S. markets for 1976 to 2001 and reports the standard error in each estimate.[7]

Table 7.4 Risk Premiums for Non-U.S. Markets: 1976 to 2001

Country	Weekly Average	Weekly Standard Deviation	Equity Risk Premium	Standard Error
Canada	0.14%	5.73%	1.69%	3.89%
France	0.40%	6.59%	4.91%	4.48%
Germany	0.28%	6.01%	3.41%	4.08%
Italy	0.32%	7.64%	3.91%	5.19%
Japan	0.32%	6.69%	3.91%	4.54%
UK	0.36%	5.78%	4.41%	3.93%
India	0.34%	8.11%	4.16%	5.51%
Korea	0.51%	11.24%	6.29%	7.64%
Chile	1.19%	10.23%	15.25%	6.95%
Mexico	0.99%	12.19%	12.55%	8.28%
Brazil	0.73%	15.73%	9.12%	10.69%

7 Salomons, R. and H. Grootveld, 2003, "The equity risk premium: Emerging vs. developed markets," *Emerging Markets Review*, v4, 121–144.

Before we attempt to come up with a rationale for why the equity risk premiums vary across countries, it is worth noting the magnitude of the standard errors on the estimates, largely because the estimation period includes only 25 years. Based on these standard errors, we cannot even reject the hypothesis that the equity risk premium in each of these countries is greater than zero, let alone attach a value to that premium. If the standard errors on these estimates make them close to useless, consider how much more noise there is in estimates of historical risk premiums for even younger emerging-market equity markets. These often have a reliable history of ten years or less and very large standard deviations in annual stock returns. Historical risk premiums for emerging markets may provide for interesting anecdotes, but they clearly should not be used in risk-and-return models.

- **Fundamentally flawed premiums**: When analysts use limited historical data to derive equity risk premiums and book interest rates to arrive at costs of debt, they may end up with numbers that are not only implausible, but also impossible. For instance, the risk premium derived for equity over the risk-free rate using only five or ten years of data can be negative if equity markets have declined sharply. While the actual equity risk premium can be negative, the expected equity risk premium cannot. An investor who can receive 4% in a risk-free investment will not invest in equities unless she believes she can earn a higher return. Similarly, when analysts use the book interest rate as the cost of debt, because companies are not rated and have no bonds, the number they derive can be less than the risk-free rate if the firm has old, low-cost, or short-term debt on its books. No firm should be able to borrow money at less than the risk-free rate and pushing through with a cost of debt that assumes that a firm can do so will result in flawed valuations.
- **Switch to a mature market currency/ inputs**: Some analysts in emerging markets, when confronted with an absence of historical data and bond ratings in those markets, switch the currency that they do the valuation in to a mature market currency (say, U.S. dollars). Then they use the equity risk premium from that market in valuation. Thus, an Indonesian company will be valued in U.S. dollars, using the historical risk premium of 3.88% from the U.S., in computing cost of equity. The problem with doing this is that country risk does not disappear just because you switch currencies. Also, the risk premium for Indonesia (in U.S. dollar terms) should be higher than the risk premium in the U.S., whether you do your analysis in Indonesian rupiah or U.S. dollars.

Solutions

When little or no historical data exists for computing equity risk premiums, and no default spreads are available to compute the cost of debt, there are solutions that yield reasonable approximations. For equity risk premiums, we can start with a mature market equity risk premium and build up to a country risk premium. For the cost of debt and default spreads, we can come up with our own estimates of bond ratings for companies (synthetic ratings) and extend mature market default spreads to come up with a cost of borrowing money.

Equity Risk Premiums: Mature Market Plus

With emerging markets, we will almost never have access to as much historical data as we do in the U.S. If we combine this with the high volatility in stock returns in these markets, the conclusion is that historical risk premiums can be computed for these markets, but they will be useless because of the large standard errors in the estimates. Consequently, it makes sense to build equity risk premium estimates for emerging markets from mature market historical risk premiums.

$$\text{Equity Risk Premium}_{\text{Emerging Market}} = \text{Equity Risk Premium}_{\text{Mature Market}} + \text{Country Risk Premium}$$

To estimate the base premium for a mature equity market, we will argue that the U.S. equity market is a mature market and that the U.S. has sufficient historical data to make a reasonable estimate of the risk premium. In the following example, we estimate the equity risk premium for an emerging market in September 2008. Looking at the historical data for the U.S., we estimated the geometric average premium earned by stocks over Treasury bonds of 4.79% between 1928 and 2007. To estimate the country risk premium, we can use one of three approaches:

- **Country bond default spreads**: One of the simplest and most easily accessible country risk measures is the rating assigned to a country's debt by a ratings agency. (S&P, Moody's, and IBCA all rate countries.) These ratings measure default risk (rather than equity risk), but they are affected by many of the factors that drive equity risk—the stability of a country's currency, its budget and trade balances, and its political stability, for instance.[8] The other advantage of ratings is that they can be used to estimate default spreads over a riskless rate. For instance, Brazil was rated Ba1 in September 2008 by Moody's. The Brazilian ten-year dollar-denominated bond was priced to yield 5.95%, 2.15% more than the interest rate (3.80%) on a ten-year Treasury bond at the same time.[9] Analysts who use default spreads as measures of country risk typically add them to both the cost of equity and debt of every company traded in that country. If we assume that the total equity risk premium for the U.S. and other mature equity markets is 4.79%, the risk premium for Brazil would be 6.94%.[10]
- **Relative standard deviation**: Some analysts believe that the equity risk premiums of markets should reflect the differences in equity risk, as measured by the volatilities of equities in these markets. A conventional measure of equity risk is the standard deviation in stock prices; higher standard deviations are generally associated with more risk. If we scale the standard deviation of one market against another, we obtain a measure of relative risk:

$$\text{Relative Standard Deviation}_{\text{Country X}} = \frac{\text{Standard Deviation}_{\text{Country X}}}{\text{Standard Deviation}_{\text{US}}}$$

8 The process by which country ratings are obtained is explained on the S&P website at http://www.ratings.standardpoor.com/criteria/index.htm.

9 These yields were as of September 1, 2008. While this is a market rate and reflects current expectations, country bond spreads are extremely volatile and can shift significantly from day to day. To counter this volatility, the default spread can be normalized by averaging the spread over time or by using the average default spread for all countries with the same rating as Brazil in September 2008.

10 If a country has a sovereign rating and no dollar-denominated bonds, we can use a typical spread based on the rating as the default spread for the country. These numbers are available on my website, http://www.damodaran.com.

This relative standard deviation when multiplied by the premium used for U.S. stocks should yield a measure of the total risk premium for any market:

$$\text{Equity Risk Premium}_{\text{Country X}} = \text{Risk Premium}_{\text{US}} * \text{Relative Standard Deviation}_{\text{Country X}}$$

Assume, for the moment, that we are using a mature market premium for the U.S. of 4.79%. The annualized standard deviation in the S&P 500 between 2006 and 2008, using weekly returns, was 15.27%. In contrast, the standard deviation in the Bovespa (the Brazilian equity index) over the same period was 25.83%.[11] Using these values, the estimate of a total risk premium for Brazil in September 2008 would be as follows:

$$\text{Equity Risk Premium}_{\text{Brazil}} = 4.79\% * \frac{25.83\%}{15.27\%} = 8.10\%$$

The country risk premium can be isolated as follows:

$$\text{Country Risk Premium}_{\text{Brazil}} = 8.10\% - 4.79\% = 3.31\%$$

Although this approach has intuitive appeal, there are problems with comparing standard deviations computed in markets with widely different market structures and liquidity. There are very risky emerging markets that have low standard deviations for their equity markets because the markets are illiquid. This approach understates the equity risk premiums in those markets.

- **Default spreads plus relative standard deviations:** The country default spreads that come with country ratings are an important first step, but they still measure only the premium for default risk. Intuitively, we would expect the country equity risk premium to be larger than the country default risk spread. To address the issue of how much higher, we look at the volatility of the equity market in a country relative to the volatility of the sovereign bond used to estimate the spread. This yields the following estimate for the country equity risk premium:

  $$\text{Country Risk Premium} = \text{Country Default Spread} * \left(\frac{\sigma_{\text{Equity}}}{\sigma_{\text{Country Bond}}}\right)$$

  To illustrate, consider again the case of Brazil. As noted earlier, the default spread on the Brazilian dollar-denominated bond in September 2008 was 2.15%, and the annualized standard deviation in the Brazilian equity index over the previous year was 25.83%. Using two years of weekly returns, the annualized standard deviation in the Brazilian dollar-denominated ten-year bond was 12.55%.[12] The resulting country equity risk premium for Brazil is as follows:

  $$\text{Brazil's Additional Equity Risk Premium} = 2.15\%\left(\frac{25.83\%}{12.55\%}\right) = 4.43\%$$

11 If the dependence on historical volatility is troubling, the options market can be used to get implied volatilities for both the U.S. market (about 20%) and the Bovespa (about 38%).

12 Both standard deviations are computed on returns—returns on the equity index and returns on the ten-year bond.

Unlike the equity standard deviation approach, this premium is in addition to a mature market equity risk premium. Note that this country risk premium will increase if the country rating drops or if the relative volatility of the equity market increases. It is also in addition to the equity risk premium for a mature market. Thus, the total equity risk premium for Brazil using this approach and a 4.79% premium for the U.S. would be 9.22%. Both this approach and the previous one use the standard deviation in equity of a market to make a judgment about country risk premium, but they measure it relative to different bases. This approach uses the country bond as a base, whereas the previous one uses the standard deviation in the U.S. market. This approach assumes that investors are more likely to choose between Brazilian government bonds and Brazilian equity, whereas the previous approach assumes that the choice is across equity markets.

Cost of Debt

It is true that most companies that have bonds and bond ratings are in developed markets and that the preponderance of these companies are in the U.S. Table 7.3, which relates default spreads to bond ratings, was developed from the observed rates on traded corporate bonds in the U.S. In emerging markets and even in many developed markets (Western Europe and Japan), both inputs into the cost of debt estimation process become more difficult to obtain. Not only are most companies not rated (and debt is generally nontraded bank debt), but there are not enough companies to develop a ratings table similar to Table 7.3 in these countries.

Rather than fall back on book interest rates, which is what most analysts do, or make unrealistic estimates of the cost of debt, we propose a two-step solution:

1. **Estimate synthetic ratings.** A company's bond rating is based mostly on publicly available information on its cash flow-generating capacity, the stability of the cash flows, and the debt commitments it has made. Consequently, there is no reason why we cannot estimate a company's rating using the same financial ratios that ratings agencies use in their estimation process. We described one variation of this process in Chapter 2, where we based the rating on the firm's interest coverage ratio.

2. **Adapt U.S. default spreads to other markets.** In the first step, we extend the default spreads estimated from U.S. corporate bonds to other markets. In doing so, we make two assumptions. The first is that the price charged for default risk should be standardized across markets, since differences can be exploited by multinational companies. Thus, if the default spreads charged by European banks are consistently lower than the default spreads in U.S. corporate bonds, U.S. companies borrow from European banks rather than issue bonds. Similarly, if the default spreads in U.S. corporate bonds are consistently lower than European bank default spreads, European companies raise debt by issuing bonds in the U.S. The second assumption is that the default spreads, which are computed based on U.S. dollar-denominated bonds, can be adapted to different currencies. Thus, if the spread on a BBB-rated bond is 2.00% in the U.S., we can use the same spread over the euro risk-free rate to estimate the pre-tax cost of debt for a BBB-rated European company. This practice may work with the euro, since the risk-free rates are similar to U.S. dollar risk-free rates, but it may be dangerous if done in a currency with very different risk-free rates. For instance, it is unlikely that a BBB-rated company in Indonesia will be able to borrow at a default spread of 2% over the Indonesian risk-free rate of 12%. We

should expect the spread to increase as interest rates go up. The simplest solution to this problem is to estimate the cost of debt for the Indonesian company in U.S. dollars first, by adding the U.S. dollar default spread to the Treasury bond rate. Then we convert the U.S. dollar cost of debt into an Indonesian rupiah cost of debt by bringing in the differential inflation between the two currencies:

$$\text{Rupiah Cost of Debt} = (1 + \text{Cost of Debt}_{US\,\$})\,\frac{1+\text{Expected Inflation}_{\text{Rupiah}})}{(1+\text{Expected Inflation}_{US\,\$})} - 1$$

Thus, if the U.S. dollar cost of debt for an Indonesian company is 6%, and the expected inflation rates are 2% in U.S. dollars and 10% in rupiah, the rupiah cost of debt for that company will be the following:

$$\text{Rupiah Cost of Debt} = (1.06)\frac{(1.10)}{(1.02)} - 1 = 0.1431 \text{ or } 14.31\%$$

Historical Data Is Inconclusive

Even for markets like the U.S., which has substantial historical data stretching back decades for stock and bond returns, the historical risk premium comes with a substantial error term. This section considers some of the problems with trusting history to deliver a reasonable equity risk premium, the unhealthy responses to this uncertainty, and how we can arrive at more precise estimates of risk premiums for the future.

The Scenario

In the conventional approach for estimating the equity risk premium, we compute the average return we would have earned investing in stocks over very long time periods. Then we compare this to the average return we would have earned investing in Treasury bonds. In the process, though, we run into two issues. The first is that a historical risk premium, even over very long time periods, comes with significant estimation error. The second is that a market with a long history of returns is also likely to be a successful survivor market, which introduces bias into the estimated premium.

Noisy Estimates

In the preceding section, we pointed out the standard errors in risk premium estimates over short periods in emerging markets, and we used those standard errors as a rationale for not trusting historical premiums. As we use more historical data, the standard errors in the risk premium estimates should decline, but they remain stubbornly high even when we use 80 or 100 years of data. In fact, given the annual standard deviation in stock prices[13] between 1926 and 2008 of 20%, the standard error[14] associated with the risk premium estimate can be estimated for different estimation periods, as shown in Table 7.5.

13 For historical data on stock returns, bond returns, and bill returns, check under "updated data" at www.stern.nyu.edu/~adamodar.

14 These estimates of the standard error are probably understated, because they are based on the assumption that annual returns are uncorrelated over time. Substantial empirical evidence exists that returns are correlated over time, which would make this standard error estimate much larger.

Table 7.5 Standard Errors in Historical Risk Premiums

Estimation Period	Standard Error of Risk Premium Estimate
5 years	$20\% / \sqrt{5} = 8.94\%$
10 years	$20\% / \sqrt{10} = 6.32\%$
25 years	$20\% / \sqrt{25} = 4.00\%$
50 years	$20\% / \sqrt{50} = 2.83\%$
80 years	$20\% / \sqrt{80} = 2.23\%$

Even using the entire time period (approximately 80 years) yields a substantial standard error of 2.23%. Note that the standard errors from ten-year and 25-year estimates are likely to be almost as large as or larger than the actual risk premium estimated. This cost of using shorter time periods seems, in our view, to overwhelm any advantages associated with getting a more updated premium.

What are the costs of going back even further in time (to 1871 or before)? First, the data is much less reliable from earlier time periods, when trading was lighter and record keeping more haphazard. Second, and more important, the market itself has changed over time, resulting in risk premiums that may not be appropriate for today. The U.S. equity market in 1871 more closely resembled an emerging market, in terms of volatility and risk, than a mature market. Consequently, using the earlier data may yield premiums that have little relevance for today's markets.

Survivor Bias

Given how widely the historical risk premium approach is used, it is surprising that the flaws in the approach have not drawn more attention. Consider first the underlying assumption that investors' risk premiums have not changed over time and that the average risk investment (in the market portfolio) has remained stable over the period examined. We would be hard-pressed to find anyone who would be willing to sustain this argument with fervor. The obvious fix for this problem, which is to use a more recent time period, runs directly into a second problem—the large noise associated with historical risk premium estimates. While these standard errors may be tolerable for very long time periods, they clearly are unacceptably high when shorter periods are used.

Even if a sufficiently long period of history is available, and investors' risk aversion has not changed in a systematic way over that period, a problem remains. Markets such as the U.S., which have long periods of equity market history, represent "survivor markets." In other words, assume that you had invested in the largest equity markets in the world in 1926, of which the U.S. was one.[15] From 1926 to 2000, investments in many of the other equity markets would have earned much smaller premiums than the U.S. equity market, and some of them would have resulted in investors earning little or even negative returns over the period. Thus, the survivor bias will result in historical premiums that are larger than expected for markets like the U.S., even assuming that investors are rational and factor risk into prices.

15 Jorion, Philippe and William N. Goetzmann, 1999, "Global Stock Markets in the Twentieth Century," *Journal of Finance*, 54(3), 953–980. They looked at 39 different equity markets and concluded that the U.S. was the best-performing market from 1921 to the end of the century. They estimated a geometric average premium of 3.84% across all the equity markets they looked at, rather than just the U.S.

The Dark Side

If equity risk premiums estimated even over very long time periods have significant standard errors (noise) associated with them, how do analysts deal with the problem? Some ignore the noise and use risk premiums estimated by widely used estimation services as a shield against questions about the numbers they use. Others use the noise in the estimates to serve their purposes, essentially using whatever premium best fits their biases, and arguing that the premium falls within the range of reasonable numbers.

- **Outsource the premium**: Several services provide estimates of equity risk premiums to analysts, for a price. Perhaps the best-known and oldest service to provide this data is Ibbotson Associates, a Chicago-based service that has estimated risk premiums using historical data on stocks and bonds in the U.S. since the 1970s. Since Ibbotson equity risk premiums are widely used and are backed up by stock return data going back to 1926, analysts who use these premiums are seldom challenged. Without taking a stand on whether Ibbotson equity risk premiums are "good" estimates, it seemingly would be a dereliction of valuation duty to allow one of the most critical numbers in valuation to be a number provided by a service, and thus beyond debate.
- **Biased premium**: Earlier, we noted that the equity risk premium derived from historical data is likely to have a significant standard error associated with it. Put in more pragmatic terms, historical data on stock and bond returns provides us with a range on the equity risk premium, rather than a number. Some analysts use the fact that the equity risk premium falls within a fairly wide range to full advantage. They use the lower end of the range (or lower-risk premiums) if they want to inflate the value of a business and the higher end of the range (or higher-risk premiums) if they want to reduce the value. In either case, they let their biases dictate the risk premium to use in valuation.

Solutions

If the equity risk premium, even over periods as long as 80 years, is noisy, and it's possible that the "survivor bias" in equity markets is increasing the equity risk premium, we have to look for ways to narrow the error term on the estimates. This section considers two alternatives. In the global approach, we look at equity risk premiums in different markets globally and try to use the data to estimate a market's equity risk premium. In the implied premium approach, we abandon historical risk premiums altogether and use current stock prices to back out equity risk premiums.

Global Premiums

How can we mitigate survivor bias? One solution is to look at historical risk premiums across multiple equity markets across very long time periods. In the most comprehensive attempt at this analysis, Dimson, Marsh, and Staunton (2002, 2006) estimated equity returns for 17 markets from 1900 to 2005. Their results are summarized in Table 7.6.[16]

16 Dimson, E., P. Marsh, and M. Staunton, 2002, *Triumph of the Optimists: 101 Years of Global Investment Returns*, Princeton University Press, NJ; *Global Investment Returns Yearbook*, 2006, ABN AMRO/London Business School.

Table 7.6 Historical Risk Premiums Across Equity Markets: 1900 to 2005

	Stocks Minus Short-Term Governments				Stocks Minus Long-Term Governments			
Country	Geometric Mean	Arithmetic Mean	Standard Error	Standard Deviation	Geometric Mean	Arithmetic Mean	Standard Error	Standard Deviation
Australia	7.08	8.49	1.65	17.00	6.22	7.81	1.83	18.80
Belgium	2.80	4.99	2.24	23.06	2.57	4.37	1.95	20.10
Canada	4.54	5.88	1.62	16.71	4.15	5.67	1.74	17.95
Denmark	2.87	4.51	1.93	19.85	2.07	3.27	1.57	16.18
France	6.79	9.27	2.35	24.19	3.86	6.03	2.16	22.29
Germany	3.83	9.07	3.28	33.49	5.28	8.35	2.69	27.41
Ireland	4.09	5.98	1.97	20.33	3.62	5.18	1.78	18.37
Italy	6.55	10.46	3.12	32.09	4.30	7.68	2.89	29.73
Japan	6.67	9.84	2.70	27.82	5.91	9.98	3.21	33.06
Netherlands	4.55	6.61	2.17	22.36	3.86	5.95	2.10	21.63
Norway	3.07	5.70	2.52	25.90	2.55	5.26	2.66	27.43
South Africa	6.20	8.25	2.15	22.09	5.35	7.03	1.88	19.32
Spain	3.40	5.46	2.08	21.45	2.32	4.21	1.96	20.20
Sweden	5.73	7.98	2.15	22.09	5.21	7.51	2.17	22.34
Switzerland	3.63	5.29	1.82	18.79	1.80	3.28	1.70	17.52
U.K.	4.43	6.14	1.93	19.84	4.06	5.29	1.61	16.60
U.S.	5.51	7.41	1.91	19.64	4.52	6.49	1.96	20.16
World, minus U.S.	4.23	5.93	1.88	19.33	4.10	5.18	1.48	15.19
World	4.74	6.07	1.62	16.65	4.04	5.15	1.45	14.96

Note that the risk premiums, averaged across the 17 markets, are much lower than risk premiums in the U.S. For instance, the geometric average risk premium across the markets is only 4.04%, lower than the 4.52% for the U.S. markets (over this time period). The results are similar for the arithmetic average premium, with the average premium of 5.15% across markets being lower than the 6.49% for the U.S. In effect, the difference in returns captures the survivorship bias, implying that using historical risk premium based only on U.S. data will result in numbers that are too high for the future.

Implied Premiums

When investors price assets, they are implicitly telling you what they require as an expected return on that asset. Thus, if an asset has expected cash flows of $15 a year in perpetuity, and an investor pays $75 for that asset, he is announcing to the world that his required rate of return on that asset is 20% (15/75). It is easiest to illustrate implied equity premiums with a dividend discount model (DDM). In the DDM, the value of equity is the present value of expected dividends from the investment. In the special case where dividends are assumed to grow at a constant rate forever, we get the classic stable growth (Gordon) model:

$$\text{Value of Equity} = \frac{\text{Expected Dividends Next Period}}{(\text{Required Return on Equity} - \text{Expected Growth Rate})}$$

This is essentially the present value of dividends growing at a constant rate. Three of the four inputs in this model can be obtained or estimated: the current level of the market (value), the expected dividends next period, and the expected growth rate in earnings and dividends in the long term. The only "unknown" is the required return on equity; when we solve for it, we get an implied expected return on stocks. Subtracting the risk-free rate yields an implied equity risk premium.

To illustrate, assume that the current level of the S&P 500 Index is 900, the expected dividend yield on the index is 2%, and the expected growth rate in earnings and dividends in the long term is 7%. Solving for the required return on equity yields the following:

$$900 = (.02 * 900) / (r - .07)$$

Then we solve for r:

$$r = (18 + 63) / 900 = 9\%$$

If the current risk-free rate is 6%, this yields a premium of 3%.

To expand the model to fit more general specifications, we would make the following changes: Instead of looking at the actual dividends paid as the only cash flow to equity, we would consider *potential dividends instead of actual dividends.* In my earlier work (2002, 2006), the free cash flow to equity (FCFE)—the cash flow left over after taxes, reinvestment needs, and debt repayments—was offered as a measure of potential dividends.[17] Over the last decade, for instance, firms have paid out only about half their FCFE as dividends. If this poses too much of an estimation challenge, a simpler alternative exists. Firms that hold back cash build up large cash balances that they use over time to fund stock buybacks. Adding stock buybacks to aggregate dividends paid should give us a better measure of total cash flows to equity. The model can also be expanded to allow for a high growth phase, where earnings and dividends can grow at rates that are very different (usually higher, but not always) from stable growth values. With these changes, the value of equity can be written as follows:

$$\text{Value of Equity} = \sum_{t=1}^{t=N} \frac{E(FCFE_t)}{(1+k_e)^t} + \frac{E(FCFE_{N+1})}{(k_e - g_N)\,(1+k_e)^N}$$

17 Damodaran, A., 2002, *Investment Valuation*, John Wiley and Sons; Damodaran, A., 2006, *Damodaran on Valuation*, John Wiley and Sons.

In this equation, there are N years of high growth, $E(FCFE_t)$ is the expected free cash flow to equity (potential dividend) in year t, k_e is the rate of return expected by equity investors, and g_N is the stable growth rate (after year N). We can solve for the rate of return equity investors need, given the expected potential dividends and prices today. Subtracting the risk-free rate should generate a more realistic equity risk premium.

Given its long history and wide following, the S&P 500 is a logical index to use to try out the implied equity risk premium measure. In this section, we will begin by estimating a current implied equity risk premium (in both January and September of 2008) and follow up by looking at the volatility in that estimate over time. On December 31, 2007, the S&P 500 Index closed at 1468.36, and the dividend yield on the index was roughly 1.89%. In addition, the consensus estimate of growth in earnings for companies in the index was approximately 5% for the next five years.[18] Because this growth rate cannot be sustained forever, we employ a two-stage valuation model. We allow growth to continue at 5% for five years, and then we lower the growth rate to 4.02% (the risk-free rate) after that.[19] Table 7.7 summarizes the expected dividends for the next five years of high growth and for the first year of stable growth thereafter.

Table 7.7 Estimated Dividends on the S&P 500 Index: January 1, 2008

Year	Dividends on Index
1	29.12
2	30.57
3	32.10
4	33.71
5	34.39
6	36.81

Dividends in the first year = 1.89% of 1,468.36 (1.05)

If we assume that these are reasonable estimates of the expected dividends and that the index is correctly priced, the value can be written as follows:

$$1468.36 = \frac{29.12}{(1+r)} + \frac{30.57}{(1+r)^2} + \frac{32.10}{(1+r)^3} + \frac{33.71}{(1+r)^4} + \frac{34.39}{(1+r)^5} + \frac{36.81(1.0402)}{(r-.0402)(1+r)^5}$$

Note that the last term in the equation is the terminal value of the index, based on the stable growth rate of 4.02%, discounted back to the present. Solving for required return in this equation yields a value of 6.04%. Subtracting the ten-year Treasury bond rate (the risk-free rate) yields an implied equity premium of 2.02%.

18 We used the average of the analyst estimates for individual firms (bottom-up). Alternatively, we could have used the top-down estimate for the S&P 500 earnings.

19 The Treasury bond rate is the sum of expected inflation and the expected real rate. If we assume that real growth is equal to the real rate, the long-term stable growth rate should be equal to the Treasury bond rate.

The focus on dividends may be understating the premium, since the companies in the index have bought back substantial amounts of their own stock over the last few years. Table 7.8 summarizes dividends and stock buybacks on the index, going back to 2001.

Table 7.8 Dividends and Stock Buybacks on the S&P 500 Index: 2001 to 2007

Year	Dividend Yield	Stock Buyback Yield	Total Yield
2001	1.37%	1.25%	2.62%
2002	1.81%	1.58%	3.39%
2003	1.61%	1.23%	2.84%
2004	1.57%	1.78%	3.35%
2005	1.79%	3.11%	4.90%
2006	1.77%	3.38%	5.15%
2007	1.89%	4.00%	5.89%
Average total yield between 2001 and 2007 =			4.02%

In 2007, for instance, firms collectively returned more than twice as much cash in the form of buybacks as they paid out in dividends. Since buybacks are volatile over time, and 2007 may represent a high-water mark for the phenomenon, we recomputed the expected cash flows for the next six years (see Table 7.9). We used the average total yield (dividends plus buybacks) of 4.02%, instead of the actual dividends, and the growth rates estimated earlier (5% for the next five years and 4.02% thereafter).

Table 7.9 Cash Flows on the S&P 500 Index

Year	Dividends Plus Buybacks on Index
1	61.98
2	65.08
3	68.33
4	71.75
5	75.34
6	78.36

Using these cash flows to compute the expected return on stocks, we derive the following:

$$1468.36 = \frac{61.98}{(1+r)} + \frac{65.08}{(1+r)^2} + \frac{68.33}{(1+r)^3} + \frac{71.75}{(1+r)^4} + \frac{75.34}{(1+r)^5} + \frac{75.34(1.0402)}{(r-.0402)(1+r)^5}$$

Then we solve for the required return and the implied premium with the higher cash flows:

Required Return on Equity = 8.39%

Implied Equity Risk Premium = Required Return on Equity – Risk-Free Rate

= 8.39% – 4.02% = 4.37%

We believe that this estimate of risk premium (4.37%) is a more realistic value for January 1, 2008.

The S&P 500 had dropped to 1220 by September 15, 2008, in the aftermath of a well-publicized crisis in financial service companies. The earnings growth rate had also dropped to about 4.5%, as analysts considered the implications of a slowing economy. Factoring in the slowing down in the economy (with consequences for earnings growth) and changes in the Treasury bond rate (3.55% on September 15, 2008), we estimated the implied equity risk premium to be 4.54% in September 2008.

Risk Premiums Are Changing

In an earlier section, we noted the determinants of equity risk premiums and default spreads, including real economic uncertainty and investor risk aversion. Since the fundamentals that determine equity risk premiums and default spreads can change over time, the risk premiums for both equity and debt itself can change significantly from time period to time period. This volatility in the risk premiums over time adds volatility to the estimated value of every asset in the market.

The Scenario

Both equity risk premiums and default spreads can change over time. Since default spreads are explicit, observing changes in these spreads over time is straightforward. Equity risk premiums are more complex. While historical risk premiums tend not to dampen the volatility, the implied premium reflects changes in the equity risk premium even over short periods. In particular, movements in the index affect the equity risk premium, with higher (or lower) index values, other things remaining equal, translating into lower (or higher) implied equity risk premiums. In the same vein, default spreads also change over time. Figure 7.2 charts the default spreads of Baa-rated bonds (over the ten-year Treasury bond) and implied equity risk premiums in the S&P 500 from 1960 to 2008. Note that both jumped dramatically in 2008.

In terms of mechanics, we used potential dividends (including buybacks) as cash flows and a two-stage discounted cash flow model.[20] Note how much both default spreads and equity risk premiums have moved over time.

20 We used analyst estimates of growth in earnings for the five-year growth rate after 1980. Between 1960 and 1980, we used the historical growth rate (from the previous five years) as the projected growth, since analyst estimates were difficult to obtain. Prior to the late 1980s, the dividends and potential dividends were very similar, because stock buybacks were uncommon. In the last 20 years, the numbers have diverged.

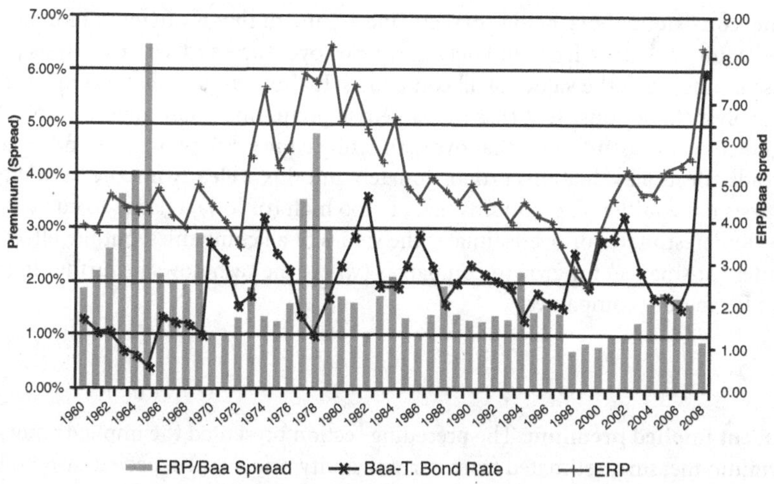

Figure 7.2: Equity Risk Premiums and Bond Default Spreads

Many analysts would look at this graph and conclude that neither equity risk premiums nor default spreads change enough over short periods to cause concern. Consequently, they argue that using the historical risk premium or a variant that yields a constant value should not be a problem. The problem, though, is that market crises can upend this conclusion and lead to sharp changes in risk premiums over short periods. Such crises are common in emerging markets, but even mature markets are not immune from sudden shifts.

The Dark Side

- **Ignorance is bliss:** Many analysts view the equity risk premium as a number that is an external input into valuation (provided by an outsider or the firm they work for), over which they have little or no control. Consequently, they are uninterested in why or how much it changes over time. Needless to say, the fact that they are unaware of changes happening does not mean that the risk premiums are not changing.
- **Trust in mean reversion:** Although most analysts would accept the proposition that equity risk premiums change over time, they stick with a constant premium, usually estimated from historical data for equity and past bond spreads, for debt. The justification that is offered is that risk premiums (equity as well as debt) will revert to these historical norms over time. While mean reversion is a powerful force in the long term, this assumption has two key problems. The first is that even if mean reversion occurs, the time it takes to revert can affect value. For instance, assume that the current equity risk premium is 7% and that the normal risk premium is 4%. If we assume that it will take five years to revert to the norm, there will be a material effect on the values we estimate. The second problem is that no consensus view exists on what comprises a normal level for either equity risk premiums or default spreads. The "mean" equity risk premium and default spread computed over the last ten years will be very different from the ones computed over the last 20 or 40 years.

- **Being consistent above being correct:** One argument that is often used for sticking with fixed equity risk premiums and default spreads over time and across analysts is that these inputs affect the values of all companies. It also is argued that it is more important for analysts to be consistent (use the same risk premiums) than correct. Implicit in this argument is the assumption that overestimating equity risk premiums and/or default spreads affects all valuations proportionately, but this is clearly not the case. When analysts use equity risk premiums that are too high (or low), relative to current levels, they underestimate (or overestimate) the values of all companies, but the effect is much greater (or smaller) for growth companies (where the cash flows lie further in the future) than for mature companies.

Solutions

- **Current implied premium:** The preceding section presented the implied equity risk premium measure, estimated from current equity prices and expected cash flows. On September 12, 2008, for instance, we estimated the implied equity risk premium in the S&P 500 to be 4.54%. Since equity prices change daily, the implied premium changes with it, allowing us to get a current value for the implied equity risk premium. The usefulness of this approach can be illustrated by looking at the time period between September 12, 2008 and January 1, 2009—a period of extraordinary volatility in the market. Figure 7.3 graphs the movements in both the S&P 500 and the implied equity risk premium on a day-to-day basis.

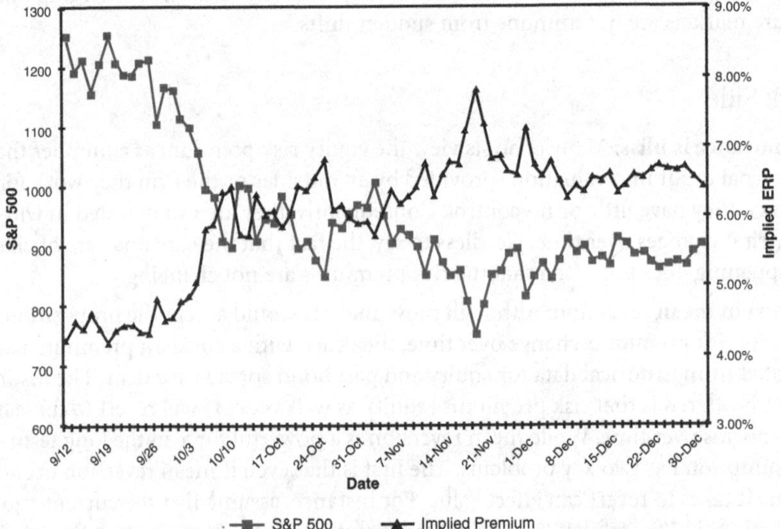

Figure 7.3: Implied Equity Risk Premium: September 12, 2008 Through January 1, 2009

Note how much the risk premiums deviated from historical norms, defined in terms of both actual returns and implied equity risk premiums in the past. If your objective is to deliver market-neutral valuations (that reflect your views of the company but none of the market), you would have used a risk premium of 4.54% on September 12 but a much higher premium of 6.5% on October 16 for the same company. On January 1, 2009, the implied equity risk premium for the U.S. market was 6.43%.

- **Default spread-based equity risk premiums:** If you're uncomfortable backing out equity risk premiums from current stock prices, you have another solution. Risk premiums should be correlated across markets. When bond investors demand higher-risk premiums for default risk, we should expect to see higher equity risk premiums. Since the former are observable (from bond prices and interest rates), we could estimate the latter if a strong relationship exists between the two. In Figure 7.2, note how much equity risk premiums have moved with default spreads over time. The average ratio of the equity risk premium to the Baa default spread from 1960 to 2007 is 2.41, but the median is approximately 2.02. Applying this ratio to the Baa default spread of 4.0% on October 16, 2008 results in the following estimate of the ERP:

  Default Spread on Baa Bonds (over Treasury) on 10/16/08 = 4.00%

  Equity Risk Premium = Default Spread * Median Ratio or ERP/Spread

  = 4.00% * 2.02 = 8.08%

  By January 1, 2009, the default spread on Baa bonds was 6% and applying the historical multiple of 2.02 to this number would have generated an equity risk premium of 12%. However, significant variation in the ratio (of ERP to default spreads) occurs over time, with the ratio dropping below 1 at the peak of the dot-com boom (when equity risk premiums dropped to 2%) and rising to as high as 2.63 at the end of 2006; the standard error in the estimate is 0.20. Whenever the ratio has deviated significantly from the average, though, reversion to that median has occurred over time.

Valuing 3M: Pre- and Post-Market Crisis

In Chapter 2, we valued 3M in September 2008 using a discounted cash flow model, and we arrived at an estimated value of $86.95 per share. In estimating the cost of equity, we used an equity risk premium of 4%, which we assumed to be a reasonable premium for mature markets. For the cost of debt, we used a default spread of 0.75%, based on the AAA rating we estimated for the company.

Figure 7.3 shows the expansion in the equity risk premium to 6% on October 16, 2008. Concurrently, the default spread on AAA-rated bonds increased to 1.40%. If we hold all the other inputs into the valuation constant and change these two inputs, the cost of capital increases to 11.16%, and the value per share decreases to $64.57. This precipitous drop in value was mirrored by a drop in the stock price from $80.00 a share on September 12 to $62.00 a share on October 16. However, this also assumes that the dramatic shift in risk premiums over the four weeks is a permanent shift that will apply in perpetuity.

An intermediate solution is to accept the reality that risk premiums have increased in the short term but will revert to or be closer to historical norms in the long term.

In effect, we could use the higher implied premium of 6% for the high-growth period (the next five years) and then change back to the mature market premium of 4% in stable growth. With default spreads, we would use the 1.40% spread for the next five years and adjust the spread to 0.75% in stable growth. If we do this, the estimate of value per share increases to $77.78 a share. If we assume only partial reversion to the average, the value per share drops to $70.52. Table 7.10 lists the assumptions about risk premiums and the effect on value per share.

Table 7.10 3M Value per Share and Risk Premiums

Timing of Valuation	Equity Risk Premium	Default Spread on AAA Rating	Cost of Capital	Value per Share
September 2008	4%	0.75%	8.63%	$86.95
October 2008	6%	1.40%	11.16%	$64.57
October 2008	6% first five years; 4% thereafter	1.40% first five years; 0.75% thereafter	11.16% first five years; 6.76% thereafter	$77.78
October 2008	6% first five years; 5% thereafter	1.40% first five years; 1% thereafter	11.16% first five years; 6.76% thereafter	$70.52

Conclusion

The prices that we assume investors charge for bearing risk in equities (equity risk premium) and being exposed to default risk in debt (default spreads) have a significant effect on the values we estimate for individual assets. In far too many valuations, analysts either depend on outside services (Ibbotson, Standard & Poor's) for these numbers or use values that are not feasible (equity risk premium less than zero, cost of debt less than the risk-free rate).

This chapter laid out the determinants of both equity risk premiums and default spreads and noted that both are likely to change over time. We also looked at three potentially problematic scenarios. First, in markets with limited or no historical data, the standard approach of using historical risk premiums for both debt and equity breaks down. In these markets, we suggested starting with premiums in more mature markets, where historical data is available, and building up to a risk premium. Second, we looked at the noise in our risk premium estimates, even in markets with substantial historical data, and the possibility that we may be overstating premiums because of a survivor bias. To counter this, we argued that we should use average equity risk premiums across multiple markets globally or an implied equity risk premium, backed out of what investors are willing to pay for stocks. Finally, we considered the possibility that risk premiums can change significantly over short periods, and we used the market crisis from September to December 2008 to illustrate this point. For analysts who are called on to value companies during market crises, the implied equity premium is most likely to reflect market realities when risk premiums are changing.

The broader lesson, though, is that the risk premiums that we use in valuation can have profound effects on the values we estimate for individual assets, with the effect being greater for high-growth companies. Consequently, we should be aware of not only the numbers we use for the equity risk premium and default spread, but also how different our estimates may be from what the market is assuming.

8

Macro Matters: The Real Economy

Companies operate in a larger economy, and the assumptions we make about macroeconomic variables affect the valuations of all companies. This chapter begins by looking at how changes in the real economy, inflation, and exchange rates affect valuation. It also looks at the historical behavior of each of these variables. We then consider how analysts deal with macroeconomic variables in valuation. They often make implicit assumptions about growth and inflation that may be unrealistic or explicit assumptions that are internally inconsistent. We evaluate whether we should be building in views on the macroeconomic variables and, if so, how best to do this.

Growth in the Real Economy

Every business is affected by the state of the economy, although the magnitude of the effect may vary across businesses. This section looks at how the growth in the real economy affects inputs into the valuation of individual companies. It also goes into some history on real economic growth.

Why Does Real Economic Growth Matter?

When valuing companies, we have to estimate growth in revenues, income, and cash flows over time. While we tend to look at the company's specific prospects while making these estimates, a company's operating numbers are influenced by the state of the economy in which the company operates. Put more simply, the revenues and earnings numbers look much better if the economy is doing well than if it is slowing down or shrinking. Because we are forecasting these numbers for the future, our estimates for individual companies are affected by how well or badly we think the economy will do over the next few years.

While all companies may be affected by the growth rate of the economy, they are not affected to the same extent. We expect companies in cyclical businesses, such as housing and automobiles, to be affected more by overall economic growth. Conversely, companies that produce staples should be affected to a lesser extent by whether the economy is in boom or recession mode. Consequently, optimism about future economic growth will result in higher values for the former, relative to the latter. The effect of changes in economic growth on company valuations can also vary, depending on whether they derive their value primarily from existing assets or growth assets. Not surprisingly, companies with significant growth assets see their values change much more dramatically in response to shifts in the overall economy than mature companies.

Finally, economic growth affects other key market-related inputs into valuation. In Chapter 6, "A Shaky Base: A 'Risky' Risk-Free Rate," we noted that risk-free rates tend to change over time and that change is often related to real economic growth. When economies are growing briskly, risk-free rates tend to rise, whereas economic slowdowns are associated with lower interest rates. In Chapter 7, "Risky Ventures: Assessing the Price of Risk," we traced the shifts in equity risk premiums and default spreads over time. We noted their tendency to rise with uncertainty about the economy and investor risk aversion.

Looking at History

How much does real economic growth change from year to year? The answer clearly depends on which economy we look at. The first part of this section focuses on real economic growth in the U.S. over time and shows how both real and nominal growth have varied across time. We will also look at how real economic growth has affected the aggregate earnings and dividends of publicly traded firms. In the second part of the section, we will expand the discussion to encompass other countries, including the fast-growing emerging markets of Asia and Latin America.

U.S. Real Economic Growth Over Time

During the 20th century, the U.S. grew to become the dominant global economic power, but the growth was not uninterrupted. Extended periods of economic decline and stagnation occurred, with the Great Depression being the most significant example. Figure 8.1 summarizes annual changes in real Gross Domestic Product (GDP) for the U.S. from 1929 to 2007.

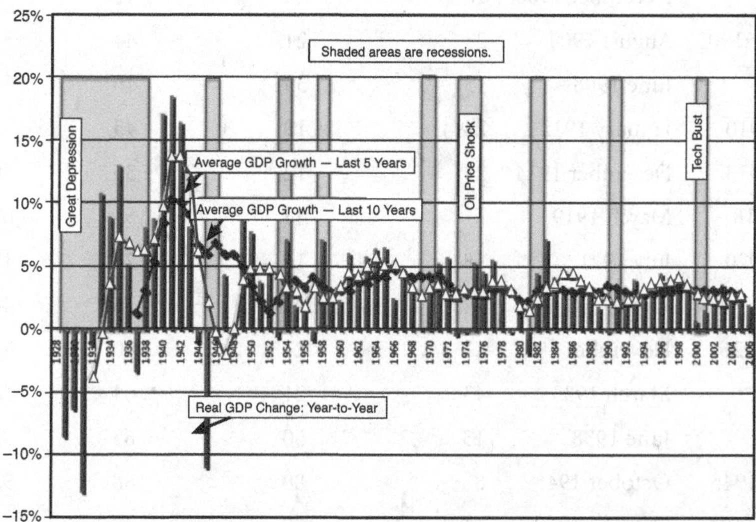

Figure 8.1: U.S. Real Economic Growth Over Time: 1929 to 2007

The shaded areas in the figure represent recessions, at least as defined by the National Bureau of Economic Research (NBER). Two consecutive quarters of negative economic growth in real GDP has become the rule of thumb for classifying recessions. Table 8.1 summarizes the business cycles since 1850 in the U.S., with the length of each cycle in months.

Table 8.1 Business Cycles (in Months) in the U.S.: 1854 to 2007

		Contraction	Expansion	Cycle	
Peak	Trough	Peak to Trough	Previous to Trough This Peak	Trough from Last Trough	Previous Peak to This Peak
June 1857	December 1858	18	30	48	—
October 1860	June 1861	8	22	30	40
April 1865	December 1867	32	46	78	54
June 1869	December 1870	18	18	36	50
October 1873	March 1879	65	34	99	52
March 1882	May 1885	38	36	74	101
March 1887	April 1888	13	22	35	60
July 1890	May 1891	10	27	37	40
January 1893	June 1894	17	20	37	30
December 1895	June 1897	18	18	36	35
June 1899	December 1900	18	24	42	42
September 1902	August 1904	23	21	44	39
May 1907	June 1908	13	33	46	56
January 1910	January 1912	24	19	43	32
January 1913	December 1914	23	12	35	36
August 1918	March 1919	7	44	51	67
January 1920	July 1921	18	10	28	17
May 1923	July 1924	14	22	36	40
October 1926	November 1927	13	27	40	41
August 1929	March 1933	43	21	64	34
May 1937	June 1938	13	50	63	93
February 1945	October 1945	8	80	88	93
November 1948	October 1949	11	37	48	45
July 1953	May 1954	10	45	55	56
August 1957	April 1958	8	39	47	49
April 1960	February 1961	10	24	34	32
December 1969	November 1970	11	106	117	116

		Contraction	Expansion	Cycle		
Peak	Trough	Peak to Trough	Previous to Trough This Peak	Trough from Last Trough	Previous Peak to This Peak	
November 1973	March 1975	16	36	52	47	
January 1980	July 1980	6	58	64	74	
July 1981	November 1982	16	12	28	18	
July 1990	March 1991	8	92	100	108	
March 2001	November 2001	8	120	128	128	
Average: 1850 to Today			**17**	**38**	**55**	**56**
Average: 1945 to 2001			**10**	**57**	**67**	**67**

Source: NBER

Looking at this long time period of history, some interesting facts emerge that may have implications for how we deal with real growth in valuation:

- **Cycle length is unpredictable**: The economic cycles have no systematic length, making it difficult to forecast the length and duration of the next cycle. The cycles of 1982 to 1990 and 1991 to 2001 have been the longest (100 months or longer), but the cycle in 1980-1981 lasted only 28 months. The average cycle lasted 55 months, but the cycles have become longer since World War II.
- **Recession length has varied**: Since the Great Depression, recessions have lasted anywhere from eight to 16 months and have ranged from mild (2001 to 2002) to strong (1981 to 1982).
- **Hindsight is 20/20**: One fact that does not come through when we look at this table is that the dates for the economic cycles are determined with the benefit of hindsight. In other words, investors and businesses were unaware in July 1990 that they were entering a recession. It was only in early 1992 that the NBER finally got around to categorizing the July 1990 to March 1991 time period as a recession.

If we accept the proposition that predicting economic cycles is impossible and that we should focus on estimating real growth over the next five or ten years rather than the growth in the next quarter, our task becomes easier (at least in hindsight). Figure 8.1 includes a smoothed-out estimate of real growth over the next five years and the next ten years to provide a contrast to the year-to-year real-growth numbers. The ten-year growth rate reported in 1954, for instance, is the average growth rate from 1954 to 1963. Note that these long-term forecasts have far more stability, especially since World War II. Both the five-year and ten-year average growth rates have been between 2 and 3%. This stability suggests that using a reasonable real-growth rate number for the long term is more important (and viable) than forecasting growth on a year-to-year basis.

Real growth affects valuation through the earnings and cash flows reported by businesses. Therefore, Figure 8.2 shows how aggregate earnings and dividends on the S&P 500 have behaved over time, as real economic growth has varied.

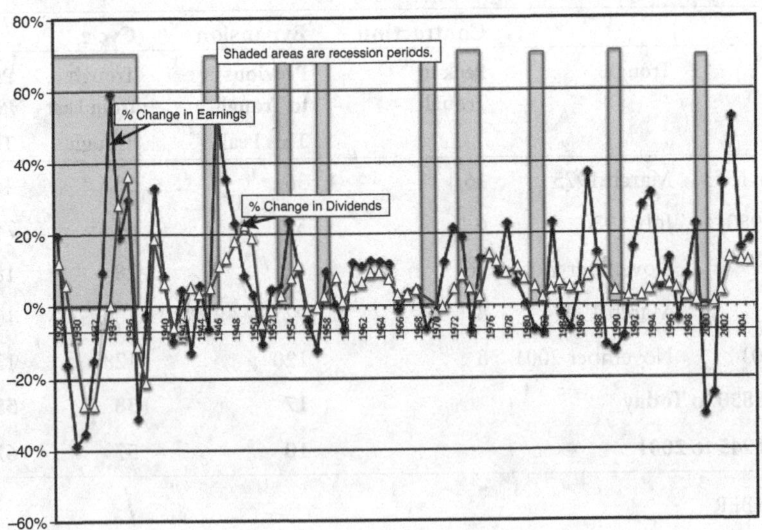

Figure 8.2: Earnings and Dividends on S&P 500 Companies

Looking back at the last 80 years of earnings and dividends on the S&P 500 companies, two trends emerge. The first is that both earnings and dividends are sensitive to economic conditions, with both declining during recessions. The second is that earnings are much more volatile than dividends over time.

As a final test, Figure 8.3 shows how the S&P 500 index has changed over time as a function of real economic growth.

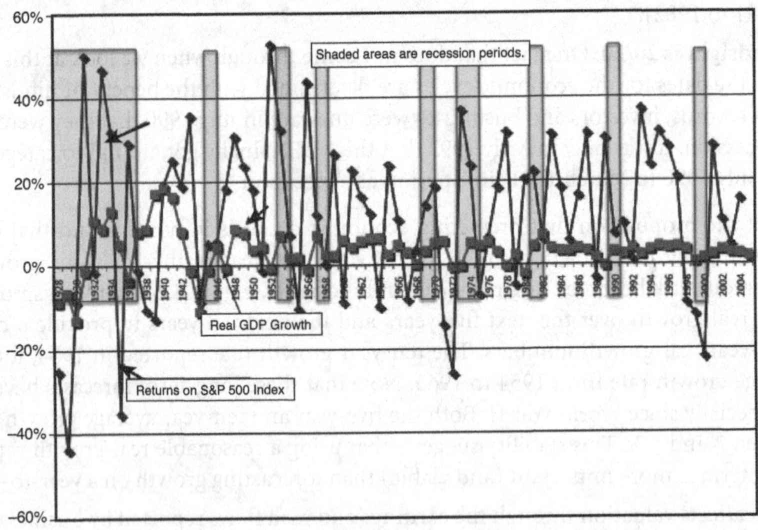

Figure 8.3: Real Economic Growth and the S&P 500

Looking at the changes in real GDP growth and changes in the S&P 500, it seems clear that the index is far more volatile than the economy. Another interesting and more subtle relationship is also visible for most of the graph. Stock prices seem to drop prior to the slowing down in the real economy and seem to start their rise prior to the actual recovery's taking hold.

Differences in Real Growth Across Countries

Estimating both short-term and long-term real growth in a mature market like the U.S. is far simpler than forecasting growth in young economies, especially ones that derive much of their growth from a commodity or specific sector. The fact that these economies are small, relative to the global economy, can allow them to grow at double-digit rates in good years and suffer catastrophic drops in bad years. Figure 8.4 summarizes real-growth rates from 1997 to 2001 and 2002 to 2006 in Brazil, India, China, and Russia and contrasts them with real-growth rates in the European Union (EU) countries, Japan, and the U.S.

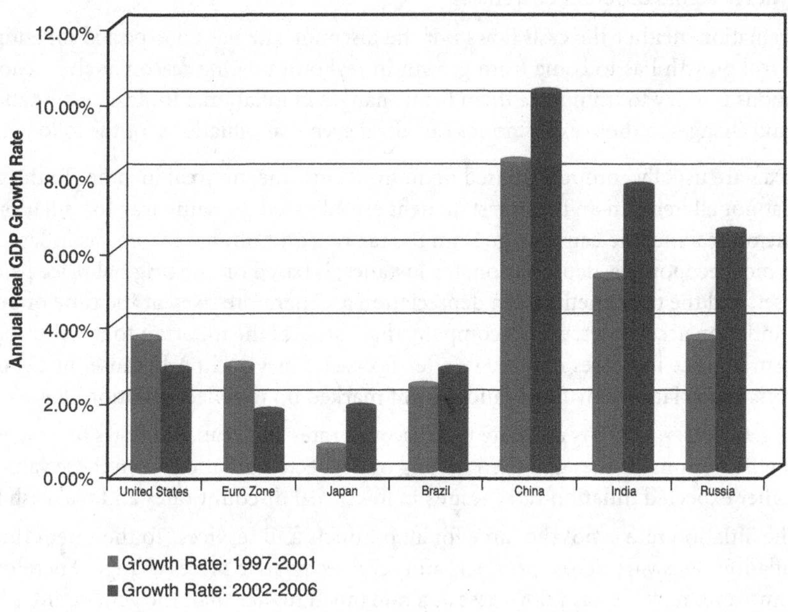

Figure 8.4: Real-Growth Rates in GDP Across Countries

Not only are real-growth rates higher in the smaller, emerging markets than in the mature economies, but they also tend to be volatile.

Expected Inflation

The valuation of every company rests on the assumptions we make about expected inflation in the future. This section begins by looking at why inflation has such an impact on value, how inflation rates have behaved in the past, and how much and why inflation rates vary across currencies.

Why Does Expected Inflation Matter?

As we noted in Chapter 6, valuations can be either nominal or real. If they're nominal, the expected inflation rate is built into both the cash flows and the discount rate. In nominal valuations, expected inflation affects key inputs that we use in our analysis:

- The risk-free rate is the interest rate on a default-free bond and thus has an expected inflation rate built into it. Consequently, the cost of equity and debt that we obtain based on this risk-free rate also have expected inflation components.
- The growth rates that we use to forecast future cash flows incorporate both the growth in real output sales and expected inflation. To the extent that higher inflation allows the firm to charge higher prices, the growth rates increase with inflation.

In other words, changing the expected inflation rate affects all aspects of a nominal valuation. That is why the currency in which we do a nominal valuation matters: expected inflation rates can vary widely across different currencies.

In a real valuation, neither the cash flows nor the discount rate has an expected inflation component, and real growth has to come from growth in real output. One reason analysts choose to do real valuations is to try to immunize them from changes in inflation. However, expectations about inflation and changes in those expectations can affect even real valuations for the following reasons:

- Taxes are usually computed based on nominal income, not real income. To the extent that not all items in an income statement are adjusted the same way for inflation, the tax rate on real income can diverge from the tax rate on nominal income as inflation rises. In most economies, depreciation, for instance, is based on the original price paid for an asset, and the tax benefits from depreciation are therefore fixed at the time of purchase. If inflation accelerates, even a company that can pass the inflation to its customers in the form of price increases may see its after-tax cash flows decline, because the tax benefits from depreciation stay fixed (and are not marked up to reflect inflation).[1]
- In many cases, analysts estimate real discount rates and real cash flows by first estimating the nominal values and then netting out expected inflation from these values. Using higher expected inflation rates results in lower real discount rates and real cash flows.
- The inflation rate is not the same for all products and services. To the extent that inflation rates vary across products and services, relative prices change. Therefore, some companies may see cash flows rise at a rate much higher than the general inflation rate, and others may see growth rates in their cash flows that lag inflation.

In summary, the value that we arrive at for a company, if we believe that expected inflation will be 3%, may be very different from the value of that same company with an expected inflation rate of 5%. Inflation is not a neutral item in valuation.

1 Assume that a firm has $100 million in EBITDA, $40 million in depreciation, and no interest expenses. Furthermore, it faces a marginal tax rate of 40% on its income. The firm reports $36 million in net income and $76 million in cash flows prior to reinvestment (net income + depreciation). Now introduce an inflation rate of 10% into the analysis, and assume that the firm can raise the prices of its products at the inflation rate. EBITDA rises to $110 million, but depreciation stays frozen at $40 million. The firm now reports net income of $42 million and cash flows of $82 million. If we convert the latter into real numbers, the real EBITDA is $100 million, the real net income is $37.8 million, and the real cash flow is $73.8 million—$2.2 million less than it used to be.

Expected inflation also has an impact on the other macro variables that go into a valuation, including real economic growth and inflation, the two other variables covered in this chapter. Expected inflation also affects risk-free rate and equity risk premiums, two inputs covered in the preceding two chapters. When expected inflation increases, the risk-free rate increases to reflect that expectation, and equity risk premiums may be ramped up as well. Uncertainty about inflation in the future can also make companies more reluctant to invest in long-term projects and thus alter both the level of real economic growth and what sectors it occurs in. Finally, if the expected inflation rate in one currency increases relative to other currencies, we should expect exchange rates to follow, with the higher inflation currency depreciating over time.

Looking at History

If expected inflation rates are constant, incorporating their effect into value is relatively simple. It is because inflation rates change over time and vary across currencies that they can wreak havoc on valuation. This section begins by looking at variation in the inflation rate in the U.S. dollar over time. Then it examines differences in inflation rates across currencies.

U.S. Inflation Rate Across Time

Before we look at variation in the inflation rate across time, we must determine how inflation is to be measured. The task is a complicated one, especially when we look at an economy as large and complex as the U.S. At least in theory, the inflation rate should measure changes in how much it costs to buy a representative basket of goods and services from period to period. Not surprisingly, inflation rates vary depending on what we put in the basket. The U.S. has three widely used measures of inflation, with a long history attached to each:

- The consumer price index (CPI) measures changes in the weighted average price paid for a specified bundle of goods by consumers. It is a reflection of price pressures at the retail level and includes imported goods and sales and excise taxes.
- The producer price index (PPI) measures the weighted average cost of the entire marketed output of US producers. Since it reflects revenues received by producers, it does not incorporate sales and excise taxes.
- The Gross National Product price deflator (GNP deflator) measures the inflation rate in the prices of the broader mix of goods and services produced by an economy, rather than the narrower mix used in the CPI.

All three measures share some common problems. The first is that the basket of goods and services that is used to compute inflation is kept stable even as relative prices change. In other words, it is assumed that the proportion of the basket that is oil remains the same, even if oil prices increase significantly relative to other items in the basket. In reality, though, consumers use less gasoline and adjust their consumption to reflect relative prices. The second problem with the basket is that it does not consider implicit costs. For instance, the cost of housing is measured by looking at the cost of renting a house rather than the implicit cost of owning one. To the extent that housing prices are increasing much faster than rental costs are, as was the case between 2002 and 2006, inflation will be understated. Figure 8.5 graphs the behavior of all three measures of inflation from 1921 to 2007.

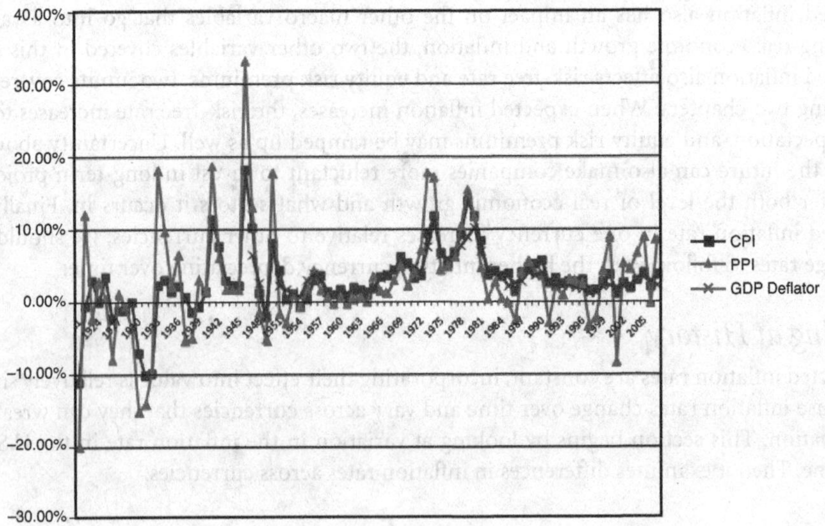

Figure 8.5: Inflation Rates in the U.S.

Note that notwithstanding the differences, the three measures move together over time. Quirks in how they are computed have sometimes caused one measure to lag the other. During much of this period, inflation in the U.S. was benign and ranged from 1 to 4%. Bouts of high inflation occurred in the 1930s and during World War II, but the volatility in inflation accelerated in the 1970s, with inflation rates hitting double digits by the last few years of the decade. The only sustained period of deflation was during the Great Depression, when prices dropped more than 10% a year in 1932 and 1933. In the last two decades, inflation has subsided again, but assuming that this stability is permanent can be dangerous.

All three measures of inflation shown in Figure 8.5 represent actual inflation. In much of valuation, our focus is on expected inflation. Two measures try to capture expectations. One comes from surveys done by the University of Michigan on inflation expectations among consumers. The other can be backed out of the ten-year nominal and inflation-indexed Treasury bond rates:

$$\text{Expected Inflation Rate} = \frac{(1 + \text{Nominal Treasury Rate})}{(1 + \text{Inflation Indexed Treasury Rate})} - 1$$

Figure 8.6 graphs both measures for the periods of time that they have been available—since 1978 for the survey and since 2003 for the Treasury rates.

The survey numbers closely track the historical inflation numbers, with expected inflation increasing in the late 1970s in response to higher observed inflation. The expected inflation rates backed out of the Treasury rates for the last six years have been consistently lower than survey expectations but have been better predictors of actual inflation during the periods.

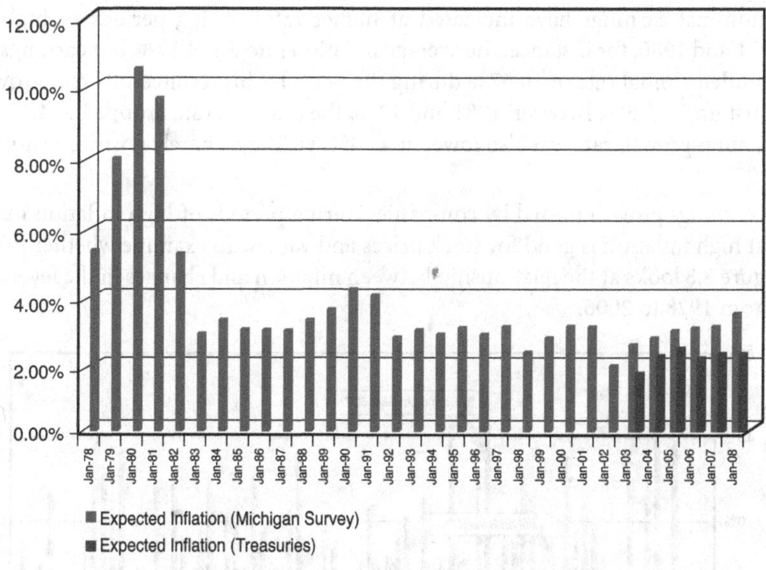

Figure 8.6: Expected Inflation: Consumer Surveys and Treasury Rates

Inflation, Earnings, and Stock Prices

As we noted at the beginning of this section, expected inflation is relevant in valuation because earnings and dividends can be affected by changes in inflation rates. To examine this relationship, Figure 8.7 shows changes in the aggregate earnings on the S&P 500 against the inflation rate (measured using the CPI) over time.

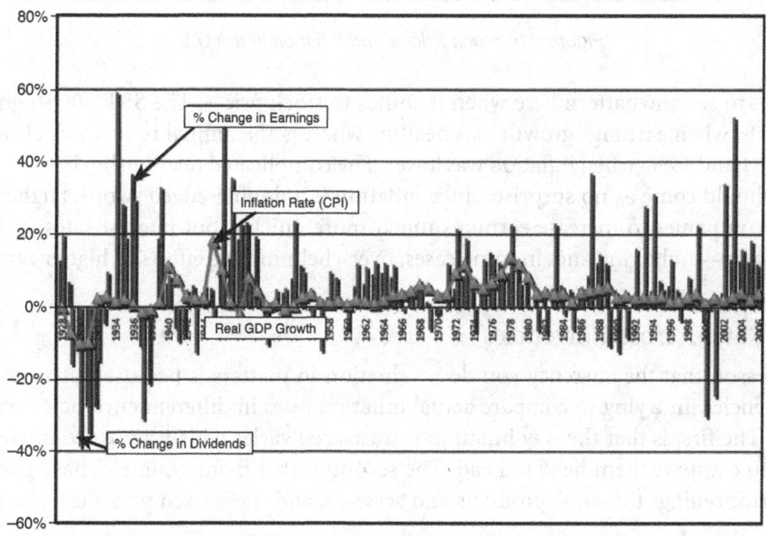

Figure 8.7: Earnings and Inflation in the U.S.

Note that nominal earnings have increased at higher rates during periods of high inflation. Between 1971 and 1980, for instance, the average inflation rate was 8.19%, but earnings increased at a compounded annual rate of 10.57% during the period. This resulted in a real-growth rate in earning of just under 2.5%. Between 1981 and 1990, the inflation rate dropped to 4.47%, and the nominal earnings growth rate was also lower at 4.74%, yielding a barely positive real-growth rate in earnings.

The higher earnings growth posted by companies during periods of high inflation may seem to indicate that high inflation is good for stock prices and values. To examine whether this is in fact the case, Figure 8.8 looks at the relationship between inflation and changes in the level of the S&P 500 index from 1928 to 2006.

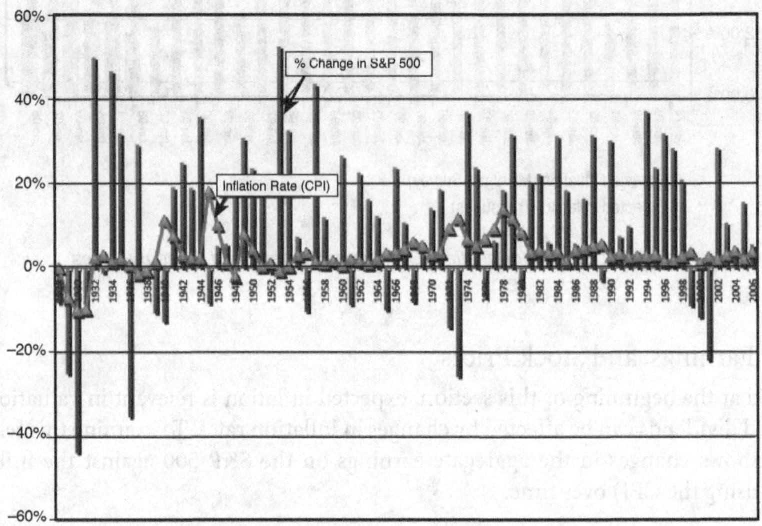

Figure 8.8: Stock Prices and Inflation in the U.S.

It is difficult to see any pattern here when it comes to stock prices. The S&P 500 stagnated during the 1970s, when earnings growth was healthy, whereas the annual return was closer to 16% between 1981 and 1990, when inflation was lower. The complicated relationship between inflation and value should come as no surprise, since inflation is a double-edged sword. Higher inflation may allow companies to increase earnings much more quickly, but interest rates and discount rates also go up—nullifying and, in some cases, overwhelming the effects of higher earnings.

Inflation Rates Across Currencies

The only reason that the currency you do a valuation in matters is because inflation rates vary across currencies. In trying to compare actual inflation rates in different currencies, we run into two issues. The first is that the way inflation is measured varies widely across countries, making it difficult to compare them head to head. The second is that many countries have government-imposed price ceilings for some products and services, and these fixed prices can skew inflation measures.

In spite of these estimation issues, it is still useful to compare inflation rates in different currencies. Figure 8.9 shows actual inflation rates in seven currencies between 2005 and 2007.

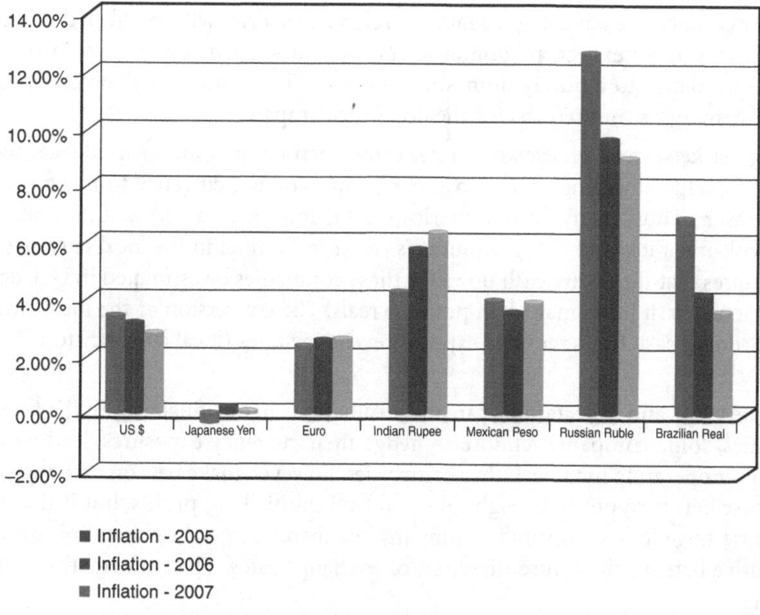

Figure 8.9: Inflation Rates in Different Currencies

Inflation rates were lowest in Japan and highest in Russia during this period. It stands to reason that interest rates are also lowest in Japan and highest in Russia and that exchange rates reflect the differences in inflation.

Exchange Rates

As with real economic growth and inflation rates, our views on exchange rates can affect the value we attach to individual companies. In this section, we will first consider why exchange rates matter, and then we will examine past history.

Why Do Exchange Rates Matter?

Changes in exchange rates in the past and expectations in the future can make a difference in valuation. For companies with foreign operations, the reported earnings are affected by changes in exchange rates. Favorable movements in exchange rates result in higher earnings, whereas unfavorable movements can result in large losses. Note, though, that what type of movement is favorable/unfavorable depends on the nature of the foreign exposure. If the firm's costs are all domestic and its revenues are overseas, a weakening of the domestic currency causes earnings to improve. On the other hand, if the firm's costs are overseas but its revenues are primarily domestic, as is the case for some software companies, a weakening in the domestic currency causes earnings to deteriorate. Expectations of future changes in exchange rates also manifest themselves in differences in expected growth. Thus, the company with foreign revenues gets a boost in growth if we expect the domestic currency to continue to depreciate over time. On the other hand, the growth rate for the company with foreign costs may have to be scaled back for the same expectation. Views on exchange rates can affect even companies with just domestic operations, because their competitive advantages against foreign adversaries will be affected by expectations of exchange rates. If we expect the domestic currency to weaken, a foreign company will be at a disadvantage relative to a purely domestic company. This, in turn, will affect expectations of future growth, margins, and returns for the domestic company.

In emerging markets, views on exchange rates can sometimes play an outsized role, because analysts choose to value emerging-market companies in a foreign currency to make some of their estimation easier. Thus, many Latin American companies are valued in U.S. dollars, because estimating risk-free rates and risk premiums is easier to do than in the local currency. However, this also requires that the future cash flows for these companies be estimated in U.S. dollars, even though the actual cash flows may be in pesos or reals. The conversion of the local currency cash flows to U.S. dollar cash flows requires expected exchange rates (local currency to U.S. dollars) in the future.

Exchange rate views and expectations can affect valuations in one final way. In the face of volatile exchange rates, some companies choose to hedge their currency exposures, leading to hedging costs that lower operating income. Other companies, however, make bets on exchange rate movements. If these bets turn out to be right, they add substantially to profits, but if they are wrong, they can cause huge losses. To value a company, we therefore need information on its hedging and speculative bets on the future direction of exchange rates. That information is not always forthcoming.

Looking at History

Until 1971, we operated in a regime of fixed exchange rates. Changes occurred only when governments chose to devalue or revalue a currency. Since these fixed exchange rates were often incompatible with the underlying fundamentals (inflation, interest rates, and real growth in the economies), black markets sprang up for the most overvalued and undervalued currencies where the intrinsic exchange rates were very different from the official rates. After the Bretton Woods Conference in 1971, the major currencies were allowed to float (and find a market price), but most emerging markets continued (and many still continue) to maintain a fixed rate structure.

The currencies that have the longest market history are the U.S. dollar, the British pound, the Swiss franc, and the Japanese yen. Figure 8.10 graphs the movements in those currencies, with the dollar as the base.

There are two things to note. The first is that different currencies often move in different directions. During this period, the dollar strengthened against the pound but weakened substantially against both the Swiss franc and the yen. Within each currency are long cycles. With the Swiss franc, for instance, the dollar weakened through 1980, strengthened for the first half of the 1980s, and reverted to weakness in the second half of the decade. Some of this movement can be traced to the underlying economic fundamentals—the strengthening of the yen reflects Japan's rise as an economic power during the 1970s and 1980s—but some of it reflects deliberate government policy. The U.S. has actively encouraged dollar depreciation since 2001 to improve the competitive position of U.S. companies in the export market.

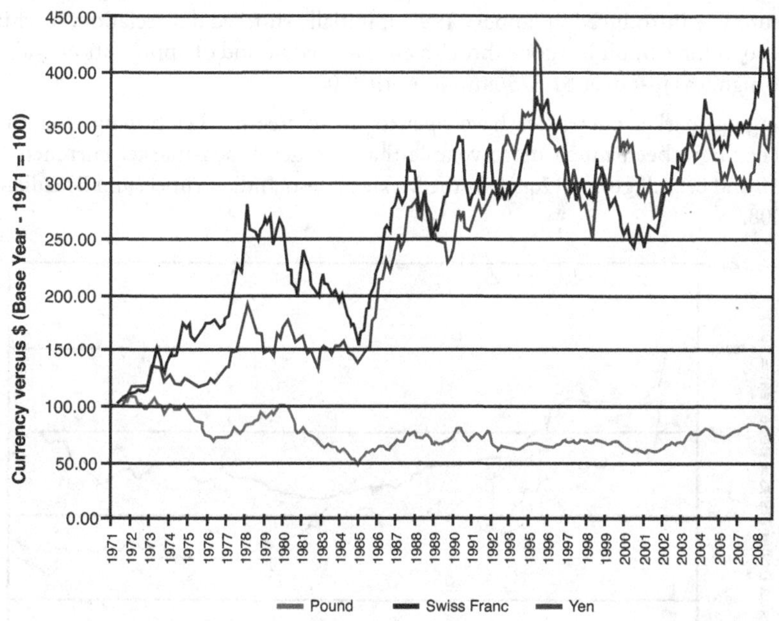

Figure 8.10: Major Trading Currencies Versus the U.S. Dollar

Figure 8.11 shows the U.S. dollar versus the euro, which replaced the individual EU currencies (such as the French franc and the Deutsche mark) in 1999.

Figure 8.11: The Euro Versus the U.S. Dollar

After the euro was introduced in January 1999, it initially suffered depreciation, reaching a value of $0.85/euro in June, but it has gone through an extended period of appreciation against the U.S. dollar. The high was just over $1.575/euro in April 2008.

Some emerging-market currencies have opened up to free-market pricing over the last two decades. They have been much more volatile than the developed-market currencies shown in Figures 8.10 and 8.11. Figure 8.12 graphs the Mexican peso, Indian rupee, and Brazilian real from 1995 to 2008.

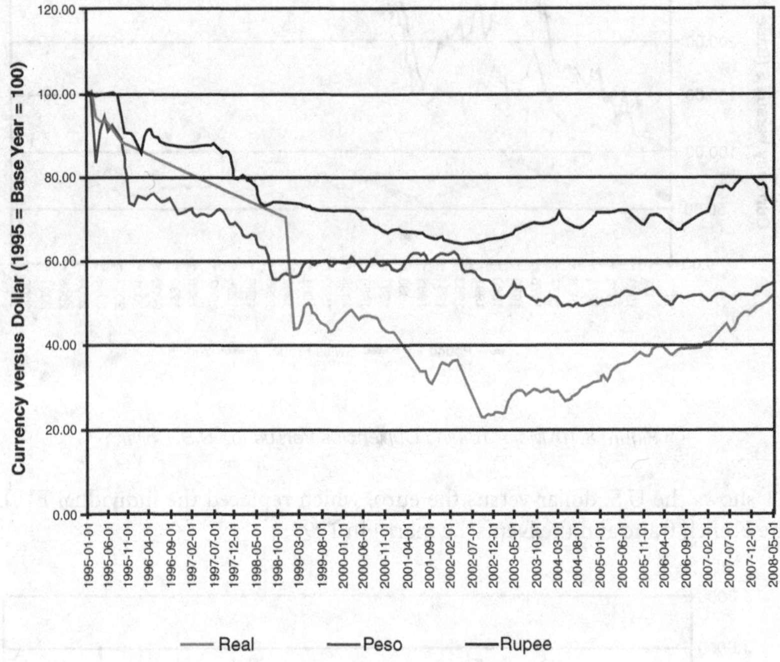

Figure 8.12: Emerging-Market Currencies Versus the U.S. Dollar

The Brazilian real lost almost 80% of its value against the dollar between 1995 and 2002 but more than doubled its value between 2002 and early 2008. The volatility in these rates should not come as a surprise. They are caused by political instability in these markets and economic variability over time.

While the conventional wisdom is that the currencies of mature economies like the U.S., Japan, and Western Europe (with similar inflation) do not go through sharp contortions, the market crisis of 2008 that we highlighted in the preceding chapter may lead to a rethinking. Figure 8.13 shows the movements in the U.S. dollar versus the euro, yen, and Brazilian real from September 12 to October 16.

While the volatility in the Brazilian Real may be predictable, the sharp devaluation of the euro (which has lost almost 8% of its value against the dollar) and the rise in the yen (up about 10%) is a sign that volatility in exchange rates is not restricted to emerging-market currencies.

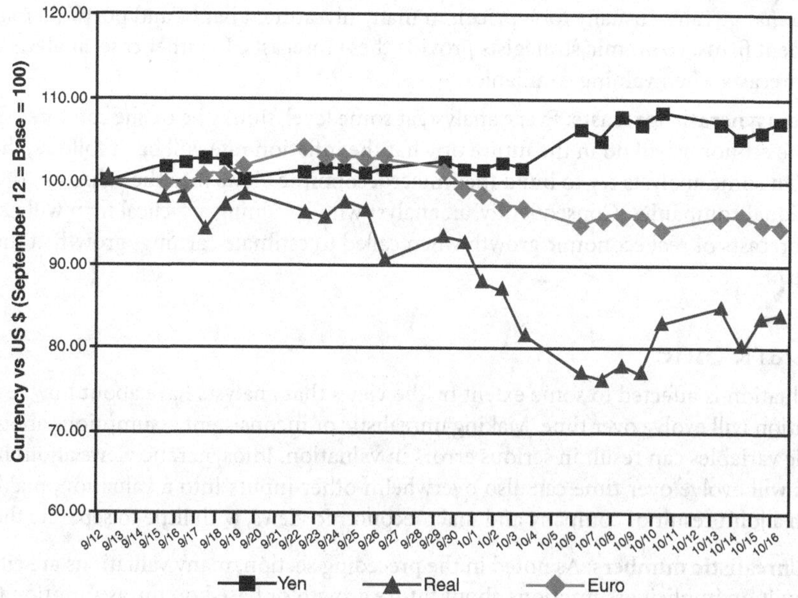

Figure 8.13: Exchange Rates During a Market Crisis

Current Practices

While changes in expectations about real economic growth, inflation, and currency movements clearly change valuations, the way in which these expectations are brought into valuation currently is surprisingly haphazard. In fact, analysts practice everything from benign neglect, where they essentially ignore the macroeconomic environment, to bringing strong and idiosyncratic views about future macroeconomic developments to every valuation they do.

- **Implicit assumptions:** Analysts often make no explicit assumptions about economic growth or inflation when doing valuations. They justify this neglect by arguing that their job is assessing a company's value and not making macroeconomic forecasts. While this argument has some merit, these analysts make implicit assumptions when they forecast company-specific inputs. For instance, estimates of earnings growth for a company, if made in nominal terms, have assumptions about expected inflation built into them. Forecasts of cash flows for cyclical companies have real-growth assumptions embedded in them. When estimating future earnings for multinationals, we make use of expected exchange rates in the future, even if we do not estimate them explicitly.
- **Base it on last year:** When asked to make forecasts of future real economic growth, inflation, and exchange rates, some analysts draw on the most recent data on these variables. Thus, the inflation and real GDP growth rate for the most recent year are used as the forecasts for the foreseeable future.
- **Use forecasts of economists:** Forecasting services employ the best economic models (and economists to run them) to provide estimates of expected growth, inflation, and

exchange rates (usually for a price). In many investment banks and portfolio management firms, economic strategists provide these forecasts. In either case, analysts use the forecasts when valuing companies.

- **Idiosyncratic forecasts:** Every analyst, at some level, thinks he or she can forecast how the economy will do in the future or what the inflation rate will be. It follows, therefore, that some analysts try to build their macroeconomic views into the valuation of individual companies. Consequently, an analyst who is valuing a cyclical firm will use his forecasts of real economic growth when called to estimate earnings growth at the cyclical firm.

The Dark Side

Every valuation is affected to some extent by the views that analysts have about how real growth and inflation will evolve over time. Making unrealistic or inconsistent assumptions about macroeconomic variables can result in serious errors in valuation. Idiosyncratic views about how these variables will evolve over time can also overwhelm other inputs into a valuation, making every valuation a joint result of company and macroeconomic views, with little to separate the two.

- **Unrealistic numbers:** As noted in the preceding section, many valuations are either built on implicit assumptions about future growth or based on the assumption that what happened last year is a good measure of what will happen in the future. With both approaches, though, the biggest danger we face is that we might be building in estimates for the future that are unsustainable for the long term. For instance, assuming that mature economies like the U.S. or Western Europe will be able to grow at 4% in real terms for the long term is unrealistic, even though that might have been the growth rate in the most recent year. Similarly, assuming that China and India will be able to maintain real-growth rates of 10% for the long term is also unrealistic.
- **Microforecasting of macroeconomic variables:** Analysts who value cyclical and commodity firms argue that these firms are affected strongly by economic cycles so that they can try to forecast the cycles in detail. An analyst valuing a cyclical firm tries to forecast not only when the next recession will begin or the current one will end but also the next full cycle of economic growth, with the effects built into earnings and cash flow forecasts. As we noted in the section "U.S. Real Economic Growth Over Time," economic cycles are unpredictable in both length and strength. Forecasts, even by the very best macroeconomists, tend to be wrong. The realism added by making these forecasts therefore is likely to be overwhelmed by the errors in these forecasts.
- **Inconsistent with other macroeconomic assumptions:** Assumptions about macroeconomic growth are embedded in many of the inputs that go into valuing a company. The expected inflation rate, in addition to affecting expected earnings growth in a company, also affects the risk-free rate. Consequently, changes in the expected inflation rate for computing earnings have to be matched by changes in the risk-free rate used in computing the discount rate. Selectively changing one set of inputs to reflect expectations about macroeconomic variables, without changes to another set, can result in valuations that are internally inconsistent.

- **Valuation driven more by macro views than by company views:** Suppose you have strong views (positive or negative) about real growth and inflation in the future, and you choose to incorporate these views into your valuation. The results will be not only predictable (more positive views about macroeconomic developments lead to higher assessments of value) but also much more difficult to evaluate. An analyst who assumes that inflation rates will decrease and that real growth will increase in the future is more likely to find a company undervalued. But that undervaluation will be more the result of the analyst's macroeconomic views than of her views on the company.

Remedies

It is difficult for analysts to keep their views on the macro economy out of their individual company valuations. To prevent these views from hijacking valuations, we suggest that you follow a few simple rules:

- **Make implicit assumptions explicit:** As noted in the preceding section, many valuations make implicit assumptions about growth, inflation, and exchange rates. While these implicit assumptions may be perfectly reasonable, the only way to tell is to make them explicit. For instance, breaking the nominal growth in revenues into growth in the units sold (real growth) and expected inflation allows us to judge whether the inflation assumptions are reasonable, given both general inflation rates and the pricing power a firm possesses. Similarly, recognizing how much of the growth in a multinational comes from its overseas operations and being cognizant of the assumptions made about exchange rates will enable us to assess whether these exchange rates are consistent with our other assumptions.
- **Don't extrapolate last year's numbers:** Extrapolating numbers from the most recent financial year is always a dangerous practice, but doing so with companies that are exposed to macroeconomic risk is doubly dangerous. When valuing cyclical companies, using a base year that is the peak (or nadir) of a cycle leads us to overestimate (or underestimate) the company's value. Forecasting the earnings for a multinational based on a base year number that is inflated because of favorable exchange rate movements will overstate earnings in future years.
- **Check for internal consistency:** As noted in the preceding section, assumptions about macroeconomic variables are interrelated. Thus, if we expect inflation rates to increase in the future, we should also adjust exchange rates and interest rates to match the expectation. The domestic currency can be expected to weaken and interest rates to rise with higher inflation. In addition, we should remain consistent with our views of the same macroeconomic variables across different inputs in a valuation. If we build in higher revenue growth rates because we anticipate higher inflation in the future, we should also factor this higher inflation into our cost variables and when making assumptions about capital expenditures.
- **Separate macro views from views on a company:** As noted in the preceding section, valuations that incorporate strong views about future real growth, inflation, and exchange rate movements are difficult to decipher, since they mix views of the company with views on macroeconomic variables. A more effective way to present views on

macro variables is to separate them from your views on an individual company. This can be accomplished by breaking the valuation into two steps. In the first step, value the company based on the assumption that the market is right about the macro variables. In effect, you value the company with inputs consistent with market views today. For inflation rates, this means using a market expectation obtained by looking at either a survey number or the difference between the nominal Treasury bond rate and the inflation-indexed Treasury rate. For exchange rates, we use forward rates and futures rates from traded currency futures as our expected exchange rates for the future. If derivatives do not exist, we use purchasing power parity to derive future exchange rates:

$$\text{Expected Exchange Rate}_{FC,\$} \text{ in Year n} = \text{Spot Rate}_{FC,\$} * \frac{(1 + \text{Expected Inflation Rate}_{FC})^n}{(1 + \text{Expected Inflation Rate}_{\$})^n}$$

Once the company has been valued using these market-determined inputs, you can consider the effects of imposing your views on these macroeconomic variables. The users of these valuations can decide whether to put more weight on your company assessments or on your macroeconomic views.

- **Use scenario analysis**: Chapter 3, "Probabilistic Valuation: Scenario Analysis, Decision Trees, and Simulations," looked at scenario analysis as one way to examine how a company's value changes as our assumptions about the company change. Scenario analysis is a useful tool in assessing the effects of changes in macroeconomic variables. For instance, we can value a cyclical company under three real-growth scenarios—economic boom, stagnation, and recession—and arrive at three different estimates of value. Applying a probability to each scenario should provide us with an estimate of value today.

Conclusion

The value of every company is affected by what we expect to happen to the overall economy, expected inflation, and exchange rates in the future. Given this centrality, it is surprising how haphazard analysts are when it comes to making reasonable assumptions about these variables. Some make implicit assumptions through the company-specific numbers they use and are unable or unwilling to make these assumptions explicit. Others build all their forecasts on last year's numbers, thus building whatever happened last year with the real economy, inflation, and exchange rates into their future estimates and value. Still others make strong assumptions about the future path of macroeconomic variables, and through these assumptions have large effects on value.

Although we cannot offer a panacea for these problems, we have three suggestions. The first is to make the implicit assumptions about real growth, inflation, and exchange rates explicit and check these assumptions for reasonability and consistency. What we assume about inflation should be consistent with what we anticipate with exchange rates. The second is to separate macroeconomic views on inflation, real growth, and exchange rates from views on individual companies when doing valuation. The third is to use scenario analysis, assign probabilities to each scenario, and estimate the value under each scenario.

9

Baby Steps: Young and Start-Up Companies

Valuing companies early in the life cycle is difficult, partly because of the absence of operating history and partly because most young firms do not make it through these early stages to success. This chapter looks at the challenges we face when valuing young companies and the shortcuts employed by many who have to estimate the value of these businesses. While some of the rules that have developed over time for valuing young businesses make sense, other rules inevitably lead to erroneous and biased estimates of value.

Young Companies in the Economy

It may be a cliché that the entrepreneurs provide the energy for economic growth, but it is also true that vibrant economies have a large number of young, idea businesses, striving to get a foothold in markets. This section begins by looking at where young companies fall in the business life cycle and the role they play in the overall economy. We will follow up by looking at some characteristics that young companies tend to share.

A Life Cycle View of Young Companies

If every business starts with an idea, young companies can range the spectrum (see Figure 9.1). Some are unformed, at least in a commercial sense. The owner of the business has an idea that he or she thinks can fill an unfilled need among consumers. Others have inched a little further up the scale and have converted the idea into a commercial product, albeit with little to show in terms of revenues or earnings. Still others have moved even further down the road to commercial success, and they have a market for their product or service, with revenues and the potential, at least, for some profits.

Since young companies usually are small, they represent only a small part of the overall economy. However, they tend to have a disproportionately large impact on the economy for several reasons.

- **Employment**: Although few studies focus just on start-ups, evidence exists that small businesses account for a disproportionate share of new jobs created in the economy. The National Federation of Independent Businesses estimates that about two-thirds of the new jobs created in recent years have been in small businesses and that start-ups account for a large share of these new jobs.[1]

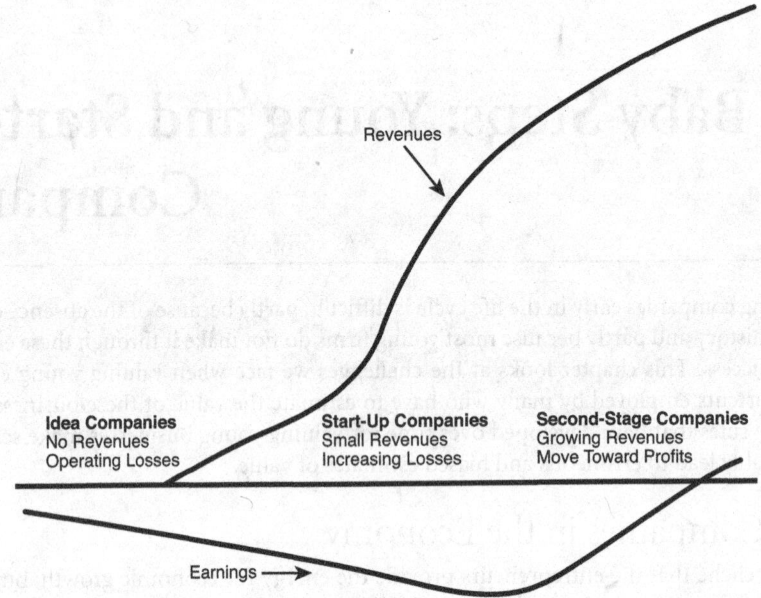

Figure 9.1: The Early Stages of the Life Cycle

- **Innovation**: In the early 1990s, Clayton Christensen, a strategy guru from the Harvard Business School, argued that radical innovation—innovation that disrupted traditional economic mechanisms—was unlikely to come from established firms. They have too much to lose from the innovation. Radical innovation was more likely to come from start-up companies that have little to lose. Thus, online retailing was pioneered by a young upstart, Amazon.com, rather than by traditional retailers.
- **Economic growth**: The economies that have grown the fastest in the last few decades have been those that have a high rate of new business formation. Thus, the U.S. generated much more rapid economic growth than Western Europe during the 1990s, primarily as a consequence of the growth of small technology companies. Similarly, much of the growth in India has come from smaller technology companies rather than from established firms.

Characteristics of Young Companies

As we just noted, young companies are diverse, but they share some common characteristics. In this section, we will consider these shared attributes, with an eye on the valuation problems and issues they create:

1 NFIB Small Business Policy Guide, Small Business Contributions in Small Business Policy Guide.

- **No history:** At the risk of stating the obvious, young companies have very limited histories. Many of them have only one or two years of data available on operations and financing. Some have financials for only a portion of a year, for instance.
- **Small or no revenues, operating losses:** The limited history that is available for young companies is rendered even less useful by the fact that they contain little operating detail. Revenues are small or nonexistent for idea companies, and the expenses often are associated with getting the business established, rather than generating revenues. In combination, they result in significant operating losses.
- **Dependent on private equity:** With a few exceptions, young businesses are dependent on equity from private sources, rather than public markets. At the earlier stages, the equity is provided almost entirely by the founder (and friends and family). As the promise of future success increases, and with it the need for more capital, venture capitalists become a source of equity capital, in return for a share of ownership in the firm.
- **Many don't survive:** Most young companies don't survive the test of commercial success. Several studies back up this statement, although they vary in the failure rates they find. A study of 5,196 start-ups in Australia found that the annual failure rate was in excess of 9% and that 64% of the businesses failed in a ten-year period.[2] Knaup and Piazza (2005, 2008) used data from the Bureau of Labor Statistics Quarterly Census of Employment and Wages (QCEW) to compute survival statistics across firms.[3] This census contains information on more than 8.9 million U.S. businesses in both the public and private sector. Using a seven-year database from 1998 to 2005, the authors concluded that only 44% of all businesses that were founded in 1998 survived at least four years and that only 31% made it through all seven years. In addition, they categorized firms into ten sectors and estimated survival rates for each one. Table 9.1 presents their findings on the proportion of firms that made it through each year for each sector and for the entire sample.

  Note that survival rates vary across sectors. Only 25% of firms in the information sector (which includes technology) survive seven years. On the other hand, almost 44% of health service businesses make it through that period.
- **Multiple claims on equity:** The repeated forays made by young companies to raise equity do expose equity investors, who invested earlier in the process, to the possibility that their value can be reduced by deals offered to subsequent equity investors. To protect their interests equity investors in young companies often demand and get protection from this eventuality. This can take the form of first claims on cash flows from operations and in liquidation. Investors also might have control or veto rights, allowing them to have a say in the firm's actions. As a result, different equity claims in a young company can vary on many dimensions that can affect their value.

2 John Watson and Jim Everett, 1996, "Do Small Businesses Have High Failure Rates?" *Journal of Small Business Management*, v34, pp. 45–63.

3 Knaup, Amy E., May 2005, "Survival and longevity in the business employment dynamics data," *Monthly Labor Review*, pp. 50–56; Knaup, Amy E. and M. C. Piazza, September 2007, "Business Employment Dynamics Data: Survival and Longevity," *Monthly Labor Review*, pp. 3–10.

Table 9.1 Survival of New Companies Founded in 1998

	Proportion of Firms That Were Started in 1998 That Survived Through...						
	Year 1	**Year 2**	**Year 3**	**Year 4**	**Year 5**	**Year 6**	**Year 7**
Natural resources	82.33%	69.54%	59.41%	49.56%	43.43%	39.96%	36.68%
Construction	80.69%	65.73%	53.56%	42.59%	36.96%	33.36%	29.96%
Manufacturing	84.19%	68.67%	56.98%	47.41%	40.88%	37.03%	33.91%
Transportation	82.58%	66.82%	54.70%	44.68%	38.21%	34.12%	31.02%
Information	80.75%	62.85%	49.49%	37.70%	31.24%	28.29%	24.78%
Financial activities	84.09%	69.57%	58.56%	49.24%	43.93%	40.34%	36.90%
Business services	82.32%	66.82%	55.13%	44.28%	38.11%	34.46%	31.08%
Health services	85.59%	72.83%	63.73%	55.37%	50.09%	46.47%	43.71%
Leisure	81.15%	64.99%	53.61%	43.76%	38.11%	34.54%	31.40%
Other services	80.72%	64.81%	53.32%	43.88%	37.05%	32.33%	28.77%
All firms	**81.24%**	**65.77%**	**54.29%**	**44.36%**	**38.29%**	**34.44%**	**31.18%**

Valuation Issues

The fact that young companies have limited histories, are dependent on equity from private sources, and are particularly susceptible to failure all contribute to making them more difficult to value. This section begins by considering the estimation issues that we run into in discounted cash flow valuations. Then we follow up by evaluating why these same issues crop up when we do relative valuation.

Intrinsic (DCF) Valuation

Chapter 2, "Intrinsic Valuation," described the four pieces that make up the intrinsic valuation puzzle:

- Cash flows from existing assets
- Expected growth from both new investments and improved efficiency on existing assets
- Discount rates that emerge from our assessments of risk in both the business and its equity
- The assessment of when the firm will become a stable growth firm (allowing us to estimate terminal value)

On each of these measures, young firms pose estimation challenges that can be traced back to their common characteristics.

Existing Assets

The standard approach to valuing existing assets is to use the firm's current financial statements and its history to estimate the cash flows from these assets and to attach a value to them. With some young firms, existing assets represent such a small proportion of the firm's overall value that it makes little sense to expend resources estimating their value. With other young firms, where existing assets may have some value, the problem is that the financial statements made available by the firm provide little relevant information in estimating that value, for the following reasons:

- The absence of historical data makes it difficult to assess how well the revenues from existing assets will hold up if macroeconomic conditions become less favorable. In other words, if all you have is one year of financial data, it is more problematic to decide whether the revenues represent a flash in the pan or are sustainable. The lack of data from prior years also makes it more difficult to analyze how revenues would change if the company changed its pricing policy or faced new competition.
- The expenses that young companies incur to generate future growth are often mixed in with the expenses associated with generating current revenues. For instance, it is not unusual to see the selling, general, and administrative (S, G, and A) expenses at some young companies be three or four times larger than revenues, largely because they include the expenses associated with lining up future customers. To value existing assets, we have to be able to separate these expenses from genuine operating expenses, and that is not easy to do.

Growth Assets

The bulk of a young company's value comes from growth assets. Consequently, the difficulties we have in assessing the value of growth assets are at the heart of whether we can value these companies in the first place. We run into several problems when valuing young companies:

- The absence of revenues in some cases, and the lack of history on revenues in others, means that we cannot use past revenue growth as an input into the estimation of future revenues. As a result, we are often dependent on the firm's own estimates of future revenues, with all the biases associated with these numbers.
- Even if we could estimate revenues in future years, we also have to evaluate how earnings will evolve in future years as revenues change. Again, the fact that young companies tend to report losses and have no history on operating income makes it more difficult to assess what future profit margins will be.
- Chapter 2 noted that it is not revenue or even earnings growth per se that determines value, but the quality of that growth. To assess the quality of growth, we looked at how much the firm reinvested to generate its expected growth. We noted that value-creating growth arises only when a firm generates a return on capital greater than its cost of capital on its growth investments. This intuitive concept is put to the test with young companies, because there is little basis for the expected return on capital on new investments. Past data doesn't provide much guidance, because the company has made so few investments in the past, and these investments have been in existence for short periods.

The current return on capital, which is often used as a starting point for estimating future returns, is generally a negative number for young companies.

In summary, we have a tough time estimating future growth in revenues and operating margins for young companies. The estimation problems are accentuated by the difficulties we face in coming up with reinvestment assumptions that are consistent with our growth estimates.

Discount Rates

The standard approaches for assessing the risk in a company and coming up with discount rates depend on the availability of market prices for the securities issued by the firm. Thus, we estimate the beta for equity by regressing returns on a stock against returns on a market index, and the cost of debt by looking at the current market prices of publicly traded bonds. In addition, the traditional risk-and-return models we use to estimate the cost of equity focus only on market risk—the risk that cannot be diversified away—based on the implicit assumption that the marginal investors in a company are diversified.

With young companies, these assumptions are open to challenge. First, most young companies are not publicly traded and have no publicly traded bonds outstanding. Consequently, there is no way we can run a regression of past returns to get an equity beta, or use a market interest rate on debt. To add to the problem, the equity in a young company is often held by investors who are either completely invested in the company (founders) or only partially diversified (venture capitalists). As a result, these investors are unlikely to accept the notion that the only risk that matters is the risk that cannot be diversified away. Instead, they will demand compensation for at least some of the firm-specific risk.

Finally, we noted that equity in young companies can come from multiple sources at different times and with very different terms attached to it. It is conceivable that the differences across equity claims can lead to different costs of equity for each one. Thus, the cost of equity for an equity claim that has a first claim on the cash flows may be lower than the cost of equity for an equity claim that has a residual cash flow claim.

Terminal Value

If the terminal value accounts for a large proportion of the overall value of a typical firm, it is an even bigger component of the value of a young company. In fact, it is not unusual for the terminal value to account for 90%, 100%, or even more than 100% of the current value of a young company. Consequently, assumptions about when a firm will reach stable growth, a prerequisite for estimating terminal value, and its characteristics in stable growth can have a substantial impact on the value we attach to a young company. Our task, though, is complicated by our inability to answer three questions:

- **Will the firm make it to stable growth?** Earlier we noted the high failure rate among young firms. In effect, these firms will never make it to stable growth, and the terminal value will not provide the large windfall to value that it does for a going concern. Estimating a firm's probability of survival early in the life cycle, therefore, is a critical component of value, but it's not necessarily an easy input to estimate.

- **When will the firm become a stable growth firm?** Even if we assume that a firm will make it to stable growth in the future, estimating when that will occur is a difficult exercise. After all, some firms reach steady state in a couple years, whereas others have a much longer stretch of high growth before settling into mature growth. The judgment of when a firm will become stable is complicated by the fact that the actions of competitors can play an important role in how growth evolves over time.
- **What will the firm look like in stable growth?** Chapter 2 noted that not just the stable growth rate determines the magnitude of terminal value. Also important are the concurrent assumptions we make about risk and excess returns during the stable phase. In effect, assuming that a firm will continue to generate excess returns forever will lead to a higher terminal value than assuming that excess returns will converge on zero or be negative. Although we must make this judgment for any firm, the absence of any historical data on excess returns at young firms complicates estimation.

Value of Equity Claims

As soon as the cash flows have been estimated, a discount rate computed, and the present value figured, we have estimated the value of the aggregate equity in the firm. If all equity claims in the firm are equivalent, as is the case with a publicly traded firm with one class of shares, we divide the value of equity proportionately among the claims to get the value per claim. With young firms, we face potential problems in making this allocation judgment, arising from how equity is generally raised at these firms. First, the fact that equity is raised sequentially from private investors, as opposed to issuing shares in a public market, can result in nonstandardized equity claims. In other words, the agreements with equity investors at a new round of financing can be very different from prior equity agreements. Second, there can be large differences across equity claims on cash flows and control rights, with some claimholders getting preferential rights over others. Finally, equity investors in each round of financing often demand and receive rights protecting their interests in subsequent financing and investment decisions made by the firm.

The net effect of these diverse equity claims is that allocating the value of equity across different claims requires us to value both the preferential cash flow and control claims and the protective rights built into some equity claims but not others.

Relative Valuation

The difficulties that we have outlined in valuing young companies in a discounted cash flow model lead some analysts to consider using relative valuation approaches to value these companies. In effect, they try to value young companies using multiples and comparables. However, this task is made more difficult by the following factors:

- **What do you scale value to?** All valuation multiples have to be scaled to some common measure. Conventional scaling measures include earnings, book value, and revenues. With young companies, each of these measures can pose problems. Since most of them report losses early in the life cycle, multiples such as price earnings ratios and EBITDA multiples cannot be computed. Since the firm has been in operation only a short while, the book value is likely to be a very small number and won't reflect the true capital invested in the company. Even revenues can be problematic, since they can be nonexistent for idea companies and miniscule for companies that have just transitioned into commercial production.

- **What are your comparable companies?** When relative valuation is used to value a publicly traded company, the comparable firms are usually publicly traded counterparts in the same sector. With young companies, the comparison would logically be to other young companies in the same business, but these companies are usually not publicly traded and have no market prices (or multiples that can be computed). We could look at the multiples at which publicly traded firms in the same sector trade at, but these firms are likely to have very different risk, cash flow, and growth characteristics than the young firm being valued.
- **What is the best proxy for risk?** Many of the proxies used for risk, in relative valuation, are market-based. Thus, beta or standard deviation of equity returns are often used as measures of equity risk, but these measures cannot be computed for young companies that are privately held. In some cases, the standard deviation in accounting numbers (earnings and revenues) is used as a measure of risk, but this too cannot be computed for a firm that has been in existence for a short time.
- **How do you control for survival?** In the context of discounted cash flow valuation, we looked at the problems created by the high failure rate of young companies. This is also an issue with using relative valuation. Intuitively, we would expect the relative value of a young company (the multiple of revenues or earnings we assign it) to increase with its likelihood of survival. However, putting this intuitive principle into practice is not easy.

In conclusion, the use of relative valuation may seem like an easy solution when faced with the estimation challenges posed in intrinsic valuation. But all the problems we face with the latter remain problems when we do the former.

The Dark Side of Valuation

With the estimation challenges that analysts face in valuing young companies, it should come as no surprise that they look for solutions that seem to, at least on the surface, offer them a way out. Many of these solutions, though, are the source of the valuation errors we see in young-company valuations. This section looks at the most common manifestations of what we view as the dark side in young-company valuations and how they play out in venture capital valuations.

- **Top line and bottom line, no detail**: It is difficult to estimate the details of cash flow and reinvestment for young companies. Consequently, many valuations of young companies focus on the top line (revenues) and the bottom line (earnings, usually equity earnings). Little or no attention is paid to either the intermediate items (that separate earnings from revenues) or the reinvestment requirements (that separate earnings from cash flows).
- **Focus on the short term, rather than the long term**: The uncertainty we feel about the estimates we make for young companies become greater as we go further out in time. Many analysts use this as a rationale for cutting short the estimation period, using only three to five years of forecasts in the valuation. "It is too difficult to forecast beyond that point in time" is the justification they offer for this short time horizon.
- **Mixing relative with intrinsic valuation**: To deal with the inability to estimate cash flows beyond short time periods, analysts who value young companies use relative valuation as a crutch. Thus, the value at the end of the forecast period (three to five years)

is often estimated by applying an exit multiple to the expected revenues or earnings in that year. The value of that multiple is itself estimated by looking at what publicly traded companies in the business trade at right now.

- **Discount rate as the vehicle for all uncertainty**: The risks associated with investing in a young company include not only the traditional factors—earnings volatility and sensitivity to macroeconomic conditions, for example—but also the likelihood that the firm will not survive to make a run at commercial success. When valuing private businesses, analysts often hike up discount rates to reflect all their concerns about the firm, including the likelihood that the firm will not make it.
- **Ad hoc and arbitrary adjustments for differences in equity claims**: As we noted in the preceding section, equity claims in young businesses can have different rights when it comes to cash flow and control. When asked to make judgments on the value of prior claims on cash flows or superior control rights, many analysts use rules of thumb that are either arbitrary or based on dubious statistical tests.

All five of these practices come into play in the most common approach used to value young firms—the venture capital approach. This approach, which we described briefly in Chapter 3, has four steps:

1. We begin by estimating the expected earnings or revenues in a future year, but not too far into the future: two to five years is the typical range. In most cases, the forecast period is set to match the point in time at which the venture capitalist plans to sell the business or take it public.
2. The value at the end of the forecast period is assessed by multiplying the expected earnings in the future year by the multiple of earnings (PE ratio) that publicly traded firms in the sector trade at. In some cases, the multiple is based on other companies in the sector that have been sold or have gone public recently.

   $$\text{Equity Value at End of Forecast Horizon} = \text{Expected Earnings}_{\text{Year n}} * \text{Forecast PE}$$

   Alternatively, the revenues at the end of the forecast period can be multiplied by the revenue multiple at which publicly traded firms trade at to arrive at an estimate of the value of the entire business (as opposed to just equity):

   $$\text{Enterprise Value at End of Forecast Period} = \text{Expected Revenues}_{\text{Year n}} * \text{Forecast EV/Sales}$$

   This approach is used for companies that may not become profitable until later in the life cycle.
3. The estimated value at the end of the forecast period is discounted back at a target rate of return. This is generally set high enough to capture both the perceived risk in the business and the likelihood that the firm will not survive. Since the latter is a high, venture capital required rates of return tend to be much higher than the discount rates we see used with publicly traded companies.

$$\text{Equity Value Today} = \frac{\text{Equity Value at End of Forecast Horizon(n)}}{(1 + \text{Target Rate of Return})^n}$$

Table 9.2 summarizes the target rates of return demanded by venture capitalists, categorized by how far along a firm is in the life cycle.

Table 9.2 Venture Capital Target Rates of Return: Stage in the Life Cycle

Stage of Development	Typical Target Rates of Return
Start-up	50 to 70%
First stage	40 to 60%
Second stage	35 to 50%
Bridge / IPO	25 to 35%

How do we know that these rates of return have survival risks built into them? In addition to the intuitive rationale that they decrease as firms move through the life cycle and the chance of failure drops off, the actual returns earned by venture capitalists at every stage of the process are much more modest. Table 9.3 summarizes the actual returns earned by venture capitalists (VC) in the aggregate for investments across the life cycle.

Table 9.3 Returns Earned by Venture Capitalists in 2007

	Three-Year	Five-Year	Ten-Year	20-Year
Early/seed VC	4.90%	5.00%	32.90%	21.40%
Balanced VC	10.80%	11.90%	14.40%	14.70%
Later-stage VC	12.40%	11.10%	8.50%	14.50%
All VC	8.50%	8.80%	16.60%	16.90%
NASDAQ	3.60%	7.00%	1.90%	9.20%
S&P	2.40%	5.50%	1.20%	8.00%

Note that the long-term returns earned by venture capitalists, especially on early-stage investments, are significantly higher than the returns earned by investors in equity in public markets over the same period. But they're nowhere near the target returns listed in Table 9.2. For instance, early-stage VC investors earned an annual return of 21.4% over the last 20 years, well below the 50 to 70% target returns. In effect, the high target rates of return that are used in analysis are not delivered by most investments (usually the ones that fail to make it to the exit valuation).

4. Venture capitalists receive a proportion of the business in return for the capital they bring to the firm. To decide what proportion of the firm they are entitled to, the new capital

brought in is added to the estimated value from step 3 (called the pre-money value) to arrive at the firm's post-money valuation.

$$\text{Post-Money Valuation} = \text{Pre-Money Valuation from Step 3} + \text{New Capital Infusion}$$

The proportion of equity that the venture capitalist is entitled to is then computed by dividing the capital infusion by the post-money valuation:

$$\text{Proportion of Equity to New Capital Provider} = \frac{\text{New Capital Provided}}{\text{Post-Money Valuation}}$$

As we see it, the venture capital approach has several problems. Many of them are rooted in the practices we listed before:

- By focusing on revenues and earnings, and ignoring both the intermediate items and those that come after, venture capital valuations encourage game playing. Since value increases as the projected earnings (revenues) increase, the existing owners of the business try to push up these values, without having to flesh out the consequences in terms of future capital investment. On the other side of the bargaining table, venture capitalists will argue for using lower numbers for earnings and revenues, since this pushes down the estimated value (and gives them a greater share of equity for the same capital investment). Consequently, the projected value becomes a bargaining point between the two sides rather than the subject of serious estimation.
- Venture capital valuations try to avoid the challenges of estimating operating details for the long term by cutting off the estimates prematurely (with a short forecast period) and using a multiple that is usually based on what comparable companies are trading at currently. However, the multiple of earnings or revenues that a business will trade at three years from now will be a function of the cash flows after that point. Not estimating those cash flows or dealing with the uncertainty in the cash flows does not mean that the uncertainty has gone away.
- A degree of sloppiness is associated with the use of a target rate to discount the firm's future value. This target rate is the rate demanded by venture capitalists, who are equity investors in the firm. It incorporates the likelihood that the business will fail. Using this number as the discount rate on the future value of the business creates two problems. The first is that the future value discounted has to be an equity value. Of course, this is the case when we use expected equity earnings and a PE ratio, but it is not so if we use revenues and enterprise value multiples. In the latter case, we should consider the cost of capital as the discount rate and not the rate demanded by just equity investors. The second problem is that building in a probability that the business will not survive into the discount rate also implies that this rate will not change over time, as a firm moves through the life cycle.
- Although the rationale for adding the new capital infusion to the pre-money value is simple, it works only if the new capital raised stays in the firm to be used to fund future investments. If some or all of the new capital is used by existing equity investors to cash out of their ownership in the firm, the portion that is removed from the firm should not be added back to get to the post-money value.

Valuing Secure Mail Software: the Venture Capital Approach

Secure Mail Software is a small company that has developed a new computer virus screening program that it believes will be more effective than existing antivirus programs. The company is fully owned by its founder and has no debt outstanding. The firm has been in existence only a year. It offers a beta version of the software for free to online users but has never sold the product (revenues are zero). During its year of existence, the firm has incurred $15 million in expenses, thus recording an operating loss for the year of the same amount. As a venture capitalist, you have been approached about providing $30 million in additional capital to the firm, primarily to cover the commercial introduction of the software and expand the market for the next two years. To value the firm, you decide to employ the venture capital approach:

1. The founder believes that the virus program will quickly find a market and that revenues will be $300 million by the third year.
2. Looking at publicly traded companies that produce antivirus software, you come up with two companies you feel are relevant comparables:

Company	Market Cap	Debt Outstanding	Cash	Enterprise Value	Revenues	EV/Sales
Symantec	$9,388	$2,300	$1,890	$9,798	$5,874	1.67
McAfee	$4,167	$0	$394	$3,773	$1,308	2.88

You decide to use the average across the two companies, which yields an enterprise value of 2.275 times revenues:[4]

Estimated Value in Three Years = RevenuesYear 3 * EV/Sales
= 300 * 2.275 = $682.89 million

3. Since this business has a product ready for the market, but it also has no history of commercial success, you decide to use a target rate of return of 50%. Since the firm has no debt outstanding, the estimated value is entirely equity, and the value today can be estimated as follows:

$$\text{Value Today} = \frac{\text{Estimated Value in Year 3}}{(1+\text{Target Return})^3} = \frac{682.89}{1.50^3} = \$202.34 \text{ million}$$

4 As the venture capitalist, you would probably argue for an even lower number (Symantec's multiple). To counter, the founder of Secure Mail would probably argue that his company will be priced more like McAfee.

4. To estimate the post-money valuation, you add the cash proceeds that you will be bringing into the firm to the pre-money value of $202.34 million:

$$\text{Post-Money Value} = \text{Pre-Money Value} + \text{Capital Infusion}$$
$$= \$202.34 \text{ million} + \$30 \text{ million} = \$232.34 \text{ million}$$

The proportion of the equity in the firm that you will receive for your capital infusion can then be computed as follows:

$$\text{Proportional Share of Equity} = \frac{\text{Capital Infusion}}{\text{Post-Money Value}} = \frac{30}{232.34} = 12.91\%$$

Note that these numbers are subject to negotiation and that this is the minimum share that the venture capitalist would accept. The venture capitalist will push for lower future revenues, a more conservative multiple of those revenues in the final year, and a higher target rate of return. All of these lower the firm's value and give him a higher share of the equity (for the same capital investment). The firm's existing owner will push for higher future revenues, a higher multiple of these revenues in the final year, and a lower target rate of return. This is all in the interest of pushing up value and giving up less equity ownership for the capital invested.

The Light Side of Valuation

While it is understandable that analysts, when confronted with the myriad uncertainties associated with valuing young companies, look for shortcuts, there is no reason why young companies cannot be valued systematically. This section begins by describing the foundations for estimating the intrinsic value of a young company. Then we will move on to consider how best to adapt relative valuation for the special characteristics of young companies. We will close with a discussion of how real options may be useful—at least when valuing some small businesses.

Discounted Cash Flow Valuation

To apply discounted cash flow models to valuing young companies, we will move systematically through the process of estimation, considering at each stage how best to deal with the characteristics of young companies.

Estimating Future Cash Flows

The preceding section noted that many analysts who value young companies forecast just the top and bottom lines (revenues and earnings) for short periods. They offer the defense that there are far too many uncertainties in the long term to do estimation in detail. We believe that it is important, uncertainties notwithstanding, to look at operating expenses in the aggregate and to go beyond earnings to estimate cash flows. We can approach the estimation process in two ways. In the first, which we call the *top-down* approach, we begin with the total market for the product or service that a company sells, and we work down to the firm's revenues and earnings. In the *bottom-up* approach, we work within the firm's capacity constraints, estimate the number of units that will be sold, and then derive revenues, earnings, and cash flows from those units.

The Top-Down Approach

In the top-down approach, we start by estimating the total market for a product or service and then derive the rest of the numbers from that top line. In effect, we estimate the revenues first and then consider how much we need as capacity (and capital to create this capacity) to sustain these revenues. The steps involved in the process are as follows:

1. **Potential market for the product/service:** The first step in deriving the firm's revenues is estimating the total potential market for its products and services. At this juncture, we face two challenges:

   Defining the product/service offered by the firm: If the product or service offered by the firm is defined narrowly, the potential market will be circumscribed by that definition and will be smaller. If we use a broader definition, the market will expand to fit that definition. For example, defining Amazon.com as a book retailer, which is what it was in 1998, would have yielded a total market of less than $10 billion in that year, representing total book retailing sales in 1998. Categorizing Amazon.com as a general retailer would have yielded a much larger potential market. While that might have been difficult to defend in 1998, it became more plausible as Amazon expanded its offerings in 1999 and 2000.

   Estimating the market size: Having defined the market, we face the challenge of estimating the size of that market. For a product or service that is entering an established market, the best sources of data tend to be trade publications and professional forecasting services. Almost every business has a trade group that tracks the operating details of that business. The U.S. alone has almost 7,600 trade groups, tracking everything from aerospace to telecommunications equipment.[5] In many businesses, firms specialize in collecting information about the businesses for commercial and consulting purposes. For instance, the Gartner Group collects and provides data on different types of information technology businesses, including software.

   Evolution in total market over time: Since we have to forecast revenues into the future, it would be useful to get a sense of how the total market is expected to change or grow over time. This information usually is available from the same sources that provide the numbers for the current market size.

2. **Market share**: Once we have a sense of the overall market size and how it will change over time, we have to estimate the share of that market that will be captured by the firm being analyzed, both in the long term and in the time periods leading up to steady state. Clearly, these estimates will depend on both the quality of the product or service that is being offered and how well it measures up against the competition. A useful exercise in estimation is to list the largest players in the targeted market currently and to visualize where the firm being valued will end up as soon as it has an established market. However, two other variables must be considered concurrently. One is the *capacity of the management of the young company* to deliver on its promises. Many entrepreneurs have brilliant ideas but do not have the management and business skills to take them to commercial fruition. That is part of the reason that venture capitalists look for entrepreneurs who have a track record

5 Wikipedia has an excellent listing of industry trade groups, with links to each one. See http://en.wikipedia.org/wiki/List_of_industry_trade_groups_in_the_United_States.

of past success. The other variable is the *resources that the young company can draw on* to get its product/service to the desired market share. Optimistic forecasts for market share have to be coupled with large investments in both capacity and marketing; products don't produce and sell themselves.

3. **Operating expenses/margins**: Revenues may be the top line, but for investors, a firm can have value only if it ultimately delivers earnings. Consequently, the next step is estimating the operating expenses associated with the estimated revenues. We are stymied in this process with young companies, both by the absence of history and the fact that these firms usually have very large operating losses at the time of the estimate. Again, we would separate the estimation process into two parts. In the first part, we would focus on estimating the operating margin in steady state, primarily by looking at more established companies in the business. Once we have the target margin, we can look at how we expect the margin to evolve over time. This "pathway to profitability" can be rockier for some firms than others, with fixed costs and competition playing significant roles in the estimation. One final issue that has to be confronted at this stage is the level of detail that we want to build into our forecasts. In other words, should we just estimate the operating margin and profit, or should we try to forecast individual operating expense items such as labor, materials, selling, and advertising expenses? As a general rule, the level of detail should decrease as we become more uncertain about a firm's future. While this may seem counterintuitive, detail in forecasts leads to better estimates of value, if and only if we bring some information into that detail that otherwise would be missed. An analyst who has a tough time forecasting revenues in year 1 really is in no position to estimate labor or advertising costs in year 5 and should not even try. In valuing young companies, less (detail) is often more (precision).

4. **Investments for growth**: When owners are asked for forecasts of revenues and earnings (steps 2 and 3), it is natural that they go for optimistic values. Revenues increase at exponential rates, and margins quickly move toward target values. In any competitive business, though, neither revenue growth nor margin improvement is delivered for free. Consequently, it is critical that we estimate how much the firm is reinvesting to generate the forecast growth. With a manufacturing firm, this takes the form of investments in additional production capacity. With a technology firm, it includes not only investments in R&D and new patents, but also human capital (hiring software programmers and researchers). There are two reasons to pay attention to this step of the process. The first is that these investments require cash outflows and thus affect the final bottom line, which is the cash flow that can be delivered to investors. The second reason (and this is especially so with young firms) is that this reinvestment often results in negative cash flows, which then have to be covered with new capital infusions. Thus, existing equity investors either see their share of the ownership reduced (when new equity investors come in) or are called on to make fresh investments to keep the business going.

5. **Compute the tax effect**: With healthy firms, computing the tax effect is usually a simple exercise of multiplying the expected pre-tax operating income by the tax rate. The only real estimation question we face is what tax rate to use—marginal or effective. Young firms that are losing money have two estimation challenges. The first is that these firms have generally never paid taxes in the past (since they have never generated earnings)

and thus have no effective tax rates. The second challenge is that the losses that have been made in the past and that you often expect in the near future create net operating losses that can be carried forward and used to shelter positive earnings in future years. The most direct way of dealing with these losses is to cumulate them as they are expected to occur over time and to keep track of the net operating loss (NOL) carryforward. In the first few years of positive earnings, we can draw on this NOL and essentially not pay taxes. When the NOL is exhausted, we should move to a marginal tax rate based on the statutory tax codes. This is a conservative solution. The alternative is to use the average effective tax rate paid by healthy firms in the sector.

6. **Check for internal consistency**: One of the perils of the top-down approach is that operating income and reinvestment are estimated separately, so these numbers might not be internally consistent. In other words, we may be reinvesting too little, given our forecasts of expected revenue growth, or too much. One simple test that can be used to check for consistency is to compute an imputed return on capital, based on the earnings and reinvestment forecasts:

$$\text{Imputed Return on Capital} = \frac{\text{Expected Operating Income after Tax}_t}{\text{Capital Invested in Firm}_{t-1}}$$

The numerator is the forecast operating income, and the denominator is computed as the cumulated total of all reinvestment (net capital expenditures and change in noncash working capital) over time, through period t −1, added to the initial capital invested (at the time of the valuation):

$$\text{Capital Invested}_{t-1} = \text{Capital Invested}_0 + \sum_{n=1}^{n=t-1} \text{Reinvestment}_n$$

The imputed return on capital, as you approach steady state, can then be compared to both the industry average return on capital (to ensure that you are not making your company an outlier) and to the company's own steady state cost of capital. An imputed return on capital well above the industry average and the cost of capital is an indication that the reinvestment forecast for the firm over the forecast period is insufficient, given the expected earnings. Conversely, an imputed return on capital below the cost of capital would indicate that the reinvestment numbers are too high, given the revenue and earnings forecasts.

Estimating Cash Flows for a Young Business: Secure Mail Software

We will illustrate the top-down approach with Secure Mail Software, the company that we used earlier to illustrate the venture capital approach.

1. **Total market**: Secure Mail is planning to sell antivirus software. We use the estimates of total size of the security software market (which includes the antivirus software) globally, from Gartner in 2008. Table 9.4 summarizes the estimate of the market size in 2008 and the forecasts from 2009 to 2012.

Table 9.4 **Forecast Global Market for Security Software (in Millions of U.S. Dollars)**

Year	Current (2008)	2009	2010	2011	2012	2013
Market growth rate	NA	5.50%	5.50%	5.50%	5.50%	5.50%
Overall market	$10,500	$11,078	$11,687	$12,330	$13,008	$13,723

Beyond 2012, we estimate a growth rate, in the overall market, of 5% from 2013 to 2018 and 3% afterwards.

2. **Market share**: To estimate the market share, we look at the largest antivirus software firms in the market in 2008, in terms of market share. Table 9.5, also from Gartner, lists the largest firms, with their market share.

Table 9.5 **Largest Antivirus Software Companies in 2007**

Company	2007 Revenues	Market Share
Symantec	$2,789 million	26.6%
McAfee	$1,226 million	11.8%
Trend Micro	$810 million	7.8%
IBM	$608 million	5.8%
CA	$419 million	4.0%
EMC	$415 million	4.0%
Others	$4,171 million	40.0%

Secure Mail's software offering measures up well against the competition, both in terms of features and price. In addition, the management of the company includes the founder, who has had experience in other successful software start-ups. Consequently, we estimate that Secure Mail will be able to capture a 10% market share in steady state (expected in ten years).

3. **Operating income/margins**: To estimate the expected operating margin in ten years, we examine the pre-tax operating margins and after-tax returns on invested capital of the largest publicly traded competitors that operated primarily in the antivirus business in 2007 (see Table 9.6).

Table 9.6 **Pre-Tax Profitability Measures: Antivirus Software Business**

Company	Operating Margin (Pre-Tax)	Return on Invested Capital (After-Tax)
Symantec	13.05%	17.07%*
McAfee	12.91%	22.80%
Trend Micro	14.50%	17.89%

*Symantec had $11 billion in goodwill on the balance. We netted out a portion of this goodwill in computing return on capital.

We assume that Secure Mail's pre-tax operating margin would converge to 13%, close to the margins reported by Symantec and McAfee, by 2018. However, the pathway to profitability is likely to be rocky, with margins staying negative for at least three years. Table 9.7 lists the estimated revenues and operating margins for Secure Mail for the next ten years.

Table 9.7 Expected Revenues, Operating Margins, and Earnings for Secure Mail Software

Year	Total Market	Market Share	Revenues	Pre-Tax Operating Margin	Pre-Tax Operating Income
2009	$11,078	0.50%	$55	–10.00%	–$5.54
2010	$11,687	1.50%	$175	–5.00%	–$8.77
2011	$12,330	2.50%	$308	–1.00%	–$3.08
2012	$13,008	4.00%	$520	5.00%	$26.02
2013	$13,723	5.00%	$686	10.00%	$68.62
2014	$14,409	6.00%	$865	10.60%	$91.64
2015	$15,130	7.00%	$1,059	11.20%	$118.62
2016	$15,886	8.00%	$1,271	11.80%	$149.97
2017	$16,680	9.00%	$1,501	12.40%	$186.15
2018	$17,515	10.00%	$1,751	13.00%	$227.69

4. **Taxes**: In computing taxes for Secure Mail, we start with the fact that the firm has already accumulated net operating losses of $15 million over its lifetime. In the first three years, where we are anticipating operating losses, we add the losses to the NOL, and then we use this NOL to shelter income in year 4 and partially in year 5. We will use the marginal U.S. tax rate of 40% as the tax rate on income thereafter. Table 9.8 lists the NOL and taxes paid each year, based on the 40% tax rate.

Table 9.8 NOLs, Taxes, and After-Tax Operating Income

Year	Pre-Tax Operating Income	NOL at Start of Year	NOL at End of Year	Taxable Operating Income	Taxes	After-Tax Operating Income
2009	–$5.54	$15.00	$20.54	$0.00	$0.00	–$5.54
2010	–$8.77	$20.54	$29.30	$0.00	$0.00	–$8.77
2011	–$3.08	$29.30	$32.39	$0.00	$0.00	–$3.08
2012	$26.02	$32.39	$6.37	$0.00	$0.00	$26.02

2013	$68.62	$6.37	$0.00	$62.24	$24.90	$43.72
2014	$91.64	$0.00	$0.00	$91.64	$36.66	$54.99
2015	$118.62	$0.00	$0.00	$118.62	$47.45	$71.17
2016	$149.97	$0.00	$0.00	$149.97	$59.99	$89.98
2017	$186.15	$0.00	$0.00	$186.15	$74.46	$111.69
2018	$227.69	$0.00	$0.00	$227.69	$91.08	$136.61

5. **Reinvestment**: We are assuming that revenues will increase to $1.75 billion in ten years, as Secure Mail expands its market share of this growing market. To estimate how much Secure Mail will need to reinvest to generate this additional revenue, we use the ratio of revenues to capital invested in this sector of 1.95 (based on revenues and book capital at publicly traded firms in the business). We also use a one-year lag between reinvestment and growth to estimate the reinvestment in each year. Table 9.9 summarizes our estimates.

Table 9.9 Estimated Reinvestment by Year

Year	Revenues	Change in Revenues in the Next Year	Sales/Capital	Reinvestment
2009	$55	$120	1.95	$61.49
2010	$175	$133	1.95	$68.17
2011	$308	$212	1.95	$108.75
2012	$520	$166	1.95	$85.05
2013	$686	$178	1.95	$91.49
2014	$865	$195	1.95	$99.76
2015	$1,059	$212	1.95	$108.62
2016	$1,271	$230	1.95	$118.13
2017	$1,501	$250	1.95	$128.31
2018	$1,751	$53	1.95	$26.95*

*Revenues in 2019 at $1,804 million are 3% higher than revenues in 2018.

Note that the reinvestment in year 1 is computed based on the change in revenues from year 1 to year 2 and using the sales-to-capital ratio of 1.95:

$$\text{Reinvestment in Year 1} = \frac{(\text{Revenues}_2 - \text{Revenues}_1)}{\text{Sales to Capital Ratio}} = \frac{(175 - 55)}{1.95} = \$61.49 \text{ million}$$

The process is repeated for the ensuing periods.

6. **Internal consistency check**: As a final check on our estimates, we compute the capital invested each year, starting with the initial capital investment of $5 million and adding to this amount the reinvestment each year to get to cumulated capital invested at the end of each period. Dividing by the after-tax operating income each year yields the after-tax return on capital, as shown in Table 9.10.

Table 9.10 Estimated Capital Invested and ROIC

Year	After-Tax Operating Income	Reinvestment	Capital Invested at Start of Year	Capital Invested at End of Year	Return on Capital
2009	–$5.54	$61.49	$5.00	$66.49	–110.78%
2010	–$8.77	$68.17	$66.49	$134.67	–13.18%
2011	–$3.08	$108.75	$134.67	$243.42	–2.29%
2012	$26.02	$85.05	$243.42	$328.47	10.69%
2013	$43.72	$91.49	$328.47	$419.96	13.31%
2014	$54.99	$99.76	$419.96	$519.71	13.09%
2015	$71.17	$108.62	$519.71	$628.34	13.69%
2016	$89.98	$118.13	$628.34	$746.46	14.32%
2017	$111.69	$128.31	$746.46	$874.78	14.96%
2018	$136.61	$26.95	$874.78	$901.72	15.62%

We computed the return on capital each year, based on the capital invested at the start of the year.[6] The return on capital in 2018 is 15.62%, below the industry average return on capital reported in Table 9.6, but close to what we will assume Secure Mail's return on capital to be for stable growth of 15%. The end result of these assumptions is Table 9.11, which summarizes the expected cash flows, after taxes and reinvestment needs, to Secure Mail as a business for the next ten years.

6 The alternative is to use the average capital invested over the period. In keeping with the fact that we are using end-of-the year cash flows (rather than mid-year cash flows), we chose the capital invested at the start of each year.

Table 9.11 Expected Free Cash Flow to the Firm for Secure Mail Software

Year	After-Tax Operating Income	Reinvestment	FCFF
2009	–$5.54	$61.49	–$67.03
2010	–$8.77	$68.17	–$76.94
2011	–$3.08	$108.75	–$111.84
2012	$26.02	$85.05	–$59.03
2013	$43.72	$91.49	–$47.77
2014	$54.99	$99.76	–$44.77
2015	$71.17	$108.62	–$37.45
2016	$89.98	$118.13	–$28.15
2017	$111.69	$128.31	–$16.62
2018	$136.61	$26.95	$109.67

Note that earnings become positive well before cash flows do; the latter are weighed down by the reinvestment made to sustain future growth.

The Bottom-Up Approach

The bottom-up approach is a more contained way of estimating the expected cash flows on a business. In the top-down approach, we started with the total market and built down to estimates of revenues and cash flows for the firm. This time we begin with an estimate of investment in capacity and then build up to estimates of revenues and cash flows, based on this capacity constraint. In general, we can break the approach into the following steps:

1. **Capacity size/investment:** The process begins with an estimate of what we will need to invest to get the business off the ground; this also determines the production capacity. A trade-off is inherent in this step. Investing in more capacity allows us to produce and sell more in the future, but the capital (both financial and human) needed to sustain this capacity will also be greater. To the degree that either human or financial capital is limited, we may have to settle for less capacity over more.
2. **Unit sales/revenues:** Once we have chosen a capacity constraint, we have to estimate how many units we can sell each period, for the forecast period, and the price that will be charged per unit. At this stage, we have to consider not only the potential market for the product or service we offer, but also the competition (both current and potential) in this market. The choices we make on pricing can determine the number of units sold. Lower prices generally translate into more sales, but not necessarily higher profits.

3. **Operating costs:** With the number of units sold each period as an input, we can estimate the costs of production in each period. These estimates should include not only the costs of inputs that go into the product, but also selling, administrative, and other costs. The latter must be consistent with the unit sales assumptions in step 2.

4. **Taxes:** The revenue and expense estimates are used to estimate the taxable income that the firm will generate each period and the resulting taxes. At this stage, we also have to separate capital from operating expenses, and estimate depreciation and amortization on the former. We also must separate operating expenses from financial expenses (interest expenses) to determine cash flows to the firm and cash flows to equity. The former is before financial expenses, whereas the latter is after.

5. **Additional reinvestment:** Although we estimated the initial investment in step 1, we might have to make additional investments over time to augment or preserve the earning capacity of the business. We need to determine what the business will have to reinvest to preserve its income-generating capacity. If the business requires working capital, growth in revenues may also lead to investments in working capital (inventory and accounts receivable) that have to be considered as reinvestment.

As a general rule, bottom-up approaches of cash flows yield lower expected cash flows and earnings, because we work with capacity constraints. Consequently, these approaches are more suited for businesses that either face significant restrictions on raising additional capital (because they are too small and/or in the wrong type of business) or are dependent on a key person or people for their success. As a general rule, personal-service businesses (medical practices, a plumbing business, restaurants) are better valued using this approach rather than the top-down approach, unless the service can be franchised or replicated easily.

Estimating Cash Flows for Healthy Meals, an Organic Restaurant

Charles Black, a chef at a five-star restaurant in New York City, has decided to leave his job and start a new business. He will make and deliver healthy family meals, created with organic produce, in a suburban town in New Jersey.[7] To estimate the cash flows, we will go through the steps in the bottom-up approach:

1. **Capacity investment**: The business, Healthy Meals, will be run out of a storefront on Main Street. It will be converted into a state-of-the-art kitchen with an investment of $80,000. Licensing, legal, and other setup costs are expected to amount to $20,000, with the entire initial cost ($100,000) being tax-deductible immediately.[8] Half of the initial cost ($50,000) will be covered by a bank loan, with an interest rate of 7%. The kitchen (with Mr. Black as chef) can produce up to 60 family meals a day.

7 Mr. Black has lived in the town for a long time and is a local celebrity.

8 Mr. Black has enough taxable income this year to claim the tax deduction immediately.

2. **Unit sales/revenues**: The family meals, which will come prepackaged and ready to serve up to six people, will be priced at $60 a meal next year. The price is expected to rise with the inflation rate in subsequent years (with inflation assumed to be 2% a year). The expectation is that the restaurant will sell about 20 meals a day, on average, next year. It is also expected that sales will increase each year after that to hit a peak of 50 meals a day in five years.[9] The restaurant plans to be open approximately 250 days a year for the first 2 years and then 300 days a year for the remaining period. Table 9.12 summarizes the expected revenues at the restaurant for the next five years.

Table 9.12 Expected Revenues for Healthy Meals

	Year 1	Year 2	Year 3	Year 4	Year 5
Number of meals per day	20	30	40	45	50
Number of days per year	250	250	300	300	300
Price per meal	$60.00	$61.20	$63.67	$67.57	$73.14
Revenues	$300,000	$459,000	$764,070	$912,192	$1,097,095

3. **Operating costs**: Several fixed operating costs are involved in running the restaurant. These include a rental expense of $25,000 for next year for the storefront, and selling, general, and administrative expenses that are expected to amount to $100,000 next year. These expenses will increase at the inflation rate after next year. The cost of the ingredients for the meals will amount to 30% of the revenues, whereas labor costs (kitchen help, delivery people) are anticipated to be 20% of revenues. The latter does not include a salary for Mr. Black, but he would have earned a salary of $80,000 next year if he had stayed on as a restaurant chef in Manhattan. This salary would have grown with inflation over time. Table 9.13 estimates the operating costs and profits for Healthy Meals for the next five years.

Table 9.13 Expected Operating Income for Healthy Meals

	Year 1	Year 2	Year 3	Year 4	Year 5
Revenues	$300,000	$459,000	$764,070	$912,192	$1,097,095
– Rental expense	$25,000	$25,500	$26,010	$26,530	$27,061
– Cost of ingredients	$90,000	$137,700	$229,221	$273,657	$329,128
– Labor costs	$60,000	$91,800	$152,814	$182,438	$219,419
– Imputed chef salary (owner)	$80,000	$81,600	$83,232	$84,897	$86,595
– S, G, and A expenses	$100,000	$102,000	$104,040	$106,121	$108,243
Operating income	–$55,000	$20,400	$168,753	$238,548	$326,649

9 Although the kitchen can produce 60 meals a day, it is unrealistic to expect it to produce and sell this many meals every day of the year.

4. **Taxes**: To compute the taxes, we use a marginal tax rate of 40% to cover federal, state, and local taxes. Since all of the initial investment is tax-deductible, we have no depreciation charges to consider. Table 9.14 summarizes expected taxes paid and after-tax operating income for the restaurant.

Table 9.14 Expected Taxes and After-Tax Operating Income for Healthy Meals

	Year 1	Year 2	Year 3	Year 4	Year 5
Operating income	–$55,000	$20,400	$168,753	$238,548	$326,649
– Taxes	–$22,000	$8,160	$67,501	$95,419	$130,660
Operating income after taxes	–$33,000	$12,240	$101,252	$143,129	$195,989

We are assuming that Mr. Black will be able to claim the loss on the restaurant as a tax deduction in year 1 against his imputed salary.

5. **Additional reinvestment**: Since Mr. Black intends to keep the business going after year 5, he will have to invest in updating the kitchen appliances and renovating the storefront. While the precise timing of the investment is unclear, we will assume that he will need to set aside 10% of his after-tax operating income each year to cover these costs. Table 9.15 summarizes the expected after-tax cash flows, prior to debt payments, from the restaurant.

Table 9.15 Expected After-Tax Cash Flow to Healthy Meals

	Year 0	Year 1	Year 2	Year 3	Year 4	Year 5
EBIT (1–t)		–$33,000	$12,240	$101,252	$143,129	$195,989
– Reinvestment	$60,000	–$3,300	$1,224	$10,125	$14,313	$19,599
FCFF	–$60,000	–$29,700	$11,016	$91,127	$128,816	$176,390

Note that the initial investment is the after-tax initial investment cost. The initial investment of $100,000 is tax-deductible and delivers a tax benefit of 40%. In addition, we assume that the chef takes money out of the business ($3,300) to cover potential losses. That assumption can be modified to make the reinvestment zero in year 1.

Estimating Discount Rates

Chapter 2 described the inputs that go into discount rates. To summarize, we estimated the cost of equity by looking at the beta (or betas) of the company in question and the cost of debt from a measure of default risk (an actual or synthetic rating). Then we applied the market value weights for debt and equity to come up with the cost of capital. Both conceptual and estimation issues make each of these ingredients difficult to deal with when it comes to young companies:

- **Beta and cost of equity**: Young companies are often held by either undiversified owners or partially diversified venture capitalists. Consequently, it does not make sense to assume that the only risk that should be priced in is the market risk. The cost of equity must incorporate some (in the case of venture capitalists) or maybe even all (for completely undiversified owners) of the firm-specific risk. The standard practice of estimating betas from stock prices will not work, because young firms are generally not publicly traded.

- **Cost of debt:** Young firms almost never have bonds outstanding; instead, they are dependent on bank loans for debt. Consequently, no bond rating will measure default risk. Even though we may be able to use the process described in Chapter 2 to estimate a synthetic rating, the resulting cost of debt may not appropriately capture the interest rates actually paid by these small and risky businesses, since banks may charge them a premium.
- **Debt ratio**: Since the equity and debt in young companies are not traded, no market values can be used to weight the debt and equity to arrive at the cost of capital.

The confluence of these problems is used to justify the use of arbitrary "target rates" by venture capitalists. We suggest an alternative process built around the following steps:

1. **Sector averages**: While the company being valued may not be traded, there are generally other companies in the same business that have made it through the early stage in the life cycle and are publicly traded. We would use the betas of these firms to arrive at an estimate of the market risk associated with being in this business. Generally, this requires taking an average of the regression betas across the publicly traded firms and unlevering the beta to arrive at the beta of the business:

$$\text{Unlevered Beta for Sector} = \frac{\text{Average Regression Beta for Publicly Traded Firms}}{(1 + (1 - \text{Tax Rate})\ \text{Average Market D/E Ratio for Publicly Traded Firms})}$$

2. **Adjust for diversification or its absence.** As noted earlier, the owners of young businesses tend not to be diversified. In fact, the entire firm may be held by the founder, who, in turn, has all of his or her wealth tied up in that investment. To account for this absence of diversification, we will again draw on the publicly traded firm sample. The same regressions that yielded the market betas for these firms also provide an estimate of how much of the risk in these firms comes from the market (through the R-squared and correlation coefficients in the regressions). Dividing the market beta by the correlation of the publicly traded firms with the market gives us a scaled-up version of beta (that we will call the total beta) that captures all the risk of being in a specific business, rather than just the market risk:

$$\text{Total Beta} = \frac{\text{Market Beta}_{\text{Publicly Traded Firms in Business}}}{\text{Correlation with Market}_{\text{Publicly Traded Firms in Business}}}$$

This total beta will be much higher than the market beta. The resulting cost of equity will reflect the cost of equity to an investor who is completely invested only in this business. As the firm expands and taps into venture capitalists, it attracts investors who have some diversification. Venture capitalists tend to hold investments in multiple companies, but often in the same sector or a few sectors. The portfolio of investments held by a venture capitalist will be more highly correlated with the market than an individual company is, and the resulting total beta to a venture capitalist will be lower:

$$\text{Total Beta}_{VC} = \frac{\text{Market Beta}_{\text{Publicly Traded Firms in Business}}}{\text{Correlation with Market}_{\text{VC Portfolio}}}$$

Thus, as firms move through the life cycle and attract larger and more diversified venture capitalists into the fold, they should see lower costs of equity. Ultimately, the cost of equity will converge on the market beta measure if the firm goes public or is sold to a publicly traded entity.

3. **Consider the use of debt and its cost.** The absence of a rating should not be used as an excuse to use book interest rates or arbitrary costs of debt. As described in Chapter 6, "A Shaky Base: A 'Risky' Risk-Free Rate," synthetic bond ratings can be estimated for any firm based on financial ratios that are available even for private businesses. Thus, an interest coverage ratio can be computed for a small business and used to come up with a synthetic rating and a pre-tax cost of debt (by adding the default spread based on the rating to the risk-free rate). The one additional adjustment we would consider making to this cost of debt is to add a spread to capture the small size of these businesses. It is likely that a bank would charge more for a BBB-rated firm with revenues of $1 million than for a BBB-rated firm with revenue of a billion.
4. **Look at management proclivities and industry averages.** There are some young businesses where the owners come in with strong views on using (or, more commonly, never using) debt. In these cases (and they are unusual), we can use the target debt ratio specified by management to compute the cost of capital. In the more common scenario, where the owners are unclear about how much they will use debt, especially as they grow, it is best to revert to the publicly traded firms in the business and use their average market debt ratio as the debt ratio for the firm being analyzed.
5. **Build in expected changes in all of these inputs over time.** As firms move through the life cycle, we should expect their risk and cash flow characteristics to change. In fact, we build in these expected changes in the earnings and cash flows we forecast. To preserve consistency, we should allow the cost of equity, debt, and capital to change over time. Thus, a firm that is all equity-funded and owned entirely by its founder, with a cost of equity of 30%, as a start-up, should not only see its cost of equity decline over time as it attracts more diversified investors into the mix but also should be more open to the use of debt as earnings become larger and more stable.

Estimating Discount Rates for Secure Mail Software

To estimate the cost of equity and capital for Secure Mail, we begin with the unlevered beta of the virus software business. We estimate this number by first averaging the regression betas of publicly traded security software firms and then adjusting this beta for the typical financial leverage at these firms:[10]

10 We use a sample of 12 companies involved in the security software business, rather than stick with the stricter sample of firms that just produce antivirus software. We assume a marginal tax rate of 40% applied to all of these firms.

Average Beta Across Public Security Software Firms = 1.24

Average Debt-to-Equity Ratio for Security Software Firms = 6%

Unlevered Beta for Security Software Firms = 1.24 / (1 + (1 – 0.4) (.06)) = 1.20

While we leave this unlevered beta untouched for the entire ten-year time horizon, we assume that the only equity investor in the business in the first two years is the founder, who is completely undiversified (and fully invested in the firm). We compute the average R-squared across the security software company regressions and use this number to estimate a total beta for Secure Mail:

Average R-Squared of Security Software Firms with Market = 0.16

Average Correlation of Security Software Firms with Market = 0.40

Total Beta: Years 1 and 2 = Market Beta / Average Correlation = 1.20 / 0.40 = 3.00

At the start of year 3, we expect the firm to approach a venture capitalist who, while not fully diversified, has a portfolio of several software companies. The correlation between this portfolio and the market is expected to be 0.50, which results in a lower total beta after year 3:

Total Beta: Years 3 and 4 = Market Beta / Correlation of VC Portfolio = 1.20 / 0.50 = 2.40

At the end of year 4, we expect larger venture capitalists to invest in the firm. Their portfolios, which include growth companies from multiple sectors, have a correlation of 0.75 with the market:

Total Beta: Years 5 to 10 = Market Beta / Correlation of Larger VC Portfolio = 1.20 / 0.75 = 1.60

Finally, we expect the firm to go public at the end of year 10, at which point the market beta will apply.

Since the owners of the firm are dead set against the use of debt, and the sector itself is lightly levered (D/E ratio = 6%), we will assume that the firm will be all equity funded over time. Using a risk-free rate of 4% and a market risk premium of 5% yields the costs of equity by year for Secure Mail, as shown in Table 9.16.

Table 9.16 Costs of Equity and Capital for Secure Mail Software

Year	Market Beta	Correlation with Market	Total Beta	Cost of Equity	Debt Ratio	Cost of Capital
2009	1.2	0.40	3.0000	19.00%	0.00%	19.00%
2010	1.2	0.40	3.0000	19.00%	0.00%	19.00%

Table 9.16 Costs of Equity and Capital for Secure Mail Software (continued)

Year	Market Beta	Correlation with Market	Total Beta	Cost of Equity	Debt Ratio	Cost of Capital
2011	1.2	0.50	2.4000	16.00%	0.00%	16.00%
2012	1.2	0.50	2.4000	16.00%	0.00%	16.00%
2013	1.2	0.75	1.6000	12.00%	0.00%	12.00%
2014	1.2	0.75	1.6000	12.00%	0.00%	12.00%
2015	1.2	0.75	1.6000	12.00%	0.00%	12.00%
2016	1.2	0.75	1.6000	12.00%	0.00%	12.00%
2017	1.2	0.75	1.6000	12.00%	0.00%	12.00%
2018	1.2	0.75	1.6000	12.00%	0.00%	12.00%
After 2018	1.2	1.00	1.2000	10.00%	0.00%	10.00%

Note that in the absence of debt, the cost of equity is also the cost of capital for the firm.

Estimating Discount Rates for Healthy Meals

To estimate the cost of equity for Healthy Meals, we begin with the betas of publicly traded firms in the restaurant business and cleanse them of the financial leverage effect:[11]

Average Regression Beta Across Public Restaurants = 0.902

Average Debt-to-Equity Ratio for Public Restaurants = 25%

Unlevered Beta for Restaurants = 0.902 / (1 + (1 – .4) (.25)) = 0.782

As with the beta for Secure Mail, we adjust this beta for the owner/chef's lack of diversification by estimating the average correlation of publicly traded restaurants with the market:

Average Correlation of Restaurant Firms with the Market = 0.333

Total Unlevered Beta for Restaurants = 0.782 / 0.333 = 2.346

Unlike Secure Mail, where we assumed that the firm would depend entirely on equity, the owner of Healthy Meals plans to borrow $50,000 (from a bank, with an interest rate of 7%) and will continue to borrow as he expands the business.

11 The sample had 22 publicly traded restaurants, and we assumed a marginal tax rate of 40% applied to them.

Rather than trust a book debt ratio, we will assume that Healthy Meals will adopt a debt ratio similar to publicly traded restaurants (a 25% debt-to-equity ratio and a 20% debt-to-capital ratio). The resulting levered beta is computed as follows:

Levered Beta for Healthy Meals = 2.346 (1 + (1 – .4) (.25)) = 2.70

Sticking with the risk-free rate of 4% and an equity risk premium of 5%, we can estimate the cost of equity from this beta. We will use the interest rate on the bank loan as the pre-tax cost of debt.[12] Table 9.17 summarizes costs of equity and capital for Healthy Meals.

Table 9.17 Costs of Equity and Capital for Healthy Meals

	Year 1	Year 2	Year 3	Year 4	Year 5
Total beta	2.70	2.70	2.70	2.70	2.70
Cost of equity	17.50%	17.50%	17.50%	17.50%	17.50%
Cost of debt (after-tax)	4.20%	4.20%	4.20%	4.20%	4.20%
Debt-to-capital ratio	20.00%	20.00%	20.00%	20.00%	20.00%
Cost of capital =	14.84%	14.84%	14.84%	14.84%	14.84%

Since there are no other equity investors in the picture, we will leave the cost of equity and capital unchanged over time at 14.84%.

Estimating Value Today and Adjusting for Survival

The expected cash flows and discount rates, estimated in the last two steps, are key building blocks toward estimating the value of the business and equity today. However, we must deal with three more components at this stage to get to the firm's value. The first is determining what happens at the end of our forecast period—the assumptions we make lead to the value that we assign the business at the end of the period. The second component is adjusting for the likelihood that the business will not survive. This issue has added relevance for young firms, because so many fail early in the process. The third factor that we have to deal with, at least in businesses that depend on one or a few key people for their success, is how best to incorporate into the value the effects of their loss.

Terminal Value

Earlier we considered how best to estimate earnings and cash flows for a forecast period for a young firm. At some point in the future, we have to stop estimating cash flows, partly because of increasing uncertainty and partly for practical reasons. Whatever the reason for stopping, we have to then estimate what we expect the value of the business to be at that point in time. This "terminal value" estimate represents a big chunk of the value of any business, but it's an even bigger component of value for a young firm that has small or negative cash flows in the near years. We can estimate the terminal value of young firms in three ways:

12 Because this is a fresh bank loan, we assume that the bank is charging a fair interest rate, given perceived default risk.

- We can value the firm as a going concern, making reasonable assumptions about cash flows growing in perpetuity. Chapter 2 noted that the terminal value could then be written as a function of the perpetual growth rate and the excess returns accompanying the growth rate (with excess returns defined as the difference between returns on invested capital and the cost of capital).
- If the assumption of cash flows continuing in perpetuity is too radical for the firm being valued, either because the firm is dependent on a key person or persons for survival, or because it is a small business, we can make an assumption about how long we expect cash flows to continue beyond the forecast horizon and estimate the present value of these cash flows.
- The most conservative assumption that we can make about terminal value is that the firm will be liquidated at the end of the forecast period and that the salvage value of any assets that the firm may have accumulated over its life is the terminal value.

Note that using relative valuation (multiples) to estimate terminal value, as is often the practice, is inconsistent with the notion of intrinsic value. Of the three approaches described, the right approach for estimating terminal value depends on the characteristics of the firm being valued. When valuing firms, where success translates into an initial public offering or sale to a publicly traded firm, the perpetual growth model makes the most sense. For smaller, less ambitious firms, where success is defined as surviving the forecast period and delivering cash flows beyond, assuming a finite life for the cash flows will yield the most reasonable value. Finally, liquidation value is best suited for businesses that come with time limits on their operating lives, such as an operating license that will end in five years.

Estimating Terminal Value and Value Today for Secure Mail Software

We estimate the terminal value for Secure Mail at the end of year 10 for three reasons:

- It is the first year with a growth rate (3%) that is consistent with stable growth. In other words, it is less than the risk-free rate and the nominal growth rate in the economy.
- Operating margins do not reach the target level (13%) until year 10.
- The firm is assumed to be ready for an initial public offering, allowing us to settle on betas and costs of equity and capital in perpetuity.

Reviewing the year 10 numbers, Secure Mail is expected to generate $136.61 million in after-tax operating income on revenues of $1.751 billion. We first estimate revenues and after-tax operating income in year 11:

$$\text{Revenues}_{11} = \text{Revenues}_{10}\ (1 + \text{Stable Growth Rate})$$

$$= \$1{,}751\ (1.03) = \$1{,}804 \text{ million}$$

$$\text{After-Tax Operating Income}_{11} = \text{Revenues}_{11}\ (\text{Stable Operating Margin})\ (1 - \text{Tax Rate})$$
$$= \$1{,}804\ (0.13)\ (1 - .4) = \$140.71 \text{ million}$$

To estimate how much the firm will need to reinvest to sustain a 3% growth rate forever, we assume that the return on capital at Secure Mail in stable growth is 15%. (Note that we made reinvestment assumptions during the high-growth phase with the intent of pushing toward this return. It is lower than the industry average but higher than the cost of capital of 10% in stable growth.)

$$\text{Reinvestment in Stable Growth} = \frac{\text{Stable Growth Rate}}{\text{Stable ROC}} = \frac{3\%}{15\%} = 20\%$$

$$\text{Free Cash Flow to the Firm}_{11} = \text{After-Tax Operating Income}_{11} * (1 - \text{Reinvestment Rate})$$
$$= \$140.71\ (1 - .20) = \$112.57$$

Finally, using the stable period cost of capital of 10% (see Table 9.16), we estimate the terminal value:

$$\text{Terminal Value}_{10} = \frac{\text{FCFF}_{11}}{(\text{Cost of Capital}_{\text{Stable}} - \text{Stable Growth Rate})} = \frac{112.57}{(.10 - .03)} = \$1608.13$$

Incorporating this value into the expected free cash flows to the firm (estimated in Table 9.11) and discounting back at the year-specific costs of capital (from Table 9.16), we can arrive at the value of the operating assets today (see Table 9.18).

Table 9.18 Expected Cash Flows and Value Today for Secure Mail Software

Year	FCFF	Terminal Value	Cost of Capital	Cumulated Cost of Capital	Present Value
2009	–$67.03		19.00%	1.19000	–$56.33
2010	–$76.94		19.00%	1.41610	–$54.33
2011	–$111.84		16.00%	1.64268	–$68.08
2012	–$59.03		16.00%	1.90550	–$30.98
2013	–$47.77		12.00%	2.13416	–$22.38
2014	–$44.77		12.00%	2.39026	–$18.73
2015	–$37.45		12.00%	2.67710	–$13.99

Table 9.18 Expected Cash Flows and Value Today for Secure Mail Software

Year	FCFF	Terminal Value	Cost of Capital	Cumulated Cost of Capital	Present Value
2016	–\$28.15		12.00%	2.99835	–\$9.39
2017	–\$16.62		12.00%	3.35815	–\$4.95
2018	\$109.67	\$1,608.13	12.00%	3.76113	\$456.72
					\$177.56

Note that the cost of capital is cumulated to reflect the changes in the cost over time. Thus, the cost of capital in year 5 is computed as follows:

Cost of Capital in Year 5 = $(1.19)^2 (1.16)^2 (1.12) = 2.13416$

Based on the expected cash flows and discount rates, the value of the operating assets today is \$177.56 million.

Estimating Terminal Value and Value Today for Healthy Meals

We use a much shorter growth period for Healthy Meals because it will run into its capacity constraint (both physical and financial) by the end of year 5. As a privately owned restaurant, we are unwilling to assume that the business will generate cash flows forever or that there is the possibility of public investors in the company. Consequently, we make the following assumptions:

- The after-tax operating income (\$195,989) and free cash flow to the firm (\$176,390) in year 5 (see Table 9.15) will continue to grow at the inflation rate of 2% for ten more years. At the end of year 15, we will assume that the business is shut down and that there are no assets to salvage.
- The owner will continue to be the only equity investor in the business, and the debt ratio we assumed for the first five years will hold for the next 10 years. The cost of capital therefore will remain at 14.84% (see Table 9.17) for the entire period.

With these assumptions, we can estimate the terminal value at the end of year 5 using an equation for a growing annuity:[13]

13 This equation is a shortcut. You can obtain the same answer by estimating the cash flows each year for ten years and discounting back at the cost of capital.

$$\text{Terminal Value} = \frac{FCFF_5(1+g)(1-\frac{(1+g)^n}{(1+r)^n}}{(r-g)} = \frac{176,390(1.02)(1-\frac{(1.02)^{10}}{(1.1484)^{10}}}{(.1484-.02)} = \$973,098$$

Including this estimate with the cash flows for each year estimated in Table 9.15 and discounting back at the cost of capital of 14.84% yields the estimate of value for the firm's operating assets of $632,212, as shown in Table 9.19. (Note also that replacing the negative reinvestment in year 1 with reinvestment of zero changes the value only slightly to just below $630,000.)

Table 9.19 Cash Flows and Value Today for Healthy Meals

	Year 0	Year 1	Year 2	Year 3	Year 4	Year 5
EBIT (1 – t)		–$33,000	$12,240	$101,252	$143,129	$195,989
– Reinvestment	$60,000	–$3,300	$1,224	$10,125	$14,313	$19,599
FCFF	–$60,000	–$29,700	$11,016	$91,127	$128,816	$176,390
Terminal value						$973,098
Cost of capital		14.84%	14.84%	14.84%	14.84%	14.84%
Present value	–$60,000	–$25,862.07	$8,352.91	$60,167.98	$74,062.28	$575,491.14
Value of operating assets today =	$632,212					

Survival

Many young firms succumb to the competitive pressures of the marketplace and don't make it. Rather than try to adjust the discount rate for this likelihood (a difficult exercise), we suggest a two-step approach. In the first step, we would value the firm on the assumption that it survives and makes it to financial heath. This, in effect, is what we are assuming when we estimate a terminal value and discount cash flows back to today at a risk-adjusted discount rate. In the second step, we would bring in the likelihood that the firm will not survive. The probability of failure can be assessed in one of three ways:

- **Sector averages:** Earlier in the chapter, we noted a study by Knaup and Piazza (2007). It used data from the Bureau of Labor Statistics to estimate the probability of survival for firms in different sectors from 1998 to 2005. We could use the sector averages from this study as the probability of survival for individual firms in the sector. For a software firm that has been in existence for one year, for instance, the likelihood of failure (from Table 9.1) over a five-year period would be assessed at 40.07% (the difference between the probability of surviving two years [64.85%] and the probability of surviving seven years [24.78%]). We are painting with a broad brush, in this case, and generalizing findings from a very specific time period (1998–2005) to all firms.
- **Probits:** A more sophisticated way to estimate the probability of failure is to look at firms that have succeeded or failed over a time period (say, the last ten years). Then we can try to build a model that can predict the probability of a firm's failing as a function

of firm-specific characteristics—the firm's cash holdings, the age and history of its founders, the business it is in, and the debt it owes.

- **Simulations:** Chapter 3 noted that simulations can be put to good use when confronted with uncertainty. If we can specify probability distributions (rather than just expected values) for revenues, margins, and costs, we may be able to specify the conditions under which the firm will face failure (costs exceed revenues by more than 30% and debt payments are coming due, for example) and estimate the probability of failure.

After the probability of failure has been assessed, the firm's value can be written as an expected value of the two scenarios—the intrinsic value (from the discounted cash flows) under the going-concern scenario and the distress value under the failure scenario:

Expected Value = Value of Going Concern (1 – Probability of Failure) + Distress Sale Value (Probability of Failure)

Adjusting the Valuation of Secure Mail Software for Survival

Earlier we estimated the value of Secure Mail, assuming that it survives to become a going concern and becomes a publicly traded firm. Since the firm has no revenues today, this is an inherently optimistic assumption. There is a strong possibility that the firm will not survive. To estimate the probability of survival, we begin by looking at the Knaup/Piazza data that suggests that only 25% of software firms survive past year 5. But we adjust this probability upward to 60% to reflect the fact that Secure Mail has a solid antivirus product (albeit in beta form) and that its founder has been involved with other start-ups that have succeeded in the past. In the event of failure, we assume that distress sale proceeds will be close to zero, since there are few tangible assets to sell and salvage. The expected value of the operating assets can then be written as follows:

Expected Value of Operating Assets = Value of Going Concern
(1 – Probability of Failure) + Distress Sale Value (Probability of Failure)
= \$177.56 (1 – .4) + 0 (.4) = \$106.54 million

This is clearly much lower than the value we assessed using the venture capital approach of \$202.34 million. In this case, at least, the lower intrinsic value can be traced to three factors:

- The high costs of equity in the early years, resulting from the lack of diversification of the early equity investors
- The negative cash flows that the firm is expected to experience for much of the high-growth phase
- The high chance of failure

This firm's value will change significantly with each year of survival, because the probability of failure will drop off over time, the costs of equity decrease, and the positive cash flows get closer to fruition. Table 9.20 estimates the value of Secure Mail each year until its expected initial public offering in year 10.

Table 9.20 Future Values of Secure Mail Software

End of Year	PV of Future Cash Flows	Probability of Failure	Value
Current	$177.56	40%	$106.54
1	$278.33	35%	$180.91
2	$408.15	30%	$285.71
3	$585.29	25%	$438.97
4	$737.97	15%	$627.28
5	$874.30	10%	$786.87
6	$1,023.98	5%	$972.78
7	$1,184.32	0%	$1,184.32
8	$1,354.58	0%	$1,354.58
9	$1,533.75	0%	$1,533.75
10	$1,608.13	0%	$1,608.13

Note that the value of the end of each period is estimated by discounting subsequent cash flows at the cumulated cost of capital from that point. The probability of failure remains high for the first three years (when the firm is reporting losses) but decreases after that.

Key Person Discounts

Young companies, especially in service businesses, are often dependent on the owner or a few key people for their success. Consequently, the value we estimate for these businesses can change significantly if one or more of these key people will no longer be associated with the firm. To assess a key person discount in valuations, we suggest that the firm be valued first with the status quo (with key people involved in the business) and then be valued again with the loss of these individuals built into revenues, earnings, and expected cash flows. To the extent that earnings and cash flows suffer when key people leave, the value of the business will be lower with the loss of these individuals. The key person discount can then be estimated as follows:

$$\text{Key Person Discount} = \frac{(\text{Value of Firm}_{\text{Status Quo}} - \text{Value of Firm}_{\text{Key Person Lost}})}{\text{Value of Firm}_{\text{Status Quo}}}$$

No simple formula will help determine how many cash flows will be lost as a result of the loss of key personnel, because this varies not only across businesses but also across the personnel involved. One way to assess it is to survey existing customers to see how they will respond if the key personnel leave and then build this impact into operating forecasts.

Adjusting the Valuation of Healthy Meals for Key Person Discount

Earlier we estimated the value of Healthy Meals, an organic restaurant, using expected cash flows of $632,212. A key factor in its expected success are the networking connections that Charles Black, the founder/chef, has in the suburban town in which Healthy Meals will be located. The value of the restaurant is therefore very dependent on Mr. Black's health and continued involvement. To estimate how much of an impact his absence would have on the value, we must estimate the impact on both cash flows and value. We assume that although a replacement chef could be found for Mr. Black (for a salary equivalent to the $80,000 that we estimated for him), the revenues will drop by 20% every year as a result of his absence. Table 9.21 summarizes the cash flows and value with the lower revenues.

Table 9.21 Value of Healthy Meals Without the Key Person

	Initial	Year 1	Year 2	Year 3	Year 4	Year 5
Revenues		$240,000	$367,200	$611,256	$729,753	$877,676
– Rental expense		$25,000	$25,500	$26,010	$26,530	$27,061
– Cost of ingredients		$72,000	$110,160	$183,377	$218,926	$263,303
– Labor costs		$48,000	$73,440	$122,251	$145,951	$175,535
– Imputed chef salary (owner)		$80,000	$81,600	$83,232	$84,897	$86,595
– S, G, and A expenses		$100,000	$102,000	$104,040	$106,121	$108,243
Operating income		–$85,000	–$25,500	$92,346	$147,329	$216,939
– Taxes		–$34,000	–$10,200	$36,938	$58,932	$86,776
Operating income after taxes		–$51,000	–$15,300	$55,408	$88,397	$130,164
– Reinvestment	–$60,000.00	–$5,100	–$1,530	$5,541	$8,840	$13,016
Free cash flow to firm	$60,000.00	–$45,900	–$13,770	$49,867	$79,558	$117,147
Terminal value						646,270

	Initial	Year 1	Year 2	Year 3	Year 4	Year 5
Cost of capital		14.84%	14.84%	14.84%	14.84%	14.84%
Present value	$60,000	–$39,968.65	–$10,441.13	$32,925.46	$45,741.38	$382,204.58
Value of firm today =	$470,462					

We value the firm using the lower revenues and earnings, arising from these estimates at $470,462. The key person discount, in this case, can then be estimated as 25.58%.

$$\text{Key Person Discount} = \frac{(\text{Value of Firm}_{\text{Status Quo}} - \text{Value of Firm}_{\text{Key Person Lost}})}{\text{Value of Firm}_{\text{Status Quo}}}$$

$$= \frac{(632{,}212 - 470.462)}{632{,}212} = 25.58\%$$

Clearly, this will come into play if Mr. Black ever decides to sell the restaurant. To the extent that the buyer will have to build in the discount, he would be willing to pay about 25.58% less than the estimated value. Mr. Black can ease the effect by agreeing to stay on for a transition period as the chef and provide an easier transition for the new owner.[14]

Valuing Equity Claims in the Business

The path from firm value to equity value in publicly traded firms is simple. We add back cash and marketable securities, subtract debt, and divide by the number of shares outstanding to estimate value of equity per share. With young private businesses, each phase has complications.

From Operating Asset to Firm Value: Cash and Capital Infusions

Unlike mature companies, where the cash balance represents what the firm has accumulated from operations and is generally static, cash balances at young companies are dynamic for two reasons. The first is that these firms use the accumulated cash, rather than earnings from ongoing operations, to fund new investments. The resulting "cash burn" can quickly eat through the cash balances. The second reason is that young firms raise new capital at regular intervals. These capital infusions can not only augment the cash balance but also represent a significant proportion of overall firm value.

To deal with the former, we suggest caution. Rather than add the cash balance from the most recent financial statements to operating asset value, we recommend obtaining an updated value (reflecting the cash balance today). To deal with capital infusions, we would revert to the concept of pre-money and post-money valuations that we introduced in the section on venture capital valuation. When we discount free cash flows to the firm, where reinvestment needs are treated as

14 Needless to say, the buyer will want Mr. Black to sign an agreement that he will not compete with the existing owner for the customer base.

cash outflows, we are in effect computing a value of the operating assets, with no consideration for the cash that we may have on hand to make these investments. Adding the company's prevailing cash balance yields a pre-money valuation of the firm:

$$\text{Pre-Money Firm Value} = \sum_{t=1}^{t=\infty} \frac{E(FCFF_t)}{(1 + \text{Cost of Capital})^t} + \text{Cash \& Marketable Securities}$$

$$\text{Pre-Money Equity Value} = \text{Pre-Money Firm Value} - \text{Debt}_{\text{Existing}}$$

If the firm raises additional capital in the form of either debt or equity, the portion of that capital infusion that stays in the firm (as opposed to being used by owners who want to cash out their ownership) augments value to yield a post-money valuation:

$$\text{Post-Money Firm Value} = \text{Pre-Money Firm Value} + (\text{Equity}_{\text{New}} + \text{Debt}_{\text{New}} - \text{Owner Cash-Out})$$

$$\text{Post-Money Equity Value} = \text{Post-Money Firm Value} - \text{Debt}_{\text{Existing}} - \text{Debt}_{\text{New}}$$

From Firm Value to Equity Value: Dealing with Debt

Many young firms do not borrow money. Those that do often have to add special features to make them acceptable to lenders. Convertible debt is far more common at young firms than at mature firms. Since convertible debt is a hybrid—the conversion option is equity, and the rest is debt—it makes the process of getting from firm value to equity value a little trickier. Strictly speaking, we should subtract only the debt portion of the convertible debt from firm value to arrive at equity value:

$$\text{Equity Value} = \text{Value of the Firm} - \text{Debt Portion of Convertible Debt}$$

After we estimate the equity value, we can apportion the value between the option holders (in the convertible debt or elsewhere) and standard equity investors.

Differences in Equity Claims

After we have the aggregate equity value in a young firm, we have to allocate the value of the equity across various claim holders. This part of the process is complicated by the fact that equity claims in a young firm are seldom homogeneous, as is the case with publicly traded firms, with one class of shares. Instead, some equity claim holders have first claim on the cash flows of the business, and other claim holders get control claims, which give them more power over how the firm is operated. To apportion the value of equity across different claim holders, we have to value these cash flow and control rights.[15]

Cash Flow Claims

Two types of preferential cash flow rights can be embedded in equity claims. The first allows some equity investors to claim a share of the operating cash flows, usually in the form of preferential

15 This chapter offers a compressed version of how best to value cash flow and control claims. A more comprehensive paper on this topic is Damodaran, A., 2008, "Claims on Equity: Voting and liquidity differences, cash flow preferences and financing rights."

dividends, before other claim holders get paid. The second gives priority to some equity investors if the firm is liquidated and the cash flows are distributed to investors.

To value first claim on the cash flows from operations (preferred dividends), the simplest mechanism to use is to discount these dividends back at a lower rate than other cash flows to equity. This should lead to a premium for those owning these claims. The practical issue is coming up with an appropriate discount rate. If we accept the premise that preferred equity is similar to a debt issue, we can approach this question in much the same way that we estimate the pre-tax cost of debt. In effect, the risk-adjusted rate for fixed preferred dividend-paying equity is as follows:

Risk-Adjusted Discount Rate = Risk-Free Rate + Spread Capturing Default Risk (of Defaulting on Dividend Payment)

The default spread can be estimated using an approach that is often used to estimate the cost of debt for nonrated companies. We estimate a synthetic rating for a company based on its financial ratios and then use that rating to come up with a default spread. In fact, one ratio that is widely used for synthetic bond ratings is the interest coverage ratio:

Interest Coverage Ratio = Operating Income / Interest Expenses

This ratio can be adapted to incorporate preferred dividends in the denominator (treated like interest expenses):

Preferred Coverage Ratio = Operating Income / (Interest Expenses + Preferred Dividends)

The resulting number should yield a synthetic rating for preferred stock. In turn, this can be used to estimate the default spread and the risk-adjusted cost of preferred stock. The resulting number should be higher than the pre-tax cost of debt, because preferred dividends are paid after interest expenses. But it should be lower than the cost of equity, because preferred stockholders get their dividends before common stockholders.

$$\text{Pre-Tax Cost of Debt} < r_{\text{Preferred Dividends}} < \text{Cost of Equity}$$

The question of whether the dividend is cumulative or noncumulative can be examined in this context as well, with the rate on cumulative preferred stock being lower than the rate on non cumulative preferred stock.

In some cases, preferred stockholders also get first claim on the firm's cash flows on liquidation. Unlike dividends, which represent an ongoing claim, liquidation is a one-time event, and the valuation approaches we use reflect the difference. One approach to bring in liquidation cash preferences is to try to incorporate the likelihood of and expected cash flows from liquidation into a discounted cash flow model and arrive at a value today. The simplest way to do this is to create two scenarios. In the first, you value the equity claims assuming that the firm is a going concern. In effect, you assume that the cash flows (dividends or free cash flows) continue forever and compute the present value. In the second scenario, you assume that the firm will be liquidated at a specific point in time (say, five years from now). Then you compute the value of the equity claims on the firm based on the cash flows each period during operations and the cash flows in liquidation. Once the claims have been valued under both scenarios, you estimate the probability of each scenario (going concern and liquidation) and compute an expected value. This approach is predicated on the assumption that liquidation will occur only at the specified point in time and that the probability of its occurrence can be estimated with reasonable ease.

Control Claims

There are two ways in which control claims can vary across equity investors in young businesses. In the first, one class of equity may have the power to operate the firm and make the day-to-day decisions that determine value, whereas the other class represents passive equity investors. This is the case, for instance, in partnerships with limited partners, who supply capital but do not have a role in running the firm, and general partners, who control the operations. In the second way, some classes of equity may be given powers, but only if a specified event occurs, such as an acquisition or public offering. These powers can be classified loosely into two groups. With veto powers, the equity class can prevent the event from occurring if it feels that its interests are not being served. With protective powers, the equity class obtains special protection against its value or ownership claim being diluted.

Veto power—the power to keep an event from occurring—does protect the rights of the equity claim endowed with the power, but it does so at the expense of overall firm value. By reducing the probability of a specific event (acquisition, initial public offering) that may increase overall firm value at the expense of a specific claim on equity, it reduces the expected value of the business and thus the value of all claims on the business. For instance, assume that a firm's value, run by existing managers, is \$10 million, the value to an acquirer is \$15 million, and the probability of an acquisition is 40%. If the firm has only one class of shares outstanding, and there are ten million shares, the value per share can be estimated as follows:

$$\text{Value per Share} = \frac{\text{Status Quo Value } (1 - \text{Prob}_{\text{Acq}}) + \text{Acquisition Value } (\text{Prob}_{\text{Acq}})}{\text{Number of Shares}}$$

$$= \frac{10\,(1 - .4) + 15\,(.4)}{10} = \$1.20/\text{Share}$$

Now assume that there are two classes of equity—5 million class A shares with no special rights, and 5 million class B shares with veto rights over acquisitions. As a consequence, the probability of an acquisition drops to 20%. The estimated value of equity per share reflects this change:

$$\text{Value per Generic Share} = \frac{10\,(1 - .2) + 15\,(.2)}{10} = \$1.10/\text{Share}$$

Note that the class B shareholders are costing the firm a million dollars in value. It is possible that they could negotiate to give up their veto rights for approximately that amount. Consequently, the value per class B share can be computed as follows:

$$\text{Value per Class B Share} = \text{Value per Share} + \frac{\text{Value Loss}}{\text{\# Class B Shares}} = \$1.10 + \frac{(\$12 - \$11)}{5}$$

$$= \$1.30 \text{ per Share}$$

The veto power that the class B shareholders have gives them a higher value than the class A shareholders, but they can monetize this value only if they are willing to give up their veto power.

Protective rights can be more complicated to value, because the right extends beyond the power to say no. In effect, the equity claim holders who have the right receive cash flows to compensate for the loss of value from the event. It is more akin to an option, providing protection against negative consequences, and it can be valued as such.

Valuing Equity Claims in Secure Mail Software

To get from the value of the operating assets to the value of equity in Secure Mail, we will first consider the firm's cash balance and debt. The former is $5 million, and no debt is outstanding. The pre-money valuation can be computed as follows:

Expected Value of Operating Assets (Adjusted for Survival) =	$106.54 million
+ Existing Cash Balance =	$5.00 million
Firm's Pre-Money Value =	$111.54 million
– Existing Debt =	$0.00 million
Pre-Money Value of Equity =	$111.54 million

If a venture capitalist is planning to bring $30 million in additional capital into the firm, and all the capital is assumed to stay in the firm, the post-money value of both the firm and its equity will be altered:

Pre-Money Value of the Firm =	$111.54 million
+ Capital Infusion =	$30.00 million
– Cash Withdrawn by Owner =	$0.00 million
Post-Money Value of Firm =	$141.54 million

One possible modification may be to the probability of failure. The addition of $30 million to the cash balance may reduce the possibility of failure in the firm. If we assume, for instance, that the probability of failure will decrease from 40% to 30% as a result of the capital infusion, the firm's post-money value will be $154.29 million.[16]

Relative Valuation

The essence of relative valuation is that you value a firm based on how much the market is paying for similar firms. This premise is clearly more challenging with young firms, which often have little to show in terms of operations and are private businesses. Notwithstanding these problems, analysts have tried to extend the relative valuation practices that have been developed for public

16 It is unlikely that the venture capitalist will accept the higher valuation, unless he gets full credit for the increase in value, since it is his capital infusion that creates the increase.

companies into the private business space. In general, the biggest area of difference across analysts who value private businesses lies in where they go to get the comparable firms. Some analysts focus on transaction prices paid for other private businesses, arguing that these businesses are likely to have more in common with the young business being valued. Other analysts, distrustful of private transaction prices, draw on the market prices of publicly traded companies in the same business and try to adjust for differences in fundamentals.

Private Transaction Multiples

Since we are valuing a young, private business, it seems logical that we should look at what others have paid for similar businesses in the recent past. That is effectively the foundation on which private transaction multiples are based. In theory, at least, we pull together a dataset of other young, private businesses, similar to the one we are valuing (same business, similar size, and at the same stage in the life cycle), that have been bought/sold and their transaction values. We then scale these values to a common variable (revenues, earnings, or even something sector-specific) and compute a typical multiple that acquirers have been willing to pay. Applying this multiple to the same variable for the company being valued should yield an estimated value for the company.

Problems

The biggest problem used to be the absence of organized databases of private business transactions, but that is no longer the case. Many private services offer databases (for a price) that contain this data, but other problems remain:

- **Arm's-length transactions**: One of the perils of using prices from private transactions is that some of them are not arm's-length transactions, where the price reflects just the business being sold. In effect, the price includes other services and side factors that may be specific to the transaction. Thus, a doctor selling a medical practice may get a higher price because he agrees to stay on for a period of time after the transaction to ease the transition.
- **Timing differences**: Private business transactions are infrequent and reflect the fact that the same private business will not be bought and sold dozens of time during a particular period. Unlike public firms, where the current price can be used to compute the multiples for all firms at the same point in time, private transactions are often staggered across time. A database of private transactions can therefore include transactions from June 2008 and December 2008, a period when the public markets lost almost 45% of their value.
- **Scaling variable**: To compare firms of different scale, we generally divide the market price by a standardizing variable. With publicly traded firms, this can take the form of revenues (price/sales, EV/sales), earnings (PE, EV/EBITDA), or book value. While we could technically do the same with private transactions, there are two potential roadblocks. The first is that young firms have little to show in terms of current revenues and earnings, and what they do show may not be a good indication of their ultimate potential. The second is that there are broad differences in accounting standards across private businesses, and these differences can result in bottom lines that are not quite equivalent.
- **Nonstandardized equity**: As we noted in the preceding section, equity claims in young, private businesses can vary widely in terms of cash flow and control claims. The transaction price for equity in a private business reflects the claims that are embedded in

the equity in that business. It may not easily generalize to equity in another firm with different characteristics.

- **Non-U.S. firms**: Most of the transaction databases that are available and accessible today are databases of transactions of private businesses in the U.S. As we are called on increasingly to value young businesses in other markets, some of which are riskier, emerging markets, it is not clear how or even whether this data can be used in that context.

Usefulness and Best Practices

So, when is it appropriate to use private transaction data to value a young, private business? As a general rule, this approach works best for small businesses that plan to stay small and private, rather than expand their reach and perhaps go public. It also helps if the firm being valued is in a business where there are a large number of other private businesses and also where transactions are common. For instance, this approach should work well for valuing a medical/dental practice or a small retail business. It will get more difficult to apply for firms that are in unique or unusual businesses.

If we decide to employ private company transactions to value a young business, some general practices can help deliver more dependable valuations:

- **Scale to variables that are less affected by discretionary choices**: As a counter to the problem of wide differences in accounting and operating standards across private companies, we can focus on variables where discretionary choice matters less. For instance, multiples of revenues (which are more difficult to fudge or manipulate) should be preferred to multiples of earnings. We could even scale value to units specific to the business being valued, such as the number of patients for a general medical practice or the number of customers for a landscaping business.
- **Value businesses, not equity**: Chapter 4 classified multiples into equity multiples (where equity value is scaled to equity earnings or book value) and enterprise value multiples (where the value of the business is scaled to operating earnings, cash flows, or the book value of capital). Given the wide differences in equity claims and the use of debt across private businesses, it is better to focus on enterprise value multiples rather than equity multiples. In other words, it is better to value the entire business and then work out the value of equity than it is to value equity directly.
- **Start with a large dataset**: Since transactions with private businesses are infrequent, it is best to start with a large dataset of companies and collect all transaction data. This allows us to screen the data for transactions that look suspicious (and thus are likely to fail the arm's-length test).
- **Adjust for timing differences**: Even with large datasets of private transactions, timing differences will occur across transactions. While this is not an issue in a period where markets are stable, we should make adjustments to the value (even if they are crude) to account for the timing differences. For instance, using June 2008 and December 2008 as the transaction dates, we would reduce the transaction prices from June 2008 by the drop in the public market (a small cap index like the Russell 5000 dropped by about 40% over that period) to make the prices comparable.

- **Focus on differences in fundamentals:** The notion that the value of a business depends on its fundamentals—growth, cash flows, and risk—cannot be abandoned just because we are doing relative valuation. The estimated value is likely to be more reliable if we can collect other measures of the transacted private businesses that reflect these fundamentals. For instance, it would be useful to obtain not only the transaction prices of private businesses but also the growth in revenues recorded in these businesses in the period prior to the transactions and the age of the business (to reflect maturity and risk). We can explore the data to see if a relationship exists between transaction value and these variables. If there is one, we can build it into the valuation.

Public Multiples

It is far easier to obtain timely data on pricing and multiples for publicly traded firms. In fact, for analysts who do not have access to private transaction data, this is the only option when it comes to relative valuation. The peril, though, is that we are extending the pricing lessons we learn from looking at more mature, publicly traded firms to a young, private business.

Problems

The issues we face in applying public market multiples to private businesses, especially early in the life cycle, are fairly obvious:

- **Life cycle affects fundamentals**: If we accept the premise that only young firms that make it through the early phase of the life cycle and succeed are likely to go public, we also have to accept the reality that public firms will have different fundamentals than private firms. Generally, public firms are larger, have less potential for growth, and have more established markets than private businesses. These differences manifest themselves in the multiples that investors pay for public companies.
- **Survival:** A related point is that young firms have a high probability of failure. However, this probability of failure should decrease as firms establish their product offerings. Firms that go public should have a greater chance of surviving than younger private firms. The former should therefore trade at higher market values, for any given variable such as revenues, earnings, or book value, holding all else (growth and risk) constant.
- **Diversified versus undiversified investors**: Earlier we discussed estimating risk and discount rates for young, private businesses. We noted the different perspectives on risk that diversified investors in public companies have, relative to equity investors in private businesses. That difference can manifest itself as higher costs of equity for the latter. When we use multiples of earnings or revenues, obtained from a sample of publicly traded firms with diversified investors, to value a private business with undiversified investors, we overvalue the latter.
- **Scaling variable:** Assuming that we can obtain a reasonable multiple of revenues or earnings from our public company dataset, we face a final problem. Young firms often have very little revenues to show in the current year, and many will be losing money, so the book value is usually meaningless. Applying a multiple to any of these measures will result in strange valuations.

Usefulness and Best Practices

What types of private businesses are best valued using public company multiples? Generally, young companies that aspire to reach a larger market and either go public or be acquired by a public company are much better candidates for this practice. In effect, we are valuing the company for what it wants to be, rather than what it is today.

Some simple practices can prevent egregious valuation errors and lead to better valuations:

- **Use forward revenues/earnings**: One of the problems we noted with using multiples on young companies is that the company's current operations do not provide much in terms of tangible results: Revenues are very small, and earnings are negative. One solution is to forecast the firm's operating results later in the life cycle and to use these forward revenues and earnings as the basis for valuation. In effect, we will estimate the value of the business in five years, using revenues or earnings from that point in time.
- **Adjust the multiple for your firm's characteristics at time of valuation**: If we are valuing the firm five years down the road, we have to estimate a multiple that is appropriate for the firm at that point in time, rather than today. Consider a simple illustration. Assume that you have a company that is expected to generate a compounded revenue growth of 50% a year for the next five years, as it scales from being a very small firm to a more established enterprise. Assume that revenue growth after year 5 will drop to a more moderate compounded annual rate of 10%. The multiple we apply to revenues or earnings in year 5 should reflect an expected growth rate of 10%, not 50%.
- **Adjust for survival**: When we estimated the intrinsic value for young firms, we allowed for the possibility of failure by adjusting the value for the probability that the firm would not make it. We should stick with that principle, because the value based on future revenues/earnings is implicitly based on the assumption that the firm survives and succeeds.
- **Adjust for nondiversification**: The value estimated for the firm or equity, based on future earnings and revenues, must be discounted back to the present to arrive at the value today. We can use the techniques we developed for adjusting the beta and cost of equity for private businesses in the intrinsic value section. We can discount for the forecast future value of the business by a high-enough rate to reflect the nondiversification of equity investors today. In effect, we are assuming that the firm will go public in the future year (where the multiple is applied) and that the nondiversification issue will dissipate.

Valuing Secure Mail Software: Relative Valuation

We will use publicly traded firms as comparable firms in the relative valuation of Secure Mail for two reasons:

- It aspires to become a much larger firm and eventually go public.
- Very few transactions involve young, private software companies.

In coming up with a sample of comparable firms, we initially looked at only the three antivirus firms that we used in the venture capital approach—Symantec, McAfee, and Trend Micro—but we decided that we could not base a valuation on a sample this small. Consequently, we expanded our sample to include publicly traded software companies with a market capitalization less than $100 million. We regressed the ratio of enterprise value to sales at these companies against three variables: the beta (as a measure of risk), the expected growth in revenues over the next five years (to capture growth differences), and the return on capital (as a measure of the quality of growth):

EV/Sales = 0.33 – 0.6 (Beta) + 7.6 (Revenue Growth) + 5.3 (Return on Capital)

We then applied this regression to get a predicted EV/sales ratio for Secure Mail in year 5, using the following inputs as independent variables: the firm's total beta in year 5 (1.60), the expected growth rate in revenues from years 6 to 10 (which is computed to be 21.2%, based on the forecasts in Table 9.7), and the return on capital in year 5 (estimated to be 13.31% in year 5, from Table 9.10):

Predicted EV/SalesSecure Mail, Year 5 = 0.33 – 0.6 (1.6) + 7.6 (0.212) + 5.3 (0.1331) = 1.7466

Applying this multiple to revenues of $686 million in year 5, we obtain a value for the firm of $1,198 million in year 5. We make two adjustments to get to value today:

- We adjust for the probability that the firm will fail before the fifth year (40%) and arrive at an expected value:

Expected Value = Estimated Value in Year 5 (1 – Probability of Failure)

= 1,198 (1 – .40) = $561.56 million

$$\text{Value Today} = \frac{561.56}{(1.19)^2\ (1.16)^2\ 1.12} = \$338.93 \text{ million}$$

- We discount the estimated value in year 5 back to today using the higher costs of equity that we estimated in the intrinsic valuation for years 1 to 5:

The final value that we obtain for the operating assets at Secure Mail, using this approach, is $339 million. It is higher than the intrinsic value, partly because we are ignoring the possibility of negative cash flows from years 1 through 5. Consequently, the number of shares we divide this value by should be modified to reflect expectations that more equity will be issued to cover capital requirements.

Real Options

Chapter 5 introduced the concept of real options. It argued that the option to expand into new businesses can sometimes result in a premium being attached to intrinsic value. With young companies, this real-options argument sometimes has resonance. We will explore its applicability in this section.

The Option to Expand in Young Companies

In both discounted cash flow and relative valuation, we build in our expectations of what success for a young firm looks like in terms of revenues and earnings. Thus, it can be argued that the potential upside is already reflected in the value. The counter to this argument is that success in one business or market can sometimes be a stepping-stone to success in other businesses or markets:

- **New products**: Success with an existing product or service can sometimes provide an opening for a firm to introduce a new product. A classic example is Microsoft building off the operating systems (MS-DOS and Windows) it developed for the PC to produce Microsoft Office, an immensely profitable addition to its product line. Another example is Apple's introduction of the iPhone, which took advantage of the customer base Apple developed with the iPod. While neither new product (Microsoft Office and the iPhone) could have been predicted at the time of the original product's introduction, the success of the initial product was clearly the launching pad for these offerings.
- **New markets:** In some cases, companies that succeed with a product in one market may be able to expand into other markets, with similar success. The most obvious example of this is expanding into foreign markets to build on domestic market success, a pathway adopted by companies like Coca-Cola, McDonald's, and many retail companies. The more subtle examples are products that are directed at one market but that serendipitously find new markets. An ulcer drug that reduces cholesterol is a good example.

Why can't we build expectations about new products and new markets into our cash flows and value? We can try, but there are two problems. The first is that our forecasts about these potential product and market extensions will be very hazy at the time of the initial valuation, and the cash flows will reflect this uncertainty. In other words, neither Microsoft nor Apple would have been able to visualize the potential markets for Microsoft Office or the iPhone at the time they were introducing MS-DOS and the iPod. The second problem is that the information gleaned and lessons learned during the initial product launch and subsequent development allow firms to take full advantage of the follow-up offerings. This learning and adaptive behavior give rise to the option value.

Valuing the Option to Expand in Young Companies

Given that we are valuing the option to expand today, when the uncertainties are greatest, how can we about go about estimating a value? Four steps are involved in putting a number (and a premium) to real options:

1. **Estimate the expected value and cost of going ahead with the expansion option today.** The process of valuing real options begins with a fairly counterintuitive first step. We determine what the present value of the expected cash flows would be if we expanded into the new product today, and the cost of that expansion. In other words, this would have required Apple to consider the possibility and the potential cash flows of introducing the iPhone at the time it introduced the iPod. Many analysts resist making these estimates, arguing that they know too little about the potential product and market. But that is precisely where the option value is derived.

2. **Assess the uncertainty in the estimated value of the expansion option.** In the second step in the process, we not only confront the inherent uncertainty in the process, but we also try to measure this uncertainty in the form of a standard deviation in the value of the cash flows. There are two ways in which we can do this. The first is to fall back on a market-based measure. The standard deviation of publicly traded firms in the business could be used as a proxy. The other way is to run simulations on the expansion investment and derive a standard deviation in the value of the expected cash flow across simulations.
3. **Determine the point in time when the firm will have to make the expansion choice.** The option to expand into new markets and products cannot be open-ended. Practically speaking, there must be a date by which the firm must decide to either expand or abandon that option. In some cases, this time period may be a function of specified factors, such as a patent expiring or a license renewal, and in others it may be self-imposed.
4. **Value the option to expand.** The inputs to value the option are now in place, with the following pieces going into value. The present value of the expected cash flows from expansion, assuming we expand now, becomes the value of the underlying asset, and the cost of expansion today becomes the strike price. The standard deviation in value is the volatility in the underlying assets, and the life of the option is the point in time by which the expansion decision must be made. In theory, binomial option pricing models should work better at pricing real options, because they allow for early exercise, but the traditional Black-Scholes model provides reasonable approximations for most real options.

Limits

The argument we use to justify a real-options premium (that what we learn from existing products and markets can be used to add value down the road by expanding into new products and markets) can be made for any young firm. However, a key test must be passed before we assess a value for the option to expand and augment our traditional estimates of value. That is the test of exclusivity. In other words, the learning and adaptive behavior must be restricted to the firm in question and not open to the rest of the market.

Consider, for instance, the two examples we used to illustrate the real-options argument in the first part of this section. Microsoft's exclusivity in developing Office arose from its control of the operating system. Thus, it had a significant advantage over the competition (Lotus, WordPerfect) when developing its software. Apple's exclusivity came from a reputation for innovation and coolness it developed with the iPod. Both were critical components in the adoption of the iPhone.

The allure of the real-options argument is the premium you can add to traditional discounted cash flow valuation. Some people push the use of this argument to its logical limit and beyond. Thus, some analysts argue that discounted cash flow valuations undervalue all young companies and that we should add option premiums to all of them. Other analysts mistake opportunities for options, using the real-options argument to add premiums to any company that has high growth potential. These range from technology companies in growing markets (software and alternative energy, for example) to small companies in large, emerging markets (such as India and China). In the process, they often double-count the value of growth—once through the expected cash flows in discounted cash flow valuation, and again when they add the premium. While real options are a powerful and effective tool for assessing value, they have to be used selectively. They can be used only when the expected expansion opportunities cannot be adequately captured in the expected cash flows, and when the company in question has significant competitive advantages over the competition.

Valuing the Option to Expand into Database Systems: Secure Mail Software

We have valued Secure Mail based on the potential cash flows from its antivirus software program. However, the company might be able to use the customer base it develops for the antivirus software and the technology on which the software is based to create a database software program sometime in the ***next five years***.

- It will cost Secure Mail about $500 million to develop a new database program if it decides to do so today.
- Based on the information that Secure Mail has right now on the market for a database program, the company can expect to generate about $40 million a year in after-tax cash flows for ten years from the program. The cost of capital for private companies that provide database software is 12%.
- The annualized standard deviation in firm value at publicly traded database companies is 50%.
- The five-year Treasury bond rate is 3%.

To value the expansion option, we use this information to derive the option inputs:

S = Value of the underlying asset

= PV of expected cash flows from entering the database software market today

$$= \frac{40\left(1 - \frac{1}{(1.12)^{10}}\right)}{0.12} = \$226 \text{ million}$$

K = Exercise price = Cost of entering the database software market = $ 500 million

t = Life of the option = Period over which expansion opportunity exists = 5 years

s = Standard deviation of underlying asset = 50%

r = Riskless rate = 3%

Inputting these numbers into the Black-Scholes model, we obtain the following:[17]

17 The values we derive for d1 and d2 are as follows:

$$d_1 = \frac{\ln\left(\frac{226}{500}\right) + \left(0.03 + \frac{(0.50)^2}{2}\right)(5)}{0.50\sqrt{5}} = 0.0171$$

$$d_2 = 0.0171 - 0.50\sqrt{5} = -1.1351$$

$$\text{Value of Call} = S\,N(d1) - K\,e^{-rt}\,N(d2)$$

$$= 226\,(0.4932) - 500\,e^{-(.03)}\,(5)\,(0.1282) = \$56.30 \text{ million}$$

Note that the numbers do not justify developing the database program today. The present value of the expected cash flows ($226 million) is well below the cost. However, Secure Mail has two factors in its favor. The first is that it can refine its assessments of the market based on how its antivirus program performs. The second is that it can adapt the database program, based on the information it collects, to increase the potential market and cash flows.

If we accept this value for the expansion option, we should add it to the value we derived for Secure Mail earlier in the intrinsic valuation of $111.54 million. We would justify the use of the option pricing model in this case by arguing that Secure Mail derives its exclusivity from its proprietary technology and access to customer lists (from its antivirus program).

Conclusion

There is no denying that young companies pose the most difficult estimation challenges in valuation. A combination of factors—short and not very informative histories, operating losses, and the possibility of failure—feed into valuation practices that try to avoid dealing with the uncertainty by using a combination of forward multiples and arbitrarily high discount rates.

This chapter has described processes that can be used to apply conventional valuation models to young companies. While these approaches require us to estimate inputs that are often difficult to nail down, they are still useful insofar as they force us to confront the sources of uncertainty, learn more about them, and make our best estimates. While we may be tempted to add premiums to these values for potential opportunities we see in the future, the use of real-options premiums should be limited to companies that have some degree of exclusivity in exploiting these opportunities.

10

Shooting Stars? Growth Companies

In the preceding chapter, we looked at the estimation challenges associated with valuing young idea companies. One of the issues we confronted was the question of survival, since many young companies fail early in their lives. But what about firms that make it through the test of competition and become successful businesses? This chapter looks at a subset of these firms that become growth companies. A few of these firms stay private, but many of them enter public markets, partly because of their need for capital and partly to allow owners to cash in on their success.

This chapter examines the issues we face when valuing growth companies. Many of the concerns we saw with young companies—short and volatile operating histories, uncertainty about future growth, and changing risk profiles—remain problems when we value growth companies, especially in their initial phases. However, the data and tools we use to deal with them do become better. The existing concerns are joined by new concerns about how growth rates may change as companies get larger and how access and exposure to public capital markets will change financing and investment decisions at the firm.

Growth Companies

Companies at every stage of the life cycle aspire to be growth companies. The young idea businesses in the preceding chapter hope to make it through the rigors of the marketplace to become growth companies, and mature firms keep trying to reinvent themselves as growth companies. This section looks at why growth companies are appealing and the role that growth companies play in the economy and in public markets.

A Life Cycle View of Growth Companies

While investors and managers often talk about growth and mature companies as distinct groups, the differences are hazier in the real world. So, what is a growth company? Many definitions for growth companies are used in practice, but they all tend to be subjective and have significant flaws:

- **Sector-based measures:** Many analysts categorize companies as growth companies or mature companies based on the sector they operate in. Thus, technology companies in the U.S. are treated as growth companies, whereas steel companies are considered mature. This definition clearly misses the vast differences in growth prospects across companies within any given sector. Technology companies like Intel and Microsoft may be more mature businesses than growth businesses at this stage of their corporate evolution.

- **Analyst growth estimates/growth history**: A second categorization of companies into growth and mature companies is based on expected growth in future earnings, usually based on forecasts by equity research analysts. In the absence of forecast growth, some services use past growth in earnings as the growth measure. In both cases, firms that have high growth rates are considered growth companies; how high is a matter of both judgment and overall market growth. For instance, if earnings for the entire market are growing at 10% a year, companies may need to deliver 25% growth to be considered growth companies. With market earnings growth of only 5%, a 15% growth rate in earnings may qualify a company as a growth company. The limits of this approach are that it is circumscribed by its focus on earnings, as opposed to revenues or units sold. After all, many young high-growth companies may have exponential growth in revenues while losing money. Similarly, mature companies can post healthy earnings increases with improved efficiency and relatively little operating unit growth.
- **Market-based measures:** Morningstar, as part of its mutual fund tracking service, categorizes mutual funds into those investing in growth stocks and those investing in mature companies. Morningstar bases its categorization on the market multiples that companies trade at. It argues that companies that are perceived to be growth companies will trade at higher multiples of earnings, revenues, and book value than mature companies. Given that our focus in valuation is to decide whether markets are pricing stocks correctly, this process seems to work backwards by implicitly assuming that the market is right.

All three definitions—industry groupings, earnings growth, and market multiples—lead to miscategorization. Although we cannot offer a perfect alternative, we suggest using the financial balance sheet we introduced in Chapter 1 to make this judgment. Figure 10.1 focuses on the asset side of the financial balance sheet, where assets are broken into existing investments and growth assets.

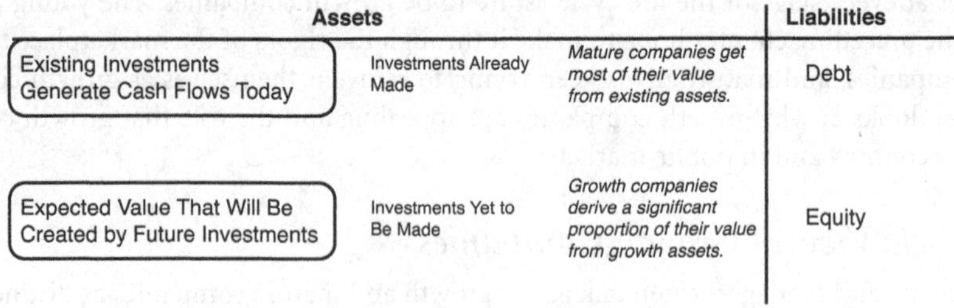

Figure 10.1: The Asset Side of the Financial Balance Sheet

Growth firms get a significant portion of their value from growth assets—investments they expect to make in the future. While this may seem like a restatement of the growth categorization described earlier, where firms with high growth rates are treated as growth companies, there is an important difference. As we noted in Chapter 2, the value of growth assets is a function of not only how much growth is anticipated but also the excess returns that accompany that growth. Specifically, growth investments have no value if the firm earns a return on capital equal to the cost of capital on these investments. The problem with this categorization is that it can be made only after you value a company, since you need to assess a company's fundamentals (prospective returns on new investments and cost of capital) to make the judgment.

No matter how we decide to categorize companies into growth and mature businesses, we still think about growth in terms of a firm's life cycle. Chapter 9 was our attempt to value firms in their infancy, at the earliest stages of the life cycle. The firms in this chapter have made it through perhaps the most difficult part of the life cycle and are reaping some of the benefits of surviving the early phase. Since the growth phase can extend over many years, the companies we will consider in this chapter are diverse. Some are small and risky and bear a resemblance to the young firms we analyzed in Chapter 9. Others are further along in the growth cycle and have more in common with the mature firms we will value in Chapter 11 than young firms.

Growth companies play a key role in any economy, with an impact that is often larger than their economic output. Growth companies collectively may account for a smaller portion of the real economy (output and employment) than mature companies. But they are the engines of economic growth because they account for a much larger proportion of changes in the real economy over time. In the U.S., for instance, where traditional manufacturing has retreated from its central role, much of the growth in employment and economic output the last two decades has come from technology and health care businesses, many of which would be categorized as growth companies.

Finally, if we look at publicly traded companies, the proportion of overall market value that is from growth companies will be much higher than the proportion of the real economy they account for. The disparity between market value and current operating assets depends on a number of factors, including the level of interest rates, risk premiums, and optimism about future economic growth. In early 2000, at the peak of the technology boom, technology companies represented almost 35% of the overall market capitalization of the S&P 500. One year later, after the collapse in the sector, technology stocks accounted for only 17% of the overall index.

Characteristics of Growth Companies

Growth companies are diverse in size and growth prospects and can be spread out over very different businesses. But they share some common characteristics that make an impact on how we value them. This section looks at some of these shared features:

- **Dynamic financials**: Much of the information we use to value companies comes from their financial statements (income statements, balance sheets, and statements of cash flows). One feature shared by growth companies is that the numbers in these statements are in a state of flux. Not only can the numbers for the latest year be very different from numbers in the prior year, but they can change dramatically, even over shorter time periods. For many smaller, high-growth firms, for instance, the revenues and earnings from the most recent four quarters can be dramatically different from the revenues and earnings in the most recent fiscal year (which may have ended only a few months ago).
- **Private and public equity**: It is accepted as conventional wisdom that the natural path for a young company that succeeds at the earliest stages is to go public and tap capital markets for new funds. There are three reasons why this transition is neither as orderly nor as predictable in practice. The first is that the private-to-public transition varies across different economies, depending on both institutional considerations and the development of capital markets. Historically, growth companies in the U.S. have entered public markets earlier in the life cycle than growth companies in Europe, partly because this is the preferred exit path for many venture capitalists in the U.S. The second reason

is that even within any given market, access to capital markets for new companies can vary across time as markets ebb and flow. In the U.S., for instance, initial public offerings increase in buoyant markets and drop in depressed markets. During the market collapse in the last quarter of 2008, initial public offerings came to a standstill. The third reason is that the pathway to going public varies across sectors. Companies in some sectors, such as technology and biotechnology, get access to public markets much earlier in the life cycle than firms in other sectors, such as manufacturing and retailing. The net effect is that the growth companies we cover in this chapter draw on a mix of private equity (venture capital) and public equity for their equity capital. Put another way, some growth companies are private businesses, and some are publicly traded. Many of the latter group will still have venture capitalists and founders as large holders of equity.

- **Size disconnect**: The contrast we drew in Chapter 1 between accounting and financial balance sheets, with the former focused primarily on existing investments and the latter incorporating growth assets into the mix, is stark in growth companies. The market values of these companies, if they are publicly traded, are often much higher than the accounting (or book) values because the former incorporate the value of growth assets and the latter often do not. In addition, the market values can seem discordant with the firm's operating numbers—revenues and earnings. Many growth firms that have market values in the hundreds of millions or even billions can have small revenues and negative earnings. Again, the reason lies in the fact that the operating numbers reflect the firm's existing investments, and these investments may represent a very small portion of the firm's overall value.
- **Use of debt**: While the usage of debt can vary across sectors, the growth firms in any business tend to carry less debt, relative to their value (intrinsic or market), than more stable firms in the same business. This is simply because they do not have the cash flows from existing assets to support more debt. In some sectors, such as technology, even more mature growth firms with large positive earnings and cash flows are reluctant to borrow money. In other sectors, such as telecommunications, where debt is a preferred financing mode, growth companies generally have lower debt ratios than mature companies.
- **Market history is short and shifting**: We are dependent on market price inputs for several key components of valuation—especially for estimating risk parameters (such as betas). Even if growth companies are publicly traded, they tend to have short and shifting histories. For example, an analyst looking at Google in early 2009 would have been able to draw on about four years of market history (a short period). But even those four years of data may not be particularly useful or relevant, because the company changed dramatically over that period. It went from revenues in the millions to revenues in the billions, from operating losses to operating profits, and from a small market capitalization to a large one.

While the degree to which these factors affect growth firms can vary across firms, they are prevalent in almost every growth firm.

Valuation Issues

The shared characteristics of growth firms—dynamic financials, a mix of public and private equity, disconnects between market value and operating data, a dependence on equity funding, and a short and volatile market history—have consequences for both intrinsic and relative valuations.

Intrinsic (DCF) Valuation

If a company's intrinsic value comes from its cash flows and risk characteristics, we will run into problems while valuing growth companies that can be traced back to where they are in the life cycle. This section breaks down the valuation issues specific to growth companies by the key components of intrinsic value—existing asset value, growth asset value, risk (discount rates), terminal value, and equity value per share.

Existing Assets

To value existing assets, we start with the cash flows generated by these assets and discount back at an appropriate risk-adjusted rate. Two considerations can make this measurement complicated:

- **Poorly measured earnings**: With growth firms, existing assets tend to be a small part of overall value and can easily be swamped by what a firm expends to sustain and nurture its growth assets. Consider, for instance, the standard assumption that we make in discounted cash flow valuation that the existing operating income can be attributed to existing assets and thus be the basis for valuing those assets. With any company, the existing operating income (or loss) will be after selling, advertising, and other administrative expenses. While we assume that these expenses are associated with existing assets, that assumption may not hold up in a growth company. After all, the sales force in a growth company may be less interested in pushing existing products and more focused on cultivating a customer base for future products. By treating all sales expenses as operating expenses, we are understating the earnings from and consequently the value of existing assets.
- **Shifting profitability**: If one of the key inputs into value is the measure of the firm's future profitability, the fact that margins and returns at growth firms change significantly over time can make it difficult to make forecasts. Unlike mature firms, where margins usually move within a narrow range and returns are stable, using past margins and returns to forecast future values for a growth firm may not yield reasonable numbers.

Growth Assets

The bulk of a value for a growth company obviously comes from growth assets, making it imperative that we assess the value correctly. The challenges we face in attaching a reasonable value to growth assets in a growth company can also be daunting:

- **The scaling effect on growth**: One of the biggest questions we have to answer about a company's expected growth rates is how they will be affected by the company's changing size. Consider, for instance, a company that has posted a growth rate of 80% over the last five years. The company today is obviously much larger (by a factor of 18) than it was five years ago.[1] It is extremely unlikely that it will be able to maintain an 80% growth rate for the next year, given its larger size. In general, delivering a given growth rate becomes more difficult as a company gets bigger.

- **Success attracts competition**: A small company can operate under the radar and sometimes show exceptional profitability. As the company grows, though, its success attracts attention from larger and more predatory competitors, often possessing more significant resources. This competition, in turn, results in lower profitability and value for growth.
- **Macroeconomic effects**: While all companies are susceptible to macroeconomic shocks, small companies are more exposed to economic downturns, because their products are often niche products that are discretionary. While customers may be inclined to buy them in good book economic times, they are likely to hold back during recessions or economic slowdowns.

Questions about how quickly growth rates will scale down, how profitability will survive competitive assaults, and the effects of overall economic growth will have to be answered if we intend to attach a value to growth assets.

Discount Rates

The two key determinants of discount rates are the risk in the underlying investments of a business and the mix of debt and equity used to fund the business. On both dimensions, growth companies pose a challenge in valuation:

- **Risk of existing assets versus risk of growth assets**: Since growth companies derive significant value from both growth assets and existing assets, delineating the risk in each category can make a big difference in how we value them. In other words, if growth assets are riskier than existing assets, we should be using higher discount rates for expected cash flows from the former and lower discount rates for cash flows from the latter. However, it is difficult to make this judgment on risk from the historical information, especially using stock price data, since it is for the consolidated firm (and not for existing or growth assets as individual groupings).
- **Market value versus book value ratios and volatile market value**: The conventional practice of estimating the weights to use for debt and equity in the cost of capital computation is to use market values for both. With growth firms, we should follow the same practice, but the volatility in stock prices can result in weights that change with the prices. In particular, a drop in the stock price can lead to a much higher debt ratio and potentially a lower cost of capital for a firm; this will strike some as counterintuitive.
- **Changing risk for the firm over time**: If computing the current risk parameters and debt ratio for a growth firm is difficult, the task is complicated further by a simple fact. On both dimensions, growth firms can be expected to change over time, leading to discount rates that vary across the years. To be more specific, as a firm becomes larger over time (as it will in future periods, with growth), we should expect existing assets to

1 Applying a compounded growth rate of 80% for five years to $1 results in an end value of almost $19, an overall increase of 1,800% over five years.

become a larger proportion of overall value and risk measures to change to reflect the firm's increasing (and more stable) earnings. Concurrently, the firm's capacity to borrow money will increase. If it exploits this capacity, its debt ratio will change as well. Generally speaking, the discount rates used to value growth firms should be higher in the earlier periods and decrease in later periods toward mature company levels.

Terminal Value

Two key questions that overhang the valuation of any firm relate to *when* the firm will become a stable growth firm and the *characteristics* it will possess in this phase. The answer to the first question will determine the length of the high-growth period, with the terminal value being computed on the assumption that growth beyond that point will be sustained forever. The answer to the second question, especially on risk and the returns generated on new investments, will influence the value we assign to the firm, for any given level of growth. Again, while these are estimation issues that arise in any valuation, they can be more problematic for growth companies for the following reasons:

- **Terminal value is a bigger proportion of value**: Since growth companies generate relatively low cash flows from existing assets, the terminal value comprises a much larger proportion of their overall value. Thus, the assumptions we make about terminal value will matter more in any assessment of current value for a growth firm than at a mature firm.
- **More uncertainty about terminal value assumptions**: Concurrent with the terminal value being a larger proportion of the value of a growth company than for a mature firm is the fact that there is significantly more uncertainty about assessing that value for two reasons. First, we are looking at a young and often untested firm and assessing not only how quickly it will continue to grow but also how it will respond to more aggressive competition. Second, the fact that the firm is evolving makes it difficult to evaluate what market it is aspiring to be in or even who its direct competitors are.
- **Terminal value characteristics**: Earlier in this section, we noted the difficulties we face in arriving at the current cash flows, returns, and discount rates for a growth firm. We will be called on to estimate all these numbers again, when we put the firm into stable growth, in 10 or 15 years. If we cannot estimate the current cost of capital for a growth firm, it seems unreasonable to believe that we can estimate this and other numbers for the same firm 10 or 15 years in the future.

The irony of terminal value estimation for growth firms is that it is more important that we get it right and that we have far less basis for making the estimate in the first place. How we resolve this contradiction will play a key role in whether the value we arrive at for a growth firm is a reasonable one.

Value of Equity per Share

To get from the value of the operating assets to the value of equity per share, we generally add the value of cash and cross-holdings, subtract debt and nonequity claims, and then divide by the number of shares in the firm. While these steps stay intact for growth companies, we face issues at each step:

- **Cash balances and cash burn ratios**: In most firm valuations, we get information on cash balances from financial statements (usually the most recent balance sheet). For growth firms, especially early in the growth phase, where reinvestment needs can be substantial, cash balances can be dissipated very quickly. The pace of cash usage, generally called the "cash burn" rate, can result in a cash balance today (which is when we are valuing the company) that is very different from the cash balance on the most recent fiscal statement.
- **Convertible debt and preferred stock**: When growth firms raise funds from nonequity investors, they seldom use conventional debt—bank loans and straight bonds. More common is the use of the convertible debt, either in the form of bank loans with equity sweeteners or convertible bonds. The key advantage of using hybrids such as these is that interest payments are kept low in return for providing equity options to lenders. Because only debt should be subtracted to get to equity values, we should break convertible debt into debt and equity components, with the equity options going into the latter.
- **Voting and nonvoting shares**: Voting and nonvoting shares are not unique to growth firms, but they are much more common in these companies than in mature firms. This is largely because these firms are young, and the founders are still not only significantly stockholders but also value being able to control the firms they have created. One way to maintain control, while raising equity from the general public, is to create two classes of share and to preserve a hold on the company by retaining the voting shares. When estimating the value of equity per share, we therefore must determine how (if at all) we will differentiate shares with higher voting rights from shares without (or with lower) voting rights.

In summary, getting from the value of operating assets to the value of equity per share can pose a series of roadblocks and diversions with growth firms.

Relative Valuation

Many analysts, when confronted with the intrinsic valuation problems outlined earlier, decide that relative valuation is a much easier path to follow with growth companies. Not surprisingly, the issues that make discounted cash flow valuation difficult also crop up when we do relative valuation:

- **Comparable firms**: The conventional practice of using other publicly traded companies in the same sector can be dangerous for a couple reasons. The first is that a growth company in a mature sector will (and should) bear little or no resemblance on either fundamentals or pricing multiples to the rest of the firms in the sector. The second reason is that even if every firm in the sector has growth potential, growth firms can vary widely in terms of risk and growth characteristics, thus making it difficult to generalize from industry averages.
- **Base year values and choice of multiples**: Most multiples are stated as a function of base year values for revenues, earnings, and book value. To estimate the PE ratio, for instance, we divide the stock price today by the earnings per share in the most recent fiscal year or four quarters. If a firm is young, the current values for these numbers will bear little resemblance to the firm's future potential. Using PE ratios to illustrate this point, this

can lead to either very high PE ratios (since current earnings per share will be small relative to stock prices today) or not meaningful values (because earnings currently are negative and PE ratios cannot be computed) for many growth companies. Moving up the income statement to EBITDA or revenues offers little solace, because the values for these items will also be low relative to future potential.

- **Controlling for growth differences:** Since growth potential is the key dimension on which these firms vary, it becomes critical that we control for growth when comparing firms or extrapolating from industry averages. Unfortunately, the relationship between growth and value is too complex to lend itself to the simplistic generalizations that make relative valuation so attractive to both analysts and investors. Not only does the level of growth make a difference to value, but so does the length of the growth period and the excess returns that accompany that growth rate. Put another way, two companies with the same expected growth rate in earnings can trade at very different multiples of these earnings, because they vary on other dimensions.
- **Controlling for risk differences:** Growth and risk are twin variables, with higher values for one generally going with higher values for the other. Determining how the net trade-off will affect value is difficult to do in any valuation, but it is doubly so in relative valuation, where many companies have both high growth and high risk. Furthermore, as risk and growth characteristics change over time, as they inevitably do for any growth company, the multiple we will apply to the company's operating numbers should also change.

Analysts who use multiples and comparables to value growth firms may feel a false sense of security about their valuations, since their assumptions are often implicit rather than explicit. The reality, though, is that relative valuations yield valuations that are just as subject to error as discounted cash flow valuations.

The Dark Side of Valuation

Given the many estimation issues we face when valuing growth companies, it is not surprising that the dark side of valuation manifests itself in many ways when analysts value these firms. In this section, we will consider the ways in which valuations of growth firms can be skewed by unrealistic or unreasonable assumptions about the future, first in the context of discounted cash flow valuation and then in relative valuation.

Discounted Cash Flow Valuation

The estimation issues with valuing growth companies, outlined earlier in the chapter, generate heartburn among analysts, who then look for shortcuts, often devised from their valuation experiences with more mature firms, to get to a valuation.

Using Current Numbers as a Base

Most valuations start with a set of base year numbers, which usually come from the current financial statements. Analysts who follow this process with young companies will be building valuations on a shifting and unreliable foundation for several reasons. The first is that the numbers can be very small and not very meaningful for growth firms earlier in the life cycle. Many growth companies that have small revenues report operating losses, and extrapolating from either number can be dangerous. The second reason is that the hazy lines between operating and capital expenses at young companies can skew both earnings and reinvestment (capital expenditures) numbers. For instance, if much of selling expenses are really for generating future growth, and they are treated as operating expenses, both income and capital expenditures will be understated. The third reason is that the volatility in the numbers can cause big changes from year to year in items like operating margin and return on capital that are fundamental inputs into any valuation.

Scaling Issues

In the earlier sections, we pointed out our concerns about the sustainability of growth—how quickly the growth rates at growth firms will decrease as the firm becomes larger—because of the scaling effect and due to competition. Analysts who use historical growth rates as forecasts of future growth are susceptible to overvaluing their firms, since they are extrapolating growth rates posted by the firm when it was much smaller, to a much larger firm. In fact, this overoptimism about growth manifests itself in two ways: a higher growth rate for the growth period than the firm can sustain, and a much longer growth period than is likely. In fact, it is not uncommon to see growth companies valued with growth rates of 25% or higher for ten years or longer.

Growth and Scale: Under Armour and Evergreen Solar

To illustrate the effect of using high growth rates as firms become larger, we will use two companies that we will value in detail later in this chapter. Under Armour is a company with a very successful line of microfiber apparel for athletes. Evergreen Solar is a company that manufactures solar panels and cells. It benefited from high oil prices from 2004 to 2008.

Under Armour, headquartered in Baltimore, was founded by Kevin Plank in 1996. It capitalized on its success by going public in 2006. Revenues at the firm tripled from $205 million in 2004 to $607 million in 2007. Over the three-year period, the company had a compounded growth rate in revenues of 44% a year. If we assume that the firm will continue to grow at a compounded rate of 44% a year for the next five years, we would expect revenues to increase to $3,758 million in 2012. While that may be possible under the best scenario, it is also unlikely. To see why, Figure 10.2 compares the revenues at the largest firms in the apparel business in the U.S., based on 2008 revenues, to Under Armour. The figure shows both revenues in the most recent 12-month period (ending in September 2008) and the forecast revenue in 2012.

Note that with our forecasts, Under Armour will become the ninth largest apparel firm in the U.S. in five years—a difficult, but not impossible, task in a very competitive business.

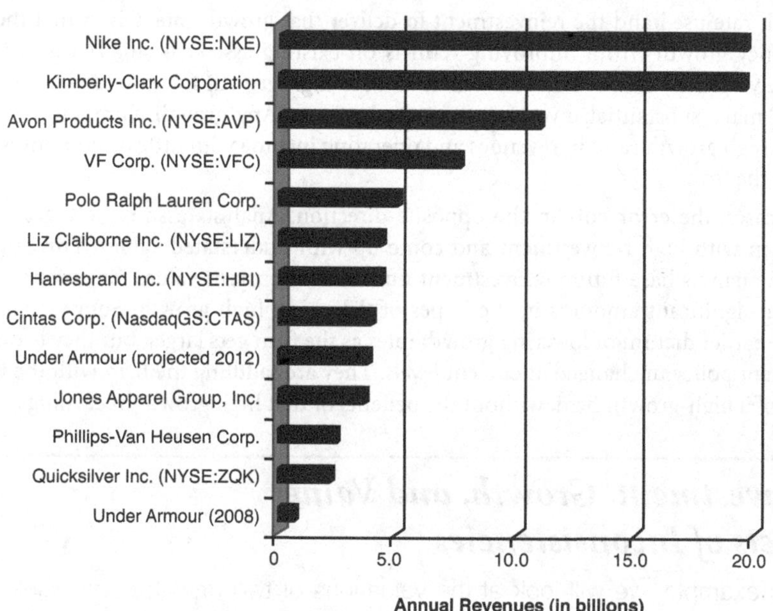

Figure 10.2: Under Armour Versus Apparel Firms

Evergreen Solar, a Massachusetts-based manufacturer of solar power cells, was founded in 2003. Revenues at the firm increased from $24 million in 2004 to $70 million in 2007, yielding a compounded growth rate of 43% a year. With Evergreen Solar, we feel comfortable allowing the growth rate to continue to be about 40% a year at least for the next five years, for two reasons. The first is that the company's total revenue in the most recent period is only $70 million, much lower than revenues at Under Armour. Allowing this revenue to grow at a 40% compounded rate will result in revenues that are still less than $500 million in five years. The second reason is that the potential market for energy products (of which solar cells are one component) is huge. Even with a high growth rate over the next five years, Evergreen will remain a very small firm in a business dominated by behemoths.

Growth, Reinvestment, and Excess Returns

The focus on growth rates in revenues and earnings at growth firms often diverts attention from a variable that is just as critical in determining value. This variable is the reinvestment that the firm must make to deliver this growth. Chapter 2 argued that growth without excess returns (returns over and above the cost of equity and capital) adds no value to the firm. When valuing growth firms, it becomes critical that we pay heed to the excess returns that accompany a specified growth rate.

In many discounted cash flow valuations, this lack of care in estimating (or even thinking about) excess returns manifests itself as inconsistencies between two key inputs into the valuation—

the growth rate used and the reinvestment to deliver that growth rate. Given that the potential for efficiency growth (from improving returns on existing assets) is small at growth firms, it is extremely unlikely that a firm can deliver double-digit growth for extended periods without having to make substantial investments in the business. Any growth company valuation that combines high growth rates in revenues and operating income with little or no reinvestment will overvalue the firm.

In some cases, the error cuts in the opposite direction. Analysts assume low growth rates in conjunction with high reinvestment and come up with understated values. This is usually the case when analysts base future reinvestment numbers on current values for companies that are reinvesting significant amounts in the hopes of delivering high growth. Suppose analysts then follow the earlier dictum of lowering growth rates as the firm gets larger, but they leave the firm's reinvestment policy unchanged at current levels. They are saddling the firm with the investment outflows of a high-growth firm, without the benefits of that high growth in earnings.

Reinvestment, Growth, and Value: Effects of Inconsistencies

In this example, we will look at the valuations of two growth companies, where inconsistent assumptions are made about growth and reinvestment, and consider the consequences for value.

In the first example, assume that an analyst is valuing a growth company with $10 million in after-tax operating income in the current year, and a reinvestment of $1 million in that year.[2] Also assume that the analyst is forecasting a growth rate of 20% a year for the next five years and 4% thereafter and is using a cost of capital of 10% in perpetuity. If the firm's current reinvestment rate is used to forecast future cash flows, we arrive at the numbers shown in Table 10.1.

Table 10.1 Expected Free Cash Flows to the Firm

	Year 1	Year 2	Year 3	Year 4	Year 5
After-tax operating income	$12.00	$14.40	$17.28	$20.74	$24.88
– Reinvestment	$1.20	$1.44	$1.73	$2.07	$2.49
FCFF	$10.80	$12.96	$15.55	$18.66	$22.39
Terminal value					$388.18
PV	$9.82	$10.71	$11.68	$12.75	$254.93
Value of firm today =	$299.89				

2 Reinvestment may be low in a given year for a high-growth firm for several reasons. One is that reinvestment is lumpy. In other words, the firm may have reinvested a very large amount in the previous year and is taking a break this year. The other reason is that the accounting number for capital expenditure may not capture what the firm is reinvesting to generate growth, either because the reinvestment is embedded in an operating expense (selling expenses) or is misclassified as an operating expense (R&D).

Note that the cash flow used to estimate the terminal value is the cash flow in year 5, grown out one year at 4%. This is not a good practice, but it's a common one.

$$\text{Terminal Value} = \frac{FCFF_5\,(1+g_{stable})}{(r-g)} = \frac{22.39(1.04)}{(.10-.04)} = \$388.18$$

The firm's value, based on these numbers, is $299.89 million. This vastly overstates the true value, because the analyst has underestimated the firm's reinvestment needs. How do we know? Using the growth rates and reinvestment rates estimated each year, we can back out the return on capital that the firm must make to justify these assumptions, on a year-by-year basis, as shown in Table 10.2.

Table 10.2 Implied Return on Capital

	Year 1	Year 2	Year 3	Year 4	Year 5	Year 6
Reinvestment rate	10.00%	10.00%	10.00%	10.00%	10.00%	10.00%
Expected growth rate	20.00%	20.00%	20.00%	20.00%	20.00%	4.00%
Implied return on capital	200.00%	200.00%	200.00%	200.00%	200.00%	40.00%

While some of the higher growth in the early years may be justified using the "higher efficiency" argument, the fact that existing assets are small relative to growth investments undercuts this claim.

In the second example, consider an analyst valuing a growth company with $10 million in after-tax operating income and a reinvestment of $8 million in the most recent year. Assume that the analyst uses the same parameters for growth and cost of capital as in the first example—20% growth rate for the next five years, followed by a growth rate of 4%, and a cost of capital of 10%. Again, assuming that the current reinvestment rate remains unchanged, we estimate the cash flows as shown in Table 10.3.

Table 10.3 Expected Free Cash Flow to the Firm

	Year 1	Year 2	Year 3	Year 4	Year 5
After-tax operating income	$12.00	$14.40	$17.28	$20.74	$24.88
– Reinvestment	$9.60	$11.52	$13.82	$16.59	$19.91
FCFF	$2.40	$2.88	$3.46	$4.15	$4.98
Terminal value					$86.26
PV	$2.18	$2.38	$2.60	$2.83	$56.65
Value of firm today =	$66.64				

Again, the terminal value is estimated by growing the cash flow in year 5 by 4%:

$$\text{Terminal Value} = \frac{FCFF_5(1 + g_{stable})}{(r - g)} = \frac{4.98(1.04)}{(.10 - .04)} = \$86.26$$

The firm's value today is $66.64. This understates the true value, because the analyst has locked into a reinvestment rate. Although this is reasonable for the high-growth phase, it's much too high for stable growth. Again, this can be seen when we back out the return on capital implied by the reinvestment rate and growth rates, as shown in Table 10.4.

Table 10.4 Implied Return on Capital

	Year 1	Year 2	Year 3	Year 4	Year 5	Terminal Year (6)
Reinvestment rate	80.00%	80.00%	80.00%	80.00%	80.00%	80.00%
Expected growth rate	20.00%	20.00%	20.00%	20.00%	20.00%	4.00%
Implied return on capital	25.00%	25.00%	25.00%	25.00%	25.00%	5.00%

Note that the return on capital assumed for the high-growth phase is 25%. This is high but not unreasonable for a firm with investment opportunities. However, the return on capital built into the terminal value is 5%, well below the cost of capital. Unless there is a clear reason to believe that the managers of this firm are hell-bent on destroying value in the long term, this is clearly an unrealistic assumption. The bottom line is that estimating the cash flow for the terminal value computation by growing the prior year's computation one extra year is always a dangerous practice, but it becomes doubly so with growth companies.

Growth and Risk

Just as growth and reinvestment are linked by our estimates of excess returns, risk and growth tend to move together. As we move through the forecast period, lowering the expected growth rate as the company gets larger and more stable, we should expect to see the risk of the business decrease. In too many growth company valuations, the cost of capital is estimated up front for the entire valuation and remains unchanged as the firm makes its transition from high growth to mature company. Holding all else equal, this will result in growth companies being undervalued. In effect, as we reduce growth, we are giving the company all the negatives of being a mature company without any of the positives.

Trusting Market-Based Risk Measures

Risk parameters in valuations, including betas and costs of equity, are often estimated using historical data. For instance, we estimate a firm's beta by regressing the returns on the stock against return on a market index. With growth firms, this practice can lead to misleading estimates for two reasons. First, the stock has been listed only a short time, and the estimate that emerges from the data has a large error estimate. Second, the company's characteristics have changed over the listing period, thus rendering the historical beta estimate useless as an estimate of the beta for the future.

Consider the beta estimate for Under Armour, using historical returns on the stock from January 2007 to January 2009, as shown in Figure 10.3.

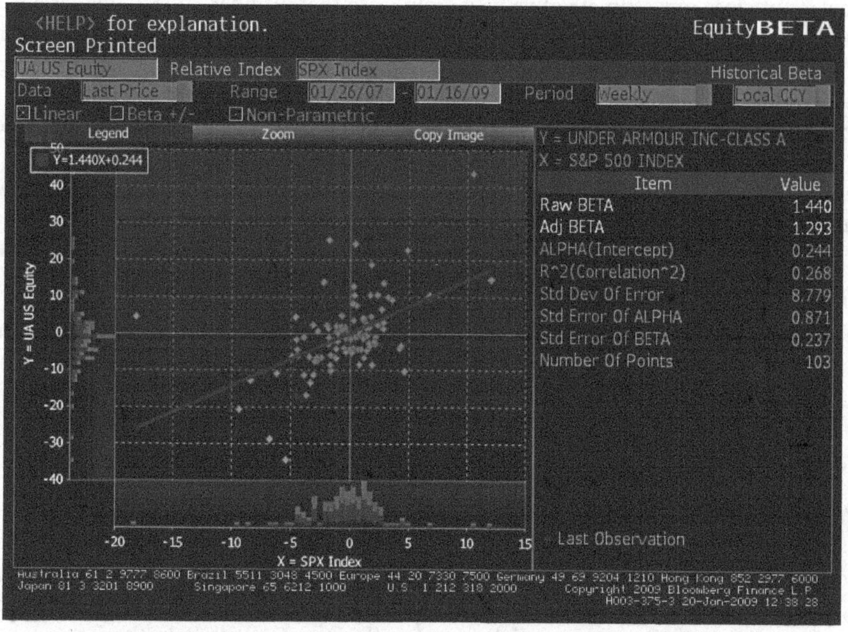

Figure 10.3: Historical Beta Estimate for Under Armour

The regression beta is 1.44, but the standard error on the estimate is 0.24. Furthermore, the beta reflects risk in 2007 and 2008, during which the firm doubled its revenues and operating income. Using this beta to estimate the cost of equity for future years puts us at risk of using a regression estimate that has substantial standard error associated with it. It's also possible that the number will not reflect the changes in the company's fundamentals over time.

Shortcuts for Dealing with Convertibles and Voting Shares

In the section outlining the estimation issues associated with valuing growth companies, we noted that these firms are far more likely to issue convertible debt than straight debt when borrowing, and they have different classes of shares when it comes to voting rights. Analysts valuing growth companies look for simplifying assumptions when dealing with both phenomena. They tend to treat convertible debt as all debt until it gets converted, at which point it becomes all equity. At best, they assume that convertible bonds will get converted to shares, and they use the resulting total number (fully diluted) as the basis for computing value per share.

With voting and nonvoting shares, the practice is often either benign neglect, where the differences in voting rights are just overlooked or viewed as worthless, or the use of simple rules of thumb, where voting shares are assumed to command a fixed premium (such as 5%).

The Market Must Know Something I Don't: The Market Price Magnet

When valuing publicly traded firms, it is difficult not to be aware of the stock's market price and how far or close our estimate of value is from or to that number. In fact, there is a feedback mechanism, where a big difference between the price and the value leads an analyst to revisit the assumptions used in the valuation, with the inevitable narrowing of the difference. With growth companies, this feedback loop can take on a life of its own, partly because analysts are so uncertain about their future estimates. Consider an analyst who makes what she thinks are reasonable assumptions about growth, cash flows, and risk and arrives at a value that is one quarter of the market price. She will be tempted to go back and increase growth rates and returns, and lower the discount rate, to arrive at a value closer to the stock price.

Relative Valuation

At the risk of generalizing, analysts who go down the relative valuation path are looking for even more simplistic ways of dealing with growth than analysts who wrestle with discounted cash flow valuation. Not surprisingly, the errors that we see in the relative valuations of growth companies reflect the errors of these time-saving assumptions.

Sector-Based Comparables

Much of relative valuation in practice is built around the practice of building comparable firms from other firms in the sector. Thus, software firms are compared to other software firms and energy firms to other energy firms. Adopting this practice when valuing growth companies can be dangerous, especially in sectors with diverse growth characteristics. Take the software business as an example. Although this segment has high-growth firms, they coexist with firms like Microsoft that are more mature. Using industry average multiples to value individual software firms will lead to poor estimates of values.

Sector-Specific Multiples

One of the problems we face with valuing some growth firms using multiples is the absence of an operating variable of any substance that can be used to scale value. Many growth firms, early in the growth cycle, have negative net income, operating income, and EBITDA, making it impossible to apply any earnings-based multiple. Rather than fall back on revenues, the only operating variable that cannot be negative, some analysts fall back on multiples of operating measures that are specific to the sector. In the late 1990s, with nascent Internet companies, analysts estimated value as a multiple of website visitors. With cable TV and telecommunications companies, value was computed as a multiple of the company's subscribers.

While the push toward sector-specific multiples can be justified by arguing that the company's operating variables fall short, it does expose you to some significant valuation problems. The first is that few people have a sense of what is high, low, or reasonable for a sector-specific multiple.

Put another way, while we may hold back from paying 100 times revenues for a company (since we know that this is a high value), we may not hold back from paying $3,000 per subscriber. This is partly because we have little or no sense of what a reasonable value per subscriber is. The second problem is that assessing what fundamentals, if any, we should be controlling for becomes more difficult with sector-specific multiples. Thus, while we know the variables that cause PE ratios to vary across companies (see Chapter 4), we have little sense of the key factors that cause the value per subscriber to vary across firms.

Unrealistic Growth/Value Relationships

Most analysts valuing growth companies are aware that growth affects multiples. They know that higher-growth companies should trade at higher multiples of earnings, revenues, or any other operating variable than lower-growth companies. At the same time, they want to stick with the simplicity of multiples and not deal with the complexity of analyzing the effect of changing growth rates on value. This manifests itself in valuation in two ways:

- **Storytelling:** Rather than deal with differences in growth rates quantitatively, some analysts argue for the use of higher multiples for higher-growth companies, without being explicit about the relationship between growth and value, with a "growth story." Consequently, they argue that Chinese consumer products companies should trade at higher multiples of earnings than European companies because China has more potential growth. But they are fuzzy on how much more growth exists and what premium it justifies.
- **Modified multiple:** A compromise that takes into account growth while preserving simplicity would be to incorporate growth into the multiple. But this requires us to make unreasonable assumptions about the relationship between growth and value. Consider, for instance, the price earnings ratio. We know that higher-growth companies trade at higher PE ratios than lower-growth companies and that investing in the lowest PE stocks will bias you toward lower-growth companies. It was to counter this bias that analysts developed the PEG ratio—the ratio of PE to expected growth:

  PEG = PE / Expected Growth in Earnings per Share

For example, a firm with a PE ratio of 20 and an expected growth rate in earnings per share of 10% would have a PEG ratio of 2. Companies that trade at low PEG ratios represent bargains, because you get growth at a lower price.

All shortcuts in valuation have a price. The PEG ratio comes with a hefty price tag. First, it ignores the effects of risk. If two firms have the same expected growth rate in earnings, the higher-risk firm should trade at a lower PE (and a lower PEG) ratio. Second, it assumes that PE increases proportionately with growth; as growth doubles, the PE ratio doubles. In reality, though, value increases less than proportionately with growth. Value increases by less than 100% when growth is doubled. Figure 10.4 shows the intrinsic PEG ratio for a hypothetical firm at different expected growth rates. It shows how undervalued (or overvalued) the firm will look using the conventional PEG ratio. The intrinsic PEG ratio reflects the complicated relationship between PE and growth, whereas the conventional approach assumes that it remains unchanged (at 1) as growth changes.

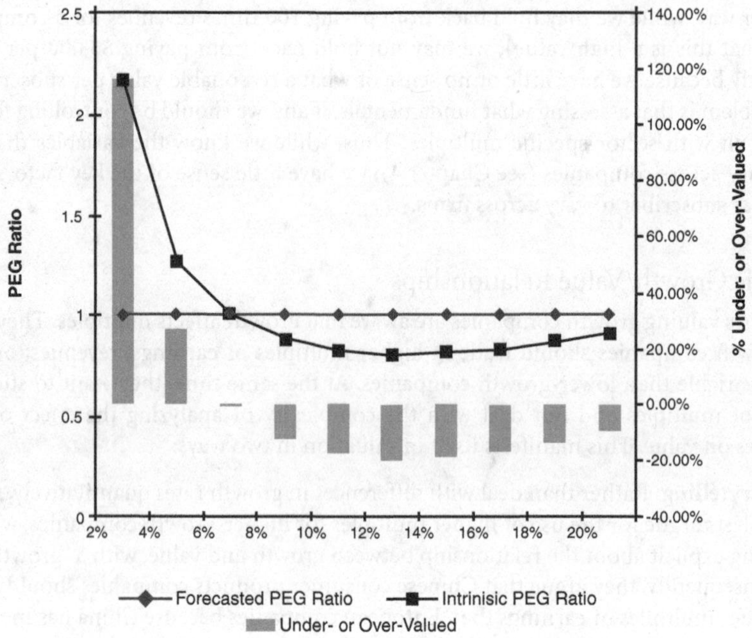

Figure 10.4: Intrinsic Versus Conventional PEG Ratio

Using the conventional PEG ratio, with its flawed assumptions of growth and PE, leads us to conclude that the firms are overvalued at low growth rates (by more than 100% at a 2% growth rate) and undervalued at higher growth rates.

Forward Multiples and Changing Fundamentals

When confronted with current year numbers for revenues and earnings that are either too small or negative, some analysts use forecast values for revenues and earnings to compute forward multiples for comparison. This practice makes sense, and we recommended it in the preceding chapter on young growth companies. However, remember that the multiple we attach to revenues or earnings in a future year should reflect the characteristics of the company in that year rather than its current characteristics. Many analysts use multiples that are based on current growth characteristics to arrive at forward values and thus double-count growth. Consider, for instance, a firm that has revenues of $50 million today and a forecast revenue growth of 50% a year for the next five years; the revenues in year 5 will be $380 million. A valuation that applies a high multiple to the revenues in year 5, with the high multiple justified by the high growth rate of 50%, in effect double-counts growth. A more reasonable valuation would use a multiple more in line with growth after year 5 (likely to be much lower than 50%).

The Light Side of Valuation

While growth companies raise thorny estimation problems, we can navigate our way through them to arrive at values for these firms that are less likely to be contaminated by internal inconsistencies. This section describes the steps to follow in discounted cash flow and relative valuations of growth companies.

Discounted Cash Flow Valuation

The objective in discounted cash flow valuation is to arrive at reasonable estimates of the cash flows and discount rates. Therefore, the following sections describe some of the considerations that should enter into the process when we value growth companies.

Choice of Model

Chapter 2 described the choices we face with discounted cash flow models. We can either value the entire business (by discounting cash flows to the firm at the cost of capital) or value the equity directly (by discounting cash flows to equity at the cost of equity). While both approaches should yield the same value for the equity, estimating cash flows to equity, if we expect the debt ratio to change over time, is much more difficult than estimating the cost of capital. The former requires us to forecast new debt issues, debt repayments, and interest payments each period, as the dollar debt changes, whereas the latter is based on changing debt ratios.

Since many growth companies have little or no debt in their capital structure, analysts often fall back on equity valuation models, using the absence of debt as justification. However, this assumes that growth companies will continue with their policy of not using debt in perpetuity, even as growth decreases and the companies become more mature. If we make the more reasonable assumption that growth companies will become mature companies over time and adopt the financing practices of the latter, firm valuation models provide analysts with more flexibility to reflect these changes.

Needless to say, the discounted cash flow models used need to allow for high growth and even changing operating margins over time. As a general rule, rigid models that lock in the company's current characteristics do not perform as well as more flexible models, where analysts can change the inputs over time in valuing growth companies.

Valuing the Operating Assets

If we accept the premise that firm valuation models work better than equity valuation models when valuing growth companies, the first step in the process is valuing the firm's operating assets, incorporating both existing assets and growth assets.

Revenue Growth Rates

The valuation process starts with estimating future revenues. In making these estimates, many of the considerations we raised in Chapter 9 for young companies come into play. The biggest issue, and one we have emphasized repeatedly in this chapter, is the scaling factor. Revenue growth rates will decrease as companies get larger, and every growth company will get larger over time if our forecasts of growth come to fruition. In a test of how growth changes as firms get larger,

Metrick (2006) examined the revenue growth rate for high-growth firms, relative to growth rate in revenues for the sector in which they operate, in the immediate aftermath of their initial public offerings.[3] The results are shown in Figure 10.5.

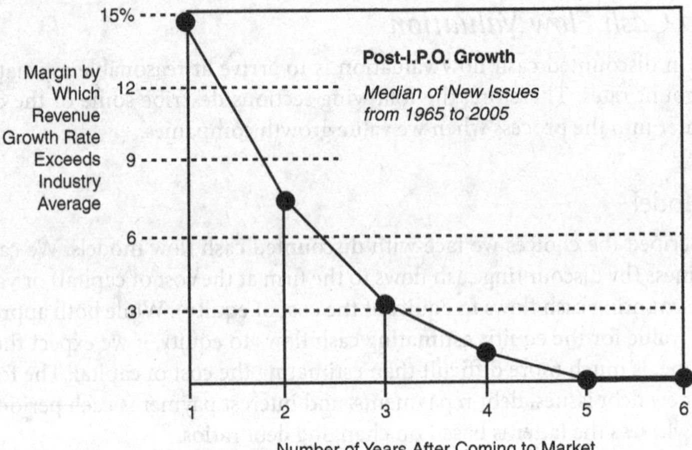

Figure 10.5: Revenue Growth in the Years After the Initial Public Offering

Source: Andrew Metrick, *The New York Times*

When they go public, firms have growth rates that are much higher than the industry average. Note how quickly the revenue growth at these high-growth firms moves toward the industry average. They go from a 15% higher revenue growth (than the industry average) one year after the IPO to 7% higher in year 2 to 1% higher in year 4 to the industry average in year 5. We are not saying that this will happen at every high-growth firm. However, the aggregate evidence suggests that growth firms that can maintain high-growth rates for extended periods are the exception rather than the rule.

The question of how quickly revenue growth rates will decline at a given company can generally be addressed by looking at the company's specifics. These include the size of the overall market for the company's products and services, the strength of the competition, and the quality of its products and management. Companies in larger markets with less aggressive competition (or protection from competition) and better management can maintain high-revenue growth rates for longer periods.[4]

We can use a few tools to assess whether the assumptions we are making about revenue growth rates in the future for an individual company are reasonable:

3 Metrick, A., 2006, *Venture Capital and the Finance of Innovation*, John Wiley & Sons.

4 For an extended discussion of this issue, see Damodaran, A., 2008, *The Origins of Growth*, working paper, SSRN.

- **Absolute revenue changes:** One simple test is to compute the absolute change in revenues each period, rather than to trust the percentage growth rate. Even experienced analysts often underestimate the compounding effect of growth and how much revenues can balloon over time with high growth rates. Computing the absolute change in revenues, given a growth rate in revenues, can be a sobering antidote to irrational exuberance when it comes to growth.
- **Past history:** Looking at past revenue growth rates for the firm in question should give us a sense of how growth rates have changed as the company size changed in the past. For those who are mathematically inclined, clues in the relationship can be used to forecast future growth.
- **Sector data:** The final tool is to look at revenue growth rates of more mature firms in the business to get a sense of what a reasonable growth rate will be as the firm becomes larger.

In summary, expected revenue growth rates tend to drop over time for all growth companies but the pace of the drop off will vary across companies.

Current Margins Versus Target Margins

To get from revenues to operating income, we need operating margins over time. The easiest and most convenient scenario is one in which the current margins of the firm being valued are sustainable and can be used as the expected margins over time. In fact, if this is the case, we can dispense with forecasting revenue growth and instead focus on operating income growth, since the two are equivalent. In most growth firms, though, it is more likely that the current margin will to change over time.

Let's start with the most likely case, which is that the current margin is either negative or too low relative to the sustainable long-term margin. This can happen for three reasons. One is that the firm has up-front fixed costs that have to be incurred in the initial phases of growth, with the payoff in terms of revenue and growth in later periods. This is often the case with infrastructure companies such as energy, telecommunications, and cable TV. The second reason is the mingling of expenses incurred to generate growth with operating expenses. We noted earlier that selling expenses at growth firms are often directed toward future growth rather than current sales but are included with other operating expenses. As the firm matures, this problem will get smaller, leading to higher margins and profits. The third reason is that there might be a lag between expenses being incurred and revenues being generated. If the expenses incurred this year are directed toward much higher revenues in three years, earnings and margins will be low today.

The other possibility, where the current margin is too high and will decrease over time, is less likely, but it can occur, especially with growth companies that have a niche product in a small market. In fact, the market may be too small to attract the attention of larger, better-capitalized competitors, thus allowing the firms to operate under the radar for the moment, charging high prices to a captive market. As the firm grows, this will change, and margins will decrease. In other cases, the high margins may come from owning a patent or other legal protection against competitors, and as this protection lapses, margins will decrease.

In both of the latter two scenarios—low margins converging to a higher value or high margins dropping to more sustainable levels—we have to make judgment calls on what the target margin should be and how the current margin will change over time toward this target. The answer to the first question usually can be found by looking at both the average operating margin for the industry in which the firm operates and the margins commanded by larger, more stable firms in that industry. The answer to the second question depends on the reason for the divergence between the current and target margin. With infrastructure companies, for instance, it reflects how long it will take the investment to be operational and capacity to be fully utilized.

Reinvest to Sustain Growth

A constant theme in the earlier chapters was the insistence that growth is not free and that firms have to reinvest to grow. As we noted earlier in this chapter, it is dangerous to base reinvestment assumptions on a growth company's history of reinvestment. In other words, taking the net capital expenditures and working capital changes from the most recent year and assuming that these items will grow at the same rate as revenues can result in reinvestment numbers that are both unrealistic and inconsistent with our assumptions about growth.

To estimate reinvestment for a growth firm, we will follow one of three paths, depending largely on the characteristics of the firm in question:

- **For growth firms earlier in the life cycle**, we will adopt the same road map we used for young growth companies, where we estimated reinvestment based on the change in revenues and the sales-to-capital ratio:

  $\text{Reinvestment}_t = \text{Change in Revenues}_t / (\text{Sales/Capital})$

  The sales-to-capital ratio can be estimated using the company's data (which is more stable than the net capital expenditure or working capital numbers) and the sector averages. Thus, assuming a sales-to-capital ratio of 2.5 in conjunction with a revenue increase of $250 million results in reinvestment of $100 million. We can build lags between the reinvestment and revenue change into the computation by using revenues in a future period to estimate reinvestment in the current one.

- **With a growth firm that has a more established track record of earnings and reinvestment,** we can use the relationship between fundamentals and growth rates described in Chapter 2:

  Expected Growth Rate in Operating Income = Return on Capital * Reinvestment Rate + Efficiency Growth (as a Result of Changing Return on Capital)

  In the unusual case where margins and returns and capital have settled into sustainable levels, the second term drops out of the equation.

- **Growth firms that have already invested in capacity for future years** are in the unusual position of being able to grow with little or no reinvestment for the near term. For these firms, we can forecast capacity usage to determine how long the investment holiday will last and when the firm will have to reinvest. During the investment holiday, reinvestment can be minimal or even zero, accompanied by healthy growth in revenues and operating income.

With all three classes of firms, though, the leeway that we have in estimating reinvestment needs during the high-growth phase should disappear as soon as the firm has reached its mature phase. The reinvestment in the mature phase should hew strictly to fundamentals:

$$\text{Reinvestment Rate in Mature Phase} = \frac{\text{Growth Rate}_{\text{Stable}}}{\text{Return on Capital}_{\text{Stable}}}$$

In fact, even in cases where reinvestment is estimated independently of the operating income during the growth period, and without recourse to the return on capital, we should keep track of the imputed return on capital (based on our forecasts of operating income and capital invested). Doing so ensures that it stays within reasonable bounds. The process for doing so is described in Chapter 9.

Risk Profile Consistent with Growth and Operating Numbers

The components of the cost of capital—the beta(s) and the cost of equity, the cost of debt, and the debt ratio—are the same for a growth company as they are for a mature company. However, what sets growth companies apart is that their risk profiles shift over time. The key to maintaining balance in growth company valuations is to adjust the discount rates over time to keep them consistent with the growth and margin assumptions that we make in each period. Here are two general rules:

- Growth firms should have high costs for equity and debt when revenue growth is highest, but the costs of debt and equity should decline as revenue growth moderates and margins improve.
- As earnings improve and growth drops, another phenomenon comes into play. The firm generates more cash flows than it needs, which it can use to both pay dividends and service debt financing. Firms are not required to use this debt capacity, and some of them do not, but the tax advantages of debt lead some firms to borrow, causing debt ratios to increase over time.

In summary, the cost of capital for a growth company should almost never be a number that remains unchanged over the entire time horizon. Instead, it should be a year-specific number that keeps pace with the rest of the changes we forecast at the firm.

In terms of estimating risk parameters (betas), we would steer as far as we can from using the limited price data that is available on growth companies. The standard errors on the estimates are likely to be huge. Instead, we would use estimates of betas obtained by looking at other publicly traded firms that share the same risk, growth, and cash flow characteristics as the firm being valued. If the case for using these bottom-up betas (industry average as opposed to a regression beta) is strong with any firm, it is even stronger with growth firms.

For growth firms that have operating losses carried forward from prior years or that are expected to keep losing money in the future, a final factor must be considered when computing discount rates. The tax advantage of debt, manifested as an after-tax cost of borrowing, depends on having positive earnings to offset interest expenses. With operating losses (and carryforwards), there may be no or limited tax benefits from interest expenses, and the after-tax cost of debt should reflect this fact.

Stable Growth Assumptions: What Will the Firm Look Like, and When?

The assumptions we make about terminal value loom large with a growth company, because it comprises a much larger portion of the firm's current value than is the case with a mature firm. When will a growth firm become a mature, stable-growth firm? While we have a little more information than we did with young companies, making this assessment is difficult. It's akin to looking at a teenager and wondering what he or she will look like or be doing in middle age.

Although no one answer or approach will work with every growth company, we will draw on the discussions in Chapter 2 and this chapter to develop the following general propositions:

- **Do not wait too long to put a firm into stable growth.** As we noted in the section on the dark side of valuing growth companies, analysts often allow for very long growth periods for growth firms and justify this assumption by pointing to past growth. As shown in Figure 10.5, both scale and competition conspire to lower growth rates quickly at even the most promising growth companies. Growth periods that exceed ten years, especially when accompanied by high growth rates over these periods, are difficult to defend, because only a handful of companies have been able to accomplish this over time.
- **When you put your firm into stable growth, give it the characteristics of a stable growth firm.** In keeping with the emphasis on preserving internal consistency, we should change the company's characteristics to reflect stable growth. With discount rates, as noted in the preceding section, this takes the form of using lower costs of debt and equity and a higher debt ratio. With reinvestment, the key assumption is the return on capital that we assume for the stable growth phase. While some analysts believe that the return on capital should be set equal to the cost of capital in stable growth, we would preserve some company-specific flexibility. We suggest that the difference between return on capital and cost of capital should narrow during stable growth to a sustainable level (less than 4 or 5%).

The nature of cash flows at growth companies—low or negative in the early years and higher later—will ensure that the terminal value is a high proportion of value, accounting for 80.90% or even more than 100% of value. Some analysts use this fact as ammunition against using discounted cash flow valuations, suggesting that assumptions about the high-growth phase will be drowned out by terminal value assumptions. This is not true. The base year value for the terminal value calculation (earnings and cash flows in year 5 or 10) is a function of the assumptions during the high-growth phase. Changing these assumptions will have dramatic effects (as it should) on value.

Valuing Operating Assets: Evergreen Solar

To value Evergreen Solar, we first update the operating numbers to reflect the firm's operations through the end of September 2008, the most recent quarter for which we have financial data. Table 10.5 summarizes the estimates.

Table 10.5 Trailing 12-Month Operating Numbers for Evergreen Solar

	Last 10K: 2007	9 Months Ended September 2007	9 Months Ended September 2008	Trailing 12 Month*
Pre-tax operating income	$(25.58)	–$20.66	–$44.80	$(49.72)
Interest expense	$3.41	$2.75	$2.86	$3.52
Capital spending	$50.74	$20.68	$250.79	$280.85
Depreciation and amortization	$7.86	$5.34	$15.69	$18.21
Revenues	$69.87	$47.68	$67.70	$89.89

*Trailing 12-month number = last 10K – 9-month 10Q Sept. '07 + 9-month 10Q Sept. '08

In summary, Evergreen Solar became a larger firm on every dimension—revenues, operating income, and reinvestment—between the end of 2007 and the third quarter of 2008.

The two key assumptions that will determine the value of Evergreen Solar are about revenue growth in future years and expected pre-tax operating margins. Table 10.6 summarizes these estimates, as well as our estimates of taxes and after-tax operating income each year.

Table 10.6 Revenues and Operating Income for Evergreen Solar

Year	Revenues	Revenue Growth Rate	Pre-Tax Margin	Pre-Tax Operating Income	NOL	Taxes	After-Tax Operating Income
Trailing 12 month	$89.89		–55.31%	–49.72	$98.00	$0.00	–$49.72
1	$125.85	40.00%	–31.87%	–$40.11	$138.11	$0.00	–$40.11
2	$176.18	40.00%	–16.25%	–$28.63	$166.74	$0.00	–$28.63
3	$246.66	40.00%	–5.83%	–$14.39	$181.13	$0.00	–$14.39
4	$345.32	40.00%	1.11%	$3.84	$177.29	$0.00	$3.84
5	$483.45	40.00%	5.74%	$27.75	$149.54	$0.00	$27.75
6	$628.48	30.00%	8.83%	$55.48	$94.06	$0.00	$55.48
7	$785.61	25.00%	10.88%	$85.51	$8.55	$0.00	$85.51
8	$942.73	20.00%	12.26%	$115.55	$0.00	$42.80	$72.75

Table 10.6 continued

Year	Revenues	Revenue Growth Rate	Pre-Tax Margin	Pre-Tax Operating Income	NOL	Taxes	After-Tax Operating Income
9	$1,084.14	15.00%	13.17%	$142.79	$0.00	$57.12	$85.68
10	$1,192.55	10.00%	13.78%	$164.34	$0.00	$65.74	$98.60
Terminal year	$1,219.38	2.25%	15.00%	$182.91	$0.00	$73.16	$109.74

Note that Evergreen had a net operating loss (NOL) carryforward of $98 million coming into the valuation. We track and use this to compute the taxes and after-tax operating income each year. The net operating loss carried forward is augmented by the expected losses in the first three years, reaching a peak of $181.13 million at the end of year 3. It shelters the expected operating income from taxes for the next few years. By our estimates, Evergreen does not pay its full marginal tax rate of 40% until the ninth year.

To ensure that we reinvest enough to sustain this expected growth, we estimate Evergreen's reinvestment needs using a sales-to-capital ratio of 2.50.[5] The resulting reinvestment and free cash flows are summarized in Table 10.7.

Table 10.7 Expected Free Cash Flow to the Firm for Evergreen Solar

Year	After-Tax Operating Income	Change in Revenues	Sales to Capital	Reinvestment	FCFF	Capital Invested	Implied ROC
Trailing 12 month	–$49.72					$884.82	
1	–$40.11	$35.96	2.50	$14.38	–$54.50	$899.20	–4.53%
2	–$28.63	$50.34	2.50	$20.14	–$48.76	$919.34	–3.18%
3	–$14.39	$70.47	2.50	$28.19	–$42.58	$947.53	–1.57%
4	$3.84	$98.66	2.50	$39.47	–$35.63	$986.99	0.40%
5	$27.75	$138.13	2.50	$55.25	–$27.50	$1,042.24	2.81%
6	$55.48	$145.03	2.50	$58.01	–$2.54	$1,100.26	5.32%
7	$85.51	$157.12	2.50	$62.85	$22.66	$1,163.11	7.77%

5 We did not build in a lag between reinvestment and revenue change. If we had, the reinvestment numbers would have been higher, because they would have been tied to revenue change in future years.

Year	After-Tax Operating Income	Change in Revenues	Sales to Capital	Reinvestment	FCFF	Capital Invested	Implied ROC
8	$72.75	$157.12	2.50	$62.85	$9.90	$1,225.95	6.25%
9	$85.68	$141.41	2.50	$56.56	$29.11	$1,282.52	6.99%
10	$98.60	$108.41	2.50	$43.37	$55.24	$1,325.88	7.69%

There are two trends to note in the cash flows. The first is that the reinvestment outflows in the first three years are accompanied by operating losses, creating negative cash flows in those periods. Even after the firm starts generating positive earnings in year 4, the reinvestment needs make the cash flows negative in years 4 through 6. To check on our reinvestment numbers, we compute two numbers. The first is the capital invested in each year, which we estimate by adding the reinvestment during the year to the previous year's capital invested. The second number is the return on capital, estimated by dividing the after-tax operating income in each year by the capital invested at the end of the prior year.[6] Not surprisingly, the returns on capital are negative at the start of the estimation period, but they climb to a more respectable 7.69% by the end of our estimation period.

To estimate the costs of capital to use to discount these cash flows, we begin with the assumption that the firm's beta will be 1.60 (based on the average beta of other alternative energy companies). Using a risk-free rate of 2.25% and an equity risk premium of 6% yields a cost of equity of 11.85% to start the valuation. Since the firm has substantial default risk and significant debt outstanding, we assign it a cost of debt of 8.25%, with no tax benefit to offset the cost for the first five years. As the firm's revenues grow and margins improve, we lower the beta to 1.00 (in stable growth) and assume that the debt ratio will move down toward a more sustainable level of 20%, with a lower pre-tax cost of 5.25%. These changes, in conjunction with interest expenses finally benefiting from tax savings, show up as a lower cost of capital in future years, as shown in Table 10.8.

Table 10.8 Costs of Debt, Equity, and Capital for Evergreen Solar

Year	Beta	Cost of Equity	Pre-Tax Cost of Debt	Tax of Savings	After-Tax Cost of Debt	Debt Ratio	Cost of Capital
1	1.60	11.85%	8.25%	0.00%	8.25%	41.20%	10.37%
2	1.60	11.85%	8.25%	0.00%	8.25%	41.20%	10.37%
3	1.60	11.85%	8.25%	0.00%	8.25%	41.20%	10.37%
4	1.60	11.85%	8.25%	0.00%	8.25%	41.20%	10.37%

6 Current Capital Invested = Current Book Value of Debt + Current Book Value of Equity

Table 10.8 continued

Year	Beta	Cost of Equity	Pre-Tax Cost of Debt	Tax of Savings	After-Tax Cost of Debt	Debt Ratio	Cost of Capital
5	1.60	11.85%	8.25%	0.00%	8.25%	41.20%	10.37%
6	1.48	11.13%	7.65%	0.00%	7.65%	36.96%	9.84%
7	1.36	10.41%	7.50%	0.00%	7.50%	35.90%	9.37%
8	1.24	9.69%	7.25%	37.04%	4.56%	34.13%	7.94%
9	1.12	8.97%	6.75%	40.00%	4.05%	30.60%	7.46%
10	1.00	8.25%	5.25%	40.00%	3.15%	20.00%	7.23%
After year 10	1.00	8.25%	5.25%	40.00%	3.15%	20.00%	7.23%

As the firm matures, the cost of capital drops from 10.37% in year 1 to 7.23% in year 10 (and beyond).

To provide closure on the valuation, we assume that Evergreen Solar as a stable firm (after year 10) will earn a return on capital of 7.23% in perpetuity, equal to its cost of capital. We believe it will be difficult for any firm in this business to earn excess returns in perpetuity. We also assume that the growth rate after year 10 will be capped at the risk-free rate of 2.25% that we have used in the analysis. Furthermore, we assume that the reinvestment rate and terminal value can be computed as follows:

Reinvestment Rate (After Year 10) = Stable Growth Rate/Stable Return on Capital

= 2.25%/ 7.23% = 31.12%

$$\text{Terminal Value} = \frac{\text{EBIT}_{11}(1-t)(1-\text{Reinvestment Rate})}{(\text{Cost of Capital}_{\text{Stable}} - g_{\text{Stable}})}$$

$$= \frac{\$182.91(1-.40)(1-.3112)}{(.0723-.0225)} = \$1517.90 \text{ million}$$

Now that we have the cash flows and the costs of capital for Evergreen Solar, we can estimate the value of the operating assets today, as shown in Table 10.9.

Table 10.9 Cash Flows, Discount Rates, and Value Today for Evergreen Solar

Year	Cost of Capital	Cumulated Cost of Capital	FCFF	Terminal Value	Present Value
1	10.37%	1.1037	–$54.50		–$49.38
2	10.37%	1.2181	–$48.76		–$40.03
3	10.37%	1.3444	–$42.58		–$31.67
4	10.37%	1.4837	–$35.63		–$24.01
5	10.37%	1.6375	–$27.50		–$16.79
6	9.84%	1.7987	–$2.54		–$1.41
7	9.37%	1.9672	$22.66		$11.52
8	7.94%	2.1234	$9.90		$4.66
9	7.46%	2.2819	$29.11		$12.76
10	7.23%	2.4469	$55.24	$1,517.90	$642.92
		Sum of the PV of cash flows =			**$508.56**

Note two details in the computations. The first is that the cash flows are discounted back at the cumulated cost of capital, reflecting the changing cost of capital over time. For instance, the cumulated cost of capital in year 7 is computed as follows:

$$\text{Cumulated Cost of Capital in Year 7} = (1.1037)^5 * (1.0984) * (1.0937) = 1.9672$$

The second detail is that the value of the firm's operating assets is $509 million, with the terminal value tipping the balance. In fact, the present value of cash flows for the first 10 years is –$112 million, largely because of the extended string of negative cash flows in the early years. Intuitively, this represents the loss in ownership (or dilution, if you prefer that term) to existing stockholders, accruing from the firm's need to raise additional capital, from debt and equity, in future years. Incidentally, this is also why we do not try to adjust the number of shares today for future equity issues—that would be double counting.

Valuing Operating Assets: Under Armour

To value Under Armour's operating assets, we begin by updating the numbers to reflect the most recent data. Table 10.10 summarizes the most recent 12 months of data for Under Armour (as of January 2009).

Table 10.10 Updated 12-Month Numbers for Under Armour

	Last 10K	Last Year Through January 2008	This Year Through January 2009	Trailing 12 Month
Current EBIT =	$86.27	$58.01	$54.05	$82.31
EBIT (adjusted for leases)				$88.28
Current interest expense =	$0.80	$0.53	$0.86	$1.13
Current capital spending	$33.96	$26.24	$30.85	$38.57
Current depreciation and amortization =	$14.62	$10.00	$15.48	$20.10
Current revenues =	$606.56	$431.72	$545.97	$720.81

The updated numbers reflect the higher revenues and lower operating income at the firm over the last 12 months, relative to the last annual report.

As in the previous valuation, we begin with our estimates of revenues and operating income, as shown in Table 10.11.

Table 10.11 Revenues and Operating Income for Under Armour

Year	Revenues	Revenue Growth Rate	Pre-Tax Margin	Pre-Tax Operating Income	NOL	Taxes	After-Tax Operating Income
Trailing 12 month	$720.81		12.25%	$88.28	$0.00	$35.31	$52.97
1	$973.09	35.00%	12.46%	$121.22	$0.00	$48.49	$72.73
2	$1,216.37	25.00%	12.57%	$152.95	$0.00	$61.18	$91.77
3	$1,459.64	20.00%	12.64%	$184.48	$0.00	$73.79	$110.69
4	$1,678.59	15.00%	12.67%	$212.76	$0.00	$85.10	$127.66
5	$1,846.44	10.00%	12.69%	$234.41	$0.00	$93.76	$140.64
6	$1,994.16	8.00%	12.71%	$253.38	$0.00	$101.35	$152.03
7	$2,113.81	6.00%	12.71%	$268.71	$0.00	$107.49	$161.23

Year	Revenues	Revenue Growth Rate	Pre-Tax Margin	Pre-Tax Operating Income	NOL	Taxes	After-Tax Operating Income
8	$2,208.93	4.50%	12.72%	$280.88	$0.00	$112.35	$168.53
9	$2,275.20	3.00%	12.72%	$289.35	$0.00	$115.74	$173.61
10	$2,343.46	3.00%	12.72%	$298.06	$0.00	$119.22	$178.83
Terminal year	$2,396.18	2.25%	12.72%	$304.79	$0.00	$121.92	$182.88

Since the firm has no operating losses to carry forward, we assume that the taxes in future years will be based on a marginal tax rate of 40%. The Evergreen Solar estimates have two key contrasts. One is that we reduce revenue growth rates far more precipitously with Under Armour than with Evergreen Solar for three reasons: Under Armour currently is a larger firm (in terms of revenues), the overall market is smaller, and competition is much more intense. The other is that unlike Evergreen Solar, Under Armour is generating profits and has a healthy pre-tax operating margin. While we move it toward the industry average of 12.72% over the next ten years, the number remains relatively stable.

To estimate how much the firm will have to reinvest in future years, we assume that the sales-to-capital ratio (1.83 in January 2009) of the entire apparel business will apply to Under Armour going forward. Table 10.12 estimates the free cash flows to the firm using these reinvestment numbers.

Table 10.12 Reinvestment and Cash Flows for Under Armour

Year	After-Tax Operating Income	Revenue Change	Sales to Capital	Reinvestment	FCFF	Capital Invested	Implied ROC
1	$72.73	$252.28	1.83	$137.86	–$65.13	$495.05	20.36%
2	$91.77	$243.27	1.83	$132.94	–$41.17	$627.99	18.54%
3	$110.69	$243.27	1.83	$132.94	–$22.25	$760.92	17.63%
4	$127.66	$218.95	1.83	$119.64	$8.01	$880.57	16.78%
5	$140.64	$167.86	1.83	$91.73	$48.92	$972.29	15.97%
6	$152.03	$147.72	1.83	$80.72	$71.31	$1,053.01	15.64%
7	$161.23	$119.65	1.83	$65.38	$95.85	$1,118.39	15.31%
8	$168.53	$95.12	1.83	$51.98	$116.55	$1,170.37	15.07%
9	$173.61	$66.27	1.83	$36.21	$137.40	$1,206.58	14.83%
10	$178.83	$68.26	1.83	$37.30	$141.54	$1,243.88	14.82%

Under Armour has positive cash flows from day 1, because it is already generating profits and reinvesting less than its entire earnings. As with Evergreen Solar, we check the reinvestment numbers by computing the return on capital implied by our forecasts of operating income and reinvestment.[7] The return on capital exceeds 20% to begin the valuation but drifts down to 14.82% by the end of the tenth year, a number in line with what mature firms in the business (like Nike) generate as returns on capital.

To estimate the cost of equity today for Under Armour, we use a beta of 1.30 (the industry average for apparel firms that offer niche products at high prices) and keep the risk-free rate of 2.25% and an equity risk premium of 6%. While the firm has little conventional debt, we convert lease commitments and other fixed commitments (related to sponsorships) to debt, resulting in an initial debt ratio of 16%. Over time, we move the beta down toward 1.10, move the cost of debt from 6.25% to 4.25%, and increase the debt ratio toward the industry average of 25%. Table 10.13 summarizes the costs of debt, equity, and capital for Under Armour.

Table 10.13 Costs of Debt, Equity, and Capital for Under Armour

Year	Beta	Cost of Equity	Pre-Tax Cost Of Debt	Tax Savings	After-Tax Cost of Debt	Debt Ratio	Cost of Capital
1	1.30	10.05%	6.25%	40.00%	3.75%	12.44%	9.27%
2	1.30	10.05%	6.25%	40.00%	3.75%	12.44%	9.27%
3	1.30	10.05%	6.25%	40.00%	3.75%	12.44%	9.27%
4	1.30	10.05%	6.25%	40.00%	3.75%	12.44%	9.27%
5	1.30	10.05%	6.25%	40.00%	3.75%	12.44%	9.27%
6	1.26	9.81%	5.85%	40.00%	3.51%	14.95%	8.87%
7	1.22	9.57%	5.75%	40.00%	3.45%	15.58%	8.62%
8	1.18	9.33%	5.58%	40.00%	3.35%	16.62%	8.34%
9	1.14	9.09%	5.25%	40.00%	3.15%	18.72%	7.98%
10	1.10	8.85%	4.25%	40.00%	2.55%	25.00%	7.28%
After year 10	1.10	8.85%	4.25%	40.00%	2.55%	25.00%	7.28%

7 We start the process of estimating capital invested with the current book value of capital (debt + equity), or $357.19 million.

While the change in the cost of capital is not as dramatic as it was for Evergreen Solar, the cost of capital for Under Armour drops from 9.27% to 7.28% over the next 10 years.

As a final step, we assess what Under Armour will look like as a stable-growth firm. As a slightly less risky business, with more debt in its capital structure, it should have a lower cost of capital (7.28%). We will assume that the firm will be able to use the magic of its brand name to generate returns on capital of 9% in perpetuity on new investments, above the cost of capital. The firm's reinvestment rate and terminal value can be computed as follows:

$$\text{Reinvestment Rate (After Year 10)} = \text{Stable Growth Rate/Stable Return on Capital}$$
$$= 2.25\%/\ 9\% = 25\%$$

$$\text{Terminal Value} = \frac{EBIT_{11}(1-t)(1-\text{Reinvestment Rate})}{(\text{Cost of Capital}_{Stable} - g_{Stable})}$$

$$= \frac{178.83(1-.25)}{(.0728-.0225)} = \$2729.50 \text{ million}$$

As the final step, we pull together the expected free cash flows to the firm and the costs of capital in Table 10.14. We intend to compute the value of the firm's operating assets.

Table 10.14 Cash Flows, Discount Rates, and Value for Under Armour

Year	Cost of Capital	Cumulated Cost of Capital	FCFF	Terminal Value	Present Value
1	9.27%	1.0927	–$65.13		–$59.60
2	9.27%	1.1939	–$41.17		–$34.48
3	9.27%	1.3046	–$22.25		–$17.05
4	9.27%	1.4254	$8.01		$5.62
5	9.27%	1.5575	$48.92		$31.41
6	8.87%	1.6957	$71.31		$42.05
7	8.62%	1.8418	$95.85		$52.04
8	8.34%	1.9953	$116.55		$58.41
9	7.98%	2.1545	$137.40		$63.77
10	7.28%	2.3112	$141.54	$2,729.50	$1,242.22
		Sum of PV of cash flows =			$1,384.40

The value that we estimate for the firm's operating assets is $1.384 billion.

From Operating Asset Value to Equity Value per Share

Navigating from operating asset value to equity value per share for growth companies can be fraught with dangers, many of which we outlined in earlier sections. In this section, we will outline precautions that can protect against some of these dangers (at least partially).

Cash and Nonoperating Assets

Earlier in this chapter, we noted how quickly growth firms can burn through cash balances and how using the cash balance from the most recent financial statements can lead to misleading values. At least in theory, it would be useful to know what the cash balance is today when valuing a firm. While investors in public equity markets have no way to access this information, an acquirer (or at least a friendly acquirer) should be able to get this information from the target firm and use it to estimate an updated value. Even public investors can make judgments about current cash balances by using two pieces of public information—the firm's cash flows and any new financing during the period since the last financial statement. For instance, assume that the last cash balance (from three months ago) is \$100 million for a firm that reported EBITDA of negative \$80 million in the most recent 12-month period. If the firm has not raised any new financing in the last three months (through either equity issues or new debt), the firm's current cash balance is likely to be closer to \$80 million than \$100 million. (We are reducing the cash balance by the estimated EBITDA of –\$20 million—one quarter of –\$80 million.)

Debt and Other Nonequity Claims

If convertible debt is the preferred mode of borrowing for a growth firm, we should treat it as what it is—a hybrid security that is part debt and part equity. Since the conversion option is equity and the rest is debt, the easiest way to decompose convertible debt into debt and equity is to value the convertible debt as if it were straight debt and to treat the resulting number as debt. For instance, assume that a growth firm has five-year convertible debt outstanding, with a face value of \$50 million and a coupon rate of 4%. Also assume that the firm's current pre-tax cost of debt, assuming it uses conventional debt, is 10%. The value of the convertible bond, treated like a conventional bond, would be as follows:[8]

$$\text{Debt Value of Convertible Bond} = (50 * .04)\left(\frac{1-(1.10)^{-5}}{.10}\right) + \frac{50}{(1.10)^5} = \$38.63 \text{ million}$$

Subtracting this value from the market value of convertible bond yields the value of the conversion option. Thus, if the convertible debt is trading at \$52 million, the conversion option (equity) will be valued at \$13.37 million.[9] When valuing this company, we would treat this part as equity and the rest as debt in computing the current cost of capital. We would subtract only the debt portion from the firm's value to arrive at the overall value of equity.

Another aspect of debt that is potentially problematic is that debt ratios change over time, and with those changes come changes in the debt outstanding at the firm. Since the value of equity is the firm's value, net of debt, analysts often get caught up in the question of whether they should subtract the debt outstanding today (which may be negligible) or the expected debt outstanding

8 For simplicity, we have assumed annual interest payments. This equation can easily be modified to allow for semi-annual payments.

9 If the market value of the debt is unavailable, an approximation would be to use the face value.

in the future (which may be very large). The answer, when valuing the firm, is that we should subtract only the current debt outstanding, even though that value may be miniscule relative to future debt issues.

Post-Valuation Corrections

After we have derived the value of equity in a growth firm, the final step is to allocate the value of equity across the shares outstanding in the firm. In making this final judgment, three considerations must be kept in mind.

Survival and Illiquidity

The first two considerations are issues that were raised with young growth companies. The probability of survival must be factored into the value, and illiquidity can cause discounts to this value. Neither of these factors is as significant with growth firms. The probability of survival for growth firms is much higher than for nascent businesses. The equity is usually more liquid—especially if the growth firm is publicly traded. Even publicly traded growth firms have to shut down operations, especially if they run out of cash. Shares in these firms may trade far less frequently (and with much higher transaction costs) than shares in more mature companies.

If survival is truly a concern, we suggest using the approaches we developed in the last chapter. In summary, you estimate the probability that the growth firm will fail and the consequences (in terms of what equity investors will receive) if it does. The expected value of equity will then reflect the weighted average of the going concern and failure values, weighted by the probabilities of success and failure. Similarly, if illiquidity is weighing down value, using one of the approaches described in the preceding section—adjusting the cost of capital or applying a post-valuation illiquidity discount—will help.

Voting Right Differentials

The final factor to consider in arriving at value of equity per share is differences in voting rights across shares. While we would expect voting shares to trade at a premium on nonvoting shares, the magnitude of the difference should be a function of the value of voting rights and consequently varies across firms.

How much are voting rights worth? The earliest studies of voting share premiums were done with U.S. companies that had different voting share classes. Lease, McConnell, and Mikkelson (1983) found that voting shares in that market trade, on average, at a relatively small premium of 5 to 10% over nonvoting shares.[10] They also found extended periods where the voting share premium disappeared or voting shares traded at a discount to nonvoting shares. This surprising finding can be explained partially by the relative illiquidity of voting shares (since only a small percentage are available for public trading). Reilly (2005) updated this study to look at 28 companies with voting and nonvoting shares in 1994 and 1999 and concluded that the median voting share premium increased from 2% in 1994 to 2.8% in 1999.[11]

10 Lease, R. C., J. J. McConnell, and W. H. Mikkelson, 1983, "The market value of control in publicly-traded corporations," *Journal of Financial Economics*, v11, pp. 439–471.

11 Reilly, R. F., 2005, "Quantifying the Valuation Discount for Lack of Voting Rights and Premium," *American Bankruptcy Institute Journal.*

Studies in recent years have expanded the analysis of voting share premiums to other markets, where differential voting rights are more common. Premiums of a magnitude similar to those found in the U.S. (5 to 10%) were found in the U.K. and Canada. Much larger premiums are reported in Latin America (50 to 100%), Israel (75%), and Italy (80%). In a comparative study of voting premiums across 661 companies in 18 countries, Nenova (2003) found that the median value of control block votes varies widely across countries, ranging from less than 1% in the U.S. to 25% or greater in France, Italy, Korea, and Australia. She concluded that the legal environment is the key factor in explaining differences across countries. She also concluded that the voting premium is smaller in countries with better legal protection for minority and nonvoting stockholders and is larger for countries without such protection.[12]

The most common way to allocate value across voting and nonvoting shares is to use the evidence from these studies to justify a premium. In the U.S., for instance, voting share premiums have generally been set between 5 and 10%. Although we are not entirely convinced about this rule of thumb, we will stick with it for this chapter and return to examine it in the next.

From Operating Asset to Equity Value per Share: Evergreen Solar and Under Armour

To get from operating asset to equity value, we have to add back cash and subtract debt. With Evergreen Solar, we have to consider how best to deal with the fact that all its debt is convertible (and thus has an equity component). We also must decide whether to take the cash balance reported in the September 2008 financial statements as the cash balance today. With Under Armour, we have to examine the consequences of the debt primarily taking the form of lease and sponsorship commitments and the existence of two classes of shares with different voting rights.

Evergreen Solar

Earlier we valued the operating assets of Evergreen Solar at $509 million. To get to value of equity per share, we have to add back the current cash balance and subtract debt owed:

- **Cash balance**: Evergreen Solar reported a cash balance of $285.23 million in its most recent financial statements, from September 2008. This represents a big jump from the cash balance of $99.7 million, reported at the end of 2007. The reason for the increase, though, was that the firm raised almost $492 million from new financing ($166 million from equity and the balance from the issue of a convertible bond).[13] If we consider the new funding raised and the cash balances from December 2007 and September 2008, we can estimate the cash that the firm is "burning" each month:

12 Nenova, T., 2003, "The value of corporate voting rights and control: A cross-country analysis," *Journal of Financial Economics*, v68, pp. 325–351.

13 We use the statement of cash flows from September 2008 and the cash from financing activities for the first three quarters of 2008.

$$\text{Cash Burn/Month} = \frac{(\text{Cash}_{\text{Dec 2007}} + \text{New Financing}_{\text{Dec to Sept}} - \text{Cash}_{\text{Sept 2008}})}{\text{Number of Intervening Months}}$$

$$= \frac{(99.7 + 492.44 - 285.23)}{9} = \$34.10 \text{ million}$$

- Because three months have elapsed since the last financial statements, the updated cash balance can be computed as follows:

Updated Cash Balance = Most Recent Cash Balance – Cash Burn per Month * Number of Months Since Last Financials = 285.23 – (34.10 * 3) = $182.92 million

- Adding this amount to the estimated value of the operating assets yields the value for Evergreen Solar as a firm:

Value of Firm = Value of Operating Assets + Updated Cash Balance
= $509 million + $183 million = $692 million

- **Debt**: During 2008, Evergreen Solar retired its existing debt and replaced it with five-year convertible debt, with a face value of $373.75 million and a coupon rate of 4%. To break this debt into debt and equity components, we value this debt as if it were conventional debt, using the pre-tax cost of debt of 8.25% we estimated earlier for the firm. Discounting the expected semiannual coupons of $14.95 million (4% of $373.75 million) and the face value at 8.25% yields a value for the bond of $312 million:

$$\text{Debt Value} = (373.75 * .04)\left(\frac{1-(1.0825)^{-5}}{.0825}\right) + \frac{373.75}{1.0825^{5}} = \$312 \text{ million}$$

- We consider this to be the debt portion of the convertible debt. We attribute the difference between the market value of the convertible bond ($360 million) and the debt amount to the conversion option, which is equity.

Conversion Option (Equity) = Market Value – Straight Debt Value
= $360 million – $312 million = $48 million

- Subtracting the debt amount alone from the firm's value yields the value of equity of $380 million:

Value of Equity in Evergreen Solar = Value of Firm – Debt
= $692 – $312 = $380 million

- **Equity value per share**: To estimate the value of equity per share, we consider the two claims on equity—one from the option holders (valued at $48 million) and one from common stockholders:

$$\text{Value of Equity (in Common Stock)} = \text{Value of Equity} - \text{Value of Equity Options} = 380 - 48 = \$332 \text{ million}$$

- Since we have already netted out the value of equity options, this number can be divided by the actual number of shares outstanding (as opposed to a diluted number) to arrive at a value per share of $2.01 per share:

$$\text{Value per Share} = \frac{\text{Value of Equity in Common Stock}}{\text{Primary Shares Outstanding}} = \frac{332}{164.875} = \$2.01/\textit{Share}$$

Under Armour

Getting from operating asset value to equity value for Under Armour poses fewer challenges than it did at Evergreen Solar. The cash balance of $40.15 million reported by the firm in its most recent financial statements in September 2008 is very similar to the cash balance of $40.59 million it reported in December 2007. Since the firm is generating positive earnings, we feel comfortable assuming that the cash balance is intact at the time of the valuation in January 2009. With debt, the only confounding detail is that the bulk of the debt takes the form of leases and sponsorship commitments. Of the total debt of $133 million, $95.5 million represents the present value of future commitments. From a valuation perspective, though, we see no need to separate the two types of debt. Consequently, the value of equity at Under Armour can be estimated as follows:

$$\text{Value of Equity} = \text{Value of Operating Assets} + \text{Cash} - \text{Debt} = \$1{,}384 \text{ million} + \$40 \text{ million} - \$133 \text{ million} = \$1{,}292 \text{ million}$$

To get from this value to the value of equity per share, two final details must be taken care of. The first is to consider the overhang of equity options that have been granted in the past to management. We estimated the value of the 2.13 million options outstanding at the firm, with an average strike price of $8.26 and an average expiration of 3.7 years, to be $23 million after taxes.[14] (We will return to this issue in Chapter 15, when we look at technology firms.) The second detail is that the firm has two classes of shares—36.791 million class A shares that are held by the investing public and are traded, and 12.5 million class B shares that are held by Kevin Plank, the firm's founder. Class B shares have ten times the voting rights of class A shares. If we attribute no value to voting rights, the value per share that we estimate is $25.73.

$$\text{Value per Share} = \frac{\text{Value of Equity}}{(\text{\# Class A Shares} + \text{\# Class B Shares})} = \frac{(\$1{,}292 - \$23)}{(36.791 + 12.5)} = \$25.73$$

14 We use the standard Black-Scholes model and adjust for the potential dilution and tax savings that will accrue to the firm when the options are exercised.

Note that the control component should give class B shares a premium, but the fact that the shares are not traded results in an illiquidity discount. If we assume that class B shares have a 10% premium on class A shares, we can estimate the value of equity per share for class A and class B shares as follows:

$$\text{Value per Class A Share} = \frac{\text{Value of Equity}}{(\#\text{Class A Shares} + \text{Value Premium} * \#\text{Class B Shares})}$$

$$= \frac{(\$1{,}292 - 23)}{(36.791 + 1.1 * 12.5)} = \$25.09 / Share$$

$$\text{Value per Class B Share} = \text{Value of Class A Share} * 1.1 = \$27.60$$

Note that the cumulative market value stays at $1,263 million and that all we are doing is reallocating the value across the two classes of shares. The 10% premium is based on past studies of voting shares. We will consider a more nuanced approach to estimating the value of control (and voting/nonvoting shares) in the coming chapters.

Dealing with Uncertainty

It is almost a given that the value of a growth company, no matter how much we pay attention to the details and how much information we use, will be less precisely estimated than the value of a mature company. This uncertainty can lead to post-valuation angst in which analysts second-guess themselves and try to reconcile differences not only between their estimates and the market price but also across different valuations (done by different analysts).

Note, though, that much of this uncertainty comes not from the quality of the information or the precision of the valuation model used, but from the real world. The future is full of surprises, and for growth firms, where so much of the value lies in the future, this translates into big changes in value. This is small consolation to the analyst who gets the value of equity in a growth company wrong and is held accountable. Chapter 3 presented probabilistic approaches including decision trees, simulations, and scenario analysis that can be used to enrich valuations. These approaches offer some promise for growth companies, not because they provide more precise estimates of value or even because they generate risk measures, but because they allow analysts to be more comfortable with their own estimates of value. However, they are not particularly useful for a simple reason. The uncertainty in the estimates will result in distributions in value that reflect that uncertainty. Thus, a simulation of Evergreen's value, even if well done, tells us that the value per share for Evergreen can range from a very low number to a very high number. It also tells us that the market price falls well within that range.

A more useful technique for grappling with uncertainty with growth companies is to focus on one of two key drivers of value for that company. We also look at not only the effects on value of varying assumptions about those drivers but also break-even points in terms of the current price. For instance, assuming that revenue growth is the key determinant of value for a firm, we can ask what the revenue growth rate would have to be to justify the current market price. We can then follow up by looking whether we are comfortable as investors with the market-implied revenue growth rate.

Consider the valuation of Evergreen Solar. From our perspective, we feel comfortable with the revenue growth assumption, since the market is such a large one. But we're uncertain about what the operating margins will be in stable growth (since so few alternative energy companies have made it to stable growth). Figure 10.6 shows our estimates of value per share against the target pre-tax operating margin, varying it from our base-case assumption of 15%.

To justify its current stock price of $2.70 a share, Evergreen Solar would have to generate a pre-tax operating margin of 17% in steady state.

With Under Armour, where margins are fairly close to industry averages already, the key question is whether revenues will continue to grow at high rates. Figure 10.7 shows the value per share for Under Armour as a function of the compounded revenue growth over the next ten years.

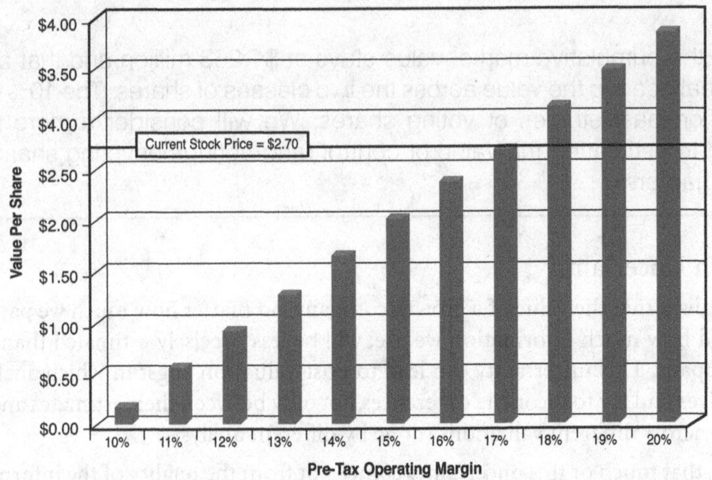

Figure 10.6: Value per Share for Evergreen Solar: Target Operating Margin

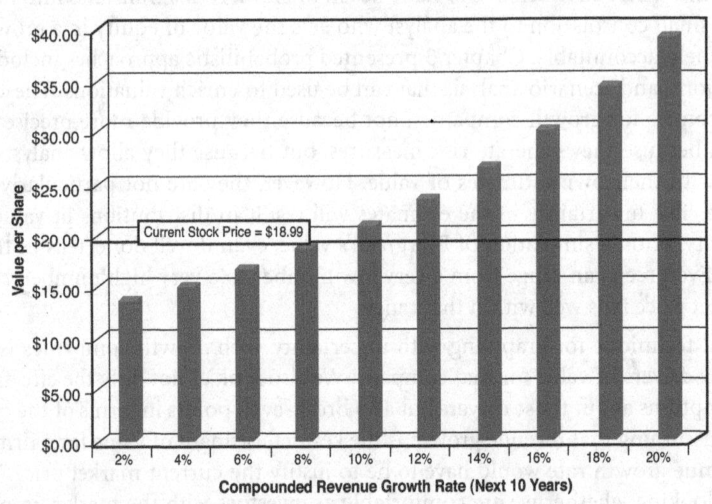

Figure 10.7: Value per Share for Under Armour: Compounded Revenue Growth Rate

The compounded revenue growth rate over the next ten years has to be above 8% to justify paying the current stock price of $19 a share.

Relative Valuation

There is no reason why relative valuation cannot be used to arrive at an independent estimate of the value of equity in a growth firm—as long as we keep two key factors in mind. The first is that using multiples and comparables cannot reduce the uncertainty inherent in valuing growth companies. The second is that relative valuation techniques have to be adapted to meet the limitations of growth companies—the paucity and unreliability of current operating numbers and the shifting risk/growth characteristics over time.

Comparable Firms

Optimally, we would like to assess how the market values a growth firm by comparing its pricing with that of otherwise similar growth firms. In a business like software, which has growth firms aplenty, this can be accomplished by staying within the traditional framework of defining comparable firms as those in the same industry. In businesses like retailing and automotive parts, a growth firm may be the exception in a sector where the bulk of the firms are either mature or in decline. In these cases, we may have to abandon the conventional practice and define growth firms in terms of fundamentals rather than business. The pricing of a retail firm with growth prospects should be compared to how the market is pricing growth firms in other sectors rather than more mature firms in its own industry. There is no reason why the PE ratio for a high-growth retail firm should not be comparable to the PE ratio for a high-growth software firm.

Choice of Multiples and Base Year

As we noted in the section on the dark side as it relates to relative valuation, analysts valuing growth companies tend to use either revenues in the current year or estimates of operating performance in future years (forward earnings or revenues) to compute multiples. Each carries some danger:

- **Revenue multiples** are troubling simply because they gloss over the fact that the company being valued could be losing significant amounts of money. Consequently, we suggest bringing the expected future profit margins (which will be estimates) into the discussion of what comprises a reasonable multiple of revenues. Other things held constant, we would expect firms with higher expected profit margins (in the mature phase) to trade at higher multiples of current revenues than firms with lower expected profit margins.
- **Forward earnings multiples** implicitly assume that the firm being valued will survive to the forward year and that the estimates of earnings for that year are reasonable. If forward multiples are used, controlling for survival becomes a critical component of the analysis. Firms that have a greater chance of surviving to the forward year should trade at a higher multiple of earnings than firms that have a greater chance of failure.

As a general rule, we suggest steering away from multiples of either current book value or current earnings with growth companies early in the growth cycle, simply because these numbers are likely to be small and unstable.

Adjusting for Differences in Growth and Risk

No matter how careful we are about constructing a set of comparable firms and picking the right multiple, there will be significant differences across the firms on their fundamentals. As we noted earlier in the chapter, the two ways in which analysts control for these differences—storytelling and assuming that multiples increase proportionately with growth—yield misleading results. In fact, both approaches break down when we have to control for more than one variable when making comparisons.

When dealing with large differences in growth and risk across companies, the approach that offers the most flexibility is a multiple regression. The chosen multiple is the dependent variable and growth, risk, and any other fundamentals we want to control for representing independent variables. With large enough samples of comparable firms, not only can we control for as many variables as we want, but the approach lets us allow for complex relationships between growth and each variable.

A Relative Valuation of Under Armour

To evaluate how Under Armour is being priced relative to other firms in the sector, we extracted information on 34 publicly traded apparel firms in the U.S., with earnings growth rate estimates available for the next five years from analysts following the companies.[15] Table 10.15 provides the PE ratios, expected growth rates, and two-year betas for these companies.

Table 10.15 PE, Growth, and Risk for Apparel Companies

Company Name	Market Capitalization	PE	Expected Growth Rate in EPS in the Next Five Years	Beta	PEG Ratio
Nike, Inc. (NYSE:NKE)	$22,102.80	11.91	13.10%	1.04	0.91
Kimberly-Clark Corporation (NYSE:KMB)	$21,830.00	12.64	7.33%	0.603	1.72
Avon Products, Inc. (NYSE:AVP)	$8,896.80	11.53	13.00%	0.966	0.89
VF Corp. (NYSE:VFC)	$5,996.90	9.21	10.60%	1.02	0.87
Polo Ralph Lauren Corp. (NYSE:RL)	$3,781.30	8.00	13.60%	1.25	0.59

15 There were 84 companies in the overall sample. Only 34 had positive earnings (to compute PE) and expected growth rates in earnings for the next five years.

Company Name	Market Capitalization	PE	Expected Growth Rate in EPS in the Next Five Years	Beta	PEG Ratio
Cintas Corp. (NasdaqGS:CTAS)	$3,627.20	11.26	10.80%	0.999	1.04
Guess?, Inc. (NYSE:GES)	$1,472.40	6.67	16.00%	1.25	0.42
Gildan Activewear, Inc. (NYSE:GIL)	$1,291.90	8.93	12.50%	1.1	0.71
Tupperware Brands Corporation (NYSE:TUP)	$1,285.10	8.54	12.00%	1.45	0.71
Columbia Sportswear Company (NasdaqGS:COLM)	$1,083.70	8.87	9.70%	0.664	0.91
Warnaco Group, Inc. (NYSE:WRC)	$969.80	11.21	20.00%	1.91	0.56
Under Armour, Inc. (NYSE:UA)	$969.10	20.71	20.90%	1.44	0.99
Phillips-Van Heusen Corp. (NYSE:PVH)	$968.30	6.05	14.00%	1.25	0.43
Carters, Inc. (NYSE:CRI)	$964.70	12.64	15.00%	1.19	0.84
Wolverine World Wide, Inc. (NYSE:WWW)	$929.80	9.56	12.60%	0.693	0.76
Hanesbrands, Inc. (NYSE:HBI)	$918.00	5.77	15.30%	1.44	0.38
Fossil, Inc. (NasdaqGS:FOSL)	$814.70	5.62	16.50%	1.35	0.34
Polaris Industries, Inc. (NYSE:PII)	$772.50	6.50	11.20%	1.5	0.58
Timberland Co. (NYSE:TBL)	$642.50	11.92	12.00%	1.06	0.99
UniFirst Corp. (NYSE:UNF)	$551.20	8.69	13.00%	0.906	0.67
Jos. A. Bank Clothiers, Inc. (NasdaqGS:JOSB)	$529.10	9.71	15.00%	1.11	0.65
Iconix Brand Group, Inc. (NasdaqGS:ICON)	$511.20	7.08	17.00%	1.74	0.42

Table 10.15 PE, Growth, and Risk for Apparel Companies

Company Name	Market Capitalization	PE	Expected Growth Rate in EPS in the Next Five Years	Beta	PEG Ratio
Bebe Stores, Inc. (NasdaqGS:BEBE)	$507.30	8.61	13.00%	1.55	0.66
Raven Industries, Inc. (NasdaqGS:RAVN)	$415.40	12.94	14.50%	1.08	0.89
K-Swiss, Inc. (NasdaqGS:KSWS)	$382.00	11.24	19.00%	1.17	0.59
G&K Services, Inc. (NasdaqGS:GKSR)	$347.10	9.86	10.70%	0.922	0.92
Ennis, Inc. (NYSE:EBF)	$301.40	7.32	10.00%	1.21	0.73
True Religion Apparel, Inc. (NasdaqGS:TRLG)	$284.30	7.00	17.00%	1.3	0.41
Volcom, Inc. (NasdaqGS:VLCM)	$225.20	5.99	20.00%	1.9	0.30
Maidenform Brands, Inc. (NYSE:MFB)	$211.70	7.40	14.50%	1.45	0.51
American Apparel, Inc. (AMEX:APP)	$157.10	18.33	30.00%	0	0.61
Cherokee, Inc. (NasdaqGS:CHKE)	$133.70	9.03	12.00%	1.27	0.75
Oxford Industries, Inc. (NYSE:OXM)	$104.90	20.61	13.00%	1.54	1.59
G-III Apparel Group, Ltd. (NasdaqGS:GIII)	$85.80	4.47	18.30%	1.32	0.24
Lacrosse Footwear, Inc. (NasdaqGM:BOOT)	$64.90	8.78	13.50%	0.283	0.65
Perry Ellis International, Inc. (NasdaqGS:PERY)	$60.80	3.27	13.50%	1.57	0.24
Sector average	**$2,288.25**	**9.70**	**15.00%**	**1.15**	**0.70**

First let's consider the two most common approaches used by analysts following growth companies:

- **Subjective**: The PE ratio for Under Armour in January 2009 is 20.71, well above the average PE ratio for the sector (9.70). An optimistic analyst would undoubtedly point to Under Armour's higher expected growth in earnings (20.90% versus the industry average of 15%) as justification for a higher PE. A pessimistic analyst would draw attention to Under Armour's higher risk (a beta of 1.44 versus the industry average of 1.15) to suggest that the stock was overvalued.

- **PEG ratio**: A simple way to control for differences in growth is to compute the PEG ratio we described earlier. Lower PEG ratios indicate an undervalued company. The PEG ratio for Under Armour is a shade under 1.00:

$$PEG_{\text{Under Armour}} = \frac{PE}{\text{Expected Growth Rate in EPS}} = \frac{20.71}{20.90} = 0.99$$

- Since the average PEG ratio for the sector is much lower at 0.70, this would seem to indicate that Under Armour is overvalued.

Since neither approach captures the effects of both growth and risk satisfactorily, and the PEG ratio assumes that PE increases in lockstep with growth, Figure 10.8 graphs the PE ratios of apparel firms against expected EPS growth in the next five years.

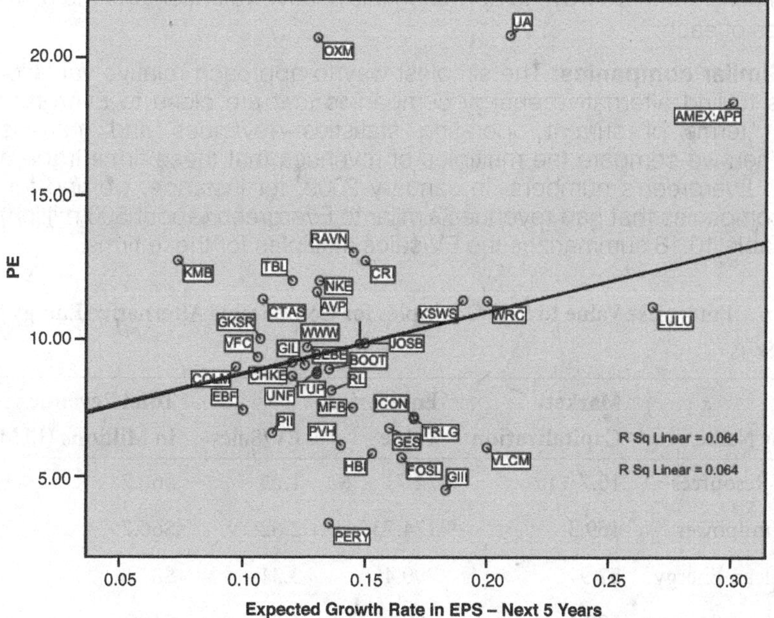

Figure 10.8: PE Versus Expected Growth for Apparel Companies

Note that Under Armour (UA) has the highest PE ratio in the group, but it also has a high growth rate. We regressed PE ratios against the expected growth rate and betas, weighting each firm by market capitalization. The results are as follows (with t statistics in parentheses below the coefficients):

$$\text{PE} = 13.78 + 32.04 \text{ (expected growth rate)} - 6.60 \text{ Beta } R^2 = 25.9\%$$
$$(10.88) \quad (3.49) \qquad\qquad\qquad (1.91)$$

In keeping with intuition, higher-growth firms have higher PE ratios, and higher risk pushes down the PE, and both relationships are statistically significant. Using the expected growth in earnings per share of 20.9% that analysts are forecasting for Under Armour for the next five years and the two-year beta estimate of 1.44, we can estimate the expected PE ratio for the firm:

$$\text{Expected PE}_{\text{Under Armour}} = 13.78 + 32.04\ (.209) - 6.60\ (1.44) = 10.98$$

At its existing PE ratio of 20.71, Under Armour looks overvalued, on a relative valuation basis, by almost 48%.

A Relative Valuation of Evergreen Solar

With small revenues, miniscule book value, and big operating losses, Evergreen Solar presents more of a challenge when it comes to relative valuation. To begin with, the only multiple that we can use, with current numbers, is a revenue multiple. We will consider three ways to approach this relative valuation and the pluses and minuses of each:

- **Similar companies**: The simplest way to approach relative valuation is to find alternative energy companies that are close to Evergreen in terms of current operating statistics—revenues and margins. Then we compare the multiples of revenues that these firms trade at to Evergreen's numbers. In January 2009, for instance, we find four companies that had revenues similar to Evergreen (about $90 million). Table 10.16 summarizes the EV/sales multiples for these firms.

Table 10.16 Enterprise Value to Sales Multiples for Comparable Alternative Energy Companies

Company Name	Market Capitalization	Enterprise Value	EV/Sales	Total Revenue in Millions (LTM)
Sumatec Resources	10.7	74.71	1.23	$60.7
China Windpower	169.3	174.73	2.62	$66.7
Viridis Clean Energy	52.9	290.4	3.31	$87.8
Terna Energy SA	580.1	580.1	5.51	$105.3
Average			**3.17**	

Note that the average EV/sales ratio across these firms is 3.17. Applying this to Evergreen Solar's revenues of $90 million in 2007 would have yielded an enterprise value today of $285.3 million. In using this sample, we are implicitly assuming that these firms have the same growth and profit potential in steady state. Note also how much variation there is in the EV/sales ratio across these four firms.

- **Forward values**: One reason why we have trouble using multiples with growth companies is that the current numbers are not representative of what we expect the firm to look like in the future. One way around this problem is to use the forecast revenues and other operating numbers to estimate value. With Evergreen, we draw on our earlier estimates of future revenues and earnings. In Table 10.6, we forecast Evergreen's revenues in year 5 to be $483 million and its pre-tax operating income to be $27.75 million. Looking across the larger publicly traded firms that are listed under alternative energy, we estimated an average EV/sales ratio of 1.55. Applying this to the revenues in year 5 yields an expected enterprise value (in year 5) of $749 million:

Expected Enterprise Value in Year 5 = $483 * 1.55 = $749 million

- Discounting this value back at Evergreen's cost of capital of 10.37% for the first five years (see Table 10.8), we estimate an enterprise value today of $457 million:

Enterprise Value Today = $749 million / 1.1037^5 = $457 million

This approach is based on three premises. The first is that the firm will survive and make it to year 5. This may or may not happen, given operating losses and the overlay of debt. The second premise is that our forecasts of revenues and operating income in year 5 are reasonable numbers. If we have over- or underestimated these numbers, the resulting estimates of values will also be affected. The third premise is that the firm being valued will look like larger firms in the industry in five years, thus making it all right to use the industry average multiple.

- **Melded approach**: In this approach, we take elements of the second approach, where we use forward revenues/earnings but superimpose two factors. The first is risk, captured in the discount rate used to bring the value back to today and also in the probability that the firm will not make it. The second factor is the use of a multiple that is not the industry average; instead, we would use a multiple that will reflect the company's characteristics in the forward year. To estimate this value, we would look at the relationship between the multiple and fundamentals across the sector today.

Consider the last component first. To measure how the multiple of revenues changes as the expected growth rate changes in this sector, we ran a regression of EV/sales against expected revenue growth rates and operating margins across the sector today. The resulting output is summarized as follows:

$$EV/Sales_{Evergreen} = 0.85 + 7.41\ (\text{Operating Margin}) + 3.56\ (\text{Expected Growth})$$

To estimate the multiple of revenues at which Evergreen Solar will trade at the end of the fifth year, we estimate the revenue growth rate of 20.32% from years 6 through 10 in Table 10.6 and the pre-tax operating margin of 5.74% in year 5. Plugging these values into the regression provides us with a forecast EV/sales ratio at the end of year 5:

$$\text{Forecast EV/Sales in year 5} = 0.85 + 7.41\ (0.0574) + 3.56\ (0.2032) = 2.00$$

Applying this multiple to the revenues in year 5 yields the enterprise value. Discounting back to today provides us with an estimate of the enterprise value today:

$$Revenues_{Evergreen\ in\ Year\ 5} = \$483\ \text{million}$$

$$\text{Enterprise Value}_{Evergreen\ in\ Year\ 5} = \$483 * 2.00 = \$966\ \text{million}$$

$$\text{Enterprise Value}_{Evergreen\ Today} = \$966 / 1.1037^5 = \$589\ \text{million}$$

This is much closer to the $509 million we estimated in the discounted cash flow model for Evergreen Solar's enterprise value today.

Conclusion

When valuing a growth company, we confront many of the issues we faced with young idea companies, albeit on a lesser scale. Data on past operations provides a short, volatile, and not particularly useful basis for forecasting the future. Much of the company's value comes from expectations about how high growth will be in the future, how long this growth can be sustained, and the quality of this growth, all of which are difficult to forecast. In particular, the rate at which growth rates will drop as the company becomes bigger will be a key factor determining its value. Estimating risk parameters from stock price data can yield strange values, and the firm's risk profile will change as its growth rate changes.

Analysts, confronted with these challenges, often adopt shortcuts that may save them time but yield misleading values. They fail to adjust growth rates as the company gets bigger, allowing firms to grow for too long at high rates. They make assumptions about risk and reinvestment that are inconsistent with their own growth estimates. Finally, they are often cavalier about when they put their firms into stable growth and the assumptions they make to get terminal value. When doing relative valuation, they stick with the standard practices used to value mature companies.

They use other firms in the industry as comparable companies and use revenue or forward earnings multiples. They don't adjust for differences across firms, or they do so subjectively or in the most simplistic fashion.

Valuing growth companies well, in a discounted cash flow framework, has three key components. The first is to ensure that the assumptions we are making about growth and margins reflect not only market potential and competition, but also change to reflect the firm's changing size over time. The second component is to reinvest enough into the business to sustain the forecast growth rates. The third component is to modify the firm's risk profile to match its growth characteristics. The costs of equity, debt, and capital are all likely to decrease as the firm goes from high growth to stable growth. With relative valuation, controlling for differences in growth and risk when comparing companies is essential.

11

The Grown-Ups: Mature Companies

Attrition occurs at each stage of the life cycle of the firm. Most young companies fail to make it through early tests to become growth companies. A large number of growth companies find that growth is short-lived and either go out of business or are acquired by larger firms. This chapter focuses on the companies that survive these grueling phases of competition and become mature companies. They are mature not only in terms of growth rates but also in terms of risk profiles and return characteristics.

Companies in the mature phase of the life cycle should present the least problems in valuations. They have long periods of operating and market history, allowing us to estimate most of the inputs for valuation from historical data. They have also settled into established patterns of investment and financing, resulting in fundamentals (risk and returns) that are stable over time, giving us more confidence in our estimates of these numbers. However, these established patterns may present a problem, because not all long-standing practices are good. Put another way, some mature firms make financing and investment choices that are not optimal or sensible, and they have been doing so for a long time. It is possible that these firms, with new management in place, could be run differently (and better) and have higher values. Analysts valuing mature companies have to juggle two values—the status quo value and an optimal value. How analysts deal with these values will in large part determine the quality of the valuation.

Mature Companies in the Economy

Mature companies represent the backbone of most economies. While growth companies may capture our imagination and attention, mature companies deliver most of the current output and employment in an economy. This section begins by looking at how we can categorize companies as mature. It also examines characteristics that mature companies tend to share.

A Life Cycle View of Mature Companies

In the life cycle view of a firm, a business starts as an idea business. If it survives, it goes from being a young growth company, often privately held, to a more established growth company, generally in public markets. As we noted in the preceding chapter, even the best growth companies eventually run into a wall when it comes to growth, partly because their success makes them larger and partly because they attract competition. Consequently, it is not a question of whether a company becomes a mature company, but when it happens.

One way to categorize companies as growth and mature companies is to look at the growth rate, with lower-growth companies being treated as mature. This approach has two problems. First, given that growth is a continuum, any growth rate that we adopt as a cutoff point will be subjective. We will find more mature companies if we adopt a 6% growth rate cutoff rather than a 4% growth rate. Second, not all operating measures grow at the same rate. We have to decide whether the growth rate we use for the categorization will be growth in revenues, units, or earnings. It is conceivable for a company with low growth in revenues to deliver high earnings growth, at least over short periods.

A better way of thinking about growth is to use the financial balance sheet construct we developed in the preceding chapter (see Figure 11.1). Rather than focus on operating measures such as revenue or earnings growth, we can look at the proportion of a firm's value that comes from existing investments as opposed to growth assets. If growth companies get the bulk of their value from growth as growth assets, mature companies must get the bulk of their value from existing investments.

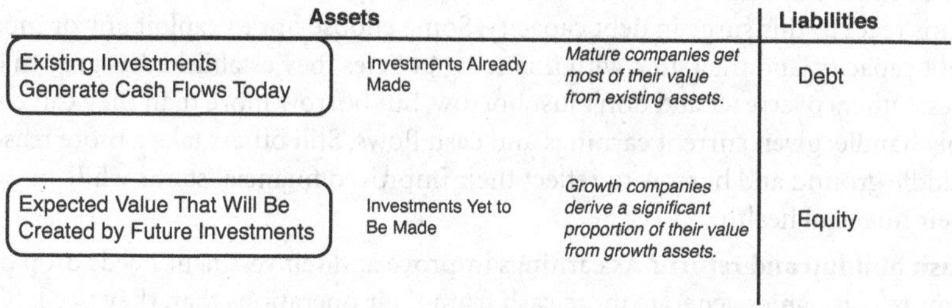

Figure 11.1: Existing Investments on the Balance Sheet

We can use the distribution, across all companies, of the proportion of value that comes from mature assets to determine our threshold for mature companies. Thus, suppose we define mature companies as the top 20% of all companies, in terms of proportion of value from mature assets. The threshold for being a mature company will vary across markets. It will be lower in growth economies like India and China than in the U.S. or Western Europe. It also will vary across time. The threshold will be higher when economies slow down, as they did in 2008 and 2009, and it's lower when economies are booming.

Characteristics of Mature Companies

There are clear differences across mature companies in different businesses, but they share some common characteristics. This section looks at what they have in common, with an eye on the consequences for valuation:

- **Revenue growth is approaching the growth rate in the economy:** The preceding section noted that there can be a wide divergence between growth rate in revenues and earnings in many companies. While the growth rate for earnings for mature firms can be high as a result of improved efficiencies, the revenue growth is more difficult to alter. For the most part, mature firms register growth rates in revenues that, if not equal to, will converge on the economy's nominal growth rate.
- **Margins are established:** Another feature shared by growth companies is that they tend to have stable margins. The exceptions are commodity and cyclical firms, where margins

vary as a function of the overall economy. Although we will return to take a closer look at this subgroup later in the book, even these firms have stable margins across the economic or commodity price cycle.

- **Competitive advantages?** The dimension on which mature firms reveal the most variation is in the competitive advantages they hold on to, manifested by the excess returns they generate on their investments. While some mature firms see excess returns go to zero or become negative with the advent of competition, other mature firms retain significant competitive advantages (and excess returns). Since value is determined by excess returns, the latter retain higher values relative to the former, even as growth rates become anemic.
- **Debt capacity**: As firms mature, profit margins and earnings improve, reinvestment needs drop off, and more cash is available for servicing debt. As a consequence, debt ratios should increase for all mature firms, although there can be big differences in how firms react to this surge in debt capacity. Some choose not to exploit any or most of the debt capacity, and they stick with financing policies they established as growth companies. Others overreact and don't just borrow, but borrow more than they can comfortably handle, given current earnings and cash flows. Still others take a more reasoned middle ground and borrow to reflect their improved financial status while preserving their financial health.
- **Cash buildup and return?** As earnings improve and reinvestment needs drop off, mature companies generate more cash from their operations than they need. If these companies do not alter their debt or dividend policies, cash balances will start accumulating in these firms. The question of whether a company has too much cash and, if so, how it should return this cash to stockholders becomes a standard one at almost every mature company.
- **Inorganic growth**: The transition from a growth company to a mature company is not an easy one for most companies (and the managers involved). As companies get larger and internal investment opportunities do not provide the growth boost that they used to, it should not be surprising that many growth companies look for quick fixes that will allow them to continue maintaining high growth. One option, albeit an expensive one, is to buy growth. Acquisitions of other companies can provide a boost to revenues and earnings.

One final point that needs to be made is that not all mature companies are large companies. Many small companies reach their growth ceiling quickly and essentially stay small, mature firms. A few growth companies have extended periods of growth before they reach stable growth. These companies tend to be the large companies that we find used as examples of typical mature companies. Coca-Cola, IBM, and Verizon are all good examples.

Valuation Issues

As with young businesses and growth firms, the characteristics of mature companies can create estimation challenges during valuations. This section first focuses on the valuation issues in the discounted or intrinsic valuation of mature companies. Then it looks at manifestations of the same problems when we do relative valuation.

Intrinsic (DCF) Valuation

If a firm's intrinsic value is the present value of the expected cash flows from its investments, discounted back at a risk-adjusted rate, it would seem that mature firms should be easiest to value on that basis. While this is generally true, problems can still lurk under the surface of these firms' long and seemingly stable histories.

Existing Assets

We categorized mature companies as those that get the bulk of their value from existing assets. Consequently, measuring the value of these assets correctly becomes far more critical with mature firms than it was with the growth firms that we analyzed in the last two chapters. Since a key input into valuing existing assets is estimating the cash flows they generate, we encounter two issues when valuing mature companies:

- **Managed earnings**: Mature companies are particularly adept at using the discretionary power offered in accounting rules to manage earnings. They are not necessarily committing accounting fraud or even being deceptive. But this does imply that the earnings reported from existing assets by companies that aggressively approach accounting choices will be much higher than the earnings reported by otherwise similar conservative companies. Failing to factor in the differences in the "accounting" mind-set can lead us to overvalue the existing assets of aggressive companies and undervalue those of conservative companies.
- **Management inefficiencies**: Mature companies have long periods of stable operating history. This fact can lull us into believing that the numbers from the past (operating margins, returns on capital) are reasonable estimates of what existing assets will continue to generate in the future. However, past earnings reflect how the firm was managed over the period. To the extent that managers may not have made the right investment or financing choices, the reported earnings may be lower than what the existing assets would be able to produce under better or optimal management. If there is the possibility of such a management change on the horizon, we will undervalue existing assets using reported earnings.

In summary, the notion that existing assets can be easily valued at a mature company, because of its long operating history, is defensible only at well-managed companies or at companies where existing management is so entrenched that there is no chance of a management change.

Growth Assets

Companies can create growth assets in two ways. One is to invest in new assets and projects that generate excess returns; this is generally called organic growth. The other is to acquire established businesses and companies and thus short-circuit the process; this is inorganic or acquisition-driven growth. While both options are available to companies at any stage in the life cycle, mature companies are far more likely to take the "acquired growth" route for three reasons. The first is that as companies mature, internal investments start to become scarce, relative to what the firm has available to invest. The second reason is that as companies get larger, the new investments they make also have to grow to have any impact on overall growth. While it is difficult to find multibillion-dollar internal projects, it is easier to find acquisitions of that size, and these affect the growth rate almost immediately. The third reason applies in businesses that have a long lead time between investment and payoff. In these businesses, there will be a lag between the initial investment in a new asset and the growth generated by that investment. With an acquisition, we are in effect speeding up the payoffs.

So what are the consequences for intrinsic valuation? As a general rule, the value of acquisition-driven growth is much more difficult to assess than the value of organic growth. Unlike organic growth, where firms take several small investments each period, acquisitions tend to be infrequent and lumpy. A multibillion-dollar acquisition in one year may be followed by two years of no investments, followed by another acquisition. The consequences of this lumpiness can be seen if we relate growth to fundamentals:

Expected Growth Rate = Reinvestment Rate * Return on Capital

Since reinvestment and returns on capital should reflect both organic and acquisition-driven growth, we think it is far more difficult to estimate these numbers for acquisitive companies. If we follow the standard practice of using the reinvestment numbers from the most recent financial statement, we risk overstating the value (if there was a large acquisition during the period) or understating it (if it was a period between acquisitions). Computing the return on capital on investments is much more difficult with acquisitions, partly because of the accounting treatment of the price paid and its allocation to goodwill, and partly because we have far fewer observations to base our judgments on.

Discount Rates

When estimating discount rates, we start from a position of more strength when analyzing mature companies because we have more data to work with. Most mature companies have been publicly traded for extended periods, giving us access to more historical price data. They also have settled risk profiles, which stabilizes the data. Thus, estimating equity risk parameters from historical data is more defensible with this group of companies than it was with the growth companies we analyzed in the preceding two chapters. In addition, many mature companies, at least in the U.S., use corporate bonds to raise debt, which yields two benefits. The first is that we can get updated market prices and yields on these bonds, which are an input into the cost of debt. The second is that the bonds are accompanied by bond ratings, which provide not only measures of default risk but also pathways to default spreads and costs of debt.

However, three estimation issues can affect discount rate estimates. The first is that mature companies accumulate debt from multiple places, leading to a complex mix of debt—fixed- and floating-rate, in multiple currencies, senior and subordinated, and with different maturities. Since they often carry different interest rates (and even different ratings), analysts are left with the challenge of how to deal with this complexity when computing debt ratios and costs of debt. The second issue is that discount rates (costs of debt, equity, and capital) are affected by the firm's mix of debt and equity. The estimates we obtain from the current price data and ratings reflect the firm's current financing mix. If that mix is altered, the discount rate must be reestimated. The third factor comes into play for firms that follow the acquisitive route to growth. Acquiring a firm in a different business or with a different risk profile can alter the firm's discount rate.

Terminal Value

As in any intrinsic valuation, the terminal value accounts for a large share of the overall value of a mature firm. Since mature firms have growth rates that are close to that of the economy, the computation of terminal value may seem both more imminent and simpler with a mature company than with a growth company. While this may be true, two factors can still cause distortions in the computation:

- **Stable growth rates, unstable risk, and investment profile**: Many mature companies have growth rates low enough to qualify for stable growth (by being less than the economy's growth rate and the risk-free rate). However, the other inputs into the valuation may not reflect this maturity. Thus, a firm with a 2% growth rate in revenues and earnings would qualify as a stable firm based on its growth rate, but not if its beta is 2.00 and it is reinvesting 90% of its after-tax operating income into the business. To qualify as a stable-growth firm that can be valued using the terminal value equation, the firm needs a sustainable growth. It also should have the risk profile of a stable firm (close to average risk) and should behave like a stable firm (in terms of reinvestment).
- **Lock in inefficiencies in perpetuity**: The cash flows from existing assets and the discount rates we obtain from past data will reflect the choices the firm makes. To the extent that the firm is not managed optimally, the cash flows may be lower and the discount rate higher than it would have been for the same firm with a different management. If we lock in current values (margins, returns on investment, and discount rates) when estimating terminal value, and the firm is poorly run, in effect we undervalue the firm by assuming that the current practices will continue forever.

The assumption that a firm is in stable growth and can be valued using a terminal value equation cannot be made easily, even for mature firms.

Relative Valuation

With mature companies, with positive revenues and earnings and meaningful book values, we have a luxury of riches when it comes to relative valuation. We can estimate revenues, earnings, and book-value multiples and compare how a company is priced relative to other companies like it:

- **Too many values?** Finding a multiple that works and comparable companies is easier with mature firms than with the growth firms we analyzed in the preceding two chapters. However, the fact that each multiple we use gives us a different estimate of value can be problematic. Put another way, relative valuation is a subjective process. The same company can be assigned very different values, depending on whether we are using a firm or equity multiple; whether that multiple is stated as a function of revenues, earnings, and book value; and the companies we pick to be its comparables. With mature firms, the problem we face is not that we cannot estimate a relative value, but that there are too many values to choose from.
- **Management change**: The multiples that we compute for revenues, earnings, and book value reflect the mature firm as it is managed today. To the extent that changing the firm's management could change all these numbers, we are faced with the same problem

that we were with discounted cash flow valuation. How do we best reflect, in a relative valuation, the potential for management change and the consequent increase in value? The problem is magnified, though, because the same issue of how different management can affect operating numbers also affects all the other companies that are used as comparable firms.

- **Acquisition noise**: Acquisition-driven growth, a source of intrinsic valuation angst, contaminates relative valuation. The accounting aftermath of acquisitions—the creation of goodwill as an asset and its subsequent treatment—can affect both earnings and book value, making multiples based on either number dicey.
- **Changing financial leverage**: The other factor that can throw a wrench into relative valuations is changing financial leverage. Mature companies can make large changes to their debt ratios overnight—debt for equity swaps, recapitalizations—and some multiples can be affected dramatically by such actions. In general, equity multiples, such as PE and price-to-book ratios, change more as financial leverage changes than enterprise value or firm multiples, which are based on the collective value of both debt and equity. A stock buyback, using borrowed funds, can reduce market capitalization dramatically (by reducing the shares outstanding), but it will have a much smaller impact on enterprise value (since we are replacing equity with debt). For the same reason, equity earnings (earnings per share, net income) will change when firms alter debt ratios.

The Dark Side of Valuation

The dark side of valuation manifests itself less often with mature companies than with growth or declining companies, but it still shows up with surprising frequency. This section looks at some of ways in which mature-company valuations are skewed by inconsistent or unrealistic assumptions.

Growth in Mature Companies

If we categorize companies as mature based on whether they get the bulk of their value from existing assets, it would seem unlikely that growth assumptions significantly alter value at these companies. However, three common mistakes that are related to growth can be damaging to valuations:

- **Mistaking bottom-line growth for top-line growth**: We noted that earnings growth and revenue growth can diverge at many mature companies, at least over short time periods. Thus, a firm that improves the efficiency with which it operates existing assets can post growth rates in earnings that are much higher than growth rates in revenues. Analysts who focus on the former without paying much attention to the latter sometimes use earnings growth rates to estimate revenues and overvalue mature companies.
- **Stable growth rate models with unstable growth rates**: The advantage of assuming that a growth rate is sustainable forever is that it allows us to dispense with cash flow estimates beyond that point and compute a terminal value. Chapter 2 noted that the

stable-growth model comes with two constraints. The first is that the growth rate cannot exceed the economy's nominal growth rate, with the nominal risk-free rate operating as a proxy for this growth rate. The second constraint is that the firm's risk profile and investment returns should also be consistent with stable growth, with risk converging on the average firm's risk, and excess returns moving toward, if not to, zero. Analysts valuing mature companies sometimes overlook one or both of these assumptions, using stable-growth models for firms with growth rates higher than the risk-free rate and/or accompanying this growth rate with risk-and-return assumptions that are incompatible with a growth firm. They often justify the first action by arguing that the growth rate is close enough to the economy's growth rate to employ a shortcut: the mature firm is growing at only 4%, and the economy is growing at 3%. What they fail to consider is that even small violations of the stable-growth rate cap (it cannot exceed the risk-free rate) can create large effects on value.

Stable Growth, Unstable Inputs

Hormel Foods, which sells packaged meat and other food products, has been in existence as a publicly traded company for almost 80 years. In 2008, the firm reported after-tax operating income of $315 million, reflecting a compounded growth of approximately 5% over the previous five years. In addition, the firm had capital expenditures of $126 million, matching its depreciation amount for the year, and working capital had increased about $44 million a year on average, for the previous five years. The firm's beta was 0.83, and its debt ratio was 10.39%. The risk-free rate at the time of the analysis was 2.35%, the marginal tax rate was estimated to be 40%, and we used an equity risk premium of 6%. The cost of capital was computed as follows:

Cost of Equity = Risk-Free Rate + Beta * Equity Risk Premium
= 2.35% + 0.83 (6%) = 7.33%

Cost of Debt = Risk-Free Rate + Default Spread (Based on Rating)
= 2.35% + 1.25% = 3.60%

Cost of Capital = 7.33% (.8961) + 3.60% (1 – .40) (.1039) = 6.79%

Assume that the analyst decides to treat Hormel as a stable-growth firm. He argues that its growth rate of 5% is low enough to be a stable-growth rate and that it is behaving like a stable-growth firm, with capital expenditures offsetting depreciation.[1] The value he would assign the firm would be as follows:

1 The analyst justifies the claim that 5% is a stable-growth rate by noting that the average nominal growth rate in the U.S. economy between 1981 and 2008 was approximately 5% a year.

Free Cash Flow to the Firm = After-Tax Operating Income – (Cap Ex – Depreciation) – Change in Noncash Working Capital = $315 - (126 - 126) - $44 = $271 million

$$\text{Value of Hormel's Operating Assets} = \frac{\text{FCFF}_{\text{Last year}}(1+g)}{(\text{Cost of Capital} - g)}$$

$$= \frac{271(1.05)}{(.0683 - .05)} = \$15{,}897 \text{ million}$$

Adding the existing cash balance ($155 million) and subtracting debt ($450 million) yields the value of equity in the firm:

$$\text{Value of Equity} = \text{Value of Operating Assets} + \text{Cash} - \text{Debt}$$
$$= 15{,}897 + 155 - 450 = \$15{,}602 \text{ million}$$

Dividing this value by the number of shares outstanding (134.53 million) yields a value per share of $115.97, well above the stock price of $32 at the time of the analysis.

Before jumping on this investment opportunity, we should note that internal inconsistencies in this valuation make it fatally flawed. The first is that while a growth rate of 5% may have been perfectly reasonable as a stable-growth rate in 1983 or 1995, it is inappropriate in January 2009. In fact, the risk-free rate of 2.35% signals dramatically lower inflation and/or real growth in the economy looking forward. Consequently, the stable-growth rate should not have been set higher than 2.35%. The second inconsistency is that although the cost of capital may be consistent with a stable-growth firm—the beta of 0.83 is well within a stable range (0.80 to 1.20)—the reinvestment that the analyst is building into the cash flows in perpetuity is incompatible with the growth rate he is using:

$$\text{Reinvestment Rate} = \frac{(\text{Cap Ex} - \text{Depreciation} + \text{Change in WC})}{\text{After-Tax Operating Income}}$$

$$= \frac{(126 - 126 + 44)}{305} = 14.49\%$$

With the assumed growth rate of 5%, this would imply that Hormel would be able to generate returns on capital on its new investments of 34.5%, well above its current return on capital of about 14%:

$$\text{Implied Return on Capital} = \frac{g}{\text{Reinvestment Rate}} = \frac{.05}{.1449} = 34.5\%$$

In summary, the use of too high a growth rate (for stable growth) and an unrealistically high return on capital to accompany that growth rate is skewing the valuation.

Acquisition Inconsistencies

When firms grow by acquiring other firms, rather than through internal investments, we noted the collateral damage that is created to the numbers we depend on for valuation. Growth rates, risk measures, and accounting return computations can all be skewed by acquisitions.

The most common error made by analysts valuing acquisitive companies is their failure to look past the accounting numbers. When valuing a firm, analysts often use historical growth rates in revenues and earnings as a basis for future projections and use the capital expenditure numbers reported in the statement of cash flows. Implicit here is a mismatch. The growth rate in operating numbers reflects the acquisitions that a firm has made over the time period, but the accounting definition of capital expenditures does not incorporate acquisitions. Consequently, using these numbers in unison essentially gives a firm the benefits of future acquisition in the form of higher expected growth without factoring in the cost of making these acquisitions.

A secondary error is an overreliance on the most recent period's financial statements when estimating inputs such as reinvestment and returns on capital. As we noted, acquisitions tend to be lumpy and infrequent, and the most recent year's numbers can be skewed as a consequence. This error can cut both ways, resulting in overvaluations of some acquisitive companies and undervaluations of others.

Acquisition Inconsistency: Valuing Cisco

The 1990s belonged to Cisco, a firm that rode the networking and Internet wave to increase its market capitalization from $4 billion in 1991 to more than $400 billion in 1999. During this period, it adopted a growth strategy that paid off richly. Rather than develop new technologies internally, it acquired small companies with promising technologies and developed them commercially. While the success of this strategy has waned, Cisco still gets the bulk of its growth from acquisitions. Table 11.1 summarizes revenues and earnings each year from 2005 to 2008, with the reported numbers for depreciation, capital expenditures, and acquisitions each year.

Table 11.1 Cisco's Revenues, Earnings, and Reinvestment

	2005	2006	2007	2008	Aggregate	Growth Rate
Revenues	$24,801	$28,484	$34,922	$29,540	$117,747	6.00%
Operating income	$7,416	$6,996	$8,621	$9,442	$32,475	8.38%
After-tax operating income	$5,298	$5,114	$6,682	$7,414	$24,508	11.85%
Net income	$5,741	$5,580	$7,333	$8,052	$26,706	11.94%
Capital expenditures	$692	$772	$1,251	$1,268	$3,983	
Depreciation	$1,020	$1,293	$1,413	$1,744	$5,470	

Table 11.1 continued

Change in working capital	–$34	–$81	–$36	–$57	–$208
Reinvestment	–$362	–$602	–$198	–$533	–$1,695
Acquisitions	$911	$5,399	$3,684	$398	$10,392
Modified reinvestment	$549	$4,797	$3,486	–$135	$8,697

In the last column of the table, we report on the growth rates in revenues and earnings over the period. They indicate healthy growth—6% annually for revenues and almost 12% in after-tax operating income and net income. The reinvestment numbers based on internal investment—net capital expenditures and change in working capital—seem inconsistent with a growing company, since the reinvestment over the entire period was negative (–$1,695 million). Only when we consider the $10.392 billion spent on acquisitions over the period do we see the full picture. Including that cost in reinvestment would result in a total reinvestment over the period of $8.7 billion.

To illustrate the dangers of mismatching growth and reinvestment, consider the consequences of estimating the future growth in operating measures from historical data and using only traditional capital expenditures in computing the reinvestment. Table 11.2 summarizes the projected cash flows for the next five years, based on these assumptions.

Table 11.2 Cash Flows and Reinvestment Mismatching Effect

	Base	Growth Rate	Year 1	Year 2	Year 3	Year 4	Year 5
Revenues	$29,540	6.00%	$31,313	$33,192	$35,185	$37,296	$39,535
After-tax operating income	$7,414	6.00%	$7,859	$8,330	$8,830	$9,360	$9,922
Depreciation	$1,744	6.00%	$1,849	$1,960	$2,077	$2,202	$2,334
Capital expenditures	$1,268	6.00%	$1,344	$1,425	$1,510	$1,601	$1,697
Change in working capital	–$57	6.00%	–$60	–$64	–$68	–$72	–$76
FCFF	$7,947	6.00%	$8,424	$8,929	$9,465	$10,033	$10,635

To be conservative, we have used historical revenue growth as the basis for projecting growth in all the numbers. Note that the free cash flows to the firm exceed the after-tax operating income in each year, because we are assuming that reinvestment will stay negative and become even more so. Even if we make reasonable assumptions about growth and reinvestment in the terminal value computation, we will overvalue Cisco, because we have in effect allowed the company the benefits of acquisition-driven growth without the cost.

Unreal Restructuring

Mature companies can be mismanaged or managed less than optimally. Analysts valuing these companies sometimes try to reflect the potential for management change in the values they assign to companies, but the adjustments they make are not always reasonable.

The most damaging way of dealing with the possibility of a management change is to add an arbitrary premium to the firm's estimated value. This addition, often called a control premium, can increase a firm's value by 20 to 25%. Analysts who use this adjustment generally base it on premiums paid by acquiring companies for target firms over and above the market price. If acquiring companies pay 20% more than the current price, on average, they argue that this must reflect how much they can increase the value of the target company. The problem with this argument is that the premium paid on an acquisition reflects not only control expectations but two other variables—the expected value of the synergy that is anticipated from the merger and any overpayment by the acquirer.

In some cases, analysts recognize the need to consider the effects of a new management team on the firm's operating characteristics. However, the adjustments they make to operating margins and returns on capital do not reflect reality. In fact, the only thing they have in common is that they are more favorable than the current numbers. For instance, the firm's operating margin will be increased from its current value of 10 to 14%, with no attention paid to whether this is feasible or even possible in the sector in which the firm operates.

The last scenario is if the firm being valued has been explicitly targeted for an acquisition and the analyst is familiar with the acquirer. If the acquirer is viewed as a "smart money" investor—a KKR, Blackstone, or Carl Icahn—analysts allow the halo effect of past deals done to color their valuation. Put another way, the argument is that if a smart investor thinks a firm is worth $200 million more than its existing price, it must be, because the smart investor knows what he or she is doing. In effect, a company's value becomes whatever a smart investor is willing to pay for the company.

Debt and Value

In addition to having less-than-optimal operations, mature firms may be less than optimally financed. They might use too much or too little debt to fund the assets or might mismatch debt and assets (using short-term debt to fund long-term assets, for example).

In trying to deal with the potential for a changing financing mix, analysts sometimes fall into the trap of keeping the cost of equity and debt fixed and changing the mix of debt and equity. Since equity is generally much more expensive than debt, this assumption has a predictable outcome. The cost of capital will decrease (and firm value will increase) as we increase the debt ratio.

The other approach used by many analysts is to compute the tax benefits of debt and to add this number to the firm's value with no debt. This is a version of adjusted present value (APV), which counts the benefits of debt while ignoring the costs. Again, the firm's value increases as the firm borrows more money.

As a final quirk, even analysts who include the costs of borrowing money in their analysis by adjusting the costs of debt and equity as the debt ratio increases or bringing in the expected bankruptcy costs of debt (in the adjusted present value approach) often value a company with a target debt ratio instead of an actual debt ratio. The choices of financial leverage are made by the firm's existing managers, and their views on what comprises a reasonable debt ratio may diverge from the target debt ratios used in the valuation. Therefore, there is a very real chance that we will misvalue the firm using a target debt ratio.

Debt and Value: The Upside of Debt and No Downside

In the first sidebar, we estimated a current cost of capital of 6.79% for Hormel Foods, based on its current cost of equity of 7.33%, an after-tax cost of debt of 2.16%, and a debt-to-capital ratio of 10.39%. Since this debt ratio is much lower than the industry average debt ratio of 25%, an analyst decides to use the industry average debt ratio as the target debt ratio and recomputes the cost of capital. In making the computation, though, he decides to keep the cost of equity and debt at the current levels:

Cost of Capital = 7.33% (.75) + 2.16% (.25) = 6.04%

Even if we accept the presumption that Hormel will move to the target debt ratio (and there is no guarantee that it will), this cost of capital understates the true cost. If Hormel increases its debt ratio, its equity will become riskier (leading to a higher cost of equity), and the default risk of its debt will increase (pushing up the cost of debt). We will return to examine the mechanics of this estimation later in this chapter.

Relative Valuation

The inconsistencies that contaminate the intrinsic valuations of mature companies show up in subtle ways when the companies are valued using multiples and comparables. In addition to all the standard issues that are part of any relative valuation—finding comparable firms and adjusting for differences in growth and risk—the potential for a change in operating efficiency and differences in financial leverage can skew relative valuations.

Consider first the question of how best to reflect the possibility of management change. Many analysts who use relative valuation to value mature companies that they believe are poorly run compute market multiples based on comparable firms and then add control premiums (of the same 20% magnitude we mentioned in the intrinsic value section). The problem with this approach is not just the arbitrary nature of the premium but the base on which it is applied. To the extent that the market prices for companies already reflect the likelihood of management change, the market multiples at which comparable companies trade already has at least a portion of the control premium built into them. Augmenting the relative value for control is double counting. To illustrate, assume that we are valuing a cement company with EBITDA of $100 million by looking at publicly traded cement companies (all of which are similar to the company we are valuing in terms of fundamentals) and that they are trading at 6 times EBITDA. The estimated enterprise value for the firm, on a relative basis, is then $600 million:

$$\text{Enterprise Value} = \text{EBITDA}_{\text{Company}} * \text{EV/EBITDA}_{\text{Comparables}}$$

Now assume that you believe that all these companies are poorly managed and that earnings could be higher under a different management team. At first sight, it seems reasonable that we should add a premium to the $600 million to reflect this potential for improvement. However, here is a reality that should make us pause. If the market agrees with our assessment that the firms are poorly managed, but it also believes that there is a good chance (say, 50%) that management will change, the market price will reflect this expectation. Thus, the EV/EBITDA multiple already reflects half of the control premium. As a consequence, relative valuation is difficult when firms are poorly run and have the potential for increased value. Adjusting the observed prices (and market multiples) requires us to make judgments not only on the company being valued but on the comparable companies and what the market is building into prices.

The possibility of large changes in debt ratios at mature firms can also have consequences for the relative valuation of these firms. Analysts who use equity multiples to value mature firms are likely to find their numbers upended by a recapitalization, where debt is raised to buy back equity, or skewed when large differences exist in the use of debt across the comparable companies. In the latter scenario, firms that use higher debt ratios may look cheap in good times on a PE ratio basis, since increased leverage can improve earnings per share. When the firm is doing poorly, the higher debt ratios hurt these firms, with earnings going down more than for the rest of the sector.

The Light Side of Valuation

Looking at estimation issues related to valuation and the dark side as it manifests itself in the valuation of mature companies, we must be able to deal with two aspects of mature companies in order to value them correctly. The first is how best to value growth at mature companies, especially when the growth is generated by acquisitions. The other is how to assess the impact on value of changing how a mature company is run. As we noted earlier, mature firms that have endured for long periods under existing management can have significant operating and financial inefficiencies.

Growth and Acquisitions

Some firms grow primarily through acquisitions; valuing these firms poses challenges. However, we can follow some simple rules to minimize the fallout from the acquisitions:

1. Assess whether the acquisitions done by the firm in the past represent unusual transactions or are part of a long-term strategy. This judgment is subjective and is based on the motivation for the acquisitions and management views. If we conclude that the acquisition or acquisitions in the past represent unique events that will not be repeated in the

future, we can ignore acquisitions in our valuation, both in the reinvestment and in the growth rate. In practical terms, this implies that our future growth rate for the firm will be lower than the past growth rate (which was augmented by the acquisition) and that the reinvestment rate will reflect only internal investments.

2. If acquisitions are part of the firm's long-term strategy, collect data on what the acquisitions have cost the firm (including acquisitions paid for with stock) over a long period (three to ten years).[2] As acquisitions become more infrequent, we have to extend the time period over which we make this estimate.
3. Estimate the firm's reinvestment rate, with acquisitions counting as part of capital expenditures, over the period:

$$\text{Modified Reinvestment Rate} = \frac{(\text{Cap Ex} + \text{Acquisitions} - \text{Depreciation})}{\text{After-Tax Operating Income}}$$

Looking at this rate over a longer period allows us to adjust it for the lumpiness of acquisitions.

4. The conventional measure of return on capital that we derived in Chapter 2, obtained by dividing the after-tax operating income by the book value of capital invested (equity plus net debt), can be skewed after acquisitions by the presence of and adjustments to goodwill. If we assume that goodwill represents a premium paid for the growth assets of the target firm, the adjustment is a simple one:

$$\text{Return on Capital} = \frac{\text{After-Tax Operating Income}}{(\text{BV of Debt} + \text{BV of Equity} - \text{Cash} - \text{Goodwill})}$$

Since operating income is generated by existing assets and not by growth assets, we are removing goodwill from capital invested to preserve consistency. However, this can be too generous to acquisitive firms that consistently overpay on acquisitions. Goodwill, after all, includes not only a premium for growth assets but premiums for control and synergy, as well as any overpayment on the acquisition. In a full information world, we would subtract only that portion of goodwill that is due to growth assets and leave behind the portions attributable to synergy, control, and overpayment. The first two should be part of capital invested, because they should generate higher earnings if true. The last should be part of capital invested, because a firm that consistently overpays on acquisitions will continue to deliver poor investment returns and destroy value.[3]

2 To account for an acquisition paid for with stock, we need information on the number of shares that were issued to cover the acquisition and the stock price at the time of the acquisition.

3 Although no firm will ever be willing to break goodwill into these components, we can make our own estimates based on the target company characteristics at the time of the acquisition or even by looking at the history of the acquiring company. If an acquiring firm has a history of making large acquisitions, followed by regret and goodwill impairments, it seems reasonable to conclude that a significant portion of goodwill should be left in capital invested.

Valuing an Acquisitive Mature Company: Revisiting Cisco

While Cisco's glory days of growth are behind it, the firm continues to make acquisitions and report a growth rate that is too high to qualify as stable. Earlier we looked at the consequences of mismatching growth and acquisitions in a valuation. Here we will look at how to incorporate acquisition growth and costs into a valuation.

To Cisco, acquisitions are clearly an integral part of growth. A valuation of Cisco that ignores acquisitions for both growth and reinvestment estimates may be consistent, but it does not reflect reality. To assess how much acquisitions will affect cash flows, we begin in Table 11.3 by looking at the total reinvestment in the firm over the last four years, with acquisitions considered as capital expenditures.

Table 11.3 Cisco's Reinvestment Rate from 2005 to 2008

	2005	2006	2007	2008	Aggregate
After-tax operating income	$5,298	$5,114	$6,682	$7,414	$24,508
Capital expenditures	$692	$772	$1,251	$1,268	$3,983
Depreciation	$1,020	$1,293	$1,413	$1,744	$5,470
Change in working capital	–$34	–$81	–$36	–$57	–$208
Conventional reinvestment	–$362	–$602	–$198	–$533	–$1,695
Reinvestment rate	**–6.83%**	**–11.77%**	**–2.96%**	**–7.19%**	**–6.92%**
Acquisitions	$911	$5,399	$3,684	$398	$10,392
Modified reinvestment	$549	$4,797	$3,486	–$135	$8,697
Modified reinvestment rate	10.36%	93.80%	52.17%	–1.82%	35.49%

The average reinvestment rate over the four-year period, with acquisitions counted as part of capital expenditures, is 35.49%. Years of frenetic activity (2006 and 2007) are interspersed with years of inactivity (2005 and 2008).[4]

Since the other piece of the growth puzzle is the return on capital earned on investments, we estimate the return on capital for Cisco as a company using two different measures of invested capital. In the first, we leave the entire goodwill in the invested capital, and in the second, we net out the entire goodwill:

4 Because Cisco does a large number of small acquisitions every year, it probably poses less of a challenge than a company that does much larger but more infrequent assumptions. With the latter, both averaging across time and making judgments about the future become more difficult.

$$ROC_{\text{No Goodwill Netted}} = \frac{\text{After-Tax Operating Income}_{2008}}{(\text{BV of Debt}_{2007} + \text{BV of Equity}_{2007} - \text{Cash}_{2007})}$$

$$= \frac{9445\,(1-.375)}{(6408+31490-3728)} = 16.82\%$$

$$ROC_{\text{All Goodwill Netted}} = \frac{\text{After-Tax Operating Income}_{2008}}{(\text{BV of Debt}_{2007} + \text{BV of Equity}_{2007} - \text{Cash}_{2007} - \text{Goodwill}_{2007})}$$

$$= \frac{9445\,(1-.375)}{(6408+31490-3728-12121)} = 25.53\%$$

Given Cisco's good record of acquisitions, and since its targets are young technology firms, with little in terms of revenues and earnings, we will stick with the measure computed with 100% of goodwill subtracted from invested capital. If we assume that the reinvestment rate and returns on capital just estimated are sustainable, the resulting growth rate is 9.06%:

$$\text{Expected Growth Rate} = \text{Reinvestment Rate} * \text{Return on Capital}$$
$$= 35.49\% * 25.53\% = 9.06\%$$

We assume that Cisco will be able to maintain this growth rate for the next five years and preserve its current risk profile and cost of capital. With a beta of 1.73 and a debt ratio of 7.46%, the cost of capital is 11.95%.[5] Table 11.4 summarizes the expected cash flows for the next five years, with the present value computed for each year.

Table 11.4 Expected Cash Flows for Cisco's High-Growth Phase

	Current	Year 1	Year 2	Year 3	Year 4	Year 5
EBIT * (1 – tax rate)	$5,978	$6,520	$7,111	$7,755	$8,458	$9,225
– Reinvestment	–$135	$2,314	$2,524	$2,752	$3,002	$3,273
Free cash flow to firm	$6,113	$4,206	$4,587	$5,003	$5,456	$5,951
Cost of capital		11.95%	11.95%	11.95%	11.95%	11.95%
Present value		$3,757	$3,660	$3,566	$3,474	$3,384
Reinvestment rate	–1.82%	35.49%	35.49%	35.49%	35.49%	35.48%

After year 5, the growth rate will drop to 2.35% (set at the risk-free rate cap). We will also assume that Cisco's beta will decrease to 1.20 (the cap for the stable-growth phase) and that the debt ratio and the cost of debt will remain unchanged.

5 We used a risk-free rate of 2.35% and an equity risk premium of 6%, in making our cost of equity estimates. The cost of debt was assumed to be 3.60%, reflecting a synthetic rating of AAA for the firm. The marginal tax rate used is 37.5%.

This will cause the cost of capital to drop to 6.86%. Assuming also that Cisco maintains a return on capital of 10%, higher than its cost of capital in perpetuity, allows us to estimate the reinvestment rate and terminal value:

$$\text{Reinvestment Rate} = \frac{g_{Stable}}{ROC_{Stable}} = \frac{2.35\%}{10\%} = 23.5\%$$

$$\text{Terminal Value} = \frac{\text{After-Tax Operating Income}_5\ (1+g_{Stable})(1-\text{Reinvestment Rate})}{(\text{Cost of Capital}_{Stable} - g_{Stable})}$$

$$= \frac{9225(1.0235)(1-.235)}{(.0686-.0235)} = \$160{,}102$$

Discounting this value back to today at the current cost of capital of 11.95% and adding it to the present value of the cash flows over the first five years, the value we obtain for the operating assets of the firm is $108,901 million.[6]

To get to the value of equity per share, we add the current cash balance ($5,191 million), subtract debt ($7,758 million) and the value of management options outstanding ($1,621 million), and divide by the number of shares outstanding (5,855.09 million shares) to arrive at a value per share of $17.88:

$$\text{Value per Share} = \frac{108{,}901 + 5{,}191 - 7758 - 1621}{5855.09} = \$17.88/\text{Share}$$

In January 2009, Cisco was trading at $16.15 a share, about 10% below our estimated value.

Changing Management

If the key to valuing mature companies is assessing the potential change in value from changing how they are run, it is critical that we come up with better ways of assessing that effect. This section begins by looking at the potential to enhance value at any firm, first by focusing on changes in operations and then by examining how financing policy and strategy can alter value. We will extend the discussion by bringing both the potential for value change and the possibility of making that change into a measure of the expected value of control. We will close the section by evaluating the implications of the expected value of control on valuing mature companies and on estimating the premium we should pay for voting rights.

Operating Restructuring

When we value a company, our forecasts of earnings and cash flows are built on assumptions about how the company will be run. If these numbers are based on existing financial statements,

6 Although the terminal value is computed using the stable period cost of capital of 6.86%, it must be discounted back at the high-growth period cost of capital. Investors must be exposed to higher risk for the next five years to get to the terminal value.

we are, in effect, assuming that the firm will continue to be run the way it is now. In this section, we will look at how changes in operations manifest themselves in valuation, using the intrinsic value framework we have already used extensively in this book. In this approach, the value of a firm is a function of five key inputs. The first is the *cash flow from assets in place* or investments already made. The second is the *expected growth rate in the cash flows* during what we can call a period of both high growth and excess returns (during which the firm earns more than its cost of capital on its investments). The third is the *length of time before the firm becomes a stable-growth firm*. The fourth is the *discount rate*, reflecting both the risk of the investment and the financing mix used to fund it. The final element represents *cash, cross-holdings, and other nonoperating assets* that the firm may hold that augment the value of operating assets. Figure 11.2 captures all five elements.

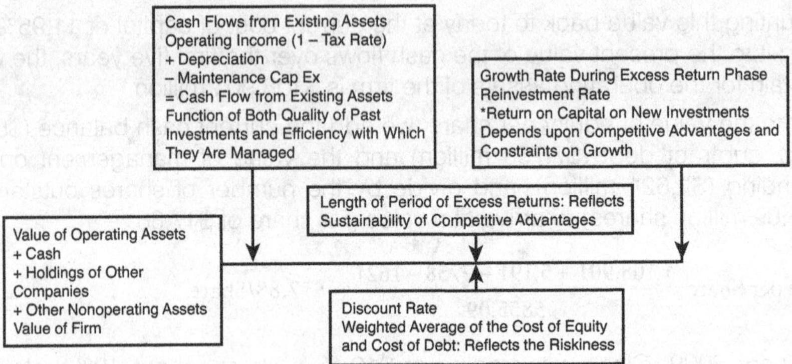

Figure 11.2: Determinants of Value

A firm can increase its value by increasing cash flows from current operations, by increasing expected growth and the period of high growth, by reducing its composite cost of financing, and by managing its nonoperating assets better. In this section, we will focus on all these inputs, except for the cost of financing.

Increase Cash Flows from Assets in Place

The first place to look for value is in the firm's existing assets. These assets reflect investments that have already been made and that generate the firm's current operating income. To the extent that these investments earn less than the cost of capital, or are earning less than they could if optimally managed, there is potential for value enhancement. In general, actions taken to increase cash flows from assets in place can be categorized into the following groups:

- **Asset redeployment:** To the extent that the assets of a business are poorly invested, you can increase the firm's cash flows and value by divesting poorly performing assets[7] or by

7 At first sight, divesting businesses that are earning poor returns or losing money may seem like the ticket to value creation. However, the real test is whether the divestiture value exceeds the value of continuing in the business. If it does, divestiture makes sense. After all, when a business is earning poor returns, it is unlikely that a potential buyer will pay a premium for it.

moving assets from their existing uses to ones that generate higher value. One example is a retail firm that owns its stores deciding that the store spaces would be worth more developed as commercial real estate instead of being used in retailing.

- **Improved operating efficiency**: When a firm's operations are riddled with inefficiencies, reducing or eliminating these inefficiencies translates into an increase in operating cash flows and value. Thus, a telecommunications firm that is overstaffed should be able to generate value by reducing the size of its workforce. A steel company that is losing money because of outdated equipment in its plants may be able to increase its value by replacing the equipment with something newer and more efficient. In recent years, manufacturing companies in developed markets like the U.S. and Western Europe have been able to generate substantial savings by moving their operations to emerging markets, where labor costs are lower.
- **Reduced tax burden:** It is every firm's obligation to pay taxes, but it shouldn't pay more than its fair share. If a firm can legally reduce its tax burden, it should do so. A multinational firm may be able to reduce its taxes by moving more of its operations (and the ensuing earnings) to lower tax locales. Risk management can also play a role in reducing taxes by smoothing out earnings over periods; spikes in income can subject a firm to higher taxes.
- **Reduced capital maintenance and working capital investments**: A significant portion of after-tax operating income is often reinvested in the firm not to generate future growth but to maintain existing operations. This reinvestment includes capital maintenance (which is capital expenditure designed to maintain and replace existing assets) and investments in inventory or accounts receivable. Much of this reinvestment may be unavoidable, because assets age and firms need working capital to generate sales. Some firms, though, may have potential for savings, especially in working capital. A retail firm that maintains inventory at 10% of sales, when the average for the sector is only 5%, can increase cash flows substantially if it can decrease its inventory levels to industry standards.

Increase Expected Growth

A firm with low current cash flows can still have high value if it can grow quickly during the high-growth period. As noted earlier, higher growth can come from either new investments or more efficiently utilizing existing assets:

- With new investments, higher growth has to come from either a *higher reinvestment rate or a higher return on capital on new investments, or both*. Higher growth does not always translate into higher value, since the growth effect can be offset by changes elsewhere in the valuation. Thus, higher reinvestment rates usually result in higher expected growth, but at the expense of lower cash flows, since more reinvestment reduces free cash flows, at least in the near term.[8] To the extent that the return on capital on the new investments

8 Acquisitions have to be considered as part of capital expenditures for reinvestment. Thus, it is relatively easy for firms to increase their reinvestment rates, but it's very difficult for these firms to maintain high returns on capital as they do so.

is higher (or lower) than the cost of capital, the value of the business will increase (or decrease) as the reinvestment rate rises. Similarly, higher returns on capital also cause expected growth to increase, but value can still go down if the new investments are in riskier businesses and there is a more-than-proportionate increase in the cost of capital.

- With existing assets, the effect is more unambiguous, with higher returns on capital translating into higher growth and higher value. A firm that can increase its return on capital on existing assets from 2 to 8% over the next five years will report healthy growth and higher value.

Which of these two avenues offers more promise for value creation? The answer depends on the firm in question. For mature firms with low returns on capital (especially when they are less than the cost of capital), extracting more growth from existing assets is likely to yield quicker results, at least in the short term. For smaller firms with relatively few assets in place, generating reasonable returns, growth has to come from new investments that generate healthy returns.

Lengthen the Period of High Growth

As noted, every firm, at some point in the future, becomes a stable-growth firm, growing at a rate equal to or less than the economy in which it operates. In addition, growth creates value only if the return on investments exceeds the cost of capital. Clearly, the longer high growth and excess returns last, other things remaining equal, the greater the firm's value. Note, however, that no firm should be able to earn excess returns for any length of time in a competitive product market, since competitors will be attracted by the excess returns into the business. Thus, implicit in the assumption that high growth occurs in conjunction with excess returns is the assumption that some barriers to entry prevent firms from earning excess returns for extended time periods.

Given this relationship between how long firms can grow at above-average rates and the existence of barriers to entry, one way firms can increase value is by augmenting existing barriers to entry and coming up with new barriers to entry. Another way of saying this is to note that companies that earn excess returns have significant competitive advantages. Nurturing these advantages can increase value.

Manage Nonoperating Assets

In the first three components of value creation, we focused on ways in which a firm can increase its value from operating assets. A significant chunk of a firm's value can derive from its nonoperating assets—cash and marketable securities, holdings in other companies, and pension fund assets (and obligations). To the extent that these assets are sometimes mismanaged, potential for value enhancement exists.

Cash and Marketable Securities

In conventional valuation, we assume that the cash and marketable securities a firm holds are added to the value of operating assets to arrive at the firm's value. Implicitly, we assume that cash and marketable securities are neutral investments (zero NPV investments) earning a fair rate of return, given their risk. Thus, a cash balance of $2 billion invested in treasury bills and commercial paper may earn a low rate of return, but that return is what you would expect to earn on these investments.

However, there are two scenarios in which a large cash balance may not be value-neutral and thus provide opportunities for value enhancement. The first is when *cash is invested at below market rates.* A firm with $2 billion in a cash balance held in a non-interest-bearing checking account is clearly hurting its stockholders. The second scenario arises when investors are concerned that *management will misuse cash to make poor investments or acquisitions.* In either case, a discount is applied to cash to reflect the likelihood that management will misuse the cash and the consequences of such misuse. Returning to the example of the company with $2 billion in cash, assume that investors believe that there is a 25% chance that this cash will be used to fund an acquisition and that the firm will overpay by $500 million on this acquisition. The value of cash at this company can be estimated as follows:

Value of Cash = Stated Cash Balance – Probability of Poor Investment * Cost of Poor Investment = $2 billion – 0.25 * 0.5 billion = $1.875 billion

If cash is being discounted, returning some or all of this cash to stockholders in the form of dividends or stock buybacks will make stockholders better off.

Holdings in Other Companies

When firms acquire stakes in other firms, the value of these holdings will be added to the value of operating assets to arrive at the value of the firm's equity. In conventional valuation, again, these holdings have a neutral effect on value. As with cash, potential problems with these cross-holdings can cause markets to discount them (relative to their true value).

Cross-holdings are difficult to value, especially when they are in subsidiary firms with different risk and growth profiles than the parent company. It is not surprising that firms with substantial cross-holdings in diverse businesses often find these holdings being undervalued by the market. In some cases, this undervaluation can be blamed on *information gaps*, caused by the failure to convey important details on growth, risk, and cash flows on cross-holdings to the markets. In other cases, the undervaluation may reflect market skepticism about the parent company's *capacity to manage its cross-holdings portfolio*; consider this a conglomerate discount.[9] If such a discount applies, the prescription for increased value is simple. Spinning off or divesting the cross-holdings and thus exposing their true value should make stockholders in the parent company better off.

Pension Fund Obligations (and Liabilities)

Most firms have large pension obligations and matching pension assets. To the extent that both the obligations and assets grow over time, they offer both threats and opportunities. A firm that mismanages its pension fund assets may find itself with an unfunded pension obligation, which reduces the value of its equity. On the other hand, a firm that generates returns that are higher than expected on its pension fund assets could end up with an overfunded pension plan and higher equity value.

There are ways of creating value from pension fund investments, but some are more questionable from an ethical perspective than others. The first is to invest pension fund assets better, generating

9 Studies looking at conglomerates conclude that they trade at a discount of between 5 and 10% on the value of the pieces they are composed of.

higher risk-adjusted returns and higher value for stockholders. The second (and more questionable) approach is to reduce pension fund obligations, either by renegotiating with employees or by passing on the obligation to other entities (such as the government) while holding on to pension fund assets.

Financial Restructuring

The one element of value that we did not address in the preceding chapter was the cost of financing. In this chapter, we will look at two aspects of financing that affect the cost of capital, and through it, the value we derive for a firm. First, we will look at how best to reflect changes in the mix of debt and equity used to fund operations in the cost of capital. Second, we will look at how the choices of financing (in terms of seniority, maturity, currency, and other add-on features) may affect the cost of funding and value.

Changing the Financing Mix

The question of whether changing the mix of debt and equity can alter the value of a business has long been debated in finance. Although the answer may seem obvious—debt, after all, is always less expensive than equity—the choice is not that simple. This section first describes the trade-off of debt versus equity in qualitative terms. Then we consider three tools that can be used to assess the effect of financing mix on value.

Debt Versus Equity: The Trade-Off

Debt has two key benefits, relative to equity, as a mode of financing. First, the interest paid on debt financing is tax-deductible, whereas cash flows to equity (such as dividends) generally are not.[10] Therefore, the higher the tax rate, the greater the tax benefit of using debt. This is absolutely true in the U.S. and is partially true in most other parts of the world. The second benefit of debt financing is more subtle. The use of debt, it can be argued, induces managers to be more disciplined in project selection. In other words, the managers of a company funded entirely by equity, and with strong cash flows, have a tendency to become lazy. For example, if a project turns sour, the managers can hide evidence of their failure under large operating cash flows, and few investors notice the effect in the aggregate. But if those same managers use debt to fund projects, bad projects are less likely to go unnoticed. Since debt requires the company to make interest payments, investing in too many bad projects can lead to financial distress or even bankruptcy, and managers may lose their jobs.

Relative to equity, the use of debt has three disadvantages—an expected bankruptcy cost, an agency cost, and the loss of future financing flexibility:

- The expected bankruptcy cost has two components. One is simply that as debt increases, so does the probability of bankruptcy. The other component is the cost of bankruptcy, which can be separated into two parts. One is the direct cost of going bankrupt, such as legal fees and court costs, which can eat up a significant portion of the value of the assets of a bankrupt firm. The other (and more devastating) cost is the effect on operations of

10 This is clearly the case in the U.S. In some other markets, such as Brazil, equity cash flows also provide tax advantages. Even in those markets, the tax advantages for debt tend to be higher than the tax advantages for equity.

being perceived as being in financial trouble. Thus, when customers learn that a company is in financial trouble, they tend to stop buying the company's products. Suppliers stop extending credit, and employees start looking for employment elsewhere. Borrowing too much money can create a downward spiral that ends in bankruptcy.

- Agency costs arise from the different and competing interests of equity investors and lenders in a firm. Equity investors see more upside from risky investments than lenders do. Consequently, left to their own devices, equity investors tend to take more risk in investments than lenders would want them to. They also alter financing and dividend policies to serve their interests. As lenders become aware of this potential, they alter the terms of loan agreements to protect themselves in two ways. One is by adding covenants to these agreements, restricting investing, financing, and dividend policies in the future; these covenants create legal and monitoring costs. The other way is by assuming that there will be some game-playing by equity investors and by charging higher interest rates to compensate for expected future losses. In both instances, the borrower bears the agency costs.
- As firms borrow more money today, they lose the capacity to tap this borrowing capacity in the future. The loss of future financing flexibility implies that the firm may be unable to make investments that it otherwise would have liked to make, simply because it will be unable to line up financing for these investments.

Table 11.5 captures the trade-off inherent in the use of debt as opposed to equity.

Table 11.5 Trade-Off on Debt Versus Equity

Advantages of Debt	Disadvantages of Debt
Tax benefits of debt: As tax rates increase, the tax benefits of debt increase.	Expected bankruptcy costs: As firms borrow more, the probability of bankruptcy increases. Multiplying by the cost of going bankrupt yields the expected bankruptcy cost.
Added discipline: Debt can make managers at all equity-funded firms with significant cash flows more prudent about the investments they make.	Agency costs: As conflicts between equity investors and lenders increase, the costs to borrowers rise (from monitoring costs and higher interest payments).
	Loss of future financing flexibility: As firms use their debt capacity today, they lose the capacity to use that debt capacity in the future.

In the special case where there are no taxes, no default risk, and no agency issues (between managers and stockholders as well as between stockholders and bondholders), debt has neither advantages nor disadvantages. This, of course, is the classic Miller-Modigliant world, where debt has no effect on value. In the real world, which has tax benefits and agency problems and default looms as a possibility, there is clearly an optimal mix of debt and equity for a firm. Firms can borrow too much as well as too little; both have adverse effects on value.

Tools for Assessing the Effect of the Financing Mix on Value

Three basic tools can help you determine how much debt a company can take on. The basic cost-of-capital approach ignores indirect bankruptcy costs. The enhanced cost-of-capital approach tries to incorporate indirect bankruptcy costs. The adjusted present value (APV) approach tries to capture the benefits of debt separately in value.

- In the cost-of-capital approach, the optimal debt-to-equity ratio is the one that minimizes a company's cost of capital. In effect, we keep operating cash flows fixed and assume that changing debt changes only the cost of capital. By minimizing the cost of capital, we maximize firm value.
- The enhanced cost-of-capital approach introduces indirect bankruptcy costs into the analysis. In this case, the optimal debt ratio creates a combination of cash flows and cost of capital that maximizes a company's value.
- In the adjusted present value approach, debt is separated from operations, and the company is valued as if it has no debt. Then, the positive and negative value effects of debt are considered as separate components.

To illustrate all three approaches, we will revisit the cost-of-capital computation for Hormel Foods from the first sidebar.

Cost-of-capital approach: The cost-of-capital approach has its roots in the discounted cash flow model for valuing a firm, where expected cash flows to the firm (prior to debt payments but after taxes and reinvestment needs) are discounted back at the cost of capital. If a company can keep its cash flows unchanged and lower its cost of capital, it will increase its present value. Therefore, the optimal debt ratio is the one at which the cost of capital is minimized.

At first glance, the answer to what will happen to the cost of capital as the debt ratio is increased seems trivial. The cost of debt is almost always lower than the cost of equity for a business. However, that solution misses the dynamic effects of introducing debt into a business. To see these effects, consider the two components that drive the cost of capital—the cost of equity and the cost of debt:

$$\text{Cost of Capital} = \text{Cost of Equity}\left(\frac{\text{Equity}}{\text{Debt} + \text{Equity}}\right) + \text{Pre-Tax Cost of Debt}\,(1 - \text{Tax Rate})\left(\frac{\text{Debt}}{\text{Debt} + \text{Equity}}\right)$$

As the company borrows more money, its equity becomes riskier. Even though it has the same operating assets (and income), it now has to make interest payments, and financial leverage magnifies the risk in equity earnings. Thus, the cost of equity is an increasing function of the debt ratio. Furthermore, as borrowing increases, so does default risk, which, in turn, increases the cost of debt. The trade-off on debt's effect on the cost of capital can be summarized as follows: Replacing equity with debt has the positive effect of replacing a more expensive mode of funding with a less expensive one. But in the process, the increased risk in both debt and equity pushes up the costs of both components, creating a negative effect. Whether the cost of capital increases or decreases is a function of which effect dominates. Figure 11.3 captures the trade-off.

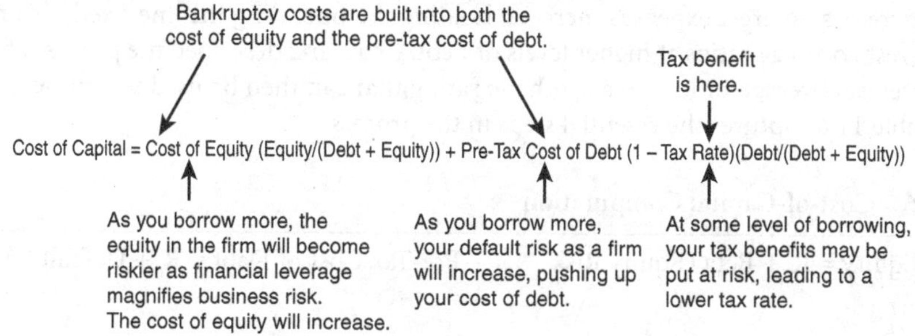

Figure 11.3: Trade-Off on Cost of Capital and Debt

To understand the mechanics of the cost-of-capital approach, we will work through it in steps:

1. Start with a risk-and-return model to estimate the cost of equity. For instance, with the capital asset pricing model, we use the following:

   Cost of Equity = R_f + Equity Beta (Equity Risk Premium)

   In this equation, R_f is the risk-free rate. Neither this number nor the equity risk premium will change as the debt ratio changes, leaving us with only one input to estimate—the equity beta. To estimate this number, you should start with an asset or unlevered beta.[11] As the company increases borrowing, recompute the debt-to-equity ratio, and compute a levered beta based on this recomputed ratio:[12]

   $$\text{Levered Beta} = \text{Unlevered Beta}\left[1+(1-t)\left(\frac{\text{Debt}}{\text{Equity}}\right)\right]$$

   The levered beta is the equity beta and will rise inexorably as the firm borrows more money. As the equity beta climbs, so will the cost of equity.

2. Consider the cost of debt, which is the rate at which you can borrow money long term today, given the firm's default risk:

   Pre-Tax Cost of Debt = R_f + Default Spread

   As the firm borrows more money, its default risk (and the default spread) goes up. To get a simple measure of default risk, estimate the interest expense at each debt level, and compute an interest coverage ratio based on expense:

   $$\text{Interest Coverage Ratio} = \frac{\text{Operating Income}}{\text{Interest Expense}}$$

11 The simplest way to estimate an unlevered beta is by looking at publicly traded firms in the business, computing an average regression beta across these firms, and then cleaning up these companies' debt-to-equity ratios. The process is described in more detail on my website.

12 This is one variation on the levered beta equation. Others assume a beta for debt, and still others ignore the tax effect. Using any of these approaches consistently yields similar results.

As debt increases, interest expenses increase; holding the operating income fixed, this results in lower interest coverage ratios at higher levels of debt. Chapter 2 described the process of converting the interest coverage ratio into a synthetic rating that can then be used to compute a default spread. Table 11.6 captures the essential steps in the process.

Table 11.6 Cost-of-Capital Computation

Cost of Equity = R_f + Beta (Equity Risk Premium)	Pre-Tax Cost of Debt = R_f + Default Spread
Start with the beta of the business (asset or unlevered beta).	Estimate the interest expense at each debt level.
As the firm borrows more, recompute the debt-to-equity (D/E) ratio.	Compute an interest coverage ratio based on expense: Interest Coverage Ratio = Operating Income / Interest Expense
Compute a levered beta based on this debt-to-equity ratio: Levered Beta = Unlevered Beta (1 + (1 – t) (D/E))	Estimate a synthetic rating at each level of debt.
Estimate the cost of equity based on the levered beta.	Use the rating to come up with a default spread that, when added to the risk-free rate, should yield the pre-tax cost of debt.

As powerful as the cost-of-capital approach is, it clearly has flaws that may lead firms to choose the wrong financing mix. In particular, three elements of the analysis are troublesome:

- **Indirect bankruptcy costs:** One flaw is the assumption that cash flow can remain fixed even as the debt ratio is increased. Indirect bankruptcy costs should preclude a company with a rising debt ratio (and lower bond ratings) from maintaining the operating income at its existing level.
- **Static approach in a dynamic world:** A second flaw is that the approach itself is static; it is based on the previous year's operating income and prevailing values for interest rates and default spreads. But conditions change. A recession for a cyclical firm, the loss of a major contract, or an increase in competition can all change a firm's optimal debt ratio.
- **Risk-bearing assumptions:** This approach makes rigid assumptions about the ways in which market risk and default risk are borne by different claimholders as a company continues to increase debt. For instance, the approach that we have used for levering and unlevering betas assumes that all market risk is borne only by the equity investors.

The Cost-of-Capital Approach: Hormel Foods

In the first sidebar, we looked at Hormel Foods in January 2009 and computed a cost of capital of 6.79%, based on the existing debt ratio of 10.39%. The cost-of-capital approach, in conjunction with the default spreads in January 2009, was used to derive the costs of debt and equity for Hormel at different debt ratios. Table 11.7 summarizes the results.

Table 11.7 Costs of Equity, Debt, and Capital for Hormel Foods

Debt Ratio	Beta	Cost of Equity	Bond Rating	Debt	Rate	Cost of Debt (After-Tax)	WACC	Value
0%	0.78	7.00%	AAA	3.60%	40.00%	2.16%	7.00%	$4,523
10%	0.83	7.31%	AAA	3.60%	40.00%	2.16%	6.80%	$4,665
20%	0.89	7.70%	AAA	3.60%	40.00%	2.16%	6.59%	$4,815
30%	0.97	8.20%	A+	4.60%	40.00%	2.76%	6.57%	$4,834
40%	1.09	8.86%	A–	5.35%	40.00%	3.21%	6.60%	$4,808
50%	1.24	9.79%	B+	8.35%	40.00%	5.01%	7.40%	$4,271
60%	1.47	11.19%	B–	10.85%	40.00%	6.51%	8.38%	$3,757
70%	1.86	13.52%	CCC	12.35%	40.00%	7.41%	9.24%	$3,398
80%	2.70	18.53%	CC	14.35%	38.07%	8.89%	10.81%	$2,892
90%	5.39	34.70%	CC	14.35%	33.84%	9.49%	12.01%	$2,597

We use the unlevered beta of 0.78 to estimate the levered beta at 10% increments on the debt ratio, up to 90% debt. The table also shows the effect of the rising debt ratio on the company's bond ratings, interest rate on debt, tax rate, cost of debt, weighted average cost of capital (WACC), and firm value. The firm value at each cost of capital is computed by taking the existing firm value and adding to it the present value of the change in annual financing costs that would accrue from moving to the new debt ratio. Thus, the firm value at a 30% debt ratio (the optimal) would be computed as follows:

$$\text{Firm Value @ 30\%} = \text{Existing Firm Value} + \frac{(\text{Cost of Capital}_{\text{Existing}} - \text{Cost of Capital}_{\text{30\% Debt}})\ \text{Existing Firm Value}}{(\text{Cost of Capital}_{\text{30\% Debt Ratio}} - \text{Stable Growth Rate})}$$

$$= \$4{,}672 \text{ million} + \frac{(.0679 - .0657)\,4672}{(.0657 - 0.0022)} = \$4{,}834 \text{ million}$$

The cost of equity and cost of debt both rise as debt increases, but the cost of capital drops and the firm value increases, at least initially. The benefits of debt exceed its costs, until the debt reaches 30%, at which point the cost of capital starts climbing again and the firm value begins to drop. To minimize the cost of capital for Hormel, the optimal debt ratio would be about 30%, or $1.4 billion in debt.

Enhanced cost-of-capital approach: Through the enhanced cost-of-capital approach, we introduce three innovations. First, indirect costs are built into the expected operating income. As the company's rating declines, the operating income is adjusted to reflect the loss in operating income that will occur when customers, suppliers, and investors react. Thus, we account for distress costs, such as indirect bankruptcy costs. Second, we can make the analysis more dynamic. Rather than examining a single, static number for operating income, we allow for the use of a distribution of operating income, thus allowing for a range of optimal debt ratios. Third, the levered beta formulations can be modified to reflect the fact that debt holders sometimes bear market risk (the beta of debt is greater than 0). Since the latter two modifications have little effect on the optimal debt ratio, we will describe just the first modification in this section.

To quantify the distress costs, we tie operating income to a company's bond rating. As shown in Table 11.8, once a company's rating drops below A (that is, below investment grade), distress costs occur in the form of a percentage decrease in earnings.

Table 11.8 Operating Income and Bond Rating

Rating	Drop in EBITDA
A or higher	No effect
A–	2.00%
BBB	5.00%
BB+	10.00%
BB	15.00%
B+	20.00%
B	20.00%
B–	25.00%
CCC	40.00%
CC	40.00%
C	40.00%
D	50.00%

The result of this enhancement to the cost-of-capital approach is shown in Table 11.9, where we compute the costs of capital, operating income, and firm values at different debt ratios for Hormel.

Table 11.9 Firm Value, Cost of Capital, and Debt Ratios: Enhanced Cost of Capital

Debt Ratio	Beta	Cost of Equity	Bond Rating	Debt	Rate	Cost of Debt (After-Tax)	WACC	Firm Value
0%	0.78	7.00%	AAA	3.60%	40.00%	2.16%	7.00%	$4,524
10%	0.83	7.31%	AAA	3.60%	40.00%	2.16%	6.80%	$4,665
20%	0.89	7.70%	AAA	3.60%	40.00%	2.16%	6.59%	$4,815
30%	0.97	8.20%	CCC	12.35%	40.00%	7.41%	7.96%	$1,987
40%	1.20	9.53%	D	22.35%	18.41%	18.24%	13.01%	$903
50%	1.44	10.97%	D	22.35%	14.73%	19.06%	15.01%	$781
60%	1.80	13.12%	D	22.35%	12.27%	19.61%	17.01%	$688
70%	2.39	16.72%	D	22.35%	10.52%	20.00%	19.01%	$615
80%	3.59	23.90%	D	22.35%	9.20%	20.29%	21.01%	$556
90%	7.18	45.45%	D	22.35%	8.18%	20.52%	23.01%	$507

As long as the bond ratings remain investment grade, Hormel's value remains intact. Its value, in fact, achieves its highest level at an AAA rating and a debt ratio of 20%. But as soon as the rating drops below investment grade, the distress costs begin to take effect, and Hormel's value drops precipitously. Thus, the debt ratio of 30% that seemed optimal under the unmodified cost-of-capital approach now appears entirely imprudent. The optimal debt ratio is now 20%, which means that Hormel should borrow about $1.2 billion, not $934 million.

Adjusted present value approach: In the adjusted present value approach, we explicitly add the value added by the tax benefits from the use of debt. We also subtract the value destroyed by higher bankruptcy costs from the value of the firm with no debt (unlevered firm value):

Firm Value = Unlevered Firm Value + (Tax Benefits of Debt – Expected Bankruptcy Costs from Debt)

As in the other two approaches, the optimum debt level is the one that maximizes the firm's value. Three steps are needed for the adjusted present value approach. First, the value of the unlevered company must be estimated. This can be done in two different ways:

- Estimate the unlevered beta, which is the cost of equity based on the unlevered beta. Then value the company using this cost of equity (which is also the cost of capital in an unlevered company).
- Start with the company's current market value, subtract the current tax benefits of debt, and add the expected bankruptcy costs from debt. In effect, you remove the components of market value that reflect the influence of the debt that the firm currently has on its books.

Second, calculate the present value of tax benefits at different levels of debt. The simplest assumption is that the tax benefits are perpetual, in which case the following equation applies:

Tax Benefits = Dollar Debt * Tax Rate

Note that this equation can be easily adapted to meet more general descriptions of the debt. The key is that the interest tax savings are being discounted at the pre-tax cost of debt to arrive at the value of the tax savings. (In some modifications of the APV approach, the tax benefits are discounted back at the unlevered cost of equity.)

Third, estimate a probability of bankruptcy at each debt level. Then multiply that by the cost of bankruptcy (including direct and indirect costs) to estimate the expected bankruptcy cost. The probability of bankruptcy can usually be estimated using the synthetic ratings process described earlier in computing the cost of debt. However, estimating direct and indirect costs of bankruptcy is the most difficult task in the APV exercise, so it is often skipped. But if these costs, which represent the disadvantages of debt, are not estimated, the optimal debt ratio will be 100%. This is why adjusted present value is the approach preferred by many proponents of high financial leverage.

Assuming that direct and indirect bankruptcy costs are roughly 25% of Hormel's firm value, we can compute the firm's value at different debt ratios, as shown in Table 11.10.

Table 11.10 Adjusted Present Value for Hormel Foods

Debt Ratio	Debt	Tax Rate	Unlevered Firm Value	Tax Benefits	Bond Rating	Probability of Default	Expected Bankruptcy Cost	Value of Levered Firm
0%	$0	40.00%	$4,477	$0	AAA	0.07%	$1	$4,476
10%	$467	40.00%	$4,477	$187	AAA	0.07%	$1	$4,663
20%	$934	40.00%	$4,477	$374	AAA	0.07%	$1	$4,850
30%	$1,402	40.00%	$4,477	$561	A+	0.60%	$8	$5,030
40%	$1,869	40.00%	$4,477	$748	A–	2.50%	$33	$5,192
50%	$2,336	40.00%	$4,477	$934	B	36.80%	$498	$4,913
60%	$2,803	40.00%	$4,477	$1,121	CCC	59.01%	$826	$4,772
70%	$3,271	40.00%	$4,477	$1,308	CC	70.00%	$1,012	$4,773
80%	$3,738	38.07%	$4,477	$1,423	CC	70.00%	$1,032	$4,867
90%	$4,205	27.99%	$4,477	$1,177	C	85.00%	$1,201	$4,452

Note that the unlevered firm value stays the same at every debt ratio. Up to a point, the tax benefits increase as debt increases, but they level off as soon as the interest expenses exceed the operating income. The expected bankruptcy costs also increase as the probability of bankruptcy rises at high debt ratios. The value of the firm reaches its highest point at a 40% debt ratio.

A summary of debt assessment tools: All three of these approaches rely on sustainable cash flow to determine the optimal debt ratio. They do not rely on market value or growth prospects, and I believe that is appropriate. The more stable and predictable a company's cash flow and the greater the magnitude of these cash flows—as a percentage of enterprise value—the higher the company's optimal debt ratio can be. Furthermore, the most significant benefit of debt is the tax benefit. Higher tax rates should lead to higher debt ratios.

Based on the insights offered so far, the best candidates for large amounts of financial leverage are mature or declining companies that have large, reliable cash flows. Growth companies—companies with their best days ahead of them—are not good candidates for high financial leverage. Such companies have high market values relative to cash flows. They usually need to plow these cash flows back into the business (rather than pay interest expenses) to generate future growth.

Finally, the macro environment has relatively little effect on optimal debt ratios. Two myths often asserted by market observers need to be dispelled. The first is that optimal debt ratios increase as interest rates decline. Certainly, it is true that lower interest rates decrease the cost of debt, but they also decrease the cost of equity, and it is the relative costs that determine financing choices. The second myth is that optimal debt ratios increase as default spreads decline. It is true that lower default spreads lower the cost of debt, but periods where default spreads decrease are also usually periods when equity risk premiums also go down. In other words, the cost of debt and equity both decline when default spreads and equity risk premiums decline. It is only when one measure declines while the other remains unchanged that one mode of financing dominates the other. The 2003 to 2007 period was an aberration in that sense, because default spreads decreased while equity risk premiums remained relatively stable. Not surprisingly, this provided an incentive for firms to borrow more money and for leveraged deals.

Financing Type

The fundamental principle in designing a firm's financing is to ensure that the cash flows on the debt match as closely as possible the cash flows on the asset. Firms that mismatch cash flows on debt and cash flows on assets (by using short-term debt to finance long-term assets, debt in one currency to finance assets in a different currency, or floating-rate debt to finance assets whose cash flows tend to be adversely impacted by higher inflation) end up with higher default risk, higher costs of capital, and lower firm values. To the extent that firms can use derivatives and swaps to reduce these mismatches, firm value can be increased.

Converting this intuitive statement about matching financing to assets and its effect on default risk into specifics can be difficult. In many cases, mismatching financing to assets shows up only after it has created a crisis. A firm that has used short-term funding to finance long-term assets is unable to refinance its debt and has to put its assets up for sale. We suggest that a much simpler lesson is embedded in the financing matching principle. Companies often use a bewildering array of debt and justify this complexity on the basis of cheapness, defined purely in terms of interest payments. Note that, if we follow this path, short-term debt will be cheaper than long-term debt in most periods, just as borrowing money in lower-inflation currencies (yen, dollar, euro) will be cheaper than borrowing money in high-inflation currencies (peso, ruble). Rather than trying to assign different costs to each layer of debt, we recommend a consolidation of all debt with a composite cost of debt attached to it. This composite cost should reflect the firm's overall default risk (rather than the default risk of a specific bond or debt) and the cost of borrowing long term (even if the firm uses short-term debt).

The Expected Value of Control

By considering the effects of operating and financing changes on value explicitly, rather than attaching an arbitrary control premium, we can get a much better handle on the value of control. In this section, we will first consolidate and summarize the effects of changing management on value. Then we will look at the likelihood that we can make this change. The product of these analyses is the expected value of control, which we then will use to examine a wide array of valuation issues.

The Value of Changing Management

If we consider value to be the end result of the investment, financing, and dividend decisions a firm makes, the firm's value is a function of how optimal (or suboptimal) we consider a firm's management to be. Suppose we estimate a value for the firm, assuming that existing management practices continue, and call this a status quo value. Also suppose we reestimate the value of the same firm, assuming that it is optimally managed, and call this estimate the optimal value. The value of changing management can be written as follows:

Value of Management Change = Optimal Firm Value – Status Quo Value

The value of changing management is a direct consequence of how much we can improve how the firm is run. The value of changing management will be zero in a firm that is already optimally managed but will be substantial for a firm that is badly managed.

Retracing the steps through value, it should also be quite clear that the pathway to value enhancement will vary for different firms. Suboptimal management can manifest itself in different ways for different firms. For firms where existing assets are poorly managed, the increase in value will be primarily from managing those assets more efficiently—higher cash flows from these assets and efficiency growth. For firms where investment policy is sound but financing policy is not, the increase in value will come from changing the mix of debt and equity and a lower cost of capital. Table 11.11 considers potential problems in existing management, fixes to these problems, and the value consequences.

Table 11.11 Ways of Increasing Value

Potential Problem	Manifestations	Possible Fixes	Value Consequence
Existing assets are poorly managed.	Operating margins are lower than the peer group, and return on capital is lower than the cost of capital.	Manage existing assets better. This may require divesting some poorly performing assets.	Higher operating margin and return on capital on existing assets, leading to higher operating income. Efficiency growth in near term as return on capital improves.

Potential Problem	Manifestations	Possible Fixes	Value Consequence
Management is underinvesting. (It is too conservative in exploiting growth opportunities.)	Low reinvestment rate and high return on capital in high-growth period.	Reinvest more in new investments, even if it means lower return on capital (albeit > cost of capital).	Higher growth rate and higher reinvestment rate during high-growth period, creating higher value because growth is value-creating.
Management is overinvesting. (It is investing in value-destroying new investments.)	High reinvestment rate and return on capital that is lower than cost of capital.	Reduce reinvestment rate until marginal return on capital is at least equal to cost of capital.	Lower growth rate and lower reinvestment rate during high-growth period, resulting in higher value, because growth is no longer value-destroying.
Management is not exploiting possible strategic advantages.	Short or nonexistent high-growth period with low or no excess returns.	Build on competitive advantages.	Longer high-growth period, with larger excess returns, leading to higher value.
Management is too conservative in its use of debt.	Debt ratio is lower than optimal (or industry average).	Increase debt financing.	Higher debt ratio and lower cost of capital, resulting in higher firm value.
Management is overusing debt.	Debt ratio is higher than optimal.	Reduce debt financing.	Lower debt ratio and lower cost of capital, generating higher firm value.
Management is using the wrong type of financing.	Cost of debt is higher than it should be, given the firm's earning power.	Match debt to assets using swaps, derivatives, or refinancing.	Lower cost of debt and cost of capital, creating higher firm value.
Management holds excess cash and is not trusted by the market with the cash.	Cash and marketable securities are a large percentage of firm value. The firm has poor track record on investments.	Return cash to stockholders, either as dividends or stock buybacks.	Firm value is reduced by cash paid out, but stockholders gain because the cash was discounted in the firm's hands.

Table 11.11 continued

Potential Problem	Manifestations	Possible Fixes	Value Consequence
Management has made investments in unrelated companies.	Substantial cross-holdings in other companies that are being undervalued by the market.	As a first step, try to be more transparent about cross-holdings. If that is insufficient, divest cross-holdings.	Firm value is reduced by divested cross-holdings but is increased by cash received from divestitures. When cross-holdings are undervalued, the latter should exceed the former.

A Valuation of Hormel Foods: Status Quo Versus Optimal

To value control at Hormel, we value the firm twice—first with existing management continuing to run the firm, and then with an optimal management team in place. For the status quo value, we assume that the firm will stay with its existing financing mix (10.5% debt). We also assume that the firm will stay with its existing investment policy, thus preserving current reinvestment rates and returns on capital for the next three years. At the end of the third year, we assume that the firm will be in stable growth and that excess returns will fade to zero. Table 11.12 summarizes the assumptions used to value Hormel Foods under the status quo.

Table 11.12 Inputs for Valuation: Hormel Foods Status Quo

	High-Growth Period	Stable-Growth Phase
Length of high-growth period	3	After year 3
Growth rate	2.75%	2.35%
Debt ratio used in cost-of-capital calculation	10.39%	10.39%
Beta used for stock	0.83	0.90
Risk-free rate	2.35%	2.35%
Risk premium	6.00%	6.00%
Cost of debt	3.60%	4.50%
Tax rate	40.00%	40.00%
Cost of capital	6.79%	7.23%
Return on capital	14.34%	7.23%
Reinvestment rate	19.14%	32.52%

There are two things to note about the high-growth phase. The first is that the high-growth period is short and the growth rate during the period is anemic (2.75%). This reflects the conservative reinvestment policy of the existing management. The return on capital on existing investments is healthy (14.34%), but the firm reinvests only 19.14% of its after-tax operating income. The second thing to note is that the low growth rate we have estimated by itself is insufficient to allow us to use a stable-growth model, because it is higher than the risk-free rate, and the excess returns generated currently (almost 7.45%) are incompatible with a stable firm. Table 11.13 summarizes our estimates of cash flows for the first three years and the present value of these cash flows for Hormel Foods.

Table 11.13 Hormel Foods Cash Flows and Value Today

	Current	Year 1	Year 2	Year 3
EBIT * (1 – tax rate)	$315	$324	$333	$342
– Reinvestment	$60	$62	$64	$65
Free cash flow to firm	$255	$262	$269	$276
Cost of capital		6.79%	6.79%	6.79%
Present value		**$245**	**$236**	**$227**

In stable growth, we not only move the growth rate down to the risk-free rate; we also assume that the return on capital drops to equal the cost of capital of 7.23%. The cost of capital increases marginally because we increase the beta in stable growth:

$$\text{Reinvestment Rate} = \frac{g_{Stable}}{ROC_{Stable}} = \frac{2.35\%}{7.23\%} = 32.52\%$$

$$\text{Terminal Value} = \frac{\text{After-Tax Operating Income}_3\ (1+g_{Stable})(1-\text{Reinvestment Rate})}{(\text{Cost of Capital}_{\text{Stable}} - g_{\text{Stable}})}$$

$$= \frac{342(1.0235)(1-.3252)}{(.0723-.0235)} = \$4{,}840 \text{ million}$$

Adding the present value of the terminal value, discount back three years at the current cost of capital of 6.79%, to the present value of the cash flows for the first three years, gives us a value for the operating assets of $4,682 million. Adding the firm's cash holdings ($155 million), subtracting debt ($491 million), and the value of management options outstanding ($53 million) yields the value of equity in common stock. When divided by the number of shares outstanding (134.53 million), this generates a value per share of $31.91:

$$\text{Value per Share} = \frac{4682 + 155 - 491 - 53}{134.53} = \$31.91 / Share$$

To value the firm under optimal management, we make three key changes:

- **More debt-based financing**: Based on our analysis of Hormel's financing mix in the preceding section, we increase the debt ratio from 10.56% to 20%. Even allowing for the higher risk in equity (the beta goes up to 0.90), the firm's cost of capital decreases to 6.63% in the high-growth phase and to 6.74% in stable growth.
- **Higher reinvestment rate**: We assume that the firm will be more aggressive in seeking out new investments, using a higher reinvestment rate of 40%, but we assume that the return on capital will drop to 14% as a result.
- **Longer growth period**: Hormel has several key brand names in its stable. We will assume that it can exploit these brand names to generate excess returns for a longer time period—five years instead of three.

The resulting valuation inputs are summarized in Table 11.14.

Table 11.14 Valuation Inputs: Hormel Foods Optimal Management

	High Growth	Stable Growth
Length of high-growth period	5	Forever
Growth rate	5.60%	2.35%
Debt ratio used in cost-of-capital calculation	20.00%	20.00%
Beta used for stock	0.90	0.90
Risk-free rate	2.35%	2.35%
Risk premium	6.00%	6.00%
Cost of debt	3.60%	4.50%
Tax rate	40.00%	40.00%
Cost of capital	0.10%	6.74%
Return on capital	14.00%	6.74%
Reinvestment rate	40.00%	34.87%

Table 11.15 shows the cash flows, terminal value, and value of the firm today that emerge from these assumptions.

Table 11.15 Cash Flows and Value Today: Optimal Management

	Current	Year 1	Year 2	Year 3	Year 4	Year 5
EBIT * (1 – tax rate)	$315	$333	$351	$371	$392	$414
– Reinvestment	$131	$133	$141	$148	$157	$165
Free cash flow to firm	$184	$200	$211	$223	$235	$248
Terminal value						$6,282
Cost of capital		6.63%	6.63%	6.63%	6.63%	6.63%
Present value		$187	$185	$184	$182	$5,655
Value of operating assets	$5,474					

To complete the story, we make the same adjustments for cash, debt, and management options that we did in the status quo valuation to arrive at a value per share:

$$\text{Value per Share} = \frac{5474 + 155 - 491 - 53}{134.53} = \$37.80/\text{Share}$$

The value per share that we obtain for Hormel Foods, with a different management team in place, is $37.80, an increase of $5.89 over the status quo value per share. That would represent the overall value of control at Hormel Foods.

The Probability of Changing Management

Although the value of changing management in a badly managed firm can be substantial, increased value will be created only if management policies are changed. While this change can sometimes be accomplished by convincing existing managers to modify their ways, all too often it requires replacing the managers themselves. If the likelihood of management change is low, the expected value of control also is low. In this section, we first consider the mechanisms for changing management, and then we discuss some of the factors that determine the likelihood of management change.

Mechanisms for Changing Management

It is difficult to change how a company is run, but in general, it can be done in four ways:

- **Activist investors** are a variation on moral or at least economic suasion. One or more large institutional investors introduce shareholder proposals designed primarily to improve corporate governance, holding the threat of more extreme action over the heads of managers. A mix of pension funds and private investors has shown a willingness to confront incumbent managers. These activist investors, with the weight of their large stockholdings, can present proposals to stockholders to change policies that they feel are inimical to shareholder interests. Often, these proposals are centered on corporate governance. Changing how the board of directors is chosen and removing anti-takeover clauses in the corporate charter are common examples.

- **Proxy contests** are where an investor who is unhappy with how the firm is being run challenges the incumbent managers for proxy votes. With sufficient votes, the investor can get representation on the board and may be able to change management policy. In most companies, investors vote with their feet—selling their stockholdings when dissatisfied—and thus concede power to incumbent managers. In some companies, however, activist investors compete with incumbent managers for the proxies of individual investors, with the intent of getting their nominees for the board elected. While they may not always succeed at winning majority votes, they do put managers on notice that they are accountable to stockholders. Evidence exists that proxy contests occur more often in companies that are poorly run, and that they create significant changes in management policy and improvements in operating performance.
- **Replacing management**: The third method is to try to replace the existing managers in the firm with more competent ones. In publicly traded firms, this requires a board of directors who are willing to challenge management. Top management turnover at most firms is usually a consequence of retirement or death, and the successor usually follows in the incumbent's footsteps. In some cases, though, top managers are forced out by the board because of displeasure over their performance, and new management is brought in to head the firm. This provides an opening for a reassessment of the firm's current management policies and for significant changes. While forced management turnover was uncommon outside the U.S. until recent years, it is becoming more frequent.
- **Hostile acquisition**: The fourth and most extreme method is a hostile acquisition of the firm by an investor or another firm. The incumbent management is usually replaced after the acquisition, and management policy is revamped. Investor pressure, CEO turnover, and proxy contests are all internal processes for management discipline. When these fail, the only weapon stockholders have left is to hope the firm will become the target of a hostile acquisition, where the acquirer will take over the company and change how it is run. For hostile acquisitions to be effective as a management disciplining mechanism, several pieces have to fall into place. First, firms that are badly managed and run should be targeted for acquisitions. Second, the system should give potential hostile acquirers a reasonable chance of success; the bias toward incumbency should be negligible or small. Third, the acquirer has to change both the managers and the management policies of the target company after the acquisition.

Determinants of Management Change

There is a strong bias toward preserving incumbent management at firms, even when there is widespread agreement that the management is incompetent or does not have the interests of stockholders at heart. Some of the difficulties arise from the institutional tilt toward incumbency, and others are put in place to make management change difficult, if not impossible. In general, there are four determinants of whether management will be changed at a firm:

- **Institutional concerns:** The first group of constraints on challenging incumbent management in companies that are perceived to be badly managed and badly run is institutional. Some of these constraints can be traced to difficulties associated with raising the capital needed to fund the challenge, some to state restrictions on takeovers, and some to inertia:
  - You need to raise capital to acquire firms that are poorly managed, and any constraints on that process can impede hostile acquisitions. It should come as no surprise that hostile acquisitions are rare in economies where capital markets—equity and debt—are not well-developed. In general, then, we would argue that the likelihood of changing the management in badly managed firms is greater when financial markets are open and funds are accessible at low cost to a wide variety of investors (not just to large corporations in good credit standing).
  - Many financial markets outside the U.S. impose significant legal and institutional restrictions on takeover activity. Few markets forbid takeovers, but the cumulative effect of the restrictions is to make hostile takeovers just about impossible.
  - If the stockholders in these firms are passive and don't respond to the pleas of acquirers or other investors by tendering their shares in an acquisition or their proxies in a proxy contest, it is very likely that incumbent managers will stay entrenched.
- **Firm-specific constraints:** In some firms, incumbent managers, no matter how incompetent, are protected from stockholder pressure by actions taken by these firms. This protection can take the form of anti-takeover amendments to the corporate charter, elaborate cross-holding structures, and the creation of shares with different voting rights. In some cases, the incumbent managers may own large-enough stakes in the firm to stifle any challenge to their leadership.

  The time-honored way to protect incumbent management is to issue shares with different voting rights. In its most extreme form, the incumbent managers hold all the shares with voting rights and issue only nonvoting shares to the public. This is the rule rather than the exception in much of Latin America and Europe,[13] where companies routinely issue nonvoting shares to the public and withhold voting shares for the controlling stockholders and managers. In effect, this allows the insiders in these firms to control their destiny with a small percentage of all outstanding stock. More generally, firms can accomplish the same objective by issuing shares with different voting rights.
- **Corporate holding structures:** Control can be maintained over firms with a variety of corporate structures, including pyramids and cross-holdings. In a pyramid structure, an investor uses control in one company to establish control in other companies. For instance, company X can own 50% of company Y and use the assets of company Y to buy 50% of company Z. In effect, the investor who controls company X ends up

13 Faccio, M. and L. Lang, 2002, "The Ultimate Ownership of European Corporations," *Journal of Financial Economics*, v65, pp. 365–396. They analyzed 5,232 firms in Europe and found that although 37% are widely held, 44% are family controlled, with dual class shares and pyramid structures.

controlling companies Y and Z as well. Studies indicate that pyramids are a common approach to consolidating control in family-run companies in Asia and Europe. In a cross-holding structure, companies own shares in each other, thus allowing the group's controlling stockholders to run all the companies with less than 50% of the outstanding stock. The vast majority of Japanese companies (keiretsus) and Korean companies (chaebols) in the 1990s were structured as cross-holdings, immunizing management at these companies from stockholder pressure.

- **Large shareholder/managers**: In some firms, the presence of a large stockholder as a manager is a significant impediment to a hostile acquisition or management change. Consider a firm like Oracle, where founder/CEO Larry Ellison owns almost 30% of the outstanding stock. Even without a dispersion of voting rights, he can effectively stymie hostile acquirers. Why would such a stockholder/manager mismanage a firm when it costs him or her a significant portion of market value? The first reason can be traced to hubris and ego. Founder CEOs, with little to fear from outside investors, tend to centralize power and can make serious mistakes. The second reason is that what is good for the inside stockholder, who often has all of his or her wealth invested in the firm, may not be good for the other investors in the firm.

What May Cause the Likelihood of Management Changing to Shift?

If there is one constant in markets, it is change. Managers who are viewed as impervious to outside challenge can find their authority challenged. In this section, we consider some of the factors that may cause this shift:

- The first is that the rules governing corporate governance do change over time, sometimes in favor of incumbent managers and sometimes in favor of stockholders. In recent years, for instance, many emerging-market economies have made it easier for stockholders in companies to challenge managers. A similar trend can be seen in Europe, where incumbent managers clearly had the upper hand until a few years ago. The impetus for this reform has come from institutional investors who have grown tired of being ignored by managers when confronted with clear evidence of poor decisions.
- Even when the rules allow investors to challenge management decisions, most investors take the passive route of voting with their feet. It is here that the presence of activist investors who are willing to take large positions in companies and use these holdings as a platform to challenge and change management practices makes a difference. In the U.S., these investors made their presence felt in the 1980s.[14] Although it has taken a little longer in the rest of the world, activist investors are part of the investment landscape in more and more countries now.

14 Del Guercio, D. and J. Hawkins, 1999, "The Motivation and Impact of Pension Fund Activism," *Journal of Financial Economics*, v52, pp. 293–340. The authors studied five activist pension funds: CREF, CALPERS, CALSTRS, SWIB, and NYC. These accounted for 20% of all pension fund investment between 1987 and 1993. The authors concluded that companies activist investors own stock in are more likely to be targets of hostile takeovers and management change than other companies.

- Nothing changes the perceptions of management's vulnerability to an outside challenge more than a well-publicized hostile takeover or the ouster of a CEO of a large firm in the same market. In the late 1990s, for instance, the hostile acquisition of Telecom Italia by Olivetti changed the landscape in Europe and changed the perception that the managers at large European firms were immune from stockholder challenges.

Estimating the Probability of Management Change

While the determinants of management change can be listed, it is far more difficult to quantitatively estimate the probability that change will occur. One statistical approach that is promising is a logit or probit, where we assess the probability of management change by contrasting the characteristics of firms where management has changed in the past with firms where that has not occurred. Researchers have applied this technique to look at both acquisitions and forced CEO change.

In one of the first papers to assess the likelihood of takeovers by comparing target firms in acquisitions to firms that were not targets, Palepu (1986) noted that target firms in takeovers were *smaller* than nontarget firms and *invested inefficiently*.[15] In a later paper, North (2001) concluded that firms with *low insider/managerial ownership* were more likely to be targeted in acquisitions.[16] Neither paper specifically focused on hostile acquisitions, though. Nuttall (1999) found that target firms in hostile acquisitions tended to *trade at lower price-to-book ratios* than other firms. Weir (1997) added to this finding by noting that target firms in hostile acquisitions also earned lower returns on invested capital.[17] Finally, Pinkowitz (2003) finds no evidence to support the conventional wisdom that firms with substantial cash balances are more likely to become targets of hostile acquisitions.[18] In summary, target firms in hostile acquisitions tend to be smaller, trade at lower multiples of book value, and earn relatively low returns on their investments.[19]

While many CEO changes are voluntary (retirement or job switching), some CEOs are forced out by the board. In recent years, researchers have examined when forced CEO turnover is most likely to occur:

15 Palepu, K. G., "Predicting Take-Over Targets : A Methodological and Empirical Analysis," *Journal of Accounting and Economics*, 8 (1986), pp. 3–35.

16 North, D. S., 2001, "The Role of Managerial Incentives in Corporate Acquisitions: the 1990s Evidence," *Journal of Corporate Finance*, 7, pp. 125–149.

17 Nuttall, R., "Take-Over Likelihood Models for UK Quoted Companies," Nuffield College working paper, Oxford University (1999); Weir, C. "Corporate Governance, Performance and Take-Overs: An Empirical Analysis of UK Mergers," *Applied Economics*, 29 (1997), pp. 1465–1475.

18 Pinkowitz, L., 2003, "The Market for Corporate Control and Corporate Cash Holdings," working paper, SSRN. His study of hostile acquisitions between 1985 and 1994 concluded that firms with large cash balances are less (not more) likely to be targets of hostile acquisitions.

19 In a contrary finding, Franks and Mayer (1996) found no evidence of poor performance in target firms in hostile acquisitions in the UK. Franks, J. and C. Mayer, "Hostile Takeovers and the Correction of Management Failure," *Journal of Financial Economics*, v40, pp. 163–181.

- The first factor is *stock price and earnings performance*, with forced turnover more likely in firms that have performed poorly relative to their peer group and to expectations.[20] One manifestation of poor management is overpaying on acquisitions. Evidence exists that CEOs of acquiring firms that pay too much on acquisitions are far more likely to be replaced than CEOs who do not do such acquisitions.[21]
- The second factor is the *structure of the board*, with forced CEO changes more likely to occur when the board is small[22] and composed of outsiders,[23] and when the CEO is not also the chairman of the board of directors.[24]
- The third and related factor is the *ownership structure*; forced CEO changes are more common in companies with high institutional and low insider holdings.[25] They also seem to occur more frequently in firms that are more dependent on equity markets for new capital.[26]
- The final factor is industry structure, with CEOs more likely to be replaced in competitive industries.[27]

In summary, firms where you see forced CEO change share some characteristics with firms that are targets of hostile acquisitions. They are poorly managed and run. But they tend to have much more effective boards of directors and more activist investors who can change management without turning over the firm to a hostile acquirer.

A widely held misconception is that control is an issue only when you do acquisitions. To the contrary, we argue that the stock price of every publicly traded firm includes an expected value for control, reflecting both the likelihood that the firm's management will be changed and the value of making that change.

20 Warner, J., R. Watts, and K. Wruck, 1988, "Stock Prices and Top Management Changes," *Journal of Financial Economics*, v20, pp. 461–492; Murphy, K. and J. Zimmerman, 1993, "Financial Performance Surrounding CEO Turnover," *Journal of Accounting and Economics*, v16, pp. 273–316; Puffer, S. and J. B. Weintrop, 1991, "Corporate Performance and CEO Turnover: The Role of Performance Expectations," *Administrative Science Quarterly*, v36, pp. 1–19.

21 Lehn, K. and M. Zhao, 2004, "CEO Turnover After Acquisitions: Do Bad Bidders Get Fired?," working paper, University of Pittsburgh.

22 Faleye, O., 2003, "Are large boards poor monitors? Evidence from CEO turnover," working paper, SSRN. Using a proportional hazard model, he found that every additional director on the board reduces the probability of a forced CEO change by 13%.

23 Weisbach, M., 1988, "Outside Directors and CEO Turnover," *Journal of Financial Economics*, v20, pp. 431–460.

24 Goyal, V. K. and C. W. Park, 2001, "Board Leadership Structure and CEO Turnover," *Journal of Corporate Finance*, v8, pp. 49–66.

25 Dennis, D. J., D. K. Dennis, and A. Sarin, 1997, "Ownership Structure and Top Executive Turnover," *Journal of Financial Economics*, v45, pp. 193–221.

26 Hillier, D., S. Linn, and P. McColgan, 2003, "Equity Issuance, Corporate Governance Reform and CEO Turnover in the UK," working paper, SSRN. They found that CEOs are more likely to be forced out just before new equity issues or placings.

27 DeFondt, M. L. and C. W. Park, 1999, "The effect of competition on CEO turnover," *Journal of Accounting and Economics*, v27, pp. 35–56.

The Probability of Control Changing: Hormel Foods

Although making a precise estimate of the probability of control changing may be difficult with Hormel Foods, the fact that the Hormel Foundation holds 47.4% of the outstanding stock in the company is a key factor. The foundation is run by independent trustees, but it retains strong links with the incumbent managers and is unlikely to acquiesce to a hostile acquisition that will change key parts of the company. Management change, if it does come, will have to occur with the agreement of the foundation. Consequently, we will estimate a probability of only 10% of the change occurring. In effect, the firm must be under extreme duress before the foundation will step in and agree to a change.

Implications

Once we have a measure of the expected value of control, it is useful not just to acquirers who are trying to buy a firm, but also to any investor in the firm. The market price we observe for a publicly traded stock should reflect the expected value of control, as should the premium we observe for voting shares, relative to nonvoting shares.

Expectations and Stock Prices

To see how the expected value of control shows up in stock prices, assume that you live in a world where management change never happens and that the market is reasonably efficient about assessing the values of the firms it prices. In this scenario, every company trades at its status quo value, reflecting both the strengths and weaknesses of existing management. Now assume that you introduce the likelihood of management change into this market, in the form of either hostile acquisitions or CEO changes. If the market remains reasonably efficient, the stock price of every firm should rise to reflect this likelihood:

Market Value = Status Quo Value + (Optimal Value – Status Quo Value) * Probability of Management Changing

The degree to which this affects stock prices varies widely across firms. The expected value of control is greatest for badly managed firms that have a high likelihood of management turnover. It is lowest for well-managed firms and for firms that have little or no chance of management change.

Many people are skeptical about the capacity of markets to make these assessments with any degree of accuracy and whether investors actually try to estimate the expected value of control. The evidence indicates that although markets may not use sophisticated models to make these assessments, they do try to value and price in control.

To the extent that the expected value of control is already built into the market value, there are important implications for acquirers, investors, and researchers:

- **Paying a premium over the market price can result in overpayment.** If the current market price incorporates some or all of the value of control, the effect of management change on market value (as opposed to status quo value) will be small or nonexistent. In a firm where the market already assumes that management will be changed and builds this into the stock price, acquirers should be wary of paying a premium on the current market price, even for a badly managed firm. Consider an extreme example. Assume that you have a firm with a status quo value of $100 million and an optimally managed value of $150 million. Also assume that the market is already building in a 90% chance that the firm's management will change in the near future. The market value of this company will be $145 million. If an acquirer decides to pay a substantial premium (say, $40 million) for this firm, based on the fact that the company is badly managed, he will overpay substantially. In this example, he will pay $185 million for a company with a value of $150 million.

- **Anything that causes market perception of the likelihood of management change to shift can have large effects on all stocks.** A hostile acquisition of one company, for instance, may lead investors to change their assessments of the likelihood of management change for all companies, and this can cause an increase in stock prices. Since hostile acquisitions often are clustered in a particular sector—oil companies in the 1980s, for instance—it is not surprising that a hostile acquisition of a single company often leads to increases in stock prices for companies in its peer group.
- **Poor corporate governance equals lower stock prices.** The price of poor corporate governance can be seen in stock prices. After all, the essence of good corporate governance is that it gives stockholders the power to change the management of badly managed companies. Consequently, stock prices in a market where corporate governance is effective will reflect a high likelihood of change for bad management and a higher expected value for control. In contrast, it is difficult, if not impossible, to dislodge managers in markets where corporate governance is weak. Stock prices in these markets therefore incorporate lower expected values for control. The differences in corporate governance are likely to manifest themselves most in the worst-managed firms in the market.

Market Prices and the Expected Value of Control

Consider the earlier valuation of Hormel Foods. We estimated both the status quo and the optimal value of the equity in the company and arrived at the following results:

	Value of Equity	Value per Share
Status quo	$4,293 million	$31.91 per share
Optimally managed	$5,085 million	$37.80 per share

We estimated the probability of management change happening at only 10%. If we assume that these are all reasonable estimates, the expected value per share for Hormel is as follows:

Expected Value per Share = $31.91 (.90) + $37.80 (.10) = $32.51

If our assessments are correct, the stock should be trading at $32.51. The actual market price at the time of this valuation was about $32.25. Assuming that both the market price and our values per share are correct, the market price can be written in terms of a probability of control changing and the expected value of control:

Expected Value per Share = Status Quo Value + Probability of Control Changing * (Optimal Value – Status Quo Value)

$32.25 = $31.91 + Probability of Control Changing ($37.80 – $31.91)

The market is attaching a probability of 5.6% that management policies can be changed.

Voting and Nonvoting Shares

To link the premium on voting shares to the expected value of control, let's begin with an extreme and very simple example. Assume that you have a company with n_v voting shares and n_{nv} nonvoting shares and that the voting shareholders have total control of the business. Thus, they are free to ignore the views of nonvoting shares in the event of a hostile takeover, and they negotiate the best deal that they can for themselves with the acquirer.[28] Assume further that this firm has a status quo value of V_b and an optimal value of V_a and that the likelihood of management changing in this firm is π. Since the nonvoting shares have absolutely no say in whether the management can be changed, the value per nonvoting share is based purely on the status quo value:

$$\text{Value per Nonvoting Share} = V_b / (n_v + n_{nv})$$

The voting shares will trade at a premium that reflects the expected value of control:

$$\text{Value per Voting Share} = V_b / (n_v + n_{nv}) + (V_a - V_b)\, \pi / n_v$$

The premium on voting shares should therefore be a function of the probability that there will be a change in management at that firm (π) and the value of changing management ($V_a - V_b$). To the extent that nonvoting shareholders are protected or can extract some of the expected value of control, the difference between voting and nonvoting shares will be lower. It is possible, for instance, for nonvoting shares to gain some of the value of control if this is accomplished by changing managers, rather than by a hostile takeover. In that case, the value of the firm increases, and all shareholders benefit.

One special category of voting shares is called golden shares. We sometimes see this in government-owned firms that have been privatized. These shares are retained by the government after the privatization; essentially they give the government veto power over major decisions made by the firm. In effect, they allow the government to retain some or a great deal of control over how the firm is run. While golden shares are not traded, they affect the values of shares that are traded by reducing the expected value of control.

28 In reality, even nonvoting shareholders receive at least partial protection in the event of a takeover, and they share in some of the benefits.

If the primary reason for the voting share premium is the value of control, several conclusions follow:

- The difference between voting and nonvoting shares should go to zero if there is no chance of changing management/control. This is clearly a function of the concentration of ownership of the voting shares. If there are relatively few voting shares, held entirely by insiders, the probability of management change may very well be close to zero, and voting shares should trade at the same price as nonvoting shares. On the other hand, if a significant percentage of voting shares is held by the public, the probability of management change should be higher, and the voting shares should reflect this premium.
- Other things remaining equal, voting shares should trade at a larger premium over nonvoting shares at badly managed firms than well-managed firms. Since the expected value of control is close to zero in well-managed firms, voting shares and nonvoting shares should trade at roughly the same price in these firms. In a badly managed firm, the expected value of control is likely to be higher, as should the voting share premium.
- Other things remaining equal, the smaller the number of voting shares relative to nonvoting shares, the higher the premium on voting shares should be. Since the expected value of control is divided by the number of voting shares to get the premium, the smaller that number, the greater the value attached to each share. This has to be weighed against the reality that when the number of voting shares is small, it is more likely to be held entirely by incumbent managers and insiders, thus reducing the likelihood of management change.
- Other things remaining equal, the greater the percentage of voting shares that are available for trading by the general public (float), the higher the premium on voting shares should be. When voting shares are entirely or predominantly held by managers and insiders, the probability of control changing is small, and so is the expected value of control.
- Any event that illustrates the power of voting shares relative to nonvoting shares is likely to affect the premium at which all voting shares trade. The expected value of control is a function of perceptions that management at these firms can be changed. In a market where incumbent managers are entrenched, voting shares may not trade at a premium, because investors assess no value to control. A hostile acquisition in this market or a regulatory change providing protection to nonvoting shareholders can increase the expected value of control for all companies and, with it, the voting share premium.

In summary, we would expect the voting share premium to be highest in badly managed firms where voting shares are dispersed among the public. We would expect it to be smallest in well-managed firms and in firms where the voting shares are concentrated in the hands of insiders and management.

Valuing Voting and Nonvoting Shares

To value voting and nonvoting shares, we will consider two companies—Embraer, the Brazilian aerospace company, in 2004, and Under Armour in 2009, to complete the valuation we commenced in Chapter 10. As is typical of most Brazilian companies, Embraer has common (voting) shares and preferred (nonvoting shares). Under Armour has two classes of shares, with all the voting shares held by founder Kevin Plank.

Embraer

We value the company twice—first under the status quo, and then under optimal management. With existing management in place, we estimate a value of 12.5 billion Brazilian Reais ($R) for the equity. This is based on the assumption that the company will continue to maintain its conservative (low-debt) financing policy and high returns on investments (albeit with a low reinvestment rate), at least for the near term. We then revalue the firm at 14.7 billion $R, assuming that the firm will be more aggressive both in its use of debt and in its reinvestment policy.

The company has 242.5 million voting shares and 476.7 nonvoting shares. The probability of management change is relatively low, partly because the bulk of the voting shares are held by insiders[29] and partly because the Brazilian government has significant influence in the company.[30] Assuming a probability of 20% that management will change, we estimate the value per nonvoting and voting share:

Value per Nonvoting Share = Status Quo Value / (Number of Voting Shares + Number of Nonvoting Shares)
= 12,500 / (242.5 + 476.7) = 17.38 $R per Share

Value per Voting Share = Status Quo Value per Share + Probability of Management Change * (Optimal Value – Status Quo Value) = 17.38 + 0.2 * (14,700 – 12,500) / 242.5 = 19.19 $R per Share

With our assumptions, the voting shares should trade at a premium of 10.4% over the nonvoting shares.

Under Armour

In Chapter 10, we arrived at a status quo value of $1.268 million for the equity in common stock in Under Armour. We revalued Under Armour, with two changes—a compounded revenue growth of 15% (instead of 12.5%) and a higher return on capital of 10% (instead of 9%) in perpetuity, from augmenting brand name. The value of equity, with these changes, is $1,444 million. There are 36.791 million class A shares, with one voting right per share, and 12.5 million class B shares with ten voting rights per share. Since all the class B shares are held by the founder, we will assume that the probability of change is only 10%. We can compute the expected value of control and the value per voting right as follows:

29 Of the 242.5 million voting shares, 80% are equally held by four entities: Cia Bozano, Previ, Sistel, and the European Group. Effectively, they control the company.

30 The Brazilian government owns only 0.8% of the voting shares, but a significant portion of Embraer's customer financing is provided by the Brazilian development bank (BNDES), which also owns 9.6% of the nonvoting shares.

$$\text{Status Quo Value per Share} = \frac{\text{Status Quo Value}}{(\#\text{ Class A Shares} + \#\text{ Class B Shares})}$$

$$= \frac{\$1{,}268}{(36.791 + 12.5)} = \$25.72$$

$$\text{Expected Value of Control} = (\text{Optimal Value} - \text{Status Quo Value})\ \text{Probability}_{\text{Change}}$$

$$= (1444 - 1268)\ (.10) = \$17.6 \text{ million}$$

$$\text{Value per Voting Right} = \frac{\text{Expected Value of Control}}{\#\text{ Voting Rights}} = \frac{17.6}{(36.791 * 1 + 12.5 * 10)} = \$0.1088$$

$$\text{Value per Class A Share} = \text{Status Quo Value per Share} + \text{Value of One Voting Right}$$

$$= \$25.72 + \$0.11 = \$25.83$$

$$\text{Value per Class B Share} = \text{Status Quo Value per Share} + \text{Value of 10 Voting Rights}$$

$$= \$25.72 + \$0.11 * 10 = \$26.82$$

Conclusion

In general, it is easier to value mature companies than high-growth companies, because we have more relevant historical data on earnings, cash flows, and revenues. That does not mean, however, that mature companies pose no challenges. This chapter looked at two aspects of mature companies that may create problems in valuations. We considered the shift that some mature firms make to acquisitions to jump-start growth, and the possibility that a change in management could create a change in value.

Valuing acquisitive companies requires us to deal with two estimation issues. The first is the lumpiness of acquisitions, where a big acquisition in one year is followed by inactivity in the other. The second is the accounting treatment of acquisitions, which is inconsistent with the treatment of internal investment, and which skews key measures such as return on capital. Rather than treat acquisitions separately, we included them with capital expenditures when estimating reinvestment, and used averages over extended periods to overcome the year-to-year volatility. When measuring returns, we removed goodwill from invested capital, assuming that it represents a premium for growth assets.

To deal with the possibility of management change and the consequences for value, we value a firm twice. We value it once with the incumbent management (status quo) and again with different and better management in place (optimal). The difference between the two numbers is the overall value of control. When multiplied by the probability of management changing, it yields the expected value of control. This has consequences not only in acquisitions, but also in valuing any publicly traded company and in assigning premiums to voting shares.

12

Winding Down: Declining Companies

Chapter 9 examined firms at the earliest stages in the life cycle and wrestled with how best to build in the reality that most young idea firms do not survive to become healthy businesses. Chapter 10 moved forward in the life cycle to look at growth firms, and our biggest challenge became estimating growth rates as firms become larger and competition enters the business. In Chapter 11, we continued further up the life cycle to look at mature companies, a grouping that most growth companies seek to avoid but inevitably join. We discussed the valuation consequences of acquisitions and management changes. In this chapter, we turn to the final phase of the life cycle—decline—and examine the key questions that drive the value of firms that enter this phase.

This chapter examines many issues related to decline, but an overriding problem that most analysts face with valuing companies in decline is a psychological one. As human beings, we are hardwired for optimism, and we reflect that with positive growth rates and higher cash flows in the future for the companies we value. When valuing declining firms, we have to go against the grain and estimate cash flows for the future that may be lower than cash flows today. We will examine the process of estimating cash flows for declining firms in the first part of the chapter. We will spend the second half looking at one possible consequence of decline—distress—and how best to build its likelihood into value.

Declining Companies in the Economy

Every economy has companies whose best days are behind them. They tend to be clustered in a few sectors. Some of these firms can be large companies that account for a significant share of economic output and employment. In the U.S., for instance, the automobile and steel companies, which at one time represented the heart of the economy, have been in decline for decades. But they still employ large numbers of people and account for a significant portion of the overall economy.

A Life Cycle View of Declining Companies

As we noted in Chapter 11, growth companies do not want to become mature companies, and mature companies constantly try to rediscover their growth roots. By the same token, no mature company wants to go into decline, with the accompanying loss of earnings and value. So how do we differentiate between mature firms and firms in decline? We use the financial balance sheet, as we did in the earlier chapters, to illustrate the difference (see Figure 12.1).

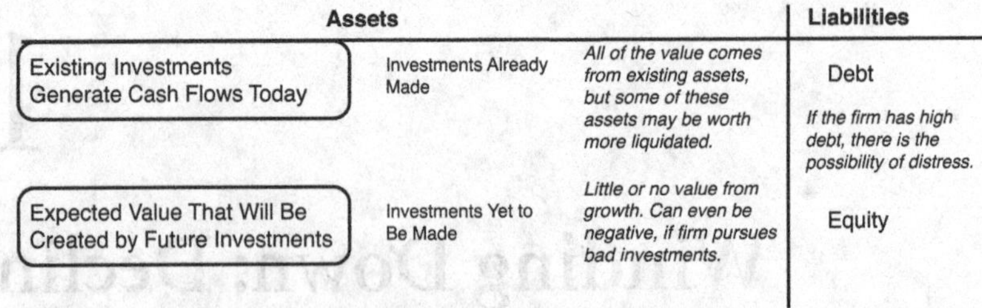

Figure 12.1: The Part of the Financial Balance Sheet for Mature Companies

Mature companies differ from companies in decline in two key areas. The first is on the asset side of the balance sheet. If mature companies get the bulk of their value from existing assets and less from growth assets, declining companies get none (or close to none) of their value from growth assets. In fact, it is not uncommon for declining companies to actually lose value from growth investments, especially if they decide to reinvest at rates well below their cost of capital. Not only do existing assets represent all the value of declining firms, but some firms may actually get more from liquidating or divesting these assets than from continuing operations. On the liability side, declining firms face much more dire consequences from being overleveraged. They cannot count on higher earnings in the future to cover debt obligation. In other words, decline and distress often go hand in hand.

Characteristics of Declining Companies

In this section, we will look at characteristics that declining companies tend to share, with an eye toward the problems they create for analysts trying to value these firms. Note again that not every declining company possesses all these characteristics, but they do share enough of them to make the following generalizations:

- **Stagnant or declining revenues**: Perhaps the most telling sign of a company in decline is its inability to increase revenues over extended periods, even when times are good. Flat revenues or revenues that grow at less than the inflation rate indicate operating weakness. It is even more telling if these patterns in revenues apply not only to the company being analyzed but also to the overall sector. This would eliminate the explanation that the revenue weakness is due to poor management (and thus can be fixed by bringing in a new management team).
- **Shrinking or negative margins**: The stagnant revenues at declining firms are often accompanied by shrinking operating margins, partly because firms are losing pricing power and partly because they are dropping prices to keep revenues from falling further. This combination results in deteriorating or negative operating income at these firms, with occasional spurts in profits generated by asset sales or one-time profits.
- **Asset divestitures**: If one of the features of a declining firm is that existing assets are sometimes worth more to others, who intend to put them to different and better uses, it stands to reason that asset divestitures will be more frequent at declining firms than at firms earlier in the life cycle. If the declining firm has substantial debt obligations, the need to divest becomes stronger, driven by the desire to avoid default or to pay down debt.

- **Big payouts—dividends and stock buybacks:** Declining firms have few or any growth investments that generate value, existing assets that may be generating positive cash flows, and asset divestitures that result in cash inflows. If the firm does not have enough debt for distress to be a concern, it stands to reason that declining firms not only pay out large dividends, sometimes exceeding their earnings, but also buy back stock.
- **The downside of financial leverage:** If debt is a double-edged sword, declining firms often are exposed to the wrong edge. With stagnant and declining earnings from existing assets and little potential for earnings growth, it is not surprising that many declining firms face overwhelming debt burdens. Note that much of this debt was probably acquired when the firm was in a healthier phase of the life cycle, and at terms that cannot be matched today. In addition to difficulties these firms face in meeting the obligations they have committed to meet, they face additional trouble in refinancing the debt, because lenders will demand more stringent terms.

Valuation Issues

The issues we face in valuing declining companies come from their common characteristics. Most of the valuation techniques we use for businesses, whether intrinsic or relative, are built for healthy firms with positive growth. Sometimes they break down when a firm is expected to shrink over time or if distress is imminent.

Intrinsic (DCF) Valuation

A company's intrinsic value is the present value of the company's expected cash flows over its lifetime. Although that principle does not change with declining firms, practical problems can impede valuations.

Existing Assets

When valuing the firm's existing assets, we estimate the expected cash flows from these assets and discount them back at a risk-adjusted discount rate. Although this is standard valuation practice in most valuations, two aspects of declining companies may throw a wrench into the process:

- **Earning less than cost of capital:** In many declining firms, existing assets, even if profitable, earn less than the cost of capital. The natural consequence is that discounting the cash flows back at the cost of capital yields a value that is less than the capital invested in the firm. From a valuation perspective, this is neither surprising nor unexpected: assets that generate subpar returns can destroy value.
- **Divestiture effects:** If existing assets earn less than the cost of capital, the logical response is to sell or divest these assets and hope that the best buyer will pay a high price for them. From a valuation perspective, divestitures of assets create discontinuities in past data and make forecasts more difficult. To see how divestitures can affect past numbers, consider a firm that divested a significant portion of its assets midway through last year. All the operating numbers from last year—revenues, margins, and reinvestment—are affected by the divestiture, but the numbers for the year reflect the

operating results from the portion of the year before the divestiture. Similarly, risk parameters such as betas, where we use past prices or returns, can be skewed by divestitures of assets midway through the time period. For the forecasting consequences, try estimating the revenues and earnings for a firm that is expected to divest a large portion of its assets over the next few years. Not only do we have to pinpoint the assets that will be divested and the effects of the divestiture on operating revenues and earnings, but we also have to estimate the proceeds from the divestitures. Put another way, a divestiture by itself does not affect value, but what we expect to receive in comparison to the divested assets can affect value.

Thus, what makes the valuation of existing assets of a declining firm difficult is that the value you derive from these assets in cash flows may be lower than the value you obtain from divesting the assets.

Growth Assets

Declining firms derive little from growth assets, so the valuation of these assets should not have a significant impact on value. While this is generally true, we have to consider the possibility that some declining firms are in denial about their status and continue to invest in new assets, as if they had growth potential. If these assets earn less than the cost of capital, the value of adding new assets will be negative, and reinvestment will lower the firm's value.

We can actually go further. If we view divestitures as reductions in capital invested, the reinvestment rate for a declining firm can be negative in future years. This will lead to negative growth rates, at least for the foreseeable future. Analysts who have learned their valuation fundamentals at healthier companies often are uncomfortable with the notion of negative earnings growth rates and cash flows that exceed earnings—but that combination characterizes many declining firms.

Discount Rates

If the cost of capital is a weighted average of the costs of debt and equity, what is it about declining firms that makes it difficult to estimate these numbers? First, the large dividends and buybacks that characterize declining firms can have an effect on the overall value of equity and debt ratios we use in the computation. In particular, returning large amounts of cash to stockholders reduces the market value of equity, through the market price, with dividends, and the number of shares, with stock buybacks. If debt is not repaid proportionately, the debt ratio increases, which affects of costs of debt, equity, and capital.

Second, the presence of distress can have significant effects on both the cost of equity and debt. The cost of debt increases as default risk increases, and some rated firms will see their ratings drop to junk status—BB, B, or lower. If operating earnings drop below interest expenses, the tax benefits of debt also dissipate, leading to further upward pressure on the after-tax cost of debt. As debt-to-equity ratios climb, the cost of equity should also increase as equity investors see much more volatility in earnings. From a measurement standpoint, analysts who use regression betas, which reflect changes in equity risk on a lagged basis, may find themselves facing the unusual scenario of a cost of equity that is lower than the pre-tax cost of debt.[1]

Terminal Value

The standard procedures for estimating terminal value were examined in detail in earlier chapters. We first estimate a growth rate that a firm can sustain forever, with the caveat that the growth cannot exceed the growth rate of the economy, with the risk-free rate acting as a proxy. We follow up by making reasonable assumptions about what a firm can generate as excess returns in perpetuity, and we use this number to forecast a reinvestment rate for the firm. We complete the process by estimating a discount rate for the terminal value computation, with the qualifier that the risk parameters used should reflect the fact that the company will be a more stable one.

At each stage of this process, declining and distressed firms pose special challenges. At the first stage, we have to consider the significant possibility that the firm being valued will not make it to stable growth. Many distressed firms will default and go out of business or be liquidated. Even if a firm is expected to survive to reach steady state, not only will the expected growth rate in perpetuity be well below the growth rate of the economy and inflation, but in some cases, it can even be negative. Essentially, the firm will continue to exist, but it will get progressively smaller over time as its market shrinks. At the second step, the biggest estimation issues we face will arise with declining firms that are earning well below their cost of capital currently, with no reason for optimism about the future. In effect, the most reasonable assumption to make about such a firm may be that it will continue to earn a return on its capital that is below the cost of capital in perpetuity. This will have consequences for both reinvestment and the terminal value. Finally, the problems we mentioned in the previous section relating to discount rates can spill over into the terminal value computation. In other words, a distressed firm can have sky-high costs of equity and debt at the moment. Leaving these numbers at or even close to current levels can cause terminal values to implode.

From Operating Assets to Equity Value per Share

The process of getting from operating assets to equity value per share follows the standard script. We add cash and other nonoperating assets, subtract debt outstanding and the value of any equity options granted by the firm (either in financing or to management), and divide by the number of shares outstanding. However, we face three problems, especially with the distressed subset of declining firms.

The first is a familiar problem that we have run into with firms earlier in the life cycle that are losing money. A firm's cash balance today may bear little resemblance to the cash balance reported on the balance sheet. Declining firms with negative earnings can very quickly deplete cash balances. Failing to account for this will result in an overvaluation of equity.

1 Regression betas may not adequately capture the risk in the equity of a firm in financial distress for two reasons. The first is that they are computed using a long period of historical returns. To the extent that the firm was healthy (or healthier than it is today) over some of that period, the regression beta understates the true beta. The second reason is that during periods of distress, the stock prices of companies tend to be volatile, but often with no relation to the market; they may move up and down as a function of debt restructuring talks or rumors of impending bankruptcy. Because the regression beta captures how a stock moves with the market, it may actually decrease during periods of financial distress.

The second problem is that the market value of debt in distressed firms trades (or is valued) at a discount to the book value. This is not surprising, since the debt was borrowed and recorded in past periods, when the firm was healthy. Now that default risk has risen, that debt has a lower value. Note that this is true even if the firm has no corporate bonds, only bank loans outstanding. The difference is that the drop in value is visible with bonds, since they are traded, and is implicit with bank loans, which are not. So what are the consequences for valuing equity? Consider a simple example, in which you have valued a firm's operating assets at $800 million. Assume that the firm has debt outstanding, with a book value of $1 billion but a market value of only $500 million. In discounted cash flow valuation, the notion of a going concern requires us to stick with market value. We do this both for computing debt ratios in the cost of capital and for subtracting from firm value to get to the value of equity. However, with the example just cited, this puts us in the uncomfortable position of attaching a value of $300 million for equity (firm value minus market value of debt). This is simply because the market perceives a high chance of default in the firm. The tenuous nature of this solution can be illustrated by reestimating the value of equity in this firm if the firm is acquired by a healthy suitor who also assumes the debt. Since the acquirer is perceived as having less default risk, the value of the debt rises toward the book value, which, holding firm value constant, will very quickly reduce or even eliminate the value of equity.

The third troublesome component in estimating equity value is that the line between debt and equity in a distressed firm is a gray one. Not only does distressed debt take on the characteristics of equity on its own, but lenders often demand and get equity stakes either in the form of equity options or as privileges to convert to equity. These equity options have to be valued and netted out from overall equity value to arrive at the value of common stock. In fact, debt renegotiation talks at distressed firms can alter the debt, equity option, and common stock numbers in the firm overnight. When a large lender agrees to accept shares in the company in exchange for the debt, the consequences for the value of equity per share are unpredictable.

Relative Valuation

Analysts who fall back on relative valuation as a solution to the problems of valuing declining or distressed firms, using intrinsic valuation, will find themselves confronting the estimation issues we listed in the earlier sections either explicitly or implicitly when they use multiples and comparables:

- **Scaling variable:** All multiples have to be scaled to common variables, which can be broadly categorized into revenues, earnings, book value, or sector-specific measures. With distressed companies, earnings and book values can become inoperative very quickly—the former because many firms in decline have negative earnings, and the latter because repeated losses can drive down the book value of equity, into negative territory. We can scale value to revenues, but we are then implicitly assuming that the firm will be able to turn around its operations and deliver positive earnings.
- **Comparable firms:** We can face two possible scenarios when valuing declining firms. One is when we are valuing a declining firm in a business where the remaining firms are all healthy and growing. Since markets value declining firms very differently from healthy firms, the challenge in this case is working out how much of a discount the declining firm should trade at, relative to the values being attached to healthy firms. We face the second scenario when we value a declining/distressed firm in a sector where

many or even all of the firms share the same characteristic. In this case, not only do our choices of what multiple to use become more limited, but we have to consider how best to adjust for the degree of decline in a firm. For instance, in early 2009, Ford, GM, and Chrysler all showed signs of distress, but GM was in the worst shape, followed by Chrysler and Ford.

- **Incorporating distress:** While analysts often come up with creative solutions to the first two problems—using multiples of future earnings and controlling for differences in decline, for instance—the presence of distress puts a wild card in the comparison. Put another way, when firms are not only in decline but are viewed as distressed, we should expect firms that have a higher likelihood of distress to trade at lower values (and hence at lower multiples) than firms that are more likely to make it. Unless we explicitly control for distress, we will find ourselves concluding, based on relative valuation, that the first group of firms are undervalued and the second group are overvalued.

By now, the message should be clear. Any issues that skew intrinsic valuations also skew relative valuations. The symptoms of decline (negative growth rates, poor or negative margins, flat revenues, and the potential for failure), caused by too much debt and declining earnings, will not disappear as issues just because we base our value on a revenue multiple.

The Dark Side of Valuation

Analysts who value declining and distressed firms often find that the tools and approaches that served them adequately with healthy companies fail them. This problem is worse when a sector with a history of financial health becomes troubled, since analysts are slow to let go of old rules of thumb and metrics. This section considers some of the resulting problems in valuing declining and distressed companies.

Autopilot Optimism

At the start of this chapter, we argued that one of the biggest problems that analysts face in valuing declining companies is that they have to fight the optimism that is inherent in valuation. This optimism manifests itself in the valuation of distressed companies in three places:

- **Growth rates:** Analysts hold on to their standard practice of estimating positive growth rates, not only for the short term, but also in perpetuity for most firms. Thus, it is not unusual to see a declining company being valued with current earnings growing at positive rates in the future, simply because that is the way it is for most companies. However, this view of the future is at war with reality, because flat revenues and declining margins are incompatible with positive earnings growth in the future. The consequence of using positive growth rates for distressed companies is that we overestimate future earnings and cash flows and, in the process, overvalue these companies.
- **Discount rates:** Many distressed company valuations are based on the assumption that the company in question will move to its target debt—instantaneously in many cases—and replace its distressed debt and risky equity with much safer alternatives. In effect, the firms are valued using the cost of capital of healthy firms in their sector. The assumption is that no matter the current problems that are causing distortions in the discount rate, they will go away quickly.

- **Excess returns and margins**: In addition to estimating positive growth rates in earnings, analysts assume that the firm being valued will revert to historic averages in terms of margins and excess returns—if not immediately, at least over time. While this may be possible for some declining companies, it may be unlikely for others and infeasible for still others.

Combining positive growth rates in revenues with improving margins and healthy company discount rates leads to the obvious conclusion that most declining and distressed companies are undervalued.

Valuing Sears: An Overoptimistic Valuation in September 2008

Sears, a retailer with a long and distinguished history, has seen its fortunes fade over the last ten years. Its core customer base has abandoned it for retailers like Target and Wal-Mart. In the fiscal year ending in February 2008, Sears reported revenues of $50.7 billion, just 3.2% higher than its revenues in 2006, and operating income of $1.54 billion, about 17.7% lower than its operating income in 2006. During the 2008 fiscal year, Sears reduced the number of stores it operated and bought back almost $2.9 billion of its own stock. Finally, Sears generated a return on capital of 4.99% on its retail operations for the year, well below its cost of capital of 7.50%. In summary, Sears has all the hallmarks of a company in decline.

For an overoptimistic valuation of Sears, we could make the following assumptions:

- Revenues will grow at 6% a year for the next five years and then drop to a stable growth rate of 4%. Over the period, the pre-tax operating margins will revert to the 5% level that the firm commanded when it was healthy.
- The firm's cost of capital will drop to the industry average of 7.13% immediately and remain at that level forever. (In September 2008, the treasury bond rate was 4.09%, and the equity risk premium was 4.5%.)
- The firm's return on capital will jump back to 12%, which is the retail industry average, for new investments made by Sears. This will be the return on capital in perpetuity.

With these assumptions in place, we first estimate the cash flows for the first five years, as shown in Table 12.1, and discount these cash flows back at the cost of capital of 7.13%.

Table 12.1 Expected Free Cash Flow to the Firm in the Next Five Years

	Current	Year 1	Year 2	Year 3	Year 4	Year 5
Revenue growth rate		6%	6%	6%	6%	6%
Revenues	$50,703	$53,745	$56,970	$60,388	$64,011	$67,852
Operating margin	3.05%	3.44%	3.83%	4.22%	4.61%	5%
EBIT	$1,548	$1,850	$2,183	$2,549	$2,951	$3,393
EBIT * (1 – tax rate)		$1,147	$1,353	$1,580	$1,830	$2,103
– Reinvestment		$574	$677	$790	$915	$1,052
Free cash flow to firm		$574	$677	$790	$915	$1,052
Present value		$535	$590	$643	$695	$745

Tax rate = 38%

Note that as revenues grow and pre-tax operating margins increase from 3.05% (current) to the target of 5% (in linear increments), operating income grows substantially. The reinvestment during the five-year period is estimated to be 50% of after-tax operating income, based on the revenue growth rate of 6% and the return on capital of 12%. At the end of year 5, we put the firm into stable growth, using a 4% growth rate forever, and estimating the reinvestment rate from the return on capital of 12%:

$$\text{Reinvestment Rate} = \frac{g_{Stable}}{ROC_{Stable}} = \frac{4\%}{12\%} = 33.33\%$$

$$\text{Terminal Value} = \frac{\text{After-Tax Operating Income}_5\ (1+g_{stable})(1-\text{Reinvestment Rate})}{(\text{Cost of Capital}_{Stable} - g_{Stable})}$$

$$= \frac{2103\ (1.04)(1-.333)}{(.0713-.04)} = \$45,797$$

Discounting back the terminal value and adding it to the present value of the cash flows generates a value for the operating assets of $35,663 million:

$$\text{Value of Operating Assets} = \$535 + \$590 + \$643 + \$695 + \$745 + \frac{\$45,797}{1.0713^5} = \$35,663$$

Adding cash ($1,622 million) and subtracting debt ($7.728 million) yields a value of equity per share of $223.90, significantly higher than the stock price of $76.25 at the time of the analysis

$$\text{Value per Share} = \frac{35,663 + 1,622 - 7728}{132.01} = \$223.90/\text{Share}$$

Discount Rate Contortions

In the preceding section, we noted that optimists who value declining and distressed companies replace the company's current risk parameters with those of healthier companies in the business. These analysts, though, are on more solid ground than those who use today's debt numbers, estimate parameters for the company from historical data (book interest rates for debt and regressions for betas), and then lock up these numbers in perpetuity for the following reasons:

- Many declining and distressed companies have debt ratios that are vastly higher than the industry average and are not sustainable in the long term or compatible with a going concern. Thus, the valuation of an airline that uses a market debt-to-capital ratio of 90% and leaves it at that value, while assuming that the airline will return to financial health, is being internally inconsistent.
- Following the standard practice for estimating the cost of debt, which is to look at the current market interest rate on a firm's bonds, can result in extremely high costs of debt. In January 2009, for instance, the yield to maturity on bonds issued by many firms with substantial default risk was in excess of 20%. If analysts estimate the cost of equity from a regression beta, they can find themselves facing a quandary, where the cost of equity is well below the pre-tax cost of debt. To overcome this problem, analysts try creative solutions, but many of these solutions have no basis in either theory or evidence. One is to use the book interest rate, obtained by dividing the interest expense by the book value of debt. Since much of the debt on the books was acquired when the firm was healthier, the book interest rate yields numbers for the cost of debt that seem more reasonable. The other is to arbitrarily hike the cost of equity above the pre-tax cost of debt, using the logic that equity is riskier than debt. While the logic is impeccable, the arbitrary nature of the adjustment is not.
- It is true that interest expenses are tax-deductible and that the after-tax cost of debt for most firms is much lower than the pre-tax cost of debt. We capture the benefit by multiplying the pre-tax cost by (1 – tax rate). Analysts who follow this practice with declining or distressed firms are missing a key part of the tax benefit argument. For interest expenses to deliver tax benefits, we need operating income that is sufficient to cover these interest expenses. To the extent that the firm has lost money, is losing money right now, and is expected to keep losing money, we may get no tax benefits from debt for extended periods.

In summary, the discount rates for distressed companies should reflect their distress and should change over time to be consistent with our assumptions about future profitability and financial health.

Discount Rate Contortions: Las Vegas Sands

Las Vegas Sands owns and operates the Venetian Casino and Sands Convention Center in Las Vegas and the Sands Macau Casino in Macau, China. While the firm does not fit the classic profile of a declining company—its revenues increased from $1.75 billion in 2005 to $4.39 billion in 2008, and it had two other casinos in development—it ran into significant financial trouble in the last quarter of 2008.

Fears about whether the firm would be able to meet its debt obligations pushed down both stock prices (by almost 90%) and bond prices (by about 40%) in 2008.

By January 2009, the firm was operating under the threat of defaulting on its debt, and both its debt and equity prices reflected that fear:

- The debt was rated B2 by Moody's (and B+ by S&P). A bond issued by Las Vegas Sands, expiring in 2015, was trading at a yield to maturity of 19.82%. The firm did report an operating income of $164 million for 2009, but the net loss for the year was $229 million, primarily due to interest expenses that amounted to $422 million during the course of the year. Thus, while the marginal tax rate is 38%, the firm got only a portion of the tax benefits on interest expenses:

$$\text{Tax Benefit (Rate)} = \text{Marginal Tax Rate} * \frac{(\text{Interest Expenses} - \text{Net Loss})}{\text{Interest Expenses}}$$

$$= = 38\%\left[\frac{(422-229)}{422}\right] = 17.37\%$$

- The regression beta, estimated using two years of weekly returns from January 2007 to January 2009, was 2.78. Using a risk-free rate of 3% (the ten-year bond rate at the time of the analysis) and an equity risk premium of 6%, we derive a cost of equity of 19.03% for the firm:

$$\text{Cost of Equity} = 3\% + 2.78\ (6\%) = 19.68\%$$

- The firm's market value of equity in January 2009 was $2.727 billion, higher than the book value of equity of $2.28 billion. The book value of debt was $10.47 billion, well above the market value of $7.57 billion, reflecting the increase in default risk since the debt was issued. The weights based on market values are as follows:

$$\text{Debt} / (\text{Debt} + \text{Equity}) = 7.57 / (7.57 + 2.727) = 73.57\%$$

- If we take these numbers at face value, we arrive at a cost of capital of 17.25%:

$$\begin{aligned}\text{Cost of Capital} &= \text{Cost of Equity } (E / (D + E)) + \text{After-Tax Cost of Debt } (D / (D + E)) \\ &= 19.68\%\ (0.2643) + 19.82\%\ (1 - .1737)\ (0.7357) = 17.25\%\end{aligned}$$

In addition to being much higher than the industry average cost of capital of 9% for the casino business, this estimate has a couple of unsettling characteristics. The first is that the pre-tax cost of debt is higher than the cost of equity. The second is that the debt ratio at 74% is too high for a healthy firm.

To overcome the problems in the estimate, the analyst valuing the company decides to replace the conventional measures with more "reasonable" numbers:

- Rather than use the current cost of borrowing, a "book interest rate" is computed by dividing the total interest expense by the book value of debt. Using the interest expense of $422 million in 2008 and the book value of debt of $10,470 million at the end of 2008, we arrive a book cost of debt of 4.03%. Assuming that the tax benefits will be derived at some point in time, we estimate an after-tax cost of debt of 2.50%, based on a marginal tax rate of 38%:

After-Tax Cost of Debt = Pre-Tax Book Interest Rate (1 – Marginal Tax Rate)
= (422 / 10,470) (1 – .38) = 2.50%

- To estimate the cost of equity, the sector beta of 1.78, estimated by averaging regression betas across all publicly traded casino companies, was used to estimate a cost of equity of 13.68%:

Cost of Equity = 3% + 1.78 (6%) = 13.68%

- To estimate the weights, the market values are replaced with book values for debt and equity, resulting in a debt ratio of 82.1%:

Debt Ratio = Book Value of Debt / (Book Value of Debt + Book Value of Equity)
= 10.47 / (10.47 + 2.28) = 82.1%

- With these numbers in place, the cost of capital for Las Vegas Sands is only 8.11%, much closer to the industry average:

Cost of Capital = Cost of Equity (E / (D + E)) + After-Tax Cost of Debt (D / (D + E))
= 13.68% (0.179) + 2.50% (0.821) = 4.50%

This estimate of the cost of capital bears no resemblance to reality. Las Vegas Sands is a company in significant trouble. The original estimate of 17.25% for the cost of capital is reflective of the perils it faces.

Divestiture Follies

Declining and distressed firms often have divested assets in the past and can be expected to divest more assets in the future. These divestitures will generate cash flows for the firm, but incorporating these cash flows into a valuation requires us to be both realistic and consistent.

When divestitures of assets are expected in the future, analysts valuing the firm are often dependent on managers telling them both which assets they plan to divest and what they expect to get in return. If analysts take them at their word on both dimensions, a real danger exists that managers may be overestimating what they will able to get in asset sales from buyers. In distressed scenarios, where firms have to sell assets to meet urgent cash flow needs, their bargaining positions are weak. It is unlikely that they will be able to extract fair value, let alone a premium. As a general rule, the greater the proportion of a firm's assets that have to be divested, and the more dependent the firm is on the divestitures to meet its obligations, the more conservative we have to be about estimating divestiture proceeds.

The other point about divestitures is an obvious one, but it needs to be made anyway. When a firm divests an asset or division, it can no longer keep the earnings and cash flows from that division. In far too many valuations, analysts seem to count on having their cake and eating it too. They count the cash proceeds from the divestiture in the early years while not reflecting the loss of earnings in their forecasts in subsequent years.

Book Capital

A tactic that is common in valuations of declining or distressed firms is to assume that the firms will be liquidated and estimating a liquidation value as an alternative or supplement to discounted cash flow valuation. While this is legitimate, it is sullied by the dependence on book value for the assets as a proxy for liquidation value. By this reasoning, any firm that trades at a market value less than the book value is undervalued, at least relative to its liquidation value. As justification, analysts argue that the liquidation value is difficult to obtain and that the book value does reflect what the firm has invested in the assets. Even if we accept the latter part of the argument, this does not imply that book value is a good measure of liquidation value. The reason lies in the nature of the firms we are valuing. As we noted near the beginning of this chapter, declining and distressed firms often have existing asset bases that earn well below their costs of capital, and that shortfall cannot be attributed entirely to poor management. If this is the case, the fair or intrinsic value of these assets should be well below the book value.

The dependence on book value can also show up in a different place in the valuation—in the computation of debt and equity weights for computing the cost of capital. Many people use book value weights for debt and equity, arguing that they are more stable and dependable, especially in periods of market turmoil. With distressed companies, these analysts sometimes are faced with the absurdity of this argument, since the book value of equity can become negative at a firm after a period of extended losses. Using this book equity will result in a debt-to-capital ratio that exceeds 100% and will yield a meaningless cost of capital.

Dealing with Distress

Distress is a constant undercurrent in some declining companies. The analysts valuing these companies cannot help but be aware of the rumors and news items attesting to the worry. However, how they deal with the possibility of distress does not seem to reflect this concern:

- **Denial**: Earlier in this chapter, we noted that many valuations of declining and distressed companies use excessively optimistic assumptions about growth (that it will be positive), discount rates (that they will resemble those of healthy companies), and profitability (that margins and returns will revert to predistress days). In this fairy-tale universe, a happy ending (a large terminal value) always results, and no company is ever forced into default.
- **Discount rate excuses**: Analysts who use the current costs of equity and debt, both of which are likely to be elevated for distressed companies, argue that their valuations already reflect distress. There are two reasons to be skeptical. The first is that the cost of capital is not very responsive to distress in many firms. In other words, changing the costs of debt and equity, even by large amounts, often does not show up as a

dramatically higher cost of capital.[2] The second is that the risk parameters we estimate for cost of capital—betas and default spreads—are designed to capture risk in going concerns; they reflect uncertainty about future cash flows. The risk of distress is a truncation risk (for example, this firm may not be in existence six months from now) and is much more difficult to capture in the discount rate. We will return to examine this theme later in the chapter.

- **Post-valuation storytelling:** In many valuations, distress is brought into the picture after the valuation is complete and takes the form of either an arbitrary discount (reducing the value by 20 to 30%) or a cautionary note. (The stock looks undervalued, but don't buy it, because there is a chance of distress.)

Relative Valuation

Two tactics are used to value distressed companies. The first is to stay with current values for operations (revenues, earnings, book value) and to try and scale market value to those variables that are still viable (revenues and book value). The second is to use estimated revenues or earnings in a future year and to compute a forward multiple, which is then compared across companies.

Consider the use of current revenues and book value multiples to analyze declining companies. If these companies are outliers in their sectors (they are declining companies in sectors with primarily healthy companies), the results of this relative valuation will be predictable. The declining company will look cheap, because it will trade at lower multiples than the rest of the sector. To make a legitimate comparison, we have to examine differences in risk, revenue growth, and expected profitability over time.

With forward numbers, the problems shift to the distress issue. To see why, assume that you are valuing a firm that is in severe financial trouble, with stagnant revenues, negative earnings, and substantial debt obligations. You forecast a turnaround in the firm's fortunes and predict that the EBITDA in five years will be $150 million and that the firm will be healthy, trading at roughly the same multiple of EBITDA that other healthy firms in the sector are trading at right now (6 times EBITDA). The forward estimate of value for this company is $900 million, but there is a catch. This works only if you assume that good health is guaranteed and that there is no chance of default. To the extent that there is a significant chance of bad things happening to the firm over the next five years, we would have to reduce the estimated value.

The Light Side of Valuation

If the key issues that drive declining and distressed companies are dealing with negative growth (and making consistent assumptions) and distress, we have to develop better ways of dealing with both in practice. This section begins by establishing a framework for analyzing declining firms. Then it examines the details of valuing these firms.

A Framework for Dealing with Decline and Distress

We will build our analysis of declining firms around two key questions. The first is whether the decline that we are observing in a firm's operations is reversible or permanent. In some cases, a

2 Part of the reason is that these higher costs of debt and equity are accompanied by higher debt ratios. Since debt is cheaper than equity, it pushes down the cost of capital.

firm may be in a tailspin but could pull out of it with a new management team. The second question relates to whether the firm faces a significant possibility of distress; not all declining firms are distressed.

To assess the question of reversibility, we can look at a firm's own history as well as the state of other companies in the sector. A firm that has gone through cycles of good and bad times, as is often the case with cyclical and commodity companies, is more likely to be able to move back to health than a firm that has not been subject to these cycles. Similarly, it can be argued that a firm that is doing badly in a sector filled with healthy firms has problems that are more attributable to poor management than to fundamentals. With better management, the firm may be able to revert to health, if not growth. In contrast, a firm that is doing badly in a sector filled with poorly performing firms, with no obvious macroeconomic reasons for the problems, has problems that will not be remedied by changing managers.

To evaluate distress, the place to start is the debt load that the firm may have accumulated over time. Declining firms with significant debt obligations are more likely to face default, resulting in cessation of operations and liquidation by creditors. If the firm is rated by a bond ratings agency, we would expect to see a low credit rating, generally below investment grade. Declining firms that do not face these fixed obligations should be able to survive even with poor earnings and no or even negative growth. How we estimate value will depend on the combination of reversibility and decline that we observe in a given firm. Here are four possible combinations:

- **Reversible decline, low distress**: If a firm has flat revenues and declining margins, but the problems can be fixed, we would follow the framework we developed in Chapter 11 for valuing control. We would first value the firm, run by existing management, with continuing decline in operations; the resulting status quo value will be low. We would then revalue the firm, assuming that better management is in place and that the decline is reversed; this optimal value should be much higher. Finally, we would estimate a probability of management changing and compute an expected value based on the status quo and optimal values:

  expected value = status quo value (1 – probability of management change) + optimal value (probability of management change)

- **Irreversible decline, low distress**: If a firm's poor performance cannot be attributed to poor management and cannot easily be fixed, we cannot revalue the firm with operating improvements. However, the assets that the firm deploys may be put to better use by others (in other businesses) and thus be worth more in a divestiture. Since the firm is under no pressure to sell its assets to meet fixed obligations, it can liquidate the assets in an orderly manner, waiting for both the best time and the highest bidder for each asset. The expected proceeds from this orderly liquidation will provide an alternative estimate of value for the firm. The final value that we would attach to the firm would be the higher of the two numbers:[3]

Expected Value = Maximum (Status Quo Value, Orderly Liquidation Value)

3 We are assuming that managers in this firm will take the right action and liquidate, if that is the course that will deliver higher value. If they don't, we will have to estimate probabilities, just as we did for firms with management deficiencies.

- **Reversible decline, high distress:** For firms that have a high probability of distress, we will consider two courses of action. In the first one, we will try to bring the probability of distress into the expected cash flows and discount rates and derive distress-adjusted values. In the second strategy, we will compute the expected values, just as we did in the low-distress scenario, and then estimate the probability of distress separately. Following this with an estimate of the proceeds that we can expect to receive in a distress sale will yield the firm's distress-adjusted value. The fact that decline is reversible, though, may give equity investors in this firm the possibility of large payoffs, if distress is avoided and the firm recovers its bearings, thus giving equity the characteristics of an option.
- **Irreversible decline, high distress:** When decline is inevitable and is overlaid with distress, we have a toxic combination for value. As with the preceding case, we have to adjust expected values for distress by either changing the inputs to discounted cash flow or adjusting the expected no-distress value for the probability of distress. Two significant differences, from the reversible decline scenario, can depress value. The first is that, if distress occurs, the proceeds from a distress sale with irreversible decline will be lower, both because the pool of buyers is thin (if most firms in the sector are troubled) and because buyers don't see much potential upside. The second difference is that equity investors have less to gain from the option to liquidate, since the best-case value is constrained by the poor quality of the assets.

Table 12.2 summarizes the four scenarios.

Table 12.2 A Framework for Dealing with Decline and/or Distress

	No or Low Distress (Not Much Debt, Investment Grade Rating)	**High Distress (High Debt Commitments, Low Rating)**
Irreversible (sector in trouble)	Value the firm with existing management and expected decline (going-concern value). Value the firm assuming orderly liquidation of all its assets. Expected Value = Maximum (Going-Concern Value, Orderly Liquidation Value)	Start with the expected value (irreversible, no distress). Estimate the probability of distress and proceeds from forced liquidation of the firm. Recompute the expected value, adjusting for distress.
Reversible (firm outlier in healthy sector)	Value the firm with existing management and expected decline. Value the firm with better management and recovery. Expected Value = Status Quo Value (Probability of No Management Change) + Optimum Value (Probability of Management Change)	Start with the expected value (reversible, no distress). Estimate the probability of distress and proceeds from distress sale of the firm. Recompute the expected value, adjusting for distress. If equity investors run the firm, value the option to liquidate.

Irreversible Decline, Low Distress

With some firms, the symptoms of operating decline—flat revenues and declining margins—have deep roots that cannot be easily remedied for three reasons. The first is that the overall market for the firm's products and services is shrinking and is expected to keep doing so over time. The second reason is that all the firms in the sector share some or many of the same symptoms as the firm being valued. The third reason is that no macroeconomic factor can be pointed to as the reason for the decline, as is the case with an economic recession for a cyclical firm or the price cycle for a commodity company. A good example is the airline business in much of the developed world since deregulation. In this business, the healthy company has been the exception, rather than the rule, and most companies seem to teeter on the edge of bankruptcy, even in good economic times.

The first step in valuing such companies is to estimate the value as a going concern, notwithstanding the fact that the assets, as invested currently, may be earning less than the cost of capital. In effect, we are valuing the businesses on the assumption that they will continue to be operated, while destroying value for existing investors. This status quo value may be well below the firm's book value, but that is not surprising given the negative excess returns that we are projecting on existing assets. The value will be depressed further if management insists on adding to its asset base with new investments in the same business.

The second step is to consider a logical alternative to continuing in business. If the assets deployed by the firm can be used elsewhere (in other businesses or by other firms) to generate higher returns, we can consider divesting these assets and liquidating the business over time. Since distress is not a concern, the firm can wait until the right time and the right bidder and extract the maximum value from divestiture. Hence, we will call this an *orderly liquidation*, which can occur over many years. As for estimating what the divestiture proceeds will be, the answer will vary across sectors and for different assets, but we can develop a few general propositions. The first is that the expected proceeds should be higher than the present value of the cash flows that would have been generated by the assets in the existing usage. If this is not the case, the divestiture would not make sense in the first place. Thus, if the asset is expected to generate \$50 million in perpetuity, in its existing use, with a risk-adjusted discount rate of 10%, the divestiture proceeds should exceed \$500 million. The second proposition is that little or no illiquidity discount should be applied to the divestiture value, because no urgency is associated with the sale.

Once we have both values in hand—the value of the firm as a going concern and the value from an orderly liquidation of the firm over time—we would expect the firm to trade at the higher of the two values. In fact, an intermediate solution exists. A portion of the firm, composed of assets that are more valuable to others, is liquidated, but the rest of the firm continues as a going concern.

Valuing a Company in Irreversible Decline: Sears in September 2008

We will revisit our earlier valuation of Sears, where we used overoptimistic assumptions and derived a value of $223 a share. We will not assume that Sears will be able to quickly move back to growth and financial health. Instead, we will assume that the firm, while not under any significant threat of default, will shut down less-profitable stores over time. It will liquidate some of its real estate holdings in the process and become a smaller firm with higher-quality assets.

Revenues will decrease 5% a year each year for the next five years, from the current level of $50.7 billion to $39.2 billion in the fifth year, as the firm shuts down stores. After year 5, we will assume that the shrinkage will stop and that revenues will grow 2% a year forever.

The pre-tax operating margin will improve from 3.05% to 4% in linear increments over the next five years, reflecting both the cost savings from shutting down unprofitable stores and a reversal to health at the other stores. The tax rate is assumed to remain unchanged at 38%.

For the first five years, we will use the current cost of capital for Sears, which we estimate to be 7.50%. To arrive at this number, we use a beta of 1.22 for the stock, based on the unlevered beta for retailers and the debt-to-equity ratio for Sears (which is higher than the industry average), and a pre-tax cost of borrowing of 7.74%, based on a synthetic rating of BB and a default spread of 3.65%. (The treasury bond rate was 4.09% and the equity risk premium was assumed to be 4.5% at the time of this analysis.)

Cost of Equity = 4.09% + 1.22 (4.5%) = 9.58%

After-Tax Cost of Debt = 7.74% (1 – .38) = 4.80%

Debt Ratio[4] = 7,725 / (7,725 + 10,066) = 43.42%

Cost of Capital = 9.58% (1 – .4342) + 4.80% (.4342) = 7.50%

During the five-year period, as stores are being closed and assets divested, Sears will reduce its capital invested and collect proceeds from the divestitures. To estimate the proceeds, we first assume that the return on capital at Sears will increase from the current level of 4.99% to 7.50%, in linear increments, over the next five years. Then we back out the book value of capital invested based on the after-tax operating income and the return-on-capital estimate. Using the change in book capital each year as the basis, we then estimate the divestiture proceeds as a proportion of the book value. Table 12.3 reports the numbers by year.

4 Included in the debt is the estimated market value of interest-bearing debt ($3,084 million) and the present value of future lease commitments ($4,644 million). The market value of equity is based on the stock price of $76.25 at the time of the analysis.

Table 12.3 Divestiture Proceeds by Year

	Current	Year 1	Year 2	Year 3	Year 4	Year 5
Growth rate		–5%	–5%	–5%	–5%	–5%
Revenues	$50,703	$48,168	$45,759	$43,471	$41,298	$39,233
Operating margin	3.05%	3.24%	3.43%	3.62%	3.81%	4.00%
EBIT	$1,548	$1,562	$1,570	$1,574	$1,574	$1,569
EBIT * (1 – tax rate)	$960	$968	$974	$976	$976	$973
Return on capital	4.99%	5.50%	6.00%	6.50%	7.00%	7.50%
Capital invested	$19,234	$17,606	$16,227	$15,015	$13,939	$12,973
Change in book capital		–$1,628	–$1,379	–$1,212	–$1,077	–$965
Divestiture proceeds as % of book value		54.08%	58.9%	61.9%	64.7%	67.2%
Divestiture proceeds ($)		$880	$811	$751	$697	$649

Since we are assuming that the most unprofitable stores will be closed first, we also assume that the divestiture proceeds, as a percentage of book value, will be lower in the earlier years and increase over time. Note, though, that we receive well below 100% of capital invested in every year, ranging from 54% of capital in year 1 to 67% of capital in year 5. This reflects the fact that the investments being sold are delivering poor returns.[5]

To apply closure in the valuation, we assume that the divestitures end in year 5 and that Sears will revert to a more traditional, stable-growth firm after year 5. In keeping with this assumption, the cost of capital after year 5 drops to 7.13%, and the return on capital stays at 7.50% in perpetuity. Finally, we assume that the after-tax operating income will grow 2% a year in perpetuity, thus allowing us to estimate a reinvestment rate and terminal value:

$$\text{Reinvestment Rate} = \frac{g_{stable}}{ROC_{stable}} = \frac{2\%}{7.5\%} = 26.7\%$$

$$\text{Terminal Value} = \frac{\text{After-Tax Operating Income}_5\ (1+g_{\text{stable}})(1-\text{Reinvestment Rate})}{(\text{Cost of Capital}_{\text{stable}} - g_{\text{stable}})}$$

$$= \frac{973\ (1.02)(1-.267)}{(.0713-.02)} = \$14,187$$

Table 12.4 summarizes the cash flows for the next five years, the terminal value at the end of the fifth year, and the present values of these cash flows (discounted back at the cost of capital of 7.50%).

5 It is possible that we are being too conservative in this estimate, because the buyers of these assets may have no intention of preserving them as retail stores.

Table 12.4 **Expected Cash Flows and Value Today**

	Current	Year 1	Year 2	Year 3	Year 4	Year 5	Terminal Year
EBIT * (1 – tax rate)	$960	$968	$974	$976	$976	$973	$992
– Reinvestment		–$880	–$811	–$751	–$697	–$649	$265
Free cash flow to firm		$1,849	$1,785	$1,727	$1,673	$1,622	$728
Terminal value						$14,187	
Present value		$1,720	$1,545	$1,390	$1,252	$11,012	
Cost of capital		7.50%	7.50%	7.50%	7.50%	7.50%	7.13%

Summing up the present values over time yields a value of $16,918 million for the operating assets. Adding cash ($1,622 million), subtracting debt ($7,728 million), and dividing by the number of shares outstanding (132.01) yields a value per share of $81.91, about 10% higher than the prevailing market price ($76.25):

$$\text{Value per Share} = \frac{16,918 + 1,622 - 7728}{132.01} = \$81.91/\text{Share}$$

Reversible Decline, Low Distress

The corporate world has seen its share of rebirths, where firms that were viewed as in decline reversed the process and returned to growth or mature status. One example is Harley Davidson, the manufacturer of the cult-classic motorcycle. The firm saw sales slip to 32,400 motorcycles in 1982 and reported a loss of about $30 million that year. While many analysts were writing its epitaph, a new management team devised a strategy built around a loyal customer base and an iconic brand, and Harley rebounded to profitability and financial health.

It is worth noting, however, that most troubled firms never turn around and that righting the ship is not easy. Consequently, we should be realistic in our assessments of when decline is reversible and when it is not. Decline is more likely to be reversible if one or more of the following conditions are true:

- The company being analyzed has a history of operating ups and downs and has come back from decline before. Cycles in revenue growth and margins may then be part of the company's makeup and should be considered when valuing it.
- The sector or industry to which the company belongs is, for the most part, healthy, and the firm being analyzed is more the exception than the rule. When most of a firm's competitors are growing and making reasonable returns, and the firm is not, it seems reasonable to conclude that decline is the result of choices made by the firm, and that new management could conceivably turn the company around.

- The company is in a business that can benefit from macroeconomic trends. Even declining companies in a very cyclical business can see their operating results improve if the economy booms.

Note that while we may conclude that decline is likely to be reversed, there are no guarantees that it will.

The first step in valuing declining companies, where reversal is possible, is to estimate a value with existing policies and strategies, notwithstanding past failures. Since we are assuming continuing decline, it is entirely possible that the firm's revenues will stay flat, margins will decrease over time, and the returns on capital invested on both existing assets and new investments will be less than the cost of capital (are value-destroying). In effect, we are valuing the firm under the status quo, assuming that it is unable to turn itself around.

The second step is to assume that the firm's fortunes can be turned around either by new management/ownership or by existing management changing its policies. Assuming that the firm will revert to financial health, if not immediately, but in the near future, we can reestimate the firm's value, with the operating improvements built into the cash flows. If the rest of the sector is healthy, we could assume that the firm's margins and returns on invested capital will revert to industry averages. If not, we can look at the company's history to get a sense of what it will look like if it reverts to health. With these improvements in place, we should derive a higher value for the firm, under new or optimal management, than we did with the status quo.

The third step is estimating a probability of change occurring, using some of the techniques that we described in Chapter 11. Using a mix of subjective judgment and quantitative techniques, we can compute the likelihood that management will change. This estimate, though, will change as a function of the external environment, with the entrance of an activist investor into the mix changing the assessment. The firm's expected value will then reflect the weighted average of the status quo and optimal values, based on the probability of change.

Distress

Not all declining firms are distressed, nor are all distressed firms in decline, but distress and decline seem to go together. We will begin this section by arguing that distress occurs frequently and has serious consequences for value. We will then examine ways in which we can bring distress into discounted cash flow valuations. We also will examine the notion that equity investors may be able to derive value from the option to liquidate the firm. We will close the section by looking at how best to adapt relative valuation approaches to deal with distress.

The Possibility and Consequences of Financial Distress

Growth is not inevitable, and firms may not remain going concerns. In fact, even large publicly traded firms sometimes become distressed, and the consequences for value can be serious. This section first considers how often firms become distressed; it follows up by looking at the costs they face as a consequence. We will close the section by examining why, given the frequency with which firms face distress, we have historically not paid attention to distress in valuation.

The Possibility of Distress

Financial distress is far more common in the real world than most of us assume. In fact, even casual empirical observation suggests that a large number of firms do not survive and go out of business. Some fail because they borrow money to fund their operations and then are unable to make these debt payments. Others fail because they do not have the cash to cover their operating needs.

To get a measure of the probability of distress, we have to begin by defining distress. If we define it as companies that enter Chapter 11 bankruptcy, relatively few publicly traded firms at any point in time can be considered distressed. If we define distress more broadly as firms that have trouble making interest payments and meeting other contractual commitments, distress is much more common. Kahl (2001) examined all publicly traded firms in the U.S. between 1980 and 1983 and found that 1,346 firms had trouble making their interest expenses from operating income in at least one year. In addition, 151 firms could be considered distressed, in the sense that they were renegotiating with lenders to restructure debt.[6] Following up on these firms, he found that while less than half of these firms declare Chapter 11, only a third of them survive as independent companies. The rest get either acquired or liquidated.

The Consequences of Distress

What are the consequences of financial failure? Firms that are unable to make their debt payments have to liquidate their assets, often at bargain-basement prices, and use the cash to pay off debt. If any cash is left over, which is highly unlikely, it is paid to equity investors. Firms that are unable to make their operating payments also have to offer themselves to the highest bidder, with the proceeds distributed to the equity investors. In effect, these "liquidation costs" can be considered the direct costs of bankruptcy.

In fact, the costs of distress stretch far beyond the conventional costs of bankruptcy and liquidation. The perception of distress can do serious damage to a firm's operations, as employees, customers, suppliers, and lenders react. Firms that are viewed as distressed lose customers (and sales), have higher employee turnover, and have to accept much tighter restrictions from suppliers than healthy firms. These indirect bankruptcy costs can be catastrophic for many firms and essentially make the perception of distress into a reality. The magnitude of these costs has been examined in studies; it can range from 10 to 23% of firm value.[7]

In summary, the possibility and costs of distress are far too substantial to be ignored in valuation. The question then becomes not whether we should adjust firm value for the potential for distress, but how best to make this adjustment.

Distress in Discounted Cash Flow Valuation

Consider how we value a firm in a discounted cash flow world. We begin by projecting expected cash flows for a period. Then we estimate a terminal value at the end of the period that captures what we believe the firm will be worth at that point in time. Finally, we discount the cash flows

6 Kahl, M., 2001, "Financial Distress as a Selection Mechanism," SSRN working paper.

7 For an examination of the theory behind indirect bankruptcy costs, see Opler, T. and S. Titman, 1994, "Financial Distress and Corporate Performance," *Journal of Finance*, 49, pp. 1015–1040. For an estimate of how large these indirect bankruptcy costs are in the real world, see Andrade, G. and S. Kaplan, 1998, "How Costly Is Financial (Not Economic) Distress? Evidence from Highly Leveraged Transactions That Become Distressed," *Journal of Finance*, 53, pp. 1443–1493. They look at highly levered transactions that subsequently became distressed and conclude that the magnitude of these costs ranges from 10 to 23% of firm value.

back at a discount rate that reflects the riskiness of the firm's cash flows. This approach is extraordinarily flexible. It can be stretched to value firms ranging from those with predictable earnings and little growth to those in high growth with negative earnings and cash flows. Implicit in this approach, though, is the assumption that a firm is a going concern, with potentially an infinite life. The terminal value is usually estimated by assuming that earnings grow at a constant rate forever (a perpetual growth rate). Even when the terminal value is estimated using a multiple of revenues or earnings, this multiple is derived by looking at publicly traded firms (usually healthy ones).

Given the likelihood and consequences of distress, it seems foolhardy to assume that we can ignore this possibility when valuing a firm—particularly when we are valuing firms in poor health and with substantial debt obligations. So, you might wonder, what arguments are offered by proponents of discounted cash flow valuation for not explicitly considering the possibility of firms failing? We will consider five reasons often provided to explain this oversight. The first two are offered by analysts who believe that there is no need to consider distress explicitly in valuation. The last three reasons come from those who believe that discounted cash flow valuations already incorporate the effect of distress.

We value only large, publicly taded firms, and distress is very unlikely for these firms.

It is true that the likelihood of distress is lower for larger, more established firms, but experience suggests that even these firms can become distressed. The last few months of 2008 saw the demise of several large, publicly traded firms across the globe. At the end of 2008, analysts were openly discussing the possibility that GM and Ford would be unable to make their debt payments and may have to declare bankruptcy. The other problem with this argument, even if we accept the premise, is that smaller, high-growth firms are traded and need to be valued just as much as larger firms. In fact, we could argue that the need for valuation is greater for smaller firms, where the uncertainty and possibility of pricing errors are greater. With these firms, it is clearly foolhardy to ignore the potential for distress.

We assume that access to capital is unconstrained.

In valuation, as in much of corporate finance, we assume that a firm with good investments has access to capital markets and can raise the funds it needs to meet its financing and investment needs. Thus, firms with great growth potential will never be forced out of business, because they will be able to raise capital (more likely equity than debt) to keep going. In buoyant and developed financial markets, this assumption is not outlandish. Consider, for instance, the ease with which new-economy companies with negative earnings and few if any assets were able to raise new equity in the late 1990s. However, even in a market as open and accessible as the U.S., access to capital can dry up during a market crisis; in the last quarter of 2008, even GE had trouble rolling over its commercial paper. In summary, in 1998 and 1999 we may have been able to get away with assuming that firms with valuable assets will not be forced into a distress sale, but that assumption is untenable in 2009.

We adjust the discount rate for the possibility of distress.

The discount rate is the vehicle we use to adjust for risk in discounted cash flow valuation. Riskier firms have higher costs of equity, higher costs of debt, and usually higher costs of capital than safer firms. A reasonable extension of this argument would be that a firm with a greater possibility of distress should have a higher cost of capital and thus a lower firm value. The argument has merit up to a point. The cost of capital for a distressed firm, estimated correctly, should be higher than the cost of capital for a safer firm. If the distress is caused by high financial leverage, the cost of equity should be much higher. Since the cost of debt is based on current borrowing rates, it should also climb as the firm becomes more exposed to the risk of bankruptcy. The effect is exacerbated if the tax advantage of borrowing also dissipates (as a result of operating losses). Ultimately, though, the adjustment to value that results from using a higher discount rate is only a partial one. The firm is still assumed to generate cash flows in perpetuity, although the present value is lower. A significant portion of the firm's current value still comes from the terminal value. In other words, the biggest risk of distress—the loss of all future cash flows—is not adequately captured in value.

We adjust the expected cash flows for the possibility of distress.

To better understand this adjustment, it is worth reviewing what the expected cash flows in a discounted cash flow valuation are supposed to measure. The expected cash flow in a year should be the probability-weighted estimate of the cash flows under all scenarios for the firm, ranging from the best case to the worst case. In other words, if there is a 30% chance that a firm will not survive the next year, the expected cash flow should reflect both this probability and the resulting cash flow. In practice, we tend to be far sloppier in our estimation of expected cash flows. In fact, it is not uncommon to use an exogenous estimate of the expected growth rate (from analyst estimates) on the current year's earnings or revenues to generate future values. Alternatively, we often map out an optimistic path to profitability for unprofitable firms and use this path as the basis for estimating expected cash flows. We could estimate the expected cash flows under all scenarios and use the expected values in our valuation. Thus, the expected cash flows would be much lower for a firm with a significant probability of distress. Note, though, that, contrary to conventional wisdom, this is not a risk adjustment. We are doing what we should have been doing in the first place—estimating the expected cash flows correctly. If we wanted to risk-adjust the cash flows, we would have to adjust the expected cash flows downward even further using a certainty equivalent.[8] If we do this, though, the discount rate used would have to be the risk-free rate, not the risk-adjusted cost of capital. As a practical matter, it is very difficult to adjust expected cash flows for the possibility of distress. Not only do we need to estimate the probability of distress each year, we have to keep track of the cumulative probability of distress as well. This is because a firm that becomes distressed in year 3 loses its cash flows not just in that year but also in all subsequent years.

8 A certainty equivalent cash flow replaces an uncertain cash flow with an equivalent riskless cash flow. Thus, an expected cash flow of $125 million will be replaced by a riskless cash flow of $100 million. The more uncertain the cash flow, the greater the downward adjustment.

We assume that, even in distress, the firm will be able to receive the present value of expected cash flows from its assets as proceeds from the sale.

The problem with distress, from a DCF standpoint, is not that the firm ceases to exist, but that all cash flows beyond that point in time are lost. Thus, a firm with great products and potentially a huge market may never see this promise converted into cash flows, because it goes bankrupt early in its life. If we assume that this firm can sell itself to the highest bidder for a distress sale value that is equal to the present value of expected future cash flows, however, distress does not have to be considered explicitly. This is a daunting assumption. We are not only assuming that a firm in distress has the bargaining power to demand fair market value for its assets. We also are assuming that it can do this not only with assets in place (investments it has already made and products it has produced) but also with growth assets (products it may have been able to produce in the future).

In summary, the failure to explicitly consider distress in discounted cash flow valuation does not have a material impact in value if any the following conditions are true:

- There is no possibility of bankruptcy, either because of the firm's size and standing or because of a government guarantee.
- Easy access to capital markets allows firms with good investments to raise debt or equity capital to sustain themselves through bad times, thus ensuring that these firms will never be forced into a distress sale.
- We use expected cash flows that incorporate the likelihood of distress and a discount rate that is adjusted for the higher risk associated with distress. In addition, we have to assume that the firm will receive sale proceeds that are equal to the present value of expected future cash flows as a going concern in the event of a distress sale.

If these conditions do not hold, and it is easy to argue that they will not for some firms at some points in time, discounted cash flow valuations overstate firm value.

Discounted Cash Flow Valuation

When will the failure to consider distress in discounted cash flow valuation have a material impact on value? If the likelihood of distress is high, access to capital is constrained (by internal or external factors), and distress sale proceeds are significantly lower than going-concern values, discounted cash flow valuations will overstate firm and equity value for distressed firms. This is true even if the cash flows and discount rates are correctly estimated. This section considers several ways of incorporating the effects of distress into the estimated value.

Simulations

In traditional valuation, we estimate the expected values for each of the input variables. For instance, in valuing a firm, we may assume an expected growth rate in revenues of 30% a year and that the expected operating margin will be 10%. In reality, each of these variables has a distribution of possible values, which we condense into an expected value. Chapter 3 noted that simulations use the information in the entire distribution, rather than just the expected value. By doing so, they give us an opportunity to deal explicitly with distress.

Before we begin running the simulations, we have to decide the circumstances that will constitute distress and what will happen in the event of distress. For example, we may determine that cumulative operating losses of more than $1 billion over three years will push the firm into distress and that it will sell its assets for 25% of book value in that event. The parameters for distress will vary not only across firms, based on size and asset characteristics, but also on the state of financial markets and the overall economy. A firm that has three bad years in a row in a healthy economy with rising equity markets may be less exposed to default than a similar firm in the middle of a recession.

The simulations follow the standard steps described in Chapter 3. First we choose the variables we want to assign distributions to. Some of these, such as revenue growth and margins, are specific to the firm. Others, such as interest rates, relate to the overall economy. Then we estimate the probability distributions for these variables. In each simulation, we draw one outcome from each distribution (revenue growth rate, margin, and interest rate) and estimate the firm's earnings and cash flows. If the distress constraint is triggered, we assume that the firm will become distressed, and we estimate a distress sale value. If distress is not triggered, we value the firm as a going concern. The average across all simulated values is the firm's value. We should also be able to assess the probability of default from the simulation and the effect of distress on value. The primary limitation of simulation analysis is the information that is required for it to work. In practice, it is difficult to choose the right distribution to describe a variable and the parameters of that distribution. When these choices are made carelessly or randomly, the output from the simulation may look impressive, but it actually conveys no valuable information.

Modified Discounted Cash Flow Valuation

We can adapt discounted cash flow valuation to reflect some or most of the effects of distress on value. To do this, we will bring the effects of distress into both expected cash flows and discount rates.

Estimating Expected Cash Flows

To build the effects of distress into a discounted cash flow valuation, we have to incorporate the probability that a firm will not survive into the expected cash flows. In its most complete form, this requires that we consider all possible scenarios, ranging from the most optimistic to the most pessimistic. It also requires that we assign probabilities to each scenario and cash flows under each scenario, and estimate the expected cash flows each year:

$$\text{Expected Cash Flow} = \sum_{j=1}^{j=n} \pi_{jt}\,(\text{Cash Flow}_{jt})$$

π_{jt} is the probability of scenario j in period t. Cash flow$_{jt}$ is the cash flow under that scenario and in that period. These inputs have to be estimated each year, because the probabilities and cash flows are likely to change from year to year. Note that the adjustment for distress is a cumulative one and will have a greater impact on the expected cash flows in the later year. Thus, if the probability of distress is 10% in year 1, the expected cash flows in all subsequent years have to reflect the fact that if the firm ceases to exist in year 1, there will be no cash flows later. If the probability of distress in year 2 is 10% again, there is now only an 81% chance that the firm will have cash flows in year 3.[9]

9 The probability of surviving into year 3 = (1 – .10) (1 – .10) = 0.81.

Estimating Discount Rates

In an earlier section, we noted the problems with estimating costs of capital for distressed firms. Regression betas often lag distress, because they are estimated over long time periods. Also, the cost of debt can be skewed upward (if we use the market interest rate on bonds issued by the company) or downward (if we stick with book interest rates). To estimate discount rates that truly reflect the firm's distress risk, we have to look past the standard approaches:

- To estimate the cost of equity, we have two options that provide more reasonable estimates than regression betas. Instead of using regression betas, we could use the bottom-up unlevered beta and the firm's current market debt-to-equity ratio. Since distressed firms often have high debt-to-equity ratios, brought about largely as a consequence of dropping stock prices, this leads to levered betas that are significantly higher than regression betas.[10] If we couple this with the reality that most distressed firms are in no position to get any tax advantages from debt, the levered beta becomes even higher:

Levered Beta = Bottom-Up Unlevered Beta (1 + (1 – Tax Rate) (Debt-to-Equity Ratio))

Note, though, that it is reasonable to reestimate debt-to-equity ratios and tax rates for future years based on our expectations for the firm and to adjust the beta to reflect these changes.[11] The other choice is to estimate the cost of equity, using a beta more reflective of a healthy firm in the business, and then add an additional premium to reflect distress:

Cost of Equity = Risk-Free Rate + $\text{Beta}_{\text{Healthy}}$(Equity Risk Premium) + Distress Premium

We compute the distress premium in one of two ways. We can look at historical data on returns earned by investing in the equity of distressed firms. Or we can compare the company's own pre-tax cost of debt to the industry average cost of debt. Thus, if the industry average cost of debt is 8% and a company has a pre-tax cost of debt of 16%, we would add 8% to the conventional cost-of-equity estimate.

- To estimate the cost of debt for a distressed firm, we recommend using a default spread based on the firm's bond rating:

Pre-Tax Cost of Debt = Risk-Free Rate + Default Spread Based on Bond Rating

If the firm is not rated, we would estimate a synthetic rating for it. This will still yield a high cost of debt, but it is more reasonable than the yield to maturity when default is viewed as imminent.[12]

- To compute the cost of capital, we need to estimate the weights on debt on equity. In the initial year, we should use the current market debt-to-capital ratio (which may be very high for a distressed firm). As we make our forecasts for future years and build in our

10 For more on bottom-up betas, see Damodaran, A., 2002, *Applied Corporate Finance*, John Wiley and Sons.

11 There are other variations on this leverage adjustment. Some analysts, for instance, prefer a more complete version that allows debt to carry systematic risk and have a beta. Others prefer to eliminate the tax adjustment. Still others argue for other ways of adjusting betas for distress risk.

12 The yields to maturity on bonds issued by companies that have a significant probability of distress will be stratospheric, because they are based on the promised cash flows on the bond, rather than expected cash flows.

expectations of improvements in profitability, we should adjust the debt ratio toward more reasonable levels. The conventional practice of using target debt ratios for the entire valuation period (which reflect industry averages or the optimal mix) can lead to misleading estimates of value for firms that are significantly overlevered.

- The biggest roadblock to using this approach is that even in its limited form, it is difficult to estimate the cumulative probabilities of distress (and survival) each year for the forecast period. Consequently, the expected cash flows may not completely incorporate the effects of distress. In addition, it is difficult to bring both the going concern and the distressed firm assumptions into the same model. We attempt to do so using probabilities, but the two approaches make different and sometimes contradictory assumptions about how markets operate and how distressed firms evolve over time.

Dealing with Distress Separately

An alternative to the modified discounted cash flow model presented in the preceding section is to separate the going-concern assumptions and the value that emerges from them from the effects of distress. To value the effects of distress, we estimate the cumulative probability that the firm will become distressed over the forecast period, and the proceeds that we estimate we will get from the distress sale. The value of the firm can then be written as follows:

$$\text{Firm Value} = \text{Going-Concern Value} * (1 - \pi_{\text{Distress}}) + \text{Distress Sale Value} * \pi_{\text{Distress}}$$

where π_{distress} is the cumulative probability of distress over the valuation period. In addition to making valuation simpler, it allows us to make consistent assumptions within each valuation. You may wonder about the differences between this approach and the far more conventional one of estimating liquidation value for deeply distressed firms. You can consider the distress sale value to be a version of liquidation value. If you assume that the probability of distress is 1, the firm value will, in fact, converge on liquidation value. The advantage of this approach is that it allows us to consider the possibility that even distressed firms have a chance of becoming going concerns.

Going-Concern DCF

To value a firm as a going concern, we consider only scenarios in which the firm survives. The expected cash flow is estimated only across these scenarios and thus should be higher than the expected cash flow estimated in the modified discounted cash flow model. When estimating discount rates, we assume that debt ratios will, in fact, decrease over time if the firm is overlevered and that the firm will derive tax benefits from debt as it turns the corner on profitability. This is consistent with the assumption that the firm will remain a going concern. Most discounted cash flow valuations that we observe in practice are going-concern valuations, although they may not come with the tag attached.

A less precise, albeit easier, alternative is to value the company as if it were healthy today. This requires estimating the cash flows that the firm would have generated if it were a healthy firm. This task is most easily accomplished by replacing the firm's operating margin with the average operating margin of healthy firms in the business. The cost of capital for the distressed firm can be set to the average cost of capital for the industry, and the firm's value can be computed. The danger of this approach is that it will overstate firm value by assuming that the return to financial health is both painless and imminent.

Estimating the Probability of Distress

A key input to this approach is the estimate of the cumulative probability of distress over the valuation period. This section considers three ways in which we can estimate this probability. The first is a statistical approach. Here we relate the probability of distress to a firm's observable characteristics—firm size, leverage, and profitability, for instance—by contrasting firms that have gone bankrupt in prior years with firms that did not. The second is a less data-intensive approach, where we use a firm's bond rating, and the empirical default rates of firms in that rating class, to estimate the probability of distress. The third way is to use the prices of corporate bonds issued by the firm to back out the probability of distress:

- **Statistical approaches**: The fact that hundreds of firms go bankrupt every year provides us with a rich database that can be examined to evaluate both why bankruptcy occurs and how to predict the likelihood of future bankruptcy. One of the earliest studies that used this approach was by Altman (1968), where he used linear discriminant analysis to arrive at a measure he called the Z score. In this first paper, which he has since updated several times, the Z score was a function of five ratios:

Z = 0.012 (Working Capital / Total Assets) + 0.014 (Retained Earnings / Total Assets) + 0.033 (EBIT / Total Assets) + 0.006 (Market Value of Equity / Book Value of Total Liabilities) + 0.999 (Sales / Total Assets)

Altman argued that we could compute the Z scores for firms and use them to forecast which firms would go bankrupt, and he provided evidence to back up his claim. Since his study, both academics and practitioners have developed their own versions of these credit scores.[13] Notwithstanding its usefulness in predicting bankruptcy, linear discriminant analysis does not provide a probability of bankruptcy. To arrive at such an estimate, we use a close variant—a probit. In a probit, we begin with the same data that was used in linear discriminant analysis—a sample of firms that survived a specific period and firms that did not. We develop an indicator variable that takes on a value of 0 or 1, as follows:

Distress Dummy = 0 for Any Firm That Survived the Period
= 1 for Any Firm That Went Bankrupt During the Period

We then consider information that would have been available at the beginning of the period that may have allowed us to separate the firms that went bankrupt from those that did not. For instance, we could look at the debt-to-capital ratios, cash balances, and operating margins of all the firms in the sample at the start of the period. We would expect firms with high debt-to-capital ratios, low cash balances, and negative margins to be more likely to go bankrupt. Finally, using the dummy variable as our dependent variable and the financial ratios (debt to capital and operating margin) as independent variables, we look for a relationship:

13 Altman, E. I., 1968, "Financial Ratios, Discriminant Analysis and the Prediction of Corporate Bankruptcy," *Journal of Finance*. For a more updated version of the Altman Z score and its relationship to default probabilities, take a look at Altman, E. I., 1993, *Corporate Financial Distress and Bankruptcy*, 2nd ed., John Wiley & Sons, New York.

Distress Dummy = a + b (Debt to Capital) + c (Cash Balance / Value) + d (Operating Margin)

If the relationship is statistically and economically significant, we have the basis for estimating probabilities of bankruptcy.[14] One advantage of this approach is that it can be extended to cover the likelihood of distress at firms without significant debt. For instance, we could relate the likelihood of distress at young technology firms to the cash-burn ratio, which measures how much cash a firm has on hand relative to its operating cash needs.[15]

- **Based on bond rating**: Many firms, especially in the U.S., have bonds that are rated for default risk by the ratings agencies. These bond ratings not only convey information about default risk (or at least the ratings agency's perception of default risk), but they also come with a rich history. Since bonds have been rated for decades, we can look at the default experience of bonds in each ratings class. Assuming that the ratings agencies have not significantly altered their ratings standards, we can use these default probabilities as inputs into discounted cash flow valuation models. Altman (2007) has estimated the cumulative probabilities of default for bonds in different ratings classes over five- and ten-year periods, following issuance. These estimates appear in Table 12.5.[16]

Table 12.5 Bond Rating and Probability of Default: 1971 to 2007

Rating	Cumulative Probability of Distress	
	5 Years	**10 Years**
AAA	0.04%	0.07%
AA	0.44%	0.51%
A+	0.47%	0.57%
A	0.20%	0.66%
A–	3.00%	5.00%
BBB	6.44%	7.54%
BB	11.9%	19.63%
B+	19.25%	28.25%
B	27.50%	36.80%
B–	31.10%	42.12%

14 This looks like a multiple regression. In fact, a probit is a more sophisticated version of this regression with constraints built in, ensuring that the probabilities do not exceed 1 or become negative.

15 Cash-Burn Ratio = Cash Balance / EBITDA. With negative EBITDA, this yields a measure of how long it will take the firm to burn through its cash balance.

16 Altman, E. I., 2008, Altman High-Yield Bond Default and Return Report, Citi Research.

Table 12.5 Bond Rating and Probability of Default: 1971 to 2007

Rating	Cumulative Probability of Distress	
	5 Years	**10 Years**
CCC	46.26%	59.02%
CC	54.15%	66.6%
C+	65.15%	75.16%
C	72.15%	81.03%
C–	80.00%	87.16%

As elaboration, the cumulative default probability for a bond rated BB at the start of the period is 19.63% over the next ten years. What are the limitations of this approach? The first is that we are delegating the responsibility of estimating default probabilities to the ratings agencies, and we assume that they do it well. The second is that we are assuming that the ratings standards do not shift over time. The third is that Table 12.5 measures the likelihood of default on a bond, but it does not indicate whether the defaulting firm goes out of business. Many firms continue to operate as going concerns after default. We can illustrate the use of this approach with Delta Airlines and Las Vegas Sands, two operating companies with significant probability of default at the start of 2009:

Company	Bond Rating	Estimated Probability of Distress
Delta Airlines	BBB–	13.58%
Las Vegas Sands	B+	28.25%

- **Based on bond price:** The conventional approach to valuing bonds discounts back promised cash flows at a cost of debt that incorporates a default spread to come up with a price. Consider an alternative approach. We could discount the expected cash flows on the bond, which would be lower than the promised cash flows because of the possibility of default, at the risk-free rate to price the bond. If we assume a constant annual probability of default, we can write the bond price as follows for a bond with a fixed coupon maturing in N years:

$$\text{Bond Price} = \sum_{t=1}^{t=N} \frac{\text{Coupon } (1-\pi_{Distress})^t}{(1+\text{Risk-Free Rate})^t} + \frac{\text{Face Value of Bond}(1-\pi_{Distress})^N}{(1+\text{Risk-Free Rate})^N}$$

This equation can now be used in conjunction with the price on a traded corporate bond to back out the probability of default. We are solving for an annualized probability of default over the life of the bond. We are ignoring the reality that the annualized probability of default will be higher in the earlier years and will decline in the later years. While this approach has the attraction of being simple, we hasten to add the following caveats in using it. First, note that we not only need to find a straight bond issued by the company—special features such as convertibility will render the approach unusable—but the bond price has to be available. If the corporate bond issue is privately placed, this will not be feasible. Second, the probabilities that are estimated may be different for different bonds issued by the same firm. Some of these differences can be traced to the assumption we have made that the annual probability of default remains constant, and others can be traced to the mispricing of bonds. Third, as with the previous approach, failure to make debt payments does not always result in the cessation of operations. Finally, we are assuming that the coupon is either paid fully or not at all. If there is a partial payment of either the coupon or the face value in default, we will overestimate the probabilities of default using this approach.

Estimating the Probability of Bankruptcy Using Bond Price: Las Vegas Sands

In January 2009, Las Vegas Sands had a 6.375% coupon bond, maturing in February 2015, trading at $529. The following estimates the probability of default (with a Treasury bond rate of 3% used as the risk-free rate):

$$529 = \sum_{t=1}^{t=7} \frac{63.75\,(1-\pi_{Distress})^t}{(1.03)^t} + \frac{1000(1-\pi_{Distress})^7}{(1.03)^7}$$

Solving for the probability of bankruptcy, we get the following:

$\pi_{Distress}$ = Annual Probability of Default = 13.54%

Here's how we estimate the cumulative probability of distress over ten years:

Cumulative Probability of Surviving 10 Years = $(1 - .1354)^{10}$ = 23.34%

Cumulative Probability of Distress over 10 Years = 1 – .2334 = .7666 or 76.66%

Estimating Distress Sale Proceeds

Once we have estimated the probability that the firm will be unable to make its debt payments and cease to exist, we have to consider the logical follow-up question. What happens then? As noted earlier in the chapter, it is not distress per se that is the problem, but the fact that firms in distress have to sell their assets for less than the present value of the expected future cash flows from existing assets and expected future investments. Often, they may be unable to claim even the present value of the cash flows generated by existing investments. Consequently, a key input we need to estimate is the expected proceeds in the event of a distress sale. We have three choices:

- Estimate the present value of the expected cash flows in a discounted cash flow model, and assume that the distress sale will generate only a percentage (less than 100%) of this value. Thus, if the discounted cash flow valuation yields $5 billion as the value of the assets, we may assume that the value will be only $3 billion in the event of a distress sale.

- Estimate the present value of expected cash flows only from existing investments as the distress sale value. Essentially, we are assuming that a buyer will not pay for future investments in a distress sale. In practical terms, we would estimate the distress sale value by considering the cash flows from assets in place as a perpetuity (with no growth).
- The most practical way of estimating distress sale proceeds is to consider them as a percentage of book value of assets, based on the experience of other distressed firms.

Note that many of the issues that come up when estimating distress sale proceeds—the need to sell at below fair value, the urgency of the need to sell—are issues that are relevant when estimating liquidation value.

Estimating Distress Sale Proceeds in January 2009: Las Vegas Sands

To estimate the expected proceeds in the event of a distress sale, we consider several factors. First, the poor state of the economy in January 2009 and the ongoing credit crisis clearly do not bode well for any firm trying to liquidate its assets in a hurry. Second, Las Vegas Sands assets are primarily real estate, and that segment of the economy is in even worse shape than the rest of the market. To estimate the proceeds in a distress sale, we consider two alternatives:

- We use the average operating income of $401.91 million, estimated using four years of data from 2005 to 2008 for Las Vegas Sands, as a reasonable measure of earnings from existing assets. We use a corporate tax rate of 38% and the cost of capital of 9% of healthier casino companies to estimate the value of existing assets:

$$\text{Value of Existing Assets} = \frac{\text{EBIT}(1-t)}{\text{Cost of Capital}} = \frac{401.91(1-.38)}{.09} = \$2{,}769 \text{ million}$$

  Note that we assume no growth and that any depreciation charges accrued will be plowed back into the firm to preserve earning power. A healthy casino firm should be willing to pay $2.769 billion to buy the existing assets.

- The book value of Las Vegas Sands' fixed assets at the end of 2008 was $11.275 billion. This represents the company's investments in both its ongoing assets (the Venetian and Sands Macau Casinos and the Las Vegas convention center) and its new developments. Since this book value represents real estate prices at the time of the original investment, we make two adjustments. First, we reduce the value by 40% to reflect the drop in real estate prices reported for Las Vegas between 2007 and 2008. Second, we estimate a relatively modest illiquidity discount of 10%, resulting in the following distress sale value:

Distress Sale Value = Book Value (1 – Price Depreciation) (1 – Illiquidity Discount)
= 11,275 (1 – .40) (1 – .10) = $6,089 million

To both estimates of distress sale proceeds, we would add the current cash balance of $3.04 billion to arrive at the total proceeds. Since the firm has debt outstanding with a face value of $10.47 billion, the equity investors would receive nothing in the event of a distress sale.

Although the two approaches yield very different estimates of distress sale value, we are wary of the book-value-based estimate. While it is true that the bulk of the company's investments are in real estate, it is also true that any buyer of this real estate would have to continue to operate the properties primarily as casinos. Consequently, the earnings power approach, which yields the lower value of $2.769 billion, is the one we would trust more in our analysis.

The Shifting Debt Load

In addition to having a substantial amount of debt, distressed firms often have very complicated debt structures. Not only do they owe money to a number of different creditors, but the debt itself often is complex—convertible, callable, and filled with special features demanded by the creditors for their own protection. In addition, distressed firms are often in the process of negotiating with debt holders, trying to convince them to change the terms of the debt and, in some cases, convert their debt into equity. Consequently, the value of the debt can change dramatically from day to day, thus affecting the value of equity, even if the enterprise value does not.

When estimating the value of debt in a distressed firm, we should consider doing the following:

- Rather than relying on the last available financial statements for the available debt, we should try to obtain an updated estimate of the outstanding debt. This may be difficult when the debt negotiations are private (between the distressed firm and the lenders).
- We should update the estimated market value of debt frequently, since the default risk of distressed firms can change substantially from period to period. Even if the debt is not traded, it is never appropriate with distressed firms to use the book value of debt as a proxy for the market value of debt. Instead, we should estimate the market value of debt, treating book debt like a corporate bond.
- When confronted with convertible debt, we should strip the conversion option from the debt and treat it as equity. Again, a simple way to do this is to value the convertible debt as if it were straight debt—this yields the debt portion of the convertible debt—and consider the difference between the market value of the convertible debt and the straight debt portion as equity.

In general, valuing a distressed firm is far easier than valuing equity in the same firm, largely because the debt outstanding will vary over time.

Valuing Las Vegas Sands with Distress Valued Separately

To value Las Vegas Sands with distress valued separately, we begin with a going-concern valuation of Las Vegas Sands, assuming that the firm survives and reverts to financial health.

For the fiscal year ended December 2008, Las Vegas Sands reported revenues of $4,390 million and pre-tax operating income of $209 million, yielding a pre-tax operating margin of 4.76%.[17] The capital invested in the company at the start of the year was $9,832 million, yielding an abysmal after-tax return on capital of 1.72% (assuming the firm's effective tax rate of 26%):

$$\text{Return on Capital} = \frac{209(1-.26)}{8975} = 1.72\%$$

To map out a path to recovery, first we have to estimate what we believe to be reasonable profitability measures if Las Vegas Sands can turn things around. To make these estimates, we first look at the operating margins and returns on capital reported by the firm over the last five years, as shown in Table 12.6.

Table 12.6 Revenues, Margins, and Return on Capital for LVS: 2003 to 2008

Year	Revenues	Operating Income	Pre-Tax Margin	Capital Invested	ROC
2004	1,197	233	19.47%	1,575	9.17%
2005	1,741	491	28.20%	1,810	16.82%
2006	2,237	577	25.79%	2,791	12.82%
2007	2,951	331	11.22%	2,049	10.02%
2008	4,390	209	4.76%	8,975	1.72%

Both the margins and returns earned in 2008 represent a break from a generally profitable past for Las Vegas Sands. We follow by estimating the average pre-tax operating margin (16.96%) and after-tax return on capital (approximately 10%) for casino firms in the U.S. at the start of 2009. Based on these numbers, we will assume that Las Vegas Sands, assuming it makes it as a healthy firm, will have a pre-tax operating margin of 17% and earn an after-tax return on capital of 10%.

To project operating results into the future, we will assume that revenues will grow only 1% next year and 2% the year after. We also will assume that the revenue growth rate will pick up, especially as two new casinos in development come online. The revenue growth rate will increase to 20% in years 3 through 5 before dropping

17 The reported operating income of $163 million was after an impairment charge for disposal of assets of $46 million. The adjusted operating income is $209 million.

to 5% a year for years 6 through 10. We will also assume that the recovery to the targeted margin will occur gradually over the next ten years. Pre-tax operating margins will improve to 10% by year 5 and then post a further increase to 17% by year 10; the changes in each period occur in linear increments. Table 12.7 summarizes our forecasts of revenues, margins, and operating income each year for the next ten years. We use a 26% effective tax rate to estimate the after-tax operating income for the first five years but gradually move that number up to the marginal tax rate of 38% by year 10.

Table 12.7 Expected Revenues and Operating Income for LVS

Year	Revenue Growth	Revenues	Operating Margin	Operating Income	Tax Rate	After-Tax Operating Income
Current		$4,390	4.76%	$209	26.00%	$155
1	1%	$4,434	5.81%	$258	26.00%	$191
2	2%	$4,523	6.86%	$310	26.00%	$229
3	20%	$5,427	7.90%	$429	26.00%	$317
4	20%	$6,513	8.95%	$583	26.00%	$431
5	20%	$7,815	10.00%	$782	26.00%	$578
6	5%	$8,206	11.40%	$935	28.40%	$670
7	5%	$8,616	12.80%	$1,103	30.80%	$763
8	5%	$9,047	14.20%	$1,285	33.20%	$858
9	5%	$9,499	15.60%	$1,482	35.60%	$954
10	5%	$9,974	17.00%	$1,696	38.00%	$1,051

Since much of the capital for the new casinos has already been invested, we will hold down capital expenditures for much of the high-growth period; in effect, the company is living off past investments.[18] As a consequence, the reinvestment rate will be negative for the next two years, because there will be significant cash inflows from depreciation charges. Then it will increase in the rest of the high-growth period.[19] Table 12.8 lists the free cash flows to the firm each year for the next ten years.

18 LVS had invested almost $3 billion in new developments in January 2009 that still had not commenced operations.

19 Since the cost of capital changes over time, we must compute a cumulated cost. For instance, the cost of capital in year 7 = $1.0988^5 * 1.979 * 1.0950 = 1.9261$.

Table 12.8 Expected Free Cash Flow to Firm for LVS

Year	After-Tax Operating Income	Reinvestment Rate	Reinvestment	FCFF
1	$191	–10.00%	–$19	$210
2	$229	–5.00%	–$11	$241
3	$317	0.00%	$0	$317
4	$431	5.00%	$22	$410
5	$578	10.00%	$58	$520
6	$670	10.00%	$67	$603
7	$763	20.00%	$153	$611
8	$858	25.00%	$215	$644
9	$954	30.00%	$286	$668
10	$1,051	33.30%	$350	$701

We will begin the valuation with a cost of capital for Las Vegas Sands that reflects its tenuous hold on going-concern status. We use the unlevered beta of 1.15 for casino companies as a starting point and compute the levered beta, based on the company's existing debt-to-equity ratio of 277.34%. This is computed based on the estimated market value of equity and debt at the time of the analysis. The market value of equity, based on the prevailing stock price of $4.25 and the 641.839 million shares outstanding, is $2.728 billion. To estimate the market value of debt, we first estimate the cost of debt. We add a default spread of 6% (based on its rating of B+, from S&P) to the risk-free rate of 3%. Then we use the current interest expenses ($422 million) and face value of debt ($10.47 billion) to arrive at a present value for the debt of $7.57 billion:

$$\text{Estimated Market Value of Debt} = \text{Interest Expense}\left[\frac{1-\frac{1}{(1+r)^n}}{r}\right] + \frac{\text{Face Value of Debt}}{(1+r)^n}$$

$$= 422\left[\frac{1-\frac{1}{(1.09)^{8.1}}}{.09}\right] + \frac{10,470}{(1.09)^{8.1}} = \$7,565m$$

Market Debt / Equity Ratio = 7,565 / 2,728 = 277.34%

Market Debt / Capital Ratio = 7,565 / (7,565 + 2,728) = 73.5%

Levered Beta = 1.15 (1 + (1 – .38) (2.7734)) = 3.14

Cost of Equity = Risk-Free Rate + Beta (Equity Risk Premium)

= 3% + 3.14 (6%) = 21.82%

Since the firm still has positive operating income and is expected to recover, we will assume that it will be able to get the full tax benefits of debt (based on the marginal tax rate of 38%):

Pre-Tax Cost of Debt = Risk-Free Rate + Default Spread = 3% + 6% = 9%

After-Tax Cost of Debt = 9% (1 – .38) = 5.58%

Using the current debt ratio of 73.50%, we estimate a cost of capital of 9.88% for Las Vegas Sands:

Cost of Capital = Cost of Equity (1 – Debt Ratio) + After-Tax Cost of Debt (Debt Ratio)

= 21.82% (.265) + 5.58% (.735) = 9.88%

However, we will assume that as the firm becomes healthier, its debt ratio will converge on the casino industry average of 50%. We also will assume that its cost of capital will move down to 7.43% to reflect the return to financial health. Table 12.9 lists the resulting numbers.

Table 12.9 Costs of Equity, Debt, and Capital for LVS

Year	Beta	Cost of Equity	Pre-Tax Cost of Debt	Debt Ratio	Cost of Capital
1	3.14	21.82%	9.00%	73.50%	9.88%
2	3.14	21.82%	9.00%	73.50%	9.88%
3	3.14	21.82%	9.00%	73.50%	9.88%
4	3.14	21.82%	9.00%	73.50%	9.88%
5	3.14	21.82%	9.00%	73.50%	9.88%
6	2.75	19.50%	8.70%	68.80%	9.79%
7	2.36	17.17%	8.40%	64.10%	9.50%
8	1.97	14.85%	8.10%	59.40%	9.01%

Year	Beta	Cost of Equity	Pre-Tax Cost of Debt	Debt Ratio	Cost of Capital
9	1.59	12.52%	7.80%	54.70%	8.32%
10	1.20	10.20%	7.50%	50.00%	7.43%

As operating margins improve, we will keep track of the firm's return on capital. We will compute the capital invested each year (based on the reinvestment) and check to make sure that we are moving toward our targeted return on capital of 10% over time. Table 12.10 summarizes the year-by-year estimates of capital invested and after-tax return on capital for Las Vegas Sands.

Table 12.10 Capital Invested and Return on Capital for LVS

Year	After-Tax Operating Income	Reinvestment	Capital Invested	Return on Capital
Current	$155		$8,975	1.72%
1	$191	–$19	$8,956	2.13%
2	$229	–$11	$8,944	2.57%
3	$317	$0	$8,944	3.55%
4	$431	$22	$8,966	4.81%
5	$578	$58	$9,024	6.41%
6	$670	$67	$9,091	7.37%
7	$763	$153	$9,243	8.26%
8	$858	$215	$9,458	9.07%
9	$954	$286	$9,744	9.79%
10	$1,051	$350	$10,094	10.41%

Capital Invested in Year n = Capital Invested Year n – 1 + Reinvestment in Year n

Note that the return on capital in year 10 is 10.41%, close to the target return on capital of 10%.

To complete the valuation, we will assume that Las Vegas Sands will be in stable growth after year 10, growing at 3% a year (set equal to the risk-free rate cap) forever. We will also assume that the return on capital will be 10% in perpetuity and that the stable period cost of capital is 7.43% (from Table 12.9). The terminal value can then be computed:

$$\text{Reinvestment Rate} = \frac{g_{stable}}{ROC_{stable}} = \frac{3\%}{10\%} = 30\%$$

$$\text{Terminal Value} = \frac{\text{After-Tax Operating Income}_5\,(1+g_{stable})(1-\text{Reinvestment Rate})}{(\text{Cost of Capital}_{stable} - g_{stable})}$$

$$= \frac{1051\,(1.03)(1-.30)}{(.0743-.03)} = \$17{,}129$$

Bringing together the free cash flows from Table 12.8, the terminal value just shown, and the cost of capital from Table 12.9, we can compute the value of the operating assets, as shown in Table 12.11.

Table 12.11 Value of Operating Assets for LVS

Year	FCFF	Terminal Value	Cost of Capital	Cumulated Cost of Capital	PV
1	$210		9.88%	1.0988	$190.79
2	$241		9.88%	1.2075	$199.54
3	$317		9.88%	1.3268	$239.25
4	$410		9.88%	1.4579	$281.12
5	$520		9.88%	1.6021	$324.88
6	$603		9.79%	1.7590	$342.71
7	$611		9.50%	1.9261	$316.98
8	$644		9.01%	2.0997	$306.52
9	$668		8.32%	2.2744	$293.72
10	$701	$17,129.27	7.43%	2.4433	$7,297.83
			Value of operating assets =		$9,793.34

Adding cash ($3,040 million), subtracting the market value of debt ($7,565 million), and dividing by the number of shares outstanding (641.839 million) yields a value per share of $8.21:

$$\text{Value per Share} = \frac{9793 + 3040 - 7565}{641.839} = \$8.21/\text{Share}$$

Note that the market value of debt is significantly lower than the face value of almost $10.47 billion. However, it is consistent with our assumption that LVS will make it as a going concern.

We can now bring the probability of distress and the consequences into our final estimate of equity value. Earlier we estimated the probability of distress from the bond market to be 76.66%. We concluded that the distress sale value of the assets would be lower than the debt outstanding, making equity worthless. The expected value of equity per share in LVS can then be computed:

Expected Value per Share = Value per Share as Going Concern (1 – Probability of Distress) + Value per Share in Distress (Probability of Distress)
= \$8.21 (.2334) + \$0.00 (1 – .2334) = \$1.92

If we adjust for the possibility of distress, the value per share is only $1.92, about half the stock price of $4.25 in February 2009. However, using the probability of distress, based on the B+ rating, of 28.25% yields a value of $5.89 per share, about 40% higher than the stock price. The question of whether Las Vegas Sands is under- or overvalued therefore becomes one of assessing the likelihood of distress at the firm.

Adjusted Present Value (APV)

With the APV approach, described more fully in Chapter 11, we begin with the value of the firm without debt. As we add debt to the firm, we consider the net effect on value by considering both the benefits and the costs of borrowing. To do this, we assume that the primary benefit of borrowing is a tax benefit and that the most significant cost of borrowing is the added risk of bankruptcy. With distressed firms, the advantage of separating the value impact of debt from the value of the operating assets is that more attention can be paid to the cost and probability of distress.

Reviewing the steps in the APV approach, we estimate the firm's value in three steps. We begin by estimating the firm's value with no leverage by discounting the expected free cash flow to the firm at the unlevered cost of equity. In the special case where cash flows grow at a constant rate in perpetuity, the firm's value is easily computed:

$$\text{Value of Unlevered Firm} = \frac{FCFF_0(1+g)}{\rho_u - g}$$

$FCFF_0$ is the current after-tax operating cash flow to the firm, ρ_u is the unlevered cost of equity, and g is the expected growth rate. In the more general case, we can value the firm using any set of growth assumptions we believe are reasonable for the firm.

We then consider the present value of the interest tax savings generated by borrowing a given amount of money. This tax benefit is a function of the firm's tax rate and is discounted at the cost of debt to reflect the riskiness of this cash flow. If the tax savings are viewed as a perpetuity, the value is as follows:

$$\text{Value of Tax Benefits} = \frac{(\text{Tax Rate})(\text{Cost of Debt})(\text{Debt})}{\text{Cost of Debt}}$$

$$= (\text{Tax Rate})(\text{Debt})$$

$$= t_c D$$

For a distressed firm, this value is depressed if the firm has substantial operating losses and does not expect to get tax benefits for the foreseeable future.

The third step is to evaluate the effect of the given level of debt on the firm's default risk and on expected bankruptcy costs. This requires estimating the probability of default with the additional debt and the direct and indirect costs of bankruptcy. If π_a is the probability of default after the additional debt, and BC is the present value of the bankruptcy cost, the present value of the expected bankruptcy cost can be estimated:

$$\text{PV of Expected Bankruptcy Cost} = (\text{Probability of Bankruptcy})(\text{PV of Bankruptcy Cost}) = \pi_a BC$$

We can use the approaches described in the preceding section to arrive at an estimate of the probability of bankruptcy. We can also consider the difference between the value of a firm as a going concern and the distress sale value as the cost of bankruptcy. Thus, if the present value of expected cash flows is \$5 billion—the going-concern value—and the distress sale proceeds are expected to be only 25% of the book value of \$4 billion, the bankruptcy cost is \$4 billion:

Expected Bankruptcy Cost = \$5 billion – .25 (4 billion) = \$4 billion

Again, with distressed firms, the present value of expected bankruptcy costs is likely to be a large number. The combination of low tax benefits and large bankruptcy costs is likely to reduce firm value.

Almeida and Philippon (2005) suggest a variation on the adjusted present value model. They argue that the conventional measure of distress costs understates its magnitude because it does not factor in the reality that distress costs are often systematic (market- and economy-driven). They present two ways of adjusting distress cost value to reflect this systematic risk. In the first, they derive probabilities of default from corporate bond spreads, akin to what we did earlier. In the second, they derive the risk adjustment from historical data on distress probabilities and asset-pricing models. They conclude that the expected bankruptcy costs are substantial and have a large impact on value.

Valuing Las Vegas Sands: Adjusted Present Value

To value Las Vegas Sands on an adjusted present value basis, first we need to value the firm as an unlevered entity. We can do this by using the unlevered cost of equity as the cost of capital:

Unlevered Beta for Las Vegas Sands = 1.1535

We use the risk-free rate of 3% and the market risk premium of 6%:

Unlevered Cost of Equity for Las Vegas Sands = 3% + 1.1535 (6%) = 9.92%

We use this cost of equity as the cost of capital and discount the expected free cash flows to the firm, shown earlier in Table 12.8. Table 12.12 summarizes the present value of the cash flows at the unlevered cost of equity. (Note that the terminal value is left unchanged. We will continue to assume that the firm will earn its cost of capital on investments after year 10.)

Table 12.12 Present Value of FCFF at Unlevered Cost of Equity

Year	FCFF	Terminal Value	Present Value
1	$210		$191
2	$241		$199
3	$317		$239
4	$410		$281
5	$520		$324
6	$603		$342
7	$611		$315
8	$644		$302
9	$668		$285
10	$701	$10,952	$4,525
Terminal year	$758		
Unlevered value of operating assets =			$7,003

The unlevered value for the operating assets is $7,003 million. To this we should add the expected tax benefits of debt, computed by taking 38% of the debt outstanding ($7,565 million).[20] To estimate the bankruptcy cost, we consider the difference between the going-concern value of $7,003 million and the distress sale estimate of $2,769 million (estimated earlier) to be the bankruptcy cost. Multiplying this by the probability of bankruptcy (76.66%) estimated earlier yields the expected cost of bankruptcy:

Adjusted Present Value of LVS's Assets = Unlevered Firm Value + Present Value of Tax Benefits – Expected Bankruptcy Costs

= 7,003 + 0.38 * 7,565 – 0.7666 (7003 – 2,769)

= $6,632 million

Adding back the cash and marketable securities and subtracting debt yields a value of equity for Las Vegas Sands:

20 We use the market value of debt to capture the possibility that tax benefits will be lost if the firm defaults on its debt.

APV of LVS Assets = $6,632 million

+ Cash and Marketable Securities = $3,040 million

– Market Value of Debt = $7,565 million

Value of Equity = $2,107 million

Value per Share = $2,107 million / 355.27 = $3.28

This value is already distress-adjusted and can be compared to the market price of $4.25 a share.

Equity as an Option

In most publicly traded firms, equity has two features. The first is that the equity investors run the firm and can choose to liquidate its assets and pay off other claimholders at any time. The second is that the liability of equity investors in some private firms and almost all publicly traded firms is restricted to their equity investments in these firms. This combination of the option to liquidate and limited liability gives equity the features of a call option. In firms with substantial debt and a significant potential for bankruptcy, the option value of equity may be in excess of the discounted cash flow value of equity.

The Payoff on Equity as an Option

The equity in a firm is a residual claim. In other words, equity holders lay claim to all cash flows left after other financial claimholders (debt, preferred stock) have been satisfied. If a firm is liquidated, the same principle applies. Equity investors receive the cash that is left in the firm after all outstanding debt and other financial claims have been paid off. With limited liability, if the firm's value is less than the value of the outstanding debt, equity investors cannot lose more than their investment in the firm. The payoff to equity investors on liquidation therefore can be written as follows:

Payoff to Equity on Liquidation = $V - D$ if $V >$ = 0 if $V \leq D$

where

V = the firm's liquidation value

D = face value of the outstanding debt and other external claims

Equity thus can be viewed as a call option on the firm. Exercising the option requires that the firm be liquidated and the face value of the debt (which corresponds to the exercise price) be paid off. The firm is the underlying asset, and the option expires when the debt comes due. The payoffs are shown in Figure 12.2.

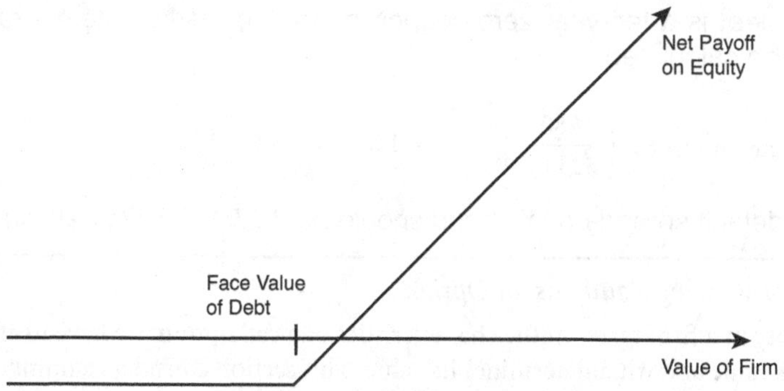

Figure 12.2: Payoff on Equity as an Option on a Firm

Valuing Equity as an Option

Assume that we are valuing the equity in a firm whose assets are currently valued at $100 million; the standard deviation in this asset value is 40%. The face value of debt is $80 million (it is zero-coupon debt with ten years left to maturity). The ten-year treasury bond rate is 10%. We can value equity as a call option on the firm, using the following inputs for the option pricing model:

Value of the Underlying Asset = S = Value of the Firm = $100 million

Exercise Price = K = Face Value of Outstanding Debt = $80 million

Life of the Option = t = Life of Zero-Coupon Debt = 10 years

Variance in the Value of the Underlying Asset = σ^2 = Variance in Firm Value = 0.16

Riskless Rate = r = Treasury Bond Rate Corresponding to Option Life = 10%

Based on these inputs, the Black-Scholes model provides the following value for the call:

$d_1 = 1.5994 \quad N(d_1) = 0.9451$

$d_2 = 0.3345 \quad N(d_2) = 0.6310$

Value of the Call = $100\ (.9451) - 80\ e^{-(.10)(10)}\ (.6310)$ = $75.94 million

Since the call value represents the value of equity and the firm value is $100 million, the estimated value of the outstanding debt can be calculated:

Value of the Outstanding Debt = $100 – $75.94 = $24.06 million

Since the debt is a ten-year zero-coupon bond, the market interest rate on the bond can be calculated:

$$\text{Interest Rate on Debt} = \left(\frac{\$80}{\$24.06}\right)^{\frac{1}{10}} - 1 = 12.77\%$$

Thus, the default spread on this bond should be 2.77% (12.77% –10%).

Implications of Viewing Equity as an Option

When the equity in a firm takes on the characteristics of a call option, we have to change how we think about its value and what determines its value. This section considers a number of potential implications for equity investors and bondholders in the firm.

When Will Equity Be Worthless?

In discounted cash flow valuation, we argue that equity is worthless if what we own (the firm's value) is less than what we owe. The first implication of viewing equity as a call option is that equity will have value even if the firm's value falls well below the face value of the outstanding debt. Although the firm will be viewed as troubled by investors, accountants, and analysts, its equity is not worthless. Deep out-of-the-money traded call options command value because of the possibility that the value of the underlying asset may increase above the strike price in the option's remaining lifetime. Similarly, equity commands value because of the time premium on the option (the time until the bonds mature and come due) and the possibility that the value of the assets may increase above the face value of the bonds before they come due.

Firm Value and Equity Value

Revisiting the preceding example, assume that the firm's value drops to $50 million, below the face value of the outstanding debt ($80 million). Also assume that all the other inputs remain unchanged. The parameters of equity as a call option are as follows:

Value of the Underlying Asset = S = Value of the Firm = $50 million

Exercise Price = K = Face Value of Outstanding Debt = $80 million

Life of the Option = t = Life of Zero-Coupon Debt = 10 years

Variance in the Value of the Underlying Asset = σ^2 = Variance in Firm Value = 0.16

Riskless Rate = r = Treasury Bond Rate Corresponding to Option Life = 10%

Based on these inputs, the Black-Scholes model provides the following value for the call:

$d_1 = 1.0515 \quad N(d_1) = 0.8534$

$d_2 = -0.2135 \; N(d_2) = 0.4155$

Value of the Call (Equity) = 50 (0.8534) – 80 $\exp^{(-0.10)(10)}$ (0.4155) = \$30.44 million

Value of the Bond= \$50 – \$30.44 = \$19.56 million

As we can see, the equity in this firm retains value, because of the option characteristics of equity. In fact, equity continues to have value in this example, even if the firm value drops to \$10 million or less.

Increasing Risk Can Increase Equity Value

In traditional discounted cash flow valuation, higher risk almost always translates into lower value for equity investors. When equity takes on the characteristics of a call option, we should not expect this relationship to continue to hold. Risk can become our ally when we are equity investors in a troubled firm. In essence, we have little to lose and much to gain from swings in firm value.

Equity Value and Volatility

Let us revisit the valuation from two sidebars ago. The value of the equity is a function of the variance in firm value, which we assume to be 40%. If we change this variance, holding all else constant, the value of the equity will change, as shown in Figure 12.3.

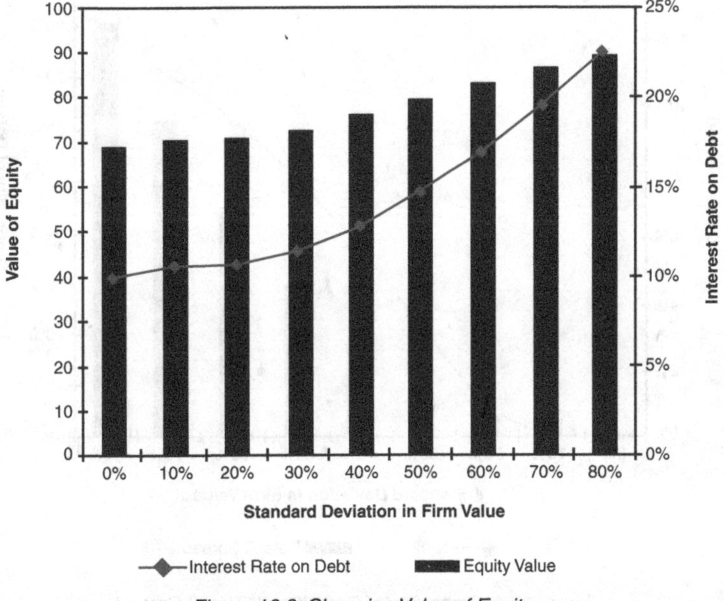

Figure 12.3: Changing Value of Equity

Note that the value of equity increases if we hold firm value constant, as the standard deviation increases. The interest rate on debt also increases as the standard deviation increases.

Probability of Default and Default Spreads

One of the more interesting pieces of output from the option pricing model is the risk-neutral probability of default that we can obtain for the firm. In the Black-Scholes model, we can estimate this value from $N(d_2)$, which is the risk-neutral probability that $S > K$. In this model, this is the probability that the value of the firm's asset will exceed the face value of the debt:

$$\text{Risk-Neutral Probability of Default} = 1 - N(d_2)$$

In addition, the interest rate from the debt allows us to estimate the appropriate default spread to charge on bonds.

You can see the potential of applying this model to bank loan portfolios to extract the probability of default and to measure whether you are charging a high-enough interest rate on the debt. In fact, there are commercial services that use fairly sophisticated option-pricing models to estimate both values for firms.

Probabilities of Default and Default Spreads

Now we will estimate the probability of default as $N(d_2)$. The default spread is measured as the difference between the interest rate on a firm's debt and the risk-free rate as a function of the variance. These values are graphed in Figure 12.4.

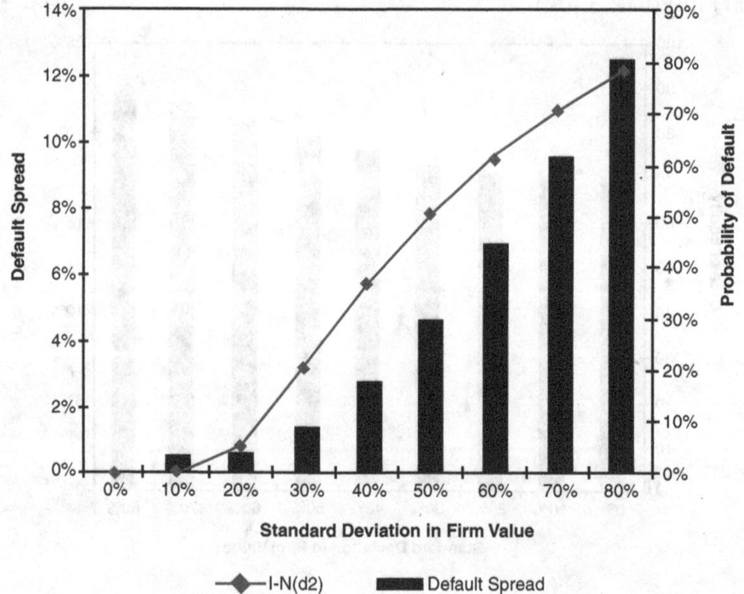

Figure 12.4: Probability of Default and Default Spread

Note that the probability of default climbs very quickly as the standard deviation in firm value increases and the default spread follows it.

Estimating the Value of Equity as an Option

The examples we have used thus far to illustrate the application of option pricing to value equity have included some simplifying assumptions:

- The firm has only two claimholders—debt and equity.
- Only one issue of debt is outstanding, and it can be retired at face value.
- The debt has a zero coupon and no special features (convertibility, put clauses, and so on).
- The value of the firm and the variance in that value can be estimated.

Each of these assumptions is made for a reason. First, by restricting the claimholders to just debt and equity, we make the problem more tractable. Introducing other claimholders such as preferred stock makes it more difficult, albeit not impossible, to arrive at a result. Second, by assuming only one zero-coupon debt issue that can be retired at face value any time prior to maturity, we align the features of the debt more closely to the features of the strike price on a standard option. Third, if the debt is coupon debt, or more than one debt issue is outstanding, the equity investors can be forced to exercise (liquidate the firm) at these earlier coupon dates if they do not have the cash flows to meet their coupon obligations.

Finally, knowing the value of the firm and the variance in that value makes option pricing possible, but it also raises an interesting question about the usefulness of option pricing in equity valuation. If the firm's bonds are publicly traded, the market value of the debt can be subtracted from the firm's value to obtain the value of equity much more directly. The option pricing approach does have its advantages, however. Specifically, when a firm's debt is not publicly traded, option pricing theory can estimate the value of the firm's equity. Even when the debt is publicly traded, the bonds may not be correctly valued, and the option pricing framework can be useful in evaluating the values of debt and equity. Finally, relating the values of debt and equity to the variance in firm value provides some insight into the redistributive effects of actions taken by the firm.

Inputs for Valuing Equity as an Option

Since most firms do not fall into the neat framework just developed (such as having only one zero-coupon bond outstanding), we have to make some compromises to use this model in valuation.

Value of the Firm

We can obtain the value of the firm in one of four ways. In the first, we cumulate the market values of outstanding debt and equity, assuming that all debt and equity are traded, to obtain firm value. The option pricing model then reallocates the firm value between debt and equity. This approach, while simple, is internally inconsistent. We start with one set of market values for debt and equity and, using the option pricing model, end up with entirely different values for each.

In the second approach, we estimate the market values of the firm's assets by discounting expected cash flows at the cost of capital. The one consideration we need to keep in mind is that the firm's value in an option pricing model should be the value obtained on liquidation. This may be less than the total firm value, which includes expected future investments, and it may also be reduced to reflect the cost of liquidation. If we estimate the firm value using a discounted cash flow model, this suggests that only existing investments should be considered while estimating firm value. The biggest problem with this approach is that financial distress can affect operating income, so the value we obtain by using current operating income may be too low.

In the third approach, we estimate a multiple of revenues by looking at healthy firms in the same business and apply this multiple to the revenues of the firm we are valuing. Implicitly, we are assuming that a potential buyer, in the event of liquidation, will pay this value.

We can use the fourth approach for firms that have separable assets that are individually traded. Here, we cumulate the value of the assets' market values to arrive at firm value. For example, we can value a troubled real estate firm that owns five properties by valuing each property separately and then aggregating the values.

Variance in Firm Value

We can obtain the variance in firm value directly if both stocks and bonds in the firm are traded. Defining σ_e^2 as the variance in the stock price, σ_d^2 as the variance in the bond price, w_e as the market-value weight of equity, and w_d as the market-value weight of debt, we can write the variance in firm value as follows:[21]

$$\sigma^2_{firm} = w_e^2\sigma_e^2 + w_d^2\sigma_d^2 + 2w_e w_d \rho_{ed}\sigma_e\sigma_d$$

where ρ_{ed} is the correlation between the stock and the bond prices. When the bonds of the firm are not traded, we can use the variance of similarly rated bonds as the estimate of σ_d^2 and the correlation between similarly rated bonds and the firm's stock as the estimate of ρ_{ed}.

When companies get into financial trouble, this approach can yield misleading results, because both its stock prices and bond prices become more volatile. An alternative that often yields more reliable estimates is to use the average variance in firm value for other firms in the sector. Thus, the value of equity in a deeply troubled steel company can be estimated using the average variance in firm value of all traded steel companies.

Maturity of the Debt

Most firms have more than one debt issue on their books, and much of the debt comes with coupons. Since the option pricing model allows for only one input for the time to expiration, we have to convert these multiple bond issues and coupon payments into one equivalent zero-coupon bond:

- One solution, which takes into account both the coupon payments and the maturity of the bonds, is to estimate the duration of each debt issue and calculate a face-value-weighted average of the durations of the different issues. This value-weighted duration is then used as a measure of the option's time to expiration.
- An approximation is to use the face-value-weighted maturity of the debt converted to the maturity of the zero-coupon bond in the option pricing model.

21 Earlier we used the weighted average maturity of this debt of 8.1 years to compute the market value of debt. The duration of debt is lower than its maturity, because of the interest payments in earlier years.

Face Value of Debt

When a distressed firm has multiple debt issues outstanding, we have three choices when it comes to what we use as the face value of debt:

- We can add up the principal due on all the firm's debt and consider it to be the face value of the hypothetical zero-coupon bond we assume the firm has issued. The limitation of this approach is that it understates what the firm will truly have to pay out over the life of the debt, since there will be coupon payments and interest payments during the period.
- At the other extreme, we could add the expected interest and coupon payments that will come due on the debt to the principal payments to come up with a cumulated face value of debt. Since the interest payments occur in the near years and the principal payments are due only when the debt comes due, we are mixing cash flows at different points in time when we do this. However, this is the simplest approach to dealing with intermediate interest payments coming due.
- We can consider only the principal due on the debt as the face value of the debt. The interest payments each year, specified as a percentage of firm value, can take the place of the dividend yield in the option pricing model. In effect, each year that the firm remains in existence, we would expect to see the firm's value decline by the expected payments on the debt.

Valuing Equity as an Option: Las Vegas Sands in January 2008

Earlier we estimated the value of Las Vegas Sands as a going concern. We arrived at a value for the firm of $9,793 million for the firm's operating assets. For the standard deviation in this value, we used the casino industry average of 31%, computed using returns from 2007 and 2008. The firm has debt outstanding, with a face value of almost $10.47 billion and a market value of $7.57 billion. Much of the debt is long-term debt, with a weighted average duration of 5.4 years.[22] In summary, the inputs to the option pricing model are as follows:

Value of the Underlying Asset = S = Value of the Firm = $9,793 million

Exercise Price = K = Face Value of Outstanding Debt = $10,470 million

Life of the Option = t = Weighted Average Duration of Debt = 5.4 years

Variance in the Value of the Underlying Asset = σ^2 = Variance in Firm Value = $(0.31)^2$

Riskless Rate = r = Five-Year Treasury Bond Rate Corresponding to Option Life = 2.5%

22 Earlier we used the weighted average maturity of this debt of 8.1 years to compute the market value of debt. The duration of debt is lower than its maturity because of the interest payments in earlier years.

Based on these inputs, we estimate the following value for the call:

$d_1 = 0.4548 \quad N(d_1) = 0.6754$

$d_2 = -0.2655 \quad N(d_2) = 0.3953$

$$\text{Value of the Call} = 9{,}793(0.6754) - 10{,}470e^{(-0.025)(5.4)}(0.3953) = \$2{,}998 \text{ million}$$

If we treat this as the value of equity, it yields a value per share of $4.67 a share, which is higher than the going-concern estimate of value of $1.92 per share that we estimated earlier; the actual stock price of $4.25 is close to this price.

The option pricing framework, in addition to yielding a value for LVS equity, yields some valuable insight into the drivers of value for this equity. While it is certainly important that the firm try to bring costs under control and increase operating margins, the two most critical variables determining equity value are the duration of the debt and the variance in firm value. Any action that increases (or decreases) the debt duration will have a positive (or negative) effect on equity value. Thus, the results of debt renegotiation talks that were ongoing at the time of this analysis could have a significant effect on value.

Relative Valuation

Most valuations in practice, including those of distressed firms, are relative valuations. In particular, firms are valued using multiples and groups of comparable firms. An open question then becomes whether the effects of distress are reflected in relative valuations and, if not, how best to do so.

Distress in Relative Valuation

It is not clear how distress is incorporated into an estimate of relative value. Consider how relative valuation is most often done. We choose a group of firms that we believe are comparable to the firm we are valuing. Usually, we pick firms in the same business that our firm is in. We then standardize prices by computing a multiple—price earnings, price to book, enterprise value to sales, or enterprise value to EBITDA. Finally, we examine how our firm measures up on this multiple, relative to the comparable firms. While this time-honored approach is used for distressed firms as well, the following issues generally are unique to distressed firms:

- Revenue and EBITDA multiples are used more often to value distressed firms than healthy firms. The reasons are pragmatic. Multiples such as price earnings or price to book value often cannot even be computed for a distressed firm. Analysts therefore move up the income statement, looking for a positive number. For firms that make heavy infrastructure investments, where depreciation and amortization are significant charges against operating income and there are substantial interest expenses, the EBITDA is often positive, and net income is negative. For some firms, even EBITDA is negative, and revenue multiples are only multiples that yield positive values.
- Analysts who are aware of the possibility of distress often consider it subjectively when they compare the multiple for a distressed firm to the industry average. For example,

assume that the average telecom firm trades at 2 times revenues and the firm we are analyzing trades at 1.25 times revenues. Also assume that the firm has substantially higher default risk than the average telecom firm. We may conclude that the firm is not undervalued, even though it trades at a significant discount on the average, because of the potential for default. The perils of subjective adjustment are obvious. Barring the most egregious misvaluations, analysts will find a way to justify their prior biases about firms.

Adapting Relative Valuation to Distress

Is there a way in which relative valuation can be adapted to cover distressed firms? We believe so, although the adjustments tend to be much more approximate than those described in the discounted cash flow section. We'll consider two ways of building distress explicitly into relative valuations. In the first, we compare a distressed company's valuation to the valuations of other distressed companies. In the second, we use healthy companies as comparable companies, but we find a way to adjust for the distress that the firm we are valuing is facing.

Choosing the Comparables

To value a distressed firm, we can find a group of distressed firms in the same business and look at how much the market is willing to pay for them. For instance, we could value a troubled telecom firm by looking at the enterprise value to sales (or book capital) multiples at which other troubled telecom firms trade. Although this approach has promise, it works only if a large number of firms in a sector slip into financial trouble at the same time. In addition, by categorizing firms as distressed or not distressed, we run the risk of lumping together firms that are distressed to different degrees.

One possible way to expand this approach is to look at distressed firms across the whole market, rather than just the sector in which the firm operates. This allows for a larger sample. But there is the possible disadvantage that a troubled grocery store may be in a better position (in terms of generating distress sale proceeds) than a troubled technology company.

Choosing Distressed Comparables

To value Las Vegas Sands, we consider only casino firms with high financial leverage (market debt-to-capital ratios that exceed 60%). Our objective is to arrive at a sample of casino firms that have a significant likelihood of distress. We use the EBITDA in the most recent trailing 12 months and compute the enterprise value by adding the market value of equity to the book value of debt and subtracting cash. Table 12.13 summarizes the resulting EV/EBITDA ratios for these firms.

Table 12.13 Distressed Casino Firms

Company	Market Cap	Total Debt	Cash	EV	EBITDA	EV/ EBITDA
Codere, S.A.	516.6	1,072.8	144.1	1,445.3	295.2	4.90
Ameristar Casinos, Inc.	561.1	1,615.7	68.2	2,108.6	289.4	7.29
Las Vegas Sands Corp.	2,729	1,0470	1276	11,628.9	812.5	14.31
Groupe Partouche S.A.	139.1	675	146.9	667.2	178.2	3.74
Boyd Gaming Corp.	431.2	2,624.1	123.6	2,931.7	372.5	7.87
MGM Mirage (NYSE:MGM)	1,548.4	13,288.3	250.1	14,586.6	1,959.6	7.44
Wynn Resorts, Ltd.	2,747	4,917.7	1,713.7	5,951	714.4	8.33
				Average across firms =		7.70
				Average (without LVS) =		6.60

The average EV/EBITDA multiple, not including LVS, across these firms is 6.60. Las Vegas Sands clearly looks overvalued relative to the rest of the group. However, we offer a caveat. The use of book value of debt clearly overstates the enterprise value computations, and more so for companies that are more distressed. For instance, using the estimated market value of debt of $7.57 billion instead of the book value would lower LVS's multiple to about 10 times EBITDA.

Considering the Possibility of Distress Explicitly

One of the adaptations we suggested for discounted cash flow valuation was an explicit assessment of default risk and a firm value that was a weighted estimate of a going-concern value and a distress sale value. For a distressed firm in a sector where the average firm is healthy, this approach offers promise. We can estimate the value of the distressed firm using the comparable firms and consider it the going-concern value. For instance, if healthy firms in the business trade at 2 times revenues, we would multiply the firm's revenues by 2 to arrive at the going-concern value. We could then estimate the firm value as follows:

$$\text{Firm Value} = \text{Going-Concern Relative Value} * (1 - \pi_{\text{Distress}}) + \text{Distress Sale Value} * \pi_{\text{Distress}}$$

The probability of distress and the distress sale value would be estimated just as they were in the preceding section. This approach makes the most sense when valuing a firm that is distressed in a sector containing mostly healthy firms, because the prior two approaches could not be used here.

In some cases, we may have to use forecast values for revenues and operating income to arrive at the going-concern value. This is especially true if current revenues and operating income are adversely impacted by the overhang of distress.

Forward Multiples and Distress

Consider the forecasts of revenues and EBIT made in Table 12.7 for Las Vegas Sands. Although the firm is not currently generating a large operating income, we are anticipating an improvement in margins and growth in revenues, resulting in an expected operating income of $1,696 million in year 10. Adding the expected depreciation charge of $572 million to this value yields an expected EBITDA of $2,268 million.[23] Using the average enterprise value/EBITDA multiple of 8.25 at which healthy casino firms trade, we can estimate an expected enterprise value in year 10:[24]

$$\text{Expected Enterprise Value in Year 10} = \text{EBITDA}_{10} * \text{EV/EBITDA}_{\text{Current for Healthy Casino Firms}}$$
$$= 2{,}268 * 8.25 = \$18{,}711 \text{ million}$$

We can estimate the present value of this estimated value by discounting back at Las Vegas Sands' cumulated cost of capital, computed earlier to be 2.4433:

$$\text{Enterprise Value Today} = 18{,}711 / 2.4433 = \$7{,}658 \text{ million}$$

This, of course, is based on the assumption that Las Vegas Sands will become a healthy firm. Using the probability of survival (23.34%) and distress (76.66%) estimated earlier, we can value LVS's operating assets today:

$$\text{Estimated Enterprise Value} = \text{Going-Concern Value } (\pi_{\text{Going Concern}}) + \text{Distress Sale Value } (1 - \pi_{\text{Going Concern}})$$
$$= 7{,}658\ (.2334) + 2{,}769\ (.7666) = \$3{,}910 \text{ million}$$

Note that the estimate of the distress sale value of $2,769 million was made earlier. By ignoring the cash flows over the next ten years, we are also significantly understating the value of LVS as a going concern.[25] Adding back the firm's cash balance ($3,040 million) and subtracting debt ($7.565 million) yields a value for the equity:

Enterprise Value = $3,910 million

+ Cash and Marketable Securities = $3,040 million

– Debt = $7,565 million

Value of Equity = –$605 million

23 Although we have not explicitly forecast depreciation, the depreciation in the current year is $509 million, and the book capital invested in year 10 is about 25% higher than today's book capital. We scaled up depreciation by the same proportion.

24 We define healthy casino firms as those with market debt ratios lower than 50%.

25 We could always add back the present value of cash flows, but if we do, we are mixing up intrinsic and relative valuations.

Effectively, the value per share would be 0. It is only if we use the lower probability of distress, estimated from the bond rating, that we get a positive value for equity.

Conclusion

Looking across the life cycle, the firms at either end of the life cycle seem to pose the most valuation challenges—sometimes for the same reasons. If the question with young firms is whether they will survive to become profitable businesses, a key issue with declining firms is whether they will survive deteriorating operations and large debt obligations and emerge as going concerns.

In this chapter, we looked at the interplay between decline and distress to develop a framework for valuing declining companies. When decline is irreversible, but distress is not imminent, we argued for valuing the firm twice—once as a going concern, and again in an orderly liquidation—and using the higher of the two numbers. When the decline is attributable to poor management and thus is reversible, and no distress is overhanging the firm, we again argued for two valuations—once with existing management and again with better management—and estimating an expected value based on the probability of management change.

When distress is a distinct possibility, we have three choices. In the first, we can develop probability distributions for key variables and run simulations, with distress built into the process. In the second, we can try to adjust the expected cash flows and discount rates in a valuation to reflect the probability of distress occurring and the resulting cash flows. In the third, we value the firm as a going concern and then adjust for the likelihood of distress separately. The contrast here between reversible and irreversible decline shows up in two places with distressed firms. One is that the proceeds from a distress sale are likely to be higher for the first group, where buyers see a potential for turnaround for the assets, than for the second group. The other is that equity in distressed firms with the potential for a turnaround can have option characteristics.

13

Ups and Downs: Cyclical and Commodity Companies

Uncertainty and volatility are endemic to valuation, but cyclical and commodity companies have volatility thrust on them by external factors. These include the ups and downs of the economy with cyclical companies, and movements in commodity prices with commodity companies. As a consequence, even mature cyclical and commodity companies have volatile earnings and cash flows. When valuing these companies, the danger of focusing on the most recent fiscal year is that the resulting valuation will depend in great part on where in the cycle (economic or commodity price) that year fell. If the most recent year was a boom (or down) year, the value will be high (or low).

This chapter looks at how best to deal with the swings in earnings that characterize commodity and cyclical companies in both discounted cash flow and relative valuations. We argue that trying to forecast the next cycle is not only futile but dangerous, and that it is far better to normalize earnings and cash flows across the cycle.

The Setting

This chapter looks at two groups of companies. The first group is cyclical companies—those whose fortunes rest in large part on how the economy is doing. The second group is commodity companies. They derive their earnings from producing commodities that may become inputs to other companies in the economy (oil, iron ore) or be desired as investments in their own right (gold, platinum, diamonds).

Cyclical Companies

We usually define cyclical firms in relation to the overall economy. Firms that move up and down with the economy are considered cyclical companies. There are two ways to identify these firms:

- We can categorize industry sectors into cyclical and noncyclical, based on historical performance, and assume that all firms in the sector share the same characteristics. For instance, the housing and automobile sectors have historically been considered cyclical, and all firms in these sectors share that label. While the approach is low-cost and simple, we run the risk of tarring all firms in a sector with the same brush. Thus, Wal-Mart and Abercrombie & Fitch would both be categorized as cyclical firms, because they are in the retailing business. In addition, categorizing some sectors, such as technology, as cyclical or noncyclical has become much more difficult.

- We can look at a company's own history, in conjunction with overall economic performance, to make a categorization. Thus, a company that has historically reported lower earnings/revenues during economic downturns and higher earnings/revenues during economic boom times would be viewed as cyclical. This approach allows for more nuance than the first one because it works only when the companies being analyzed have long operating histories. Furthermore, factors specific to the firm can cause volatility in earnings that can make this analysis misleading.

In general, the shift from manufacturing-based economies to service-based economies has made it more difficult to categorize firms. At the same time, though, every economic recession reminds us that some firms are affected more negatively than other when the economy slows down. In other words, it is not that there are fewer cyclical firms today than there were two or three decades ago. It is that we have a more difficult time pinpointing these firms ahead of the fact.

Commodity Companies

We can categorize commodity companies into three groups. The first group has products that are inputs to other businesses but are not consumed by the general public. Included in this group are mining companies such as Vale, Rio Tinto, and BHP Billiton. The second group generates output that is marketed to consumers, although other intermediaries may be involved in the process. In this group are most of the food and grains companies. The third group includes firms whose output serves both other businesses and consumers. Oil and natural gas businesses come to mind, but gold mining companies can also be considered part of this group.

The key characteristic that commodity companies share is that they are producers of the commodity and thus are dependent on the price of the commodity for their earnings and value. In some emerging market economies, with rich natural resources, commodity companies can represent a significant portion of overall value. In the Middle East, for instance, oil companies and their satellites account for the bulk of the overall value of traded companies. In Australia and Latin America, agricultural, forestry, and mining companies have accounted for a disproportionate share of both the overall economy and market value.

Characteristics

Commodity companies can range the spectrum from food grains to precious metals, and cyclical firms can be in diverse businesses. However, they share some common factors that can affect how we view them and the values we assign to them:

- **The economic/commodity price cycle**: Cyclical companies are at the mercy of the economic cycle. It is true that good management and the right strategic and business choices can make some cyclical firms less exposed to movements in the economy. However, the odds are high that all cyclical companies will see revenues decrease in the face of a significant economic downturn. Unlike firms in many other businesses, commodity companies are, for the most part, price takers. In other words, even the largest oil companies have to sell their output at the prevailing market price. Not surprisingly, the revenues of commodity companies are heavily impacted by the commodity price. In fact, as commodity companies mature and output levels off, almost all the variance in revenues can be traced to where we are in the commodity price cycle. When commodity prices are on the upswing, all companies that produce that commodity benefit, whereas during a downturn, even the best companies in the business see the effects on operations.

- **Volatile earnings and cash flows**: The volatility in revenues at cyclical and commodity companies are magnified at the operating income level because these companies tend to have high operating leverage (high fixed costs). Thus, commodity companies may have to keep mines (mining), reserves (oil), and fields (agricultural) operating even during low points in price cycles, because the costs of shutting down and reopening operations can be prohibitive.
- **Volatility in earnings flows into volatility in equity values and debt ratios**: While this does not have to apply for all cyclical and commodity companies, the large infrastructure investments that are needed to get these firms started has led many of them to be significant users of debt financing. Thus, the volatility in operating income that we referenced earlier manifests itself in even greater swings in net income.
- **Even the healthiest firms can be put at risk if a macro move is very negative**: Cyclical and commodity companies are exposed to cyclical risk over which they have little control. This risk can be magnified as we move down the income statement, resulting in high volatility in net income, even for the healthiest and most mature firms in the sector. It is easy to see why we have to be more concerned about distress and survival with cyclical and commodity firms than with most others. An extended economic downturn or a lengthy phase of low commodity prices can put most of these companies at risk.
- **Finite resources**: Commodity companies have one final shared characteristic. This planet has a finite quantity of natural resources. If oil prices increase, we can explore for more oil, but we cannot create oil. When valuing commodity companies, this will not only play a role in what our forecasts of future commodity prices will be, but it may also operate as a constraint on our normal practice of assuming perpetual growth (in our terminal value computations).

In summary, then, when valuing commodity and cyclical companies, we have to grapple with the consequences of economic and commodity price cycles and how shifts in these cycles will affect revenues and earnings. We also have to come up with ways of dealing with the possibility of distress, induced not by bad management decisions or firm-specific choices, but by macroeconomic forces.

The Dark Side of Valuation

The volatility in earnings at cyclical and commodity firms, with macro factors at play rather than firm-specific issues, can make it difficult to value even the most mature and largest firms in the sector. In many cases, errors in valuation arise either because analysts choose to ignore the economic or commodity price cycle or because they fixate on it.

Base Year Fixation

When valuing companies, we tend to put a great deal of weight on current financial statements. In fact, we would not be exaggerating if we said that most corporate valuations are built with the current year as the base year, with little attention paid to the firm's own history or the performance of the overall sector.

While this fixation on the current year's numbers is always dangerous, it is doubly so with cyclical and commodity firms for a simple reason. The most recent year's numbers for a steel or oil company are, for the most part, determined by where we are in the cycle. Put another way, the earnings at all oil companies are elevated if oil prices increase 30% during the course of a year, just as earnings at steel companies collectively are depressed if the economy goes into a steep downturn. The consequences of using the most recent year's numbers as a base become obvious. If the base year is at or close to the peak of a cycle, and we use the numbers from that year as the basis for valuation, we overvalue companies. If the base year represents the bottom or trough of a cycle, and we use the earnings from that year to value companies, we consistently underestimate their values.

Note that it is not just the base year earnings that are skewed by where we are in the cycle. Other inputs into the valuation can also be affected:

- **Profitability measures:** Any ratios or measures based on earnings—profit margins and returns on equity or capital, for instance—also are a function of whether we are closer to the peak or bottom of the cycle.
- **Reinvestment measures:** If we measure reinvestment as capital expenditures and investments in working capital, these numbers also ebb and flow with earnings. For instance, oil companies spend more on exploring for and developing new oil reserves if oil prices are high, and cyclical manufacturing companies are more likely to invest in new factories in good economic times.
- **Debt ratios and cost of funding:** To the extent that we use market debt ratios and costs of debt and equity to arrive at the cost of capital, changes in the cost of funding can occur as we move through the cycle, although the direction of the movement can be unpredictable. As we noted in Chapters 6 and 7, risk-free rates and risk premiums change over the economic cycle, with the former decreasing and the latter increasing as the economy slows. If we superimpose the fact that the preferences for debt and equity can also shift over the cycle, we can see the cost of financing changing from period to period.

In summary, locking in earnings, reinvestment, and cost-of-capital numbers from the most recent year for a cyclical or commodity firm is a recipe for erroneous valuations.

Valuing Exxon Mobil with 2008 Earnings

Exxon Mobil had a banner year in 2008, reporting $66.29 billion in operating income and $45.22 billion in net income. During the year, the firm reported net capital expenditures of about $6.939 billion and negligible working capital investments. Using the effective tax rate of 35%, from the 2008 financial statements, on the income, we estimate a free cash flow to the firm of $36.15 billion:

Free Cash Flow to the Firm = $66.290 billion (1 – .35) – $6.939 = $36.15 billion

To estimate Exxon Mobil's cost of equity in January 2009, we use a regression beta of 1.10, estimated using weekly returns from January 2007 to December 2008, and an equity risk premium of 6.5% (the Treasury bond rate is 2.5%):

Cost of Equity = 2.5% + 1.1 (6.5%) = 9.65%

Exxon has $9.4 billion in debt outstanding, resulting in a debt ratio of about 2.85%. Attaching a cost of debt of 3.75% (based on an AAA rating) to this debt yields a cost of capital of 9.44%:

Cost of Capital = Cost of Equity (E / (D + E)) + After-Tax Cost of Debt (D / (D + E))
= 9.65% (0.9715) + 3.75% (1 – .35) (.0285) = .0944 or 9.44%

If we assume a growth rate of 2% in perpetuity, we arrive at a value for Exxon Mobil's operating assets of $495.34 billion:

$$\text{Value of Operating Assets} = \frac{\text{Expected FCFF Next Year}}{(\text{Cost of Capital} - g)} = \frac{36.15(1.02)}{(.0944 - .02)} = \$495.34 \text{ billion}$$

Adding the cash balance ($32.01 billion) and subtracting debt ($9.4 billion) yields a value for equity of $517.95 billion:

Value of Equity = Value of Operating Assets + Cash – Debt
= $495.34 + $32.01 – $9.4 = $517.95 billion

At its existing market value of $320.37 billion for equity, Exxon Mobil seems significantly undervalued.

The Macro Crystal Ball

If some analysts are guilty of ignoring the effects of economic and commodity price cycles on valuation fundamentals, other analysts are guilty of the opposite. When valuing cyclical and commodity companies, these analysts spend almost all their time forecasting not only the current cycles but also future cycles. They then use these to estimate earnings and cash flows for their companies. On the face of it, their logic is impeccable. Cyclical and commodity companies have earnings and cash flows that have gone up and down with cycles in the past. Thus, any forecasts of earnings and cash flows should have the same characteristics. However, there are two problems with this reasoning:

- The cash flows and earnings estimate that are built on forecasts of future cycles may look more realistic to an outside observer, but that is deceptive. After all, the cash flow estimates are only as good as the macro forecasts that underlie them. Thus, the valuation of a cyclical company in 2009 that is built on forecasts of recessions in 2013 and 2018 will unravel if the recessions actually occur in 2011 and 2020.

- If time is a constraint in any endeavor, an analyst who spends more time looking at macro variables will have less time to spend analyzing the company. Unless there is good reason to believe that this analyst has some special skills at forecasting macroeconomic movements or access to special macroeconomic data, it is difficult to see how the payoff can be positive.

Note that we are not arguing that no cycles will occur in the future. On the contrary, economic and commodity price cycles will continue to drive earnings and cash flows. However, if we cannot forecast economic and commodity price cycles with any accuracy, and even professional forecasters admit that their crystal balls are hazy even in the short term, trying to build in long-term forecasts of cycles adds noise to the valuation and may actually undercut the quality of the overall estimate.

Macro Point of View (POV) Valuations

Most analysts and investors have views on the overall economy or commodity prices. Some of us may have very strong views on both. Analysts with strong views on the economy and the direction of commodity prices often find it difficult to leave their views behind when valuing these companies. Thus, they insert their predictions of future oil prices into the valuation of oil companies and their forecasts of real economic growth into the valuation of cyclical companies, even if (and perhaps especially if) these views are very different from those held by the rest of the market.

Any valuation that follows will be a joint reflection of the analyst's views on the specific company and his or her macroeconomic views. Put another way, an analyst who expects stronger economic growth in the future more than most other market participants is more likely to find a cyclical company to be undervalued. But a person looking at this valuation will have no way of disentangling how much of this undervaluation is due to the analyst's views on the company and how much is due to his views on the economy. Similarly, an appraiser who believes that oil prices, at $45 a barrel in March 2009, will bounce back to $100 a barrel by year's end and who builds this forecast into the valuation of an oil company will find it undervalued.

Selective Normalization

This section argues that one of the remedies for cyclical earnings is normalization. Many analysts who value cyclical and commodity companies take this lesson to heart but make two common errors in putting it into practice:

- **Incomplete normalization**: To do normalization right, we have to carry it to its logical extreme. In addition to normalizing earnings, we have to normalize return on capital, reinvestment, and cost of financing. In many cases, the only number that is normalized in a valuation is the earnings number, but the rest of the inputs are left at their current-year figures. Thus, with a cyclical firm that has reported depressed earnings in a recessionary environment, we replace these earnings with normalized earnings. But we combine these earnings with capital expenditure, working capital, and cost of financing numbers extracted from the recessionary year.

- **Inconsistent growth**: Consider the cyclical company with low earnings that we discussed in the preceding section. If the problems are entirely the result of the aggregate economy's sluggishness, we should expect robust growth in earnings as the economy recovers. In fact, the estimates of earnings growth for cyclical companies often reflect this optimism, especially at the start of the recovery. If we decide to replace the current earnings for this firm with normalized (and higher) earnings, and we use external estimates of earnings growth (from analysts or management) to forecast future earnings, we overestimate these earnings and the company's value. In effect, we are double-counting growth—once by normalizing earnings, and again by using a higher growth rate.

We will look at normalization as a way out of the difficulties of valuing cyclical and commodity companies, but makeshift approaches to normalization will not necessarily yield better estimates of value.

False Stability

It is human nature, when confronted with volatility in an input, to look for a more stable alternative. Analysts who value cyclical and commodity companies using relative valuation (multiples and comparables) try to get more stability in their valuations by doing the following:

- **Moving up the income statement:** As we move up the income statement, we generally find more stability. Operating income is less volatile than net income, and revenues have less variance than operating income. Using EBITDA or revenue multiples for cyclical companies therefore offers two advantages. The first is that these multiples generally can be computed for most cyclical and commodity firms, even in the midst of a downturn. On the other hand, multiples like PE ratios become impossible to estimate for large portions of the sample as earnings become negative. The second advantage is that these multiples will be more stable over time, since the denominator is less volatile.
- **Using normalized earnings**: In the preceding section, we talked about how analysts use normalized earnings in discounted cash flow valuation to value cyclical and commodity companies. Normalized earnings, usually estimated by looking at average earnings over a period (five to ten years), are also commonly used with multiples to value companies in these sectors.

While the search for a more stable base makes sense, we have to recognize that investors cannot lay claim to revenues or EBITDA and that they ultimately still care about the bottom line (earnings and cash flows). Failing to control for differences in volatility in these numbers across companies can lead us to make poor judgments about which companies are under- and overvalued.

EBITDA Multiples: Specialty Chemical Companies

To illustrate the potential problems with relying on multiples of operating income, Table 13.1 lists the enterprise value, EBITDA, and resulting multiples for specialty chemical companies at the start of March 2009.

Table 13.1 EV/EBITDA: Specialty Chemical Companies

Company Name	Enterprise Value	EBITDA	EV/EBITDA
Airgas Inc.	$3,812.40	$855.70	4.46
American Vanguard Corp.	$374.90	$56.20	6.67
Arch Chemicals	$464.70	$192.10	2.42
Ashland Inc.	–$402.30	$449.00	–0.90
Balchem Corp	$374.80	$38.70	9.68
Cabot Microelectronics	$238.30	$94.10	2.53
Ecolab Inc.	$8,325.90	$1,270.80	6.55
Ferro Corp.	$554.70	$272.60	2.03
Fuller (H.B.)	$672.70	$161.40	4.17
ICO, Inc.	$76.30	$39.40	1.94
International Flavors & Fragrances	$3,049.90	$543.50	5.61
KMG Chemicals, Inc.	$103.80	$22.90	4.53
Lubrizol Corp.	$2,854.80	$802.70	3.56
Lydall, Inc.	$30.50	$46.50	0.66
Minerals Technical	$492.80	$270.80	1.82
NewMarket Corp.	$534.20	$164.90	3.24
OM Group	$326.00	$262.70	1.24
Park Electrochemical	$82.60	$51.90	1.59
Penford Corp.	$95.20	$43.80	2.17
Praxair, Inc.	$21,065.90	$3,331.00	6.32
Quaker Chemical	$120.70	$54.30	2.22
Rohm and Haas	$13,171.70	$2,018.00	6.53
RPM International	$2,032.40	$544.90	3.73
Schulman (A.)	$341.30	$105.20	3.24
Sherwin-Williams	$5,415.40	$1,327.80	4.08
Sigma-Aldrich	$4,384.80	$668.10	6.56
SurModics, Inc.	$277.30	$39.40	7.04
Tredegar Corp.	$540.30	$152.30	3.55
Valspar Corp.	$2,362.40	$455.00	5.19
Zep, Inc.	$190.30	$51.40	3.70

Note that the EBITDA is from 2007 for most of these firms, whereas the enterprise values have been updated to reflect current numbers. Because these firms are cyclical companies, their earnings will undoubtedly wither as a result of the recession. Comparing the value today to these earnings measures tells us little about which companies are undervalued and which are overvalued.

Even as the 2008 numbers come out, note that the multiples may not revert to more reasonable numbers. The effect on earnings will lag with some firms and lead with others and will vary in intensity across companies. Since the earnings are unstable, controlling for differences across companies becomes much more difficult.

The Light Side of Valuation

If volatility in earnings is a given at cyclical and commodity companies, and forecasting the cycles that cause the volatility is often impossible, how can we value such companies? This section examines healthy responses to the volatility in the valuation of these companies.

Discounted Cash Flow Valuation

Chapter 2 noted that a company's discounted cash flow value rests on four inputs—earnings and cash flows from existing assets, the growth in these cash flows in the near term, a judgment about when the company will become mature, and a discount rate to apply to the cash flows. Using this framework, we will develop two ways of adapting discounted cash flow valuations for cyclical and commodity companies. In the first, we will normalize our estimates for all four of these inputs using normalized cash flows, growth rates, and discount rates to estimate a normalized value for a firm. In the second, we will try to adjust the growth rate in the cash flows to reflect where we are in the cycle—setting it to low or even negative values at the peak of a cycle (reflecting the expectation that earnings will decline in the future) and high values at the bottom of a cycle.

Normalized Valuations

The easiest way to value cyclical and commodity companies is to look past the year-to-year swings in earnings and cash flows and to look for a smoothed-out number underneath. This section begins by defining what comprises a normal value. Then it considers different techniques that can be used to estimate this number.

What Are Normal Numbers?

If a company's current financial statements answer our questions about how much it earned, reinvested, and generated as cash flows in the most recent period, the normalized versions of these numbers answer a different question: How much earnings, reinvestment, and cash flow would this company have generated in a normal year?

If we are talking about cyclical companies, a normal year would be one that represents the midpoint of the cycle, where the numbers are neither puffed up nor deflated by economic conditions. With commodity companies, a normal year would be one in which commodity prices reflect the intrinsic price of the commodity, reflecting the underlying demand and supply. Each of these definitions conveys the subjective component of this process, because two analysts looking at the same economy or commodity can make very different judgments about what is normal.

Measuring Normalized Values for Cyclical Companies

If we accept the proposition that normalized earnings and cash flows have a subjective component, we can begin laying out procedures for estimating them for individual companies. With cyclical companies, three standard techniques usually are employed for normalizing earnings and cash flows:

- **Absolute average over time**: The most common approach used to normalize numbers is to average them over time, although over what period remains in dispute. At least in theory, the averaging should occur over a period long enough to cover an entire cycle. Chapter 8 noted that economic cycles, even in mature economies like the U.S., can range from short periods (two to three years) to very long ones (more than ten years). The advantage of this approach is its simplicity. The disadvantage is that the use of absolute numbers over time can lead to normalized values being misestimated for any firm that becomes larger or smaller over the normalization period. In other words, using the average earnings over the last five years as the normalized earnings for a firm that doubled its revenues over that period will understate the true earnings.
- **Relative average over time**: A simple solution to the scaling problem is to compute averages for a scaled version of the variable over time. In effect, we can average profit margins over time, instead of net profits, and apply the average profit margin to revenues in the most recent period to estimate normalized earnings. We can employ the same tactics with capital expenditures and working capital by looking at ratios of revenue or book capital over time, rather than the absolute values.
- **Sector averages**: In the first two approaches to normalization, we are dependent on the company's having a long history. For cyclical firms with a limited history or a history of operating changes, it may make more sense to look at sector averages to normalize. Thus, we will compute operating margins for all steel companies across the cycle and use the average margin to estimate operating income for an individual steel company. The biggest advantage of this approach is that sector margins tend to be less volatile than individual company margins. However, this approach fails to incorporate the characteristics (operating efficiencies or inefficiencies) that may lead a firm to be different from the rest of the sector.

Valuing Toyota: Normalized Earnings

By most accounts, in early 2009 Toyota was considered the best-run automobile company in the world. However, the firm was not immune to the ebbs and flows of the global economy. It reported a loss in the last quarter of 2008. This was a precursor to much lower and perhaps negative earnings in its 2008–2009 fiscal year (stretching from April 2008 to March 2009).

To normalize Toyota's operating income, Table 13.2 shows its operating performance from 1998 to 2008.

Table 13.2 Toyota's Operating Performance: 1998 to 2009 (in Millions of Yen)

Year	Revenues	Operating Income	EBITDA	Operating Margin	EBITDA/ Revenues
FY1 1998	¥11,678,400	¥779,800	¥1,382,950	6.68%	11.84%
FY1 1999	¥12,749,010	¥774,947	¥1,415,997	6.08%	11.11%
FY1 2000	¥12,879,560	¥775,982	¥1,430,982	6.02%	11.11%
FY1 2001	¥13,424,420	¥870,131	¥1,542,631	6.48%	11.49%
FY1 2002	¥15,106,300	¥1,123,475	¥1,822,975	7.44%	12.07%
FY1 2003	¥16,054,290	¥1,363,680	¥2,101,780	8.49%	13.09%
FY1 2004	¥17,294,760	¥1,666,894	¥2,454,994	9.64%	14.20%
FY1 2005	¥18,551,530	¥1,672,187	¥2,447,987	9.01%	13.20%
FY1 2006	¥21,036,910	¥1,878,342	¥2,769,742	8.93%	13.17%
FY1 2007	¥23,948,090	¥2,238,683	¥3,185,683	9.35%	13.30%
FY1 2008	¥26,289,240	¥2,270,375	¥3,312,775	8.64%	12.60%
FY 2009 (estimated)	¥22,661,325	¥267,904	¥1,310,304	1.18%	5.78%
Average		¥1,306,867		7.33%	

Each year, we report the operating income or loss, the EBITDA, and the margins relative to revenues. We consider three different normalization techniques:

- **Average income**: Averaging the operating income from 1998 to 2009 yields a value of 1,306.9 billion yen. Since the revenues over the period more than doubled, this understates the firm's normalized operating income.
- **Industry average margin**: The average pre-tax operating margin of automobile firms (global) over the same time period (1998 to 2008) is about 6%. In 2009, however, many of these firms were in far worse shape than Toyota, and many were likely to report large losses. While we could apply the industry-average margin to Toyota's 2009 revenues to estimate a normalized operating income (6% of 22,661 billion yen = 1,360 billion yen), this will also understate the normalized operating income. It will not reflect the fact that Toyota has been among the most profitable firms in the sector.
- **Historical margin**: Averaging the pre-tax operating margin from 1998 to 2009 yields an average operating margin of 7.33%. Applying this margin to the revenues in 2009 yields a normalized operating income of 1,660.7 billion yen (7.33% of 22,661 billion yen). This estimate

captures both the larger scale of the firm today and its success in this business. We will use this value as our normalized operating income.

To value the firm, we also make the following assumptions:

- To estimate Toyota's cost of equity, we use a bottom-up beta (estimated from the automobile sector) of 1.10. Using the ten-year Japanese yen government bond rate of 1.50% as the risk-free rate and an equity risk premium of 6.5%, we compute a cost of equity of 8.65%:[1]

$$\text{Cost of Equity} = \text{Risk-Free Rate} + \text{Beta} * \text{Equity Risk Premium}$$
$$= 1.50\% + 1.10\ (6.5\%) = 8.65\%$$

- In early 2009, Toyota had 11,862 billion yen in debt outstanding, and its market value of equity was 10,551 billion (3.448 billion shares outstanding at 3,060 yen per share). Using a rating of AA and an associated default spread of 1.75% over the risk-free rate, we estimate a pre-tax cost of debt of 3.25%. Assuming that the current debt ratio is sustainable, we estimate a cost of capital of 5.09%. The marginal tax rate for Japan in 2009 was 40.7%:

$$\text{Debt Ratio} = 11{,}862\ /\ (11{,}862 + 10{,}551) = 52.9\%$$
$$\text{Cost of Capital} = 8.65\%\ (.471) + 3.25\%\ (1 - .407)\ (.529) = 5.09\%$$

- We examine the cost of capital for Toyota over time. Because neither the debt ratio nor the cost of capital has moved substantially over time, we use this as the normalized cost of capital.
- Since Toyota is already the largest automobile firm in the world, in terms of market share, we assume that the firm is in stable growth, growing at 1.50% (capped at the risk-free rate) in perpetuity. We also assume that the firm will be able to generate a return on capital equal to its cost of capital on its investments.[2] The reinvestment rate that emerges from these two assumptions is 29.46%:

$$\text{Stable Period Reinvestment Rate} = \frac{g}{ROC} = \frac{.015}{.0509} = .2946$$

Bringing together the normalized operating income (1,660.7 billion yen), the marginal tax rate for Japan (40.7%), the reinvestment rate (29.46%), the stable growth

1 We are using a mature market equity risk premium of 6.5% for Toyota. An argument can be made that we should be adding a country risk premium to reflect Toyota's sales exposure in emerging markets in Asia and Latin America.

2 Our reasoning is as follows. By most indicators, Toyota is the most efficiently run automobile firm. We are assuming that it will not generate excess returns but will be able to break even. In fact, the return on capital we computed based on the normalized income and the capital invested at the end of 2008 was 4.98%, very close to the estimated value of 5.09%.

rate of 1.5%, and the cost of capital of 5.09%, we can estimate the value of the operating assets at Toyota:

$$\text{Value}_{\text{Operating Assets}} = \frac{\text{Operating Income}(1+g)(1-\text{Tax Rate})(1-\text{Reinvestment Rate})}{(\text{Cost of Capital}-g)}$$

$$= \frac{1660.7(1.015)(1-.407)(1-.2946)}{(.0509-.015)} = 19{,}640 \text{ billion Yen}$$

Adding in cash (2,288 billion yen) and nonoperating assets (6,845 billion yen), subtracting debt (11,862 billion yen) and minority interests in consolidated subsidiaries (583 billion yen), and dividing by the number of shares (3.448 billion) yields a value per share of 4,735 yen per share.[3]

$$\text{Value per Share}$$

$$= \frac{\text{Operating Assets} + \text{Cash} + \text{Non-Operating Assets} - \text{Debt} - \text{Minority Interest}}{\text{Number of Shares}}$$

$$= \frac{19640 + 2288 + 6845 - 11862 - 583}{3.448} = 4735 \text{ Yen/Share}$$

Based on the normalized income, Toyota looks significantly undervalued at its stock price of 3,060 yen per share in early 2009.

Measuring Normalized Earnings for Commodity Companies

With commodity companies, the variable that causes the volatility is the price of the commodity. As it moves up and down, it impacts not only revenues and earnings but also reinvestment and financing costs. Consequently, normalization with commodity companies has to be built around a normalized commodity price.

Normalized Commodity Prices

What is a normalized price for oil? For gold? There are two ways to answer this question:

- One is to look at history. Commodities have a long trading history. We can use the historical price data to come up with an average, which we can then adjust for inflation. Implicitly, we are assuming that the average inflation-adjusted price over a long period of history is the best estimate of the normalized price.

3 The nonoperating assets include marketable securities and holdings in other companies. Absent detailed information, we are assuming that the book value of these assets is the market value. The minority interests are also taken at book value, but the amount is small enough that using a market value would have made little difference in our final value per share.

- The other approach is more complicated. Since the price of a commodity is a function of demand and supply for that commodity, we can assess (or at least try to assess) the determinants of that demand and supply and try to come up with an intrinsic value for the commodity.

After we have normalized the price of the commodity, we can assess what the revenues, earnings, and cash flows would have been for the company being valued at that normalized price. With revenues and earnings, this may require just multiplying the number of units sold at the normalized price and making reasonable assumptions about costs. With reinvestment and cost of financing, it requires some subjective judgments about how much (if any) the reinvestment and cost-of-funding numbers would have changed at the normalized price.

Market-Based Forecasts

Using a normalized commodity price to value a commodity company does expose us to the critique that the valuations we obtain will reflect our commodity price views as much as they do our views of the company. For instance, assume that the current oil price is $45 and that we use a normalized oil price of $100 to value an oil company. We are likely to find the company to be undervalued, simply because of our view about the normalized oil price. If we want to remove our views of commodity prices from valuations of commodity companies, the safest way to do so is to use market-based prices for the commodity in our forecasts. Since most commodities have forward and futures markets, we can use the prices for these markets to estimate cash flows in the next few years. For an oil company, then, we will use today's oil prices to estimate cash flows for the current year and the expected oil prices (from the forward and futures markets) to estimate expected cash flows in future periods.

The advantage of this approach is that it comes with a built-in mechanism for hedging against commodity price risk. An investor who believes that a company is undervalued but is shaky on what will happen to commodity prices in the future can buy stock in the company and sell oil price futures to protect herself against adverse price movements.

Valuing Exxon Mobil: Normalized Commodity Prices

Exxon Mobil may be the largest of the oil companies, with diversified operations in multiple locations, but it is as dependent on oil prices as the rest of the companies in its sector. Figure 13.1 shows Exxon's operating income as a function of the average oil price each year from 1985 to 2008.

The operating income clearly increases (or decreases) as the oil price increases (or decreases). We regress the operating income against the oil price per barrel over the period and obtain the following:

$$\text{Operating Income} = -6{,}395 + 911.32\,(\text{Average Oil Price}) \quad R^2 = 90.2\%$$
$$(2.95) \quad (14.59)$$

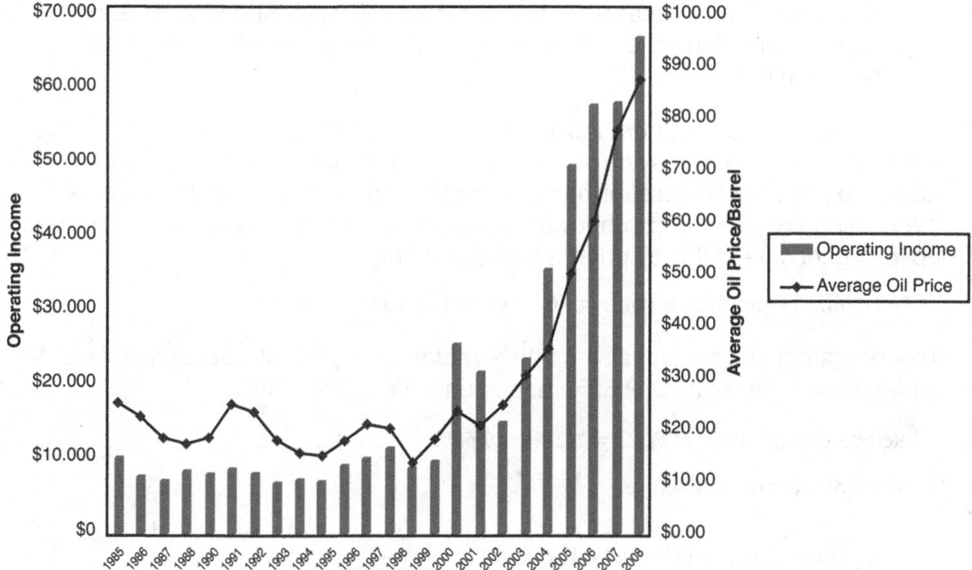

Figure 13.1: Operating Income Versus Oil Prices for Exxon Mobil: 1985 to 2008

Put another way, Exxon Mobil's operating income increases about $9.11 billion for every $10 increase in the price per barrel of oil, and 90% of the variation in Exxon's earnings over time comes from movements in oil prices.[4]

To get from operating income to equity value at Exxon, we make the following assumptions:

- We estimate a bottom-up beta of 0.90 for Exxon Mobil. Then we use the Treasury bond rate of 2.5% and an equity risk premium of 6.5% to estimate a cost of equity:

  Cost of Equity = 2.5% + 0.90 (6.5%) = 8.35%

- Exxon has $9.4 billion of debt outstanding and a market capitalization of $320.4 billion (4,941.63 million shares, trading at $64.83 per share), resulting in a debt ratio of 2.85%. As an AAA-rated company, its cost of debt is expected to be 3.75%, reflecting a default spread of 1.25% over the risk-free rate. Using a marginal tax rate of 38% (rather than the effective tax rate), we estimate a cost of capital of 8.18% for the firm:

  Cost of Capital = 8.35% (.9715) + 3.75% (1 – .38) (.0285) = 8.18%

- Exxon Mobil is in stable growth, with the operating income growing at 2% a year in perpetuity. New investments are expected to generate

4 The relationship is very strong at Exxon because it has been a large and stable firm for decades. It is likely that the relationship between earnings and oil prices will be weaker at smaller, evolving oil companies.

a return on capital that reflects the normalized operating income and current capital invested. This return on capital is used to compute a reinvestment rate.

Exxon reported pre-tax operating income in excess of $60 billion in 2008, but that reflects the fact that the average oil price during the year was $86.55. By March 2009, the price per barrel of oil had dropped to $45, and the operating income for the coming year will be much lower. Using the regression results, the expected operating income at this oil price is $34,614 billion:

$$\text{Normalized Operating Income} = -6{,}395 + 911.32\ (\$45) = \$34{,}614$$

This operating income translates into a return on capital of approximately 21% and a reinvestment rate of 9.52%, based on a 2% growth rate:[5]

$$\text{Reinvestment Rate} = g/\ ROC = 2/21\% = 9.52\%$$

Value of Operating Assets

$$= \frac{\text{Operating Income}\,(1+g)\,(1-\text{Tax Rate})\,(1-\frac{g}{ROC})}{(\text{Cost of Capital} - g)}$$

$$= \frac{34614\,(1.02)\,(1-.38)\,(1-\frac{2\%}{21\%})}{(.0818-.02)} = \$320{,}472 \text{ million}$$

Adding the current cash balance ($32,007 million), subtracting debt ($9,400 million), and dividing by the number of shares (4,941.63 million) yields the value per share:

$$\text{Value per Share} = \frac{\text{Operating Assets} + \text{Cash} - \text{Debt}}{\text{Number of Shares}}$$

$$= \frac{320472 + 32007 - 9400}{4941.63} = \$69.43/\textit{Share}$$

At its current stock price of $64.83, the stock looks slightly undervalued. However, this reflects the assumption that the current oil price (of $45) is the normalized price. Figure 13.2 shows the value of Exxon Mobil as a function of the normalized oil price.

5 To compute the return on capital, we aggregate the book value of equity ($126,044 million), the book value of debt ($9,566 million), and netted-out cash ($33,981 million) from the end of 2007 to arrive at an invested capital value of $101,629 million. The return on capital is computed as follows:

return on capital = operating income (1 – tax rate) / invested capital = 34,614 (1 – .38) / 101,629 = 21.1%

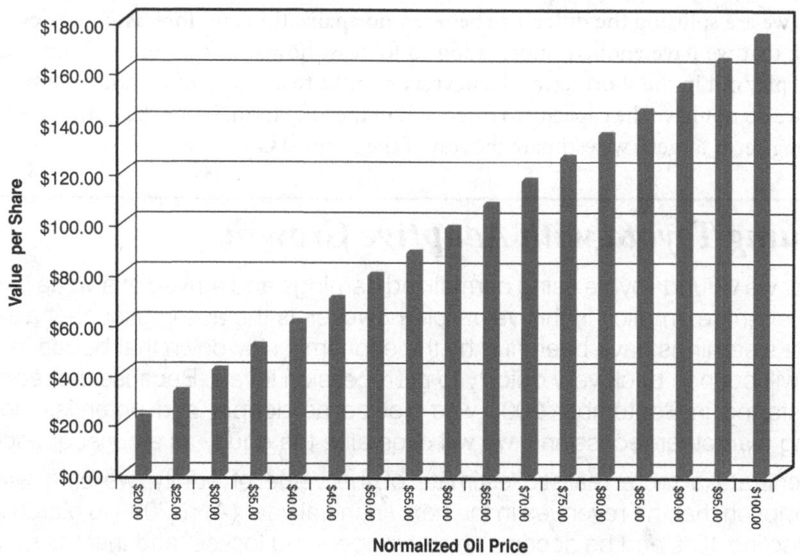

Figure 13.2: Normalized Oil Price and Value per Share for Exxon Mobil

As the oil price changes, the operating income and the return on capital change. We keep the capital-invested number fixed at $101,629 million and reestimate the return on capital with the estimated operating income. If the normalized oil price is $42.52, the value per share is $64.83, equal to the current stock price. Put another way, any investor who believes that the oil price will stabilize above this level will find Exxon Mobil to be undervalued.

Adaptive Growth

One of the perils of normalization, no matter what approach you use, is that we are replacing a company's current numbers with what we believe the company will generate in earnings and cash flows if the cycle rights itself. Since cycles can last for long periods, the danger is that normalization, even if warranted, may be a long time coming. One compromise is to assume normalization in the long term, but to allow earnings to follow the current cycle for the short term, and to use the growth rate as a mechanism to bring us back to normalcy.

Consider first the case of a cyclical company, with the economy mired in recession, or a commodity company, when the price is at the low point in the cycle. The earnings will be negative or low in the most recent time period and may get worse before they get better. We can allow for the deterioration by lowering revenues, earnings, and cash flows in the near term (the first year). We can allow for the improvement by allowing for higher revenue growth and improved margins in the medium term, as the company takes advantage of the economic cycle. With a cyclical company at the peak of the economic cycle or a commodity company when commodity companies have peaked, we reverse the process. We allow for short-term prosperity from the cycle before reducing revenues and profit margins as the cycle reverts to historic norms.

In effect, we are splitting the difference between normalization and forecasting the cycle. We are assuming that we have enough information to forecast how the economic or commodity price cycle will play out in the short term (the next six months to a couple of years). We also are assuming that we do not have the capacity to forecast it in the long term. Using the normalized numbers as our long-term targets, we estimate the rest of the numbers.

Valuing Toyota with Adaptive Growth

Earlier we valued Toyota using normalized earnings and arrived at a value of 4,735 yen per share. Implicit in this valuation, however, is the assumption that although Toyota's earnings have been hurt by the economic slowdown that began in 2008, they will bounce back very quickly to prerecession levels. Because the recession that started in September 2008 was viewed as deeper and potentially longer-lasting than other recessions, we will overvalue the equity as a consequence.

To generate a more realistic estimate of the value of equity, we start with the assumption that the revenues in the next financial year (April 2009 to March 2010) will decline 10% and be accompanied by operating losses, and that the recovery will gradually begin the following year before picking up steam in the third year. In year 4, we assume that Toyota will reach the stable state that we assumed earlier, earning its historical average operating margin of 7.33% on revenues and generating a return on capital of 5.09% (equal to the cost of capital). Table 13.3 summarizes the year-by-year estimates of revenues, operating income, and cash flows for the next three years and for the terminal year (year 4).

Table 13.3 Toyota's Expected Free Cash Flow to the Firm

	Current	Year 1	Year 2	Year 3	Terminal Year
Revenue growth rate		–10%	4%	8%	1.50%
Revenues	¥22,661	¥20,395	¥21,211	¥22,908	¥23,251
Operating margin	1.18%	–3%	1%	4%	7.33%
Operating income	¥268	–¥612	¥212	¥916	¥1,704
Taxes	¥93	¥0	¥0	¥203	¥694
After-tax operating income	¥175	–¥612	¥212	¥714	¥1,011
– Reinvestment	–¥79	–¥200	¥300	¥400	¥298
FCFF	¥254	–¥412	–¥88	¥314	¥713
Terminal value				¥19,856	
Present value		–¥392	–¥80	¥17,378	

	Current	Year 1	Year 2	Year 3	Terminal Year
Capital invested	¥14,945	¥14,745	¥15,045	¥15,445	
Return on capital	1.79%	–4.15%	1.41%	5.93%	5.09%
Tax rate	34.73%	36.22%	37.72%	39.21%	40.70%
NOL			¥611.85	¥399.74	
Cost of capital	5.09%	5.09%	5.09%	5.09%	5.09%
Value of operating assets =	¥16,907				
+ Cash and other nonoperating assets	¥9,133				
– Debt	¥11,862				
– Minority interest	¥583				
Value of equity =	¥13,595				
Value per share =	¥3,943				

$$\text{Capital Invested}_t = \text{Capital Invested}_{t-1} + \text{Reinvestment}_t$$

You should note several things about the projections. The first is that revenue growth is negative in year 1 but bounces back sharply in years 2 and 3, reflecting the climb back to normalcy. The second is that the operating loss that we forecast for year 1 creates a net operating loss (NOL) carryforward that shelters the firm entirely from taxes in year 2 and partially in year 3. The tax rate also climbs from the current effective rate of 34.73% to the marginal rate of 40.7% in year 4. The third is that Toyota pulls back from reinvesting in the first year but returns strongly to reinvest (again making up for lost ground) in years 2 and 3, before settling into its steady state reinvestment rate of 29.46%:

$$\text{Stable Period Reinvestment Rate} = \frac{g}{\text{ROC}} = \frac{.015}{.0509} = .2946$$

We keep the cost of capital unchanged at 5.09% over the period. The present value of the cash flows over the next three years and the terminal value yield a value for the operating assets of 16,907 billion yen. Making the identical adjustments for cash, nonoperating assets, debt, and minority interests that we used earlier, we estimate a value of equity per share of 3,943 yen. Although this is lower than the 4,735 yen per share we estimated, with instant normalization, it is still significantly higher than the price per share of 3,060 yen in February 2009.

Probabilistic Approaches

Chapter 3 considered probabilistic approaches to valuation. Since the earnings, cash flow, and value of cyclical and commodity firms are determined to a great extent by what happens to a few macroeconomic variables, probabilistic approaches work well with these firms:

- **Scenario analysis:** In its simplest form, we can categorize the economy or commodity prices into discrete scenarios: economic boom, stagnation, or recession with cycles, for instance. We can value the firm under each scenario and use either the expected value across scenarios (which would require probability assessments of the scenarios) or the range in values across the scenarios (as a measure of risk) to make our investment judgments.
- **Simulations**: If we accept the premise that the key driver of earnings, cash flow, and value for a commodity company is the commodity's price, we can use simulations of the commodity price to derive the value of a commodity company. The process is made easier by the fact that commodities are publicly traded and that we can therefore estimate the parameters for the simulation far more simply than in most other simulations. The trickiest part of these simulations is to establish how the inputs to the valuation (earnings, reinvestment, and cost of financing) will change as the price of the commodity changes.

In general, probabilistic approaches work best when you have only one or two variables that determine fundamental value, and you have enough historical information on these variables to make estimates of probabilistic distributions (and parameters).

Valuing Exxon Mobil: a Simulation

Earlier we valued Exxon Mobil using normalized operating income. Since the value per share is so dependent on the oil price, it would make more sense to allow the oil price to vary and value the company as a function of this price. In Chapter 3, we introduced simulations as a tool for assessing risk. We can apply this tool for valuing commodity companies:

1. **Determine the probability distribution for the oil prices.** We use historical data on oil prices, adjusted for inflation, to both define the distribution and estimate its parameters. Figure 13.3 summarizes the distribution.

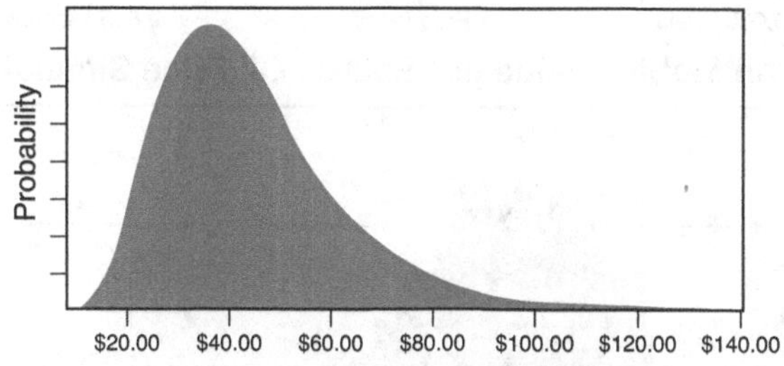

Figure 13.3: Oil Price Distribution

Note that, given historical price behavior, oil prices can vary from about $8 a barrel at the minimum to more than $120 a barrel. While we have used the current price of $45 as the mean of the distribution, we could have inserted a price view into the distribution by choosing a higher or lower mean value.[6]

2. **Link the operating results to the commodity price.** To link the operating income to commodity prices, we use the regression results from earlier:

$$\text{Operating Income} = \underset{(2.95)}{-6{,}395} + \underset{(14.59)}{911.32}\ (\text{Average Oil Price}) \quad R^2 = 90.2\%$$

As we noted earlier, the regression approach works well for Exxon, but it might not for smaller, more volatile commodity companies.

3. **Estimate the value as a function of the operating results.** As the operating income changes, the firm's value is affected in two ways. The first is that lower operating income, other things remaining equal, lowers the base free cash flow and reduces value. The second is that the return on capital is recomputed, holding the capital invested fixed, as the operating income changes. As operating income declines, the return on capital drops, and the firm will have to reinvest more to sustain the stable growth rate of 2%. While we also could have allowed the cost of capital and growth rate to vary, we feel comfortable with both these numbers and have left them fixed.
4. **Develop a distribution for the value.** We ran 10,000 simulations, letting the oil price vary and valuing the firm and equity value per share in each simulation. The results are summarized in Figure 13.4.

The average value per share across the simulations was $69.59, with a minimum value of $2.25 and a maximum value of $324.42. However, there is a greater than 50% chance that the value per share will be less than $64.83 (the current stock price).

6 We use 30 years of historical data on oil prices, adjusted for inflation, to create an empirical distribution. We then choose the statistical distribution that seems to provide the closest fit (lognormal) and choose parameter values that yield numbers closest to the historical data.

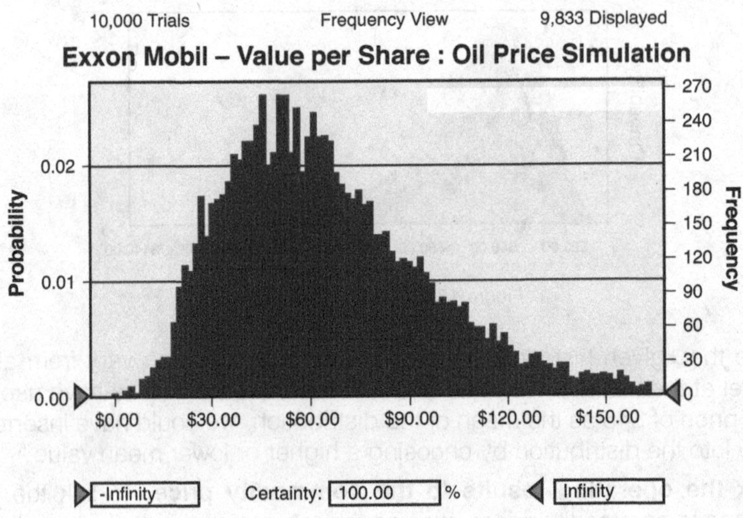

Figure 13.4: Simulation Results

Relative Valuation

The two basic approaches that we developed in the discounted cash flow approach—using normalized earnings or adapting the growth rate—are also the approaches we have for making relative valuation work with cyclical and commodity companies.

Normalized Earnings Multiples

If the normalized earnings for a cyclical or commodity firm reflect what it can make in a normal year, there has to be consistency in how the market values companies relative to these normalized earnings. In the extreme case, where there are no growth and risk differences across firms, all firms should trade at the same multiple of normalized earnings. In effect, the PE ratios for these firms, with normalized earnings per share, should be identical across firms.

In the more general case, where growth and risk differences persist even after normalization, we would expect to see differences in the multiples that companies trade at. In particular, we should expect to see firms that have more risky earnings trade at lower multiples of normalized earnings than firms with more stable earnings. We would also expect to see firms that have higher growth potential trade at higher multiples of normalized earnings than firms with lower growth potential. To provide a concrete illustration, Petrobras and Exxon Mobil are both oil companies whose earnings are affected by the price of oil. Even if we normalize earnings, thus controlling for the price of oil, Petrobras should trade at a different multiple of earnings than Exxon Mobil. Its earnings are riskier (because they are derived almost entirely from Brazilian reserves), and it has higher growth potential.

Adaptive Fundamentals

For analysts who are reluctant to replace a company's current operating numbers with normalized values, the multiples at which cyclical and commodity firms trade at change as we move through the cycle. In particular, the multiples of earnings for cyclical and commodity firms bottom out at the peak of the cycle and are highest at the bottom of the cycle. While this may seem counterintuitive, it reflects the fact that markets have to value these companies for the long term.

If the earnings of all companies in a sector (cyclical and commodity) move in lockstep, there are no serious consequences to comparing the multiples of current earnings that firms trade at. In effect, we may conclude that a steel company with a PE ratio of 6 is fairly valued at the peak of the cycle, when steel companies collectively report high earnings (and low PE). The same firm will be fairly valued at 15 times earnings at an economic trough, where the earnings of other steel companies are also down.

As with normalized earnings, the primary concern is that we control for other factors that affect the multiples. When the cycle is working in your favor (strong economy and high commodity prices), all firms in a sector may report high earnings, but some firms may have better long-term prospects and should trade at higher multiples. By the same token, all oil companies may report lower earnings when oil prices are down, but some of these companies may have more predictable earnings and therefore trade at higher multiples of earnings.

PE Ratios for Oil Companies

In February 2009, oil companies that had benefited over the prior five years of rising oil prices were shaken by the sudden drop in the price per barrel of oil, from $140 a barrel a year earlier to $45 a barrel. While the market prices of oil companies tumbled to reflect the lower oil prices, the earnings reported by these companies for the previous year reflected the high oil prices over that period. Table 13.4 lists the stock prices of oil companies in conjunction with four measures of earnings per share: earnings in the most recent (reported) fiscal year, earnings in the last four quarters, expected earnings in the next four quarters, and a measure of normalized earnings obtained by averaging earnings per share over the previous five years. The PE ratios are estimated using each measure of earnings.

Table 13.4 PE Ratios for Oil Companies in February 2009

Company Name	Stock Price	Current Price	EPS Training 12 Months	EPS Next Four Quarters	Average EPS Last Five Years	Current PE	Trailing PE	Forward PE	Normalized PE
BP PLC ADR	$37.21	$3.84	$8.18	$4.25	$6.20	9.69	4.55	8.76	6.00
Chevron Corp.	$61.22	$5.24	$11.67	$4.00	$7.30	11.68	5.25	15.31	8.39
ConocoPhillips	$37.98	$4.78	$10.69	$4.75	$6.25	7.95	3.55	8.00	6.08
Exxon Mobil Corp.	$65.77	$5.15	$8.66	$5.00	$6.50	12.77	7.59	13.15	10.12

Company Name	Stock Price	Current Price	EPS Training 12 Months	EPS Next Four Quarters	Average EPS Last Five Years	Current PE	Trailing PE	Forward PE	Normalized PE
Frontier Oil	$13.97	$0.21	$0.77	$1.35	$1.90	66.52	18.14	10.35	7.35
Hess Corp.	$57.17	$0.42	$7.24	$1.05	$3.40	136.12	7.90	54.45	16.81
Holly Corp.	$22.03	$3.06	$2.41	$2.75	$3.50	7.20	9.14	8.01	6.29
Marathon Oil Corp.	$22.59	$2.04	$4.94	$2.90	$4.20	11.07	4.57	7.79	5.38
Murphy Oil Corp.	$41.00	$2.88	$8.73	$2.85	$5.50	14.24	4.70	14.39	7.45
Occidental Petroleum	$55.59	$3.18	$8.97	$3.05	$5.50	17.48	6.20	18.23	10.11
Petroleo Brasileiro ADR	$30.47	$4.05	$4.44	$4.05	$4.15	7.52	6.86	7.52	7.34
Repsol-YPF ADR	$15.76	$1.48	$3.49	$2.45	$3.70	10.65	4.52	6.43	4.26
Royal Dutch Shell "A"	$43.32	$5.42	$10.15	$5.10	$6.40	7.99	4.27	8.49	6.77
Sunoco, Inc.	$28.33	$5.68	$7.48	$3.65	$4.30	4.99	3.79	7.76	6.59
Tesoro Corp.	$13.67	$2.60	$1.76	$2.10	$2.80	5.26	7.77	6.51	4.88
Total ADR	$49.85	$5.84	$9.16	$5.65	$7.15	8.54	5.44	8.82	6.97

As you can see, each version of the PE ratio tells a different story. With the current PE (based on earnings per share in the most recent fiscal year), the cheapest stock is Sunoco, with a PE of 4.99. Hess is off the charts with its PE ratio of 136. But the fact that the most recent fiscal year is different for different firms—2007 for some, midway through 2008 for others, and the end of 2008 for a handful—gives us pause. With trailing PE, the cheapest stock is ConocoPhillips, and the most expensive is Frontier Oil, and there are relatively few outliers. If we assume that all oil companies benefited equally from the oil price boom in the last four quarters and that there are no significant differences in growth and risk across oil companies, this would suggest that ConocoPhillips is cheap. However, perusing the expected growth rates in earnings per share, we find that Conoco has an expected growth rate of only 4% for the next five years, whereas analysts are forecasting growth of 8.5% a year for Petrobras. With forward PE ratios, no stocks trade at PE ratios less than 6, but Repsol does have the lowest PE with 6.43. Finally, with normalized EPS, the cheapest stock remains Repsol with a PE of 4.26, and the most expensive is Hess. Our assumption that the average earnings per share over the last five years is normal can be contested.

What are we to make of this mishmash of recommendations? First, it is critical that we stay consistent in how we measure earnings with commodity and cyclical companies. If we decide to use trailing earnings, we should do so for all companies. Second, the fundamentals that determine multiples—cash flows, growth, and risk—apply just as much to commodity companies as they do to the rest of the market. To the extent that commodity companies are becoming more diverse, with large differences in growth potential and risk (especially in emerging markets), we should try to factor these differences into our analyses.

The Real Options Argument for Undeveloped Reserves

One critique of conventional valuation approaches is that they fail to consider adequately the interrelationship between the commodity price and the investment and financing actions of commodity companies. In other words, oil companies behave very differently (in terms of exploration and financing) when oil prices are $100 a barrel than they do when oil prices are only $20 a barrel. Since the managers of commodity companies get to observe the commodity price before they act, it can be argued that the learning and adaptive behavior that follows gives at least the semblance of a real options argument in these firms. If we accept this argument, the upshot in valuation is that we should be adding a premium to conventional discounted cash flow valuations to reflect this optionality, and the premium should become larger as commodity prices become more volatile.

Valuing a Natural Resources Option

The simplest application of the options approach is in the valuation of a single natural resources reserve, where the owner has the right to develop the reserve over a specified time period. The estimated value of the natural resources in the reserve—oil under the ground, timber to be harvested—is a function of the quantity of the resource and the current price. If we assume that the quantity is known, the value will be entirely a function of the current price. As the value rises and falls, the owner of the reserve compares this value to the cost of developing the reserve, with developing the reserve (exercise) making sense only if the value exceeds the development cost. If the reserve never becomes viable, the owner loses whatever was expended to acquire the reserves (exploration costs, price paid in an auction). Figure 13.5 shows the payoff diagram.

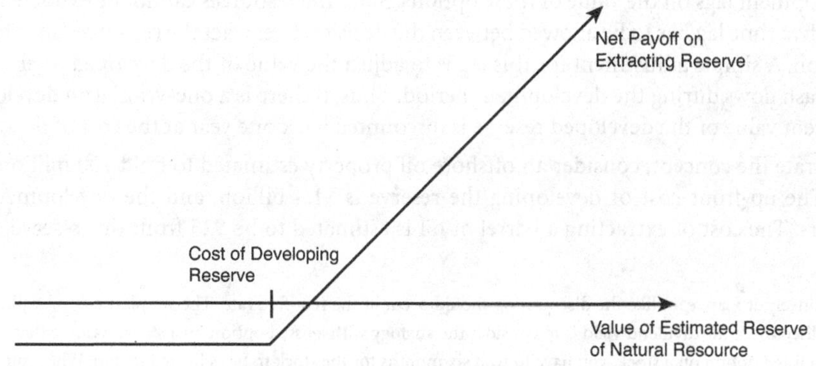

Figure 13.5: Payoff from Developing Natural Resources Reserves

If we accept the premise that natural resources reserves are options, we have to define the inputs to value them as such. Table 13.5 shows the standard option pricing inputs and how we would estimate them for a natural resources option.

Table 13.5 Inputs into Valuing a Natural Resources Option

Input	Estimation Procedure
Value of underlying asset (S)	Estimated value of natural resources in reserve. Usually estimated as the quantity of resources times the current price.
Strike price (K)	Cost of developing the reserve. Generally assumed to be known and fixed.
Life of the option (t)	Can be defined in one of two ways: If rights to the reserve are for a finite period, use that period. The number of years of production it would take to exhaust the estimated reserve. Thus, a gold mine with a mine inventory of 3 million ounces and a capacity output rate of 150,000 ounces a year will be exhausted in 20 years.
Variance in value of underlying asset	Since the quantity of the resource is assumed to be known, the variance in price of natural resources.
Dividend yield (cost of delay)	Annual cash flow as a percentage of the value of the underlying asset. Once the reserve becomes viable, this is what the firm is losing by not developing the reserve.

An important issue in using option pricing models to value natural resources options is the effect of development lags on the value of these options. Since the resources cannot be extracted instantaneously, a time lag has to be allowed between the decision to extract the resources and the actual extraction. A simple adjustment for this lag is to adjust the value of the developed reserve for the loss of cash flows during the development period. Thus, if there is a one-year lag in development, the current value of the developed reserve is discounted back one year at the cost of delay.[7]

To illustrate the concept, consider an offshore oil property estimated to hold 100 million barrels of oil. The up-front cost of developing the reserve is $1.4 billion, and the development lag is two years. The cost of extracting a barrel of oil is estimated to be $25 from this reserve, and the

7 Intuitively, it may seem like the discounting should occur at the risk-free rate. The simplest way of explaining why we discount at the dividend yield is to consider the analogy with a listed option on a stock. Assume that on exercising a listed option on a stock, you have to wait six months for the stock to be delivered to you. What you lose is the dividends you would have received over the six-month period by holding the stock. Hence, the discounting is at the dividend yield.

price per barrel of oil is \$40. The firm has the rights to exploit this reserve for the next 15 years. After the reserve is developed, the net production revenue each year will be 6.67% of the value of the reserves. The riskless rate is 5%, and the standard deviation in oil prices is 40%. Given this information, the inputs to the option pricing model can be estimated:

Current Value of the Asset = S = Value of the Developed Reserve Discounted Back the Length of the Development Lag at the Dividend Yield
$= 100\,(40 - 25) / (1.0667)^2 = \$1.318$ billion

Exercise Price = Cost of Developing the Reserve = \$1.4 billion

Time to Expiration of the Option = 15 years

Variance in the Value of the Underlying Asset = 0.16

Riskless Rate = 5%

Dividend Yield = Cost of Delay = 6.67%

Based on these inputs, the Black-Scholes model provides the following value for the call:

$d_1 = 0.5744 \quad N(d_1) = 0.7172$

$d_2 = -0.9748 \quad N(d_2) = 0.1648$

$\text{Call Value} = 1{,}318 \exp^{(-0.0667)(15)} (0.7172) - 1{,}400 (\exp^{(-0.05)(15)} (0.1648) = \$238.8 \text{ million}$

This oil reserve, although not viable at current prices, is still valuable because of its potential to create value if oil prices go up.

Valuing a Natural Resources Firm

The previous example illustrates the use of option pricing theory in valuing an individual reserve. To the extent that a firm owns multiple reserves, the preferred approach would be to consider each reserve separately as an option, value it, and cumulate the values of the options to get the firm's value. Since this information is likely to be difficult to obtain for large natural resources firms, such as oil companies, which own hundreds of such reserves, a variation on this approach is to value all the undeveloped reserves as one option. A purist would probably disagree. He or she would argue that valuing an option on a portfolio of assets (as in this approach) will provide a lower value than valuing a portfolio of options (which is what the natural resources firm really owns). Nevertheless, the value obtained from the model still provides an interesting perspective on the determinants of the value of natural resources firms.

If we decide to apply the option pricing approach to estimate the value of aggregated undeveloped reserves, we have to estimate the inputs to the model. In general terms, while the process resembles the process used to value an individual reserve, there are a few differences. Table 13.6 examines the inputs into the option pricing value.

Table 13.6 **Inputs into Valuing a Natural Resources Firm**

Input	Estimation Procedure
Value of underlying asset (S)	Cumulate all the undeveloped reserves owned by a company, and estimate the value of these reserves, based on the price of the resource today and the average variable cost of extracting these reserves today.
Strike price (K)	Aggregate cost to the company to develop all its undeveloped reserves immediately.
Life of the option (t)	Weighted average of the lives across undeveloped reserves, with weights based on reserve quantities.
Variance in value of underlying asset	Variance in the price of the underlying commodity.
Dividend yield (cost of delay)	Aggregate annual cash flow that will be generated, if reserves are developed, as a percentage of the value of the reserves.

Once we have valued the undeveloped reserves as options, we can value the developed reserves with conventional discounted cash flow models and cumulate the two to arrive at firm value. Table 13.7 summarizes the consequences.

Table 13.7 **Value of a Commodity Company: Real Options Framework**

Value of Operating Assets =	Value of Developed Reserves	+ Value of Undeveloped Reserves
Valuation approach	DCF valuation: Present value of expected cash flows from extraction and sale of natural resources in developed reserves.	Option valuation: Option value of undeveloped reserves (valued either individually or in the aggregate).
Effects of higher commodity price	Increase value.	Increase value, but reduce the time premium on the option.
Effects of higher volatility in commodity price	May reduce value by increasing the risk and discount rate.	Increase the option time premium.

Note that if we consider undeveloped reserves as options and value them separately, we cannot use the existence of these reserves to justify using higher growth rates in discounted cash flow models. That would be double counting.

The use of option pricing in valuing natural resources companies requires significant information on undeveloped reserves:

- **Quantity of undeveloped reserves:** To value undeveloped reserves as options, we need to know how much of the natural resource is in the undeveloped reserves. With oil companies, for instance, accounting convention has required disclosure of both developed reserves and proven undeveloped reserves, with the latter including only reserves that are viable given current oil prices and extraction costs. In effect, only in-the-money options are disclosed under this requirement. In recent years, some oil companies have also started disclosing probable reserves (slightly out-of-the-money options) and possible reserves (well out-of-the-money options). With other commodity companies, the information on undeveloped reserves is not as fully disclosed.
- **Variable costs:** In addition to knowing how much a company has in undeveloped reserves, we need estimates of the per-unit costs of extracting the commodity from these reserves. Thus, in addition to knowing how many barrels of oil are in undeveloped reserves, we need a measure of the average cost of extracting a barrel of oil from these reserves. Very few commodity companies provide this information. While we can make a guess, based on the location of the reserves, it will still be a very rough estimate.

In general, real options are much more useful as internal analysis tools within commodity companies, since they have access to this data. For outside investors, the information that is provided is usually too limited for us to estimate option values with any precision.

Valuing an Oil Company: Gulf Oil

Gulf Oil was the target of a takeover in early 1984 at $70 per share. It had 165.30 million shares outstanding and total debt of $9.9 billion. It had estimated reserves of 3,038 million barrels of oil. The average cost of developing these reserves at that time was estimated to be $30.38 billion dollars. The development lag was approximately two years. The average relinquishment life of the reserves was 12 years. The price of oil was $22.38 per barrel, and the production cost, taxes, and royalties were estimated at $7 per barrel. The treasury bond rate at the time of the analysis was 9.00%. If Gulf chose to develop these reserves, it was expected to have cash flows each year of approximately 5% of the value of the developed reserves. The variance in oil prices was 0.03.

Value of Underlying Asset = Value of Estimated Reserves Discounted Back for Period of

$$\text{Development Lag} = \frac{(3038)(22.38-7)}{1.05^2} = \$42{,}380 \text{ million}$$

Note that we could have used forecasted oil prices and estimated cash flows over the production period to estimate the value of the underlying asset, which is the present value of all these cash flows. We have used a shortcut of assuming that the current contribution margin of $15.38 a barrel will remain unchanged in present-value terms over the production period:

Exercise Price = Estimated Cost of Developing Reserves Today = $30,380 million

Time to Expiration = Average Length of Relinquishment Option = 12 years

Variance in Value of Asset = Variance in Oil Prices = 0.03

Riskless Interest Rate = 9%

Dividend Yield = Net Production Revenue / Value of Developed Reserves = 5%

Based on these inputs, the Black-Scholes model provides the following value for the call:[8]

$d_1 = 1.6548 \quad N(d_1) = 0.9510$

$d_2 = 1.0548 \quad N(d_2) = 0.8542$

$$\text{Call Value} = 42{,}380e^{(-0.05)(12)}(0.9510) - 30{,}380e^{(-0.09)(12)}(0.8542) = \$13{,}306 \text{ million}$$

This stands in contrast to the discounted cash flow value of $12 billion that we obtain by taking the difference between the present value of the cash flows of developing the reserve today ($42.38 billion) and the cost of development ($30.38 billion). The difference can be attributed to Gulf's option of choosing when to develop its reserves.

This represents the value of the undeveloped reserves of oil owned by Gulf Oil. In addition, Gulf Oil had free cash flows to the firm from its oil and gas production from already developed reserves of $915 million. We assume that these cash flows are likely to be constant and continue for ten years (the remaining lifetime of developed reserves). The present value of these developed reserves, discounted at the weighted average cost of capital of 12.5%, yields the following:

$$\text{Value of Already Developed Reserves} = \frac{915\left(1 - \frac{1}{1.125^{10}}\right)}{0.125} = \$5{,}066$$

Adding the value of the developed and undeveloped reserves of Gulf Oil provides the firm's value:

Value of Undeveloped Reserves	= $ 13,306 million
Value of Production in Place	= $ 5,066 million
Total Value of Firm	= $ 18,372 million
Less Outstanding Debt	= $ 9,900 million
Value of Equity	= $ 8,472 million
Value per Share	$= \frac{\$\ 8{,}472}{165.3} = \$51.25$

This analysis suggests that Gulf Oil is overvalued at $70 per share.

8 With a binomial model, we estimate the value of the reserves to be $13.73 billion.

Implications

Even if we never explicitly use option pricing models to value natural resources reserves or firms, there are implications for other valuation approaches:

- **Price volatility affects value:** The value of a commodity company is a function of not only the price of the commodity but also the expected volatility in that price. The price matters for obvious reasons—higher commodity prices translate into higher revenues, earnings, and cash flows. The variance in that price can affect value by altering the option values of undeveloped reserves. Thus, if the price of oil goes from $25 a barrel to $40 a barrel, you would expect all oil companies to become more valuable. If the price drops back to $25, the values of oil companies may not decline to their old levels, since the perceived volatility in oil prices may have changed.
- **Mature versus growth commodity companies:** As commodity prices become more volatile, commodity companies that derive more of their value from undeveloped reserves will gain in value, relative to more mature companies that generate cash flows from developed reserves. In the example used before, where oil price volatility is perceived to have changed even though the price itself has not changed, we would expect Petrobras to gain in value, relative to Exxon Mobil.
- **Development of reserves:** As commodity price volatility increases, commodity companies become more reluctant to develop their reserves. If we treat undeveloped reserves as options, and developing those reserves as the equivalent of exercising those options, higher volatility in the underlying commodity price will make exercise less likely (since we will lose the time premium on the option).
- **Optionality increases as commodity price decreases:** The time premium on an option becomes smaller (as a percentage of the option value) as it becomes in-the-money. In the context of natural resources options, this implies that the option premium is greatest when commodity prices are low (and the reserves are either marginally viable or not viable) and should decrease as commodity prices increase.

In closing, if we regard undeveloped reserves as options, discounted cash flow valuation generally underestimates the value of natural resources companies, because the expected price of the commodity is used to estimate revenues and operating profits. As a consequence, we miss the option component of value. Again, the difference is greatest for firms with significant undeveloped reserves and with commodities where price volatility is highest.

Conclusion

Cyclical and commodity companies have volatile earnings, with the volatility coming from macroeconomic factors that are not in the control of these companies. As the economy weakens and strengthens, cyclical companies see their earnings fluctuate, and commodity companies see their earnings and cash flows track the commodity price.

When valuing these companies, analysts make one of two mistakes. They either ignore the economic and commodity price cycles, and assume that the current year's earnings and cash flows (which are a function of where we are in the cycle) will continue forever, or they expend resources trying to forecast the cycle in the long term. We presented two ways of valuing these firms. In the first, we look past the cycle at the firm's normalized earnings, growth, and cash flow. In effect, we are assuming that although cycles can cause big swings in the numbers, we cannot forecast the year-to-year shifts in cycles. In the second method, we still assume normalization, but only in the long term. In the near term, we forecast revenues, earnings, and cash flows based on where we are in the cycle. While the two approaches converge when firms are in the middle of a cycle, they diverge at the top or bottom of a cycle.

In the final section of this chapter, we considered the possibility that the undeveloped reserves at commodity companies could be considered options, insofar as the company has the rights to develop these reserves but does not have to develop them. We argued that commodity companies, especially when the commodity price is volatile, can trade at a premium on their discounted cash flow values.

14

Mark to Market: Financial Services Companies

Banks, insurance companies, and other financial services firms pose special challenges for an analyst attempting to value them—for three reasons. The first is that the nature of their businesses makes it difficult to define both debt and reinvestment, making the estimation of cash flows much more difficult. The second reason is that these firms tend to be heavily regulated, and changes in regulatory requirements can have a significant effect on value. The third reason is that the accounting rules that govern bank accounting have historically been very different from the accounting rules for other firms. Assets are marked to market more frequently for financial services firms.

This chapter begins by considering what makes financial services firms unique and ways of dealing with the differences. We move on to look at how the dark side of valuation manifests itself in the valuation of financial services firms in the form of an unhealthy dependence on book values, earnings, and dividends. We then look at how best to adapt discounted cash flow models to value financial services firms by considering three alternatives—a traditional dividend discount model, a cash flow to equity discount model, and an excess return model. With each, we look at examples from the financial services arena. We move on to look at how relative valuation works with financial services firms and what multiples may work best with these firms.

Financial Services Firms: The Big Picture

Any firm that provides financial products and services to individuals or other firms can be categorized as a financial services firm. We would categorize financial services businesses into four groups from the perspective of how they make their money. A *bank* makes money on the spread between the interest it pays to those from whom it raises funds and the interest it charges those who borrow from it. It also makes money from other services it offers its depositors and lenders. *Insurance companies* make their income in two ways. One is through the premiums they receive from those who buy insurance protection from them. The other is income from the investment portfolios they maintain to service the claims. An *investment bank* provides advice and supporting products for other firms to raise capital from financial markets or to consummate deals such as acquisitions and divestitures. *Investment firms* provide investment advice or manage portfolios for clients. Their income comes from advisory fees for the advice and management and sales fees for investment portfolios. With the consolidation in the financial services sector, an increasing number of firms operate in more than one of these businesses. For example, Citigroup, created by the merger of Travelers and Citicorp, operates in all four businesses. At the same time, however, a large number of small banks, boutique investment banks, and specialized insurance firms still derive the bulk of their income from one source.

How big is the financial services sector in the U.S.? We would not be exaggerating if we said that the development of the economy in the U.S. would not have occurred without banks providing much of the capital for growth. Insurance companies predate both equity and bond markets as pioneers in risk sharing. Financial services firms have been the foundation of the U.S. economy for decades, and the results can be seen in many measures. Table 14.1 summarizes the market capitalization of publicly traded banks, insurance companies, brokerage houses, investment firms, and thrifts in the U.S. at the end of 2007. It also shows the proportion of the overall equity market they represented at the time.

Table 14.1 Financial Services Firms: Market Capitalizations on January 1, 2008 (in Millions)

Sector	Number	Market Capitalization	Proportion of Market
Bank	550	$2,404,664	4.78%
Financial services	294	$1,153,793	2.29%
Insurance	353	$4,029,009	8.00%
Securities brokerage	31	$731,343	1.45%
Thrift	234	$156,596	0.31%
All financial services	**1,462**	**$8,475,404**	**16.83%**

At the start of 2008, financial services firms accounted for about a sixth of the overall market in terms of market capitalization. In addition, the financial services sector in the 2002 economic census accounted for 6% of all full-time employees in the U.S.

Given the importance of financial services companies to the economy, the crisis of 2008 acted as a wake-up call for investors on two fronts. As stock prices at established financial services firms like AIG, Citigroup, and Bank of America collapsed, the system's fragility came to the fore. At the same time, the failure of the banking system also made us more aware of how dependent the entire economy is on the health of financial services firms. Without banks lending money, investment banks backing acquisitions and financing deals, and insurance companies pooling risk, the rest of the real economy came to a standstill. By the end of 2008, financial services firms had seen huge declines in their market capitalizations, but given the pull they exercised on the rest of the market, they preserved their proportional standing for the most part. See Figure 14.1.

In fact, while banking and security brokerages have declined as a proportion of the overall market, the other financial sectors have increased their share. This has left the total share almost unchanged after a year of unprecedented volatility.

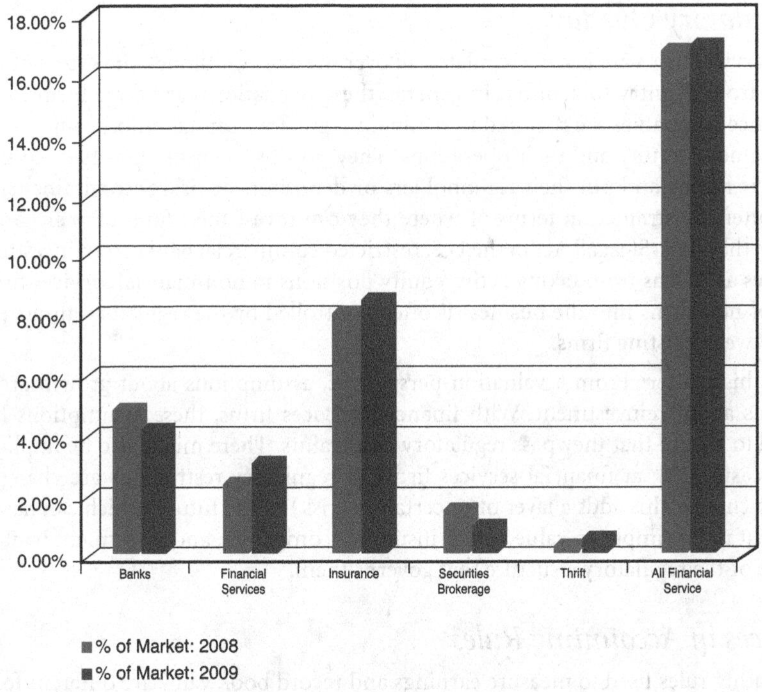

Figure 14.1: Financial Services Firms as a Proportion of the Market: January 2008 to January 2009

In emerging markets, financial services firms tend to have an even higher profile and account for a larger proportion of overall market value than they do in the U.S. If we bring these firms into the mix, it is quite clear that no one template will value all financial services firms. We have to be flexible in how we use and adapt valuation models to allow for all types of financial services firms.

Characteristics of Financial Services Firms

Financial services firms differ from other firms in the market in many ways. This section focuses on four key differences and looks at why these differences can create estimation issues in valuation. The first is that many categories (albeit not all) of financial services firms *operate under strict regulatory constraints* on how they run their businesses and how much capital they need to set aside to keep operating. The second is that accounting rules for recording earnings and asset value at financial services firms *are at variance with accounting rules for the rest of the market.* The third is that debt for a financial services firm is more akin to raw material than to a source of capital. The notion of cost of capital and enterprise value may be meaningless as a consequence. The final factor is that the *defining reinvestment* (net capital expenditures and working capital) for a bank or insurance company may be not just difficult, but impossible, and cash flows cannot be computed.

The Regulatory Overlay

Financial services firms are heavily regulated all over the world, although the extent of the regulation varies from country to country. In general, these regulations take three forms. First, banks and insurance companies are required to maintain regulatory capital ratios, computed based on the book value of equity and their operations. They do this to ensure that they do not expand beyond their means and put their claimholders or depositors at risk. Second, financial services firms are often constrained in terms of where they can invest their funds. For instance, until a decade ago, the Glass-Steagall Act in the U.S. restricted commercial banks from investment banking activities as well as from taking active equity positions in nonfinancial services firms. Third, the entry of new firms into the business is often controlled by the regulatory authorities, as are mergers between existing firms.

Why does this matter? From a valuation perspective, assumptions about growth are linked to assumptions about reinvestment. With financial services firms, these assumptions have to be scrutinized to ensure that they pass regulatory constraints. There might also be implications for how we measure risk at financial services firms. If regulatory restrictions are changing or are expected to change, this adds a layer of uncertainty (risk) to the future, which can have an effect on value. Put more simply, to value banks, insurance companies, and investment banks, we have to be aware of the regulatory structure that governs them.

Differences in Accounting Rules

The accounting rules used to measure earnings and record book value are different for financial services firms than the rest of the market, for two reasons. The first is that the assets of financial services firms tend to be financial instruments (bonds, securitized obligations) that often have an active marketplace. Not surprisingly, marking assets to market value has been an established practice in financial services firms, well before other firms even started talking about fair-value accounting. The second reason is that the nature of operations for a financial services firm is such that long periods of profitability are interspersed with short periods of large losses; accounting standards have been developed to counter this tendency and create smoother earnings.

- **Mark to market**: If the new trend in accounting is toward recording assets at fair value (rather than original costs), financial services firms operate as a laboratory for this experiment. After all, accounting rules for banks, insurance companies, and investment banks have required that assets be recorded at fair value for more than a decade, based on the argument that most of a bank's assets are traded and have market prices and therefore do not require too many subjective judgments. In general, the assets of banks and insurance companies tend to be securities, many of which are publicly traded. Since the market price is observable for many of these investments, accounting rules have tilted toward using market value (actual or estimated) for these assets. To the extent that some or a significant portion of the assets of a financial services firms are marked to market, and the assets of most nonfinancial services firms are not, we face two problems. The first is in comparing ratios based on book value (both market-to-book ratios such as price-to-book and accounting ratios such as return on equity) across financial and nonfinancial services firms. The second problem is in interpreting these ratios after they are computed. While the return on equity for a nonfinancial services firm can be considered a measure of return earned on equity invested originally in assets, the same cannot be said about return on equity at financial services firms. Here the book equity measures not what was originally invested in assets but an updated market value.

- **Loss provisions and smoothing out earnings**: Consider a bank that makes money the old-fashioned way—by taking in funds from depositors and lending these funds to individuals and corporations at higher rates. While the rate charged to lenders is higher than that promised to depositors, the risk that the bank faces is that lenders may default, and the rate at which they default will vary widely over time—low during good economic times and high during economic downturns. Rather than write off the bad loans as they occur, banks usually create provisions for losses that average out losses over time and charge this amount against earnings every year. Although this practice is logical, it has a catch, insofar as the bank is given the responsibility of making the loan loss assessment. A conservative bank will set aside more for loan losses, given a loan portfolio, than a more aggressive bank, and this will lead to the latter reporting higher profits during good times.

Debt and Equity

In the financial balance sheet that we used to describe firms, there are only two ways to raise funds to finance a business—debt and equity. While this is true for both all firms, financial services firms differ from nonfinancial services firms on three dimensions:

- **Debt is raw material, not capital**: When we talk about capital for nonfinancial services firms, we tend to talk about both debt and equity. A firm raises funds from both equity investors and bondholders (and banks) and uses these funds to make its investments. When we value the firm, we value the value of the assets owned by the firm, rather than just the value of its equity. With a financial services firm, debt has a different connotation. Rather than viewing debt as a source of capital, most financial services firms seem to view it as raw material. In other words, debt is to a bank what steel is to a manufacturing company—something to be molded into other products that can then be sold at a higher price and yield a profit. Consequently, capital at financial services firms seems to be narrowly defined as including only equity capital. This definition of capital is reinforced by the regulatory authorities, who evaluate the equity capital ratios of banks and insurance firms.
- **Defining debt**: The definition of what comprises debt also is murkier with a financial services firm than it is with a nonfinancial services firm. For instance, should deposits made by customers into their checking accounts at a bank be treated as debt by that bank? Especially on interest-bearing checking accounts, there is little distinction between a deposit and debt issued by the bank. If we do categorize this as debt, the operating income for a bank should be measured prior to interest paid to depositors. This would be problematic, because interest expenses are usually a bank's single biggest expense item.
- **Degree of financial leverage**: Even if we can define debt as a source of capital and can measure it precisely, financial services firms differ from other firms in an additional way. They tend to use more debt in funding their businesses and thus have higher financial leverage than most other firms. Although good reasons can be offered for why they have

been able to do this historically—more predictable earnings and the regulatory framework are two that are commonly cited—this high financial leverage has consequences. Since equity is a sliver of the overall value of a financial services firm, small changes in the value of the firm's assets can translate into big swings in equity value.

Estimating Cash Flows Is Difficult

We noted earlier that financial services firms are constrained by regulation in both where they invest their funds and how much they invest. If we define reinvestment as necessary for future growth, as we have so far in this book, problems are associated with measuring reinvestment with financial services firms. Note that we consider two items in reinvestment—net capital expenditures and working capital. Unfortunately, measuring either of these items at a financial services firm can be problematic.

Consider net capital expenditures first. Unlike manufacturing firms, which invest in their plant, equipment, and other fixed assets, financial services firms invest primarily in intangible assets such as brand name and human capital. Consequently, their investments for future growth often are categorized as operating expenses in accounting statements. Not surprisingly, the statement of cash flows to a bank shows little or no capital expenditures and correspondingly low depreciation. With working capital, we run into a different problem. If we define working capital as the difference between current assets and current liabilities, a large proportion of a bank's balance sheet would fall into one of these categories. Changes in this number can be both large and volatile and may have no relationship to reinvestment for future growth.

As a result of this difficulty in measuring reinvestment, we run into two practical problems in valuing these firms. The first is that we cannot estimate operating cash flows without estimating reinvestment. In other words, if we cannot identify how much a company is reinvesting for future growth, we cannot identify cash flows. The second problem is that estimating expected future growth becomes more difficult if the reinvestment rate cannot be measured.

The Dark Side of Valuation

The factors that characterize financial services firms—assets that are marked to market, earnings that are after provisions for future losses, and the difficulty we face in defining debt and reinvestment—all have an effect on how these firms are valued. This section considers some common pitfalls in valuing financial services firms.

Debt

For much of this book, we have adopted the standard practice of forecasting cash flows after taxes and reinvestment, but before debt payments, and discounting these cash flows back at a composite cost of capital. Adopting this practice with financial services firms can have disastrous consequences for several reasons, but one of the biggest is in the computation of the cost of capital. As we noted in the preceding section, defining debt in a bank or insurance company is very difficult. If we decide to treat all short-term and long-term borrowing as debt, the debt ratios we arrive at for banks will be stratospheric. If we combine these high debt ratios with the low costs of debt, we will end up with costs of capital that are unrealistically small—4% or lower for many banks.

If we decide to go with a narrower definition of debt, we have to decide what to include in debt and what to exclude, with all its subjective components. Thus, we can decide to include only long-term debt in the cost-of-capital computation and end up with more reasonable-looking numbers, but this choice has no logical rationale

Cash Flow Substitutes

In the preceding section, we noted that our inability to identify and separate capital expenditures and working capital investments in financial services firms makes it difficult, if not impossible, to estimate cash flows with any degree of precision. Some analysts plow on using either implausible variants on cash flows or the conventional definition of cash flow, in spite of the limitations.

- **Earnings as cash flows:** Some analysts value banks by discounting their earnings back to the present. They argue that banks have little or no net capital expenditure needs and that working capital needs—inventory, accounts receivable—are nonexistent. The problem, though, is that they couple the discounting of earnings with a positive (or even high) expected growth rate in these earnings. This is clearly not feasible. To see why, consider a bank that pays out 100% of its earnings as dividends. If this firm issues no new equity, its book equity stays frozen at current levels forever. If this bank continues to grow its loan portfolio, it will eventually end up with capital ratios that are lower than the regulatory minimum. That is why reinvestment has to include investments in regulatory capital, acquisitions, and other such investments that banks need to make to continue growing. That is also why even mature banks with low growth rates cannot afford to pay out 100% of their earnings as dividends.
- **Pseudo cash flow:** If analysts stick with the conventional definition of cash flows as net of reinvestment and use the capital expenditure and working capital number that they compute for banks, they can generate measures of cash flows that are even more skewed than earnings. First, the net capital expenditures at a financial services firm, at least as defined by conventional accounting statements, will be a very small or negative number. Second, defining working capital as the difference between noncash current assets and nondebt current liabilities can yield strange numbers in any given year.

In effect, analysts who claim to use cash flows to value banks are using numbers that are not good measures of cash flows, and they end up with values that reflect them.

Go with the Flow: Dividends

Many analysts accept the reality that estimating cash flows for financial services firms is not feasible and fall back on the only observable cash flow—dividends. While this makes sense, these analysts are implicitly assuming that the dividends that are paid out by a bank or insurance company are sustainable and reasonable. However, that is not always true. We know that some banks pay out less in dividends than they can and use the excess to pad their capital ratios, whereas other banks pay dividends that are far too high and then try to compensate by issuing new shares. If we value the former using actual dividends paid, we will undervalue them, since we will build in the current practice of paying too little into their cash flows in perpetuity. If we value the latter using actual dividends paid, we will overvalue them.

The focus on current dividends can also create problems when valuing financial services firms that have growth potential. If these firms hold back on paying larger dividends, given their needs to fund growth, the dividends paid will be lower than those paid by more mature firms. In some cases, there may be no dividends. If we use these dividends as our basis for valuation, and do not adjust the dividend payout as growth becomes lower, we will significantly undervalue firms. In the special case of firms that do not pay dividends, we will arrive at the result of a zero value for equity.

Dividends and Growth: Wells Fargo

Wells Fargo paid out dividends per share of $1.30 in 2008, reflecting growth of about 4% a year from 2001 to 2008. If we allow for a cost of equity for banks of approximately 9% and assume that dividends will continue to grow at 4% a year forever, we can derive the value of equity per share from a stable growth dividend discount model:

$$\text{Value of Equity per Share} = \frac{\text{Expected Dividends per Share}_{\text{Next Year}}}{(\text{Cost of Equity} - \text{Stable Growth Rate})} = \frac{1.30(1.04)}{(.09 - .04)} = \$27.04$$

Since the stock was trading at $15.75 a share at the time of this analysis, this indicates a significantly undervalued stock. However, there are reasons to be skeptical about the valuation:

- The earnings per share dropped from $4.47 in 2007 to $1.71 in 2008, with the expectation that it would drop further to $1.34 a share in 2009. In effect, we are assuming that the dividends will be higher than earnings in 2009.
- The growth in dividends between 2001 and 2008 reflected the fact that Wells Fargo was going through a boom period, with net income increasing from $3.4 billion in 2001 to $8.1 billion in 2007. In 2008, net income dropped to $2.8 billion, reflecting deteriorating business conditions. It is likely that Wells Fargo will have to cut dividends to reflect the deterioration of earnings.

Using the current dividends per share and historical growth in dividends in these circumstances will yield too high a value of equity per share.

Trusting Book Value

There are two reasons why marking assets to market value has been an accepted practice in financial services companies for years. The first is that many of the assets are financial assets that are traded, and getting market value is relatively straightforward; these assets have lesser need for estimation and subjective judgment. The second reason is that financial services firms are less likely to hold assets to maturity; banks often securitize their loan portfolios and sell them to investors. Consequently, the market prices of these securities are more relevant when analyzing firms.

Since assets reflect current market value, rather than original cost, it can be argued that analysts should be in a much better position to value financial services firms than the rest of the market. While this may be true, some costs are created in the process as well:

- **Book value equals market value**: Assets may be marked to market, but that does remove the need to assess their value independently. Analysts who equate book value to market value because of marking to market not only abandon their responsibility for estimating value but also can make significant errors for two reasons. First, even if there is an active market from which market prices are extracted, markets can make mistakes, and these mistakes will then be embedded in the book value. For instance, the book values of mortgage-backed securities at banks at the start of 2008 reflected the market prices of these securities at the time. Only when the market prices collapsed did we realize that the book values of financial services firms overstated their true values. Second, in many cases, assets are marked to market based not on an observable market price but on models used by the appraiser. In fact, the firm that holds the securities often assesses their value for accounting purposes. Not surprisingly, there is a tendency to overstate values, and a lag occurs in recognizing changes in those values.
- **Measuring investment quality**: While we can take issue with the fact that the book value of assets at many companies reflects what was originally invested in them, rather than current value, the conventional accounting approach has a benefit. One of the key determinants of a company's value is the quality of its investments, and the most widely used measures of investment quality are accounting returns—returns on equity and capital. By looking at earnings relative to original investment, we get an estimate of how much return that original investment is making. Thus, a firm that invested $800 in an asset three years ago and is generating $200 in after-tax earnings currently is earning a 25% return on its investment. By marking assets to market, we lose this important piece of information. In fact, if assets are truly marked to market, the return on equity on every asset should be equal to the cost of equity. Nothing distinguishes firms making good investments from those making bad investments.

Regulation and Risk

When investing in financial services firms, we accept the fact that we know far less about their assets than we would like to know, because they are regulated. In effect, we assume that the regulatory authorities will keep banks and insurance companies in check and ensure that they do not overreach in their risk taking. As with marking to market, this trust can expose us to significant dangers in investing. When analysts compare the price earnings ratios of banks, for instance, and do not control for the risk of the loan portfolios of these banks, they assume that all banks are equally risky. Not surprisingly, riskier banks look cheaper in this comparison.

The problem gets worse when you compare financial services firms that are covered by different regulatory regimes. A relative valuation of banks that operate in different countries is flawed if it does not control for the regulatory differences and the resulting risk differences across these countries. Even within the same market, like the U.S., investment banks, insurance companies, and commercial banks face different regulatory rules, some stricter than others. We have to consider these differences when valuing and analyzing these firms.

Discounted Cash Flow Models

In a discounted cash flow model, we consider the value of an asset to be the present value of the expected cash flows generated by that asset. In this section, we will first argue that financial services firms should be valued on an equity basis, rather than on a firm basis. We also argue that dividends, for better or worse, are often the only tangible cash flow that we can observe or estimate. Consequently, our focus will be on variants of the dividend discount model and how they can best be used to value banks and insurance companies.

Equity Versus Firm Valuation

Early in this book, we noted the distinction between valuing a firm and valuing the equity in the firm. We value firms by discounting expected after-tax cash flows prior to debt payments at the weighted average cost of capital. We value equity by discounting cash flows to equity investors at the cost of equity. Estimating cash flows prior to debt payments at a weighted average cost of capital is problematic when debt and debt payments cannot be easily identified. As we discussed earlier, this is the case with financial services firms. Equity can be valued directly, however, by discounting cash flows to equity at the cost of equity. Consequently, we would argue for the latter approach for financial services firms.

Even with equity valuation, we have a secondary problem. To value the equity in a firm, we normally estimate the free cash flow to equity. In Chapter 2, "Intrinsic Valuation," we defined the free cash flow to equity:

> Free Cash Flow to Equity = Net Income – Net Capital Expenditures – Change in Noncash Working Capital – (Debt Repaid – New Debt Issued)

If we cannot estimate net capital expenditures or noncash working capital, we clearly cannot estimate the free cash flow to equity. Since this is the case with financial services firms, we have three choices. The first is to use dividends as cash flows to equity and assume that firms over time pay out their free cash flows to equity as dividends. Since dividends are observable, we therefore do not have to confront the question of how much firms reinvest. The second choice is to adapt the free cash flow to equity measure to allow for the types of reinvestment that financial services firms make. For instance, given that banks operate under a regulatory capital ratio constraint, it can be argued that these firms have to increase regulatory capital in order to make more loans in the future. The third choice is to keep the focus on excess returns, rather than on earnings, dividends, and growth rates, and to value these excess returns.

Dividend Discount Models

In the basic dividend discount model, the value of a stock is the present value of the expected dividends on that stock. While many analysts view this model as old-fashioned, it retains a strong following among analysts who value financial services companies because of the difficulties we face in estimating cash flows. This section begins by laying out the basic model. Then it considers ways in which we can streamline its usage when valuing financial services companies.

The Standard Model

If we start with the assumption that equity in a publicly traded firm has an infinite life, we arrive at the most general version of the dividend discount model:

$$\text{Value per Share of Equity} = \sum_{t=1}^{t=\infty} \frac{DPS_t}{(1+k_e)^t}$$

where

DPS_t = Expected dividend per share in period t

k_e = Cost of equity

In the special case where the expected growth rate in dividends is constant forever, this model collapses into the *Gordon growth model*:

$$\text{Value per Share of Equity in Stable Growth} = \frac{DPS_1}{(k_e - g)}$$

In this equation, g is the expected growth rate in perpetuity, and DPS_1 is the expected dividends per share next year. In the more general case, dividends grow at a rate that is not expected to be sustainable or constant forever during a period (called the extraordinary growth period). In this case, we can still assume that the growth rate will be constant forever at some point in the future. This allows us to then estimate a stock's value, in the dividend discount model, as the sum of the present values of the dividends over the extraordinary growth period and the present value of the terminal price, which itself is estimated using the Gordon growth model:

$$\text{Value per Share of Equity in Extraordinary Growth} = \sum_{t=1}^{t=n} \frac{DPS_t}{(1+k_{e,hg})^t} + \frac{DPS_{n+1}}{(k_{e,st} - g_n)(1+k_{e,hg})^n}$$

The extraordinary growth is expected to last n years, g_n is the expected growth rate after n years, and k_e is the cost of equity (hg is high growth period and st is stable growth period).

While the dividend discount model is intuitive and has deep roots in equity valuation, dangers exist in using the model blindly. As we noted in the section on the dark side, many analysts start with the bank's current dividends as a base. Then they apply a growth rate to these earnings, based on either history or analyst forecasts, and compute a present value. For the model to yield a reasonable value, the assumptions have to be internally consistent, with the expected growth rate numbers jelling with the dividend forecasts and risk measures.

A Consistent Dividend Discount Model

Looking at the inputs into the dividend discount model, three sets of inputs determine the value of equity. The first is the cost of equity that we use to discount cash flows, with the possibility that the cost may vary across time, at least for some firms. The second input is the proportion of the earnings that we assume will be paid out in dividends. This is the dividend payout ratio. Higher payout ratios will translate into more dividends for any given level of earnings. The third input is the expected growth rate in dividends over time, which will be a function of the earnings growth rate and the accompanying payout ratio. In addition to estimating each set of inputs well, we also need to ensure that the inputs are consistent with each other.

Risk and Cost of Equity

In keeping with how we have estimated the cost of equity for firms so far in this book, the cost of equity for a financial services firm has to reflect the portion of the risk in the equity that cannot be diversified away by the marginal investor in the stock. This risk is estimated using a beta (in the capital asset pricing model) or betas (in a multifactor or arbitrage pricing model). You should keep in mind three estimation notes when estimating the cost of equity for a financial services firm:

- **Use bottom-up betas**: In our earlier discussions of betas, we argued against the use of regression betas because of the noise in the estimates (standard errors) and the possibility that the firm has changed over the period of the regression. We will continue to hold to that proposition when valuing financial services firms. In fact, the large numbers of publicly traded firms in this domain should make estimating bottom-up betas much easier.
- **Do not adjust for financial leverage**: When estimating betas for nonfinancial services firms, we emphasized the importance of unlevering betas (whether they be historical or sector averages) and then relevering them using a firm's current debt-to-equity ratio. With financial services firms, we would skip this step for two reasons. First, financial services firms tend to be much more homogeneous in terms of capital structure. They tend to have similar financial leverage primarily due to regulations. Second, and this is a point made earlier, debt is difficult to measure for financial services firms. In practical terms, this means that we will use the average levered beta for comparable firms as the bottom-up beta for the firm being analyzed.
- **Adjust for regulatory and business risk**: If we use sector betas and do not adjust for financial leverage, we are in effect using the same beta for every company in the sector. As we noted earlier, there can be significant regulatory differences across markets, and even within a market, across different classes of financial services firms. To reflect this, we would define the sector narrowly. Thus, we would look the average beta across large money center banks when valuing a large money center bank and across small regional banks when valuing one of these. We would also argue that financial services firms that expand into riskier businesses—securitization, trading, and investment banking—should have different (and higher betas) for these segments, and that the beta for the company should be a weighted average. Table 14.2 summarizes the betas for different groups of financial services companies, categorized by region, in February 2009.

Table 14.2 Betas for Financial Services Businesses

Category	U.S.	Europe	Emerging Markets
Large money center banks	0.71	0.80	0.9
Small/regional banks	0.91	0.98	1.05
Thrifts	0.66	0.75	0.85
Brokerage houses	1.37	1.25	1.5
Investment banks	1.50	1.55	1.9

Category	U.S.	Europe	Emerging Markets
Life insurance	1.17	1.20	1.1
Property and casualty insurance companies	0.91	0.95	0.9

- **Consider the relationship between risk and growth**: Throughout this book, we have emphasized the importance of modifying a company's risk profile to reflect changes that we are assuming to its growth rate. As growth companies mature, betas should move toward 1. We see no need to abandon that principle when valuing banks. We would expect high-growth banks to have higher betas (and costs of equity) than mature banks. In valuing such banks, we would therefore start with higher costs of equity, but as we reduce growth, we would also reduce betas and costs of equity.

A final point needs to be emphasized. The average betas that we get across financial services firms reflect the regulatory constraints that they operated under during that period. When significant changes to regulation are expected, we should consider the potential impact on betas across the board. For instance, the crisis of 2008 will cause banking regulations to be tightened globally and may very well push up the betas for all banks, at least for the foreseeable future.

Growth and Payout

An inherent trade-off exists between dividends and growth. When a company pays a larger segment of its earnings as dividends, it is reinvesting less and thus should grow more slowly. With financial services firms, this link is reinforced by the fact that the activities of these firms are subject to regulatory capital constraints. Banks and insurance companies have to maintain equity (in book value terms) at specified percentages of their activities. When a company is paying out more in dividends, it is retaining less in earnings; the book value of equity increases by the retained earnings. In recent years, in keeping with a trend that is visible in other sectors as well, financial services firms have increased stock buybacks as a way of returning cash to stockholders. In this context, focusing purely on dividends paid can provide a misleading picture of the cash returned to stockholders. An obvious solution is to add the stock buybacks each year to the dividends paid and to compute the composite payout ratio. If we do so, however, we should look at the number over several years, since stock buybacks vary widely across time. A buyback of billions in one year may be followed by three years of relatively meager buybacks, for instance.

To ensure that assumptions about dividends, earnings, and growth are internally consistent, we have to bring in a measure of how well the retained equity is reinvested; the return on equity is the variable that ties together payout ratios and expected growth. Chapter 2 introduced a fundamental growth measure for earnings:

Expected Growth in Earnings = Return on Equity * (1 – Dividend Payout Ratio)

For instance, a bank that pays out 60% of its earnings as dividends and earns a return on equity of 12% has an expected growth rate in earnings of 4.8%. When we introduced the fundamental equation in Chapter 2, we also noted that firms can deliver growth rates that deviate from this expectation if the return on equity is changing:

$$\text{Expected Growth}_{EPS} = (1 - \text{Payout Ratio})(\text{ROE}_{t+1}) + \frac{\text{ROE}_{t+1} - \text{ROE}_t}{\text{ROE}_t}$$

Thus, if the bank can improve the return on equity on existing assets from 10 to 12%, the efficiency growth rate in that year will be 20%. However, efficiency growth is temporary; all firms ultimately revert to the fundamental growth relationship.

The linkage between return on equity, growth, and dividends is therefore critical in determining value in a financial services firm. At the risk of hyperbole, the key number in valuing a bank is not dividends, earnings, or growth rate, but what we believe it will earn as *return on equity in the long term*. That number, in conjunction with payout ratios, will help determine growth. Alternatively, the return on equity, together with expected growth rates, can be used to estimate dividends. This linkage is particularly useful when we get to stable growth, where growth rates can be very different from the initial growth rates. To preserve consistency in the valuation, the payout ratio that we use in stable growth, to estimate the terminal value, should be as follows:

$$\text{Payout Ratio in Stable Growth} = 1 - \frac{g}{\text{ROE}_{\text{Stable Growth}}}$$

The risk of the firm should also adjust to reflect the stable-growth assumption. In particular, if betas are used to estimate the cost of equity, they should converge toward one in stable growth.

Wells Fargo Banks: February 2009

The preceding sidebar examined the effects of leaving dividends unchanged and using historical dividend growth to value Wells Fargo in early 2009. It concluded that we would overvalue the firm for two reasons. First, we are overstating the expected dividends in the future by basing them on the dividends paid in 2008. Second, the growth rate we were assuming for the future (4%) may be inconsistent with the payout ratio we assumed in the valuation. Based on the 2008 numbers, where dividends per share were $1.30 per share and earnings per share were $1.71, the payout ratio is 76%. To deliver a growth rate of 4% a year forever, the return on equity that Wells Fargo would have to deliver on its new investment is 16.67%:

$$\text{Implied Return on Equity} = \frac{g}{(1 - \text{Payout Ratio})} = \frac{4\%}{(1 - .76)} = 16.67\%$$

If we believe that Wells Fargo's future return on equity will be lower than 16.67%, we have to either lower growth or reduce dividends.

Rather than base the valuation on the 2008 dividend and earnings numbers, which are unstable and reflect the market crisis, we chose a different path. We started with the book value of equity of $47,628 million that Wells Fargo reported at the end of 2008. We then estimated what earnings and dividends would be at a normalized return on equity. For instance, consider the most optimistic scenario, in which the return on equity at Wells Fargo quickly reverts to 18.91%, the average ROE from 2001 to 2007. The normalized net income for next year would be as follows:

$$\text{Normalized Net Income} = \text{Book Value of Equity} * \text{Normalized ROE}$$
$$= \$47{,}628 \text{ million} * .1891 = \$9{,}006 \text{ million}$$

Assuming that these earnings would grow at a stable rate of 3% a year in perpetuity, we next estimate the dividend payout ratio:

$$\text{Dividend Payout Ratio} = 1 - \frac{g}{\text{ROE}} = 1 - \frac{.03}{.1891} = .8414 \text{ or } 84.14\%$$

If we assume that the cost of equity of 9% that we estimated earlier is a reasonable value, we can estimate the value of equity in Wells Fargo:[1]

$$\text{Value of Equity} = \frac{\text{Expected Dividends Next Year}}{(\text{Cost of Equity} - \text{Stable Growth Rate})}$$

$$= \frac{\text{Net Income} * \text{Payout Ratio}}{(\text{Cost of Equity} - \text{Stable Growth Rate})} = \frac{9006 * (0.8414)}{(.09 - .03)} = \$126{,}293 \text{ million}$$

Under the most optimistic scenario, Wells Fargo is significantly undervalued in February 2009 at its existing market value for equity of $66,640 million.

The two inputs that determine the value of equity at Wells Fargo are the return on equity and the cost of equity. As we lower the return on equity, the normalized net income decreases, and so does the payout ratio (for the given growth rate of 3%). The cost of equity can also change if we perceive that banks have become riskier. Following the same procedure that we did for the most optimistic scenario, we can value equity at Wells Fargo under two other scenarios. The first is an intermediate scenario in which the normalized return on equity drops to 15% and the cost of equity increases to 10%. The second is a pessimistic scenario in which the return on equity reverts to 12% and the cost of equity increases to 11%. Table 14.3 summarizes our findings under each scenario.

Table 14.3 Value of Wells Fargo Equity: February 2009

	Net Income	ROE	Payout Ratio	Cost of Equity	Value of Equity
Quick bounce back to normalcy	$9,006.45	18.91%	84.14%	9%	$126,293.58
Slow bounce back to normalcy	$7,144.20	15.00%	80.00%	10%	$81,648.00
Long-term change to lower profitability and higher risk	$5,715.36	12.00%	75.00%	11%	$53,581.50
Market cap (2/2009)					$66,643.00

1 To get to this cost of equity, we assume a beta of 1 and an equity risk premium of 6%. With a risk-free rate of 3%, we obtain a cost of equity of 3% + 6% = 9%.

While Wells Fargo continues to look undervalued, if we assume a slow bounce back to normalcy, it does not look cheap if we assume that banks will be riskier and less profitable from this point on.

Cash Flow to Equity Models

At the beginning of this discussion, we noted the difficulty in estimating cash flows when net capital expenditures and noncash working capital cannot be easily identified. It is possible, however, to estimate cash flows to equity for financial services firms if we define reinvestment differently. The cash flow to equity is the cash flow left over for equity investors after debt payments have been made and reinvestment needs met. With financial services firms, the reinvestment generally does not take the form of plant, equipment, or other fixed assets. Instead, the investment is in regulatory capital. This is the capital as defined by the regulatory authorities, which, in turn, determines the limits on future growth:

$$FCFE_{\text{Financial Services Firm}} = \text{Net Income} - \text{Reinvestment in Regulatory Capital}$$

To estimate the reinvestment in regulatory capital, we have to define two parameters. The first is the *book equity capital ratio* that will determine the investment. This is heavily influenced by regulatory requirements, but it also reflects the choices a bank makes. Conservative banks may choose to maintain a higher capital ratio than required by regulatory authorities, whereas aggressive banks may push toward the regulatory constraints. For instance, a bank that has a 5% equity capital ratio can make $100 in loans for every $5 in equity capital. When this bank reports net income of $15 million and pays out only $5 million, it is increasing its equity capital by $10 million. This, in turn, allows the bank to make $200 million in additional loans and presumably increase its growth rate in future periods. The second parameter is the *profitability of the activity*, defined in terms of net income. Staying with the bank example, we have to specify how much net income the bank will generate with the additional loans. A 0.5% profitability ratio translates into additional net income of $1 million on the additional loans.

Excess Return Models

The third approach to valuing financial services firms is to use an excess return model. In such a model, the value of a firm can be written as the sum of capital currently invested in the firm and the present value of excess returns that the firm expects to make in the future. In this section, we will consider how this model can be applied to valuing equity in a financial services firm.

Basic Model

Given the difficulty associated with defining total capital in a financial services firm, it makes far more sense to focus on just equity when using an excess return model to value a financial services firm. The value of equity in a firm can be written as the sum of the equity invested in a firm's current investments and the expected excess returns to equity investors from these and future investments:

Value of Equity = Equity Capital Invested Currently + Present Value of Expected Excess Returns to Equity Investors

The most interesting aspect of this model is its focus on excess returns. A firm that invests its equity and earns just the fair-market rate of return on these investments should see the market value of its equity converge on the book value of equity capital currently invested in it. A firm that earns a below-market return on its equity investments will see its equity market value dip below the book value of equity.

The other point that has to be emphasized is that this model considers expected future investments as well. Thus, it is up to the analyst using the model to forecast not only where the financial services firm will direct its future investments but also the returns it will make on those investments.

Inputs to the Model

Two inputs are needed to value equity in the excess return model. The first is a measure of equity capital currently invested in the firm. The second and more difficult input is the expected excess returns to equity investors in future periods.

The equity capital currently invested in a firm is usually measured as the book value of equity in the firm. While the book value of equity is an accounting measure and is affected by accounting decisions, it should be a much more reliable measure of equity invested in a financial services firm than in a manufacturing firm for two reasons. The first is that the assets of a financial services firm are often financial assets that are marked up to market. The assets of manufacturing firms are real assets, and deviations between book and market value are usually much larger. The second reason is that depreciation, which can be a big factor in determining book value for manufacturing firms, is often negligible at financial services firms. Notwithstanding this, the book value of equity can be affected by stock buybacks and extraordinary or one-time charges. The book value of equity for financial services firms that have one or both may understate the equity capital invested in the firm.

The excess returns, defined in equity terms, can be stated in terms of the return on equity and the cost of equity:

$$\text{Excess Equity Return} = (\text{Return on Equity} - \text{Cost of Equity})\ (\text{Equity Capital Invested})$$

Again, we are assuming that the return on equity is a good measure of the economic return earned on equity investments. When analyzing a financial services firm, we can obtain the return on equity from the current and past periods, but the return on equity that is required is the expected future return. This requires an analysis of the firm's strengths and weaknesses as well as the competition faced by the firm.

Excess Return Valuation: Goldman Sachs

In February 2009, Goldman Sachs, perhaps the best-regarded investment bank in the world, was trading at a market capitalization for equity of $48.7 billion, well below its book value of equity of $66 billion. A significant factor underlying the stock price collapse was the firm's decline in profitability with $2,322 million in net income in 2008, well below the $11,599 million it reported as profits in the previous year. Goldman paid out $850 million in dividends during 2008.

To value Goldman Sachs, we begin with the current cost of equity. Using the average beta of 1.50 reported by investment banks in 2008, in conjunction with a Treasury bond rate of 3% and an equity risk premium of 6%, yields a cost of equity of 12% for the firm:

Cost of Equity = 3% + 1.5 (6%) = 12%

While the return on equity at Goldman Sachs ranged from 16 to 20% between 2001 and 2007, the expected return on equity, looking forward, will be much lower. For the next five years, we will assume that the return on equity at Goldman will be 9%, well below not only the historical average return on equity but also its own cost of equity. The resulting negative excess returns and present value are summarized in Table 14.4.

Table 14.4 Excess Returns: High-Growth Period

	Year 1	Year 2	Year 3	Year 4	Year 5
Net income	$5,941.08	$6,384.60	$6,861.23	$7,373.44	$7,923.89
– Equity cost (see below)	$7,921.44	$8,512.80	$9,148.30	$9,831.25	$10,565.18
Excess equity return	–$1,980.36	–$2,128.20	–$2,287.08	–$2,457.81	–$2,641.30
Cumulated cost of equity	1.12000	1.25440	1.40493	1.57352	1.76234
Present value	–$1,768.18	–$1,696.59	–$1,627.90	–$1,561.98	–$1,498.74
Beginning BV of equity	$66,012.00	$70,939.98	$76,235.86	$81,927.08	$88,043.17
Cost of equity	12.00%	12.00%	12.00%	12.00%	12.00%
Equity cost	$7,921.44	$8,512.80	$9,148.30	$9,831.25	$10,565.18
Return on equity	9.00%	9.00%	9.00%	9.00%	9.00%
Net income	$5,941.08	$6,384.60	$6,861.23	$7,373.44	$7,923.89
Dividend payout ratio	17.05%	17.05%	17.05%	17.05%	17.05%
Dividends paid	$1,013.10	$1,088.73	$1,170.00	$1,257.35	$1,351.21
Retained earnings	$4,927.98	$5,295.87	$5,691.22	$6,116.09	$6,572.67

The net income each year is computed by multiplying the return on equity each year by the beginning book value of equity. The book value of equity each year is augmented by the portion of earnings that is not paid out as dividends. The dividend payout ratio of 17.05% is based on current dividends and normalized earnings.

To put closure on this valuation, we have to make assumptions about excess returns after year 5. We assumed that the net income would grow 3% a year beyond year 5 and that the beta for the stock would decline to 1.20. For Goldman Sachs, we will assume that the return on equity after year 5 will be 10.20%, set equal to the cost of equity in stable growth:

Cost of Equity in Stable Growth Period = 3% + 1.2(6%) = 10.20%

Net Income_6 = Book Value of Equity at Start of Year 6 * Stable ROE

= ($88,043 * 1.03) * .102 = $9,249.82 million

Note that the net income in year 6 is significantly higher than the net income in year 5, as the return on equity bounces back from 9% to 10.20%. The terminal value of excess returns to equity investors can then be computed:

$$= \frac{\text{Net Income}_6 - (\text{Cost of Equity}_6)(\text{BV of Equity}_6)}{\text{Cost of Equity} - \text{Expected Growth Rate}}$$

$$\text{Terminal Value of Excess Returns} = \frac{9{,}249.82 - (90684.47)(0.102)}{0.102 - 0.03}$$

$$= \$0$$

Since the firm earns its cost of equity after year 5, no value is gained or lost after that year. The value of equity can then be computed as the sum of the three components—the book value of equity invested today, the present value (PV) of excess equity returns over the next five years, and the present value of the terminal value of equity.

Book Value of Equity Invested Currently = $66,012

PV of Equity Excess Return in the Next 5 Years = –$8,154

PV of Terminal Value of Excess Returns = 0

Value of Equity = $57,859

Number of Shares = 461.874

Value per Share = $125.29

At the time of this valuation in February 2009, Goldman Sachs was trading at $96.45 a share. Even with the conservative estimates of return on equity that we have made, the firm looks significantly undervalued.

Asset-Based Valuation

In asset-based valuation, we value the existing assets of a financial services firm, net out debt and other outstanding claims, and report the difference as the value of equity. For example, with a bank, this would require valuing the bank's loan portfolio (which would comprise its assets) and subtracting outstanding debt to estimate the value of equity. For an insurance company, you would value the policies that the company has in force and subtract the expected claims resulting from these policies and other debt outstanding to estimate the value of the equity in the firm.

How would you value a bank's loan portfolio or an insurance company's policies? One approach would be to estimate the price at which the loan portfolio can be sold to another financial services firm, but the better approach is to value it based on the expected cash flows. Consider, for instance, a bank with a $1 billion loan portfolio with a weighted average maturity of eight years, on which it earns interest income of $70 million. Furthermore, assume that the default risk on the loans is such that the fair market interest rate on the loans would be 6.50%. This fair market rate can be estimated either by getting the loan portfolio rated by a ratings agency or by measuring the potential for default risk in the portfolio. The value of the loans can be estimated:

$$\text{Value of Loans} = \$\,70\text{ million (PV of Annuity, 8 years, 6.5\%)} + \frac{\$1{,}000\text{ million}}{1.065^{8}}$$
$$= \$\,1{,}030\text{ million}$$

This loan portfolio has a fair market value that exceeds its book value because the bank is charging an interest rate that exceeds the market rate. The reverse would be true if the bank charged an interest rate that is lower than the market rate. To value the equity in this book, you would subtract the deposits, debt, and other claims on the bank.

This approach has merit if you are valuing a mature bank or an insurance company with little or no growth potential, but it has two significant limitations. First, it does not assign any value to expected future growth and the excess returns that flow from that growth. For instance, a bank that consistently lends at rates higher than justified by default risk should be able to harvest value from future loans as well. Second, this approach is difficult to apply when a financial services firm enters multiple businesses. A firm like Citigroup that operates in multiple businesses would be difficult to value because the assets in each business—insurance, commercial banking, investment banking, portfolio management—would need to be valued separately, with different income streams and different discount rates.

Relative Valuation

In the chapters on relative valuation, we examined a series of multiples that are used to value firms, ranging from earnings multiples to book value multiples to revenue multiples. In this section, we consider how relative valuation can be used for financial services firms.

Choices in Multiples

Firm value multiples such as value to EBITDA or value to EBIT cannot be easily adapted to value financial services firms, because neither value nor operating income can be easily estimated for banks or insurance companies. In keeping with our emphasis on equity valuation for financial services firms, the multiples that we will work with to analyze financial services firms are equity multiples. The three most widely used equity multiples are price earnings ratios, price to book value ratios, and price to sales ratios. Since revenues cannot really be measured for financial services firms, price to sales ratios cannot be estimated or used for these firms. We will look, in this section, at the use of price earnings ratios and price to book value ratios to value financial services firms.

Price Earnings Ratios

The price earnings ratio for a bank or insurance company is measured much the same as it is for any other firm:

$$\text{Price Earnings Ratio} = \frac{\text{Price per Share}}{\text{Earnings per Share}}$$

In Chapter 4, "Relative Valuation," we noted that the price earnings ratio is a function of three variables—the expected growth rate in earnings, the payout ratio, and the cost of equity. As with other firms, the price earnings ratio should be higher for financial services firms with higher expected growth rates in earnings, higher payout ratios, and lower costs of equity.

An issue that is specific to financial services firms is the use of provisions for expected expenses. For instance, banks routinely set aside provisions for bad loans. These provisions reduce the reported income and affect the reported price earnings ratio. Consequently, banks that are more conservative about categorizing bad loans will report lower earnings and have higher price earnings ratios. Banks that are less conservative will report higher earnings and lower price earnings ratios.

Another consideration in the use of earnings multiples is the diversification of financial services firms into multiple businesses. The multiple that an investor is willing to pay for a dollar in earnings from commercial lending should be very different from the multiple that the same investor is willing to pay for a dollar in earnings from trading. When a firm is in multiple businesses with different risk, growth, and return characteristics, it is very difficult to find truly comparable firms and to compare the multiples of earnings paid across firms. In such a case, it makes far more sense to break down the firm's earnings by business and assess the value of each business separately.

Comparing PE Ratios: Insurance Companies

Table 14.5 compares the current price earnings ratios of life insurance companies in February 2009.

Table 14.5 **PE Ratios and Expected Growth Rates: Insurance Companies**

Company Name	PE Ratio	Expected Growth in EPS	Beta
Torchmark Corp. (NYSE:TMK)	4.11	3.60%	1.87
Odyssey Re Holdings Corp. (NYSE:ORH)	5.15	4.00%	1.53
Manulife Financial Corporation (TSX:MFC)	5.4	5.20%	2.41

Company Name	PE Ratio	Expected Growth in EPS	Beta
MetLife, Inc. (NYSE:MET)	5.45	4.50%	1.96
Assurant, Inc. (NYSE:AIZ)	5.56	5.00%	2.16
Principal Financial Group, Inc. (NYSE:PFG)	5.85	5.50%	2.15
AFLAC, Inc. (NYSE:AFL)	6.01	6.40%	2.4
Unum Group (NYSE:UNM)	6.33	6.00%	1.47
Aon Corporation (NYSE:AOC)	7.04	6.20%	1.7
The Travelers Companies, Inc. (NYSE:TRV)	7.58	6.00%	1.87
HCC Insurance Holdings, Inc. (NYSE:HCC)	7.75	7.00%	2.05
The Chubb Corporation (NYSE:CB)	7.94	10.50%	1.67
American Financial Group, Inc. (NYSE:AFG)	9.41	11.00%	1.31
ProAssurance Corporation (NYSE:PRA)	10.74	10.30%	0.89
Reinsurance Group of America, Inc. (NYSE:RGA)	11.71	11.50%	1.24
W.R. Berkley Corporation (NYSE:WRB)	12.3	12.50%	1.98
Sun Life Financial, Inc. (TSX:SLF)	12.8	10.00%	1.16
RLI Corp. (NYSE:RLI)	13.48	13.00%	1.62
Brown & Brown, Inc. (NYSE:BRO)	14.36	13.70%	1.44
Arthur J. Gallagher & Co. (NYSE:AJG)	20.21	12.67%	1.21
Transatlantic Holdings, Inc. (NYSE:TRH)	20.36	15.00%	1.22
Lincoln National Corp. (NYSE:LNC)	30.5	10.20%	0.86
The Hanover Insurance Group, Inc. (NYSE:THG)	35.52	15.00%	0.98

The PE ratios vary widely; they range from 4.11 for Torchmark Corp. to 35.52 for the Hanover Insurance Group. We also report analysts' consensus estimates of the growth rate in earnings per share over the next five years and the equity beta for each of these firms, as a proxy for risk. Some of the variation in PE ratios can be explained by differences in the expected growth rate—higher-growth firms tend to have higher PE ratios—and some of it is due to differences in risk—riskier firms have lower PE ratios. Regressing PE ratios against the expected growth rate and the standard deviation yields the following:

$$\text{PE Ratio} = \underset{(1.61)}{12.41} + \underset{(2.86)}{109.95}\ \text{Expected Growth Rate} - \underset{(-2.14)}{6.60}\ \text{Beta} \quad R^2 = 59\%$$

The regression confirms the intuition that higher-growth and lower-risk firms have higher PE ratios than other firms. Table 14.6 uses this regression to estimate predicted PE ratios for the companies in the table and reports on whether the firms are under- or overvalued.

Table 14.6 Predicted and Actual PE Ratios: Insurance Companies in February 2009

Company Name	PE Ratio	Predicted PE	% Under- or Overvalued
American Financial Group, Inc. (NYSE:AFG)	9.41	15.86	–40.66%
ProAssurance Corporation (NYSE:PRA)	10.74	17.86	–39.87%
The Chubb Corporation (NYSE:CB)	7.94	12.93	–38.61%
Unum Group (NYSE:UNM)	6.33	9.31	–31.97%
Reinsurance Group of America, Inc. (NYSE:RGA)	11.71	16.87	–30.59%
Odyssey Re Holdings Corp. (NYSE:ORH)	5.15	6.71	–23.25%
Brown & Brown, Inc. (NYSE:BRO)	14.36	17.97	–20.09%
Sun Life Financial, Inc. (TSX:SLF)	12.8	15.75	–18.72%
RLI Corp. (NYSE:RLI)	13.48	16.01	–15.81%
Aon Corporation (NYSE:AOC)	7.04	8.01	–12.08%
W.R. Berkley Corporation (NYSE:WRB)	12.3	13.09	–6.00%
Transatlantic Holdings, Inc. (NYSE:TRH)	20.36	20.85	–2.35%
Torchmark Corp. (NYSE:TMK)	4.11	4.03	2.08%
Arthur J. Gallagher & Co. (NYSE:AJG)	20.21	18.35	10.11%
The Travelers Companies, Inc. (NYSE:TRV)	7.58	6.67	13.73%
HCC Insurance Holdings, Inc. (NYSE:HCC)	7.75	6.58	17.84%
MetLife, Inc. (NYSE:MET)	5.45	4.42	23.25%
Principal Financial Group, Inc. (NYSE:PFG)	5.85	4.27	37.09%
Assurant, Inc. (NYSE:AIZ)	5.56	3.65	52.27%
The Hanover Insurance Group, Inc. (NYSE:THG)	35.52	22.43	58.33%
AFLAC, Inc. (NYSE:AFL)	6.01	3.61	66.63%
Lincoln National Corp. (NYSE:LNC)	30.5	17.95	69.93%
Manulife Financial Corporation (TSX:MFC)	5.4	2.22	143.09%

Based on this regression, Manulife Financial looks significantly overvalued, while American Financial and ProAssurance look significantly undervalued.

Price to Book Value Ratios

The price to book value ratio for a financial services firm is the ratio of the price per share to the book value of equity per share:

$$\text{Price to Book Ratio} = \frac{\text{Price per Share}}{\text{Book Value of Equity per Share}}$$

Other things remaining equal, higher growth rates in earnings, higher payout ratios, lower costs of equity, and higher returns on equity should all result in higher price to book ratios. Of these four variables, the return on equity has the biggest impact on the price to book ratio, leading us to identify it as the ratio's companion variable.

If anything, the strength of the relationship between price to book ratios and returns on equity should be stronger for financial services firms than for other firms. The book value of equity is much more likely to track the market value of equity invested in existing assets. Similarly, the return on equity is less likely to be affected by accounting decisions. The strength of the relationship between price to book ratios and returns on equity is shown in Figure 14.2. It plots the two on a scatter plot for U.S. commercial banks with market capitalization exceeding $1 billion in February 2009.

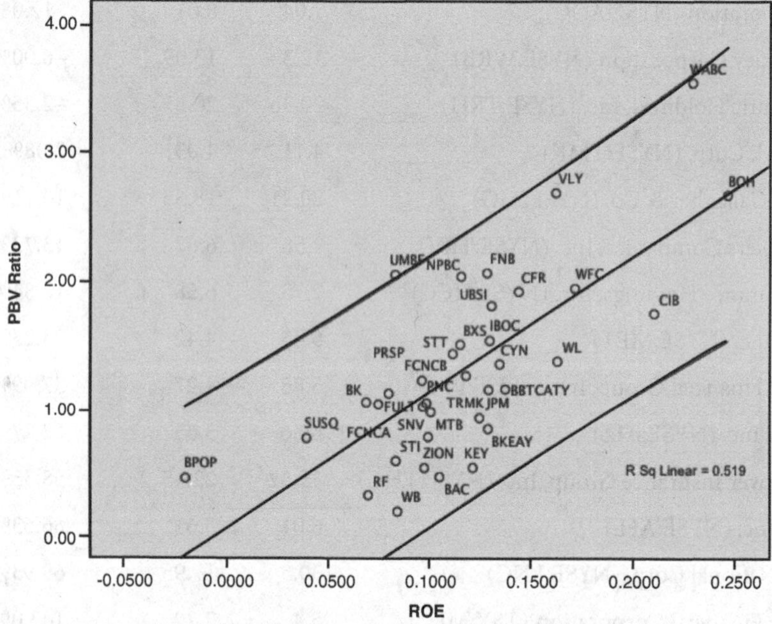

Figure 14.2: Price to Book Ratios and Returns on Equity: Banks

Regression line, with 90% confidence range on estimate

Note that these numbers were extracted in the midst of the biggest crisis in banking since the Great Depression, and in an environment where most analysts have concluded that investors are in crisis mode and that equity values in banks reflect the panic and irrationality. It is therefore astounding how close the link is between price to book ratios for banks in February 2009 and the returns on equity, based on trailing 12-month earnings. Banks such as Valley National (VLY) and WestAmerica Bancorp (WABC) that have high price to book value ratios tend to have high returns on equity. Banks such as Banco Popular (BPOP) and Wachovia (WB) that have low returns on equity trade at low price to book value ratios. The correlation between price to book ratios and returns on equity is in excess of 0.70. Put another way, there seems to be a fundamental order to the chaos that has undercut the banking sector.

While emphasizing the relationship between price to book ratios and returns on equity, we should not ignore the other fundamentals. For instance, banks vary in terms of risk, and we would expect for any given return on equity that riskier banks should have lower price to book value ratios. Similarly, banks with much greater potential for growth should have much higher price to book ratios, for any given level of the other fundamentals. In February 2009, one factor that should make a difference is the exposure that different banks have to toxic securities—mortgage-backed bonds and collateralized debt obligations (CDOs)—on their balance sheets.

Price to Book Value Ratios: Small Commercial Banks

Figure 14.2 noted the strong relationship between price-to-book ratios and returns on equity at large banks. Does the same relationship apply to smaller banks? To answer this question, Table 14.7 looks at banks with market capitalizations between $500 million and $1 billion.

Table 14.7 Price to Book Ratios and Returns on Equity: Small Commercial Banks

Company Name	P/BV Ratio	Expected Growth in EPS: Next Five Years	Standard Deviation in Stock Prices	ROE
East West Bancorp	0.76	–2.50%	57.75%	13.76%
Webster Financial	0.37	2.00%	31.06%	6.44%
NBT Bancorp	2.13	5.00%	32.72%	12.66%
PacWest Bancorp	0.60	5.00%	40.09%	7.93%
WesBanco	1.08	5.00%	41.77%	7.70%
Chemical Financial	1.12	5.00%	33.98%	7.67%
CVB Financial	2.05	6.33%	33.02%	14.26%
First Commonwealth	1.52	6.50%	30.81%	8.14%
Pacific Cap. Bancorp	1.13	6.50%	42.12%	13.26%

Table 14.7 continued

Company Name	P/BV Ratio	Expected Growth in EPS: Next Five Years	Standard Deviation in Stock Prices	ROE
Community Bank Sys.	1.43	7.30%	24.10%	8.96%
First Busey Corp.	1.17	8.00%	30.34%	5.95%
Tompkins Financial Corp.	2.75	8.00%	27.89%	13.39%
S & T Bancorp	2.70	9.00%	23.69%	16.62%
Umpqua Holdings Corporation	0.68	10.00%	30.42%	5.11%
MB Financial, Inc.	1.07	12.00%	25.50%	7.19%
PrivateBancorp, Inc.	2.17	15.60%	41.03%	2.57%
Pinnacle Financial Partners, Inc.	1.34	16.00%	33.69%	4.93%
UCBH Holdings, Inc.	0.61	24.33%	77.25%	11.35%

While the relationship between price to book ratios and returns on equity is weaker for this sample than it is for larger commercial banks, higher price to book value ratios tend to go with higher returns on equity. Since the assumption about all banks being equally risky was put to the test during this period, we used the standard deviation in stock price as a proxy for this risk. Regressing the price to book ratios against the return on equity and standard deviation yields the following:[2]

$$\text{Price to Book Ratio} = 1.527 + 8.63\ (\text{Return on Equity}) - 2.63\ (\sigma_{\text{Stock Price}}) \quad R^2 = 31\%$$
$$(2.94) \quad (1.93) \qquad (2.36)$$

Using this regression yields predicted price to book ratios for any firm in the sample. For instance, the predicted price to book ratio for Tompkins Financial, which at 2.75 times book value of equity looks expensive, would be as follows:

$$\text{Predicted P/BV for Tompkins Financial} = 1.527 + 8.63\ (0.1339) - 2.63\ (0.2789) = 1.95$$

Based on how other small banks are priced, Tompkins looks overvalued by about 30%.

2 With 18 firms in the sample, we are pushing the limits of allowable independent variables, with two. A larger sample will provide more precision.

Conclusion

The basic principles of valuation apply just as much for financial services firms as they do for other firms. However, a few aspects of financial services firms can affect how they are valued. The first is that debt, for a financial services firm, is difficult to define and measure, making it difficult to estimate firm value or costs of capital. Consequently, it is far easier to value the equity directly in a financial services firm by discounting cash flows to equity at the cost of equity. The second aspect is that capital expenditures and working capital, which are required inputs to estimating cash flows, are often not easily estimated at financial services firms. In fact, much of the reinvestment that occurs at these firms is categorized under operating expenses. To estimate cash flows to equity, therefore, we either have to use dividends (and assume that what is not paid out as dividend is the reinvestment) or modify our definition of reinvestment.

Even if we choose to use multiples, we run into many of the same issues. The difficulties associated with defining debt make equity multiples such as price earnings or price to book value ratios better suited for comparing financial services firms than value multiples. In making these comparisons, we have to control for differences in fundamentals—risk, growth, cash flows, loan quality—that affect value.

Finally, regulatory considerations and constraints overlay financial firm valuations. In some cases, regulatory restrictions on competition allow financial services firms to earn excess returns and increase value. In other cases, the same regulatory authorities may restrict the potential excess returns that a firm may be able to make by preventing the firm from entering a business.

15

Invisible Investments: Firms with Intangible Assets

In the last 20 years, we have seen a shift from manufacturing firms to service and technology firms in the global economy. The change has been greatest in the U.S. As we value more and more pharmaceutical, technology, and service companies, we are faced with two realities. The first is that the assets of these firms are often intangible and invisible—patents, know-how, and human capital. The second is that the way in which accounting has dealt with investments in these assets is inconsistent with its treatment of investments in tangible assets at manufacturing firms. As a result, many of the basic inputs that we use in valuation—earnings, cash flows, and return on capital—are contaminated.

This chapter begins by looking at the characteristics shared by firms with intangible assets and the valuation issues that follow. We then look at the dark side of valuation as it manifests itself in these companies, along with some remedies. In particular, we focus on two issues: the corrections for accounting inconsistencies in these firms, and how best to deal with the fact that many of these firms are also heavy users of employee options as compensation.

Firms with Intangible Assets

Looking at publicly traded firms, it is obvious that many firms derive the bulk of their value from intangible assets. From consumer products companies, dependent on brand names, to pharmaceutical companies, with blockbuster drugs protected by patent, to technology companies that draw on their skilled technicians and know-how, these firms range the spectrum. This section begins by looking at their place in the market and how it has shifted over time. We will follow up by identifying characteristics they share.

Intangible Assets in the Overall Economy

The simplest measure of how much intangible assets represent of the economy comes from the market values of firms that derive the bulk of their value from these assets as a proportion of the overall market. Although technology firms have fallen from their peak numbers in 2000, they still represented 14% of the overall S&P 500 index at the end of 2008. If we add pharmaceutical and consumer product companies to the mix, the proportion becomes even higher.

Other attempts have been made to capture the importance of intangible assets in the economy. In one study, Leonard Nakamura of the Federal Reserve Bank of Philadelphia provided three different measures of the magnitude of intangible assets in today's economy:

- An accounting estimate of the value of the investments in research and development (R&D), software, brand development, and other intangibles
- The wages and salaries paid to the researchers, technicians, and other creative workers who generate these intangible assets
- The improvement in operating margins that Nakamura attributes to improvements in intangible factors[1]

With all three approaches, Nakamura estimated the investments in intangible assets to be in excess of $1 trillion in 2000. The capitalized value of these intangible assets was estimated to be in excess of $6 trillion in the same year.

Characteristics of Firms with Intangible Assets

Although firms with intangible assets are diverse, they share some characteristics. This section highlights those shared factors. The consequences for valuation are described in the next section.

- **Inconsistent accounting for investments made in intangible assets**: Accounting first principles suggest a simple rule to separate capital expenses from operating expenses. Any expense that creates benefits over many years is a capital expense, whereas expenses that generate benefits only in the current year are operating expenses. Accountants hew to this distinction with manufacturing firms, putting investments in plant, equipment, and buildings in the capital expense column and labor and raw-materials expenses in the operating expenses column. However, they seem to ignore these first principles when it comes to firms with intangible assets. The most significant capital expenditures made by technology and pharmaceutical firms is in R&D, by consumer-products companies in brand-name advertising, and by consulting firms in training and recruiting personnel. Using the argument that the benefits are too uncertain, accountants have treated these expenses as operating expenses. As a consequence, firms with intangible assets report small capital expenditures, relative to both their size and growth potential.
- **They generally borrow less money**: This may be a generalization that does not hold up for some subcategories of firms with intangible assets. However, many of them tend to use debt sparingly and have low debt ratios, relative to firms in other sectors with similar earnings and cash flows. Some of the low financial leverage can be attributed to the bias that bankers have toward lending against tangible assets. Some of it may reflect the fact that technology and pharmaceutical firms are in or have just emerged from the growth phase in the life cycle.
- **Equity options**: While the use of equity options in management compensation is not unique to firms with intangible assets, these firms seem to be much heavier users of options and other forms of equity compensation. Again, some of this behavior can be attributed to where these firms are in the life cycle (closer to growth than mature). But some of it has to be related to how dependent these firms are on retaining human capital.

1 Nakamura, L., 1999, "Intangibles: What put the new in the new economy?," *Federal Reserve Bank of Philadelphia Business Review*, July/August: pp. 3–16.

Valuation Consequences

The miscategorization of capital expenses, the sparing use of debt, and equity-based compensation (options and restricted stocks) can create problems when we value these firms. This section discusses some of the issues that arise in both discounted cash flow and relative valuation:

- We generally draw on a firm's current earnings and current book value to derive a value for existing assets. The flawed accounting treatment of intangible assets renders both numbers unreliable. The reported earnings for a technology firm represent the earnings after reinvestment in R&D, rather than true operating earnings. The book value of assets (and equity) is understated because the biggest assts for these firms are off the books. If you expense an item, you cannot show it as an asset. This has consequences for discounted cash flow valuation, where these numbers become the base from which we forecast. It also has consequences for relative valuation, where we compare multiples of accounting earnings and book values across companies.
- If growth is a function of how much firms reinvest and the quality of that reinvestment, the accounting treatment of expenditures on intangible assets makes it difficult to gauge either number. The reinvestment made by the firm is often buried in the operating expenses (rather than showing up separately as capital expenditures). The failure to record the book values of intangible assets makes measures like return on equity and capital, widely used to determine the quality of a firm's investments, unreliable.
- In addition to all the standard variables that affect risk in a company, firms with intangible assets are susceptible to an additional risk. Lenders are wary of lending to firms with intangible assets, since monitoring these assets can be difficult. In addition, the values of some intangible assets, like human capital, can dissipate overnight if a firm gets into trouble or has its reputation besmirched.
- Estimating when a firm with intangible assets gets to steady state can range from simple to complex. Consider a simple scenario first. A biotechnology firm derives almost all its growth from a single blockbuster drug, with a patent expiring in seven years. Having a competitive advantage that comes with a time expiration stamp makes the judgment on when the company will hit stable growth very simple. A more complex scenario is a firm with a well-regarded brand name. Given the durability of consumer brand name as a competitive advantage, analysts face a much tougher task estimating when to put the firm into stable growth. The final and most difficult scenario is a firm whose biggest intangible asset is human capital, such as consultants at McKinsey or traders at a private equity fund. Since it is very difficult to lock in human capital, these firms can lose their best assets overnight to the highest bidder. Figuring out how or why these firms manage to hold on to their best personnel is a central component of valuing them correctly.

The defense offered by some analysts is that the rules, flawed though they might be, are the same for all firms within a sector. As we will see in the next section, that does not neutralize the problem.

The Dark Side of Valuation

How do analysts deal with the valuation issues that characterize firms with intangible assets? In many cases, they ignore these issues and trust historical data or management-provided forecasts of the numbers. In some cases, they fall back on the defense that all the firms in a sector should be equally impacted by these accounting rules and that comparisons across the firms therefore should be unaffected.

Exogenous Growth

The biggest problem with treating capital expenses (such as R&D, training, and brand advertising expenses) as operating expenses is that we lose the most potent tool that we have not only for estimating growth but also for checking for internal consistency. The growth rates we use for a firm have to be consistent with our estimates of reinvestment and return on capital for that firm. If we use conventional accounting measures of capital expenditures and capital invested for firms with intangible assets, we get measures of the reinvestment rate and return on capital that are meaningless. In fact, these conventional measures can result in negative reinvestment rates (since the biggest reinvestment is missed) and overstated returns on equity and capital (because the biggest assets are off the books).

When confronted by these numbers, analysts decide that fundamentals no longer matter, at least for these types of companies. They make their own judgments on future growth, based either on history or conversations with the company's managers. Not surprisingly, people tend to overestimate growth during good times and underestimate growth in bad times. The history of booms and busts in stock prices at these firms is a testimonial to the consequences of this behavior.

Sector Comparison

Analysts who stick with relative valuation often argue that they are unaffected by accounting inconsistencies, since all firms in their sector are affected by these inconsistencies. Thus, they argue that while comparing the PE ratio of a software firm to the PE ratio of a steel company may be difficult, comparing PE ratios across software companies is fine. After all, if every software company has R&D expenses and these expenses are all treated (incorrectly) as operating expenses, all the companies should have earnings and returns that are skewed by the treatment. The problem with this argument is that the effect of the accounting miscategorization of capital expenditures at firms can vary widely across firms within the same sector. As a general rule, the effect is much greater at younger firms, with growing investments, than at mature firms. The consequences for earnings and capital also vary, depending on the time lag between making the investment and generating earnings on the investment. Firms with shorter time lags are less affected than firms with longer time lags.

Simplistic Adjustments

Some analysts, recognizing the danger of trusting the accounting numbers at firms where expenses have been systematically miscategorized, try to look for easy solutions to the problem. For instance, rather than compare the PE ratios across technology companies, some analysts compare the multiples of market capitalization to earnings before R&D expenses at which firms trade. Similarly, with equity options, many variants of diluted earnings per share purport to capture the effect of options outstanding.

While the motivation for a simple fix is understandable, it can lull analysts into a false sense of complacency. Adding back R&D to the net income or operating income will not nullify the effects of R&D on the remaining variables. Adjusting the number of shares for options outstanding is a very sloppy way of dealing with these options. It doesn't reflect the probability of exercise or the price at which they will be exercised.

The Light Side of Valuation

To value firms with intangible assets, we have to deal with the two big problems that they share. First, we have to clean up the financial statements and recategorize operating and capital expenses. The intent is not just to get a better measure of earnings, although that is a side benefit, but to get a clearer sense of what the firm is investing to generate future growth. Second, we need to deal more effectively with equity options—the ones that were granted in the past, as well as the ones we expect to be granted in the future.

Regaining Accounting Consistency

A significant shortcoming of accounting statements is how they treat investments made in intangible assets in general, and R&D expenses in particular. Under the rationale that the products of research are too uncertain and difficult to quantify, accounting standards have generally required that all R&D expenses be expensed in the period in which they occur. This has several consequences. One of the most profound is that the value of the assets created by research does not show up on the balance sheet as part of the firm's total assets. This, in turn, creates ripple effects for the measurement of capital and profitability ratios for the firm. We will consider how to capitalize R&D expenses, and then we will extend the argument to other investmenst in intangible assests.

Capitalizing R&D Expenses

Research expenses, notwithstanding the uncertainty about future benefits, should be capitalized. To capitalize and value research assets, we have to make an assumption about how long it takes R&D to be converted, on average, into commercial products. This is called the *amortizable life* of these assets. This life varies across firms and reflects the process (legal, regulatory, and business) involved in converting research into products. To illustrate, R&D expenses at a pharmaceutical company should have fairly long amortizable lives, because the approval process for new drugs is long. In contrast, R&D expenses at a software firm, where products tend to emerge from research much more quickly, should be amortized over a shorter period.

After the amortizable life of R&D expenses has been estimated, the next step is to collect data on R&D expenses over past years, ranging back to the amortizable life of the research asset. Thus, if the research asset has an amortizable life of five years, the R&D expenses in each of the five years prior to the current one have to be obtained. Each expense then has to be amortized or written off over its amortizable life. For simplicity, it can be assumed that the amortization is uniform over time. Thus, with a five-year life, one-fifth of the expense will be written off each year. This leads to the following estimate of the residual value of the research asset today:

$$\text{Value of the Research Asset} = \sum_{t=-(n-1)}^{t=0} R\&D_t \frac{(n+t)}{n}$$

Thus, in the case of the research asset with a five-year life, you cumulate one-fifth of the R&D expenses from four years ago, two-fifths of the R&D expenses from three years ago, three-fifths of the R&D expenses from two years ago, four-fifths of the R&D expenses from last year, and this year's entire R&D expenses to arrive at the *value of the research asset*. This augments the value of the firm's assets and, by extension, the book value of equity:

Adjusted Book Value of Equity = Book Value of Equity + Value of the Research Asset

Finally, the operating income is adjusted to reflect the capitalization of R&D expenses. First, the R&D expenses that were subtracted to arrive at the operating income are added back to the operating income, reflecting their recategorization as capital expenses. Next, the cumulated amortization of the research asset is treated the same way as depreciation and is netted out to arrive at the adjusted operating income:

Adjusted Operating Income = Operating Income + R&D Expenses – Amortization of Research Asset

The adjusted operating income will generally be higher than the stated operating income for firms that have R&D expenses that are growing over time. The after-tax operating income and net income also are altered by the identical net amount (R&D Expenses – Amortization of Research Asset):

Adjusted Net Income = Net Income + R&D Expenses – Amortization of Research Asset

While we would normally consider only the after-tax portion of this amount for after-tax earnings, the fact that R&D is entirely tax-deductible eliminates the need for this adjustment.[2]

Capitalizing R&D Expenses: Amgen in February 2009

Amgen is a biotechnology/pharmaceutical firm. Like most such firms, it has a substantial amount of R&D expenses, and we will attempt to capitalize it in this example. The first step in this conversion is determining an amortizable life for R&D expenses. How long will it take, on an expected basis, for research to pay off at Amgen? Given the length of the approval process for new drugs by the Food and Drug Administration, we will assume that this amortizable life is ten years.

The second step in the analysis is collecting R&D expenses from prior years, with the number of years of historical data being a function of the amortizable life. Table 15.1 provides this information for Amgen from 1998 (year –10) to the current year (2008).

Table 15.1 Historical R&D Expenses (in Millions of Dollars)

Year	R&D Expenses
Current	$3,030.00
–1	$3,266.00
–2	$3,366.00

2 If only amortization were tax-deductible, the tax benefit from R&D expenses would be as follows:
Amortization * Tax Rate
This extra tax benefit we get from the entire R&D's being tax-deductible is as follows:
(R&D – Amortization) * Tax Rate
Adjusted After-Tax Operating Income = After-Tax Operating Income + (R&D – Amortization) (1 – t) + (R&D – Amortization) t = After-Tax Operating Income + (R&D – Amortization)

Year	R&D Expenses
–3	$2,314.00
–4	$2,028.00
–5	$1,655.00
–6	$1,117.00
–7	$864.00
–8	$845.00
–9	$823.00
–10	$663.00

The current year's information reflects the R&D in the most recent financial year (which is calendar year 2008 in this example).

The portion of the expenses in prior years that would have been amortized already and the amortization this year from each of these expenses are considered. To make estimation simpler, these expenses are amortized linearly over time; with a ten-year life, 10% is amortized each year. This allows us to estimate the value of the research asset created at the firm and the amortization of R&D expenses in the current year. This procedure is illustrated in Table 15.2.

Table 15.2 Value of the Research Asset

Year	R&D Expense	Unamortized Portion		Amortization This Year
Current	$3,030.00	100%	$3,030.00	
–1	$3,266.00	90%	$2,939.40	$326.60
–2	$3,366.00	80%	$2,692.80	$336.60
–3	$2,314.00	70%	$1,619.80	$231.40
–4	$2,028.00	60%	$1,216.80	$202.80
–5	$1,655.00	50%	$827.50	$165.50
–6	$1,117.00	40%	$446.80	$111.70
–7	$864.00	30%	$259.20	$86.40
–8	$845.00	20%	$169.00	$84.50
–9	$823.00	10%	$82.30	$82.30
–10	$663.00	0%	$0.00	$66.30
			$13,283.60	$1,694.10

Note that none of the current year's expenditure has been amortized because it is assumed to occur at the end of the most recent year (which effectively makes it today). The sum of the dollar values of unamortized R&D from prior years is $13.284 billion. This can be viewed as the value of Amgen's research asset and would also be added to the book value of equity for computing return on equity and capital measures. The sum of the amortization in the current year for all prior-year expenses is $1,694 million.

The final step in the process is adjusting the operating income to reflect the capitalization of R&D expenses. We make the adjustment by adding back R&D expenses to the operating income (to reflect its reclassification as a capital expense) and subtracting the amortization of the research asset, estimated in the last step. For Amgen, which reported operating income of $5,594 million in its income statement for 2008, the adjusted operating earnings would be as follows:

Adjusted Operating Earnings = Operating Earnings + Current Year's R&D Expense – Amortization of Research Asset

= $5,594 + $3,030 – $1,694 = $6,930 million

The stated net income of $4,196 million can be adjusted similarly:

Adjusted Net Income = Net Income + Current Year's R&D Expense – Amortization of Research Asset

= $4,196 + $3,030 – $1,694 = $5,532 million

Both the book value of equity and capital are augmented by the value of the research asset. Since measures of return on capital and equity are based on the prior year's values, we compute the value of the research asset at the end of 2007 using the same approach we used in 2008 and obtain a value of $11,948 million:[3]

$\text{Value of Research Asset}_{2007} = \$11{,}948 \text{ million}$

$\text{Adjusted Book Value of Equity}_{2007} = \text{Book Value of Equity}_{2007} + \text{Value of Research Asset}_{2007}$

= $17,869 million + $11,948 million = $29,817 million

$\text{Adjusted Book Value of Capital}_{2007} = \text{Book Value of Capital}_{2007} + \text{Value of Research Asset}_{2007}$

= $21,985 million + $11,948 million = $33,933 million

The returns on equity and capital are estimated by dividing the earnings in 2008 by the capital invested at the end of 2007. The unadjusted and adjusted numbers are as follows:

3 Note that you can arrive at this value using Table 15.2 and shifting the amortization numbers by one row. Thus, $822.80 million becomes the current year's R&D, $663.3 million becomes the R&D for year –1, 90% of it is unamortized, and so on.

	Unadjusted	Adjusted for R&D
Return on equity	$\frac{4,196}{17,869} = 23.48\%$	$\frac{5,532}{29,817} = 18.55\%$
Pre-tax return on capital	$\frac{5,594}{21,985} = 25.44\%$	$\frac{6,930}{33,933} = 20.42\%$

Although the profitability ratios for Amgen remain impressive even after the adjustment, they decline significantly from the unadjusted numbers.

Capitalizing Other Operating Expenses

Although R&D expenses are the most prominent example of capital expenses being treated as operating expenses, there are other operating expenses that arguably should be treated as capital expenses. Consumer products companies such as Gillette and Coca-Cola could make a case that a portion of advertising expenses should be treated as capital expenses, since they are designed to augment brand-name value. For a consulting firm like KPMG or McKinsey, the cost of recruiting and training its employees could be considered a capital expense, since the consultants who emerge are likely to be the heart of the firm's assets and provide benefits over many years. For many new technology firms, including online retailers such as Amazon.com, the biggest operating expense item is selling, general, and administrative (S, G, and A) expenses. These firms could argue that a portion of these expenses should be treated as capital expenses since they are designed to increase brand-name awareness and bring in new (and presumably long-term) customers.

While this argument has some merit, we should remain wary about using it to justify capitalizing these expenses. For an operating expense to be capitalized, substantial evidence should exist that the benefits from the expense accrue over multiple periods. Does a customer who is enticed to buy from Amazon based on an advertisement or promotion continue as a customer for the long term? Some analysts claim that this is indeed the case and attribute significant value added to each new customer. It would be logical, under those circumstances, to capitalize these expenses using a procedure similar to that used to capitalize R&D expenses:

1. Determine the period over which the benefits from the operating expense (such as S, G, and A) will flow.
2. Estimate the value of the asset (similar to the research asset) created by these expenses. This amount is added to the book value of equity/capital and is used to estimate the returns on equity and capital.
3. Adjust the operating and net income for the expense and amortization of the created asset.

The net effects of the capitalization will be most visible in the reinvestment rates and returns on capital that we estimate for these firms.

Capitalizing Brand-Name Advertising: Coca-Cola in 2009

Coca-Cola is widely regarded as possessing one of the most valuable brand names in the world. We know that the company has always spent liberally on advertising, partly directed at building the brand name. Table 15.3 shows the selling and advertising expenditures at Coca-Cola every year for the last 25 years, which we will assume is the amortizable life for the brand name. (In truth, we should go back much further, but data limitations get in the way.)

Table 15.3 Advertising Expenditures at Coca-Cola: 1984 to 2008

Year	Year	S, G, and A Expense	Selling and Advertising	Brand-Name Advertising	Amortization This Year	Unamortized Expense
1984	1	$2,314	$1,543	$771	$30.85	$0.00
1985	2	$2,368	$1,579	$789	$31.57	$31.57
1986	3	$2,446	$1,631	$815	$32.61	$65.23
1987	4	$2,665	$1,777	$888	$35.53	$106.60
1988	5	$3,038	$2,025	$1,013	$40.51	$162.03
1989	6	$3,348	$2,232	$1,116	$44.64	$223.20
1990	7	$4,076	$2,717	$1,359	$54.35	$326.08
1991	8	$4,604	$3,069	$1,535	$61.39	$429.71
1992	9	$5,249	$3,499	$1,750	$69.99	$559.89
1993	10	$5,695	$3,797	$1,898	$75.93	$683.40
1994	11	$6,297	$4,198	$2,099	$83.96	$839.60
1995	12	$6,986	$4,657	$2,329	$93.15	$1,024.61
1996	13	$8,020	$5,347	$2,673	$106.93	$1,283.20
1997	14	$7,852	$5,235	$2,617	$104.69	$1,361.01
1998	15	$8,284	$5,523	$2,761	$110.45	$1,546.35
1999	16	$9,814	$6,543	$3,271	$130.85	$1,962.80
2000	17	$8,551	$5,701	$2,850	$114.01	$1,824.21
2001	18	$6,149	$4,099	$2,050	$81.99	$1,393.77
2002	19	$7,001	$4,667	$2,334	$93.35	$1,680.24
2003	20	$7,488	$4,992	$2,496	$99.84	$1,896.96

Year	Year	S, G, and A Expense	Selling and Advertising	Brand-Name Advertising	Amortization This Year	Unamortized Expense
2004	21	$8,146	$5,431	$2,715	$108.61	$2,172.27
2005	22	$8,739	$5,826	$2,913	$116.52	$2,446.92
2006	23	$9,431	$6,287	$3,144	$125.75	$2,766.43
2007	24	$10,945	$7,297	$3,648	$145.93	$3,356.47
2008	25	$11,774	$7,849	$3,925	$156.99	$3,767.68
Total					$2,150.40	$31,910.23

We assume that two-thirds of the S, G, and A expenses are for selling and advertising and that 50% of the selling and advertising expenses each year are associated with building the brand name, with the balance used to generate revenues in the current year. In the next-to-last column, we compute the amortization this year of the prior year's expenditure, using straight-line amortization over 25 years. In the last column, we keep track of the unamortized portion of the prior year's expenditures. The cumulated value of this column ($31.9 billion) can be considered the capital invested in the brand name.

Potential refinements will improve this estimate. One is to use a longer amortizable life and to go back further in time to obtain advertising expenses. The other is to convert the past expenditures into current dollar expenditures, based on inflation. In other words, an expenditure of $771 million in 1984 is really much larger if stated in 2008 dollars.[4] Both of these will increase the capital value of the brand name.

The adjustments to operating income, net income, and capital invested, shown in Table 15.4, mirror those made for Amgen for R&D expenses.

Table 15.4 Capitalizing on Brand-Name Advertising at Coca-Cola

	Conventional Accounting	Capitalized Brand Name
Operating income	$8,446	$10,220
Net income	$5,807	$7,581
Equity invested	$21,744	$53,654
Capital invested	$31,073	$62,983
ROE	26.71%	14.13%
Pre-tax ROC	27.18%	16.23%

Capitalizing brand-name advertising substantially decreases both the return on equity and capital invested for Coca-Cola.

4 When we use inflation-adjusted values, the value of the brand name increases to almost $40 billion.

Capitalizing Recruitment and Training Expenses: Cyber Health Consulting

Cyber Health Consulting (CHC) is a firm that specializes in offering management consulting services to health-care firms. CHC reported operating income (EBIT) of $51.5 million and net income of $23 million in the most recent year. However, the firm's expenses include the cost of recruiting new consultants ($5.5 million) and the cost of training ($8.5 million). A consultant who joins CHC stays with the firm, on average, four years.

To capitalize the cost of recruiting and training, we obtained these costs from each of the prior four years and for the current year. Table 15.5 lists these expenses and amortizes each one over four years.

Table 15.5 Human Capital Expenses for CHC

Year	Training and Recruiting Expenses	Unamortized Portion		Amortization This Year
Current	$14.00	100%	$14.00	
–1	$12.00	75%	$9.00	$3.00
–2	$10.40	50%	$5.20	$2.60
–3	$9.10	25%	$2.28	$2.28
–4	$8.30	0%	$0.00	$2.08
Value of Human Capital =			$30.48	
Amortization This Year =				$9.95

The adjustments to operating and net income are as follows:

Adjusted Operating Income = Operating Income + Training and Recruiting Expenses – Amortization of Expenses This Year = $51.5 + $14 – $9.95 = $55.55 million

Net Income = Net Income + Training and Recruiting Expenses – Amortization of Expenses This Year = $23 million + $14 million – $9.95 million = $27.05 million

These adjusted earnings numbers in conjunction with the value of the human capital asset, estimated in Table 15.6, are used to compute the returns on equity and capital.

As with Amgen and Coca-Cola, capitalizing training expenses decreases the company's returns on equity and capital.

Table 15.6 Returns on Equity and Capital: Conventional Versus Adjusted

	Conventional Accounting	Capitalized Training Expenses
Net income	$23.00	$27.05
Operating income	$51.50	$55.55
Book equity	$125.00	$155.48
Book capital	$250.00	$280.48
ROE	18.40%	17.40%
Pre-tax ROC	20.60%	19.81%

Consequences for Valuation

When we capitalize R&D, brand-name advertising, and training expenses, there are significant consequences for both discounted cash flow and relative valuation. In discounted cash flow valuation, our estimates of cash flows and growth can be dramatically altered by the use of the adjusted numbers. In relative valuation, comparisons of firms within the same sector can be skewed by where they are in the life cycle.

Discounted Cash Flow Valuation

When we capitalize the expenses associated with creating intangible assets, we are in effect redoing the firm's financial statements and restating numbers that are fundamental inputs into valuation—earnings, reinvestment, and measures of returns:

- **Earnings:** As we noted with all three examples of capitalization (R&D, brand-name advertising, and training/recruiting expenses), a firm's operating and net income will change as a consequence. Since the adjustment involves adding back the current year's expense and subtracting the amortization of past expenses, the effect on earnings will be nonexistent if the expenses have been unchanged over time. The effect will be positive if expenses have risen over time. With Amgen, for instance, where R&D expenses increased from $663 million at the start of the amortization period to $3.03 billion in the current year, the earnings increased by more than $1.3 billion as a result of the R&D adjustment.
- **Reinvestment**: The effect on reinvestment is identical to the effect on earnings, with reinvestment increasing or decreasing by exactly the same amount as earnings.
- **Free cash flow to equity (firm)**: Since free cash flow is computed by netting reinvestment from earnings, and the two items change by the same magnitude but in offsetting directions, there will be no effect on free cash flows.
- **Reinvestment rate:** Although the free cash flow is unaffected by capitalization of these expenses, the reinvestment rate will change. In general, if earnings and reinvestment both increase as a consequence of the capitalization of R&D or advertising expenses, the reinvestment rate increases.

- **Capital invested:** Since the unamortized portion of prior year's expenses is treated as an asset, it adds to the estimated equity or capital invested in the firm. The effect increases with the amortizable life and therefore should be higher for pharmaceutical firms (where amortizable lives tend to be longer) than for software firms (where research pays off far more quickly as commercial products).
- **Return on equity (capital):** Since both earnings and capital invested are affected by capitalization, the net effects on return on equity and capital are unpredictable. If the return on equity (capital) increases after the recapitalization, it can be considered a rough indicator that the returns earned by the firm on its R&D or advertising investments are greater than its returns on its remaining investments.
- **Expected growth rates:** Since the expected growth rate is a function of the reinvestment rate and the return on capital, and both change as a result of capitalization, the expected growth rate also changes. While the higher reinvestment rate works in favor of higher growth, it may be more than offset by a drop in the return on equity or capital.

In summary, the variables that are most noticeably affected by capitalization are the return on equity/capital and the reinvestment rate. Since the cost of equity/capital is unaffected by capitalization, any change in the return on capital translates into a change in excess returns at the firm, a key variable determining the value of growth. The capitalization process gives us more realistic estimates of what these firms are investing in their growth assets and the quality of these assets. It also restores consistency to valuations by ensuring that growth rates are in line with reinvestment and return on capital assumptions. Thus, technology or pharmaceutical firms that want to continue to grow have to keep investing in R&D, while ensuring that these investments, at least collectively, generate high returns for the firm.

Valuing Amgen

Earlier we capitalized R&D expenses for Amgen and computed the adjusted operating income, reinvestment, and return on capital at the firm. We use the restated numbers to estimate the value of the firm and equity per share. The valuation, where we assume ten years of high growth, is shown in Figure 15.1.

Our estimate of value of equity per share is $62.97 a share, well above the prevailing stock price of $47.47.

An intriguing question is how the capitalization of R&D expenses affects value. To investigate, we compare the valuation fundamentals for Amgen, with conventional accounting, and with R&D treated as capital expenses, as shown in Table 15.7.

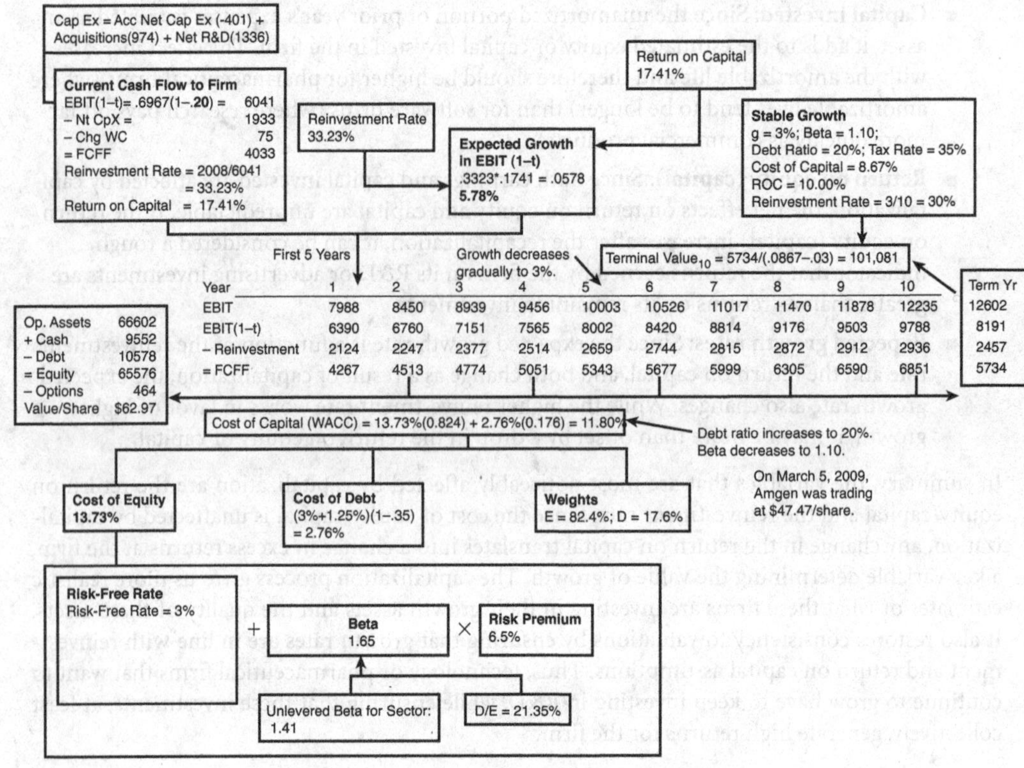

Figure 15.1: Valuing Amgen: with R&D Capitalized

Table 15.7 Valuation Fundamentals with and Without R&D Capitalization

	Conventional	Capitalized R&D
After-tax ROC	14.91%	17.41%
Reinvestment rate	19.79%	33.23%
Growth rate	2.95%	5.78%
Value per share	$43.63	$62.97

We then revalue the firm using both sets of fundamentals. As the table indicates, the value per share would have been $43.63 if we had used conventional accounting numbers. Clearly, capitalization matters, and the degree to which it matters varies across firms. In general, the effect on value per share is negative for firms that invest large amounts in R&D, with little to show (yet) in terms of earnings and cash flows in subsequent periods. It can be positive for firms that reinvest large amounts in R&D and report large increases in earnings in subsequent periods. In the case of Amgen, capitalizing R&D has a positive effect on value per share because of its track record of successful R&D. This is manifested in an increase in the return on capital and reinvestment rate, which, in turn, leads us to a higher assessment of growth (and value). For firms that have had less success in converting R&D to commercial products, capitalizing R&D can lead to dramatic drops in returns on capital, which, when accompanied with higher reinvestment rates, can lower value. For both sets of firms, though, we would argue that the reassessed value (with the capitalized R&D) is closer to the truth.

Relative Valuation

It is true that all technology and pharmaceutical companies operate under the same flawed accounting rules, expensing R&D rather than capitalizing it. That does not mean, though, that it has no consequences for relative valuation. As we noted in the preceding section, the effect of capitalizing R&D on earnings and book value can vary widely across firms and depends on the following:

- **Age of the firm and stage in the life cycle:** Generally speaking, the effects of capitalization will be much greater at young firms than at more mature firms. Consider, for instance, the capitalization of R&D expenses. Capitalizing these expenses will increase earnings far more at young firms for two reasons: R&D expenses will comprise a much larger proportion of the total expenses at these firms, and R&D expenses are more likely to have increased significantly over time.
- **Amortizable life:** The effect of capitalizing expenses will be much greater as we extend the amortizable life of R&D, especially on capital invested. If we assume that all firms in a sector share the same amortizable life for R&D, this is not an issue, but to the extent that different firms within the same business may convert research into commercial products at different speeds, the effect on earnings of capitalizing R&D can vary across firms.

If we ignore accounting inconsistencies and use the reported earnings and book values of firms in the computation of multiples, we are likely to find that younger firms or firms that have R&D with longer gestation periods are overvalued. Their earnings and book value will be understated, leading to much higher PE, EV/EBITDA, and book value multiples for these firms.

We can incorporate these factors into relative valuation in two ways. The first is to capitalize the expenses associated with investing in intangible assets for each firm and compute consistent measures of earnings and book value to use in multiples. This approach, while yielding the most precision, is also the most time- and data-intensive. The second way is to stick with the reported accounting values for earnings and book value, controlling for the factors just listed.

Valuing Large Pharmaceutical Firms with PE Ratios

To examine the effect of R&D, we estimate the PE ratios in February 2009 for pharmaceutical firms using several measures of net income, as shown in Table 15.8.

Table 15.8 PE Ratios for Pharmaceutical Companies: February 2009

Company Name	Market Cap (in Millions of Dollars)	Net Income	R&D Expense	R&D Net of Amortization	PE	P / (E + R&D)	P / (E + Net R&D)
Merck & Co.	$46,702	$7,804	$4,805	$302	5.98	3.70	5.76
AstraZeneca PLC	$44,366	$6,130	$5,179	$650	7.24	3.92	6.54
GlaxoSmith Kline ADR	$77,596	$10,619	$6,707	$225	7.31	4.48	7.16
Eli Lilly	$31,232	$3,863	$3,840	$410	8.08	4.05	7.31
Sanofi-Aventis	$67,924	$7,068	$4,575	$450	9.61	5.83	9.03
Novartis AG ADR	$79,954	$8,163	$1,834	$76	9.79	8.00	9.70
Pfizer, Inc.	$85,433	$8,104	$7,945	$550	10.54	5.32	9.87
Biogen Idec, Inc.	$12,732	$783	$1,072	$415	16.26	6.86	10.63
Wyeth	$54,391	$4,417	$3,373	$155	12.31	6.98	11.90
Bristol-Myers Squibb	$35,019	$2,165	$3,585	$710	16.18	6.09	12.18
Schering-Plough	$26,475	$1,903	$850	$135	13.91	9.62	12.99
Allergan, Inc.	$10,901	$577	$798	$255	18.89	7.93	13.10
Teva Pharmaceuticals (ADR)	$34,279	$2,374	$786	$221	14.44	10.85	13.21
Genzyme Corp.	$14,348	$421	$1,308	$622	34.08	8.30	13.76
Novo Nordisk	$28,165	$1,681	$1,368	$355	16.76	9.24	13.83
Abbott Labs	$71,357	$4,881	$2,689	$250	14.62	9.43	13.91
Gilead Sciences	$40,310	$2,011	$721	$375	20.04	14.75	16.89
Celgene Corp.	$18,302	$226	$399	$215	80.84	29.26	41.46

To contrast with the conventional PE ratio, which is based on reported net income, we compute two alternative measures of earnings. In the first, we use the simplistic adjustment of adding back R&D expenses to net income to arrive at a multiple of the market price to earnings before R&D expenses. In the second, we make the full adjustment for R&D, adding back the R&D and subtracting the amortization of R&D to arrive at an adjusted net income.

The results are revealing. On all three measures of PE, Merck looks like the most undervalued company in the group. As we add back R&D, the difference between the earnings multiples decreases, with Celgene remaining the outlier. Finally, when we compute the multiple of earnings with net R&D added back, the more mature pharmaceutical companies with less attractive growth prospects emerge with lower PE ratios. The smaller, higher-growth companies trade at higher multiples of earnings.

Dealing with Equity Options

In the last two decades, firms have increasingly turned to compensating managers using equity, with options being a key component, for several reasons. The first is to align management interests with stockholders—to make managers think like stockholders by giving them an equity stake. The second reason is that this allowed cash-poor firms with significant growth prospects to compete for employee talent against deep-pocketed rivals; young technology firms are prime users of options. The third reason is that the accounting for options woefully understated the true cost of these options, allowing these firms to report positive earnings even as they gave away big chunks of equity to managers.

Firms that pay managers and others with equity options create a second claim on the equity on top of the claim that common stockholders have. Since we are called on to estimate the value of equity per common share, we have to consider how to allocate the aggregate equity value across the two claimholders. This section examines how to deal with options that a firm may have granted to managers in the past, that have not been exercised yet; this is the option overhang. Then we will extend the analysis to look at how best to deal with options that may be granted in the future to employees. Furthermore, we will see how to bring the consequences of such grants into the value of equity per share today.

The Option Overhang

Three approaches are widely used to deal with outstanding options issued in prior periods. The crudest way is to assume that all or some of the options will be exercised in the future, adjust the number of shares outstanding, and divide the value of equity by this number to arrive at value per share. This is the diluted shares approach. The second and slightly more tempered approach is to incorporate the exercise proceeds from the options in the numerator and then divide by the number of shares that would be outstanding after exercise. This is the treasury stock approach. The third and preferred approach for dealing with options is to estimate the value of the options today, given today's value per share and the time premium on the option. After this value has been estimated, it is subtracted from the estimated equity value, and the remaining amount is divided by the number of shares outstanding to arrive at value per share.

Using Fully Diluted Number of Shares to Estimate Per-Share Value

The simplest way to incorporate the effect of outstanding options on value per share is to divide the estimated value of equity from a discounted cash flow model by the number of shares that will be outstanding if all options are exercised today—the fully diluted number of shares. While this approach has the virtue of simplicity, it will lead to too low of an estimate of value per share for three reasons:

- It considers all options outstanding, not just ones that are in the money and vested. To be fair, there are variations on this approach in which the shares outstanding are adjusted to reflect only in-the-money and vested options.
- It does not incorporate the expected proceeds from exercise, which will comprise a cash inflow to the firm.
- This approach does not build the time premium on the options into the valuation.

Fully Diluted Approach to Estimating Value per Share

To apply the fully diluted approach to estimate the per share value, we will value a company with a significant option overhang—Google. We begin by valuing equity in the aggregate, capitalizing R&D along the way (we use a four-year amortizable life for Google's R&D), and using a ten-year high-growth period. Figure 15.2 summarizes the value of equity.

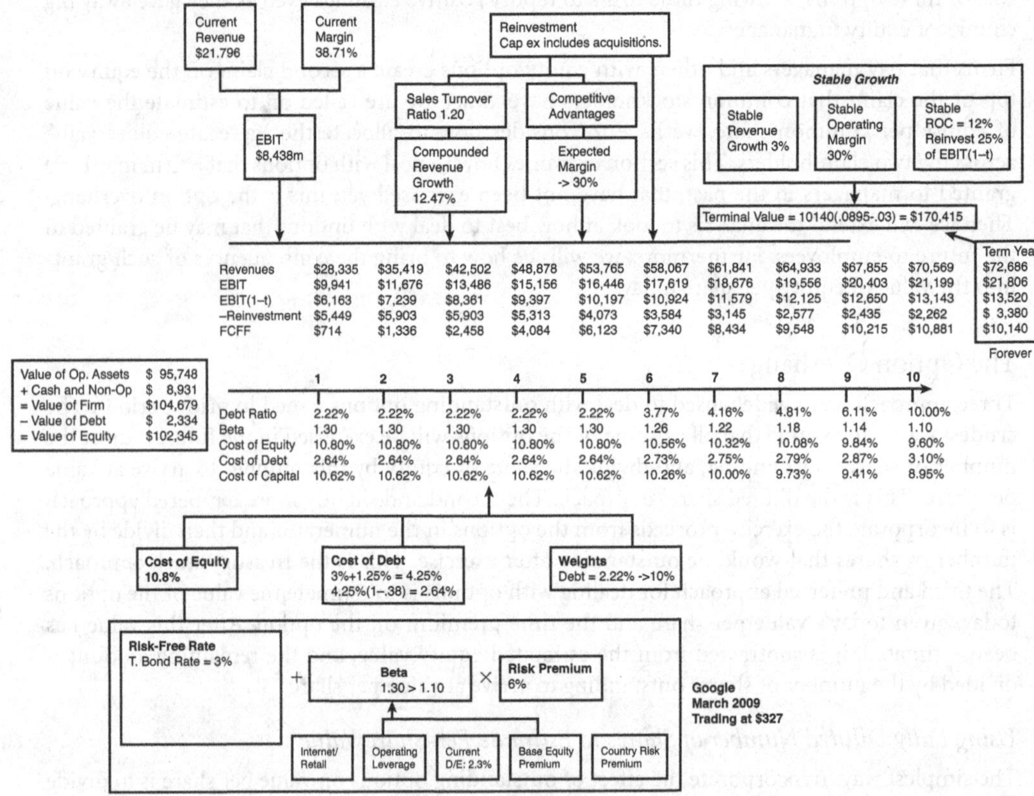

Figure 15.2: Valuing Google

In February 2009, Google had 315.29 million shares outstanding and 13.97 million in options outstanding. To estimate the value of equity per share, we divide the aggregate value of equity estimated in Figure 15.2 by the total number of shares outstanding:

Diluted Value of Equity per Share

$$= \frac{\text{Aggregate Value of Equity}}{\text{Fully Diluted Number of Shares}} = \frac{102345}{(315.29 + 13.97)} = \$310.83/Share$$

This value, however, ignores both the proceeds from the exercise of the options and the time value inherent in the options. At Google, for example, a significant number of the options issued in past years are out-of-the-money and may never be exercised.

A modified version of this approach counts only in-the-money options when computing diluted shares. Of Google's 13.97 options outstanding, 4.75 million were in-the-money, with an exercise price less than the stock price. If we count only these shares outstanding, the value of equity per share is $319.79:

Partially Diluted Value of Equity per Share

$$= \frac{\text{Aggregate Value of Equity}}{\text{Fully Diluted Number of Shares}} = \frac{102345}{(315.29 + 4.75)} = \$319.79 / Share$$

Treasury Stock Approach

This approach is a variation on the fully diluted approach. Here, the number of shares is adjusted to reflect options that are outstanding, but the expected proceeds from the exercise (the product of the exercise price and the number of options) are added to the value of equity. The limitations of this approach are that, like the fully diluted approach, it does not consider the time premium on the options, and there is no effective way to deal with vesting. Generally, this approach, by underestimating the value of options granted, overestimates the value of equity per share.

The biggest advantage of this approach is that it does not require a value per share (or stock price) to incorporate the option value into per-share value. As we will see with the last (and recommended) approach, a circularity is created when the stock price is an input into the process of estimating option value. In turn, this is needed to obtain the value per share.

Treasury Stock Approach

To use the treasury stock approach with Google, we first estimate the average exercise price across all options outstanding. Then we add the exercise proceeds to the estimated value of equity. Finally, we divide by the fully diluted number of shares outstanding. (We use the average exercise price of $391.40 across all options in making this estimate.)

Treasury Stock Value of Equity per Share

$$= \frac{\text{Value of Equity} + \text{Options Outstanding} * \text{Average Exercise Price}}{\text{Fully Diluted Number of Shares}}$$

$$= \frac{\$102{,}345 + 13.97 * \$391.40}{(315.29 + 13.97)} = \$327.44 / Share$$

As with the diluted approach, there are modified versions of this approach in which only in-the-money options are considered. This reduces the value per share for Google considerably. The average exercise price for the in-the-money options, at $185, is much lower than the weighted average exercise price of $391.40.

Treasury Stock Value of Equity per Share (Based on In-the-Money Options)

$$= \frac{\text{Value of Equity} + \text{Options Outstanding} * \text{Average Exercise Price}}{\text{Fully Diluted Number of Shares}}$$

$$= \frac{\$102{,}345 + 4.75 * \$185}{(315.29 + 4.75)} = \$314.45 / Share$$

Valuing Options

The problem with both the diluted stock and treasury stock approaches is that they miss the essence of options. After all, the value of an option should include not only the current exercise value (recognized by the treasury stock approach) but also the time premium, reflecting the fact that the option still has life and that the underlying stock is volatile. Much of the debate over dealing with options has raged around how well option pricing models work in valuing employee options. This section reviews some of this discussion and examines how to adapt conventional option pricing models to value these options.

Measurement Issues

Option pricing models have been widely used, to good effect, for almost four decades now for valuing listed and traded options on the option exchanges. In valuing employee options, however, we must confront six measurement issues:

- **Vesting**: Firms granting employee options usually require that the employee receiving the options stay with the firm for a specified period, to be able to exercise the option (at which point the employee is vested). When we examine the options outstanding at a firm, we are looking at a mix of vested and nonvested options. The nonvested options should be worth less than the vested options, but the probability of vesting depends on how in-the-money the options are and the period left for an employee to vest.
- **Illiquidity**: Employee options cannot be traded. As a result, employee options are often exercised before maturity, making them less valuable than otherwise similar traded options that are marketable. In a comprehensive study of 262,931 option exercises of employee options between 1996 and 2003 by U.S. companies, Brooks, Chance, and Cline noted that 92.3% exercise early. On average, they find that exercise takes place 2.69 years

after vesting, with 4.71 years left to expiration. Put another way, an employee option with a stated maturity of ten years is usually exercised in 5.29 years.

- **Stock price or stock value**: While conventional option pricing models are built around using the current market price as a key input, we do come up with estimates of value per share when we value companies. These estimates can be very different from current stock prices. We have to consider whether we want to use our estimates of value per share, rather than the market prices, to preserve valuation consistency.
- **Dilution**: Unlike listed options on exchanges, where the exercise of the option has no impact on the number of shares outstanding or the share price, the exercise of employee options can alter both.
- **Tax consequences**: Firms are allowed to deduct the difference between the stock and the exercise price of an option at exercise, and a potential tax saving exists at the time of the option exercise. This potential tax benefit reduces the drain on value created by having options outstanding.
- **Unobservable inputs**: The final issue relates to options granted at private firms or firms on the verge of a public offering. Key inputs to the option-pricing model, including the stock price and the variance, cannot be obtained for these firms, but the options have to be valued nevertheless.

Modifying Option Pricing Models

With all these issues affecting valuation, how do we adapt conventional option pricing models to value employee options? This question has been addressed both by academics who value options and by the Financial Accounting Standards Board (FASB) in its attempts to give guidance to firms that have to value these options for expensing.

Modified Black-Scholes

The conventional Black-Scholes model is designed to value European options on traded assets. It does not explicitly factor in the dilution inherent in employee options or the illiquidity/vesting issues specific to these options. However, adaptations of the model provide reasonable estimates of value:

- **Build expected dilution into the stock price**: One of the inputs into the Black-Scholes model is the current stock price. To the extent that the exercise of options increases the number of shares outstanding (at a price less than the current stock price), the stock price drops on exercise. A simple adjustment to the stock price can incorporate this effect:

$$\text{Adjusted Stock Price} = \text{Current Stock Price}\left[\frac{n_{\text{Shares Outstanding}}}{(n_{\text{Shares Outstanding}} + n_{\text{Options}})}\right]$$

The resulting lower adjusted stock price also reduces the option value.[5]

5 A modified version of the adjustment allocates the overall value of equity across all potential shares outstanding:

$$\text{Adjusted Stock Price} = \left[\frac{\text{Share Price} * n_{\text{Shares Outstanding}} + \text{Value per Option} * n_{\text{Options}}}{(n_{\text{Shares Outstanding}} + n_{\text{Options}})}\right]$$

- **Reduce the life of the option to reflect illiquidity and early exercise**: Earlier in this chapter, we noted that employees often exercise options well before maturity because these options are illiquid. Typically, options are exercised about halfway through their stated lives. Using a reduced life for the option reduces its value.
- **Adjust the option value for probability of vesting**: The vesting adjustment can be made in the process of calculating the option value. If we can assess the probability of vesting, multiplying this probability by the option value will yield an expected value for the option.

While purists would still resist, this model has proven remarkably resilient even in environments where its basic assumptions are violated.

Binomial Models

The possibility of early exercise and nonvesting, which is substantial in employee options, leads many practitioners to argue for the use of binomial lattice models to value employee options. Unlike the Black-Scholes, not only can these models model for early exercise, but they also can be modified to allow for other special features specific to employee options, including vesting. In addition, binomial models allow for more flexibility on inputs, with volatility changing from period to period rather than remaining constant (which is the assumption in the Black-Scholes model). The limitation of the binomial models is that they are more information-intensive, requiring the user to input prices at each branch. In any realistic version of the model, where the time intervals are short, this could translate into hundreds of potential prices.

The primary benefit of binomial models comes from the flexibility that they offer users to model the interaction between the stock price and early exercise. One example is the Hull-White Model, which proposes reducing the life used to value employee options to a more realistic level.[6] This model takes into account the employee exit rate during the vesting period (thus taking into account the probability that options will end up unvested and worthless) and the expected life of the option after they get vested. To estimate the latter, the model assumes that there will be exercise if the stock price reaches a prespecified multiple of the exercise price, thus making exercise an endogenous component of the model, rather than an exogenous component. The resulting option values are usually lower than those estimated using the unadjusted Black-Scholes model.

Simulation Models

The third choice for valuing employee options are Monte Carlo simulation models. These models begin with a distribution for stock prices and a prespecified exercise strategy. The stock prices are then simulated to arrive at the probabilities that employee options will be exercised and an expected value for the options based on the exercise. The advantage of simulations is that they offer the most flexibility for building in the conditions that may affect the value of employee options. In particular, the interplay between vesting, the stock price, and early exercise can all be built into the simulation rather than specified as assumptions. The disadvantage is that simulations require far more information than other models.

6 Hull, J. and A. White, "How to Value Employee Stock Options," *Financial Analysts Journal*, 60 (1) (2004), pp. 114–119.

How Much Does the Model Matter?

How much does the model used to value employee options matter? Are there significant differences in values when we use alternative models to value employee options? For the most part, the biggest single component determining employee option value is the life of the option. Using the stated life of employee options in the Black-Scholes models yields too high a value for these options. If we use an expected life for the option (which takes into account early exercise and vesting probabilities), the values that we arrive at are not dissimilar using different models. Ammann and Seiz (2003) show that the employee option pricing models in use (the binomial, Black-Scholes with adjusted life, and Hull-White) all yield similar values.[7] As a consequence, they argue we should steer away from models that require difficult-to-estimate inputs (such as risk-aversion coefficients) and toward simpler models.

Option Value Approach

In Table 15.9, we begin by estimating the value of the options outstanding at Google, using the Black-Scholes model, adjusted for dilution and using half the stated maturity (to allow for early exercise). To estimate the value of the options, we first estimate the standard deviation of 50% in stock prices[8] over the previous two years. Weekly stock prices are used to make this estimate, and this estimate is annualized.[9] All options, vested as well as nonvested, are valued, and there is no adjustment for nonvesting.

Table 15.9 Estimated Value of Options Outstanding

	Google
Number of options outstanding	13.97
Average exercise price	$391.41
Estimated standard deviation (volatility)	50%
Average stated maturity	7.00
Maturity adjusted for early exercise	3.50
Stock price at time of analysis	$326.6
Value per option	$103.6

7 Ammann, M. and R. Seiz, 2003, "Does the Model Matter? A Valuation Analysis of Employee Stock Options," working paper, SSRN.

8 The variance estimate is actually on the natural log of the stock prices. This allows us to cling to at least the possibility of a normal distribution. Neither stock prices nor stock returns can be normally distributed, because prices cannot fall below 0, and returns cannot be lower than –100%.

9 All the inputs to the Black-Scholes model have to be in annual terms. To annualize a weekly variance, we multiply by 52.

	Google
Value of options outstanding	$1,447
Tax rate	38.00%
After-tax value of options outstanding	$897

In estimating the after-tax value of the options at these companies, we use the marginal tax rate of 38%. Since tax law allows for tax deductions only at exercise and only for the exercise value, we are potentially overstating the possible tax benefits (and understating the costs).

The value per share is computed by subtracting the value of the options outstanding from the value of equity and then dividing by the primary number of shares outstanding:

$$\text{Value of Equity per Share} = \frac{\text{Value of Equity} - \text{Value of Options}}{\text{Primary Shares Outstanding}}$$

$$= \frac{102{,}345 - 897}{315.29} = \$321.76$$

The inconsistency referred to earlier is clear when we compare the value per share that we have estimated in this table to the price per share that we used in the previous one to estimate the value of the options. For instance, Google's value per share is $321.76, whereas the price per share used in the option valuation is $326.60. If we choose to iterate, we would revalue the options using the estimated value, which would lower the value of the options (to $1,406 million) and increase the value per share, leading to a second iteration, and a third one, and so on. The values converge to yield a consistent estimate of $321.84, close to our original estimate. That is because we estimated a value per share close to the current price; as the difference widens, the effect of doing the iterative process on value per share also increases.

Future Option Grants and Effect on Value

Just as options outstanding represent potential dilution or cash outflows to existing equity investors, expected option grants in the future will affect value per share by increasing the number of shares outstanding in future periods. The simplest way to consider why future option grants affect value is to treat them as employee compensation. The resulting increase in operating expenses will decrease operating income and after-tax cash flows in future years, thus reducing the value that we would attach to the firm today.

We should note two things here. The first is that this process is on top of the adjustment made to equity value per share for the option overhang. It does not represent double counting, because it captures two different drains on equity value per share—one from past option grants and one from expected future grants. However, if we do this, we should not also increase the number of shares outstanding to reflect future option exercise. That would be double counting. Also note that making this estimate has become immeasurably easier now that the accounting rules have changed to require firms to show option grants as expenses. The operating and net income for most firms now should be after the option expense. If we forecast future values based on these numbers, we are incorporating the expenses associated with future grants into our cash flows. The only note of caution that we would add is that as firms become larger, the option grants as a percentage of revenues or value tend to become smaller. Thus, we should move option grants for firms toward industry averages or mature firm practices as we forecast further into the future.[10]

Valuing with Expected Option Issues

When valuing Google, the current operating income is a key input. The way in which the firm has dealt with employee option expenses plays a key role in what operating income we will use in valuation. Over the past three years, the firm has shifted to expensing employee options. In its 2008 annual report, for instance, the firm highlights employee option expenses as a proportion of total revenues. Table 15.10 summarizes these numbers.

Table 15.10 Employee Option Expenses for Google

Year	Value of Employee Options Granted	As a Percentage of Revenues
2006	$458.10	4.30%
2007	$868.60	5.20%
2008	$1,119.80	5.10%

Note that the expense associated with employee options is a significant drain on income and shows no signs of abating as Google becomes larger as a company. The stated earnings, given accounting rules in 2008, already reflect these expenses.

Relative Valuation

Just as options affect intrinsic valuations, they also affect relative valuations. In particular, comparing multiples across companies is complicated by the fact that firms often have varying numbers of employee options outstanding and these options can have very different values. Failing to explicitly factor these options into the analysis will result in companies with unusually large or small (relative to the peer group) numbers of options outstanding looking misvalued on a relative basis.

To see the effect of options on earnings multiples, consider the most widely used one—the PE ratio. The numerator is usually the current price per share, and the denominator is earnings per

10 Prior to FASB 123R, the rule requiring option expensing, it was much more difficult to adjust for future option grants. In effect, we had to value option grants on our own and adjust the current earnings for the expense.

share. Analysts who use primary earnings per share are clearly biasing their analysis toward finding companies with higher option overhang to be undervalued. To see why, note that the price per share should incorporate the effect of options outstanding. The market price will be lower when more employee options are outstanding, but the denominator does not reflect the presence of options, since it reflects actual shares outstanding and does not capture potential dilution. Note that this bias does not disappear when firms switch to expensing options.

To counter this, analysts often use fully diluted earnings per share to incorporate the effect of outstanding options, thus penalizing companies with large numbers of options outstanding. The problem with this approach is that it treats all options as having an equivalent effect on value. The number of shares increases by the same unit whether the option is out-of-the-money and has three weeks left to expiration or is deep in-the-money and has five years left to maturity. Clearly, firms that have more of the latter should trade at lower market values (for any given level of earnings) and will look cheaper on a diluted basis.

What is the solution? The only way to incorporate the effect of options into earnings multiples is to value the options at fair value, using the current stock price as the basis, and add this value to the market capitalization to arrive at the total market value of equity.[11] This total market value of equity can be divided by aggregate net income to arrive at a PE ratio that incorporates (correctly) the existence of options. This allows analysts to consider all options outstanding and incorporate their characteristics into the value.

$$\text{Option-Corrected PE} = \frac{(\text{Market Capitalization} + \text{Estimated Value of Options Outstanding})}{\text{Net Income}}$$

The net income used should be the earnings estimated on the assumption that employee options are compensation and operating expenses. With the adoption of FASB 123R, this has become a little easier, although many companies still report net income before and after these expenses.

Everything we have said about earnings multiples can also be said about book value multiples. Failing to incorporate the value of equity options into the market value of equity makes option-heavy companies look cheaper, relative to companies that have fewer options outstanding. The solution is the same as it was for earnings multiples. Estimating the value of employee options and adding them to market capitalization almost always eliminates the bias in the comparison process.

Adjusting the PE Ratio for Options Outstanding

To examine the effects of options outstanding on relative valuation, we will compare Google and Cisco, two technology firms with a history of using employee options. In Table 15.11, we estimate the conventional PE ratio and contrast it with the adjusted PE ratio, using the approach just described.

11 Returning to the preceding section, the value of options used should be calculated based on the current stock price (rather than an estimated value) and on a pre-tax basis.

Table 15.11 **PE Ratio Versus Adjusted PE Ratio for Google and Cisco**

	Google	Cisco
Stock price	$326.60	$16.23
Primary shares outstanding	315.29	5,986.00
Number of options outstanding	13.97	1,199.00
Primary EPS	$13.40	$1.47
Diluted EPS	$12.83	$1.23
Primary PE	24.37	11.04
Diluted PE	25.45	13.25
Market capitalization	$102,975	$97,153
Value of options	$1,406	$3,477
Market value of equity (market capitalization + value of options)	$104,381	$100,630
Net income before option expensing	$5,347	$8,802
Net income after option expensing	$4,227	$8,052
Adjusted PE (market value of equity / net income after option expensing)	24.69	12.50

Note that for Google, incorporating options into the market value of equity and using net income after option expensing does not have a material impact on the PE ratio. For Cisco, the effects are much stronger, with the PE ranging from 11 to 13.25, depending on how we deal with options.

Conclusion

This chapter examined the two key issues we face when valuing firms with substantial intangible assets. The first is that the accounting treatment of what comprises capital expenditures at these firms is inconsistent with the accounting treatment of capital expenditures at manufacturing firms. R&D expenses, brand-name advertising, and employee recruitment and training expenses are treated as operating, rather than capital, expenses. As a result, both the earnings and book value numbers at these firms are skewed, and using them in valuation can lead to poor estimates of value. We examined ways of correcting for this accounting inconsistency and the resulting effect on value. In general, firms that can convert R&D expenditures more efficiently and profitably into commercial products will see their estimated values increase as a result of the correction. Firms that spend significant amounts on acquiring intangible assets, with little to show for it in terms of higher earnings, will see their estimated values decrease.

The second issue we considered is the use of equity options to compensate employees. We looked at two traditional approaches for dealing with these options—the diluted stock and treasury stock approaches—and discarded them. Instead, we argued for valuing these options using modified option pricing models. Then we can adjust the value of common shares today both for options that have been granted in the past (the option overhang) and for expected future option grants.

16

Volatility Rules: Emerging-Market Companies

The center of gravity for the global economy is shifting from the U.S. and Western Europe to Asia and Latin America. Increasingly, we are being called on to value emerging-market companies as they become larger players in the global economy as well as candidates for investment portfolios. This chapter focuses on issues that, although they are not unique to emerging-market companies, take on a larger role with them. In particular, many of these companies operate in markets with unstable currencies and inflation, as well as significant and shifting country risk. If we add financial statements that are not always informative and weak corporate governance, valuing emerging-market companies can pose serious valuation issues.

We will begin by looking at common errors made by analysts valuing emerging-market companies—currency mismatches, double- (or triple-) counting country risk, and failing to systematically consider the effects of different classes of shares—and to suggest ways in which we can avoid these mistakes. The bottom line, though, is that no matter how carefully we approach the valuation of these companies, our final estimates of value will be more volatile for these firms than for otherwise similar companies in developed markets.

The Role of Emerging-Market Companies

At the start of the 1990s, the U.S., Western Europe, and Japan still represented the bulk of the global economy. Asian and Latin American countries may have had high growth potential, but they accounted for only a small portion of world output. In the last two decades, emerging markets, especially India and China, have become much larger players in global economic growth. This section begins by looking at the growing clout of emerging-market companies. Then it examines why the valuation of these companies has become more critical to investors and analysts and lists factors that characterize these companies.

Emerging-Market Companies in the Global Economy

As emerging-market economies have grown, their financial markets have grown with them, and the public listings of companies have exploded. Some of the companies being listed used to be privately owned, and some are new firms. In markets like India and China, the number of publicly traded companies has doubled or even tripled over the last decade.

It is not just the number of companies that testifies to the importance of emerging-market companies. A few of these companies are now global players, with large market capitalization and operations outside their domestic markets. At the start of 1990, not a single Indian or Chinese company was in the top 100 global companies in terms of market capitalization. Today there are several. In early 2009, for instance, the three largest banks in the world, in terms of market capitalization, were all Chinese banks. Reflecting the increasingly level playing field, emerging-market companies have also gone from being the targets of acquisitions by developed-market companies to becoming acquirers of developed-market companies. In recent years, Gerdau Steel and Vale (Brazil), the Tata Group (India), and several Chinese companies have acquired developed-market counterparts.

Why Do Emerging Economies Matter?

As financial markets in emerging economies become larger and more sophisticated, we are also seeing the demand for valuation increase as investors in these markets are enticed into equity markets. The number of equity research and corporate finance analysts in Asia and Latin America has increased dramatically over the last decade, and that trend will probably continue.

Another factor also is at work. As investors in developed markets become more attuned to global diversification, they are more open to adding emerging-market companies to their portfolios, either directly or through emerging-market mutual or exchange traded funds. To smooth this process, many larger emerging-market companies have listings in New York and London, thus allowing investors to buy Infosys (an Indian company) and Embraer (a Brazilian company) in U.S. dollars or British pounds. However, this has also meant that these companies have to be valued, often by analysts in New York and London.

Finally, the increasing volume of cross-border mergers and acquisitions has also meant that developed-market companies are valuing target companies as potential targets, just as some emerging-market companies try to reverse that process.

Characteristics of Emerging-Market Companies

Emerging-market companies span different businesses and are located on various continents, but many (although not all) share certain characteristics:

- **Currency volatility**: In many emerging markets, the local currency is volatile, both in terms of what it buys of developed-market currencies (exchange rates) and in its own purchasing power (inflation). In some emerging-market economies, the exchange rate for foreign currencies is fixed, creating the illusion of stability, but significant shifts occur every time the currency is revalued or devalued. Finally, as noted in Chapter 6, the absence of long-term default-free bonds in a currency denies us one of the basic inputs into valuation: the risk-free rate.
- **Country risk**: Substantial growth is occurring in emerging-market economies, but this growth is accompanied by significant macroeconomic risk. Thus, the prospects of an emerging-market company depend as much on how the country in which it operates does as they do on the company's own decisions. Put another way, even the best-run companies in an emerging economy will find themselves hurt badly if that economy collapses, politically or economically.
- **Unreliable market measures:** When valuing publicly traded companies, we draw liberally from market-based measures of risk. To illustrate, we use betas, estimated by

regressing stock returns against a market index, to estimate costs of equity and corporate bond ratings and interest rates to estimate the cost of debt. In many emerging markets, both these measures can be rendered less useful if financial markets are not liquid and companies borrow from banks (rather than issuing market-traded bonds).

- **Information gaps and accounting differences:** While information disclosure requirements have become more stringent globally, the rules still require that much less information be disclosed in emerging markets than in developed markets. In fact, it is not unusual for significant and material information about earnings, reinvestment, and debt to be withheld in some emerging markets, making it more arduous to value firms in these markets. Along with the information gaps are differences in accounting standards that can make it difficult to compare numbers for emerging-market companies with developed-market firms. Inflation accounting, uncommon in the U.S. and Western Europe, is still used in some emerging markets, with differences in tax treatment adding to the confusion.
- **Corporate governance:** The question of how much power stockholders have over managers is a global one, but emerging-market companies pose some of the most difficult challenges, because of both history and environment. Many emerging-market companies used to be family-owned businesses. Although they might have made the transition to being publicly traded companies, the families retain control through a variety of devices—shares with different voting rights, pyramid holdings, and cross-holdings across companies. In addition, investors who challenge management at these companies often find themselves stymied by legal restrictions and absence of access to capital. As a consequence, changing the management at an emerging-market company is far more difficult than at a developed-market company.
- **Discontinuous risk:** Our earlier mention of country risk referred to the greater volatility in emerging-market economies and the effect that has on companies operating in these economies. Some emerging markets have an added layer of risk that can cause sudden and significant changes in a firm's fortunes. Included here are the threats of nationalization and terrorism. While the probability of these events may be small, the consequences are so dramatic that we ignore them at our own peril.

The Dark Side of Valuation

Analysts who have to value emerging-market companies confront more challenges than those who have to value developed-market companies. Some analysts develop coping mechanisms that, while making their jobs easier, can lead to serious valuation errors over time and across companies. This section highlights the unhealthy responses to the uncertainty we face when valuing these companies.

Currency Mismatches

If it is difficult to estimate the risk-free rate and other risk measures in the local currency, it is tempting to switch to another (more stable) currency when estimating discount rates. Many Latin American analysts, for instance, estimate the discount rates for local companies in U.S. dollars. That by itself is defensible if the cash flows for these companies are also in dollars. In many valuations, the cash flows either remain in the local currency or are converted into dollars using today's exchange rate (which effectively leaves them in the local currency). Chapter 6 highlighted the effects of this mismatch. A low inflation rate built into discount rates (through the use of U.S. dollar rates) and a high inflation rate built into cash flows (through the use of local currency cash flows or the current exchange rate) is a recipe for over-valuation.

Some emerging-market analysts also try to nullify the currency effect by doing everything in real terms. Again, while this approach is also defensible, the way in which discount rates and cash flows are adjusted for inflation can create inconsistencies.

Miscounting and Double-Counting Country Risk

Analysts who value emerging-market companies are undoubtedly aware that a layer of country-risk overlays the risk of their companies, but we see four common problems in valuation:

- **Currency switches**: As we noted in the preceding section, many analysts who value emerging-market companies decide to switch currencies and value their companies in U.S. dollars or euros. Unfortunately, some of them follow up by then ignoring country risk, arguing that the switch to a developed-market currency should make this risk go away. It is clearly not that easy to eliminate country risk. Valuations based on this assumption will generate values that are too high for emerging-market companies.
- **Mistaking expected cash flows for risk-adjusted cash flows**: Chapter 3 noted that many analysts claim to have adjusted their cash flows for country risk by building into the expected cash flows the possibility and consequences of bad outcomes. Note that computing an expected value across multiple scenarios does not comprise risk adjustment and that either the cash flow or the discount rate has to be explicitly adjusted to reflect risk.
- **Assuming that beta captures country risk**: Since beta is generally our measure of firm-specific risk, some analysts believe that it is the best place to reflect country risk. Companies in higher-risk countries, they argue, will have higher betas and higher costs of equity. The problem, however, is that there is no easy to way to incorporate country risk into the betas. If betas are estimated against the local index, the average beta across stocks in that market (no matter how risky the market is) should be 1. If betas are estimated against the S&P 500 or a global index, there is a chance that the beta might reflect country risk, but this is unlikely, given the small size of emerging-market companies (relative to the broader indices).
- **Double-counting (or triple-counting) risk**: At the other extreme are analysts who are so sensitized by country risk that they try to build it into every dimension of value. These analysts use higher risk-free rates (incorporating a default risk spread for the country into the risk-free rate) and higher equity risk premiums (augmenting mature market premiums) and haircut or reduce expected cash flows (to reflect the same country risk). Not surprisingly, they find that most emerging-market companies are overvalued.

When country risk affects multiple inputs in a valuation, not only is there the danger of double- or triple-counting the same risk, but it becomes much more difficult to determine how much country risk affects the valuation.

Risk Parameters

The preceding section described the difficulties we face in estimating risk parameters (betas and default spreads) for emerging-market companies. These stem from the volatility and illiquidity of the local equity markets and the absence of bond ratings for most companies. When valuing these companies, analysts often adopt shortcuts to get around these problems:

- **For cost of equity**: To estimate the beta, many analysts use betas estimated against broader and (what they view as) more trustworthy indices, especially if the emerging-market company has a foreign listing. For instance, many large emerging-market companies have American and Global Depositary Receipts (ADRs and GDRs) listed on the New York or London exchanges, and betas can be estimated for these listings against the S&P 500 or the FTSE indices. Figure 16.1 illustrates how different the numbers can be for Gerdau Steel, a large Brazilian company with listings on the Sao Paulo and New York exchanges.

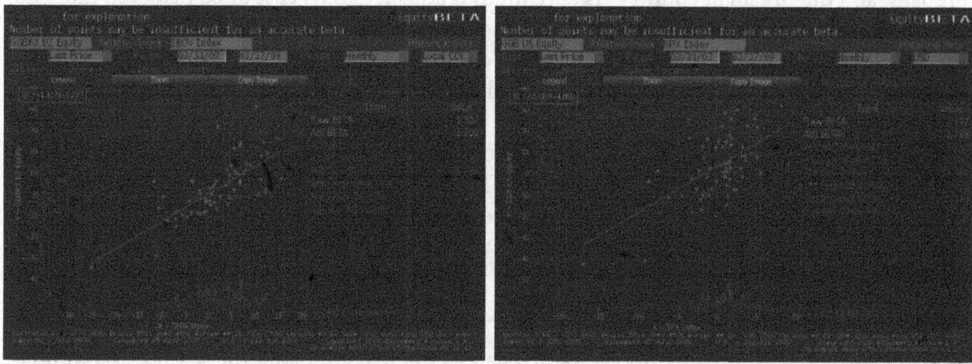

Figure 16.1: Beta Estimates for Gerdau Steel

An analyst valuing this company therefore would use the beta of 1.80, estimated against the S&P 500, as the beta for the stock. While an argument can be made that this beta provides a more reasonable measure of risk than the beta against the Bovespa, there is a cost.[1] The standard error (or noise) in the beta estimate increases as we move from the Bovespa to the S&P 500 index.

- **For cost of debt**: Using the absence of ratings and market-traded corporate bonds as an excuse, many analysts fall back on the company's book interest rate as its cost of debt:[2]

$$\text{Book Interest Rate} = \frac{\text{Interest Expenses}}{\text{Book Value of Debt}}$$

1 Some analysts justify the use of ADR betas on the grounds that they are estimating dollar costs of equity and that the beta estimated using the ADR and the S&P 500 is more consistent. This argument does not hold up to scrutiny, however. When estimating the cost of equity, we want to get as close as we can to a company's true beta, not a beta that is computed against a different index. Thus, if the marginal investor in Gerdau is a Brazilian mutual fund, there is little basis for using a beta computed against the S&P 500. If the marginal investor is an institutional investor who holds primarily U.S. stocks, we would use the beta estimated against the S&P 500, whether the valuation was in U.S. dollars or Brazilian reals.

2 Taking a weighted average of the interest rates on the firm's existing debt yields the same answer.

We described the perils of using this measure in earlier chapters, but it is doubly dangerous in emerging markets for two reasons. The first is that the book interest can change significantly if an emerging-market company borrows in dollars or euros instead of the local currency, especially if high inflation is embedded in the latter. Interest rates will be lower for dollar and euro borrowings and can reduce the book interest rate; using this interest rate for a local currency cost of debt will yield too low a number. The second reason is that much of the debt in emerging-market companies tends to be short-term debt, which can bias the book interest rate downward, since the long-term cost of debt (which is what we want) tends to be higher.

Incorporation Effect

When valuing emerging-market companies, analysts pay too much attention to where a company is incorporated and too little to where it does business. Thus, Embraer is viewed as a Brazilian company, and the Brazilian country risk premium is attached to its cost of equity, even though it gets only about 10% of its revenues in Brazil and most of its revenues in developed markets. In fact, with the conventional practice, all Brazilian companies have the entire Brazilian country risk premium added on to their costs of equity, and all Indian companies have the Indian country risk premium incorporated into their costs of equity. If we accept the proposition that different companies in an emerging market have different exposures to country risk, the consequences become obvious. We will undervalue companies that are less exposed than the typical company to country risk and overvalue companies that are more exposed. We will underestimate Embraer's value by treating it as a typical Brazilian company.

Ignoring Missing Information

When confronted with missing information, analysts often assume that the safest assumption to make is to ignore that item. Thus, if companies in an emerging market do not provide information on lease commitments (which we argued in Chapter 2 should be discounted and treated as debt), analysts ignore leases. By doing so, though, they are essentially assuming that the lease commitments in future years are zero. We would argue that this is less defensible than assuming that the current lease expenses will continue for a specified period (say, five or eight years). In fact, this pattern of ignoring items that are not reported (employee options, acquisition premiums) can be challenged on the basis that more reasonable assumptions can be made for most of these items.

Corporate Governance Mood Swings

Most analysts accept the reality that a forced change in management at many emerging-market companies is very difficult to accomplish. Rather than trying to incorporate this fact into value, they swing from one extreme to the other when valuing these companies. In good times, when markets are buoyant and the economy is doing well, they ignore the weak corporate governance rules, acting as if they have no effect on value. In bad times, when the economy is in trouble and markets are down, they use the same weak corporate governance system as justification for reducing the value at these companies, often by arbitrary amounts.

Corporate governance should matter in good and bad times. A management team that underperforms the rest of the market when the economy is doing well is destroying value just as much as a team that does the same in poor economic times. However, an arbitrary or fixed discount applied to all companies misses the differences across companies and does not reflect changes in the corporate governance rules in a market.

Post-Valuation Discounts

In emerging markets with significant risks from nationalization or terrorism, it is not uncommon to see analysts apply hefty discounts to their estimated value to reflect these risks. While the logic for these discounts is clear, the magnitude of the discounts is often "subjective," with the analysts essentially asserting their expertise as the basis. If the two inputs into the discount are the probability that the catastrophic event will occur and the cost of the event to equity investors, there is no reason why we cannot make them explicit, even if they are estimates.

The Light Side of Valuation

Emerging-market companies are not easy to value, but we can follow some commonsense rules that will both reduce the likelihood of valuation mistakes and increase transparency in the final value. We will begin by looking at techniques that are useful in discounted cash flow valuation. We will follow up by examining ways in which we can value emerging-market companies with multiples and comparables.

Discounted Cash Flow Valuation

The ingredients in a discounted cash flow valuation—cash flows and discount rates—are the same for developed-market and emerging-market companies. The challenge, then, becomes how best to incorporate the characteristics listed in the preceding section into the inputs.

Currency Consistency

Chapter 6 laid the foundations for moving from one currency to another. The key, we noted, is to ensure that the expected inflation rate built into our discount rate matches the inflation rate implicit in our cash flows. Consequently, we can work with the local currency, a foreign currency or in real terms, when valuing an emerging-market company, as long as we define our inputs accordingly all the way through the valuation. While the details of using each input are explored more fully in Chapter 6, Table 16.1 summarizes the ways of preserving internal consistency.

Table 16.1 Currency Consistency in Valuation

	Discount Rate Estimation	Cash Flow Estimation
Local currency valuation	Estimate the discount rate in the local currency, ensuring that the risk-free rate is default-free and that the equity risk premium is consistently defined. *or* Estimate the discount rate in U.S. dollars or euros, and then convert it into a local currency rate using differential inflation.	Estimate the cash flows in the local currency, building into the growth rate the expected inflation in that currency.
Foreign currency valuation	Estimate the discount rate in a foreign currency using the risk-free rate in that currency and a consistent equity risk premium.	Estimate the cash flows directly in the foreign currency, incorporating the inflation rate in that currency in the growth rate. *or* Estimate the cash flows in the local currency and convert into the foreign currency using expected exchange rates, either from forward markets or using purchasing power parity.
Real valuation	Estimate the discount rate in real terms using a real risk-free rate and a consistent equity risk premium.	Estimate the cash flows in real terms. No inflation component should be built into the growth rate. *or* Estimate the cash flows in local (foreign) currency terms, and then deflate using the expected inflation rate in local (foreign) currency.

A simple test of whether discount rates estimated in local currency, foreign currency, and real terms are consistent is to check for the following (r is the discount rate, and E(η) is expected inflation):

$$r_{\text{Local Currency}} = (1 + r_{\text{Foreign Currency}})\frac{(1+E(\eta)_{\text{Local Currency}})}{(1+E(\eta)_{\text{Foreign Currency}})} - 1 = (1 + r_{\text{real}})(1+E(\eta)_{\text{Local Currency}}) - 1$$

Thus, the only factor that causes local currency, foreign currency, and real discount rates to vary is expected inflation. The same test applies for cash flows, with expected inflation being the key driver in differences in expected growth rates over time.

Consistency in Country Risk

We must deal with two issues associated with country risk when valuing emerging-market companies. The first is how best to estimate the risk premium for a specific emerging market, reflecting its risk. The second concerns the exposure of individual companies to this country risk.

Country Risk Premium

Chapter 7 considered the question of whether there should be a country risk premium in the first place. Summarizing that discussion, we examined the argument that there should be no country risk premium, because country risk can be diversified away, and we noted that the increasing correlation across markets makes diversification unlikely. We then presented three different ways to estimate the premium for country risk—the default spread for bonds issued by the emerging-market government, the volatility of the emerging market relative to the U.S. market, and a composite measure that scales up the bond default spread by the relative volatility of the equity market (relative to the government bond).

We will value two companies in this chapter—Gerdau Steel, a Brazilian steel company, and Tata Motors, an Indian automobile company. Since we will need estimates of the country risk premiums for India and Brazil, Table 16.2 summarizes the estimates using all three approaches for both countries.

Table 16.2 Country Risk Premium Estimates for India and Brazil: March 2009

	Sovereign Rating	Default Spread	Relative Equity Market Volatility	Composite Country Risk Premium
Brazil	Ba1	3.00%	$\frac{34\%}{20\%}(6\%) - 6\% = 4.2\%$	$\frac{34\%}{21.5\%}(3\%) = 4.75\%$
India	Ba2	4.00%	$\frac{32\%}{20\%}(6\%) - 6\% = 3.6\%$	$\frac{32\%}{21.3\%}(4\%) = 6\%$

Estimated equity risk premium for the U.S. = 6%

Standard deviations: S&P 500 = 20%; Bovespa = 34%; Sensex = 32%; Brazilian bond = 21.5%; Indian bond = 21.3%

As we argued in Chapter 7, the composite estimate is the best estimate of the country risk premium; we will use those values in the valuations.

Company Risk Exposure

If we accept the proposition that country risk deserves a premium, the next question that we have to address relates to the exposure of individual companies to country risk. Intuition suggests that all companies in a country with substantial country risk should not be equally exposed to country risk. To put this intuition to practical use, we will first look at using established risk parameters such as betas to capture country risk. Then we will lay out a more general process for evaluating the country risk exposure of individual companies.

The Beta Approach

For investors who are uncomfortable with the notion that all companies in a market are equally exposed to country risk, a fairly simple alternative is to assume that a company's exposure to country risk is proportional to its exposure to all other market risk, which is measured by the beta. Thus, the cost of equity for a firm in an emerging market can be written as follows:

Cost of Equity = Risk-Free Rate + Beta (Mature Market Premium + Country Risk Premium)

In practical terms, scaling the country risk premium to the beta of a stock implies that stocks with betas greater than 1 will be more exposed to country risk than stocks with a beta less than 1. The advantage of using betas is that they are easily available for most firms. The disadvantage is that although betas measure overall exposure to macroeconomic risk, they may not be good measures of exposure to country risk.

The Lambda Approach

The more general approach to measuring a company's exposure to country risk is to allow each company to have an exposure to country risk that is different from its exposure to other market risk. For lack of a better term, let us call the measure of a company's exposure to country risk lambda (λ). Like a beta, a lambda is scaled around 1. A lambda of 1 indicates a company with average exposure to country risk. A lambda above or below 1 indicates above or below average exposure to country risk. The cost of equity for a firm in an emerging market can then be written as follows:

Expected Return = R_f + Beta (Mature Market Equity Risk Premium) + λ (County Risk Premium)

Note that this approach essentially converts our single-factor expected return model to a two-factor model. The second factor is country risk, and λ measures exposure to country risk.

Most investors would accept the general proposition that different companies in a market should have different exposures to country risk. But what are the determinants of this exposure? We would expect at least three factors (and perhaps more) to play a role:

- **Revenue source**: The first and most obvious determinant is how much of the revenues a firm derives from the country in question. A company that derives 30% of its revenues from Brazil should be less exposed to Brazilian country risk than a company that derives 70% of its revenues from Brazil. Note, though, that this then opens up the possibility that a company can be exposed to the risk in many countries. Thus, a company that derives only 30% of its revenues from Brazil may derive its remaining revenues from Argentina and Venezuela, exposing it to country risk in those countries. Extending this argument to multinationals, we would argue that companies like Coca-Cola and Nestlé can have substantial exposure to country risk because so much of their revenues come from emerging markets.

- **Production facilities:** A company can be exposed to country risk, even if it derives no revenues from that country, if its production facilities are in that country. After all, political and economic turmoil in the country can throw off production schedules and affect the company's profits. Companies that can move their production facilities elsewhere can spread their risk across several countries, but the problem is exaggerated for companies that cannot do so. Consider mining companies. An African gold mining company may export all its production, but it will face substantial country risk exposure, because its mines cannot be moved.
- **Risk management products:** Companies that would otherwise be exposed to substantial country risk may be able to reduce this exposure by buying insurance against specific (unpleasant) contingencies and by using derivatives. A company that uses risk management products should have a lower exposure to country risk—a lower lambda—than an otherwise similar company that does not use these products.

Ideally, we would like companies to provide information about all three of these factors in their financial statements.

The simplest measure of lambda is based entirely on revenues. In the preceding section, we argued that a company that derives a smaller proportion of its revenues from a market should be less exposed to country risk. Given the constraint that the average lambda across all stocks must be 1 (someone has to bear the country risk), we cannot use the percentage of revenues a company gets from a market as lambda. We can, however, scale this measure by dividing it by the percentage of revenues that the average company in the market gets from the country to derive a lambda:

$$\text{Lambda}_j = \frac{\text{\% of Revenue in Country}_{\text{Company}}}{\text{\% of Revenue in Country}_{\text{Average Company in Market}}}$$

The advantage of this approach is that the information to compute it is usually easily accessible, but the disadvantage is its focus on just revenues.

The second measure draws on a company's stock prices and how they move in relation to movements in country risk. Sovereign bonds issued by countries offer a simple and updated measure of country risk. As investor assessments of country risk become more optimistic, bonds issued by that country go up in price, just as they go down when investors become more pessimistic. A regression of the returns on a stock against the returns on a sovereign bond therefore should yield a measure of lambda in the slope coefficient:

$$\text{Return}_{\text{Stock}} = a + \lambda\ \text{Return}_{\text{Country Bond}}$$

Since stock prices should be affected by all aspects of a company's performance, this should yield a more comprehensive measure of lambda. However, it is dependent on the existence of liquid country bonds and has a large standard error associated with it.

Estimating Lambdas for Gerdau Steel and Tata Motors

To estimate the lambdas for Gerdau Steel and Tata Motors, we start with the revenue approach. In 2008, Gerdau Steel generated 51% of its revenues in Brazil and the rest of its revenues in North America. Tata Motors, on the other hand, generated about 90% of its revenues in India and the balance in other parts of the world. We scaled these numbers to what a typical Brazilian (or Indian) company generated in revenues domestically in 2008. Table 16.3 summarizes the resulting lambdas for Gerdau and Tata Motors.

Table 16.3 Revenue-Based Lambdas for Gerdau and Tata Motors

	Percentage of Revenues in Domicile	Percentage of Revenues for Typical Firm in Domicile	Lambda
Gerdau Steel	51%	72%	0.79
Tata Motors	90%	78%	1.15

We will assume that neither Gerdau nor Tata Motors has significant country risk exposure in other emerging markets—Gerdau because the bulk of its remaining revenues are in the U.S., and Tata Motors because it has very little in revenues outside India.

We also try the price-based approach for estimating lambdas for Gerdau Steel. Regressing the weekly returns on Gerdau stock between January 2007 and January 2009 on the weekly returns on the Brazilian government dollar-denominated bond yields the following:

$$\text{Return}_{\text{Gerdau}} = 0.045\% + 0.6250\ \text{Return}_{\text{Brazil \$ Bond}}$$

Based on this regression, Gerdau has a lambda of 0.625. Lacking a direct measure of country risk for India (since the Indian government does not have dollar-denominated bonds outstanding), we did not try this approach for Tata Motors.[3]

Risk Estimates in Volatile Markets

The preceding section described the problems with estimating the beta (cost of equity) and default risk (cost of debt) in volatile markets, where few companies have bond ratings. Rather than use partial solutions to this problem (such as using betas computed from ADRs), we will draw on approaches that we have used for other groups of companies in this book:

- **For equity risk parameters:** This book has repeatedly emphasized the superiority of bottom-up betas (where we start with sector averages and adjust for operating and financial leverage differences). With emerging-market companies, this approach

3 We considered running a regression of Tata Motors stock returns against the Indian government credit default swap (CDS) spreads but decided against the idea.

provides a lifeline for estimating more meaningful and precise betas. However, we would expand on the notion of "comparable firms" to include not only firms that operate in the same business in the country in which the company being valued is domiciled, but also companies listed in other markets. To analysts who worry about using the betas computed in other markets (that may be safer or riskier than the company's home market), we would present two counterpoints. The first is that beta is a relative measure of risk; no currency is attached to it. The second is that the country risk premium, rather than the beta, takes care of country risk differences. If we accept the proposition that comparable firms can include firms in other markets, the final question to address is whether we should segregate companies based on whether they are in emerging markets or developed markets. The answer depends on the sector in which the company operates. With oil and aerospace companies, where operating risks are similar across markets and the products are sold into a global market, we are open to using all companies listed globally, in both developed and emerging markets. With telecommunications and consumer products companies, it can be argued that the same product or service (water, electricity, phone service) that is nondiscretionary in a developed market can be discretionary in emerging markets, where large proportions of the population may still be lacking these services (but will acquire them if the economy does well). In these cases, we would use only emerging-market companies as our comparable firms to estimate betas.

- **For default spread estimates:** With unrated companies in the U.S., we argued that the synthetic rating should be the basis for the cost of debt. Since these synthetic ratings were computed using the interest coverage ratio, there is no reason why we cannot do the same for emerging-market companies. In effect, we could use the interest coverage ratio for an Indian or Brazilian company to compute a rating, based on the lookup table we developed in Chapter 2, and then estimate a default spread based on the rating. Two estimation issues must be confronted in the process. First, the table that we use to estimate the ratings was developed using rated companies in the U.S. If we were looking at markets that have interest rates similar to the U.S., the table should still provide reasonable ratings. However, in emerging markets that have much higher inflation and interest rates, using this table may result in ratings that are too low even for safe companies.[4] Second, the synthetic rating we obtain for a company will not reflect the default risk of the country in which the company operates. Consequently, when we compute the cost of debt for an emerging-market company, we may have to consider adding two default spreads to the risk-free rate—one for the company's default risk and another for the country's default risk:

$$\text{Cost of Debt}_{\text{Emerging-Market Company}} = \text{Risk-Free Rate} + \text{Default Spread}_{\text{Country}} + \text{Default Spread}_{\text{Company}}$$

In effect, an AA-rated Argentine company will have a higher dollar cost of debt than an AA-rated U.S. company, because the former will have the default spread for Argentina added onto its cost of debt.

4 If the risk-free rate is 12%, interest expenses will be higher for any given level of debt, which in turn lowers interest coverage ratios.

Estimating Costs of Debt and Equity for Gerdau Steel and Tata Motors

To estimate the costs of equity for Gerdau Steel and Tata Motors, we first estimate the average unlevered beta for comparable firms. For Gerdau Steel, we use the average unlevered beta for steel companies listed globally using the argument that steel is a commodity that is bought and sold in a world market. For Tata Motors, we use the unlevered beta estimated by looking at only emerging-market automobile firms (including auto parts firms), because it is very likely that automobiles are far more discretionary in emerging markets than in developed markets. (Therefore, it is likely that emerging-market auto firms should have higher betas than developed-market auto firms.) We then use the debt-to-equity ratios and marginal tax rates for Gerdau and Tata Motors to estimate the levered betas for the firms. Table 16.4 summarizes the computation. We use the marginal tax rates for Brazil (34%) and India (33.99%).

Table 16.4 Levered Betas for Gerdau Steel and Tata Motors

	Comparable Firms	Unlevered Beta	Firm's Debt-to-Equity Ratio	Marginal Tax Rate	Levered Beta
Gerdau Steel	Global steel companies	1.01	138.89%	34.00%	1.94
Tata Motors	Emerging-market auto firms	0.77	108.29%	33.99%	1.32

To estimate the dollar cost of equity for Gerdau, we use the U.S. Treasury bond rate of 3%, at the time of the analysis, as the risk-free rate, a mature market equity risk premium of 6%, the country risk premium for Brazil of 4.75%, and the lambda of 0.625 that we estimated from the regression of stock returns against returns on the dollar-denominated Brazilian bond. The resulting dollar cost of equity is 17.61%:

$$\text{Cost of Equity for Gerdau} = 3.00\% + 1.94\ (6\%) + 0.625\ (4.75\%) = 17.61\%$$

For Tata Motors, we estimate the cost of equity in rupee terms, since the valuation will be in the local currency. To estimate a risk-free rate, we start with the ten-year rupee bond issued by the Indian government that is trading at an interest rate of approximately 8% at the time of this analysis, and subtract the 4% default spread we estimated earlier for India, based on its rating, to arrive at a risk-free rate in rupees of 4.00%:

$$\begin{aligned}\text{Risk-Free Rate in Rupees} &= \text{Indian Government Bond Rate} - \text{Default Spread for India}\\ &= 8\% - 4\% = 4\%\end{aligned}$$

For the mature market risk premium, we stick with the estimate that we obtained for the U.S. (roughly 6%). To evaluate the effect of country risk, we use the lambda of

1.15 that we estimated for Tata Motors, based on its revenues, and the additional country risk premium of 6% that we estimated earlier for India. The resulting cost of capital is summarized as follows:

Cost of Equity in Rupees for Tata Motors = 4% + 1.32 (6%) + 1.15 (6%) = 18.82%

To estimate the cost of debt for the two companies, we compute the interest coverage ratios for each, using information from their 2008 financial statements and a synthetic rating based on the interest coverage ratios.[5] We add the default spreads based on these ratings to the country default spreads for Brazil and India (from Table 16.2) to obtain pre-tax costs of debt for the firms, as shown in Table 16.5.

Table 16.5 Cost of Debt for Gerdau Steel and Tata Motors

	Interest Coverage Ratio	Rating	Company Default Spread	Country Default Spread	Cost of Debt
Gerdau Steel (in U.S. dollars)	8005/1620 = 4.94	A–	3.00%	3.00%	9.00%
Tata Motors (in rupees)	19421/1756 = 11.06	AA	1.75%	4.00%	9.75%

As a final step, we use the market values of debt and equity in March 2009 to estimate the weights of the two components. The resulting costs of capital are estimated in Table 16.6.

Table 16.6 Debt Ratios and Cost of Capital

	Cost of Equity	After-Tax Cost of Debt	Debt-to-Capital Ratio	Cost of Capital
Gerdau Steel (in U.S. dollars)	17.61%	9.00% (1 – .34) = 5.94%	58.45%	10.79%
Tata Motors (in rupees)	18.82%	9.75% (1 – .3399) = 6.44%	51.92%	12.38%

For Gerdau, we will use the dollar cost of capital as our discount rate, because we will be doing our valuation in dollars. For Tata Motors, however, we derive a rupee cost of capital of 12.38%. If we wanted to convert this to a U.S. dollar cost of capital, we would have to make assumptions about expected inflation in the U.S.

5 We used the interest coverage ratio/rating relationship we developed for smaller companies in the U.S. to estimate the ratings. The default spreads reflect the spreads at the start of 2009.

and the emerging market. If we assume, for instance, that the expected inflation rate in U.S. dollars is 2% and in rupees is 3.5%, the cost of capital in U.S. dollar terms for Tata Motors can be estimated as follows:

$$\text{Cost of Capital}_\$ = (1 + \text{Cost of Capital}_{\text{Local Currency}}) \frac{(1 + \text{Exp Inflation}_\$)}{(1 + \text{Exp Inflation}_{\text{Local Currency}})}$$

$$= 1.1238 \left[\frac{1.02}{1.035}\right] - 1$$

$$= 10.75\%$$

In summary, the secret of moving consistently from one currency to another and from nominal to real numbers is to ensure that the cash flows and discount rate have the same expectation of inflation built into them.

Filling in Information Gaps

We are far more likely to find critical pieces of information missing with emerging-market companies than with developed-market companies. Rather than ignore missing items, we should make the most reasonable and consistent estimates we can for these inputs. In this endeavor, the following might help:

- **Alternative estimates**: Even if no information is provided in one part of the financial statements, perhaps clues or data in other parts can be used to plug the hole. For example, some emerging-market companies do not have statements of cash flows; they have income statements, balance sheets, and statements of changes in equity. Although normally we obtain our estimates of capital expenditures from the cash flow statement, we can estimate the gross (or net) capital expenditure from the balance sheet by looking at the change in gross (or net) fixed assets from period to period. Similarly, the absence of a reported effective tax rate can easily be remedied by looking at the taxes paid and taxable income on the income statement.
- **Current-year clues**: In earlier chapters, we argued that lease expenses are financial expenses, and that the present value of lease commitments, discounted back at the pre-tax cost of debt, should be considered debt. In the U.S. and many other developed markets, where companies report lease commitments for the future in the footnotes to the financial statements, this is easy to do. However, many emerging-market companies do not provide this information. Rather than assuming that these companies have no lease commitments, we could assume a reasonable life for the leases, given normal leasing terms in that market, and then extrapolate this year's lease or rental expense as annuities over this period.[6]

6 In most markets, lease periods are standardized. Most retail leases in the U.S., for instance, are 10 to 12 years. In emerging markets, the lease periods may be shorter.

- **Look at industry averages:** When critical information needed to value a company is missing, it may help to look at companies in the sector in the same or other markets that have more detailed information available. For a steel company that does not provide key information on inventory or accounts receivable, we could use the data from other steel companies to make estimates. Thus, if noncash working capital at the comparable companies is 3% of revenues, we can use that number to value the company with missing information.
- **Ensure consistency with your other inputs:** When valuing companies, it is just as critical that we ensure that the inputs are internally consistent as it is that we estimate each input well. Put another way, if we assume a high expected growth rate for an emerging-market company, where little or no information is provided on capital expenditures, we have to assume a high reinvestment rate to sustain that growth rate. With emerging-market companies that have missing or unreliable data, a case can be made that our inputs should be less reflective of what we see in the financial statements and more driven by the fundamentals.

In closing, we cannot let managers at emerging-market companies off the hook when they fail to provide critical information. While their defense is that information disclosure laws in their markets are weak, note that these laws put a floor on what you can reveal to investors, not a ceiling. Nothing prevents an emerging-market company from providing information on cross-holdings or leases to investors. We should be more willing to use the threat that we will assume the worst when information is withheld, and then carry through on that threat.

Dealing with Poor Corporate Governance

When deciding how best to deal with corporate governance, we should consider why governance matters. In markets with good corporate governance, bad managers are quickly replaced, and their practices reversed by new management. In Chapter 12, we estimated two values for a firm—the status quo value (based on incumbent managers running the firm) and the optimal value (based on a new and better management team running the firm). We argued that the firm's value will be a weighted average of these two numbers, with the weights reflecting the likelihood of control changing. That framework should stand us in good stead when valuing emerging-market companies that operate in weak corporate governance environments.

Consider the extreme scenario first, in which management changes are impossible (because of institutional considerations or because all the voting shares are held by incumbent managers). The value of every firm in this market is its status quo value. If a firm is badly managed, we are in effect locked into that poor management in perpetuity (or at least until they drive the firm to ruin). In practical terms, the implications of poor corporate governance on the valuation of emerging-market companies are as follows:

- **Reinvestment and growth:** If incumbent managers have made value-destroying investments in the past, they will continue to do so, essentially forever. Thus, if a firm with a cost of capital of 9% has invested in projects that generate a return on capital of 6%, it will do so in the future, and this will result in long-term value destruction.
- **Financing optimization:** Chapter 12 noted the potential for increasing value by optimizing the mix of debt and equity used to fund the business. Thus, we argued that a

firm with a debt ratio of 10% might be able to have a higher value if it employs a debt ratio of 30%. When valuing developed-market companies, analysts often use target debt ratios in valuation, with the implicit assumption that firms that are not at the target will feel pressure from stockholders to move that target. With weak corporate governance, this assumption can be dangerous. Instead, we would be better served leaving debt ratios where they are and estimating lower values for these companies.

If we incorporate the bad practices of management into our valuation inputs (through the return on capital, growth rates, and cost of capital), we have in effect already discounted the firm's value for poor corporate governance, and any additional discounts will be double counting.

The advantage of this approach is that it allows us to respond to changes in corporate governance rules and standards, both at the company level and for the entire market. Thus, a Brazilian company that eliminates voting differences across shares can be revalued easily. While the status quo and optimal values themselves might not have changed, the probability of control shifting has increased, and the firm's expected value should reflect this. As the laws and regulations governing firms changes in many emerging markets, it behooves us to be flexible in how we deal with corporate governance in valuation.

Adjusting for Discontinuous Risk

In some emerging markets, a significant concern may be that the firm will be expropriated or nationalized, leaving equity investors with a fraction of their fair value, or subject to catastrophic risk (from a terrorist attack, for instance). While we may be tempted to try to bring these risks into the costs of debt and equity, discount rates are not designed to carry this kind of risk. There is no easy way to adjust the beta or the default spread for a risk that could effectively end the cash flow streams.

In Chapter 3, we did develop an approach that may be useful in this context—decision trees. Consider the nationalization threat. We could develop a decision tree that reflects the risk and payoffs in the event of nationalization, as shown in Figure 16.2.

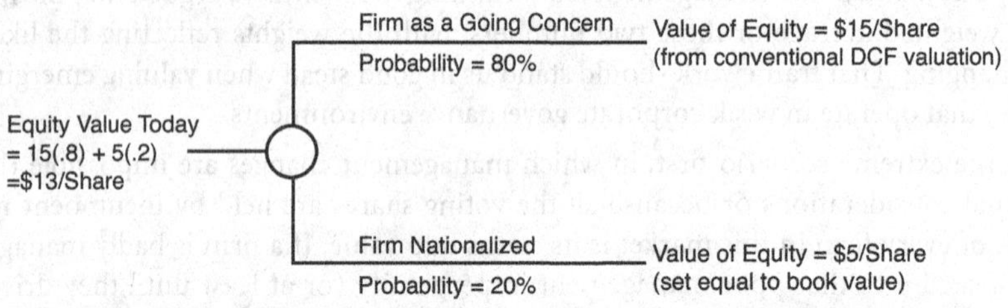

Figure 16.2: The Effect of Nationalization on Value

In valuing the firm under the "going concern" branch, we can act as if that threat does not exist. Hence, our discount rates and expected cash flows are unaffected by the possibility of nationalization. The nationalization branch is where we bring our concerns about lost value to the analysis through two inputs—the probability of nationalization and the consequences for equity value of the nationalization:

- **Probability of nationalization:** Unfortunately (or fortunately), this is not an exercise in financial analysis, but one of political assessments. By looking at a government's history, we can extract some information on what types of firms have been nationalized and how frequently. Thus, we may conclude that the threat of nationalization is greater for natural-resources firms (which are trapped by geography) than for technology firms.
- **Consequences of nationalization:** The same historical record we scoured for the probability of nationalization carries information on how much equity investors in these firms will receive in the event of nationalization. In some countries, for instance, equity investors in nationalized companies are entitled to book value (which may be well below market value). In others, they may receive nothing.

In the final assessment, we compute an expected value across both scenarios and use that as our value for the firm.

Valuing Tata Motors

We value Tata Motors in Indian rupees using the 2008 financial statements (with December 31, 2008 as the ending date) as the basis for the valuation. The steps in the valuation are as follows:

- **Base year numbers**: In 2008, Tata Motors reported pre-tax operating income of Rs 19,421 million on revenues of Rs 284,349 million. Interest expenses amounted to Rs 1,756 million, and the marginal tax rate (for India) was 33.99%. The return on capital for the year was computed to be 10.43%, based on the book values of equity (Rs 68,698 million), debt (Rs 60,130 million), and cash (Rs 5,888 million) at the beginning of the year:

$$\text{Return on Capital} = \frac{19421\,(1-.3399)}{(68698+60130-5888)} = .1043$$

Note that this number is lower than the cost of capital of 12.38% that we estimated earlier for Tata Motors. The capital expenditures for the year were augmented by the acquisition of Jaguar. They amount to Rs 22,034 million, significantly higher than the depreciation of Rs 6,478 million for the year; the noncash working capital increased by Rs 1,000 million.[7] The resulting reinvestment rate for the year is 129.14%:

$$\text{Reinvestment Rate} = \frac{(22034-6478+1000)}{19421(1-.3399)} = 129.14\%$$

7 The change in noncash working capital for the year is estimated using the noncash working capital as a percentage of revenues (5.60%) and the change in revenues from 2007 to 2008.

- **Forecast growth and cash flows**: In forecasting the growth rate, we assume that the reinvestment rate will decline to 80% for the next five years, since it is unlikely that the firm will replicate the Jaguar acquisition each year.[8] We also assume that the return on capital will stay at its existing level (10.43%) for the high-growth period, resulting in the following expected growth rate:

Expected Growth Rate = Reinvestment Rate * Return on Capital = .80 *.1043 = 8.34%

The expected free cash flows to the firm for the next five years are summarized in Table 16.7.

Table 16.7 Expected Free Cash Flows for the Next Five Years for Tata Motors

Year	Year 1	Year 2	Year 3	Year 4	Year 5
EBIT (1 – t)	Rs 13,889	Rs 15,048	Rs 16,303	Rs 17,663	Rs 19,137
– Reinvestment	Rs 11,111	Rs 12,038	Rs 13,043	Rs 14,131	Rs 15,309
FCFF	Rs 2,778	Rs 3,010	Rs 3,261	Rs 3,533	Rs 3,827

Note that the after-tax operating income is estimated using the 8.34% growth rate each year. Also note that we have consolidated the net capital expenditures and working capital investments into one item (reinvestment) and have set it to 80% of after-tax operating income.

- **Stable growth**: After year 5, Tata Motors is assumed to be in stable growth, growing 4% a year (still in Indian rupees, and capped at the Indian rupee risk-free rate). The beta is expected to drop to 1.20, the mature market equity risk premium will stay at 6%, and the country risk premium will decline to 4% (from 6%) in perpetuity. While the debt ratio remains unchanged at 51.99%, the cost of debt will decline from 9.75% to 9%, resulting in a cost of capital of 10.67%.[9] We will assume that the firm will continue to generate its current return on capital of 10.43% in perpetuity. Although this is lower than the cost of capital and thus represents permanent value destruction, the structure of governance at the company is such that little can be done to change management. The terminal value can be computed with these inputs:

8 To compute this number, we look at the average reinvestment rate over the last five years at Tata Motors.

9 Stable Cost of Equity = Risk-Free Rate + Beta (Mature ERP) + Lambda (Country Risk Premium)
= 4% + 1.20 (6%) + 1.15 (4%) = 15.80%
Stable Cost of Capital = 15.80% (.4801) + 9.00% (1 – .3399) (.5199) = 10.67%

$$\text{Reinvestment Rate} = \frac{\text{Stable Growth Rate}}{\text{Stable ROC}} = \frac{4\%}{10.43\%} = 38.36\%$$

$$\text{Terminal Value} = \frac{\text{After-Tax Operating Income}_5\,(1 + g_{Stable})(1 - \text{Reinvestment Rate})}{(\text{Cost of Capital}_{\text{Stable}} - g_{\text{Stable}})}$$

$$= \frac{19{,}137(1.04)(1-.3836)}{(.1067-.04)} = \text{Rs } 183{,}809 \text{ million}$$

- **Firm and equity valuation**: To get to the firm value, we discount back the cash flows and the terminal value at the current cost of capital of 12.38%, as shown in Table 16.8.

Table 16.8 Present Value of Cash Flows for Tata Motors

Year	Year 1	Year 2	Year 3	Year 4	Year 5
FCFF	Rs 2,778	Rs 3,010	Rs 3,261	Rs 3,533	Rs 3,827
Terminal value					Rs 183,809
Present value (at 12.38%)	Rs 2,472	Rs 2,383	Rs 2,297	Rs 2,215	Rs 104,675
Value of operating assets	Rs 114,042				

To the value of the operating assets (Rs 114,042 million) we add the current cash balance (Rs 26,644 million) and the value of Tata Motors' cross-holdings in other Tata firms, estimated to be Rs 49,103 million.[10] Subtracting the estimated market value of debt outstanding (Rs 80,933 million) and dividing by the number of shares outstanding (449.82) results in a value per share of Rs 242:

$$\text{Value per Share} = \frac{114{,}042 + 26{,}644 + 49{,}103 - 80{,}933}{449.82} = \text{Rs } 242/\text{Share}$$

Although this is significantly higher than the stock price of Rs 166 per share, prevailing in March 2009, we have two concerns about making this judgment. The first is that a large portion of the stock's value comes from cross-holdings in other Tata companies. Although we have assigned a value of Rs 49,103 million to these holdings, we have not taken a close look at any of the companies from which this value is derived. The second concern is that although we have built some of the aspects of poor corporate governance into the value, by keeping the return on capital below the cost of capital in perpetuity and the debt ratio at the existing level, we remain exposed to other actions on the part of management that may destroy value further.

10 The value of the cross-holdings is set equal to its balance sheet figure. Optimally, we would have liked to value these cross-holdings independently, but there were too many holdings and insufficient information to do this effectively.

Valuing Gerdau Steel

As we noted earlier, we chose to value Gerdau Steel in U.S. dollars, partly because of the difficulties we faced in estimating risk-free rates and risk premiums in Brazilian reals (R$). We use the 2008 financial statements and exchange rates at the time of the statements to convert the cash flows in R$ to U.S. dollars:

- **Base year numbers**: In the 2008 financial year, Gerdau reported operating income of R$8,005 million, after depreciation of R$1,896 million and interest expenses of R$1,620 million. During the year, acquisitions and internal investments combined to create capital expenditures of R$6,818 million, and noncash working capital increased by R$1,083 million. Gerdau earned an after-tax return on capital of 18.68% based on a marginal tax rate (for Brazil) of 34%, start-of-the-year book values of equity of R$17,449 million, book value of debt of R$15,979 million, and a cash balance of R$5,139 million:

$$\text{Return on Capital} = \frac{8005\,(1-.34)}{(17449+15979-5139)} = .1868$$

$$\text{Reinvestment Rate} = \frac{(6818-1896+1083)}{8005(1-.34)} = 113.66\%$$

- **Forecast growth and cash flows**: We do not believe that either the return on capital or the reinvestment rate is sustainable in the long term. Consequently, we use a reinvestment rate of 60% and a return on capital of 16% to estimate the expected growth rate of 9.60%, in R$, for the next five years:

$$\text{Expected Growth Rate} = \text{Reinvestment Rate} * \text{Return on Capital} = .60 * .16 = .096$$

We use this expected growth rate to estimate expected cash flows for the next five years in R$, as shown in Table 16.9.

Table 16.9 Expected Free Cash Flows in Reals for Gerdau Steel

Year	Year 1	Year 2	Year 3	Year 4	Year 5
EBIT (1 – t)	R$5,790	R$6,346	R$6,956	R$7,623	R$8,355
– Reinvestment	R$3,474	R$3,808	R$4,173	R$4,574	R$5,013
FCFF	R$2,316	R$2,539	R$2,782	R$3,049	R$3,342

Again, the reinvestment each year is the consolidated value of net capital expenditures, acquisitions, and investments in working capital. It amounts to 60% of after-tax operating income each year.

- **Conversion to U.S. dollars**: To convert the cash flows in R$ to U.S. dollars, we start with the current exchange rate of R$2.252/$ but forecast exchange rates for future years based on expected inflation rates of 2% in U.S. dollars and 5% in BR. The resulting expected exchange rates and cash flows in U.S. dollars are reported in Table 16.10.

Table 16.10 Expected Free Cash Flows in U.S. Dollars for Gerdau Steel

Year	Year 1	Year 2	Year 3	Year 4	Year 5
FCFF (in R$)	R$2,316	R$2,539	R$2,782	R$3,049	R$3,342
Expected exchange rate	2.32	2.39	2.46	2.53	2.60
FCFF (in U.S. dollars)	R$999	R$1,064	R$1,133	R$1,206	R$1,284

The difference in expected inflation results in R$ depreciating in value, relative to the U.S. dollar, over the five-year period.

- **Stable growth**: In stable growth, we assume that Gerdau will grow 3% a year, in dollar terms, and that its return on capital in stable growth will converge on its cost of capital (also in dollar terms). To estimate the dollar cost of capital in stable growth, we assume that the stock will have a beta of 1.20 and that the country risk premium will decline to 3%. Using a debt ratio of 50% and a cost of debt of 8%, we estimate a cost of capital of 8.68%.[11] To estimate the terminal value, we first compute the after-tax operating income in dollar terms in year 5:

$$\$EBIT\ (1-t) = \frac{EBIT\ (1-t)\ in\ R\$}{R\$/\$_{Year 5}} = \frac{8{,}355}{2.60} = \$3{,}213$$

We then compute the reinvestment rate and terminal value:

$$\text{Reinvestment Rate} = \frac{\text{Stable Growth Rate}}{\text{Stable ROC}} = \frac{3\%}{8.68\%} = 34.57\%$$

$$\text{Terminal Value} = \frac{\text{After-Tax Operating Income}_5\ (1 + g_{Stable})(1 - \text{Reinvestment Rate})}{(\text{Cost of Capital}_{Stable} - g_{Stable})}$$

$$= \frac{\$3{,}213(1.03)(1-.3457)}{(.0868-.03)} = \$\ 38{,}096 \text{ million}$$

11 Cost of Equity in Stable Growth = 3% + 1.20 (6%) + 0.625 (3%) = 12.08%
Cost of Debt in Stable Growth = 8% (1 – .34) = 5.28%
Cost of Capital in Stable Growth = 12.08% (.50) + 5.28% (.50) = 8.68%

- **Firm and equity valuation**: To complete the analysis, we first discount the expected cash flows in U.S. dollars at the cost of capital of 10.79% (as shown in Table 16.11) that we estimated earlier for Gerdau (in dollar terms):

Table 16.11 Expected Cash Flows and Present Value

Year	Year 1	Year 2	Year 3	Year 4	Year 5
FCFF (in U.S. dollars)	R$999	R$1,064	R$1,133	R$1,206	R$1,284
Terminal value					R$38,096
Present value at 10.79%	$902	$867	$833	$800	$23,595
Value of operating assets	$26,996				

To get to firm value, we add in dollar value of the firm's cash holdings ($2,404 million) and subtract the dollar value of debt ($9.788 million), with the conversion at today's exchange rate. Since Gerdau has consolidated holdings, we subtract the estimated market value of the minority interest in these holdings of $2,599 million (in dollar terms) and then divide by the number of shares outstanding (1681.12 million) to arrive at a dollar value per share of $10.12:[12]

$$\text{Value per Share} = \frac{26{,}996 + 2{,}403 - 9.788 - 2{,}599}{449.82} = \text{R\$10.12/Share}$$

Converted at today's exchange rate of 2.252 reals per dollar, we arrive at an estimate of value of R$22.79 per share, making Gerdau significantly undervalued at the price of R$9.32 per share at which it was trading in March 2009.

Relative Valuation

When valuing companies on a relative basis in emerging markets, we face two problems. The first is that there may be very few comparable firms, especially if we define comparable to mean firms in the same business and in the same emerging market. The second problem is that there can be large differences in fundamentals—risk, cash flows, and growth—across the firms, even if we stay within the same market. This is especially true if we try to expand our sample to bring in companies from other markets. This section considers ways in which we can mitigate both problems.

12 Optimally, we would have liked to value the consolidated holdings and estimated the value of the minority interests. Since we were missing much of the information to be able to do this, we applied a price-to-book ratio of 1.20 (based on the price-to-book ratio of businesses that the cross-holdings were in) to the book value of the minority interests.

Emerging-Market Comparables

When valuing an Indian retail company, it seems logical that we should look at how the market is pricing other Indian retail companies. Similarly, when pricing an Argentine bank, logic would suggest that we should look at the multiples of earnings at which other Argentine banks trade. Following up, when valuing an emerging-market company, it does make sense to start with a narrow definition of comparable firms—other companies operating in the same business in the same market. However, three considerations should enter into this process:

- **Size of the sample**: In many of the smaller emerging markets, only a handful of companies will come through as comparable if we define this group to include firms in the same market and in the same business. As a general rule, relative valuation based on sample sizes of companies are precarious, simply because we are making judgments on limited data. We can use three techniques to increase sample size. In the first, we can look at other publicly traded companies that form part of the economic chain that binds this business together. Thus, we can use auto parts manufacturers and auto distributors as comparable firms when looking at automobile companies. In the second technique, we can expand the sample geographically to include firms in the same business in other emerging markets. Thus, we can consider all retail firms in Latin America as comparable firms when analyzing a Chilean retail firm. In the third technique, we stay within the same market and consider all firms in that market to be comparable, while using regressions to control for differences in risk, growth, and cash flows.
- **Differences across firms**: Even when we can include large numbers of firms in the comparison, big differences across these firms as far as risk and growth characteristics can make any comparison that does not control for them subject to error. When comparing the Chilean retail firm to other Latin American retail firms, we have to deal with the differences in risk across Latin America. In earlier chapters on valuing growth and distressed companies, we used statistical tools (regressions) to control for these differences. In the case of emerging-market companies, we will find more use for these same tools.
- **Liquidity/pricing issues**: In many emerging markets, only the top tier of stocks are liquid and widely traded. Smaller companies often are illiquid and closely held. If the stock prices at these companies reflect illiquidity and lack of diversification on the part of their owners/managers, we can get widely divergent answers when we compare PE ratios or EV/EBITDA multiples, depending on how we define our comparable firms. In fact, we should be controlling for differences in liquidity (using trading volume or the bid/ask spread as proxies) when making comparisons across firms.

Valuing Tata Motors: Indian Auto Firms

In March 2009, Tata Motors was trading at a price of Rs166 per share, representing a multiple of 6.2 of earnings per share in the most recent 12 months. To judge its relative value, we compare Tata Motors' PE ratio to the PE ratios of other large Indian automobile companies. The results are shown in Table 16.12.

Table 16.12 Indian Automobile Companies

Company Name	Market Capitalization (in Millions of Rupees)	PE	Beta	Turnover Ratio
Atlas Honda Ltd.	Rs 2,736	9.22	0.26	1.06%
Atul Auto Ltd.	Rs 137	9.25	1.30	17.09%
Bajaj Auto Ltd.	Rs 76,781	8.54	0.80	10.02%
Hero Honda Motors Ltd.	Rs 189,072	16.25	0.44	9.26%
Hindustan Motors Ltd.	Rs 1,800	3.94	1.22	47.30%
Indus Motor Co. Ltd.	Rs 3,317	5.01	0.40	38.80%
Maharashtra Scooters Ltd.	Rs 734	7.18	0.97	6.58%
Mahindra & Mahindra Ltd.	Rs 91,954	4.88	0.79	11.94%
Majestic Auto Ltd.	Rs 230	4.86	0.85	4.81%
Maruti Suzuki India Ltd.	Rs 195,230	9.09	0.56	19.73%
Pak Suzuki Motor Co. Ltd.	Rs 2,539	2.65	0.59	21.26%
Tata Motors	Rs 74,737	3.05	1.48	24.50%

The problems with running comparisons across these companies are clear when we look at the immense difference in market capitalization and liquidity (as measured by the turnover ratio) at these firms. In fact, most of the firms in this sample are very small, lightly traded companies. Only four companies represent true comparables to Tata Motors—Hero Honda, Mahindra & Mahindra, Bajaj Auto, and Maruti Suzuki. Of these companies, Hero Honda seems to be the outlier (with a PE of 16.25), but Tata Motors has the lowest PE in this group. The small size of the sample makes us reluctant to draw any conclusions.

To expand on the analysis, we ran a regression of PE ratios against fundamentals—beta, growth rate in earnings per share (g), and payout ratio—across all publicly traded Indian companies with data available on these items in January 2009.[13] The resulting regression can be summarized as follows:

$$PE = 4.91\ g - 8.63\ (Beta) + 74.41\ (Payout\ Ratio)\quad R^2 = 95.3\%$$
$$(1.77)\quad (4.40)\quad (57.4)$$

13 Because expected growth rates were unavailable for most firms in the sample, we used the historical growth rate in earnings per share over the last five years as the proxy for growth.

Plugging the values for Tata Motors (g = 10%, beta =1.32, payout ratio = 29%) into this regression, we get a predicted PE ratio of 5.48:

$$PE = 4.91\ (.10) - 8.63\ (1.32) + 74.41\ (.29) = 10.68$$

Since this is higher than the current PE of 3.05, this would make Tata Motors significantly undervalued (by more than 70%).

Developed-Market Comparables

When valuing emerging-market companies in some sectors, analysts have to expand their sample to include developed-market firms. This would be the case, for instance, if we were valuing Embraer, a Brazilian aerospace company; almost every other publicly traded company in this business is in a developed market. In other cases, analysts choose to use only developed-market companies, simply because they do not trust the prices or multiples they observe in emerging-market counterparts.

When we value an emerging-market company, using a sample of primarily developed-market companies, we must confront three issues:

- **Accounting standards**: The first issue relates to accounting differences between emerging and developed markets and the effect they have on the scaling variable—earnings per share, EBITDA, or book value. Comparing the accounting earnings of a Brazilian firm to those of a U.S. firm may not represent a fair comparison, because accounting standards vary across these two countries.
- **Risk differences**: Earlier in this chapter, we noted that the difference in country risk and the resulting country risk premiums can cause companies in the same business in emerging and developed markets to have very different discount rates (even in the same currency). The higher discount rates at emerging-market companies should lead them to trade at lower multiples of earnings, revenues, and book value than otherwise similar developed-market companies.
- **Macro differences**: To the extent that expected inflation and interest rates vary across markets, there can be significant differences in the multiples at which firms trade at markets. In general, we would expect companies to trade at much higher multiples of earnings in low-interest-rate environments than in high-interest-rate environments.

Therefore, to legitimately compare emerging-market companies to developed-market companies in the same business, we have to do the following:

- **Adjust the scaling variable to reflect accounting differences**: If the emerging-market company has a depositary receipt (ADR) listed in the U.S., the company has to restate its earnings using U.S. accounting standards, thus bringing it in line with the developed-market companies in the sample. If it does not have a developed-market listing, we have to attempt to make the numbers more comparable by restating the earnings of the emerging-market company to reflect at least the biggest differences in accounting
- **Control for country risk**: We can adjust for country risk in two ways. One is to bring country risk into the comparison explicitly using country ratings or default spreads as proxies for this risk. In effect, we can examine whether and how much of the differences

in PE ratios across companies can be explained by differences in country ratings or default spreads. Another method is to divide the overall sample of comparable firms into developed- and emerging-market subgroups and to examine what the market is charging as a discount for emerging-market risk. Thus, if the average PE ratio for developed-market chemical companies is 10.50 and the average PE ratio for emerging-market chemical companies is 7.00, the market discount for emerging-market companies is 33%.

- **Control for interest rates and inflation**: As we noted earlier in this chapter, differences in interest rates and inflation become an issue only when we use different currencies for different companies. Comparing the PE ratio for an Indian company, computed using Indian rupee market price and earnings, to the PE ratio for a U.S. company, where both numbers are stated in U.S. dollars, can be problematic. If the company has an ADR listed in the U.S., the problem resolves itself, since all the numbers are stated in U.S. dollar terms. If not, we have to explicitly adjust for differences across markets.

Valuing Gerdau Steel: Steel Companies Listed in the U.S.

Gerdau Steel has an ADR listed on the New York Stock Exchange. Table 16.13 compares the EV/EBITDA multiple for Gerdau to the multiples of EBITDA of other steel companies listed in the U.S.

Table 16.13 EV/EBITDA Multiples for Steel Companies in January 2009

Company Name	EV/EBITDA	ROC	Tax Rate	Debt/Capital
AK Steel Holding	0.83	69.33%	34.43%	40.91%
Schuff International, Inc.	1.08	51.45%	34.89%	33.55%
Shiloh Industries	1.38	14.55%	44.00%	63.73%
Mueller (Paul) Co.	1.53	42.08%	37.65%	6.95%
Carpenter Technology	1.80	31.66%	32.56%	26.87%
Universal Stainless & Alloy Products	1.97	20.31%	32.74%	4.28%
Ampco-Pittsburgh	2.19	33.30%	32.78%	5.86%
Castle (A.M.) & Co.	2.28	14.78%	40.23%	26.85%
Schnitzer Steel Industries "A"	2.29	24.46%	36.39%	16.15%
ArcelorMittal	2.37	19.20%	20.41%	48.23%
Posco ADR	2.43	19.43%	26.01%	22.69%

Company Name	EV/EBITDA	ROC	Tax Rate	Debt/Capital
Reliance Steel	2.72	16.08%	37.64%	43.81%
U.S. Steel Corp.	3.07	16.42%	19.87%	45.11%
Olympic Steel, Inc.	3.37	11.85%	37.61%	9.16%
Tenaris S.A.	3.53	25.87%	28.75%	25.69%
Canam Group, Inc.	3.54	13.71%	39.26%	17.85%
Commercial Metals	3.65	13.26%	30.96%	50.53%
Samuel Manu-Tech, Inc.	3.85	9.83%	25.47%	41.25%
General Steel Holdings, Inc.	3.85	29.79%	12.32%	50.13%
Steel Dynamics	4.07	14.71%	37.39%	51.14%
Nucor Corp.	4.29	33.23%	34.68%	14.22%
Moro Corp.	4.49	11.65%	40.98%	51.28%
Gerdau Ameristeel Corp.	4.60	10.87%	30.54%	51.60%
Worthington Industries	4.64	11.57%	26.51%	30.70%
Russel Metals, Inc.	4.72	14.63%	35.42%	14.49%
Cliffs Natural Resources	5.14	22.93%	22.09%	17.70%
Gibraltar Industries	5.17	6.88%	38.55%	61.29%
Northwest Pipe Co.	7.92	7.99%	36.33%	25.20%
Great Northern Iron Ore	8.40	245.00%	0.00%	0.00%
Omega Flex, Inc.	13.52	57.23%	37.94%	0.00%

The median EV/EBITDA across the sample is 3.6, indicating that Gerdau is expensive relative to the average steel company in the U.S.

This relative valuation has several problems that are difficult to overcome. One is that the comparable companies here include both U.S. companies and foreign steel company listings. To the extent that country risk can vary across the foreign listings, the multiples will be affected. The other problem is that not only are steel companies in the U.S. mature businesses with low growth potential, but they also generate widely divergent returns on capital on existing assets.

Conclusion

As corporations and investors globalize, more and more of the companies that we value are in emerging markets. In valuing these companies, we face four issues: working with local currencies that are unstable and where risk-free rates can be difficult to estimate, an overlay of country risk, an absence of key information required for valuation, and poor corporate governance. In many emerging-market company valuations, we see either an unwillingness to confront these issues (ignoring accounting differences and corporate governance issues) or the adoption of simplistic rules (such as adding a country default spread to the cost of equity of every company in a market to reflect country risk).

This chapter developed a systematic framework for valuing emerging-market companies. We began by choosing a currency to do the valuation in and staying consistent with that choice, both in how we estimate the risk-free rate and in how we estimate the other parameters in the valuation. We followed up by measuring a country risk premium that reflects the additional risk of investing in an emerging market. Then we determined how exposed a specific company in that market is to that country risk (through the use of a beta or lambda). We also argued for using a sector-based beta to estimate the cost of equity to avoid the skewed values that will emerge from a conventional regression against a narrow, local index. With missing information, we either look for an alternative measure for the data, based on existing financial statements, or use the link between growth and fundamentals to estimate the absent inputs. We make no explicit adjustment for poor corporate governance, because the company's cash flows and discount rates today should reflect not only the quality of management but also the chance that the management can be changed. Finally, if the threat of nationalization or terrorism overhangs the value, we can account for this likelihood by first estimating the probability of the event's (nationalization, terrorism) occurring and the effect on value (firm as well as equity value).

In the last part of the chapter, we examined the relative valuation of emerging-market companies. In the event that a large number of publicly traded companies exist in the sector and in the same market in which the company operates, our task may seem simple: Estimate the multiple of earnings, book value, or revenues that investors are paying for the company being analyzed, and compare this value to the multiples at which other companies trade in the same market. The problem we face is that these companies have significant differences on both valuation fundamentals and liquidity that can lead to variance in multiples. When comparing emerging-market companies to developed-market companies, we noted the need to control for differences in accounting standards and betas.

In closing, the principles for valuing emerging-market companies are the same as those for valuing developed-market companies, but the estimation challenges are more daunting. As long as we keep the estimation issues in perspective, we should still be able to value emerging-market companies using both intrinsic and relative valuation techniques.

17

The Octopus: Multibusiness Global Companies

If globalization has been a key theme of the last decade, it should come as no surprise that the companies that we are valuing reflect that globalization. This chapter focuses on a subset of companies that are diversified not only across countries, but also across businesses. These multibusiness firms, spread out geographically, are difficult to value because they represent multiple businesses, bundled and sold as a single package. This chapter examines these firms and considers the best ways to reflect the differences in risk, cash flow, and growth characteristics across the different businesses/regions that a company may operate in.

Multinationals

The multinational, multibusiness firm is not new to markets. At the risk of arousing the ire of historians, we would argue that the colonial powers of previous centuries—the British, French, and Dutch—were the very first multinational businesses. In fact, the British were open about their commercial interests, allowing the East India Company to treat entire countries as subsidiary businesses, from which it generated profits and value. For much of the twentieth century, publicly traded firms reflected this colonial history, with firms from developed markets in the U.S. and Europe expanding into emerging markets. In the last decade, though, the equation has been muddled by the emergence of multinational, emerging-market companies that operate in developed markets. This section examines the role that complex companies play in the economy; then it looks at some characteristics they share.

Role in the Economy

Many publicly traded firms in most markets are single-business companies that derive the bulk of their revenues and earnings from domestic operations. This chapter highlights firms that are in many businesses and multiple markets. Although they represent only a small percentage of the overall number of firms, they have an outsized influence. This is because they tend to be the largest firms (in terms of revenues, earnings, and market capitalization) in many markets.

The correlation between company size and operating in multiple businesses is not an accident. After all, most firms that stay in a single business reach a saturation point in that business sooner or later, and then they have to make a choice. They can accept the fact that they are now mature companies and settle into that status, or they can aspire for more growth, usually by entering new businesses and new markets. While not every large firm is a General Electric or Siemens, most large firms have expanded beyond their original markets (in terms of both products and geography). Finally, as economies mature, companies within an economy that want to maintain high growth have to look at foreign markets. Consequently, companies in Europe and North America have aggressively expanded into emerging markets in general and Asia in particular because the potential for economic growth is greatest in those markets.

Companies in emerging markets have historically not jumped on the bandwagon of global growth for two reasons. The first is that an Indian or Chinese company has significant domestic demand, sustaining growth, and hence has less reason to look at foreign markets. The other reason is that, at least until recently, the resources available to emerging-market companies were significantly more limited (because of both their size and their lack of access to capital markets) than those available to developed-market companies. In the last decade, as equity and debt markets have opened up in Asia and Latin America, we have seen more emerging-market companies emerge as global players. This chapter is directed just as much at those companies as it is at their developed-market counterparts.

Characteristics

This section focuses on the shared characteristics of multibusiness, multinational companies, with the intent of unveiling some of the challenges they create when we value them:

- **Many different countries/markets:** If the definition of a multinational firm is that it operates in many markets, some in developed economies and some in emerging economies, the consequences for valuation are straightforward. In the preceding chapter, we noted that cash flows in emerging markets are riskier and therefore should be discounted back at a higher rate than cash flows in developed markets. For a firm that operates in only one emerging market, this implies using a higher discount rate for the expected cash flows. For firms operating in multiple markets, the discount rates used to estimate value should be higher in some markets (riskier emerging markets) than in others.
- **Risk parameters available for the aggregate but not for the pieces:** If we treat a multinational company as a portfolio of companies in different businesses and markets, we should use a weighted average of the risk parameters for each of the businesses to estimate the risk for the consolidated company to derive its value. The first problem we often encounter is that getting these risk parameters is difficult, since the consolidated company (GE, Siemens) is the one that trades, not the individual pieces. The second problem is that as the weights on businesses/countries change over time, as they will if the growth rates are different, the weighted parameters have to be adjusted to reflect these changes.
- **Taxes reflect a mix of marginal tax rates and jurisdictions:** The marginal and effective tax rates of a multinational firm reflect the different tax rates it pays on its different income sources, rather than the marginal tax rate of the domestic market. To decide which tax rates to use in estimating cash flows and discount rates, we not only have to look at where the company generates its income, but also consider whether the firm can move its income into lower tax locales and the consequences for tax rates.

- **Large centralized costs**: As a company branches into multiple businesses and many countries, it is inevitable that more and more costs will become centralized. One reason for this shift is control, as the firm tries to keep tabs on risk and cash flows and to manage risk. The other reason is economies of scale, in which replicating the same function (accounting and marketing, for instance) in multiple divisions is avoided by having one company-wide accounting or marketing department. The problem with centralized costs is not just the magnitude of these expenses, but that these expenses then have to be allocated across different businesses and regions using some operating variable as a basis. For instance, centralized general and administrative (G&A) costs can be allotted to different divisions, based on revenues generated, and employee training and recruiting costs can be divided up based on the number of employees in each division. While both allocating mechanisms are reasonable, there is no way to check what the actual costs in each division are. Consequently, any earnings measures (EBITDA, operating income, or net income) computed at the divisional or regional level can be called into question.
- **Intracompany transactions**: One troublesome aspect of firms that operate in many regions and businesses is the prevalence of intracompany transactions. For instance, a company that is in both iron ore mining and steel production will have the steel business buying its raw materials from the iron ore business. The former will report the item as a cost, and the latter will report it as revenue, and the company overall will net out the two items. Two consequences can throw off valuations. The first is that although the company's net income may be unaffected by these transactions, the revenues and costs will be inflated by the volume of the trades. The second is that the prices at which these transactions are arranged may be artificial, driven more by tax and control considerations than the economics of the marketplace. After all, setting the price of iron ore too high (relative to what you would have paid in the market) will lower the income for the steel business but inflate the income for the mining business by exactly the same amount. An analyst who tries to value just the mining business, based on its reported profits, will overestimate its value. The problems become worse when the businesses provide financing for each other, as is the case when one division lends money to another. Again, the interest rates set on the loan may not reflect market rates, with the end result being a redistribution of profits across the businesses. The presence of a financing arm within the company will exacerbate this issue.
- **Complex holding structures**: While not all multibusiness, multinational companies have complex holding structures, the structure of these firms lends itself more readily to this problem. Multibusiness companies often set up quasi-independent or independent subsidiaries for some businesses and then have holdings in these subsidiaries that can be classified in a multitude of ways. For instance, Coca-Cola split off its bottling operations into an independent company in the 1980s and reduced its holding of that company to less than 50%, allowing it to escape consolidation. In valuing Coca-Cola, though, we have to also value Coca-Cola Bottling and attribute a proportion of that value to the parent company.

All these characteristics affect the information we use when valuing a company.

Valuation Issues

When companies enter multiple businesses and many markets, we will confront the issues in the inputs that we use to value a company. We can break down the problems we face by looking at each category of inputs—first in discounted cash flow (DCF) models, and then in relative valuation.

Intrinsic (DCF) Valuation

The intrinsic or discounted cash flow value of a multibusiness company is a function of the same variables that determine the value of any company—the cash flows from existing assets, the expected growth rate and value created by new assets, the risk in these assets (as captured by a discount rate), and the period of time before the firm becomes a stable-growth firm:

- **Existing assets:** Using aggregate earnings to value the existing assets at a complex firm creates three problems. The first is that the aggregate earnings come from investments in very different businesses in different parts of the world, with currencies, risk characteristics, and capital investments varying widely across these investments. Attaching one value to these earnings/cash flows becomes very difficult because of the differences in valuation fundamentals. Second, in cases where companies do break down earnings by business and region, they also have to provide additional details on capital expenditures and investments, which is often not forthcoming. Even the earnings, broken down by division, are affected by allocation judgments made about centralized costs. Figuring out which businesses get what benefits from these costs is close to impossible. Finally, the presence of intracompany transactions and financing can create a tangle of assets, earnings, and book value that can easily lead to some assets being double-counted and others being ignored.
- **Growth assets:** As with existing earnings, not only can growth rates vary widely across businesses and regions, but the quality of growth can also be very different. To make a good assessment of the value of growth, we need information on two key variables—reinvestment amounts (and rates) by business, and the returns generated on capital invested in each. While obtaining this information for a single-business company is difficult enough, it is doubly so in complex companies where capital expenditures are often aggregated at the company level and book values of capital at the divisions level are either unavailable (because divisional balance sheets are not released) or not trustworthy (because capital has been allocated to different businesses). Furthermore, as the firm expands at different rates in different businesses and regions, the weighted growth rate changes.
- **Discount rates:** If different businesses have different risk characteristics, and operating in different parts of the world exposes companies to varying country risk, assessing risk (and cost of capital) for a multibusiness, global company creates two problems. The first is getting measures of risk for each part of the business, rather than for the firm overall. The beta of GE as a company is not very useful in assessing the risk and value of its aircraft business. The second problem is coming up with the weights to attach to each part of the business to arrive at a risk measure for the entire firm. As the growth rates in different businesses change, the weights also shift. The other input into discount

rates is financial leverage, which is just as difficult to measure at the divisional level, both because the debt used by the company is not broken down by division and because the market value of equity is accessible only for the entire firm, not individual businesses. A final dilemma we face, with both discount rates and cash flows, is that a multinational company will generate cash flows in different currencies and often issue debt in multiple currencies. Since inflation rates, risk-free rates, and discount rates can vary by currency, we face a tangle of different estimates for the same input, depending on which currency we use for the estimates.

- **Terminal value**: When a firm is in multiple businesses, it is entirely likely that some of these businesses are already in stable growth, whereas others are in high growth. If we forecast cash flows until the entire firm is in stable growth, we will be forecasting cash flows for mature businesses for extended periods. There is one added complication. Firms can spin off, split off, or divest businesses that they feel are being undervalued by the market, radically altering the firm's makeup in stable growth.

In summary, although the categories of inputs don't change for multibusiness companies, we can face more estimation questions with each of them.

Relative Valuation

If the essence of relative valuation is finding other companies that look like your company, and comparing how your company is priced relative to these comparable firms, the problems with valuing a multibusiness company that operates in many different markets become obvious. Unless we find other companies that have a similar mix of business and regional operations, which is very unlikely, we will be unable to come up with comparable companies. Thus, there is no group of companies (or a single company) that we can call comparable when valuing firms like General Electric and Siemens.

Analysts who try to evade the problem by using comparable firms within each business line will be stymied by the absence of market values for individual divisions and information on commonly used scaling variables—earnings per share, operating income, and EBITDA. Assuming that we do find a way to allocate earnings to divisions and value them, a final problem that we have to deal with is the effect of consolidating multiple businesses into one company. Thus, we have to determine whether to add a premium to our estimated value (if we believe that the consolidation leads to cost savings or other synergies) or attach a discount (if we believe that the consolidation results in lower efficiency and a lack of corporate focus), and the magnitude of the adjustment.

The Dark Side of Valuation

Given these valuation issues, analysts who value companies that have spread across businesses and countries have adopted a combination of mechanisms. Some of them are acceptable compromises given the absence of information, and others can lead to valuation fiascos. This section focuses on the latter.

Discounted Cash Flow Valuation

In valuing multibusiness, multinational companies, we face two challenges. One is dealing with the different characteristics in terms of risk, cash flows, and growth that different businesses have. The other is analyzing how to deal with different risk exposures in different countries. In many cases, analysts choose to either assume that using consolidated numbers will take care of the problem or ignore the valuation issues.

Multicountry: Incorporation Versus Operations

In Chapter 16, we noted that the focus on *where a company is incorporated* often overwhelms any analysis of *where it does business.* In the case of an emerging-market company like Embraer, a Brazil-based company with significant revenues from developed markets, this leads to an overassessment of risk premiums and costs of equity and capital. With multinational companies, the bulk of which are based in the U.S. and Europe, we see the opposite problem. Since these companies are incorporated in developed markets, analysts see no need to adjust for country or political risk, even though these firms may generate large proportions of their revenues in emerging markets. In fact, the argument that analysts use to defend this practice is that these companies, like Nestlé and GE, are in so many different regions of the world that the country risk will be diversified away. As we noted in Chapter 16, this is wishful thinking, since emerging markets have become increasingly correlated with each other.

The net effect of the practice of not adjusting discount rates of multinational companies that are based in developed markets, for risk, while allowing them to claim credit for the growth and higher profits that they may be generating in emerging markets, is that we will consistently overvalue these firms. For much of the 1980s and 1990s, analysts rewarded Coca-Cola with a growth premium for its aggressive ventures into emerging markets. It was only when confronted by a crisis, as Coca-Cola was in the late 1990s by Russia's internal turmoil, that they considered the additional risk in the strategy.

Multibusiness: The Averaging Argument

It is not just risk that varies across businesses and markets. Every input into a valuation model, including profit margins, returns capital, and growth rates, also reflects the same characteristic. Some analysts stick with using the consolidated firm figures for each of these inputs, arguing that they reflect the weighted average of the multiple ventures that the firm is in. Technically, that is correct. However, the weights that are reflected in the current values reflect the current values of the different businesses and regions. To the extent that these weights may change over time, we should change the inputs as well.

To illustrate, consider a multinational firm that reports an aggregate profit margin of 8.4% across two businesses and developed/emerging markets. Table 17.1 reflects the weights that go into the computation.

Table 17.1 **Revenue and Margin Breakdown**

		Developed	Emerging	Company
Mining	Profit Margin	12%	16%	14%
	Revenues ($)	$150	$150	$300
Steel	Profit Margin	4%	8%	6%
	Revenues ($)	$450	$250	$700
Company	Profit Margin	6%	11%	8.40%
	Revenues ($)	$600	$400	$1,000

Now assume that the mining business is expanding at the rate of 20% a year, whereas the steel business is growing only 5% a year, and that much of the growth will come from emerging markets. Given the profit margins by business and region, we can anticipate an increase in profit margins over time for the consolidated company.

The point about averaging can be extended to every other input into the valuation. The regression beta for a conglomerate, even if accurate today, will reflect the current mix of businesses for the firm and will change over time if these businesses grow at different rates. Failing to adjust the estimates of these numbers for the future, for the shifting weights, will generate distortions in value.

Ignoring Centralized Costs and Intracompany Transactions

In the preceding section, we noted the issues related to the allocation of centralized costs and the effect of intracompany transactions on reported divisional earnings. Some analysts, when valuing multinational companies, choose to ignore both items, with predictable consequences. For instance, ignoring centralized costs while valuing divisions based on preallocation divisional earnings or revenues leads to significant overvaluation. Alternatively, using post-allocation earnings at the divisional level can lock into place any allocation errors that contaminated the earnings in the first place. Similarly, failing to adjust revenues for intracompany transactions will lead us to overestimate aggregate revenues for the consolidated company and potentially cash flows in the future. If the intracompany transactions move profits from one division of a firm to another, using divisional earnings will extend this problem into the forecasts of divisional earnings and value.

Cross-Holding Valuations

As we just noted, multinational, multibusiness companies often have complicated holding structures, with minority holdings in some subsidiaries and majority holdings in others. In many cases, the information that is provided on the subsidiaries, especially in the context of minority holdings, is too scanty to actually value the subsidiaries. However, these firms often report an estimated value for the holdings on the balance sheet, although that estimated value is not necessarily a market value or even a fair value. When faced with multiple minority holdings, analysts often use these book values as estimates of the intrinsic value of the holdings.

With majority holdings, analysts face a different problem. Since companies in most countries are required to fully consolidate the subsidiaries' numbers into their own—100% of the subsidiaries' operating earnings are counted as part of the parent company's earnings, and 100% of the subsidiaries' assets are recorded on the parent company's balance sheet—the portion of the subsidiary that does not belong to the parent company is recorded as a liability (minority interest). Here again, the standard practice is to report the book value of the minority interest, rather than the market value. In many discounted cash flow valuations, analysts again reduce the value of the consolidated company by the accounting estimate of minority interest, rather than by an estimate of the fair value.

In general, analysts valuing complex multibusiness companies face large information gaps. In many cases, they trust the managers of these companies to fill in the gaps. To the extent that managers can provide misleading or optimistic estimates, these numbers get fed into the final valuations.

Relative Valuation

The relative valuations of multibusiness, multinational companies fall into two groups—treating all multibusiness companies as comparable and sum-of-the-parts valuation:

- **Diversified companies sample**: In this approach, analysts lump together all multibusiness companies and compare them to each other, even though they may operate in widely different businesses and have very different weights. These valuations, in effect, assume that all diversified companies have similar cash flow, growth, and risk characteristics and thus should trade at similar multiples of earnings or book value.
- **Sum-of-the-parts valuation**: In this approach, which is more defensible, analysts break the company into individual businesses and then try to value each business based on the pricing of comparable firms in that business. For instance, they begin with the reported revenues or EBITDA for each business, apply the average multiple at which publicly traded companies in that business trade at to that number, and then treat the sum of the values as the value of the consolidated company. The first factor that is overlooked here are the regional differences in operations that may affect risk and growth and, through these, the multiples. Thus, a U.S. multinational that has an electronics business that derives all its revenues in China is still valued using comparable electronics companies in the U.S. The second factor that is missed or misvalued is the centralized cost. Valuing the individual businesses of a large conglomerate by applying multiples to revenues generated by each of the businesses and ignoring the billions of dollars in centralized costs will result in the unsurprising conclusion that the firm will be worth more broken up than as a consolidated entity.

In summary, there is no easy way to value these complex companies using multiples and comparables.

The Light Side of Valuation

In the light side of valuation, we explicitly allow for the challenges that we have listed for complex companies and try to make the best estimates we can, given the constraints of limited information.

Discounted Cash Flow Valuation

To value firms that operate in multiple businesses and many regions, we will stick with the standard framework of estimating cash flows and discount rates. But we will modify how we come up with the numbers along the way.

Step 1: Decide Whether to Use Aggregated or Disaggregated Numbers

The first step in the process is perhaps the most critical, because it determines how we approach the remaining steps. We have to decide, at the start of the process, whether we intend to value the company as a whole (aggregated) or value its individual businesses separately (disaggregated). In a world with no information or time constraints, the choice would be an easy one. A disaggregated valuation should yield a better estimate of value than an aggregated valuation. In practice, though, the choice will be complicated by the following factors:

- **Availability of information:** The most critical variable determining whether we value the company or individual businesses is access to information. To value a company on an intrinsic basis, we need access to all the operating details (revenues, operating income, and taxes), the financing breakdown (book values of debt, equity and cash holdings, and market values of the same), and reinvestment numbers (capital expenditures, working capital). Very few companies provide this level of detail on individual businesses. One compromise solution would be to substitute industry averages (for each business) where information is lacking. Thus, we can use industry average working capital ratios to determine expected investment in working capital for each business.
- **Differences across businesses/regions:** The payoff of breaking a company into component parts is greatest when big differences exist across the parts in terms of risk, growth, and profitability. Consider a multinational company that operates only in the U.S. and Western Europe and is in the specialty retailing and apparel businesses. Since there is very little difference in country risk across the regions that this firm operates in and only small differences in profitability and growth in its two businesses, not much would be gained by breaking it into its individual parts and valuing it.
- **Number of businesses/regions:** A pragmatic consideration also will determine whether or how much you want to disaggregate a company. If a firm operates in 30 different businesses and 60 countries, we could, in theory, value each of the company's 1,800 parts (30 businesses times 60 countries) separately, but this is clearly impractical. In such cases, we may very well value the whole company and hope that the laws of averaging work in our favor.

As a final point, an intermediate solution exists, in which we break the company into the parts that are most dissimilar from the rest of the company while aggregating the rest. With GE, for instance, we may value GE Capital separately from the rest of GE, because it has fundamental differences from the rest of the company.

Step 2: Make a Currency Choice

Companies that operate in many countries have cash flows in multiple currencies. In valuing these companies, we have to decide which currency to build our valuations around:

- **Aggregated valuation**: When valuing the company as an aggregated whole, we have no choice but to pick one currency as the base currency for estimation. You cannot have one discounted cash flow valuation with different currency choices underlying different estimates. Once that currency choice has been made, all the estimates (cash flows, growth rates, and discount rates) have to be consistent with that choice. Drawing on the earlier discussion of risk-free rates in different currencies, this requires us to build the same expected inflation rate into all our estimates. While it is often easiest to work with the currency in which the parent company reports its financial statements—U.S. dollars for GE and Coca-Cola, for instance—there are two reasons why it may sometimes make sense to switch to a different currency. The first is that the company has listings in many markets, and its financial reports in a different currency may be more comprehensive or easier to work with than the domestic currency reports. Nestlé, for instance, has listings and reports financial statements in the UK and U.S., where its stock is listed, in addition to its Swiss listing. It provides more information in its foreign listings than in its domestic listings. The second reason is that getting inputs in the domestic currency for the company may be difficult. Faced with the task of valuing a Russian multinational firm, we may very well find it easier to value the company in U.S. dollars than Russian rubles.
- **Business valuations**: With disaggregated valuation, you have more flexibility. You can value each of the businesses, especially if they are located in different regions of the world, in different currencies. Then you can convert the values at the last step (when you add them together), using the current exchange rates. Alternatively, you can stick with a single currency in all your valuations, estimating cash flows and discount rates in that currency. In theory, there should be no difference in the final value assessment, but given how difficult it is to work with multiple currencies in a single company valuation, we believe that the latter is less likely to be error-prone.

Ultimately, the points we made about currency choice in earlier chapters continue to apply. A firm's value should not be a function of our currency choices. If it is, it is because of inconsistencies in our forecasts.

Step 3: Estimate Risk Parameters, Allowing for the Multiple Businesses/Regions That the Firm Operates In

Assessing risk in a multinational company that operates in many different businesses is more difficult than it is for a company in a single business operating in a single market. However, the measurement approaches we developed in earlier chapters will stand us in good stead:

- **Aggregated valuation**: There are two keys to preserving valuation consistency in aggregated valuations. The first is being cognizant of the differences in risk across businesses and regions when computing the cost of capital for a company that operates in many businesses and multiple countries. The second key is weighting these different risk estimates appropriately, given the firm's exposure to each one, to estimate the risk parameters for the consolidated firm. Breaking down the inputs into the cost of capital, we can generate the following implications:

- **Betas**: In earlier chapters, we argued for the use of bottom-up betas—sector betas adjusted for financial leverage on the basis that they are more precise than regression betas. With multibusiness companies, we can add another benefit to using bottom-up betas: the beta for a multibusiness company is a weighted average of the betas of the different businesses it operates in. If we assume that estimating the sector betas, adjusted for financial leverage, follows the same process here that it did in earlier chapters, the one estimation challenge we face with companies that operate in many businesses is in coming up with the weights for the businesses. One simple solution is to base the weights on the revenues or earnings in each business, in effect assuming that a dollar in revenues in one business is worth exactly the same amount as revenues in a different business. An alternative is to estimate an approximate value for each business, perhaps based on revenues in that business and the multiple of revenues that other publicly traded companies in that business trade at.
- **Risk premiums**: In Chapter 7, we argued that risk premiums should be higher in emerging markets than in developed markets, and we presented ways in which we could estimate the additional premium. In Chapter 16, we looked at emerging-market companies and discussed how best to estimate their country risk premiums and risk exposures. With multinational companies, which derive some of their revenues from developed markets and some from emerging markets, we face the same estimation issues that we do with emerging-market companies. We have to adjust the discount rate for the exposure that multinationals have to emerging-market risk. The simplest adjustment to make is to compute equity risk premiums for every market that a firm operates in and to take a weighted average of these numbers, using revenues or operating income as the base. A more complex adjustment would require that we compute lambdas (just as we did for emerging-market companies in Chapter 16) for the multinational against each market and then use these lambdas, in conjunction with country risk premiums, to compute a firm's cost of equity.
- **Cost of debt**: A firm's cost of debt is computed by adding the default spread to the risk-free rate and adjusting for any tax benefits generated by interest expenses:

  Cost of Debt = (Risk-Free Rate + Default Spread) (1 – Tax Rate)

  With multinational firms, we must confront three issues. The first is that the risk-free rate to use in computing the cost of debt can vary across the different currencies in which the firms may actually borrow. This is a fairly simple problem to resolve, since the risk-free rate to use will be determined by the currency you chose to do the valuation in step 2. In other words, if you decide to do your valuation in U.S. dollars, the risk-free rate will be the U.S. Treasury bond rate, no matter what currency the actual borrowing is in. The second issue is the default spread, which can vary widely across the firm's different borrowings. If the multinational firm has a rating, we can use it to compute a default spread, which can then be added to the risk-free rate to compute the costs of debt. The final issue relates to the tax rate. While it is the marginal tax rate that should use the cost of debt, the reality is that the marginal tax rates can vary across the different countries that the firm operates in. One solution is to use the marginal tax rate of the country that the multinational is incorporated in. An even better alternative is to use the highest marginal tax rate, across the countries in which the company operates, arguing that interest expenses will be directed to that country to maximize tax benefits.

- **Debt ratios:** In keeping with our objective of valuing the consolidated firm, the debt ratio we use will be based on the aggregated debt for the entire firm and the market value of all its equity.

  Using the bottom-up beta (estimated by taking a weighted average of the business betas), the consolidated equity risk premium (reflecting the country risk exposure created by operations), the cost of debt premised on the company's overall default risk, and the debt ratio for the consolidated firm, we can obtain a cost of capital. That number, though, will change over time as the firm's mix of businesses shifts.

- **Disaggregated valuations:** When we value individual businesses, we obtain more freedom in making our estimates, since the discount rates we use can vary widely across the businesses. Again, using the inputs to the discount rate as a guide, we can develop the following principles:
  - **Betas:** When valuing individual businesses, we can use bottom-up betas for those businesses in estimating the costs of equity. Since we are valuing each business individually, there is no need to compute weighted averages of the betas. For a firm with revenues from steel, mining, and technology, we would use the sector betas from each of these businesses in computing the costs of equity for each business.
  - **Risk premiums:** If we break down businesses by region and estimate each part's value separately, we should be estimating the cost of equity for each region based on the country risk premium for that region. In effect, we will be valuing Coca-Cola's Russian operations using the country risk premium for Russia in the cost-of-equity computation and its Brazilian operations using the country risk premium for Brazil.
  - **Cost of debt:** While we will stick with the principle that the cost of debt is the sum of the risk-free rate and the default spread, the costs of debt that we estimate for the same company in different businesses/divisions can be different for two reasons. One is that we may be using different currencies to value different revenue streams; this can change the risk-free rate. The other reason is that we can estimate different default spreads for different parts of the same company, basing the spreads on the riskiness and the cash flows generated by each part.
  - **Debt ratios:** As with the other inputs into the cost of capital, the debt ratio can vary across different pieces of the same firm. In some companies, where individual divisions borrow money (rather than the consolidated firm), we may be able to estimate these debt ratios based on what comparable firms do. In most companies, where debt is consolidated at the company level, we have two choices. The first is to assume that the company uses the same mix of debt and equity across all businesses, and to use the debt ratio for the company as the mix for every business. The second is to use the industry average debt ratio for publicly traded firms in the same business and to use this debt ratio in computing costs of capital for individual businesses.

The bottom line is that the cost of capital we use to discount cash flows in an aggregated valuation represents the cost of capital for the consolidated firm, given the mix of businesses and markets it operates in. On the other hand, the cost of capital we use to discount cash flows in a disaggregated valuation represents the cost of capital of being in a specific business in a specific country.

Step 4: Estimate Future Cash Flows and Value

Having picked a currency to do the valuation in and a discount rate that is consistent with that currency choice, we have to estimate expected cash flows to value a business. As with the previous sections, the way in which we approach this part of the process is determined in large part by whether we are valuing the consolidated firm or its individual parts:

- **Aggregated valuation**: When we value a company on an aggregated basis, we have to estimate the cash flows for the entire firm when valuing the firm. If we stick with fundamentals for estimating growth in the cash flow, we will base the growth on the combined reinvestment rate and return on capital for the entire firm. Given that the firm operates in different businesses, with different reinvestment rates and returns on capital in each, we are using a weighted average of the business-specific values for these numbers. As with the beta computation, we have to keep an eye on how the weights shift over time and the implications for growth and cash flows.
- **Disaggregated valuation:** When valuing the individual parts of a larger company, we acquire more flexibility. Rather than use a weighted average of the numbers across the company, we can consider each business separately, assessing the reinvestment rate and return on capital for that business as the basis of forecasting growth and expected cash flows. With large conglomerates, we may very well find that some businesses generate value from growth by earning more than their cost of capital. Other businesses within that same company destroy value, because the returns on new investments are lower than the cost of capital.

In summary, as with the other inputs into valuation, disaggregated valuation requires more of us (in terms of inputs) but also delivers more in terms of information.

Step 5: Get from Firm Value to Equity Value per Share

To get from the value of operating assets to equity value per share, we have to add cash held by the firm, subtract debt outstanding, add in the value of nonoperating assets, if any, and then divide by the number of shares. While the steps in this process are identical for a multinational, multibusiness firm, there can be significant estimation questions at each stage of the process:

- **Add cash**: In general, we would argue that a dollar in cash should be valued at a dollar, and that no discounts and premiums should be attached to cash, at least in the context of an intrinsic valuation. There are two plausible scenarios in which cash may be discounted in value—in other words, in which a dollar in cash may be valued at less than a dollar by the market:
    - The first occurs when cash held by a firm is invested at a rate that is lower than the market rate, given the riskiness of the investment. While most firms in the U.S. can invest in government bills and bonds with ease today, the options are much more

limited for small businesses and in some markets outside the U.S. When this is the case, a large cash balance earning less than a fair rate of return can destroy value over time.

- The management is not trusted with the large cash balance because of its past track record on investments. While making a large investment in low-risk or riskless marketable securities by itself is value-neutral, a burgeoning cash balance can tempt managers to accept large investments or make acquisitions even if these investments earn substandard returns. In some cases, these actions may be taken to prevent the firm from becoming a takeover target.[1] To the extent that stockholders anticipate such substandard investments, the firm's current market value reflects the cash at a discounted level. The discount is likely to be largest at firms with few investment opportunities and poor management. There may be no discount at all in firms with significant investment opportunities and good management.

- **Subtract debt**: With multinational firms, the debt we net out to derive the value of equity depends in large part on what we are valuing. If we are valuing equity in the consolidated firm, we subtract the market value of total debt outstanding to estimate the value of equity. On the other hand, if we are valuing equity in individual businesses, we should subtract the debt imputed for these individual businesses.
- **Add in values of cross-holdings**: The way in which cross-holdings are valued depends on how the investment is categorized and the motive behind the investment. In general, an investment in the securities of another firm can be categorized as a minority passive investment, a minority active investment, or a majority active investment. The accounting rules vary depending on the categorization.

  Minority passive investments: If the securities or assets owned in another firm represent less than 20% of that firm's overall ownership, an investment is treated as a minority, passive investment. These investments have an acquisition value, which represents what the firm originally paid for the securities, and often a market value. Accounting principles require that these assets be subcategorized into one of three groups—investments that will be held to maturity, investments that are available for sale, and trading investments. The valuation principles vary for each:

  - For investments that will be held to maturity, the valuation is at historical cost or book value, and interest or dividends from this investment are shown in the income statement.
  - For investments that are available for sale, the valuation is at market value, but the unrealized gains or losses are shown as part of the equity in the balance sheet and not in the income statement. Thus, unrealized losses reduce the book value of the equity in the firm, and unrealized gains increase the book value of equity.
  - For trading investments, the valuation is at market value, and the unrealized gains and losses are shown in the income statement.

1 Firms with large cash balances are attractive targets, because the cash balance can be used to offset some of the cost of making the acquisition.

In general, firms have to report only the dividends that they receive from minority passive investments in their income statements. However, they are allowed an element of discretion in how they classify investments and, subsequently, in how they value these assets. This classification ensures that firms such as investment banks, whose assets are primarily securities held in other firms for purposes of trading, revalue the bulk of these assets at market levels each period. This is called marking to market. It provides one of the few instances in which market value trumps book value in accounting statements.

Minority active investments: If the securities or assets owned in another firm represent between 20% and 50% of the overall ownership of that firm, an investment is treated as a minority active investment. While these investments have an initial acquisition value, a proportional share (based on ownership proportion) of the net income and losses made by the firm in which the investment was made is used to adjust the acquisition cost. In addition, the dividends received from the investment reduce the acquisition cost. This approach to valuing investments is called the equity approach. The market value of these investments is not considered until the investment is liquidated. At that point, the gain or loss from the sale, relative to the adjusted acquisition cost, is shown as part of the earnings in that period.

Majority investments: If the securities or assets owned in another firm represent more than 50% of the overall ownership of that firm, an investment is treated as a majority active investment.[2] In this case, the investment is no longer shown as a financial investment but is instead replaced by the assets and liabilities of the firm in which the investment was made. This approach leads to a consolidation of the balance sheets of the two firms, where the assets and liabilities of the two firms are merged and presented as one balance sheet. The share of the firm that is owned by other investors is shown as a minority interest on the liability side of the balance sheet. A similar consolidation occurs in the firm's other financial statements as well, with the statement of cash flows reflecting the cumulated cash inflows and outflows of the combined firm. This is in contrast to the equity approach, used for minority active investments, in which only the dividends received on the investment are shown as a cash inflow in the cash flow statement. Here again, the market value of this investment is not considered until the ownership stake is liquidated. At that point, the difference between the market price and the net value of the equity stake in the firm is treated as a gain or loss for the period.

Given that the holdings in other firms can be accounted for in three different ways, how do you deal with each type of holding in valuation? The best way to incorporate each of them is to value the equity in each holding separately and estimate the value of the proportional holding. This would then be added to the value of the equity of the parent company. Thus, to value a firm with holdings in three other firms, you would value the equity in each of these firms, take the percentage share of the equity in each, and add it to the value of equity in the parent company. When income statements are consolidated, you would first need to strip the income, assets, and debt of the subsidiary from the parent company's financials before you perform any of the steps just discussed. If you do not do so, you will double-count the value of the subsidiary.

2 Firms have evaded the requirements of consolidation by keeping their share of ownership in other firms below 50%.

As a firm's holdings become more numerous, estimating the values of individual holdings becomes more onerous. In fact, the information needed to value the cross-holdings may be unavailable, leaving analysts with less-precise choices:

Market values of cross-holdings: If the holdings are publicly traded, substituting the market values of the holdings for estimated value is an alternative worth exploring. While you risk building into your valuation any mistakes the market might be making in valuing these holdings, this approach is more time-efficient, especially when a firm has dozens of cross-holdings in publicly traded firms.

Estimated market values: When a publicly traded firm has a cross-holding in a private company, there is no easily accessible market value for the private firm. Consequently, you might have to make your best estimate of how much this holding is worth, with the limited information you have available. A number of alternatives exist. One way to do this is to estimate the multiple of book value at which firms in the same business (as the private business in which you have holdings) typically trade at and apply this multiple to the book value of the holding in the private business. Assume, for instance, that you are trying to estimate the value of the holdings of a pharmaceutical firm in five privately held biotechnology firms, and that these holdings collectively have a book value of $50 million. If biotechnology firms typically trade at ten times book value, the estimated market value of these holdings would be $500 million. In fact, this approach can be generalized to estimate the value of complex holdings, where you lack the information to estimate the value for each holding or if too many such holdings exist. For example, you could be valuing a Japanese firm with dozens of cross-holdings. You could estimate a value for the cross-holdings by applying a multiple of book value to their cumulative book value. Note that using the accounting estimates of the holdings, which is the most commonly used approach in practice, should be a last resort, especially when the values of the cross-holdings are substantial.

Step 6: Decide Whether You Want to Adjust the Value of Equity for Other Factors

After we estimate the value of equity in a company with investments in multiple businesses and markets, we have to consider whether (and, if so, how) to adjust for other factors that may affect equity value. The first adjustment is for the complexity of multibusiness companies, which makes them more difficult to value, thus leading to a potential discount on estimated value. The second adjustment is a positive one. It reflects the likelihood that the multibusiness company will be split into individual companies, and the value increment that you expect to follow:

- **Complexity:** Conventional valuation models have generally ignored complexity on the simple premise that what we do not know about firms cannot hurt us in the aggregate because it can be diversified away. In other words, we trust the firm's managers to tell us the truth about what they earn, what they own, and what they owe. Why would they do this? If managers are long-term investors in the company, it is argued, they would not risk their long-term credibility and value for the sake of a short-term price gain (obtained by providing misleading information). While there might be information that is unavailable to investors about these invisible assets, the risk should be diversifiable and thus should not have an effect on value.[3] This view of the world is not irrational, but it does create two fundamental problems. First, managers can make substantial short-term profits by manipulating the numbers (and then exercising options and selling their stock). This may well overwhelm whatever concerns they have about long-term value and credibility. Second, even managers who are concerned about long-term value may delude themselves into believing their own forecasts, optimistic though they may be. It is not surprising, therefore, that firms become sloppy during periods of sustained economic growth. Secure in the notion that there will never be another recession (at least not in the near future), they adopt aggressive accounting practices that overstate earnings. Investors, lulled by the rewards they generate by investing in stocks during these periods, accept these practices with few questions. The downside of trusting managers is obvious. If managers are not trustworthy and firms manipulate earnings, investors who buy stock in complex companies are more likely to be confronted with negative surprises than positive ones. This is because managers who deliberately hide information from investors are more likely to hide bad news than good news. While these negative surprises can occur at any time, they are more likely to occur when overall economic growth slows (a recession!) and are often precipitated by a shock. We could do a conventional valuation of a firm, using unadjusted cash flows, growth rates, and discount rates, and then apply a discount to this value to reflect the complexity of its financial statements. But how would we quantify this complexity discount? We have two options:

- Apply a conglomerate discount: We could estimate the discount at which complex firms trade at in the marketplace, relative to simpler firms. In the last two decades, evidence has steadily mounted that markets discount the value of conglomerates, relative to single-business (or pure-play) firms. In a study in 1999, Villalonga compared the ratio of market value to replacement cost (Tobin's Q) for diversified firms and specialized firms and reported that the former traded at a discount of about 8% on the latter.[4] Similar results were reported in earlier studies.[5]
- Measure complexity directly, and estimate a discount based on complexity: A more sophisticated option is to use a complexity scoring system to measure the complexity of a firm's financial statements and to relate the complexity score to the size of the discount. Damodaran (2006) looks at different measures of complexity, ranging from the number of pages in the company's SEC filings to complexity scores that are computed from the information in financial statements, and suggests ways of adjusting value for complexity.[6]

3 This follows from the assumption that managers are being honest. If this is the case, the information that is unavailable to investors has an equal chance of being good news and bad news. Thus, for every complex company that uncovers information that reduces its value, there should be another complex company where the information that comes out increases value. In a diversified portfolio, these effects should average out to zero.

4 Villalonga, B., 1999, "Does diversification cause the diversification discount?," working paper, University of California, Los Angeles.

5 See Berger, Philip G., and Eli Ofek, 1995, "Diversification's effect on firm value," *Journal of Financial Economics*, 37, pp. 39–65; Lang, Larry H. P. and Rene M. Stulz, 1994, "Tobin's *q*, corporate diversification, and firm performance," *Journal of Political Economy*, 102, pp. 1248–1280; Wernerfelt, Birger and Cynthia A. Montgomery, 1988, "Tobin's *q* and the importance of focus in firm performance," *American Economic Review*, 78: pp. 246–250.

6 See Damodaran, A., 2006, *Damodaran on Valuation* (Second Edition), John Wiley and Sons.

- **Potential restructuring:** One question that overhangs every multibusiness company is whether the company would be worth more if it were broken into independent businesses. This, in fact, is the motivation behind the sum of the parts valuations we described earlier. To the extent that a firm will be worth more as separate parts, we may have to add a premium to the value to reflect the probability that the firm will be broken up and the value increment that will occur as a consequence.

Valuing United Technologies on an Aggregated Basis

United Technologies is a publicly traded company in the U.S. with business interests in aerospace, defense, construction, and technology. In 2008, the firm reported operating income of $7.625 billion on revenues of $58.68 billion, with the divisional breakdown shown in Table 17.2.

Table 17.2 Divisional Breakdown for United Technologies in 2008

Division	Business	Revenues	Operating Income
Carrier	Transportation	$14,944	$1,316
Pratt & Whitney	Defense	$12,965	$2,122
Otis	Construction	$12,949	$2,477
UTC Fire & Security	Security	$6,462	$542
Hamilton Sundstrand	Industrial products	$6,207	$1,099
Sikorsky	Aircraft	$5,368	$478
Intracompany eliminations		–$214	–$1
General corporate expenses		$0	–$408
Total		$58,681	$7,625

Of the total revenues, $214 million represents intracompany transactions and is netted out to prevent double counting. Centralized corporate costs amount to $408 million, which reduces operating income. Note that we have categorized each division into a different business: Carrier (refrigeration systems for trucks) into transportation, Pratt & Whitney (aircraft engines) into defense, Otis (elevators) into construction, UTC (fire and security systems) into security, Hamilton Sundstrand (whose products service a wide array of manufacturing firms) into industrial, and Sikorsky (helicopters) into aerospace. This classification has an element of subjectivity, because some of the divisions serve more than one business.

Since the most detailed financial reports filed by UT are in the U.S., we have decided to stick with U.S. dollars as the currency for the valuation; the U.S.

Treasury bond rate is the risk-free rate used. To estimate the unlevered beta for United Technology, we use a weighted average of the unlevered betas of the businesses that the firm operates in, using operating income as the basis for the weights, as shown in Table 17.3.

Table 17.3 Weighted Average Beta for United Technologies

Division	Business	Operating Income	Weight	Unlevered Beta
Carrier	Refrigeration systems	$1,316	16.38%	0.83
Pratt & Whitney	Defense	$2,122	26.41%	0.81
Otis	Construction	$2,477	30.83%	1.19
UTC Fire & Security	Security	$542	6.75%	0.65
Hamilton Sundstrand	Manufacturing	$1,099	13.68%	1.04
Sikorsky	Aircraft	$478	5.95%	1.17
Entire firm		$8,034	100%	0.9725

To estimate the equity beta for United Technologies, we lever this beta using the market value of equity and the estimated market value of debt (with lease commitments treated as debt) in March 2009 and a marginal tax rate of 38%:

Market Value of Equity = $41,904 million

Estimated Market Value of Debt (Including Leases)[7] = $12,919 million

Levered Beta[8] = 0.9725 (1 + (1 – .38) (11,476 / 41,904)) = 1.14

United Technologies also has extensive operations outside the U.S., with more than 50% of revenues coming from foreign sales. To estimate the equity risk premium to use in valuing United Technologies, we estimate a weighted average of equity risk premiums across operating locations in Table 17.4. We use mature market equity risk premiums of 6.00% in North America and Europe, a 7.80% equity risk premium for Asia Pacific, and 8.40% for revenues from other regions.[9]

7 Conventional debt accounts for $11,476 million; the present value of lease commitments accounts for the rest.

8 Since the unlevered betas were computed using only conventional debt, we use only the conventional debt in levering the beta.

9 Unfortunately, the revenue breakdown provided in UT's filings is not very informative. Thus, sales from the Asia Pacific region include sales not only from the emerging markets of Asia (such as India and China), but also from Japan and Australia. No breakdown is provided of other markets, which could include Latin America and Canada. The equity risk premiums for the Asia Pacific and other regions are estimated by averaging the country risk premiums of countries in each area, using the sizes of the economies as weights.

Table 17.4 Equity Risk Premium for United Technologies

	Revenues	Weight	Equity Risk Premium
United States	$28,234	48.11%	6.00%
Europe	$15,819	26.96%	6.00%
Asia Pacific	$8,212	13.99%	7.80%
Other	$6,416	10.93%	8.40%
Company	$58,681	100.00%	6.51%

Using the bottom-up (levered) beta of 1.14 estimated in the preceding section, the U.S. Treasury bond rate of 3% as the risk-free rate, and the weighted average equity risk premium of 6.51%, we estimate a cost of equity for the consolidated operations of 10.43%:

Cost of Equity = 3% + 1.14 (6.51%) = 10.43%

As a final component, we estimate a cost of debt for United Technology, using an estimated rating of AA for the company and a default spread of 1.75%, reflecting this rating. The resulting after-tax cost of debt is 2.95%:

After-Tax Cost of Debt = (Risk-Free Rate + Default Spread) (1 – Marginal Tax Rate)
= (3% + 1.75%) (1 – .38) = 2.95%

Weighting the costs of debt and equity by their market values generates a cost of capital of 8.68%:

Cost of Capital = 10.43% (41,904 / (41,904 + 12,919)) + 2.95% (12,914 / (41,904 + 12,919)) = 8.68%

Since we are valuing the firm on a consolidated basis, we estimate the growth rate in the aggregated cash flows, using the return on capital for the entire firm and the reinvestment rate in 2009, both of which we assume will be sustained for the next five years:[10]

10 When estimating the return on capital and reinvestment rate, we make two adjustments to the stated earnings and book capital numbers. The first is the capitalization of operating leases, which is treated as debt for book capital purposes. The second is the capitalization of R&D expenses for the firm, which increases the book value of equity and changes the values for both the operating income and capital expenditure numbers. We also include acquisitions of $1,448 million in 2009 as part of reinvestment, because it is a standard part of United Technologies' growth strategy; the firm has done acquisitions every year for the last four years.

$$\text{Return on Capital} = \frac{\text{After-Tax Operating Income}_t}{(\text{Book Value of Equity} + \text{Book Value of Debt} - \text{Cash})_{t-1}}$$

$$= \frac{\$5{,}253}{(26{,}736 + 10{,}591 - 2904)} = 15.26\%$$

$$\text{Reinvestment Rate} = \frac{\text{Capital Expenditure} - \text{Depreciation} + \text{Change in Noncash WC}}{\text{After-Tax Operating Income}}$$

$$= \frac{4939 - 2971 + 166}{5{,}253} = 40.62\%$$

$$\text{Expected Growth Rate} = \text{Reinvestment Rate} * \text{Return on Invested Capital}$$

$$= .4062 * .1526 = 6.20\%$$

We forecast operating income, using 6.20% as the expected growth rate, and estimate the reinvestment each year, based on the reinvestment rate of 40.62%, for the next five years, as shown in Table 17.5.

Table 17.5 Expected Free Cash Flow to the Firm (in Millions of Dollars) for United Technologies

Year	Year 1	Year 2	Year 3	Year 4	Year 5
EBIT (1 – t)	\$5,578	\$5,924	\$6,253	\$6,521	\$6,717
– Reinvestment	\$2,266	\$2,407	\$2,407	\$2,233	\$2,015
FCFF	\$3,312	\$3,517	\$3,846	\$4,288	\$4,702
PV at 8.68%	\$3,048	\$2,978	\$2,996	\$3,073	\$3,101

The present value of the cash flows is computed using the cost of capital of 8.68% that we estimated earlier. The aggregated present value of the cash flows is \$15,196 million.

As the final piece in this valuation, we assume that the firm will be in stable growth, growing at 3% a year in perpetuity, beyond year 5. We also assume that although the firm's cost of capital will remain unchanged at the current level (8.68%), its return on capital will decrease to 10%, reflecting its larger size and increased competition:

$$\text{Stable Period Reinvestment Rate} = \frac{g}{ROC} = \frac{.03}{.10} = .30 \text{ or } 30\%$$

$$\text{Terminal Value} = \frac{\text{After-Tax Operating Income}_5\ (1+g)\ (1-\text{Reinvestment Rate}_{\text{Stable}})}{(\text{Cost of Capital} - g_{\text{Stable}})}$$

$$= \frac{6{,}717\ (1.03)(1-.30)}{(.0868-.03)} = \$85{,}248 \text{ million}$$

Discounting this terminal value back to the present at the current cost of capital and adding it to the present value of expected cash flows generates a value for the operating assets of $71,410 million:

$$\text{Value of Operating Assets} = \text{PV of Cash Flows during High Growth} + \frac{\text{Terminal Value}_n}{(1+\text{Cost of Capital})^n}$$

$$= \$15{,}198 \text{ million} + \frac{\$\ 85{,}248 \text{ m}}{(1.0868)^5} = \$71{,}410 \text{ million}$$

United Technologies has no minority holdings in other firms, but it does report minority interests of $1,009 million on its balance sheet. Since we know that this represents a subsidiary in the technology business, where firms typically trade at 1.75 times book value, we estimate a market value for the minority interests:

$$\text{Minority Interests}_{\text{Market Value}} = \text{Minority Interests}_{\text{Book Value}} * \text{average P/BV for Sector}$$
$$= \$1{,}009 \text{ million} * 1.75 = \$1{,}766 \text{ million}$$

We subtract this value as well as the value of debt ($12,919), while adding the cash balance ($4,327 million) to estimate the value of equity:

$$\text{Value of Equity} = \text{Value of Operating Assets} + \text{Cash} - \text{Debt} - \text{Value of Minority Interests}$$
$$= \$71{,}410 + \$4{,}327 - \$12{,}919 - \$1{,}766 = \$61{,}062 \text{ million}$$

Subtracting the estimated value of equity options outstanding (51 million options, with an average strike price of $40.35, valued at $544 million) and dividing by the number of shares outstanding (942.29 million shares), we estimate a value per share of $64.22:

$$\text{Value per Share} = \frac{\text{Value of Equity} - \text{Value of Equity Options}}{\text{Primary Number of Shares}} = \frac{(61{,}062 - 544)}{942.29} = \$64.22$$

The stock was trading at $44.47 at the time of this analysis, making it significantly undervalued.

Valuing United Technologies on a Disaggregated Basis

To value United Technologies on a disaggregated basis, we extend our search for division-specific information to include other operating items. Table 17.6 reports the breakdown of total assets, capital invested, and depreciation across the firm.

Table 17.6 Business Breakdown for United Technologies

Division	Business	Revenues	Pre-Tax Operating Income	Capital Expenditures	Depreciation	Total Assets
Carrier	Refrigeration systems	$14,944	$1,316	$191	$194	$10,810
Pratt & Whitney	Defense	$12,965	$2,122	$412	$368	$9,650
Otis	Construction	$12,949	$2,477	$150	$203	$7,731
UTC Fire & Security	Security	$6,462	$542	$95	$238	$10,022
Hamilton Sundstrand	Manufacturing	$6,207	$1,099	$141	$178	$8,648
Sikorsky	Aircraft	$5,368	$478	$165	$62	$3,985

We face two problems in using this information. The first is that the information that is provided does not quite match up to the information we need to value these businesses. Thus, we prefer to see capital invested by division, rather than total assets, and total reinvestment, which would include acquisitions and working capital, rather than capital invested. The second problem is that some information we would like to have is unavailable. For instance, we would like to see the geographic breakdown of revenues within each division and the debt used by each—the former to estimate equity risk premiums and the latter to compute levered betas and costs of capital.

We first wrestle with the estimation of cost of capital by division, a process that requires a debt ratio by division and an after-tax cost of debt. Since there is no breakdown of debt by division, we consider three options:

- **Allocate the firm's total debt** ($12,919 million) across the divisions using the total assets as the basis for the allocation. We could then use either the company's cost of debt for all the divisions or attempt to estimate synthetic ratings and costs of debt for each division. Since we would still need to estimate the market value of equity in each division, we decide that this choice would create more problems than solutions—at least for this company.

- **Use the average market debt ratio of the publicly traded firms** in each business as the debt ratio for the division. Thus, Otis, being in the construction business, would have a higher debt-to-equity ratio than Hamilton Sundstrand, in the industrial products business. The residual problem of making this choice is that the debt across the divisions will not add up to the total debt outstanding for the company. While we could use an allocation mechanism based on the industry debt ratios, the differences in the industry-average debt-to-equity ratios is not large enough for the process to pay off.
- **Use the company's debt ratio as the debt ratio for all the divisions** and the company's cost of debt as the cost for each division. While this can lead to skewed estimates for companies that have businesses with very different debt capacity, United Technologies businesses are all capital-intensive and profitable. It seems reasonable that all the divisions will carry debt ratios similar to the overall company.

Since the geographic breakdown is not provided by division, we will assume that they are identical to the company's overall exposure, leading to an equity risk premium of 6.51% (estimated earlier) for all the divisions.

Table 17.7 summarizes our estimates of levered betas and the costs of equity and capital for the businesses. We assume that the debt ratios for all the divisions match the company's debt ratio of 23.33%.

Table 17.7 Levered Betas and Costs of Equity/Capital by Business

Division	Unlevered Beta	Debt/Equity Ratio	Levered Beta	Cost of Equity	After-Tax Cost of Debt	Debt to Capital	Cost of Capital
Carrier	0.83	30.44%	0.97	9.32%	2.95%	23.33%	7.84%
Pratt & Whitney	0.81	30.44%	0.95	9.17%	2.95%	23.33%	7.72%
Otis	1.19	30.44%	1.39	12.07%	2.95%	23.33%	9.94%
UTC Fire & Security	0.65	30.44%	0.76	7.95%	2.95%	23.33%	6.78%
Hamilton Sundstrand	1.04	30.44%	1.22	10.93%	2.95%	23.33%	9.06%
Sikorsky	1.17	30.44%	1.37	11.92%	2.95%	23.33%	9.82%

Based on our estimates, the costs of capital range from 6.78% for UTC Fire & Security to 9.94% for Otis.

We allocate the total capital invested in the firm ($28,287 million) across the businesses based on the total assets and the total reinvestment for the firm in 2009 ($2,134 million) based on the capital expenditures. We use these allocated numbers as our basis for computing the after-tax return on capital and reinvestment rates by division, as shown in Table 17.8.

Table 17.8 Return on Capital and Reinvestment Rates by Division for United Technologies

Division	Total Assets	Capital Invested	Capital Expenditures	Allocated Reinvestment	Operating Income After Taxes	Return on Capital	Reinvestment Rate
Carrier	$10,810	$6,014	$191	$353	$816	13.57%	43.28%
Pratt & Whitney	$9,650	$5,369	$412	$762	$1,316	24.51%	57.90%
Otis	$7,731	$4,301	$150	$277	$1,536	35.71%	18.06%
UTC Fire & Security	$10,022	$5,575	$95	$176	$336	6.03%	52.27%
Hamilton Sundstrand	$8,648	$4,811	$141	$261	$681	14.16%	38.26%
Sikorsky	$3,985	$2,217	$165	$305	$296	13.37%	102.95%

Return on Capital = Operating Income After Taxes / Capital Invested

Reinvestment Rate = Reinvestment / Operating Income After Taxes

To estimate the expected growth rate, we assume that these reinvestment rates and returns on capital can be maintained for the near term. The resulting expected growth rates are summarized in Table 17.9, with the judgments that we made about the growth that will occur in the future.

Table 17.9 Expected Growth Rates and Growth Pattern Choices

Division	Cost of Capital	Return on Capital	Reinvestment Rate	Expected Growth	Length of Growth Period	Stable Growth Rate	Stable ROC
Carrier	7.84%	13.57%	43.28%	5.87%	5	3%	7.84%
Pratt & Whitney	7.72%	24.51%	57.90%	14.19%	5	3%	12.00%
Otis	9.94%	35.71%	18.06%	6.45%	5	3%	14.00%

Table 17.9 continued

Division	Cost of Capital	Return on Capital	Reinvestment Rate	Expected Growth	Length of Growth Period	Stable Growth Rate	Stable ROC
UTC Fire & Security	6.78%	6.03%	52.27%	3.15%	0	3%	6.78%
Hamilton Sundstrand	9.06%	14.16%	38.26%	5.42%	5	3%	9.06%
Sikorsky	9.82%	13.37%	102.95%	13.76%	5	3%	9.82%

We have assumed that all the divisions, other than UTC Fire & Security, will be able to maintain their current returns on capital and reinvestment rates for the next five years. In stable growth, the growth rate will be 3% for all divisions, with returns on capital ***moving to the cost of capital for four of the divisions***, but staying above the cost of capital for the two divisions that have the highest current returns on capital (Pratt & Whitney and Otis). With UTC Fire and Security, we assume that the firm is already in stable growth, since its growth rate (3.15%) is close to the stable growth rate (3%), and that its return on capital will be equal to the cost of capital. Equipped with these expected growth rates and costs of capital, we first compute the expected free cash flows by division for the high-growth phase, as shown in Table 17.10.

Table 17.10 Expected Free Cash Flow and Present Value by Division

Business	EBIT (1 – t)	Expected Growth Rate	Reinvestment Rate	Year 1	Year 2	Year 3	Year 4	Year 5	Present Value
Carrier	\$816	5.87%	43.28%	\$490	\$519	\$549	\$581	\$616	\$2,190
Pratt & Whitney	\$1,316	14.19%	57.90%	\$632	\$722	\$825	\$942	\$1,075	\$3,310
Otis	\$1,536	6.45%	18.06%	\$1,340	\$1,426	\$1,518	\$1,616	\$1,720	\$5,717
UTC Fire & Security	\$336	3.15%	52.27%						\$0
Hamilton Sundstrand	\$681	5.42%	38.26%	\$443	\$467	\$493	\$520	\$548	\$1,902
Sikorsky	\$296	13.76%	102.95%	–\$10	–\$11	–\$13	–\$15	–\$17	–\$49

Note that UTC has no high-growth cash flows, since it is assumed to be in stable growth. We then estimate the value at the end of the high-growth phase for each firm, as shown in Table 17.11.

Table 17.11 Estimated Terminal Value by Division

Business	After-Tax Operating Income	Stable Growth Rate	Stable ROC	Stable Reinvestment Rate	Terminal Value
Carrier	$1,085	3%	7.84%	38.28%	$13,850
Pratt & Whitney	$2,554	3%	12.00%	25.00%	$40,593
Otis	$2,099	3%	14.00%	21.43%	$23,766
UTC Fire & Security	$336	3%	6.78%	44.22%	$4,953
Hamilton Sundstrand	$887	3%	9.06%	33.10%	$9,788
Sikorsky	$565	3%	9.82%	30.54%	$5,749

For UTC Fire & Security, the terminal value is the value of the operating assets today. For the other divisions, the expected cash flows for the next five years and the terminal value have to be discounted back at the costs of capital we estimated earlier. Table 17.12 summarizes the final estimates of value for operating assets by division.

Table 17.12 Estimated Operating Asset Value by Division

Business	Cost of Capital	PV of FCFF	PV of Terminal Value	Value of Operating Assets
Carrier	7.84%	$2,190	$9,498	$11,688
Pratt & Whitney	7.72%	$3,310	$27,989	$31,299
Otis	9.94%	$5,717	$14,798	$20,515
UTC Fire & Security	6.78%	$0	$4,953	$4,953
Hamilton Sundstrand	9.06%	$1,902	$6,343	$8,245
Sikorsky	9.82%	–$49	$3,598	$3,550
Sum				**$80,250**

Finally, we have to deal with general corporate expense of $408 million, reported by the firm in 2008, that reduces the firm's overall operating income. We assume that this expense, adjusted for taxes, will continue to grow at the stable growth rate of 3% in perpetuity. Using the firm's overall cost of capital of 8.68% as the discount rate, we estimate the present value of corporate expenses in perpetuity at $4.587 billion:

$$\text{Value of Corporate Expenses} = \frac{\text{Corporate Expenses}_{\text{Current}}(1-t)(1+g)}{(\text{Cost of Capital}_{\text{Company}} - g)}$$

$$= \frac{408(1-.38)(1.03)}{(.0868-.03)} = \$4{,}587 \text{ million}$$

Reducing the cumulative value of the operating assets from Table 17.12 ($80,250 million) by this amount ($4,587 million) generates a value for the firm's operating assets of $75,663 million. This is about 6% higher than the value we obtained for the operating assets in the preceding sidebar, where we valued United Technologies on an aggregated basis of $71,420 million.

Relative Valuation

There are two ways in which we can adapt relative valuation to the complex companies we have examined in this chapter. The first is to accept the reality that we will never find comparable firms, defined in terms of business mix. If we do that, we must either find firms that have similar cash flow, growth, and risk characteristics, or control for differences on those dimensions. The second method is an extension of the sum-of-the-parts relative valuation we described earlier, with more attention paid to adjusting for the characteristics of complex companies.

Extended Relative Valuation

In most relative valuations, analysts stay within a sector to make their valuation judgments. Thus, a software company is compared to other software companies, and a steel company to other steel companies. Implicitly, we are assuming that firms within a sector share enough risk, growth, and cash flow characteristics to be priced similarly. When a company operates in many different sectors or businesses, this type of relative valuation becomes much more difficult. However, there is no reason why we cannot expand our relative valuation sample to include firms that are dissimilar from the one we are valuing, as long as we control for differences in valuation fundamentals when we make our comparisons.

In practical terms, we can try to modify the multiples we use for fundamentals or use regressions that explicitly adjust for differences across companies. In January 2009, for instance, a regression of price-to-book ratios of the 100 largest market cap companies in the U.S., against return on equity, beta, and expected growth in earnings per share (over the next five years), yielded the following output:

$$\underset{(3.83)}{\text{P/BV} = 1.57} + \underset{(8.67)}{7.67 \text{ ROE}} + \underset{(5.63)}{8.91 \text{ Expected Growth in EPS}} - \underset{(5.22)}{1.64 \text{ beta}} \quad R^2 = 62\%$$

If we wanted to value GE, a company with almost no directly comparable firms, we would plug in the values of the independent variables for GE (ROE = 11%, beta = 1.05, expected growth = 7%) into this regression to get a predicted price-to-book value multiple for GE:

$$P/BV_{GE} = 1.57 + 7.67\ (.11) + 8.91\ (.07) - 1.64\ (1.05) = 1.32$$

At the time of this analysis, GE was trading at $11.12 per share and had a book value of equity per share of $9.93, resulting in a price-to-book ratio of 1.12. This makes it undervalued by about 20%.

Modified Sum-of-the-Parts Valuation

Earlier in this chapter, we described how some analysts value companies that operate in multiple businesses by applying multiples to the earnings or revenues generated by each business. While there are significant limitations in how they use this approach, it can be adapted effectively if we go through five steps:

1. **Estimate operating numbers by business and region.** The first step is to obtain the operating numbers by business or region. While many companies provide this breakdown in their financial statements at least for the key numbers, it is better to steer away from numbers that are distorted by allocation judgments that are often arbitrary or tax considerations. Thus, the revenues or EBITDA, reported by business, generally are a more reliable base for relative valuation than the net income broken down by business.

2. **Find comparable companies by business and region.** After we have broken down the operating numbers by business and region, we can revert to the conventional practices in relative valuation. We can look for publicly traded companies that operate only or primarily in each business and obtain their market values. If we are unable to find publicly traded firms in a specific business, we may have to consolidate the businesses until we do. For example, if we break GE into the 25 or 30 different businesses it operates in, some businesses may have no comparable firms. Dividing GE into five or six primary businesses will give us a better shot of finding comparable companies.

3. **Estimate relative value by business and region, controlling for differences in risk and growth.** In this part of the process, we decide on a multiple to use and compute the summary statistics for the comparable firms. Although we could just use the median or average multiple to estimate the value of each business, a sounder approach would be to adjust the number for fundamental differences between the firms and the business being valued. It is also worth noting that we can choose different multiples for different businesses within the same company. In valuing GE, for instance, we may decide to use the PE ratio to value GE Capital, since it is in the financial services business, and EV/EBITDA to value the aircraft engines business, because of its dependence on infrastructure investment.

4. **Estimate the consolidated value.** Once we have valued the pieces of the company separately, we have to aggregate the values. When doing so, though, we have to consider what the relative values are measuring. In the GE example in the preceding step, we obtain the value of the equity in GE Capital when we use the PE ratio to value it and the value of the operating assets in GE Aircraft when we use the EV/EBITDA as our valuation metric. The former is already an equity value, whereas we need to add cash and subtract debt from the latter to get to equity value. If we are using a mix of equity and enterprise value multiples, it is safest to estimate the equity value in each business and then aggregate the equity values. But that requires us to have a measure of the debt outstanding and cash holdings of each business.

5. **Check for loose ends.** After we have valued the consolidated company by adding together the values of the individual businesses, we need to run two final checks:
   - The first is for any unallocated costs (centralized G&A, for instance) that we have not incorporated into our valuation. This is the case if we use revenues or earnings prior to allocations to value individual businesses. We can adjust the consolidated value for these costs in one of two ways. The first is look at the costs as a proportion of after-tax operating income (for the entire firm) and to reduce the value by that same amount. Thus, if centralized costs amount to $2 billion on after-tax operating income of $20 billion, we would reduce the consolidated value by 10%. The second way is to apply a multiple to the consolidated costs themselves to arrive at a value. One simple way to derive this multiple is to look at the value we are estimating for the rest of the company and the multiple of operating income it represents.
   - The second adjustment is for cross-holdings, because how they are accounted for can distort the values we obtain from relative valuation. The adjustments we make for minority holdings mirror the ones we made to intrinsic value; we have to estimate the value of these holdings and add that value to the consolidated value. With majority holdings, the income reported by business is the consolidated income; we have to subtract the estimated value of minority interests. If it is just parent company income, we have to value the majority holdings separately and add them to the consolidated value.

Sum-of-the-Parts Relative Valuation of United Technologies

Previously we valued United Technologies using discounted cash flow models. To value the company on a relative valuation basis, we will begin with a breakdown of revenues, EBITDA, operating income, and capital invested by business, as shown in Table 17.13.

Table 17.13 Scaling Variables by Division

Division	Business	Revenues	EBITDA	Operating Income	Capital Invested
Carrier	Refrigeration systems	$14,944	$1,510	$1,316	$6,014
Pratt & Whitney	Defense	$12,965	$2,490	$2,122	$5,369
Otis	Construction	$12,949	$2,680	$2,477	$4,301
UTC Fire & Security	Security	$6,462	$780	$542	$5,575
Hamilton Sundstrand	Industrial products	$6,207	$1,277	$1,099	$4,811

Division	Business	Revenues	EBITDA	Operating Income	Capital Invested
Sikorsky	Aircraft	$5,368	$540	$478	$2,217
Totals		**$58,895**	**$9,277**	**$8,034**	**$28,287**

Thus, our choices on multiples are narrowed to one of these four variables, with enterprise value (rather than equity value) being estimated. To decide which multiple (EV/revenues, EV/EBITDA, EV/EBIT, or EV/capital) to use in the valuation, we look at the publicly traded companies within each business and try to explain differences across companies (within each business) using all four multiples. We then choose the multiple that has the most significant explanatory power (the highest R-squared on the sector regression) for each business. Table 17.14 summarizes the multiple used by business, and the regression equation that generates the statistical significance.

Table 17.14 Choosing a Multiple for a Business

Business	Best Multiple	Regression	R^2
Refrigeration systems	EV/EBITDA	EV/EBITDA = 5.35 – 3.55 Tax Rate + 14.17 ROC	42%
Defense	EV/revenues	EV/Revenues = 0.85 + 7.32 Pre-Tax Operating Margin	47%
Construction	EV/EBITDA	EV/EBITDA = 3.17 – 2.87 Tax Rate + 14.66 ROC	36%
Security	EV/capital	EV/Capital = 0.55 + 8.22 ROC	55%
Industrial products	EV/revenues	EV/Revenues = 0.51 + 6.13 Pre-Tax Operating Margin	48%
Aircraft	EV/capital	EV/Capital = 0.65 + 6.98 ROC	40%

Finally, we use the multiple chosen in each business, in conjunction with the sector regression, to estimate a value for each of United Technologies' different businesses, as shown in Table 17.15.

Table 17.15 Estimated Relative Value by Business

Division	Scaling Variable	Current Value for Scaling Variable	ROC	Operating Margin	Tax Rate	Predicted Multiple	Estimated Value
Carrier	EBITDA	$1,510	13.57%	8.81%	38%	5.35 – 3.55 (.38) + 14.17 (.1357) = 5.92	$8,944.47
Pratt & Whitney	Revenues	$12,965	24.51%	16.37%	38%	0.85 + 7.32 (.1637) =2.05	$26,553.29
Otis	EBITDA	$2,680	35.71%	19.13%	38%	3.17 – 2.87 (.38) + 14.66 (.3571) = 7.31	$19,601.70
UTC Fire & Security	Capital	$5,575	6.03%	8.39%	38%	0.55 + 8.22 (.0603) = 1.05	$5,828.76
Hamilton Sundstrand	Revenues	$6,207	14.16%	17.71%	38%	0.51 + 6.13 (.1771) = 1.59	$9,902.44
Sikorsky	Capital	$2,217	13.37%	8.90%	38%	0.65 + 6.98 (.1337) = 1.58	$3,509.61
							$74,230.37

As with the disaggregated discounted cash flow valuation, we have to deal with corporate expenses of $408 million, and we have two choices. One is to use a discounted cash flow approach to estimate the value; this yielded $4,587 million. The other is to stay within a relative valuation framework and apply a multiple to this expense. In fact, the value ($74,230) that we have estimated for the operating divisions of UT in Table 17.15 is about 9.25 times the cumulated operating income ($8,034 million) across the divisions. Applying this multiple to the corporate expenses results in a capitalized value of about $3,775 million. When subtracted from the overall value, this yields a value for the operating assets of $70,565 million, a little lower than the values we estimated using the intrinsic value approaches. Note that the rest of the adjustments (adding cash, subtracting debt and minority interests, and adjusting for options outstanding) still have to be made to derive equity value per share.

Conclusion

Companies that spread their tentacles across multiple businesses and many parts of the globe are difficult to value, because their cash flows from each business or region can have very different risk and growth characteristics. This chapter looked at two ways we can approach the valuation of these. The first is to value the company as a whole, using the weighted averages of risk parameters to estimate discount rates, which we then use to discount consolidated cash flows for the firm. The dangers here are that the weights will change over time, and as they do, so will the firm's fundamentals. The second way is to value the cash flow streams separately, using different risk measures and growth rates for each stream. Thus, emerging-market and risky business cash flows will be discounted at higher rates than developed-market and safer business cash flows. The aggregated value of the different businesses should yield a better estimate of the overall company's value.

When we use relative valuation to value these companies, we run into the same valuation issues. Again, we can try to value the consolidated firm, but finding companies that are similar in business mix is almost impossible. For that reason, it makes sense to expand our definition of comparable firms to include firms that may not be similar to the multibusiness firm that we are valuing, and to control for differences in valuation fundamentals—risk, cash flow, and growth. Alternatively, we can try to find comparable firms within each business and then use the information in how the market is pricing these companies to value the pieces that make up the larger firm.

No matter what approach we use, we will be faced with more complexity and information gaps with multibusiness companies than with single-business, independent companies. We have to determine whether this complexity exposes us to more risk and, if so, how we will incorporate that concern into value.

18

Going Over to the Light: Vanquishing the Dark Side

Throughout this book, we have emphasized the importance of first principles in valuation and how they should guide us when we're faced with estimation questions and issues. The dark side of valuation, as we have described it, takes different forms with different types of firms. The remedies we offer also vary with each type. This chapter pulls together some of the core ideas that allow us to combat the pull of the dark side. In the process, we will quickly review the foundations of what we would like to portray as the enlightened side of valuation.

Enlightening Propositions

When confronted with uncertainty or missing information, we are tempted to adopt loosely backed rules of thumb and make inconsistent assumptions about growth, risk, and cash flows. The following sections outline a few propositions that can guide us in making better judgments and estimates, and result in better valuations.

Proposition 1: Be Steadfast on Principles, Open to New Tools, and Flexible on Estimates

A principle is a core idea, a tool is what you use to put that idea into practice, and an estimate is what emerges from that tool. There are a few basic principles in valuation that we should never compromise on, no matter what the counterarguments are. They include the following: (a) that an asset derives it value from its capacity to generate cash flows in the future, (b) that risk affects value, (c) that growth has to be earned (not endowed), and (d) that the laws of demand and supply cannot be repealed. An analyst who argues that firms can grow forever without reinvesting is violating a first principle.

The notion that the value of an asset should be a function of its risk is a first principle, but the capital asset pricing model (CAPM) is a tool for estimating risk. The regression beta we obtain is an estimate of that risk. We will not be swayed in our belief that an asset's value should be determined by its risk. But we should be willing to adapt, modify, or even abandon the CAPM if the data suggests that we should. As for the beta, we should use whichever approach gives us the best estimate, and that approach can vary across firms. In summary, then, we will remain steadfast in our belief that risk should affect value and be open to new developments when it comes to models for estimating that risk. Furthermore, we will always be on the lookout for better and more consistent estimates of beta or other risk parameters.

Proposition 2: Pay Heed to Markets, But Don't Let Them Determine Your Valuations

Many of the companies that we are called on to value are traded in financial markets and have market prices. Without making any judgments about markets or their efficiency, we believe that there is valuable information in how the market is pricing assets. In fact, our estimates of risk-free rates in Chapter 6 and equity risk premiums in Chapter 7 came from financial markets—the pricing of Treasury bonds for the first, and the level of equity indices for the latter. When valuing a company, we should pay attention to the market price for two reasons:

- The information we extract from markets on implied growth rates, risk, and cash flows can be used to improve our valuations.
- Ultimately, we make money not from our estimates of intrinsic values, but from the market prices moving to those intrinsic values. Thus, we need to understand why market prices deviate from value and how they will adjust over time.

At the same time, paying too much attention to markets (and prices) can lead to paralysis, since there is always an alternative set of assumptions under which the market price is justified. In other words, if we start by assuming that the market is always right, we will end up confirming that assumption in our valuations.

We face a balancing act when we use market inputs for some numbers (risk-free rates, equity risk premium, market weights for debt and equity in the cost of capital) and argue that the market is wrong on other dimensions. To derive reasonable values for companies, we have to decide early on in a valuation which inputs we will accept market inputs on and for which ones we will contest the market consensus. In Chapters 6 and 7, we argued that when valuing individual companies, we should accept the market consensus on risk-free rates and equity risk premiums and focus our attention or estimating the company's earnings and cash flows. In Chapter 13, when valuing an oil company, we made a case for using market-consensus prices for oil prices (obtained from either the spot market or the forward and futures markets). We also limited our valuation to how much oil the company would produce and its cost structure.

As a general rule, the areas where you choose to accept market wisdom and the points at which you deviate depend on two key variables. The first is in *the competitive advantages you see yourself having as an analyst* and where you think these advantages will generate the biggest payoff. If your edge is in forecasting macroeconomic movements and oil prices, you will replace the market prices for oil with your own estimates and leverage your edge to generate better valuations. On the other hand, if your biggest strength is in assessing a company's internal strengths, you should not be expending resources estimating macro parameters. The second factor is your *job description.* If your job is to assess the value of individual companies, not to assess the overall market or commodity prices, you will be doing yourself and your clients a disservice by letting your views on macroeconomic variables seep into your company valuations.

Proposition 3: Risk Matters

It is true that considerable resources have been invested in both academia and practice in coming up with models to assess risk and derive expected returns. It is also true that these models often make assumptions about the real world that do not withstand close scrutiny. In the capital asset pricing model, for instance, we assume no transaction costs and private information to derive the relationship between expected returns and betas. Analysts, looking at these models, find themselves disagreeing with the assumptions. That is perfectly understandable, but jumping from that disagreement to a conclusion that risk does not matter in value is not. Since risk assessment and measures are often at the heart of the dark side of valuation, the following list summarizes some of the ideas about risk that we have discussed in prior chapters:

- **Risk affects value**, no matter which approach you use to derive that value. In discounted cash flow models, the risk is manifested either in the discount rate or in a risk-adjusted cash flow (which is more than just an expected return). In relative valuation, firms that are riskier should trade at lower multiples of earnings, revenues, and book value than firms that are safer. While higher risk usually translates into lower value, there is a special case of assets in which higher risk can increase value. These assets have limited downside and very large upside, thus taking on the characteristics of options. We considered varied examples in earlier chapters, from young high-growth companies with proprietary technologies in Chapter 9, to equity in deeply levered, distressed companies in Chapter 12, to undeveloped oil reserves in Chapter 13.
- **Not all risk is equal**: If there is one lesson we should take away from the last few decades of examining risk, it is that all risks are not equal. Some risks affect only one firm or a few firms, whereas other risks have consequences for a wider subset of firms and sometimes for the overall market. When assessing risk for valuation, it is therefore imperative that we first identify the marginal investors (active investors with large stockholdings) in a firm and look at risk through their eyes. If the marginal investor is diversified, the only risks that should affect value are the market or macro risks that cannot be diversified away. In contrast, though, if the marginal investor is undiversified or only partially diversified, we should look at a much broader set of risks, including firm-specific risks. In Chapter 9, this was the insight we used to derive total betas and costs of equity for entrepreneurs (who tend not to be diversified) and venture capitalists (who are only partially diversified).
- **Continuous versus discrete risk**: Risk can be divided into two categories. Continuous risk affects cash flows and value continuously over time. Examples are interest rate risk and exchange rate risk. Discrete or discontinuous risk may lie dormant for long periods but affect value significantly when it occurs. The risk of default and nationalization are examples. We argued that continuous risk is best captured in discount rates, whereas discrete risk is more easily measured by assessing both the probability and consequences of the event occurring. We used the latter technique to adjust the values of young, growth companies and distressed companies for survival risk, and emerging-market companies for nationalization risk.

As we build risk into valuation models, it is also important that we adopt the following practices:

- **Isolate the risk effects**: Rather than let risk pervade all the inputs into a valuation, the effects of risk should be in one or two variables. Thus, the effect of emerging-market risk is captured in the country risk premium but does not affect risk-free rates, betas, or cash flows. There are two reasons why this is a good practice. The first is that it prevents the double or triple counting of risk. The second is that it allows for more transparency.

Thus, those who use the valuation can assess the risk adjustment made and decide whether they agree with it. If they disagree, it is relatively simple to make the change and reestimate value.

- **Be consistent**: When valuing firms, especially growth firms or firms in trouble, we have to recognize that the firm's risk profile will change over time and adjust the risk parameters accordingly. With growth firms, for instance, the high discount rates we use in the early years (reflecting the risk in those years) have to come down as growth declines. In almost all the valuations we have presented in this book, the betas and discount rates we use for the terminal value reflect this judgment.

As investors, we can invest in bonds, assets, or stocks, and in domestic or foreign markets. Therefore, we need to use the same rules when assessing expected returns across asset classes and markets.

Proposition 4: Growth Is Not Free and Does Not Always Add Value

If there is a theme to our discussions of growth across the chapters, it is that growth is not free. Ultimately, the expected growth in a company's earnings and cash flows must come from either new investments or improved efficiency. The latter is finite growth—there is a limit to how efficient you can become as a firm—whereas new investment growth can be for the long term (and potentially forever).

It is also critical to remember that growth by itself is not always a plus for a company, since the value added by growth is a function of the quality of the investments that generated that growth. That is why we have focused so intensely on excess returns, estimated by comparing the return on capital to the cost of capital, or the return on equity to the cost of equity, in our assessments of growth. A firm that grows by investing in new assets that generate a return on capital equal to its cost of capital will become larger over time, but it will not add value for its investors. A firm that grows by investing in poor investments—that is, the return on capital (or equity) is less than the cost of capital (or equity)—will become less valuable over time, even as it grows. In fact, a key test of managers is whether they can generate high excess returns while reinvesting significant amounts into the business.

In the context of relative valuation, we may not be directly focused on excess returns, but we should pay attention to them. Thus, if two companies are expected to deliver the same expected growth in earnings in the future, the company that has the higher excess returns accompanying this growth should be valued more highly.

Proposition 5: All Good Things Come to an End

In addition to looking at the value added or destroyed by growth, we often have to make estimates of future growth rates for companies. In making this assessment, we must pay attention to two key variables. The first is the *scaling effect*. As companies get bigger, it becomes more and more difficult for them to keep delivering the excess returns and growth rates they did in the past. Thus, it is almost a certainty that a firm that has grown 100% a year for the last three years will grow at a slower rate in the next three years. With the young growth companies discussed in Chapter 9, we reflected this reality by lowering expected growth rates in revenues and earnings as we move through time. The second factor is *competition*. When firms are successful, they attract attention, which in turn leads to imitation and increased competition. While firms may be successful at keeping this competition at bay for extended periods (using legal and other tools), the new competitors will inevitably chip away at profitability and growth.

One way we reflected the inevitability of declining growth is by assuming that all firms, no matter how highly regarded they might be now, eventually will become stable-growth firms. (And, at that point, we estimate a terminal value.) We captured the effects of competition over time by pushing the margins of individual firms to the industry average and the returns on capital (or equity) toward the cost of equity (or capital).

Proposition 6: Watch Out for Truncation Risk

In conventional discounted cash flow valuation, we value firms as going concerns, with cash flows continuing into perpetuity. While this may not be an unreasonable assumption for some firms, the reality is that most firms do not make it to this stable-growth phase. Many young firms run out of cash and have to shut down, some mature firms become the targets of acquirers, and most distressed firms end up defaulting on debt and going out of business. The optimism that underlies discounted cash flow valuation can lead us to overestimate the values of firms, where the risk of not making it (truncation risk) is high.

In Chapters 9–12, we argued that the risk of truncation is greatest for firms at either end of the life cycle—very young growth companies and declining or distressed companies. With these firms, we adopt a two-step approach to valuation. In the first, we assume that the firms will not only survive but also become profitable and healthy over time, and we value them on that basis. In the second step, we estimate the likelihood that they will not survive and the values for the firm and equity in the event of failure. Our final estimate of value is a weighted average of the two numbers.

Proposition 7: Look at the Past, But Think About the Future

One of the conundrums we face in valuation is that although almost all the data we have available to us is about the past, reflecting the company's history (past financial statements, betas), the sector (industry average margins and returns on capital), and macroeconomic variables (interest rates, exchange rates, stock returns), all the forecasts we have to make are for the future. While we cannot manufacture data for the future, we can follow some simple rules to minimize the damage:

- **Use historical data, but do not be bound by it**: One of the key components in valuing companies well is recognizing when to use past data and when to look at alternatives. Thus, for a profitable company with little volatility in year-to-year numbers, there is no harm in building off last year's numbers when valuing the company. For the cyclical and commodity companies we valued in Chapter 13, this base-year fixation can lead to valuations that are too high (or low) if the most recent year represents the peak (or bottom) of the cycle. Consequently, we normalized earnings for these companies using the information in the company's own history as well as in the commodity price cycle.

- **Trust in mean reversion, but watch out for structural breaks and changes:** Whenever we use historical data to make forecasts, we are assuming that mean reversion exists. In other words, both macroeconomic numbers, such as inflation and interest rates, and company-specific information, such as margins and reinvestment rates, revert to historic norms. While mean reversion has strong empirical support, two dangers are associated with assuming that it will happen. The first is that there can sometimes be significant breaks in history, where the circumstances change so much that the numbers are unlikely to revert for a very long period to past averages. This was the case, for instance, in the U.S. in the 1970s, when inflation increased and pushed up interest rates and commodity prices for almost a decade. The second danger is that there is no consensus on what exactly the historical norm is for most variables. Different analysts can look at the same data and come to very different judgments about what constitutes normalcy.
- **Use forward estimates as alternatives or checks:** With a few variables, we may be able to get forward-looking estimates that can be used either directly in valuation or to check the historical data. With equity risk premiums in Chapter 7, for instance, the implied equity risk premium we estimated, based on the current level of the equity index and the expected future cash flows, offers an alternative to historical risk premiums. With oil prices, futures and forward markets provide estimates that can be used to value companies, rather than past data. We can either replace the historical estimates with these forward-looking numbers or adjust them to reflect differences.

In closing, we should be glad that valuation is not just an exercise in taking last year's numbers and putting them through a model. After all, if this were the case, there would be no need for human intervention, since a computer could very easily accomplish this task. Our role in valuation is to look at past data, assess its usefulness, and then make our best predictions for the future.

Proposition 8: Draw on the Law of Large Numbers

One of the issues we have raised as a manifestation of the dark side is the use of rules of thumb in valuations. These rules can range anywhere from a fixed equity risk premium (obtained from a service) to adding premiums to value for control, synergy, and other "good" factors and subtracting discounts for illiquidity and poor corporate governance. In many cases, the numbers that are used in these adjustments come from looking at past data. The historical equity risk premium, for instance, is estimated by averaging the premium earned by stocks over treasuries over long time periods. The control premium (of 20%) is roughly what acquirers have paid to acquire publicly traded target firms over an extended period. Even if these estimates are constantly updated and are from services that have impeccable reputations, these numbers cannot be treated as facts. They are estimates, based on samples, and they come with substantial standard errors. Thus, a historical equity risk premium of 4%, estimated with 50 years of data in the U.S., has a standard error of about 3% associated with it, just as the acquisition premium of 20% has a standard error of about 5% attached to it.

While making estimates based on data will always be subject to noise, we can do some things to make these estimates more precise:

- **Use larger samples**: When we can, we should expand our data to include more data points. With historical risk premiums, for instance, an equity risk premium estimated over 100 years of data will have a standard error of only 2% associated with it. This push toward larger sample sizes permeates much of what we have done in this book to combat bad practices. From bottom-up betas (where we replace a single regression beta, with a large standard error, with an average of many regression betas, with much smaller standard errors) to the use of industry-average profitability measures in forecasting future earnings for a company, we substitute averages of large samples for individual company data. In relative valuation, where we look at the average multiple at which other firms in a sector trade, we suggested ways of loosening the definition of comparable firms to allow for larger samples. In effect, we would rather have a larger sample of less comparable firms than a sample of a few firms that look more like the firm we are valuing.
- **Use statistical tools to improve estimates**: In many cases, when analysts use historical data, they settle for the average. While this is a useful number, there may be ways in which the data can be utilized to deliver more precise estimates. Thus, when comparing a firm's PE ratio to the rest of the sector, using a predicted PE from a sector regression should yield a more precise estimate than just using the average PE for the sector.

We should make a final point about the law of large numbers. Since the values we obtain for individual companies are estimates, the likelihood that we will be wrong about any one company in any one period is high. However, if we assess value well, our chances of being right will improve if we extend to multiple periods (longer time horizons) and across multiple stocks (portfolios).

Proposition 9: Accept Uncertainty, and Deal with It

We noted early in this book that one of the reasons we are attracted to the dark side of valuation is because we feel overwhelmed by the uncertainties we face with some groups of companies. In fact, much of this book has been directed at developing healthier responses to uncertainty:

- **Accept uncertainty**: Accept uncertainty as a given, understanding that no matter how carefully we construct models, we cannot make uncertainty go away. Thus, adding more detail to models or making models more complicated, both of which are tactics that analysts use to reduce uncertainty, often does little to alleviate the problem and may actually make it worse.
- **Ask what-if questions, but for the right reasons**: As access to data improves and more sophisticated tools for dealing with uncertainty (Monte Carlo simulations, decision trees) are introduced, we are also seeing the potential downside of allowing analysts to subject their valuations to these tools. The first problem is that these tools often required complex inputs, and the quality of the output is a function of the quality of the inputs. Simulations, for instance, require us to choose probability distributions for our inputs and parameters for the distributions. This is a difficult task considering the data we can access. The second problem is that some analysts use these as tools for risk adjustment rather than risk assessment. In the process, they double-count risk. Consider a discounted cash flow valuation of a firm, where expected cash flows are discounted back

at a risk-adjusted rate to arrive at a value that is higher than the current market prices. Assume that you put this model through a Monte Carlo simulation, derive a distribution of values (which suggests that there is a 40% chance that the stock is overvalued), and decide not to invest in the firm on this basis. You have double-counted risk—once by using risk-adjusted rates, and again by drawing on the results of the simulation.

In summary, uncertainty and risk are part of life and investing. When valuing companies, we can demand a premium for taking this risk in the discount rate and arrive at a risk-adjusted value, but it will change as circumstances change.

Proposition 10: Convert Stories to Numbers

One of the critiques of discounted cash flow valuation is that it is so focused on numbers that it misses the qualitative variables. Included in the list of qualitative variables are items such as customer loyalty, brand name, and good management.

We hope that we have addressed this criticism directly, as we have valued individual companies. Every number in a discounted cash flow valuation should have an economic rationale—a good economic story behind it. Thus, when we set a firm's return on capital at 15%, well above its cost of capital, it behooves us to think about this firm's competitive advantages (most of which are qualitative) and how they translate into the return on capital. On the flip side, every solid economic story should find a place in the numbers. Brand name affects value, but it does so by increasing margins and excess returns, not as a premium at the end of the process.

In relative valuation, the tendency toward storytelling sometimes overwhelms the numbers. One reason for our use of statistical tools (regressions and correlations) in relative valuation is not only to assess whether the underlying story makes sense, but also to quantify the effects in our predictions. Thus, by regressing PE against expected growth, we can measure how much the PE ratio increases for every 1% increase in the growth rate, at least given how the market is pricing stocks in this sector.

Conclusion

We will end this book how we began it—by noting that valuation has only a few first principles, and that the basic structure of valuation has not changed much over time. However, the kinds of firms we are called on to value pose more challenges today than ever before. As firms and investors globalize, companies have become more complex in terms of both their operations and the financing choices they make to fund those operations.

When called on to value companies, we should recognize that rigid rules do not serve us well, since valuing individual companies requires us to be flexible and devise new rules when faced with unusual scenarios. For every rule in valuation, there are a hundred exceptions. Rather than let estimation issues overwhelm us and force us into bad choices, we should step back and assess commonsense ways, constrained by the data we have available, to deal with difficult issues.

INDEX

Page numbers followed by *n* indicate footnotes.

SYMBOLS

A

B

C

D

E

F

G

H

I

J–L

M

N

O

P

Q–R

T

U

V

W–Z